THE STORY OF
IRISH MUSEUMS
1790–2000
CULTURE, IDENTITY AND EDUCATION

You that would judge me, do not judge alone

This book or that, come to this hallowed place

Where my friends' portraits hang and look thereon;

Ireland's history in their lineaments trace;

Think where man's glory most begins and ends,

And say my glory was I had such friends.

W.B. Yeats, 'The Municipal Gallery Revisited',
New Poems, Dublin: Cuala Press, 1938, stanza 7.

THE STORY OF
IRISH MUSEUMS
1790–2000
CULTURE, IDENTITY AND EDUCATION

Marie Bourke

CORK UNIVERSITY PRESS

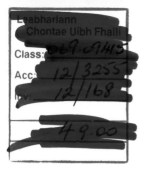
First published in 2011 by
Cork University Press
Youngline Industrial Estate
Pouladuff Road, Togher
Cork, Ireland

British Library Cataloguing in Publication Data
A CIP catalogue record for this book is available from the British Library.

ISBN 978-185918-475-1

Book design and typesetting: Anú Design, Tara
Printed in Spain by Graficas Cems

www.corkuniversitypress.com

Ollscoil na hÉireann
National University of Ireland

THE IRELAND FUNDS

Department of Arts,
Heritage and the Gaeltacht
An Rionn Ealaíon,
Oidhreacht agus Gaeltachta

An Chomhairle Oidhreachta
The Heritage Council

Contents

Abbreviations Used in Text

AAM	American Association of Museums
CEMA	Council for the Encouragement of Music and Arts
CNCI	Council of National Cultural Institutions
DCU	Dublin City University
DNB	*Dictionary of National Biography*
ICOM	International Council of Museums
IMA	Irish Museums Association
IMMA	Irish Museum of Modern Art
JRDS	*Journal of the Royal Dublin Society*
JRSAI	*Journal of the Royal Society of Antiquaries of Ireland*
MAGNI	Museums and Galleries of Northern Ireland
MoMA	Museum of Modern Art, New York
NAI	National Archives of Ireland
NCAD	National College of Art and Design
NIMC	Northern Ireland Museums Council
NGI	National Gallery of Ireland
NGIA	National Gallery of Ireland Archives
NLI	National Library of Ireland
NMI	National Museum of Ireland
NMIA	National Museum of Ireland Archives
NMNI	National Museums Northern Ireland
NPG	National Portrait Gallery, London
NUIG	National University of Ireland, Galway (also UCG)
NUIM	National University of Ireland, Maynooth
OPW	Office of Public Works
PRDS	*Proceedings of the Royal Dublin Society*
PRIA	*Proceedings of the Royal Irish Academy*
PRONI	Public Record Office of Northern Ireland
QUB	Queen's University, Belfast
RA	Royal Academy, London
RDS	Royal Dublin Society
RHA	Royal Hibernian Academy
RIA	Royal Irish Academy
RIAU	Royal Irish Art Union
RSA	Royal Society of Arts, London
RSAI	Royal Society of Antiquaries of Ireland
TCD	Trinity College, Dublin (Dublin University)
TCDA	Trinity College, Dublin Archives
UCC	University College, Cork
UCD	University College, Dublin
UCG	University College, Galway (also NUIG)
UM	Ulster Museum
V&A	Victoria & Albert Museum (*formerly* South Kensington Museum)

Chronology

A selection of museums and associated events are presented as an aid to the book.

Date	Ireland	International
1731	Dublin Society	
1733	Dublin Society Agricultural Repository	
1744	Physico-Historical Society	
1746	Dublin Society Drawing School	
1753		British Museum, opens 1759
1764	Rotunda Concert Hall, Dublin	
1765	Society of Artists	Uffizi Gallery, Florence
1768		Royal Academy of Arts, London
1773		Charleston Museum, South Carolina
1776		Albertina, Vienna
1777	Dublin University Museum (TCD)	
1781	Customs House, Dublin (1781–91)	Belvedere, Vienna
1782		Peale's Museum, Philadelphia 1886
1784	Royal College of Surgeons, Dublin	Accademia di Belle Arti, Florence
1785	Royal Irish Academy	
1786	Four Courts, Dublin (1776–86)	
1788	Linen Hall Library, Belfast	
1790	RIA Museum of Antiquities	
1791	Dublin Library Society	
1792	Dublin Society Museum, Leskean Cabinet Belfast Harp Festival Ellis's Dublin Museum Back Lane Parliament	
1793		Musée du Louvre, Paris
1795	Maynooth College	
1800	Botanic Gardens, Dublin Act of Union	Rijksmuseum, Amsterdam
1801	Dublin Society/RDS Statistical Surveys (1801–32)	

Date	Ireland	International
1815	Dublin Society acquires Leinster House	
1816	Horticultural Society of Ireland	
1819		Prado, Madrid
1820	Dublin Society receives royal charter	
1821	Belfast Natural History and Philosophical Society	
1823	Royal Hibernian Academy	
1824	Ordnance Survey, Ireland	National Gallery, London
1825		National Museum, Copenhagen (1650) established as national museum
1830	Zoological Society of Dublin	Altes Museum, Berlin
1831	Belfast Natural History Museum Board of Works/OPW Geological Society of Dublin Zoological Gardens, Phoenix Park	
1834	RDS First Industrial Exhibition First Irish railway Dublin to Kingstown (Dun Laoghaire)	
1839	Royal Irish Art Union Royal Institute of the Architects of Ireland	
1840	Irish Archaeological Society	
1844		Wadsworth Athenaeum, Hartford, Connecticut
1845	Geological Survey Act Museum of Economic Geology (renamed) Museum of Irish Industry (1847) Queen's Colleges, Cork, Belfast, Galway Great Famine (1845–50)	
1848	Irish Academy of Music	
1849	Government Schools of Design Kilkenny Archaeological Society	
1850		National Gallery of Scotland, Edinburgh
1851		Great Exhibition, Crystal Palace, London
1852	RIA moves to 19 Dawson Street Cork Industrial Exhibition	South Kensington Museum (V&A) The New Hermitage Museum, St Petersburg

Date	Ireland	International
1853	International Exhibition of Art-Industry, Dublin Ossianic Society, Dublin Irish Institution and Dargan Testimonial Committee *Ulster Journal of Archaeology*	
1854	Act of Parliament to establish NGI Catholic University, Dublin	
1855		Neues Museum, Berlin
1856		National Portrait Gallery, London
1857	Dublin Natural History Museum TCD Museum Building houses Geological Museum	
1860		Museum of Fine Arts, Montreal
1861		National Gallery of Victoria, Melbourne
1864	NGI opens	
1866		Swedish National Museum (1792) established as national museum
1867	Museum of Irish Industry becomes Royal College of Science Public Record Office of Ireland	
1869		American Museum of Natural History, New York Corcoran Art Gallery, Washington, DC
1870		Metropolitan Museum of Art, New York Museum of Fine Arts, Boston
1871	Gaiety Theatre, Dublin	
1872		Bristol Museum and Art Gallery (1823) Tokyo National Museum
1874		First Impressionist Exhibition, Paris
1876	Society for the Preservation of the Irish Language	Philadelphia Museum of Art Altes Nationalgalerie, Berlin
1877	Act of Parliament to establish Museum of Science and Art and National Library	
1878		Paris World Exposition
1879	Land League	Walker Art Gallery, Minneapolis Art Institute of Chicago

Date	Ireland	International
1882	Irish Arts and Manufactures Exhibition, Dublin	
1884	NGI National and Historical Portrait Gallery Gaelic Athletic Association	
1885	Crawford Municipal Art Gallery, Cork	
1889		First International Folklore Congress in Paris National Portrait Gallery of Scotland, Edinburgh
1890	Dublin Museum of Science and Art Kilkenny Archaeological Society renamed: Royal Society of Antiquaries of Ireland National Library of Ireland Belfast Art Gallery and Museum	
1891		Irish Literary Society, London Kunsthistorisches Museum, Vienna
1893	Gaelic League	World Exhibition, Chicago
1894		Ashmolean (1683) moves to University Galleries, 1894, merges to form Ashmolean Museum of Art and Archaeology in 1908
1895		De Young Memorial Museum, San Francisco
1896	Feis Ceoil	
1897		Tate Gallery, London Art Gallery of New South Wales, Sydney Brooklyn Museum, New York
1898	Irish Literary Theatre	Pushkin Museum of Fine Arts, Moscow
1900	Department of Agriculture and Technical Instruction	Art Gallery of Ontario, Toronto
1901		Kelvingrove Art Gallery and Museum, Glasgow
1903		Gallery Borghese, Rome
1904	Abbey Theatre, Dublin	Bode Museum, Berlin

Date	Ireland	International
1908	Municipal Gallery of Modern Art (renamed: 1975 The Hugh Lane Gallery; 2002 Dublin City Gallery The Hugh Lane) UCD Museum of Ancient History	
1909	First Dublin cinema	Dallas Museum of Art
1910	National Museum acquires RSAI collection	
1914	First World War, 1914–18	
1916	Easter Rising	
1919	War of Independence, 1919–21	Palazzo Pitti, Florence
1920		Imperial War Museum (1917) London, opens
1921	National Museum of Ireland (formerly Museum of Science and Art)	
1922	Civil War (1922–3)	
1922	Irish Free State	
1923	Public Record Office of Northern Ireland	
1924	RDS leaves Leinster House Department of Education (includes cultural institutions)	
1927		National Museum of Wales, Cardiff
1929	Belfast Municipal Museum and Art Gallery opens at Botanic Avenue Censorship of Publications Act	Museum of Modern Art, New York
1930		Pergamon Museum, Berlin
1932	Irish Academy of Letters	
1935	Irish Folklore Commission	San Francisco Museum of Modern Art
1936	Aer Lingus commences operation	
1937	Irish Constitution	
1939	Second World War, 1939–45	
1941		National Gallery of Art, Washington, DC opens
1943	Irish Exhibition of Living Art Council for the Encouragement of Music and the Arts, Northern Ireland	

Date	Ireland	International
1946		St Fagan's National History Museum, Cardiff
1949	Ireland Act – Republic of Ireland	
1951	Arts Council, Republic of Ireland Wexford Opera Festival	
1953	Chester Beatty Library Busáras	
1955	Bord Fáilte	
1958	Ulster Folk Museum	Moderna Museet, Stockholm
1959		Guggenheim, New York
1960		Scottish National Gallery of Modern Art, Edinburgh
1961	Ulster Museum, Belfast RTÉ	Los Angeles County Museum of Art
1962	Arts Council Northern Ireland Ulster Transport Museum	National Art Museum of China, Beijing
1963		Museu Picasso, Barcelona
1965		Modern Art Oxford
1968	NGI, Beit Wing Armagh Planetarium	Hayward Gallery, London Smithsonian American Art Museum (1829) re-opened 1968, renamed 2000
1971	NCAD acquires autonomy	
1972	Ulster Museum extension	
1973	Irish Republic joins EEC Merging of Ulster Folk and Transport Museum, Co. Down	
1975	Butler Gallery, Kilkenny	
1976	Irish Architectural Archive Ulster American Folk Park	
1977	James Mitchell Geological Museum (1851), UCG	Pompidou Centre, Paris
1978	Douglas Hyde Gallery, TCD	
1979	Crawford School of Art relocates to Sharman Crawford St. Druid Theatre Company, Galway	
1981	UCG Art Gallery	

Date	Ireland	International
1983		Gulbenkian Foundation, Lisbon (1956), Museum (1969), opens Modern Art Centre
1984	Cultural institutions transfer to Department of An Taoiseach	
1985	RHA Gallery, Ely Place, Dublin	
1986		Musée d'Orsay, Paris
1987		Sackler Gallery, Washington, DC
1988	National Archives of Ireland	Tate, Liverpool
1989		Louvre Pyramid
1990	Mary Robinson elected first woman President of Ireland	
1991	Irish Museum of Modern Art	Sydney Museum of Contemporary Art
1992	Tower Museum, Derry/Londonderry	Museo Renia Sofia, Madrid
1993	Department of Arts, Culture and the Gaeltacht Museums Council of Northern Ireland	Tate, St Ives
1995	Heritage Council becomes a statutory body Divorce legalized	
1997	Cultural Institutions Act NMI Decorative Arts and History, Collins Barracks, Dublin Hunt Museum, Limerick	Guggenheim, Bilbao Getty Centre, Los Angeles
1998	Museums and Galleries of Northern Ireland Good Friday Agreement	
1999	Waterford Museum of Treasures	Moscow Museum of Modern Art
2000	Chester Beatty Library opens at Dublin Castle	British Museum Great Court New Art Gallery, Walsall
2001	NMI Museum of Country Life, Castlebar Naughton Gallery, QUB Model Arts and Niland Gallery, Sligo W5 Science Discovery Centre, Belfast	Tate Modern, London
2002	NGI Millennium Wing Irish Republic joins Eurozone	Mies van der Rohe-Villa, Berlin

Date	Ireland	International
2003	Crawford Gallery extension, Cork	German Technical Museum, Berlin Peabody Essex Museum, Salem, reopens Centre for Contemporary Art, Cincinnati
2004	Lewis Glucksman Gallery, UCC	Danish Natural History Museum, Copenhagen (includes Botanical, Geological and Zoological museums) Foundling Museum, London MoMA, New York, reopens
2005	NMI and NLI acquire Board of Trustees	
2006	Dublin City Gallery, The Hugh Lane renamed (2002), extension opens Crawford Gallery, Cork, nominated national cultural institution Highlanes Municipal Art Gallery, Drogheda National Museums Northern Ireland	German Historical Museum, Berlin reopens Suzhou Museum, China Musée du Quai Branly, Paris
2007		London Transport Museum reopens
2008	Science Gallery, TCD	Museum of Islamic Art, Doha, Qatar
2009	Ulster Museum, Belfast, reopens with new extension	New Acropolis Museum, Athens Art Institute of Chicago reopens with modern wing Ashmolean Museum, Oxford reopens
2010	NMI Natural History Museum reopens The Model, Contemporary Arts Centre, Sligo, reopens Glasnevin Museum	New Museum Folkwang, Essen New art galleries at National Museum, Cardiff Mathaf Arab Museum of Modern Art, Doha

Acknowledgements

The *Story of Irish Museums* took over a decade of work and a lifetime's experience of museums. It reflects the commitment of colleagues in Ireland and overseas, who supported and encouraged the narration of a particularly Irish story. This acknowledges a debt of gratitude to all of those who assisted in the project.

I would like to acknowledge the staff of the following institutions: Armagh County Museum; Art Institute of Chicago; Arts Council; Ashmolean Museum; Boston Museum of Fine Arts; British Museum; Chester Beatty Library; Crawford Art Gallery; Dublin City Gallery The Hugh Lane; Dublin City Library & Archives; Hunt Museum; Irish Museum of Modern Art; Linen Hall Library; Louvre; Metropolitan Museum of Art, New York; National Archives of Ireland; National Botanic Gardens; National College of Art & Design; National Gallery of Art, Washington; National Gallery of Ireland; National Gallery, London; National Library of Ireland; National Museum of Ireland; National University of Ireland: Galway, Maynooth; Office of Public Works; Oireachtas Library; Queen's University, Belfast; Royal Academy; Royal Dublin Society; Royal Hibernian Academy; Royal Irish Academy; Royal Society of Antiquaries of Ireland; Tate Gallery; Trinity College, Dublin; Ulster Folk & Transport Museum; Ulster Museum; University College, Cork; University College, Dublin; University of Limerick; Victoria & Albert Museum.

Apart from others listed in the bibliography, the author gratefully acknowledges the time and help extended to her by the following: Juliana Aldeman, Helen Beaumont, Jonathan Bell, Sergio Benedetti, Eileen Black, Anne Boddaert, Bill Bolger, Karen Brown, Kieran Burns, Philomena Byrne,

Mary Cahill, Helen Carey, Brina Casey, Caroline Clarke, Timothy Collins, Professor Tom Collins, Finbarr Connolly, Pat Cooke, Pat Cronin, Professor Anne Crookshank, Peter Crowther, Ranson Davey, Barbara Dawson, Felicity Devlin, Niki Dollas, Valerie Dowling, Paul Doyle, Joanne Drum, the late Mairead Dunlevy, Professor Tom Dunne, Nieves Fernandez, Nicola Figgis, Desmond FitzGerald the Knight of Glin, Orla Fitzpatrick, Siobhan Fitzpatrick, Liz Forster, Catriona Fottrell, Lydia Furlong, Professor Raymond Gillespie, Niamh Gogan, Attracta Halpin, Peter Harbison, Christina Haywood, Roy Hewson, Nora Hickey, Anne Hodge, Michael Holland, Michael Houlihan, John Hutchinson, Aideen Ireland, Iain Wynne-Jones, Lar Joye, Fiona Kearney, Raymond Keaveney, Mary Kelleher, Monsignor J.J. Kennedy, William Laffan, Pierre le Brocquy, Adrian Le Harivel, Raffaela Lanino, Andrea Lydon, Vivienne Lynch, Aoife Lyons, Caomhán Mac Con Iomaire, Colum McCabe, Catherine McCullough, Marie McFeeley, Lynn McGrane, Jim McGreevy, Eina McHugh, Janet McLean, Brigid McManus, Niamh MacNally, Maedhbh McNamara, Maighread McParland, Donal Maguire, Hugh Maguire, Simone Mancini, Kim Mawhinney, Helen Monaghan, Nigel Monaghan, Andrew Moore, Louise Morgan, Catriona Mulcahy, Peter Murray, Sean Nolan, Jim O'Callaghan, Fr Ciaran O'Carroll, Nessa O'Connor, Colette O'Daly, Niall Ó Donnchú, Jessica O'Donnell, David O'Donoghue, Helen O'Donoghue, Homan Potterton, Jacinta Prunty, Brendan Rooney, Michael Ryan, Catherine Sheridan, Jenny Siung, Kim Smit, Michael Starrett, Matthew Stout, Tassos Tanoulas, Virginia Teehan, Geraldine Thornton, Professor John Turpin, Adriaan Waiboer, Patrick F. Wallace, Aidan Walsh, John Walsh, Gerard Whelan, Audrey Whitty, Mary Wynne, Patrick Wyse Jackson.

To the colleagues from overseas museums, including, in the UK, David Anderson, Alan Crookham, Professor Fintan Cullen, Professor Roy Foster, Rachel Hand, Nichola Johnson, Nicholas Penny, Arthur MacGregor, Neil MacGregor, and in the USA, James Cuno, Bob Eskridge, Morrison Heckscher, Professor Andrew McClellan and Ashley Williams.

I owe the greatest debt to a small group of people, whose support and assistance proved incalculable: Leah Benson, Professor John Coolahan, Professor Mary Daly, Professor Kathleen James-Chakraborty, S. Brian Kennedy, Professor Declan Kiberd, Kent Lydecker, Raghnall Ó Floinn, Giles Waterfield and Professor Kevin Whelan.

In the editing and publishing of the book, I have been guided by Rachel Pierce, whose commitment and help was exemplary, Karen Carty and Terry Foley of Anú Design, Mike Collins and Maria O'Donovan of Cork University Press.

Finally, a particular word of appreciation to my husband Barry and the supporting cast Aoife and Sinéad, *le míle buíochas*.

Published with the assistance of the Department of Arts, Heritage and the Gaeltacht, the Heritage Council, the Ireland Funds and the National University of Ireland.

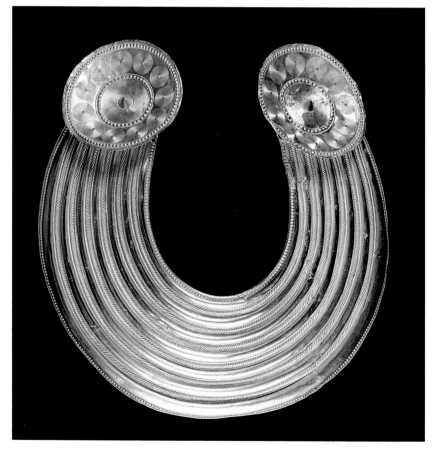

Gold Collar, Gleninsheen, County Clare, late Bronze Age 800–700 BC
W. 31.4 cm; Wt. 276 g.

Found in a rock cleft in 1932 at Gleninsheen, County Clare. National Museum of Ireland.

Foreword

The cultural institutions of Ireland, though widely admired, are not often the subject of a historical analysis. Their members have generally been too busy working and surviving from year to year to write a documentary of their own evolution. They have, in effect, been so scrupulous in recording everyone else's past that they have not managed to do full justice to their own. In the midst of her own immensely busy work at the National Gallery of Ireland, Marie Bourke has somehow made the time to write a narrative account of museums in Ireland. This is a valuable analysis, for not only does it offer the linked stories of institutions on an all-island basis, but it places their development in the wider context of Britain, Europe and the United States.

The gentlemen-scholars of the eighteenth century amassed objects on their travels at home and overseas, as part of an attempt to understand the past more fully. Many of these private scholars eventually passed their holdings on to their nations for public exhibition, in keeping with the more democratic values of the Enlightenment. The British Museum opened in 1759; and after the French Revolution of 1789, the Louvre became a place of instruction for a wider public. The notion of the past was already being linked to ideals of a revolutionary future. Some of the great libraries also passed into public hands, as literacy spread. In 1857 Henry Cole opened the South Kensington Museum for working men and women, who could buy a cup of tea or glass of beer as they studied treasures of the past.

Dr Bourke links this emergence of the modern museum to the increasingly central role of the child in social thinking. But she also astutely notes a warning from Henry Cole himself: 'if museums and galleries are made subservient to purposes of education, they dwindle into sleepy and useless institutions.' Too great an emphasis by the state on the child as apprentice adult can lead to mere schooling. A true education, on the other hand, would address itself to the intrinsic nature of the child as a thing of surpassing value in its own right.

Gifted children experience some of their earliest artistic yearnings while in the presence of radiant objects in museums. The young Oscar Wilde, who would go on to say that the energy of life is its desire for expression, always remembered his initial excitement at seeing Greek and Roman antique casts in the National Gallery; and, while still a boy, Bernard Shaw was awakened to creativity while sheltering from the Dublin rain and studying some paintings in the institution to which he would eventually bequeath so much money.

I first visited that gallery as a boy of fourteen, in the company of my younger brother and sister. This was at the Children's Christmas Art Holiday 1965, organized by the director, who had done so much to popularize Irish art on television. My memory of that event is of noisy, enthusiastic groups hard at work: according to one journalist, there were up to 4,000 parents and children in the building over the week, 'with parents kept at bay in the entrance hall'. That is a slight exaggeration, for I can distinctly remember my father (himself a keen amateur painter) standing with his head cocked in curiosity as a cheerful young woman talked the children through the completion of a painting of a clown. Many years later, I read of how a stern critic had remarked to Pablo Picasso of one of his clowns, 'a child could have done that', to which he instantly retorted, 'Yes: but could a child of forty have done it?' If play is indeed the work of the child, then that work can be a matter of lifelong learning. My father did most of his painting in the years after his retirement; and, in a world that will have more and more senior citizens, there may be entire schools of painting founded by those in their seventies and eighties.

Children are not just enthusiastic users of museums, but they also feature in any honest account as being among their greatest collectors. Dr Bourke reminds us, after all, that the Ardagh Chalice was found in Limerick earth by a boy digging potatoes. The landscape itself has a memory, as if it possessed in its layers the entire history of the human psyche, including objects that remind us of our forgotten or rejected selves. Museums, because of their origins in a period of secular enlightenment, have not always done justice to the religious experience of mankind, but somehow the uncovered earth keeps insistently restoring these elements to our human consciousness. As W.B. Yeats wrote about those who dig the earth in 'Under Benbulbin' (W.B. Yeats, *Collected Poems* (London: Macmillan, 1950), p. 398):

> A brief parting from those dear
> Is the worst man has to fear.
> Though grave-diggers' toil is long,
> Sharp their spades, their muscles strong,
> They but thrust their buried men
> Back in the human mind again.

What happens to an object taken from a grave or bog and put on display in a glass case? There is a danger that the curatorial impulse of the connoisseur, in taking that artwork out of the world, reduces it to a merely historical phenomenon. But even if the display emphasizes its integrity as a work of art, that may not be enough, unless it does so in such a way as to re-create the felt life that gave rise to it. Many great works of art were first and foremost the labour of anonymous craftspeople: for example, the Balinese told the anthropologist Margaret Mead that 'we have no art – we just do everything as well as we can'. In this context, Dr Bourke usefully reminds us of the practical as well as imaginative value of museums, which return us to this ideal of craftwork. She notes, for instance, how drawing schools in various galleries and museums were crucial in the training of architects and tradespeople, scientists and naturalists.

There are other pragmatic arguments for the proper public funding of these institutions. They may have had their origins in the international travel of gentlefolk, but are now heavily used by visitors from overseas. If culture can be used to promote tourism in Ireland, then tourism can itself help to advance the claims of culture. Dr Bourke quotes a recent report that showed that the arts' sector employed over 26,000 persons, generating €782 million in Gross Value Added and €382 in tax revenue. These are significant figures. For decades, Ireland has been playing catch-up in areas of science and technology, but in the arts, even in times of recession and unemployment, it has been a world leader. That appeal has often been underestimated by governmental authorities which, especially in the early years of the independent state, underfunded museums and galleries.

Ultimately, however, the value of such institutions to the quality of human lives cannot be quantified. All talk of making the arts the basis of some new 'smart economy' is futile. Art cannot remain art and at the same time perform as an instrument of economic policy: the 'Girl meets Tractor' posters of Soviet Russia are a depressing proof of that. To expect art to do your living for you, or indeed to revive your economy, is to risk only the humiliation of art and the frustration of the public whose expectations have been so raised. The duty of the artist, as R.P. Blackmur once said, has always been to remind the authorities of the disparate forces they have to control.

That may also, in the end, be the role of cultural institutions. If the impulse to a lofty connoisseurship was a risk in earlier centuries, there is a danger of a passive rubber-necking public experiencing a quick passing thrill at blockbuster exhibitions, rather than a more active involvement with objects. At their best, museums and galleries can reflect and even referee the contesting traditions that make up a modern society. The immigrants to Ireland from Poland, China and Africa over the past fifteen years are among the most enthusiastic users of public space; and they visit cultural institutions in great numbers to learn about the past of the people among whom they have settled. In years to come, galleries and museums will also find ways of depicting their pasts. In doing as much, they will also reflect on the experience of the Irish diaspora, whose stories cry out for further narration, not least because they would have so many points of connection with the lives of incomers.

Dr Bourke's book is an imaginative challenge as well as a scholarly history. In her quietly authoritative way, she repeats for our generation the sort of questions that were raised by those democrats who reimagined the uses of the Louvre for a more open, revolutionary future. Our present age is not revolutionary in its consciousness, and it too often encourages us to live only in the moment, as if somehow we were history's fulfilment. This is a sort of provincialism in time, which does not much encourage people to imagine what it was or will be like to live in other ages. The glory but also the restriction of democratic society is the present-tensism of its leaders' policies;

but the trust is that the interests of the dead and of the yet unborn should be registered in all our judgements.

If young people lose a sense of the past, they will also lose something even more precious: a sense of their own future. They will forget that they exist in time and that the world has many more experiences to offer than a depthless present. The gift that museums give us is a reminder that the dead and the unborn must also have votes.

What would a Museum of the Future look like? It would be exactly like current museums of the past. For that past was once somebody else's future; and it is also the most conclusive evidence we have that a future still exists.

Declan Kiberd
University College, Dublin

Godfrey Kneller (1646–1723), *Sir Hans Sloane BT,*
(1660–1753), Physician and Naturalist
(After an oil of 1716, Royal Society, London). Engraved by John Faber the Younger
(c.1684?–1756). Published J. Faber the Younger, London, 1729. Mezzotint, 36 x 26 cm.
NGI 10,160.

The collection of 'natural and artificial curiosities' forming one of the great universal collections was
left by Sloane in 1753, augmented by other bequests, to form the nucleus of the British Museum.

Introduction

A museum is a non-profit-making permanent institution in the service of society and of its development, open to the public, which acquires, conserves, researches, communicates and exhibits, for purposes of study, education and enjoyment, the tangible and intangible evidence of people and their environment.[1]

This book sets out to narrate the history of Irish museums and to examine the public role and social impact of the institutions within that context. As a contribution to the historical record, it reflects the aphorism of James Joyce: 'In the particular is contained the universal.'[2] The aim is to chart the story of Irish museums from the late eighteenth to the twenty-first century and to contextualize that story within an international framework, thereby opening up the narrative and encouraging further research and scholarship. In this way, students, academics, museum professionals and the interested onlooker will be provided with the background and perspective to engage in informed debate and discussion about the purpose and future direction of our museums.

Taking as its parameters the late eighteenth to the late twentieth century, the book adopts a cut-off point at the year 2000, focusing on growth up to that date. The story does not end with the millennium year, however, as Part V provides a brief overview of emerging trends in the twenty-first century. This approach provides the reader with a helpful chronology that is structured by century and configured with overlapping periods, so that as much of the history of the key institutions as possible can be presented, enabling the reader to keep up with unfolding events. (The list of abbreviations will clarify many of the references.[3]) By adopting this approach, questions will be raised, which may in turn encourage others to take up the mantle, as Irish museology and cultural studies are ripe for in-depth research and analysis, particularly the municipal, local authority and voluntary institutions, which were beyond the scope of this book to address.

The starting point for this study is the origins of museums as they evolved into public organizations and it explores the full range of their history as national cultural institutions. During a time when explorations around the world were producing a range of new discoveries, both artificial and from the natural world, collections were emerging in which scholars were trying to understand and to categorize the materials and specimens. The process of knowledge-gathering and discovery was prompted by private collectors, who were linked to bodies of learning and enlightenment, and who kept their curiosities and works of art in cabinets and private galleries. Sir Hans Sloane (1660–1753) is a model eighteenth-century encyclopaedic collector. A physician and naturalist, born in Killyleagh, County Down, Sloane is a prime example of a person who wanted his private cabinet (collection) to live on as a public museum after his death. In fact, Sloane's collection became the basis of the most comprehensive public museum of the Enlightenment. The British Museum, an institution financed by public funds, equipped to promote the arts and sciences within national boundaries and conceived with a 'systematic' arrangement, opened to the public in 1759, thus fulfilling Sloane's legacy.

In continental Europe, the movement that generally transformed the sovereign princely collections into museums for the public was precipitated by the French Revolution (1789–99) and exemplified by the Louvre. In Ireland, by comparison, the early Dublin Society (later Royal Dublin Society [RDS]), Trinity College, Dublin (TCD) and Royal Irish Academy (RIA) museums of the eighteenth-century Irish Enlightenment had links to the collecting era of the nineteenth century, with many of their fine art and antiquarian collections devolving to museums established under British rule, in advance of the Irish state. In this way, the private Milltown Collections at Russborough House and George Petrie's cabinet (acquired by the RIA) devolved to the National Gallery of Ireland and to the National Museum of Ireland, respectively. The latter half of the twentieth century would witness a similar pattern

**Johann Zoffany (1733–1810), *Portrait of George Fitzgerald
with his Sons George and Charles*, c.1764**
Oil on canvas, 98.5 x 123.5 cm. NGI 2007.76.

This family group portrays George Fitzgerald (d.1783) of Turlough Park, County Mayo, and his sons. The Fitzgeralds had come to Ireland with the Norman, Strongbow, and were expelled to the west of Ireland by Oliver Cromwell, where they recovered their position. A new house was built for a later member of the family by Thomas Newenham Deane. The National Museum of Country Life is now located at Turlough Park.

of museum foundation, but in the meantime, the museum had become one of the institutions of the modern state.

The significance of antiquarian collections and the establishment of a national museum underpin the historical developments. The National Museum evolved from early collections that had largely been in the care of families which were the hereditary keepers of great reliquaries, but which devolved over time to the RDS. The origins of the Irish antiquities collections resided with the RIA, which was founded in 1785. Following an Act to establish a national museum and library in 1877, these treasured Irish antiquities transferred to the Dublin Museum of Science and Art when it opened in 1890.

Within one small cultural quarter at the heart of Dublin was located TCD, the RIA and a host of institutions that devolved from the RDS: a natural history museum, a national gallery, a national library, a national museum, and a national art school.

Dublin was not alone in this coalescing of cultural and educational activity. In the north of Ireland the desire for an educated and industrious society drove the development of an early 'museum movement' that saw the foundation of a museum in 1831 first by the Belfast Natural History and Philosophical Society, followed by the opening of the Belfast Art Gallery and Museum in 1890. Similarly, a series of regional museums would develop in Cork, Limerick and elsewhere.

A critical area of study is the relationship between collecting and museums, whereby what started out as the desire by landowners or wealthy patrons to form collections for their own pleasure and enlightenment saw many of these treasures ultimately devolving to Irish museums. Much of the collecting of fine art originated with the Irish Ascendancy of the late eighteenth and early nineteenth centuries, influenced by the Grand Tourists' desire (together with the antiquarian tradition) for fine art and *objets d'art* for town houses and newly built country estates. Historians use the term 'Ascendancy' to describe the people of the upper and ruling classes in rural Ireland during the eighteenth and early nineteenth centuries, who were second- and third-generation Irish-born and 'conscious of their duty to the country that gave them birth and sustenance'. The Dublin Society Drawing Schools (1746), which eventually became the National College of Art, were pivotal in developing an interest in fine art, augmented by the newly established Royal Hibernian Academy (RHA) in 1823. The role of the Dublin International Exhibition of Art-Industry in 1853 was to provide an arena that precipitated the establishment of these museums. A number of key figures, fine arts associations, societies of artists and the Royal Irish Art Union anticipated a permanent gallery, their activities and support serving to illuminate the artistic, social and historical milieu that led to the foundation of the National Gallery of Ireland (NGI) in 1854. The Act of Parliament that established the gallery has served the institution remarkably well from its opening in 1864, up to the present day.

This book represents the first account of how the Irish museum tradition evolved, how interconnections were established between museum agencies and institutions and the links that existed between their constitution and policies. Thus, when the integration of the various institutions that led to the present-day growth of the great collections in our national cultural institutions is examined, it can be shown how these institutions, building on older traditions, sought to give expression to their role of promoting public enlightenment. In common with similar institutions overseas, it is shown how the development of museums forms an important part of the historical analysis of any nation – a point demonstrated not only in the chapters on Irish museums, but also in the two chapters dealing with the museum culture of Europe and the United States. What the research reveals is the surprising degree to which the world of museums touches on all aspects of life: war, peace, civil rights, and civilization, past, present and future. Each museum is different, due to its activities and place in history, but the impetus is always the same: the aspiration to reveal why objects are acquired, conserved, researched, exhibited, interpreted and communicated, and to give people trustworthy places in which to experience 'pleasure through enlightenment' as they discover the story of their heritage.

Scholarly publications on the international front show a range of approaches that are illustrated by two American publications. *Riches, Rivals and Radicals: 100 Years of Museums in America* (2006), by Marjorie Schwarzer, discusses the history of American museums, with an overview of developments across the full range of museum types, which is also the story of American democracy. While presenting a broad picture of the scope of the museum operation (buildings, collections, exhibitions, people and money), Schwarzer successfully distils this information so that the reader gets a genuine feeling for the American approach to museums. A different type of account is *The Art Museum: From Boullée to Bilbao* (2008), by Andrew McClellan, which portrays the art museum from its inception in the eighteenth century to the present day through the prism of museum theory and practice, ideals and mission, architecture, collecting, classification and display, the public, commercialism, restitution and repatriation. McClellan is not afraid to grasp thorny contemporary issues and many-sided debates, while presenting them in a very readable form. Other British and continental European publications employ a broad historical approach that is very effective in discussing institutional histories as well as contemporary issues. Recent studies of individual institutions include the

Guercino (Giovanni Francesco Barbieri) (1591–1666),
Jacob Blessing the Sons of Joseph, 1620
Oil on canvas, 170 x 211.5 cm. NGI 4648.

Illustrating an episode from the Book of Genesis (48: 8–20), the picture describes how Joseph brought his sons, Manasseh and Ephraim, to be blessed by their ailing grandfather, Jacob. Sir Denis Mahon endowed the NGI with eight works from his collection, of which this is a notably fine example of Italian baroque painting.

British Museum, the Victoria & Albert Museum (V&A), Tate Britain and the National Gallery, London. While some provide an overview and others a detailed account, many of these books have been published to mark anniversaries of each institution's foundation.

Irish museums, by contrast, have to date been the subject of minor scholarly attention, with little or no consideration given to the historical, theoretical or socio-political context. Some journals, including *Archaeology Ireland, Artefact, Irish Architectural & Decorative Arts Studies, Circa Contemporary Art Magazine, History Ireland, Journal of the Royal Society of Antiquaries of Ireland, Museum Ireland* and *Irish Arts Review,* are publishing articles that demonstrate the importance of the subject and the need for more research, but there is much work still to be done to bring this area of study up to international standards. Thus far, the books dealing with the history of the development of the Irish cultural institutions have been largely restricted to those produced to mark centenaries or anniversaries, leaving a gap for a much-needed comprehensive overview.[4] While these books are important additions in their own right and enjoyable to read, few of them can be said to provide major historical depth or overview. The research in this volume represents the first substantial account of the history, framework and chronological development of Irish museums and galleries during the period between the eighteenth and twentieth century, and it is hoped this will be built on substantially in the coming years.

What it does show is that Ireland is an important case study because its profile conveys the distinct textures of a particular 'national' instance, as in the case of the evolving story of the National Museum of Ireland (NMI). While the worldwide development of museums shows that they are bound up with national identity and the creation of the nation-state, the interesting situation in Ireland is that most of the major museums were established prior to the foundation of the state. Both the new and the older national museums played a significant role in the growth of a spirit of nationhood and contributed to a growing sense of Irish identity, as in the case of, for example, the national portrait collection of major Irish historical figures at the National Gallery, or the Irish antiquities and casts of Irish high crosses encapsulated in a 'cabinet of blessèd memories' at the National Museum that caught the imagination of the public.[5]

The new Irish state produced a series of modernist, avant-garde figures, including the Irish Europeans – James Joyce, W.B. Yeats, Samuel Beckett and the painter Jack B. Yeats (the poet Thomas MacGreevy was also an influential figure) – who worked mainly in a European context, but contributed to the reimagining of Irish identity. However, the initial impact of the new state on Irish cultural institutions was to limit their development through a lack of care of support, an act of negligence that was the result of the pressing demands on the government to secure economic stability for the country. This slowed down the process of expansion until the latter part of the twentieth century, when Ireland's accession in 1973 to the European Economic Community (EEC) (now European Union) reinvigorated the economy and released the funding

Dublin Society Award

The award, in the shape of an artist's palette, was presented to the painter Martin Archer Shee (1769–1850) by the Dublin Society on 15 February 1787.

necessary to invest again in museums and galleries. In this way, the national museums formed part of the manifestation of the country's national heritage.

W.B. Yeats noted that crucial to an epistemology of art is the way in which art, like music, dance, theatre, film, photography, literature and philosophy, expands understanding of ourselves as persons: 'After all one's art is not the chief end of life but an accident in one's search for reality or rather perhaps one's method of search.'[6] Through the story of the museum, this book documents an Enlightenment concept of advancement through scholarship, by means of a process of inquiry into the history and forces that shaped the evolution of Irish museums. It presents fields of study that are motivated by a desire to increase awareness of Irish museums, their public role and the place of learning that formed part of the original motivation of museums. This serves to underline the way in which Irish museums strengthen communities, offer the opportunity to be informed and inspired and provide places for people to be enriched, culturally, intellectually and emotionally.

PART I

Pre-Eighteenth Century

Jacques de Lajoue (*c.*1687–1761),
Overdoor painting from the cabinet of Bonnier de la Mosson, 1734
Oil on canvas, 132 x 160.5 cm. NGI 2002.15. Alfred Beit Foundation.

One of two overdoor paintings, modelled on a library and cabinet of natural and artificial curiosities with purpose-built rococo furnishings, formed by Bonnier de la Mosson (1702–44) at his museum in the Hôtel de Lude, Paris. It is a fanciful idea of a private cabinet prior to the emergence of public collections.

A tour guide showing visitors around a museum is used to the question, 'Where did the idea of museums come from?' The question of the origins of these spaces is one that fascinates visitors, and many are surprised to discover that the answer encompasses a long history, stretching back to antiquity. While this volume is primarily concerned with the centuries from mid-1700 to 2000, it is necessary to take a much earlier starting point in order to ground this exploration of the modern museum movement in its rightful origins. Thus it is that ancient Athens is the ideal place from which to commence the story of the public museum.

This opening chapter provides a brief overview of the story as a whole, describing an outline chronology that will be teased out in detail in the course of the book. It is helpful in that it shows how these early institutions found their shape and form and how they gradually evolved into today's public museum, a vital institution of the modern state.

1

The Story of the Public Museum

The European museum is the parent of
museums in other countries.[1]

The Ancient Origins of the Museum

The museum owes its name to the ancient Greek Temple of the Muses, the Mouseion (meaning a place or home for the Muses), which was a sacred space in which a person's mind could break free of the constraints of the everyday and reach a higher plane. The merging of the concepts of sacred temple and educational institution occurred in the Greek schools of philosophy, where the study of philosophy was seen as a divine service to the Muses. The further association of the museum with the *lyceum*, or library, arose from the idea of it being a place for collective study, with particular emphasis on the arts and sciences, which were patronized by the nine Muses (daughters of Zeus, fostered by their mother, Mnemosyne [memory]), who were the progenitors of learning and inspiration.[2] Milton left us a vision of Aristotle's Lyceum at Athens:

> See there the olive-grove of Academe …
> There … the sound
> Of bees' industrious murmur, oft invites
> To studious musing.[3]

Aristotle's Lyceum provided an important model for the Hellenistic Musaeum of Alexandria, whose scholarly community shared features in common with Plato's philosophical academy. The fabled Musaeum of Alexandria and the academies of Plato and Aristotle would be oft-cited classical sources of inspiration for the early development of museums.

At Ptolemy's musaeum at Alexandria (destroyed *c.* AD 400), the emphasis shifted from the religious and ethical to the intellectual. The fame of this musaeum was largely due to its collection of objects, renowned library and team of scholars, who formed its special community.[4] Although known only through scattered literary references, its spirit of inquiry ranged across all learning (more like a research institute than a museum in the modern sense of the word), resulting in a great stock-taking of human knowledge. The association between the museum today and the Musaeum of Alexandria is based partly on the collecting of specimens, but primarily on the concept of an encyclopaedic scope of knowledge-gathering.

By the sixteenth century the Latin word *musaeum* had, in Italy, acquired additional meanings, such as 'temple', 'gallery', 'study' and 'library', because it could accommodate so many associations.[5] In early modern France the term *musaeum* was understood to refer to the Alexandrian project, defined as a group of scholars dedicated to the study of arts, sciences, letters and the collecting of specimens.[6] The idea of public service implied in modern museums was not ushered in until the French Revolution in the late eighteenth century. Thus, from its early inception through its long evolution, the word 'museum' has had numerous meanings, but has always retained one basic characteristic: a broad, encyclopaedic outlook embracing a wide range of subjects, in which objects are the primary means of communication. Today, the museum's core functions of conservation, acquisition, scholarship and education are directed towards this all-encompassing humanist purpose.

The first repositories of works of art were treasuries formed from votive offerings made by the faithful to their goddesses in temples of ancient Greece.

The Greeks placed these gifts in buildings of the classical Acropolis in Athens, such as the Propylaea (*c.*437–32 BC, an architecturally designed gateway). The Propylaea comprised a central section flanked by two wings. The hall in the north wing was known as the Pinakotheke,[7] a recreation area displaying paintings on the walls and works by great sculptors. (Pausanias called it 'a building bearing pictures' in the second century AD,[8] while in the time of Augustus Vitruvius, the *pinacotheca* denoted a room in a great house.) The Hellenistic era saw the formation of collections of statues, precious books and *objets d'art* in libraries, with conference halls housing images of poets, philosophers and historians – a version of a historical museum.

Acropolis

Some of the first repositories of works of art were treasuries formed from votive offerings made by the faithful to their goddesses in temples in ancient Greece, such as the buildings of the classical Acropolis in Athens.

Although it was the Greeks and the Romans who conceived of museums as treasure places, the ancient world also possessed public collections of objects valued for their aesthetic, historic, religious and magical significance. In imperial Rome, the ancient cultures of Greece and Rome were venerated as a priceless legacy, the Romans wishing to own both Greek possessions and their spirit. Thus, while the recognizable constructs of museums, libraries and art collections were creations of the Hellenistic and Roman periods, the fact is that Roman civilization inherited these concepts from their Greek predecessors and developed them further. In a sense, the city of Rome itself was the archetypical museum, and indeed was described as such by the architectural historian and critic Antoine-Chrysostome Quatremère de Quincy (1755–1849): 'For a truly enquiring mind, the city of Rome is an entire world to be explored, a sort of three-dimensional mappamundi, which offers a condensed view of the ancient and modern world … The true Museum of Rome … consists of statues, temples and historical sites.'[9]

During the Middle Ages, as the Gothic world grew out of the Romanesque civilization (itself an extension of Carolingian culture), ecclesiastical treasures came to be displayed in churches as a means of encouraging devout Christian practice, as well as for their value for learning in monastic libraries. The lavish patronage of Jean, Duc de Berry (1340–1416) influenced international culture in the Gothic period, and although his collection did not survive to form a cabinet, it did herald the scope of later collections in a new continuity between the Middle Ages and the Renaissance. Florence became the centre of Italian intellectual life in the fourteenth century, as early Renaissance scholarly interest turned towards ancient Greece and Rome. The Italian Renaissance of the fifteenth century saw popes, princes and merchants recover their classical past while amassing *objets d'art* and antiquities, which they exhibited in gallery spaces that became the standard form of display for such collections. A description of the gallery (*galleria*) was provided by the Zeiller dictionary in 1632: 'a corridor where pictures hang'.[10] Thus, an Italian architect wrote about early seventeenth-century Vienna: 'In this city the gallery … following the Roman example, has been introduced into the houses of … collectors of antique marbles and bronzes, medallions, bas-reliefs and paintings.'[11]

**The Domhnach Airgid (Silver Church) Book Shrine
(eighth century AD, remodeled c. AD 1350)**

The Domhnach Airgid (Silver Church) was a venerated object made to contain relics given by St Patrick to St Macartan, patron saint of Clones, County Monaghan. The first container was a hollow yew-wood box with engraved bronze plates and a sliding lid. An inscription tells how the shrine was remade, c.1350, by John O Barden (a goldsmith who lived in Drogheda) for John O Carbry, abbot of Clones (d.1353). Decorated with cast and gilt silver plaques bearing figures of the Virgin, saints and apostles, on the lower left plate, it has been suggested a clerical scribe presents a copy of the gospels to St Macartan, founder of a church at Clogher, County Tyrone.

The word 'museum' was not universally popular, although alternatives are hard to find; earlier periods used terms such as lyceum, *guardaropa*, cabinets of curiosities, *studiolo*, libraries, *athenaeum*, and repositories that ranged from table-top cabinets (*wunderkabinette*) to entire rooms (*wunderkammern*). The actual assemblage of objects, comprising both natural and artificial curiosities, depended on the financial resources of the collector. The various types of repository, which included libraries, gardens, apothecaries' shops, and so on, formed a new construct in the field of arts and sciences and contributed to the

The *Stanzino*, or *Studiolo*, of Francesco I de' Medici (1541–87)

This *stanzino* is an example of the princely cabinet as microcosm. The sequence of images depicted on the wall cabinets allude to the contents of the cabinets.

enrichment of the eventual form of the museum, of the museum collections and of the manner of their acceptance by the public.

Natural objects, which were a source of study and wonder, were an integral part of intellectual life in early modern Europe from the sixteenth to the nineteenth century. Cabinets of curiosities developed around 1500–1650, through the acquisition, examination and display of objects, produced by a community of collectors who visited each other and met at learned societies to exchange ideas, objects and publications. The core of the enterprise centred around ports such as Amsterdam, where natural curiosities from all over the world were acquired for collections intended for the pleasure of a select few. The importance of seventeenth- and eighteenth-century European private and institutional collections, such as the earlier *studiolo* and *tribuna* of the Grand Duke Francesco I de' Medici (1541–87), lay in the transitional position they held in the evolution from private cabinets to public museums. Thus, while a number of well-formed museum collections emerged during the Renaissance period, the majority of these drew from an earlier model-proto-type for museums – the cabinet of curiosities. The Medici Palace (1445–60), with its treasure-gathering by medieval princes and newer practice of collecting classical artefacts, such as manuscripts, coins, sculpture and architectural fragments, came to be seen as a prototype of the museums of the future, and thus the origin of European museums. All of the Medici collections, including those of the famous Uffizi Palace (1560–74), became accessible to the public when they were bequeathed to the city of Florence in 1743 by the last princess of the de' Medici family, Anna Maria Luisa.[12] Throughout their history they have attracted huge visitor numbers.

Accumulations of rarities by European collectors formed the backdrop for the advancement of British collections, as the habit of forming cabinets was already widely practised in educated European society by the mid-sixteenth century. At the end of the sixteenth century, for example, Francis Bacon listed among the necessary attainments of learned gentleman, a 'goodley huge, cabinet' filled with natural and artificial wonders such as a model of the universe made private.[13] Thus, it was the seventeenth century that saw the growth of English public museum collections.

Although museums existed in Britain from the seventeenth century, many were in a poor state (for example, the Royal Society) and, apart from its

Weekly Office: Wednesday, Paradise from **Les Très Riches Heures du Duc de Berry**
Ms. 65, fol. 126f, fifteenth century, Chantilly, Musée Conde.

The Duke de Berry had a magnificent collection of *objets d'art* and precious books (of which an inventory exists) that formed part of the transition from the medieval treasury to the sixteenth–seventeenth century cabinet of curiosities.

Attributed to Domenico Remps (c.1620–99), *Cabinet of Curiosities*, 1675
Oil on canvas, 99 x 137 cm. Museo dell'Opificio delle Pietre Dure, Florence.

The theme of vanitas (the transience of life and the inevitability of death) inspired cabinet paintings such as this one. The *trompe d'œil* illusion in this work is the 'cabinet', which has been depicted opened up to reveal the curiosities inside, like a 'world in miniature'.

universities of Oxford and Cambridge, the country had no major library or museum prior to the eighteenth century. The Ashmolean Museum, attached to the University of Oxford, was founded from a private cabinet and made accessible to the public in 1683, over seventy years before the opening of the British Museum in London. The Repository of the Royal Society (1660) had an Irish successor in the Repository of the Dublin Society (1733). The purpose of the Royal Society's collections was for the study of philosophy and an exploration of human activity, rather than simply to provoke wonder. Its repository transferred to the British Museum in 1781.

The lack of royal interest in collecting contrasted with that of the landed aristocracy in Britain, who were vigorous patrons of the arts during the late eighteenth and early nineteenth centuries. This was due to the tendency in

Britain towards the decentralization of political power away from the monarch. Grand Tours of Europe educated many patrons and artists and encouraged the acquisition of works of art, which were brought back to England by discerning collectors. Connoisseurs were concerned with matters of aesthetics as the new prerequisite for collecting practices. As was the pattern in Ireland, the collections in England were accessible to anyone with genteel manners. Accordingly, Irish travellers, such as Jonathan Swift, explored the Royal Society repository.

Two major seventeenth-century figures formed collections that ended up in museums: Elias Ashmole's collection was the basis of the Ashmolean Museum; and Hans Sloane's collection was the foundation of the British Museum in 1753. While the 'Tradescant' collection (which had been bequeathed to Ashmole (1617–92) by John Tradescant the Younger and formed the basis of the collection he donated to Oxford University) moved England towards a public museum, the inscription on the tomb of the Tradescant father-and-son collectors celebrated their exploits by espousing 'A World of wonders in one closet shut'. It was, however, the British Museum that evolved into a new type of institutional museum. The British Museum's collection, formed from a private 'cabinet of curiosities', opened in 1759 and although admission was free, up to 1805 entry was by a ticket that had to be approved by the principal librarian, with a summary of the collection available by 1808. In this way the British Museum was open to scholars and ordinary people, just as Sloane had intended.

Great museums that developed in parallel with great libraries displayed objects that were gathered for aesthetic pleasure and for serious study, both in the humanities and the sciences. These had emerged as public institutions by the end of the eighteenth century, many of them established by private individuals prior to the French Revolution. The British Museum and the Louvre are typical of museums that originated in the eighteenth-century encyclopaedic movement of the European Enlightenment. By the mid-eighteenth century the practice of opening collections, to a degree, was established in France and England.

In 1710 a public gallery was opened by the Elector Palatine Johann Wilhelm in Düsseldorf. In 1750, and for about twenty years, the Luxembourg Gallery in Paris was opened to the public two days a week, for three hours per day.

Johann Zoffany (1733–1810), *The Tribuna of the Uffizi*, **1772–7**
Oil on canvas, 123.5 x 155 cm. The Royal Collection. Her Majesty Queen Elizabeth II.

This view was commissioned by Queen Charlotte about 1722 to paint highlights of the Grand Duke of Tuscany's collection shown within the *tribuna* of the Uffizi Palace. The painting omits some items and introduces others, while illustrating a large group of Grand Tourists looking at some of the great works of the Italian High Renaissance.

François I, who had an extensive cabinet at the royal palace at Fontainebleau, would see his collection forming the nucleus of the early collections of the Louvre Museum, which would eventually become a public museum. In Austria, the works of art amassed by the Habsburg princes in Vienna, Prague, Innsbruck and Antwerp were united in Vienna in the seventeenth century. The Belvedere in Vienna was partially opened about 1781, following a pedagogical reordering of the royal collection by schools and linear chronology, so that a visit to the gallery would be methodical and instructive, 'a repository where the history of art is made visible'.[14] However, access to the imperial gallery in Vienna in 1792 was limited to those with clean shoes – not a trivial matter in a city of many horses and no pavements. When the Netherlands was released from Spanish rule in the late sixteenth century, it became a republic of United

Provinces under a stadtholder, in a country where there were many quality art collections and cabinets. The collections of Russia were formed by Peter the Great (Peter I) (1672–1725) and were opened to the public as part of his drive to educate Russians. Catherine the Great (Catherine II) (1729–96) further developed the imperial collections of the Hermitage with her purchase of entire collections in Europe,[15] but as access to the collections was restricted, the number of people who actually visited the gallery tended to be small.

The papal collections also form an important part of this story. Their eventful history shows them to have developed from the Renaissance onwards, ending up in many large and small Vatican museums, which, some would argue, contain the first purpose-built museum structure. The history of the Vatican Museums begins with the election of Pope Julius II in 1503, after which he formed and displayed a collection of sculpture in the Courtyard of Statues, which was expanded by his successors and displayed as exhibits in a museum. The Vatican assumed international importance as a cultural and religious centre during the eighteenth and nineteenth centuries.

Just as the objects in these early museums originated in princely collections, so museum administrators could trace their ancestry back to eighteenth-century intermediaries such as Christian Ludwig von Hagedorn (1712–1820), the son of a Danish official who built up a private collection through careful purchases on the auction market. His *Observations on Painting*, which appeared in 1762, contained an impressive knowledge of aesthetic theory. Christian Mechel (1737–1817), the son of a Basel craftsman, set up as an art dealer, having absorbed ideas about art from Johann Joachim Wincklemann, the German art historian and archaeologist. Mechel developed a business as a printmaker and became one of the most successful art dealers in Europe. It was he who supervised the installation of the imperial collection in Vienna. Hagedorn and Mechel moved across the eighteenth-century art world and, like their contemporaries, Wincklemann and Goethe, were able to succeed, using opportunities provided to them by both the court and the public.

As access to art collections was important for artists, given that their training involved copying the works of old masters, it became standard practice to allow students and connoisseurs free access to a ruler's collections. For example, in 1786 Frederick William II of Prussia decreed that his collections should be made available to students. In Dresden, the eighteenth-century museological capital of Germany, royal paintings were displayed in the Museum of Dresden (Dresden Gemaldegalerie), a former private gallery, the nucleus of which was a Renaissance *Kunstkammer* (Kunst means art, and kammer means a small room or cabinet) of the princes of Saxony. Germany was in the vanguard of the museum movement, as almost every important German art collection was opened to the public in the eighteenth century, with details of the collections listed in J.G. Meusel's *Teutsches Kunstlerlexikon* (first published 1778, with enlarged editions in 1808 and 1814). However, this is not to say that the general public participated confidently in museum culture. Access to museums, like participation in public culture as a whole, was circumscribed by an elaborate set of rules and preconditions: one had to have the money to buy tickets, the ability to read in order to have access to books and the right appearance to be welcomed in polite society. Thus, while greater access was the impetus, in actual fact, entry to a collection was stipulated in regulations or left to the discretion of the person in charge. It, therefore, remained an elite pursuit until the violent social upheavals that marked the turn of the century.

The Emergence of the Modern Museum

It was during a crucial phase in the political history of France, between 1783 and 1805, that the modern museum emerged. This brutal period in the evolution of the French state witnessed the authority of great sovereign collections being transferred from royal, religious or private ownership to the nation, which resulted in the Louvre (a name synonymous with the very idea of a 'museum of art') becoming both the first museum in the modern sense and an institution of the modern state.

The powerful force of public ownership, through which the finest works of art were removed from their religious and royal setting, led to the development of an encyclopaedic ideal in the public museum, with education as its aim. And just as Paris became the Rome of the Enlightenment, the Louvre became its cultural epicentre. The audience would be its citizens, not believers or subjects, because ownership was no longer vested in the Church or the monarchy, but rather in the concept of national heritage presented for the benefit of the public. Thus, the name 'Louvre' summarizes the history of a

Hubert Robert (1733–1808), *View of the Grande Galerie of the Louvre, c.*1796

Established in 1793 and enlarged by Napoleon in the early 1800s, the museum at the Louvre provided the impetus for many European cities to establish national museums and galleries.

complex idea combining a broad range of concepts and expectations. To characterize it, therefore, as a 'universal survey museum', as is sometimes done, reduces the concept of universality that is embodied in the very origin of museums.[16]

The French Revolution introduced the popular museum into France. By creating the Musée Central des Arts (modern Louvre) and the Musée National d'Histoire Naturelle in 1793, a move was made towards institutional specialization by dividing collections into smaller, more practical units (illustrating a system of classifying material and according it an appropriate setting).[17] A key figure in the development of French museums was Jean-Dominique Vivant-Denon, who accompanied a commission of experts documenting Napoleon's exploits and the Imperial Museums and one of his main duties was incorporating the looted works of art that Napoleon had claimed from his European campaigns into the museums. Presiding over this enterprise,

Vivant-Denon, who was Napoleon's chief artistic advisor, was responsible for the artistic scope and historical quality of the French acquisitions. He, in turn, engaged experts to help organize, display and publicize the collections. Vivant-Denon, Europe's first great museum director, dictated the methodical systemization and hanging of the Louvre collections, which remained the model for European and American museums into the early twentieth century. Classification was by national school, in chronological sequence, guided by the history of art – 'a history course of the art of painting'.[18]

While the Congress of Vienna, 1815, required the seized materials to be returned to their owners, this phase awakened a new interest in art, in developing art collections for museums and encouraging the establishment of new museums, such as the Brera Gallery (an outgrowth of the Brera Academy) in Milan. It also provided the impetus to make some collections available to the public. This is a critical point in contemporary debates on how museum collections were formed through the deployment of military, political and economic power.

At the same time, the educational role of museums grew as the Louvre assumed significance as a centre of instruction during the French revolutionary period, when its transformation into a public museum saw its collections used as a vehicle for general education. The museum was open to everyone, free of charge, with some days reserved for students and artists, when drawing classes on Greek and Roman art took place in the gallery housing antiquities.[19] Simple guidebooks and catalogues (translated into foreign languages) were provided for visitors, who came in great numbers.[20] What began as a conservative institution, that was renamed several times, emerged as the progressive, modern Musée du Louvre. The French Revolution had served as a 'prehistory' to the evolution of the modern museum, positioning the institution in readiness to provide opportunities for self-improvement in the nineteenth century.

Between the late eighteenth and early nineteenth century the new public institution museum emerged in Europe and in the United States. The French Revolution resulted not only in the first French public museums but also provided the catalyst for change elsewhere in Europe. In Spain, the former Habsburg and Bourbon royal collections formed the basis of the Prado collection in Madrid. The history of the papal collections in Rome illustrated the evolution of Italy's private collections into public museums, the Vatican collections being some of the most significant in the world.

The German museums played a key role in the establishment of the institution, the ordering of the collections and the development of an architectural type of museum that would be influential henceforth. The Glyptothek in Munich, founded by Ludwig I of Bavaria to house his collection of ancient and modern sculptures, was designed by Leo von Klenze, opening in 1830. The Alte Pinakothek in Munich, which housed the royal collections of Bavaria, was also designed by von Klenze and when it opened in 1836 it served as a model for museums in Brussels, Kassel and St Petersburg. The public museums of Berlin emerged as part of a strategic planning process in the early nineteenth century. By 1800, the curriculum of the Berlin Academy included thirty-two hours per week to study collections in the German galleries. The Glyptothek and Alte Pinakothek in Munich competed with the earlier Vatican museums and later Altes Museum in Berlin as the first major museum buildings. As the concept of the public museum spread across Europe in the late eighteenth and early nineteenth centuries, two great Dutch museums would be expanded: the Mauritshuis (the Hague) and the Rijksmuseum (Amsterdam).

The Rijksmuseum, Amsterdam

The largest and most revered museum in the Netherlands was founded in 1800, following the French Revolution under Louis Bonaparte, King of Holland, and acquired the name Rijksmuseum under William I. The drawing illustrates Pierre Joseph Hubert Kuypers' original design completed in 1883.

Ideas about popular education prevalent in Europe were advanced in Britain by the Society for the Encouragement of Arts, Manufactures and Commerce. However, the idea of a public exhibition space grew out of concerns arising within British art at a time when painting was being elevated from a craft to a serious subject, requiring knowledge, discrimination and an awareness of the European schools.[21] The founding of the Royal Academy (RA) in London in 1768, which was critical among European academies in the influence it exerted over the progress of art in Britain, educated and shaped artistic taste, with its threefold foundation roles of art school, exhibition space and professional institution. The academy fostered public appreciation of the visual arts, while its first exhibition (1769) provided works that municipal museums could purchase – a pattern that would be emulated in Scotland and in Ireland. The RHA would instruct artists and enhance the visual arts in Ireland, just as the Dublin Society would advance the progress of Irish museums.

While the model for the American museum was mainly a European one, the revolutionary process in America meant that the contents of their new museums would be purchased, as they did not have royal or historical collections to confiscate. While these changes generated a heightened awareness of the significance of museum collections in establishing national identity, they also formed a powerful means for the instruction and education of 'public taste'. The capital city of the United States did not develop a national gallery until the twentieth century; the National Gallery of Art, in Washington, DC, was founded in 1937, opening in 1941. The Louvre provided a model other states could emulate, so that by the end of the nineteenth century virtually every Western nation housed a significant public museum that helped to articulate its national self-identity.[22] American museums, unlike those in Europe, were founded and funded by philanthropy and local government. Thus, an American grand tourist's comment that 'the European museum is the parent of museums in other countries' was ignorant of a difference of approach that grew to form the basis of American museums.[23] Charles Willson Peale (1741–1827) articulated this outlook:

> In Europe, all men of information prize a well regulated museum,
> as a necessary appendage to government, but the means of

visiting those repositories are within the reach of particular classes of society only, or open on such terms or at such portions of time, as effectually to debar the mass of society, from participating in improvement, and pleasure.[24]

The concept of art museums filled with rare objects, which had once served the interests of political or religious authority, dominated the ideology of the modern institutional museum.

From the outset, the concept of the American museum was 'neither an abandoned European palace nor a solution for storing national wealth … it is an American phenomenon developed by the people, for the people, and of the people'.[25] The growth of museums in the United States occurred in the late eighteenth century alongside a drive for learning, in a milieu where, according to an Irish visitor: 'The new world is completely derelict of objects interesting to the virtuoso in any branch of his profession.'[26] Emulating the pattern in Britain, this hunger for learning in America saw the establishment of libraries, antiquarian societies and learned bodies, together with schools and universities that created university museums. Benjamin Franklin (1709–90), in his *Proposals for Promoting Useful Knowledge among the British Plantations in America* (1743), stated that after the 'first drudgery of settling new colonies', there would be time for education and the arts. His belief in the museum's ability to produce 'an eternal image of the past' saw him visit Hans Sloane in London to see the famous Irishman's collection of natural and artificial curiosities.

The oldest museum in North America is considered to be the Charleston Museum of Natural History, which opened in 1773.[27] The Peabody Museum in Salem, Massachusetts started out as the Salem East India Marine Society in 1799, displaying decorative arts and maritime artefacts. Collections were acquired by art institutions like the Pennsylvania Academy of the Fine Arts in Philadelphia, an art school with its own important collections that opened in 1805. The Boston Athenaeum, which opened in 1807, started an annual exhibition in 1827, while the National Academy of Design, founded in New York in 1825, had collections and periodic exhibitions. And while one of the first public art museums, the Wadsworth Athenaeum, founded in Hartford, Connecticut by the collector Daniel Wadsworth in 1842 (opened

The Prado Museum, Madrid

The idea of creating a museum (natural history cabinet) emerged under Charles III (1716-88), in a building designed in 1785 by Juan de Villanueva. Under the auspices of his wife Queen Maria Isabel, Ferdinand VII transformed Villanueva's building, opening it as a museum of paintings and sculpture in 1819, named Museo del Prado in 1868.

1844), demonstrated patronage that was advanced to further the cultural education of the people, its dependency on private funding would become a factor in the everyday life of America's museums. Peale's Museum in Philadelphia, on the other hand, was the first significant American museum that emerged from a small picture gallery in 1782 to become a repository for natural curiosities, and during the time it existed in the Pennsylvania State House in 1802 it assumed the status of a major institution.[28] It was unusual in combining fine art and natural history, subjects that would be kept apart in later American museums.

American museums were quick to develop museological trends that were influenced by people with new ideas about setting up 'libraries and institutes', ideas that were enhanced by educated Americans familiar with European museums.[29] The fortuitous development of the Smithsonian Institution during the period 1826–48 was the result of a bequest by an English chemist and mineralogist. Some of the new museums began to advertise dual roles of education and entertainment, which they manifested through displays and activities that led to 'profitable reflection'.[30] Many of these museums would become known as places of learning as well as visitor attractions, a factor that became a key trend in the later twentieth century.

There were reservations about what would happen when European royal cabinets, hitherto accessible only to an elite group of learned connoisseurs and artists, became public institutions openly available to the masses. These qualms were due to the fact that the transfer of private cultural property into public ownership placed a level of genuine responsibility on the museum itself. In 1816, Quatremère de Quincy was the powerful secretary of the Académie des Beaux-Arts in Paris. His understanding of the term 'museum' went back to the original Alexandrian concept and he was sceptical: 'The public has become persuaded that the secret to making the Arts flourish lies in the virtue of these assemblages of works known as *collections, cabinets, museums.* All the nations, in emulation of one another, have made such a singular thing of them.' De Quincy's belief that the museum 'kills art to make [art] history' was a charge that persisted in the annals of museum criticism. History, however, would demonstrate how British and American museums cultivated the arts and the sciences and in so doing would become 'centres of instruction and self-improvement'.[31]

Across Europe and America examples of the modern public museum, as it is understood today, took root and grew at the Rijksmuseum, Amsterdam (1800), at the Prado, Madrid (1819), at the National Gallery, London (1824), at the Altes Museum, Berlin (1830), at the New Hermitage, St Petersburg (1852), at the National Gallery of Ireland (1854), at the Museum of Fine Arts, Boston (1870), and at the Dublin Museum of Science and Art (1877). To be responsible for this physical and mythological heritage was in itself a symbolic function, comparable in secular terms to the responsibility of a priest for the souls of his congregation. Unlike the village curate, however, the museum curator was responsible not to any localized group but to the nation as a whole. Even de Quincy might have been tempted to evince some words of sympathy for nineteenth-century museum administrators as they grappled with the implications of what becoming a 'public institution museum' actually meant.

PART II

The Eighteenth Century

Solomon Williams (fl.1777–1824), *General Charles Vallancey (1725–1812)*
Oil on canvas, 288 x 152 cm. RDS No. 177.

Vallancey was an army engineer, cartographer and antiquarian. Of Huguenot stock, he was a gentleman-connoisseur who became a manager of the Dublin Society Drawing Schools in the later eighteenth century; also chairman of the society's Committee for Fine Arts and Mechanics. Williams, a portrait painter, was a pupil of the Drawing Schools in 1771.

*T*he evocatively named 'cabinets of curiosities' were the sixteenth- to eighteenth-century precursors of museums, examples of which in Ireland were owned by, among others, R.H. Dawson, dean of St Patrick's Cathedral, the antiquarian George Petrie, the Cobbe family and the Belfast Reading Society.[1] These encyclopaedic collections of fantastic and useful objects – minerals, shells, animal specimens, objects of human art and science, clever machines, amazing toys – were stored in cabinets that had separate compartments for valued items, or private chambers (*studiolo*) for displaying works of art. Ellis's Dublin Museum, which opened in Mary Street in 1792, reputedly contained 'a collection of the arts and natural and mechanical rarities'. These collections were a combination of curiosities of scholarly, scientific, precious and strange objects, which, in effect, created a sense of wonder. Those who amassed these collections wanted to explore, discover and learn about strange objects and did so not just for contemplation but as recreational objects – or as 'toys for adults', as Joseph Cornell's late twentieth-century interpretation of this impetus would have it.

While some of the earliest museums, such as the Musaeum of Alexandria, were conceived of as a complement to an existing library, an institution people contributed to and learned from, the word 'museum' consolidated the concept of study, library and academy, placing in coexistence the aspiration to knowledge of the whole world. These early collections, which were destined solely for learned gentlemen, included geological and botanic specimens, ethnograpic and zoological artefacts, antiquities and bygones, all gathered together with the aim of capturing 'the world in miniature'. The French scholar René Huyghe (1906–97), chief curator of paintings and drawings at the Louvre, observed that museums appeared about the same time as dictionaries and encyclopaedias and demonstrated a similar desire for universal knowledge.

The somewhat eccentric, often scholarly and generally encyclopaedic nature of these cabinets led towards the gradual specialization of collections, which occurred in the wake of the French Revolution at the Musée National d'Histoire Naturelle (1793), at the Musée du Louvre (1793), at the Conservatoire National des Arts et Métiers (1794) and at the Musée des Monuments Français (1795–1816). These collections, which were dedicated by subject matter to natural history, works of art, technological progress and national history, demonstrated how museums gradually moved away from the restricted access of heretofore to assume the new shape that was to emerge in the nineteenth century:

> Many choice collections have been occasionally opened under certain regulations in the summer season, and generally there exists a most liberal feeling on the part of the proprietors of valuable galleries and collections of paintings, sculpture, virtu, etc., with respect to the admission of respectable persons who are properly introduced. This is done to a great extent, although it is sometimes attended with inconvenience to the noble and wealthy owners of these valuable possessions.[2]

When James Butler, the 1st Duke of Ormonde, arrived in Dublin as lord lieutenant in 1662, he began a building campaign that would eventually transform the medieval city into a modern metropolis (creating his own castle, 'adorn'd with paintings of great Masters', in his Kilkenny stronghold) and thus paved the way for eighteenth-century developments.[3] By the late eighteenth century the conquest of Ireland had been completed and the new landed class was producing a fresh wave of public building in Dublin, for example the Four Courts (1776–1884), the Custom House (1781–91) and Parliament House extensions (1780s).

Civil unrest in continental Europe after 1789 encouraged Irish and British tourists to turn their attentions to their own countryside, leading to a fashion for romantic landscapes and scenery, a trend supported by both the Dublin Society's and the RIA's promotion of interest in nature, 'gardening, painting and poetry'. The practical and the sublime fused as an enlightened view of nature in Edmund Burke's influential *Philosophical Inquiry into the Origin of Our Ideas of the Sublime and Beautiful* (1756), while *Reflections on the Revolution in France* (1790) demonstrated contrasting views in current philosophy. Tours of Ireland were documented by Irish and overseas visitors, including Bishop Richard Pococke, Judge Edward Willis, Richard Twiss, Arthur Young, Robert Graham and Charles Topham Bowden. As transport improved, travel books highlighted interest in the picturesque, such as William Wilson's *Traveller's Dictionary through Ireland* (1784) and George Tyner's *Traveller's Guide through Ireland* (1794). Although these tourists came to Ireland primarily to view the scenery, they also took in the collections during their visits. When Bowden visited the great houses of Ireland, he noted in his *Tour through Ireland* (1791) that it was Lord Milltown who showed his guests the collections at Russborough House, in Wicklow.

Of course, it was not only in Europe that the eighteenth century unfolded amid violence; it was a period of far-reaching unrest. The American Revolution (1775–83), the French Revolution, and the 1798 United Irishmen rebellion formed a republican triangle that linked America, France and Ireland. However, when the United Irish rising failed and the Act of Union passed in 1800, Georgian Dublin became the second city and a socially desirable capital of the British Empire. The education of the sons of the Ascendancy at universities in Utrecht, Leiden, Edinburgh and Glasgow produced a cultured class with a vested interest in developing the welfare of their countries. Both William Hamilton, who curated the Dublin Society Museum, and William Stephens, who catalogued its collections, were taught at Leiden University, together with Richard Kirwan, who would acquire the Leskean Cabinet. The gradual transition of cabinets of curiosities into early museums was taking place at three Dublin-based learning institutions: Trinity College, the Dublin Society and the RIA. Indeed, when the collections of the Dublin Society museum and library were housed at Leinster House, they would form a tangible expression of the eighteenth-century spirit of Enlightenment.

This spirit was reflected in the brisk book trade of the period, which disseminated Irish publications and texts of the French Enlightenment. It formed an important training ground for new writers, and provided a forum for established authors to discuss political, cultural, educational and ethical issues, and was a source of poems, sketches, reviews, letters, satires, obituaries and advertisements. These created a medium through which intellectuals could carry out discourses on concepts such as 'nationality', the American and French revolutions having encouraged exploration of ideas about 'Irish identity' that would be further developed in the nineteenth century. This in turn created the idea that forms of nationality and nationalism were cultural artefacts of a particular kind, which could be portrayed in the formation of a political movement or in the growth of literary journals or in the emergence of museums – the embodiment of a form of national identity. The presence of culture in this context was seen as something mobile, dynamic and contested, with imagination understood to be at the heart of its creative power.[4] These concepts were crucial to the development of forms of cultural nationalism that would emerge in the next century in political bodies such as Young Ireland, in Irish journals like *The Nation*, and in cultural institutions like the Museum of Science and Art. Thus, the growth of museums formed part of the mechanism for advancing the nation but also became an embodiment of the nation.

2

Early Museological Trends in Eighteenth-Century Ireland

Great honour is due to Ireland for having given birth to the Dublin Society, which has the undisputed merit of being the father of all the similar societies now existing in Europe.[1]

While the wider museum story can be traced back to antiquity, Irish museums have their origins in the late eighteenth century and the triumvirate of institutions that spearheaded the evolution from private collections of curiosities to public museums, namely the Dublin Society, Trinity College and the RIA. A variety of collections, mostly inspired by the work of the Dublin Society but also by that of the RIA, formed the core of these later Irish museums, but what marked out these particular institutions was the emphasis placed on, and the philosophy of education that informed, their growth. The desire for innovation and a willingness to explore were key shared features of these institutions, leading in time to the transferral of collections to the public domain, for the benefit and improvement of the Irish people.

The Dublin Society (1731)

> Thus if th' endeavours of the good and wise
> Can ought avail to make a Nation rise,
> Soon shall Hibernia see her broken statue,
> Repair'd by Arts and Industry, grow great.[2]

In 1731 a group of fourteen writers, physicians and a chemist met in the Philosophical Rooms in Trinity College and instituted 'The Dublin Society for improving Husbandry, Manufactures and other useful Arts'.[3] While learned societies existed across eighteenth-century Europe, the inspiration for this body came from the late seventeenth-century Dublin Philosophical Society (1683–1708), founded by William Molyneux, whose political tract *The Case of Ireland's being Bound by Acts of Parliament in England Stated* (Dublin, 1698) influenced the outlook of men such as Thomas Prior, recognized as the founding father of the Dublin Society, Samuel Madden, Church of Ireland clergyman and wealthy landowner, and Henry Grattan, the Patriot parliamentarian. The Dublin Philosophical Society had established a scientific tradition in Ireland and adopted procedures in common with the Royal Society in London (1660), as a result of which a close relationship was forged between intellectuals in both countries. The Royal Society attracted many Irish thinkers, with scientific discoveries conveyed to Ireland via Sir Thomas Molyneux, the physician brother of William Molyneux.

Thus the Dublin Society became one of the learned bodies that took the Royal Society as its model,[4] although the former primarily had an economic aim. By the late eighteenth century it was held in high regard and had forged links with other learned societies, including the Royal Society of Arts (RSA) (1754), the Royal Society of Edinburgh (1783), the Royal Society of Antiquaries of Scotland (1780), the Lunar Society of Birmingham (*c.*1765), the Manchester Literary and Philosophical Society (1781) and the RIA (1785). When asked to explain the ambiguous make-up of its activities, it defined itself as '... a Society *sui generis*, differing, in the nature of its establishment, from any Society that ever has existed in these, or any other countries'.[5] It acquired prestige from its distinguished membership and from its involvement in the education of Irish people and the improvement of the country. As a result of the society's

Garret Morphy (c.1655–1715/16),
William 4th Viscount Molyneux of Maryborough (c.1655–1717), c.1700
Oil on canvas, 76 x 64 cm. NGI 4151.

As a many-sided figure – philosopher, scientist and member of Parliament for Trinity College Dublin – Molyneux was well known for his celebrated book *Defending Irish Autonomy* (1698).

comprehensive approach in charting the ambitions it set itself, it became one of the most successful Irish Enlightenment bodies of the eighteenth century, from which emerged one of the earliest museums in Ireland.[6]

The Dublin Society was not an intellectual organization; rather it was a body

John van Nost (d.1780), *Bust of Thomas Prior (1682–1751)*

Marble, 68 cm high, inscribed 'John van Nost 1769'. RDS.

Prior, a prime mover in founding the Dublin Society, was its most active promoter and dedicated servant.

that disseminated practical scientific knowledge to artisans and emphasized 'useful' sciences like agriculture, in a manner that would later be emulated by the RSA (1754). As a lack of knowledge was identified as the root of many problems, tuition was communicated through publications and programmes of lectures. In true Enlightenment fashion, members of the Dublin Society wanted to see new knowledge in arts and sciences applied to the economy for the good of society, and to this end established repositories to house the latest machines and models.[7] Prior produced a pamphlet that criticized the practice of landlord absenteeism, *List of Absentees of Ireland* (1729), and promoted economic progress. A landowner and lawyer, Prior counted among his friends influential figures such as Bishop George Berkeley and Johnathan Swift and Philip Dormer Stanhope, 4th Earl of Chesterfield, PC, KG (1694–1773), English statesman, author and diplomat, briefly lord lieutenant and general governor of Ireland (1745–46). Prior's ideas were supported by William Maple, another founding member, who held the post of keeper of Parliament House and acted as the society's registrar from 1731 to 1762.

In 1731 the society's Committee of Arts met with its inaugural president, the lord lieutenant, the Duke of Dorset, in Dublin Castle. The first annual parliamentary grant of £10,000 was made by the Irish House of Commons in 1761. A second grant of £5,000 was made in 1791.[8] The society received its charter in 1750, but was not designated 'Royal' until 1820, when George IV became its patron.[9] Madden, a nephew of Sir Thomas Molyneux, became the society's first patron.

As the society's main concern was agriculture, with members, like its founders, drawn from the landowning class, it was strongly identified with the Ascendancy. This privileged class consisted of about 7,000 families, mostly of English origin and Anglican in religion, many of whom were absentee landlords. In truth, however, the society attracted people from all walks of life, including scientists, clergymen, aldermen, members of parliament, established businessmen, architects and artists. Its membership was comprised of a variety of influential people, such as Arthur Dobbs (1689–1765), member of the Irish Parliament for Carrickfergus, surveyor general of Ireland (1733–43), prospector and governor of North Carolina (1754–65), united in their concern for the economic welfare of the country.

The Dublin Society's unusual position of being a largely private institution would change in the second half of the nineteenth century, when central government realized the extent of its influence and took control of its educational, medical and economic role. Arising directly or indirectly from the society, the next century would see a number of bodies emerge to form its legacy: the Geological Survey (1845), the Royal College of Science (1867), the National Gallery (1854), the National Library and the National Museum (1877), the Botanic Gardens (1800), the Dublin Metropolitan School of Art (1877), the Veterinary College (c.1894–1900) and the first Fisheries branch (1900) of the Department of Agriculture and Technical Instruction. By the time state intervention took place in 1877, the society was already engaged in commercial exhibition activities to supplement its financial independence.

From its inception, the Dublin Society gave its greatest support by means of premiums (money awards), medals and awards towards improving home- and factory-based industries, such as linen, wool, silk, printing, earthenware, tanning and lace-making, which reflected the pragmatic, public-spirited approach of its founders. Madden proposed his own premium system, based on one he had suggested to Trinity College in his *Proposal for the General Encouragement of Learning in Dublin College* (1731). The practice of awarding premiums to inventors had been in place since 1710, having been offered under an Act of Parliament by the Irish Linen Board. Madden believed that people with means should use their wealth in an altruistic manner. One of his publications, *Reflections and Resolutions Proper for the Gentlemen of Ireland as to Their Conduct for the Service of Their Country* (1738), suggested improving

Rev. Dr Samuel Madden (1686–1765)
*Engraved by Richard Purcell (fl.1746–66), after an oil of 1755 by Robert Hunter
(fl.1745–1803). Published: W. Allen, Dublin. Mezzotint, 34.1 x 25.4 cm (2nd state), NGI 10,924.*

Hunter was 'intimate with Madden and Prior', and the print shows Madden's interest in learning
and the arts from the library and oval painting in the background.

the condition of Ireland by means of a scheme (supplementing society awards)
executed through a system of public competition for premiums. His proposal
(anonymously published in *A Letter to the Dublin Society on the Improving
Their Fund and the Manufactures and Tillage of Ireland*) was accepted by the
Dublin Society in 1739, and administered separately from the society's own

awards. As a result of this scheme, talent was fostered and progress made in the fields of painting, sculpture, lace and industry.[10]

The society's broad understanding of the requirements of eighteenth-century Irish life was demonstrated in its recognition of the need for training in drawing. Berkeley promoted the concept of art training in *The Querist* (1735): 'the annual expense of such an academy need stand the public in above two hundred pounds a year.'[11] According to W.G. Strickland, the first premium was awarded in 1741 to Susanna Drury for four watercolours of the Giant's Causeway (engraved in 1744), for which she received £25; other premiums were awarded later that year.[12] The success of the scheme encouraged the lord lieutenant to allocate an annual grant of £500 in 1746, which led to the society establishing a drawing school.[13] The society's premium system ran to the end of the century and informed practices at the RSA (1754).[14] The society's involvement in industry grew in the nineteenth century with the instigation of art and industrial exhibitions, promoting and selling products, and demonstrated its commitment to supporting employment in local industries as a means of improving the economy.

Early Museum Initiatives: Dublin Society Repository (1733) and Museum (1792)

It was the spirit of the Enlightenment and the desire to disseminate scientific knowledge that guided the formation of an agricultural repository: 'Whatever, therefore, tends, by the cultivation of the useful arts and sciences to improve and facilitate its manufactures cannot but prove of the greatest national advantage.'[15] The repository set up by the Dublin Society in 1733 was the first in a series of steps that eventually led to the formation of a museum in 1792, and illustrated the close relationship that existed between the Dublin Society and the Royal Society. 'Museum' was understood in the sense of the time: a collection of instruments or specimens for the purpose of research and often referred to, as in the case of Hans Sloane's cabinet, as being of 'natural and other curiosities'.[16] The repository was a demonstration centre for agricultural implements and was described as the earliest example 'in Great Britain or Ireland, of the formation of an agricultural museum'.[17]

In order to house the repository, the society interceded with the lords justices of the Irish Parliament for 'the use of a vault under the Parliament

House (now Bank of Ireland, College Green) for the laying up of our instruments'.[18] The space was needed to store the agricultural implements so that they could be viewed by artisans, tradesmen and other interested parties. The repository opened on 22 February 1733, with permission to carry out experiments relating to agricultural machinery at Parliament House and to leave the machines and models in the vaults.[19] The first stone of Parliament House had been laid only in 1729, so the society was among its earliest occupants. That the society was able to secure permission to admit the public twice a week, literally under the aegis of the Parliament ('the messenger attend the Parliament House ... to exhibit the machines to gentlemen that may be desirous to see them'[20]), was aided by the fact that it counted parliamentarians among its early members. Six of the founder members were MPs and nine were graduates of Dublin University, including Maple, who as keeper of Parliament House was in a position to facilitate Dublin Society meetings taking place there for twenty-six years. (Some early meetings of the committee of the Dublin Society took place at the Anne Coffee House at Essex Bridge to adjudicate Society premiums.)

The establishment of the repository is charted through the minute books, an initiative also later emulated by the RSA.[21] The repository housed bulky machinery that demanded adequate space for display and storage. The surviving records show that basic museological trends were in place, including: access – 'Garrod attend from 12.00–2.00 every Monday and Thursday to show the instruments free gratis';[22] organization – 'the times of the Messenger's attendance to show the instruments'[23]; and safe keeping – 'none of the models or instruments be lent out by the Messenger without the order of the Board'.[24] Duplicates were required for lending 'of such instruments and models as the Society most approve of to the intention that one of them be always seen at the Parliament House'.[25] Documentation was compiled – 'take a catalogue of the instruments and models belonging to the Society' – as were condition reports, – 'once in three or six months a review of the several instruments and report the state they find them'.[26] Access and security were ongoing issues: 'Brooks the Messenger be allowed the same salary ... for attending extraordinary days'; instructions were given to remove 'instruments lying in the Society's House to the vaults of Parliament House for their better security'.[27]

The educational activities of the society in relation to agriculture expanded in tandem with the repository. In 1749 John Cam instructed farmers at a time of decline in agriculture;[28] during the period 1764–73, John Wynn Baker, the English farmer and improver, wrote about agriculture and demonstrated new techniques at his farm in Celbridge, County Kildare; and the English agriculturalist Arthur Young, an authority on social and agricultural conditions in Ireland, was unstinting in his praise of the Dublin Society for improving agriculture and industry in the country.

Following its tenure at Parliament House (and one meeting at Dublin Castle, in December 1731), the society purchased a city site at Mecklenburgh Street (now Railway Street), where a meeting was held on 19 April 1739. The land, however, was unsuitable for a botanic garden and the space was relinquished in 1740.[29] In 1757 the society leased premises at Shaw's Court on Dame Street (the current site of the Central Bank), but left in 1767 after these too were deemed unsatisfactory.[30] New, purpose-built premises on Grafton Street (numbers 112–13) were acquired (1767–96), adjoining Navigation House (then home of the RIA) and opposite Trinity College's Provost's House. A contemporary report describes the Grafton Street premises:

> Over the meeting room is a library and repository for mechanical models, save those relative to husbandry, which are displayed in another place belonging to the Society. Behind the house are the Society's drawing schools, where children of indigent persons are educated in the arts of drawing, in architecture, ornament, and the human figure.[31]

Around 1781 the society began acquiring lands in the vicinity of Poolbeg Street to erect a warehouse and ultimately to construct a classic-fronted building that would remain in the society's possession until 1820 (when it would be the site of the Theatre Royal, and today the site is occupied by Hawkins House). The enlarged premises housed the repository and its growing collection of minerals, fossils, books on natural history and husbandry, and advertisements were published informing the public to this effect. The society continued to use the Grafton Street premises after 1786, but in 1796 moved to Hawkins Street, where it resided until 1820, when the premises were taken

Samuel Woolley (c.1773–1802),
The House of Lords Portico in Parliament House, Dublin, 1782
SAM WOOLLEY. 1797.
Watercolour, 40.3 x 53.8 cm. NGI 2652.

The Dublin Society met in Parliament House, in the vaults of which the Agricultural Repository was housed.

over by the Theatre Royal. According to contemporary accounts, it was here that the society built 'an edifice for their Repository, Laboratory, Galleries, Library etc.' A visitor noted the enterprise on 23 July 1802.

> spent a leisure hour with much pleasure at the Dublin Society Buildings which are nearly finished and the principal museums are open to the public ... Strangers are brought into a fine gallery of great length principally intended for sculpture and furnished with a large number of casts from the most celebrated busts and statues ... the pupils of the figure academy are at work in this gallery sketching from the sculpture ... Beyond the museums, a superb apartment of great extent ... is finishing for the annual exhibitions of the Arts, and new libraries, board

rooms are preparing, which when finished, will convey to strangers a grand idea of the plans of the Society.[32]

Strickland described the facilities as spacious and practical: the Bust Gallery was 91 feet long by 30 feet wide, the Exhibition Room was 67 feet by 29 feet and was perhaps, next to the Louvre, 'the finest exhibition room in Europe'.[33] The exhibitions were reported regularly: 'On Saturday the 25th of May 1811, the annual Exhibition of native Artists commenced at the Dublin Society house.'[34]

The society purchased Leinster House in 1815 and began the process of moving, leaving the repository *in situ* at Hawkins Street until 1820, while gradually moving the natural history material to its new home at Leinster House. The nature of the society's collections had begun to expand in the later eighteenth century:

> The Museum of the Dublin Society in Hawkins Street is really become a most useful and entertaining repository of improvements in the several mechanical arts that tend to promote agriculture and manufactures, and for which purpose a great number of the best and most approved models of modern invention are exhibited and disposed in the different chambers for the inspection of the public; nor are architectural improvements neglected, for there is a model of the famous Corn-Market in Paris to be seen with its ground plan accurately executed. A compendious and choice library of books that treat of the useful arts makes a conspicuous part of this scientific and truly rational receptacle devised with judgment and executed with taste.[35]

The growing geological and mineralogical collections at Hawkins Street led the society to make moves towards setting up a natural history museum. Scotsman Donald Stewart (an itinerant geologist by profession) was employed by the Agricultural Committee to search for minerals and fossil specimens in the counties of Dublin, Wicklow, Wexford, Waterford, Clare and Longford between 1786 and 1794. He listed his findings in 'Museum

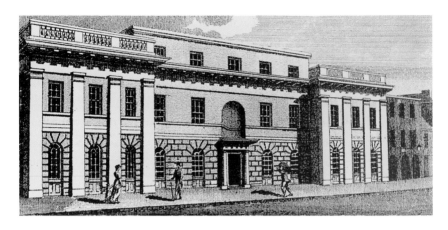

The west front of the Dublin Society's Hawkins House, 1801
Hibernia Magazine, 1801.

Hibernicum, A Catalogue of Irish Minerals in the Museum of the Royal Dublin Society', subsequently printed as 'The Report of Donald Stewart Itinerant Mineralogist', an 'imperfect sketch of Mr. Stewart's itinerary'.[36]

A new era of museum collecting had begun early in 1792 when the society set up a committee to acquire the celebrated mineralogy collection known as the Leskean Cabinet, the purpose of which was to advance mineralogical knowledge in Ireland. This collection had been acquired by Nathaniel Gottfried Leske, professor of natural history at Marburg in Germany, and had been arranged by him between 1782 and 1787 as a seventeenth-century cabinet of curiosity. Richard Kirwan was asked by the society to purchase the cabinet for the sum of £1,350 (an immense figure for this period), provided by an Act of Parliament (32 Geo III. C.14). Kirwan had been introduced to the Dublin Society by General Charles Vallancey, a military surveyor and fellow of the Royal Society. The enthusiasm of Kirwan, a well-known figure in European intellectual circles and the most eminent Irish scientist of the time, was a positive factor in the transfer of the Leskean Cabinet to Dublin in 1792. The mineralogical content of the cabinet, noted below, was the most significant element:

> External character of minerals.
> Classification of minerals.
> Earth's internal structure (or geological).

Mineralogical geography.
Economical mineralogy.[37]

In the society's 1798 catalogue the Leskean Cabinet was described by Dietrich Ludwig Gustavus Karsten[38] as a mineral history of three countries. It comprised 7,331 mineral specimens, shells, anatomical preparations of natural history together with a herbarium and botanical collection.[39] Kirwan reported on 8 November 1792 that the cabinet was lodged in Hawkins Street and he set about examining the contents, aware of the systematic arrangement of collections advocated by Carl Linnaeus as 'the most complete system of natural history'. He reported on his work in the second edition of his *Elements of Mineralogy* (1784, reprinted 1794–6).[40] The catalogue of the Leskean Cabinet, known as the 'Museum of Minerals', was translated into English by George Mitchell (1766–1803), who was friendly with Kirwan and with whom he had made collecting trips in the south of Ireland over several summers.[41]

The importance of the acquisition lay not only in the mineralogical content of the Leskean Cabinet but in the momentum it provided to build up collections for a natural history museum. It stimulated the society's members to amass geological specimens and mineral cabinets, many of which were gifted to the museum, and it was augmented by donations from the geological traveller, the Reverend George Graydon (*c.*1753–1803). Having already gifted Italian geological specimens to the RIA, Graydon approved of these being annexed to the Leskean Cabinet.[42] In 1794 the society allocated funds to extend the Hawkins Street premises, with two rooms provided for the collections – one for the Leskean Cabinet and the other for Irish specimens – and a chemical laboratory and lecture room to seat hundreds of people. A curator was procured: 'Resolved, that as Mr. Kirwan a member of the committee has recommended Mr. Higgins for the aforesaid purpose, the committee are of the opinion he should be appointed to the same.'[43]

The appointment of the chemist William Higgins led to the commencement of the extensive lecture programmes that would dominate the society's activities for the next eighty years. In 1795, when Higgins was appointed professor of chemistry and mineralogy at the Dublin Society, the Leskean Cabinet was placed under his care and he became the first professional staff member of the museum. Higgins's role was 'to assist in the arranging' of the minerals and to 'undertake the care and preservation of them hereafter', together with assisting in the chemical experiments carried out under the direction of Kirwan. The facility was open to students, albeit with special rules printed up regulating admission. Advertisements attesting to the laboratory's

William Cuming (1769–1852), Portrait of Richard Kirwan PRIA, 1813
Oil on canvas, 123 x 100 cm. RIA.

Kirwan, who was born at Cregg Castle, his family home in County Galway, assisted in the acquisition of the Leskean mineralogical collection in 1792, which he arranged and catalogued.

practical instruction appeared in *Saunders' Newsletter* and *Hibernian Journal* of 1797.[44] In 1802 a diarist commented that in the Museum, 'The apartments are very elegantly built rooms of great height, lighted by lantern skylights and appropriated to the Animal and Mineral Kingdoms … I did not examine half the curious specimens they contain.'[45]

Towards the end of the century the society began reviewing its work and, in doing so, decided to abandon the premium system, which had helped in the setting up of schools of drawing and science. Assisted by state funding, the collections had grown, to the stage where the museum was bursting at the seams with antiquities and natural history material. Contemporary with these developments was the growth of antiquities at the RIA museum and the procurement of collections for the purpose of teaching scientific subjects at Maynooth College (founded 1795) and at TCD. Meanwhile, the society's collection, including the Leskean Cabinet, was catalogued by Bernard O'Reilly in 1813 as 'Subjects of Natural History in the Museum of the Dublin Society'.[46] Fresh accommodation was needed, as an anonymous Dublin connoisseur and amateur artist, possibly a member of the Tighe family from County Wicklow (due to the fact that it was presented to the RIA by a member of the Tighe family in 1861), noted: 'The rooms are surrounded with galleries and these are filling up with glass cases.'[47] The stage was set for the foundation of the Natural History Museum in the mid-1800s.

Early Education Initiatives: The Dublin Society Drawing Schools

In order to appreciate fully the nineteenth-century growth in museums, it is helpful to examine the background to the Dublin Society Drawing Schools, together with their context within education in late eighteenth- and early nineteenth-century Ireland. The opening of a private drawing academy by Robert West in 1743 initiated professional drawing tuition in Dublin. West, 'an artist who had studied in Paris and was an accomplished draughtsman … [opened his] school in George's Lane [now South Great George's Street]'.[48] At the same time the Dublin Society was developing its broader enlightenment role in teaching programmes of botany, husbandry, philosophy, agriculture, industry and science. The society's educational enterprise formed part of a range of agencies at work in eighteenth-century Ireland, providing general instruction to the populace, to interested landowners and to entrepreneurs.

Although the majority of the rural population in the eighteenth century received no formal education, those who did attended private enterprise pay schools, known as hedge schools, until a state-funded system was put in place in the nineteenth century. Education was nonetheless a cause of parliamentary concern, the outcome of which was a plethora of commissions, reports and government documents. In a time (mainly the nineteenth century) of limited opportunity, the specialized form of drawing training provided by the society was much sought after because tuition was free and based in Dublin, plus there was the possibility of students securing work as qualified craftsmen, and draughtsmen were headhunted through the society. Students progressed through their respective industries at home, or travelled to Britain or America.

In wider terms, the role of education received a boost due to the emergence of the child onto the social radar in the eighteenth century. For the first time Irish society started to view children as rational individuals who needed an organized process of training for their complete formation. However, eighteenth-century society also expected tradesmen (like the students of the Dublin Society school) to begin their craft in workshops in their early teens and then go into trades. For parents of the better-placed families, literacy was an issue that drew them to the works of the French philosopher Jean-Jacques Rousseau and the essays of Richard and Maria Edgeworth. Published in 1798, *Essays on Practical Education* was the first full-scale Irish treatise on education, winning the Edgeworths an international reputation. The father–daughter team outlined contemporary practice, noting that 'To make any progress in the art of education it must be patiently reduced to an experimental science' requiring a comprehensively planned system, including teacher-training.[49] Maria was interested in museums and made a point of visiting them on her travels, while Richard's experiments with mechanics led to his election as an honorary member of the Dublin Society.

Literacy was much desired throughout Europe in the eighteenth century. Books and magazines were sought through libraries and reading rooms, with newspaper advertisements aimed specifically at children, 'good little Masters and Misses'.[50] Indeed newspapers, which were used to advertise the services of Dublin Society artists and art dealers, were as numerous as printers and booksellers, and included: *Dublin Intelligence, Dublin Weekly Journal, Saunders' Newsletter, Pue's Occurrences, Weekly Courant, Whalley's News Letter, Dublin*

Adam Buck (1759–1833), *Portrait of the Edgeworth Family*, 1787
Coloured pencil, watercolour and graphite on paper, 25.1 x 30.4 cm. NGI 2006.14.

This silhouette is of Richard Lovell Edgeworth (1744–1817), an improving landlord, engineer, educationalist and writer, and his family. Depicted is Richard and his eldest daughter, the writer Maria Edgeworth (1767–1849), together with his third wife, Elizabeth Sneyd, and nine of their children. He was to have four wives and twenty-two children.

Packet, and *Freeman's Journal*. While the majority were devoted to English and European news, as the century progressed the tone of many papers became patriotic, with writers turning their attention to politics rather than literature, it being the age of political pamphlets in Ireland.[51]

The type of general schooling available in Ireland at this time included Protestant parish schools (set up under the law of Henry VIII) and Quaker and Huguenot schools, which were concerned with maintaining their own cultural identity. The Charity schools (*fl.*1700–30) and the Charter schools (founded in 1733) are among the best-documented eighteenth-century educational movements. The former were based on workhouse schools (developed by the English philosopher John Locke), coinciding with the growth of industry but catering for only a fraction of children of school-going age. By the close of the eighteenth century, the teaching provided for children in

Matthew William Peters (1742–1814), *Self-Portrait with Robert West,* **1758**
Charcoal and white chalk on paper, 42.4 x 54.9 cm. NPG 2169. National Portrait Gallery, London.

Robert West drew on French influences as the first master of the Dublin Society Figure School:
'Old West was the best drawer in red chalks at Paris, for his time, and that for drawing in general he was the best scholar of Van Loo.' A high standard in drawing and pastel was a by-
product of the school. As none of West's drawings survive, this chalk portrait by Peters, a
pupil of West, traces the influence of his teacher.

hedge schools (some into young adulthood) represented rural oral education
in Ireland.[52] The teachers were poor, the standard of education varied, with
minimal reading, writing and arithmetic, and a third of the pupils were
female, as literacy was required for employment as housekeepers, governess-
es, working in shops, etc.[53] Some post-primary instruction, which focused on
numeracy and literacy, was provided by voluntary societies and endowed foundations, and was augmented by that of the Dublin Society Drawing Schools.

The impetus behind the founding of the drawing schools was clear: 'Since
a good spirit shows itself for drawing and designing which is the ground-
work of painting and is so useful in manufactures, it is intended to erect a
little academy or schools of drawing and painting.'[54] Having an interest in
West's work, the society arranged with him to instruct twelve boys in his

academy. By 1750, however, the society had taken over West's school: 'The next formal meeting of the Society took place on 15 November 1757 in the Academy for Drawing in Shaw's Court.' The school was supported by Madden's premium scheme for children under the age of fifteen, which provided the first Irish student award system for proficiency in drawing. Many students in employment were allowed time off to attend classes.

A contemporary account stated:

> There has been lately opened an Academy for Drawing and Design, erected in Shaw's Court in Dame Street, at the expense of the Dublin Society, which is furnished with several fine models in plaster imported from Paris. In which Academy pupils have already made very considerable progress both in drawing from the round and also from the life, a design, which, we hope, must show itself in the forms and elegancy of several of our manufactures.[55]

The schools were free, and subsequently marked the arrival of state-sponsored art education in Ireland by means of an annual grant towards salaries and maintenance.

Art education was important in improving the level of taste in the country and in providing craftsmen to decorate the city's fine Georgian buildings. The traditional master–apprentice system undertaken by the Dublin Guild of Cutlers, Painter-Steyners and Stationers had links with the Dublin Society.[56] Other initiatives included that instigated by John Esdall, who set out his stall in the *Daily Advertiser* on 24 August 1736: 'Drawing is the mistress of all the manual arts and masonry, carving, stucco-forming, jewellery, furniture and damask weaving.'[57] Strickland noted that 'John Esdall, of Crow Street, issued an advertisement in *Faulkner's Journal*, October 1744, and describing himself as a "face painter", announced his intention of opening an academy for instruction in painting and drawing'.[58] The same John Esdall was advertised by Langford (a London auctioneer) as a dealer: 'selling at Mr. Esdall's … a collection formed by Mr. Samuel Paris in Italy and France etc consisting of the most eminent Italian, French, Flemish and Spanish masters'.[59] William Bertrand (*fl*.1765–70) opened a school in 1765,[60] together with another French artist, Pierre Mondale Lesac,[61] whose services were promoted in 1736: 'Lesac hereby advertises the nobility and gentry that he will teach pupils … to draw from nature; copy curious pieces.'[62] None of these initiatives provided structured training like the Dublin Society, however.

While education and philanthropy were part of the story of the society's drawing schools, it was sound economics that provided the main reason for their establishment. The society's founders recognized the need to train young people to outline plans, make elevations and design fabric patterns in order to qualify for employment in the trades, to become architects, sculptors, engravers, glass-cutters, porcelain manufacturers, cabinetmakers, surveyors and engineers. This practice had originated in Europe, where drawing had formed the foundation of art education since the Renaissance. The role of the antique and the influence of Greek art encouraged the Greek Revival architectural style (influenced by the arrival and display in London in 1816 of the Elgin Marbles) and produced an emergent neo-classical style. Publications emphasized the need for drawing as a prerequisite for a career in art.[63] The society's schools differed from the European drawing tradition, however, where art academies taught the fine arts, both figure drawing and painting. This was not the case in Dublin, as Anthony Pasquin pointed out: 'The Fine Arts have never been cultivated in Ireland, with that strong attention and encouragement which is necessary to produce eminent professors: there are two reasons … the poverty of the nation, and the consequent want of illumination in the general orders of its inhabitants.'[64]

By contrast, France derived benefit from its artistic products due to the superb training of its artisans. In the mid-seventeenth century the French had set up the Écoles Gratuit de Dessin (free drawing schools) to establish drawing as a prerequisite for craftwork. In these schools tuition included the copying of casts and ornamental prints, with life drawing helping the student to master the figure for fabric design, carved and plastered panels and ceramic decoration. The French government supported an industrial school set up by Jean-Jacques Bachelier in 1762, which flourishes to this day under the name *École Nationale Supérieure des Arts Décoratifs* (ENSAD).[65] The European experience did inform the Dublin schools, however. It was the recognition that the French dominated the production of European quality craft products that led the society to form its drawing schools. Madden and

Prior understood the contribution that qualified artists in industry and design could make to the prosperity of the country, a view shared by Berkeley and Swift, who saw the arts as a step towards a more civilized way of life. Therefore, the economic considerations underpinning eighteenth-century European academies were appreciated by the society's founders, who hoped that their drawing schools would improve the archaic economy.[66]

The society established four schools, all based on practical teaching methods. The first focused on figure drawing (1746), where the primary concern was the study of ancient art, involving the idealization of the human form, a concept developed during the Italian Renaissance when there was a return to the study of Roman antiquities. Drawing was the mainstay of academic teaching and under West's tuition students would copy the features of the face and limbs from the flat (engravings), sometimes learning measurements

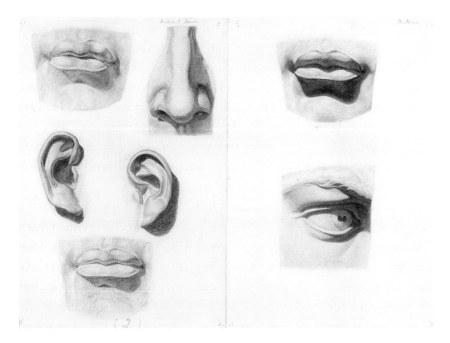

Robert Howis (nineteenth century), *Myron's Diskobolos*
Charcoal on paper, 75 x 54 cm. Signed R.Howis. NGI 19,161.

As the nineteenth-century Irish artist Robert Howis shows, the copying of antique casts was a standard part of art education. The mastering of drawing from cast collections was essential before drawing from life. This was one of many Dublin Society drawings used for teaching purposes, later transferred by the National Museum to the National Gallery.

by heart. A French innovation was the study of human expression, copied from engravings, following which the student would undertake copies from the round (plaster casts), accompanied by talks on anatomy. The final stage was the life class, where, using the *objet d'art* donations to the society, the student had the opportunity to draw from a wide range of antique sculpture casts. West's successor at the School of Figure Drawing, Jacob Ennis (his leading pupil), was appointed in 1763, followed by West's son, Francis, in 1770.

A decade later the need for further types of instruction emerged, which led to the founding of the second school, Landscape and Ornament, in 1756. It provided training to educate the designer, who was the person who made drawings for the decorative arts (following which the craftworker realized the drawings). The School of Landscape and Ornament was set up under the artist James Mannin, succeeded by John James Barralet, who acted as temporary master until the appointment of William Waldron in 1779. This school was the best attended of the four schools, being a fine art and design school in one, while the premiums awarded for landscape were the most substantial, resulting in the growth of this area and commissions for artists, such as Thomas Roberts (1748–77) and George Barret (1728/30–54), to paint views of country demesnes.

The third school, which opened in 1764, concerned itself with architectural drawing and design. It was established under the Cork-born architect Thomas Ivory, whose influence 'on the training of a generation of craftsmen' was incalculable. Ivory's conservative taste was illustrated by the purchase, in 1767, of a seventeenth-century treatise on perspective, a book on rococo designs and James Gibbs's *Book of Architecture* of 1728.[67] Ivory died in 1786 and was succeeded the following year by Henry Aaron Baker. A young woman who visited Hawkins Street in 1801–2 described the teaching method: 'The pupils of the figure academy are at work in this gallery sketching from the sculpture, for which purpose the several pedestals are furnished with rollers by which their position can be readily changed.'[68]

The fourth school, Modelling and Sculpture, was the smallest of the schools and was added in 1811, under the leading Irish sculptor Edward Smyth, to teach boys sculpture using modelling in clay. It was a useful school because modelling was used in working silver, stucco ornament, carving in wood and moulding figures in metal. Students modelled reliefs from the flat, drew and

James Barry (1741–1806), *Portrait of Edmund Burke, Statesman, Orator, c.*1774
Oil on canvas, 127 x 99 cm. NGI 128.

The Cork-born artist James Barry, a late eighteenth-century history painter, would become a founder member of the Royal Academy, London (1868). Edmund Burke (1729–97), who was an advocate of the Dublin Society Drawing Schools, sponsored Barry's five-year trip to France and Italy (1765–71).

modelled from the antique and then modelled from life using the society's plaster casts of hands and arms, friezes and mouldings and its collection of antique casts.

In effect, the four schools were departments of one Dublin Society institution, which provided free tuition and was managed through an elected Fine Arts Committee until a headmaster was appointed in 1849.[69] During the schools' early years, many old master drawings were acquired for copying, together with a collection of antique casts, augmented by drawing manuals such as Robert Dodsley's *The Preceptor* (1749). It was only later that the pupils learned to paint in oils in the studio of established artists, as the technique was not taught in Ireland at any public institution until the nineteenth century. A student at the society's School of Figure Drawing in the 1750s commented on the main influences: 'We were early familiarized to the antique in sculpture, and in painting to the style and manner of the great Italian and French masters.'[70] As a consequence: 'The close links between French designs and the applied ornament that appears in Irish rococo plasterwork, in silver chasing, and on furniture carving is the result of these sources.'[71] The society's emphasis on drawing produced high-quality Irish craftsmanship in mezzotint scraping, surveying and pastel drawing, skills that would be evident in later museum collections.

The Drawing School Collections

The formation of the Drawing School collections began with early gifts from Lord Charlemont following his Grand Tour, augmented by casts from Lord Duncannon in 1757, who was aware of prevailing academic theories: 'The art of designing was of the greatest use, not only in the polite arts but through every manufacture, which the French have proved since the establishment of the Academy by supplying almost the whole world with their fashion.'[72] The finest cast was undoubtedly a copy of the figurative group the *Laocoön*, from the original held in the Vatican, which was presented in 1790 by David La Touche and enabled tutors at the school to stress the importance of drawing as a core subject, illustrated in the perfection of Greek and Roman art.[73]

The society's concern for a basic teaching collection of antique casts was in line with European neo-classical art educational practice, which encouraged the acquisition of model drawings, Renaissance figure drawings and French landscape drawings. George Robertson, for example, presented busts copied from the Vatican collection in 1800: *Tiber*, *The Dying Alexander*, *Daphne* and *The Genius*; Sackville Hamilton gifted a figure cast of *Ganymede* in 1801; John Vernon donated antique medals and coins; Henry Hamilton presented a cast of the *Apollo Belvedere*; and the society acquired a set of casts of the Elgin Marbles, ordered in 1816.[74] The move to the Hawkins Street premises in 1796–7 resulted in Smyth being engaged 'to repair the statues and busts' so that the students could study in the exhibition gallery, which, with its coved ceiling and ornamental cornice lit by a long skylight, was ideal for displaying sculpture.[75]

A committee arranged the society's collection in the Hawkins Street exhibition gallery, together with works on loan from private collectors,

Hugh Douglas Hamilton (1740–1808), *Young Gentleman in Rome*, *c.***1790**
Oil on canvas, 93.5 x 66.3 cm.
NGI 4596.

This accomplished full-length portrait is typical of the work the artist produced for Irish and British Grand Tourists on their sejourn in Italy. The young man is standing on the Palatine Hill in Rome. Following training at the Dublin Society Drawing Schools and a successful career in London, Hamilton spent nine years in Rome, before returning to settle in Dublin.

including 'paintings, prints, natural curiosities and models' purchased from Ellis's Dublin Museum in 1810.[76] It proved to be the finest exhibition space in the city, with shows of Irish art held there up to 1819. A description dating to 1802 notes: 'Paintings on the hall and staircases. Strangers are brought into a fine gallery of great length principally intended for sculpture and furnished with a large number of casts from the most celebrated busts and statues; amongst the latter are famous *chefs d'ouvres* of antiquity.'[77]

The Irish Parliament's grant support of the Dublin Society enabled many impoverished young people to acquire training that ultimately led to employment.[78] For example, the education afforded to George Barret, a draper's son, and to Hugh Douglas Hamilton, a peruke-maker's son, led to their careers as famous artists, who were patronized by nineteenth-century Irish collectors, with their works ending up in Irish museums. (Sons of the landed gentry, on the other hand, acquired private tuition from established painters, having access to greater educational opportunities overseas.) Thus the society's schools heralded state intervention in art education prior to the schools of design in London. Their collection ultimately found its way into the NGI.

'Living Museum': The Dublin Society's Botanic Garden (1795)
Between 1790 and 1795 the Irish Parliament also provided grants for the

establishment of new botanic gardens at Glasnevin in Dublin. This was during a critical phase of the society's expansion, when educational concerns were manifest at all stages of its enterprise: agriculture, industry, drawing schools and museums. On foot of the grants received and at the behest of Parliament (in all probability effected through Parliament by Speaker John Foster), the society established the Botanic Gardens in 1795[79] with members encouraged to support the venture with gifts of seeds and plants.

By early 1796 the society had taken possession of land at Glasnevin, spending £500 on the grounds and a house. Its Committee of Agriculture asked Walter Wade, professor of botany at the Dublin Society, to arrange the gardens. He had earlier campaigned for a botanic garden, publishing a catalogue of the plants of Dublin, which was praised by Lady Kane as 'the first in Ireland under a systematic arrangement'.[80] An important aspect of the Botanic Gardens was its role in 'promoting a scientific knowledge in the various branches of agriculture'. This meant constructing a Linnaean garden, with sections on herbaceous plants and shrub fruit together with forest tree plants.[81]

Thomas Roberts (1748–77), *Lucan House and Demesne, County Dublin,*
with Figures Quarrying Stone, c.1773–5
Oil on canvas, 60.6 x 99.8 cm. NGI 4463.

This highly finished view of the house and demesne of Agmondisham Vesey was executed by Thomas Roberts, considered the finest Irish landscape painter of the late eighteenth century. Roberts had attended the Dublin Society School of Landscape and Ornament.

The Botanic Gardens opened to the public in 1800. In its inaugural year admittance was free, but the following year 'admission for non-members would be by ticket only', although members could introduce visitors at any time.[82] Once the gardens were up and running, Wade began developing his educational work by holding courses of public lectures in 1802, the syllabus for which was published in the society's *Transactions*, a practice maintained for most Dublin Society lectures. Wade's active promotion of botany as a captivating subject created genuine interest, with lectures on the history of botany followed by practical sessions, during which each classification of plant was examined and examples dissected. It became the manifestation of a form of 'living museum'. Wade delivered his botanical lectures accompanied by notes between 1802 and 1823, in addition to teaching apprentices at the Botanic Gardens and giving talks at the society's lecture theatre in Leinster House.[83] The establishment of the Botanic Gardens fulfilled one of the society's vital aims: to promote botany and science. Its significance lay in its genuine educational remit in providing research facilities, public lectures and botanical publications.

The Dublin Society's late eighteenth-century enterprise in agriculture, industry, science and education became increasingly significant in Irish life as the society became a learned body receiving financial support from the government, preserving, under the Union with Britain, the tasks entrusted to it by the Irish Parliament in the early nineteenth century. The society set out its activities in a comprehensive manner, putting structures in place that would form the foundations of many economic, cultural and educational institutions: the Agricultural Repository and its collections moved Ireland towards a natural history museum; the Drawing Schools trained artists whose works would hang in Irish museums; its drawing collection would devolve to the National Gallery. In the late eighteenth century, Ireland was on the threshold of a new era of museum foundation and collection, the success of which was largely due to the foresight and generosity of the founders and members of the Dublin Society.

Dublin University Museum (1777)

University education in eighteenth-century Ireland was confined to TCD,

The Old University Museum, Regent House, Trinity College, Dublin
Engraved by W.B. Taylor (1781–1850) and Robert Havell (fl.1800–40) after a drawing by
W.B Taylor. Published: W.B. Taylor, Dublin, 1 October 1819.
Etching and aquatint with watercolour, 33 x 37 cm. NGI 11,622.

the sole constituent college of the University of Dublin, founded by
Elizabeth I in 1592 as the College of the Holy and Undivided Trinity of
Queen Elizabeth near Dublin. (The titles Trinity College and University of
Dublin are used interchangeably.)

TCD had long been identified as the intellectual bastion of the Ascendancy,
but its position became gradually more precarious as the question of university
education became identified as a sectarian issue in nineteenth-century politics.
In addition, while Catholics had been excluded from taking qualifications at
TCD since 1637, legislation enacted in 1793 allowed them to take degrees,
although not to be eligible for scholarships or fellowships. (St Patrick's College,
Maynooth, founded in 1795 specifically for the training of student Catholic
priests, admitted lay students for a period in the nineteenth century.) The
college campus lay at the heart of Dublin city, with an impressive range of
buildings surrounding its three squares: Parliament Square, the Library
Square and Botany Bay Square.

The Dublin University Museum was established in 1777, after completion of the rebuilding of the west front of the college.[84] In fact, the university had a small geological collection in the late 1690s, described by John Dunton (a London bookseller) on a visit to the library as 'the thigh bone of a giant … manuscripts, medals and other curiosities'.[85] Regent House, where the museum was housed, had been built by late 1758, effectively a public works project since it was paid for entirely by Parliament and referred to in contemporary account books as 'Parliament Buildings'.[86] The eighteenth-century origins of the museum, according to the philosopher Ludwig Wittgenstein, derived from a background associated with 'the Protestant Ascendancy'.[87]

University collections differed from museum and private collections in their shaping of knowledge and understanding of science, giving them the unique character of being formed for instruction. The Dublin University Museum (forerunner of the present Geological Museum and Zoological Museum) was founded to house, among other items, a large collection of Polynesian artefacts collected during Captain James Cook's final two voyages.[88] The major credit for the setting up of the museum must go to the Reverend William Hamilton, who was elected a fellow of Trinity in 1779 at the age of twenty-four.[89] His appointment as 'its first curator' in 1780 was a significant step, and he expanded the collection by taking on loan antiquities from the RIA (of which he was an early member) on its establishment in 1785.[90] The RIA minute books for 1785 record the transfer of antiquities to the museum.[91] Geological specimens, such as those donated by Graydon in 1794, were used for teaching purposes. (Graydon had gathered Italian volcanic samples to demonstrate the similarities between specimens found in Antrim and in Italy.[92]) J.D. Martini, professor of German at Trinity, donated minerals from Gascony. A systematic arrangement of the cases was made by the Reverend Walter Stephens (also a member of the academy), who prepared a catalogue of 1,089 specimens, which was published in 1807.[93] However, in 1797 the eminent Scottish geologist Robert Jameson was not terribly impressed by the museum when he visited on 30 June: 'Went to the College Museum with Dr. Stokes. It is an elegant room, with a few trifling fossils, Indian dresses etc.'[94]

Accommodated in Trinity's Regent House, the museum was featured in an engraving of 1819, etched by R. Havell & Son from the drawing by William Benjamin Sarsfield Taylor, for a history of the university.[95] It was located in an upper room, over the main entrance gate in College Green, with the Cook ethnographical material on the staircase and with ready access to the natural history collections for teaching purposes. The room was 60 feet long, 40 feet wide and 30 feet high, well lit, with a deep, rich frieze cornice and stucco-panelled ceiling. The attention that had been paid to the layout of the museum was evident in the glass-fronted wooden cabinets lining the walls, with similar cases arranged at intervals and showing a systematic display of the material. An Irish harp, once reputedly the property of Brian Boroimhe, was presented to the museum by the Rt Hon. William Burton Conyngham in 1782, and a case of volcanic minerals was presented by David La Touche in 1790. The room was completed by stuffed animals adorning the walls, a tall giraffe occupying centre stage and the popular large-scale wooden model of the Giant's Causeway in County Antrim. The engraving shows the museum attracting families and friends of students, who are pictured looking at the cases and pointing at objects in the cabinets, guided by scholars and fellows. The systematic display of the collections, the publication of the catalogue in 1807 and the limited access to the museum show signs of basic museological trends. The museum was, in effect, for teaching purposes.

Royal Irish Academy Museum: Cabinet of Antiquities (1790)

In tandem with the foundation of the Dublin Society and the Dublin University Museum was the appearance of the RIA in the late eighteenth century. At this time Dublin was emerging as a city of intellectual potential, a gracious capital with a genuine architectural style, second only to London. Among the city's learned societies were the Royal College of Surgeons (1784), Apothecaries Hall (1791) and the Dublin Library Society (1791).[96] It was a time of scientific innovation. Archbishop Richard Robinson established an observatory at Armagh, enabled by an Act of Parliament that included provision for a museum (1791).[97] Key navigation networks included the Grand Canal, followed by the rival Royal Canal connecting Dublin with the upper Shannon after 1790. Improved transport and communications facilitated antiquarian research. George Taylor and Andrew Skinner published their pioneering *Maps of the Roads of Ireland* in 1790, followed by William W. Steward's directory, *Topographia Hibernia*, in 1795, used by topographers and travelling sightseers.[98] The Belfast Reading Society (1788), renamed the

Belfast Library and Society for Promoting Knowledge in 1792, had a cabinet of fossils for which scientific instruments were sought, such as a barometer, rain gauge and a Wedgwood pyrometer.[99] In Cork, Thomas Dix Hincks had begun holding talks on science and useful practical knowledge from about 1790.

William Cuming (1769–1852),
James Caulfeild Ist Earl of Charlemont (1728–99), c.1820
Oil on canvas, 127.9 x 101.7 cm. NGI 187.

Charlemont was an Irish statesman and a cultivated figure who exerted considerable social influence. He made an extensive Grand Tour from 1746 to 1754. A member of the Dublin Society, he was the first president of the Royal Irish Academy.

The RIA of 'science, polite literature and antiquities' was founded in 1785, and received its royal charter in 1786, with George III as its patron. The academy was a learned institution resembling European intellectual societies, with an added role to 'civilize the manners and refine the taste of the people'.[100] Founder members were drawn from a Protestant background and comprised academics (seven fellows of TCD), nobility and parliamentarians. The RIA grew out of previous eighteenth-century bodies, such as the Physio-Historical Society (1744–c.1756), the Medico-Philosophical Society, and the merger of the Trinity-based Palaeosophers (interested in ancient learning) (1782) with the Neophilosophers (interested in scientific problems) (1783).[101] It was influenced by the Dublin Society Committee of Antiquities (1772–4) and the lesser-known, and short-lived, Hibernian Antiquarian Society (1779), which was modelled on the Society of Antiquaries in London.[102] The establishment of the RIA in the last quarter of the century institutionalized the study of Irish antiquities.

The antiquarian tradition in Dublin was developed by Conyngham (founder of the Hibernian Antiquarian Society), who supported the setting up of the RIA and became its first treasurer. The academy set out to have a president, a treasurer, a secretary and a twenty-one-member council, to be elected at an annual general meeting. The patriot, antiquarian and improver James Caulfeild, the 1st Earl of Charlemont, who was in pursuit of a national gallery and academy of art, was a natural choice for first president. As a result of his presidency, the early academy meetings took place at his home, Charlemont House, on Parnell Square (now the Dublin City Gallery The Hugh Lane). When he died in 1799, he was replaced by Richard Kirwan.

The bishop of Killaloe, Thomas Barnard, had obtained a copy of the Royal Society's charter and statutes from its president, Sir Joseph Banks, both men agreeing that the governing of the British and Irish organizations should be 'as much as possible on aristocratic principles'.[103] Members of the RIA council were to be divided equally between three committees to focus on three branches of learning: polite literature, science and antiquities (this last committee was formed in 1785).[104] The original thirty-eight members were from the Ascendancy class and of the eighty-eight foundation members only two were Catholic. The academy was composed of practical men and its stated intention of facilitating comprehensive inquiry into literature, science and antiquities

Hugh Douglas Hamilton (1740–1808), *William Burton Conyngham (1733–1796)*
Pastel on paper, 23 x 19 cm. NGI 7242.

Teller of the Irish Exchequer and treasurer of the Royal Irish Academy (for Mezzotint no. NGI 10,182, 1780). This antiquarian, a man of taste and learning, sponsored painters to make sketches of objects of archaeological interest.

was the product of its neophilosopher origins. Its aims were clearly set out: 'Whatever, therefore tends, by the cultivation of the useful arts and sciences to improve and facilitate its manufactures … cannot but prove of the greatest advantage.'[105] Research formed the core of its activities – 'provision for all the capricious varieties of literary pursuit and embracing all the objects of rational inquiry it secures the co-operation of the learned of every description' – tempered with economy.

The academy came to rely on three areas in establishing its reputation: the strength of its collections (museum artefacts and manuscripts); influential members (antiquarians, mathematicians, physicists and astronomers); and publication of its official proceedings and lectures. The first in its long series of *Transactions* (1787–1907) appeared in 1787 and comprised essays in science, literature and antiquities. It fostered intellectual activity by means of a system of open awards for essays on subjects that included the best 'system of national education' and 'the employment of people'.[106] Charles O'Conor (1710–91)

Isaac Bond (eighteenth century),
Portrait Miniature of Charles O'Conor
***(1710–91),* 1800**
Watercolour on ivory, 4.5 x 3.3 cm. RIA.

In 1788 the antiquarian and Gaelic scholar
Charles O'Conor of Balenagare, Roscommon,
became a member of the Royal Irish Academy.
He owned a part of the original Annals of the
Four Masters, a chronicle of medieval Gaelic
history. Written in Irish, a copy of the Annals
is housed in the Royal Irish Academy.

from Belanagare, a Roscommon descendant of the high kings of Ireland, was an authority on Gaelic manuscripts and one of the academy's early and highly regarded members. The Committee of Antiquities (1785) formed a manuscript collection and decided to record overseas Irish material, starting in 1786 with O'Conor travelling to Rome to copy Irish manuscripts in the Vatican Library.[107] The council referred antiquarian matters to the Committee of Antiquities, which dealt with papers on antiquarian topics and artefacts, such as a sword exhibited by Kirwan in 1789. Papers on geological problems, such as the 'Origins of Granite, Basalt and Other Igneous Rocks', were published in the *Transactions*, copies of which were sent to learned societies in Europe to facilitate the exchange of ideas.

Dublin had become significant for the study of mineralogy and geology (the latter a science developed from a focus on the scientific study of mineralogy in the mid-1700s), ranking close to Freiburg and Edinburgh in this regard. Kirwan, president of the academy from 1799 to 1812, was a leading geologist but equally influential as a mineralogist. An early member of the academy was the distinguished figure in science, the Reverend William Hamilton (the first curator of Dublin University Museum), who contributed to the field of meteorology and geology, although his achievements were surpassed by those of Kirwan, his contemporary. Research in meteorology provided one of the academy's earliest activities, including funding barometers and thermometers for a network of weather stations around the country and involving research at Dunsink and Armagh observatories. Its scientific

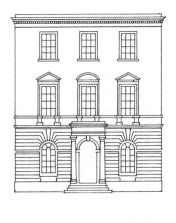

publications commanded international attention up to 1812.

Navigation House at number 114 Grafton Street was the academy's first home (1788),[108] where members met in several small rooms and a boardroom. It was located opposite Trinity College's Provost's House and next door to the Dublin Society's premises (for nine years), until the society relocated to Hawkins Street in 1796.[109] During its formative years, the academy received gifts that were loaned both to the Dublin University Museum and to the Dublin Society Museum, but as further gifts materialized the academy finally decided, in April 1790, to establish its own cabinet of antiquities, or Museum of Irish Antiquities, Geology and Natural History, ensuring there was no clash of interest with the Dublin Society.[110] Thus the formation of a museum illustrating national antiquities and heritage was one of the objects proposed in the RIA's charter of 1792. Meetings of the academy were occupied with the reading of papers, often followed by the production and examination of artefacts that would go to form the basis of the museum's collection, including coins, seals, carved stones, old mortar and original manuscripts. These first steps were extremely important in the early development of the antiquities for a national museum.

The RIA museum was located in a 'back two pair of stairs room' at Navigation House. Rev. George Graydon, a member of the Committee of Antiquities and secretary for Foreign Correspondence, was asked to procure an estimate for fitting out two rooms for the museum. He presented a plan for a cabinet of mineralogical specimens, which was accepted and in place by November 1790.[111] Graydon set about acquiring a collection in Italy (1790–1), comprising a small but 'curious collection of specimens', for which he was paid £20. The RIA museum began to acquire major archaeological material and geological specimens (which it loaned to the Dublin Society)

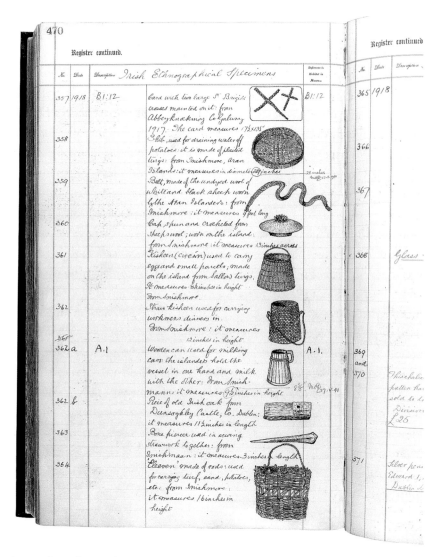

A page from the Royal Irish Academy Register of Antiquities (1886–1929) showing Irish ethnographical specimens collected 1918. From inception the academy had a Donations Book (1785–1856) and Register of Antiquities (1846–53). A fresh Register of Antiquities, starting in 1859, together with Antiquities Dockets, would form the basis of the future RIA registration system.

and became the official repository for treasure trove found in Ireland. Collecting was poorly documented, however. The increase in population from the 1780s, which continued up to the start of the Great Famine in 1845, resulted in more intensive farming. General Vallancey, a military surveyor and an authority on Irish antiquities, reported that 'multitudes of bronze celts are daily dug up in Ireland', while the field books contained entries such as 'found in breaking up new land in 1770'.[112]

The expansion of the museum and its important treasures began to attract the attention of the general public. By 1822 the academy's Library catalogue already documented more than 4,500 books, manuscripts and runs of serials. Mishaps in the early years saw the loss of objects during the course of building work and as a result of a fire at Navigation House, but enough material was beginning to emerge that had the basic components of a collection. The fire of 1837 concentrated the minds of some academicians. John Windele, wrote to the deputy keeper of manuscripts, Sir William Betham: 'Its [manuscript treasures] loss would have been a national calamity.' The issue was the lack of space to house the antiquarian and documentary collections, which were expanding due to judicious purchases by the academy and through members' donations. Eventually, the academy moved to new premises, and onto more secure footing, through a parliamentary grant, which left it in a position to advance its educational goals and acquire the major archaeological treasures that would dominate its history in the nineteenth century.

Thus, one of the most important legacies of the eighteenth century was the formalizing of basic museological trends into a more coherent museum idea and ideal. It was this organizing instinct, this desire to display treasures in an accessible way, that, allied to the growing interest in collecting (examined in detail in the next chapter), led to the museum movement of the late nineteenth century.

3

The Significance of the Eighteenth-Century Collections

I saw the cases containing casts from the antique brought from Rome, and opened, and from these in a very few years I studied.[1]

The close of the seventeenth century was marked by the defeat of King James II at the Battle of the Boyne in 1690. The Jacobite defeat consolidated the position of the Ascendancy class in Ireland and enriched the country's landlords, both present and absentee. Thus the eighteenth century opened with an air of mixed fortune and it was unclear what exactly would be the next chapter in Ireland's story.

The turning point occurred in the 1730s, when the first post-Boyne generation of landowners came to power. Industry was now focused on agriculture and linen, and rents were increasing tenfold, so the self-confident landed class, with its assured political position, built wide roads, new Georgian residential terraces and country houses with plasterwork decoration. These great houses set the tone for a century of construction, notably at Castletown House, County Kildare, the largest house ever built in Ireland at that time (1720s), and at Powerscourt (1731) and Russborough in County Wicklow (1742–8).

Nathaniel Hone (1718–1784), *The Conjurer,* **1775**
Oil on canvas, 145 x 173 cm. NGI 1790.

The Conjurer is one of the National Gallery's celebrated paintings. Originally titled *The Pictorial Conjurer displaying the Whole Art of Optical Deception*, it represents an attack on Sir Joshua Reynolds (then president of the Royal Academy). When the academy rejected the work, Hone included it in his show at 70 St Martin's Lane, one of the first one-man shows of living artists in London. Hone was one of two Irish founder members of the Royal Academy in 1768.

The century also witnessed an increase in travel to the Continent. The wealthy Irish gentry undertook Grand Tours – Paris and Italy being central to the itinerary, with Rome as the climax – and during these sojourns works of art and antiquities were acquired for their houses. The ambition of these connoisseurs was to discover the grandeur of Italy and Rome, as a result of which they were often accompanied by cultured guides and travelling companions. Lord Charlemont and La Touche viewed Italy as a museum of the past, their interest being encouraged by the exciting excavations at Herculaneum in 1738 and Pompeii in 1748, which by the 1780s played a major role in the development of neo-classical European taste.[2] Aware of these trends, Henry

Quinn (1718–91) collected cameos and intaglios.[3] Frederick Hervey, the earl-bishop of Derry, was inspired by the Villa of Lucullus, near Terracina, to propose 'a classical dog kennel … for the hounds of my eldest son',[4] the idea resurfacing in a watercolour by James Malton, *Proposal for a Triangular Building*, commissioned by Hervey.[5] In order to record and reflect their taste and affluence, the Irish invited painters to make records of themselves and their property, many of which would end up in public collections.[6]

The Irish painter Hugh Douglas Hamilton, who settled in Rome about 1780–2, was popular for his images in pastel and oil of Irish and English aristocrats, including the full-length portrait of *Frederick Augustus Hervey, Bishop of Derry and Fourth Earl of Bristol.*[7] Known for his residences at Downhill (built 1778)[8] and Ballyscullion (built 1787) in the north of Ireland, Hervey planned to display his fine collection of artworks at Ickworth House in Suffolk (built 1796),[9] the family home of the Herveys since the fifteenth century, to show 'the historical progress of the art of painting in all the five different schools [which] I deem both happy and instructive'.[10] The Earl-Bishop's collection included *The Death of General Wolfe* (1770), 'executed by the celebrated Mr. West of London – cost 500 guineas, and is thought to be the finest ever brought to Ireland … intended to be placed among his Lordship's elegant collection of paintings and statues at Downhill'.[11]

Another Grand Tourist depicted by Hamilton was the eighteen-year-old

Russborough House, County Wicklow (1742–8)

A seven-bay two-storey over basement mansion built to designs by Richard Castle (*c.* 1690–1751) and considered his finest achievement. The aim of successive members of the Leeson family, the Earls of Milltown, was to acquire art and antiquities that would enhance the beauty and comfort of Ireland's greatest Palladian mansion.

Hugh Douglas Hamilton (1740–1808), *Frederick Hervey, Bishop of Derry and 4th Earl of Bristol (1730–1803), with his Granddaughter, Lady Caroline Crichton (1779–1856) in the Gardens of the Villa Borghese, Rome,* **c.1790**
Oil on canvas, 224.4 x 199.5 cm. NGI 4350.

In what is considered one of Hamilton's finest paintings, the earl-bishop of Derry, who was a seasoned traveller and avid collector, was joined in Rome by his grandaughter, Caroline, and her mother, Lady Mary Erne (the sister of Elizabeth Foster, from whose descendants the picture was purchased). Caroline points to a relief of the seasons on the Roman Altar of the Twelve Gods, or *Ara Borghese.*

La Touche, whom Hamilton painted while he was visiting Rome in 1789, following the death of his sister, Elizabeth.[12] La Touche called at the studio of the Italian neo-classical sculptor Antonio Canova (1757–1822) in the com-

**Antonio Canova (1757–1822),
Amorino 1791.**
Marble, 142 cm high, NGI 8358.

Commissioned from Canova in 1789, by
the young John David La Touche, son of
the wealthiest Irish banker, towards the
end of his Grand Tour to Italy. The sculpture was finished in 1791, and arrived in
Dublin in 1792. This *Amorino* is considered
the most accomplished of four similar
versions.

pany of Hamilton and there he saw the *Amorino* (Cupid) being created for Colonel John Campbell, later Baron Cawdor. La Touche commissioned a copy of this sculpture, which arrived in Dublin in 1792.[13] The ultimate journey of this work, from the private La Touche collection to the NGI, is illustrative of the significance of the collections and their repatriation and place in the development of Ireland's museums.

Collecting of this nature had a key role to play in cultivating an awareness of taste in society, in encouraging patronage and in providing examples of great works for study. While Madden of the Dublin Society had a collection at Manor Waterhouse, County Fermanagh – 'fine pieces of painting several of which are originals done by the names that have been most famous over Europe' – he also left twenty works to educate the eyes of students at TCD.[14] Artists were aware of the considerable trade in pictures, many of which were imported and sold by dealers to be displayed in great houses. The collection of James Hamilton, Earl of Clanbrassil, at Tollymore Park, County Down, was printed in a catalogue that illustrated the hanging pattern of each room, with numbers identifying the paintings on the walls. Studying these collections provided a stimulus for Irish artists to travel abroad,

Claude Lorrain (1604/5–82), *Juno Confiding Io to the Care of Argus,* **1660**
Oil on canvas, 60 x 75 cm. NGI 763.

Lorrain's idealized landscapes, like this edpsode from Ovid's *Metamorphoses*, are infused with the spirit of the antique. Painted as pendant to another evening scene, both works are documented as finished drawings in the *Liber Veritas*, kept by Claude from 1635. These classical landscapes, and the realism of their Dutch counterparts, greatly influenced late eighteenth- and nineteenth-century Irish landscape painters.

resulting in a mid-century circle of painters, sculptors, dealers and antiquarians in Rome.[15] Although the finest recorders of eighteenth-century Irish life – George Barret, Thomas Roberts and William Ashford – did not paint beyond various regions of Britain, according to Barret they were aware of the instructive nature of collections: 'Pay a visit to the pictures at Holker Hall, do not be engrossed by any one master, so as to become a mimic, but think of all who have been excellent and endeavour to see nature with eyes.'[16]

Eighteenth-century prints published by artists such as Jonathan Fisher helped in the promotion of picturesque beauty spots like Killarney in County Kerry, the Giant's Causeway, and Cashel in County Tipperary. Fisher sought 'to lead the curious to points of view, where the sublime and beautiful are most picturesquely combined'.[17] It may have been Edmund Burke[18] who introduced Barret to Edward Wingfield, 2nd Viscount Powerscourt (1729–64), because early in his career the artist was working in the Powerscourt demesne. Barret also created sixteen landscapes for Joseph Leeson, later 1st Earl of Milltown, at Russborough in County Wicklow. Roberts, considered the finest Irish landscape painter of the late eighteenth century, was the son of the architect John Roberts, whose masterpiece, Waterford's Holy Trinity Cathedral, was described as 'a perfect epitome of Georgian taste'.[19] Thomas painted prospects of great Irish estates that are unfailingly refined and accomplished, as in the case of *Lucan House and Demesne* (*c*.1772).[20] William Ashford, an English artist who became the first president of the RHA, portrayed *The Opening of the Ringsend Docks, Dublin* (1796) by the lord lieutenant, Lord Camden.[21] As Dublin's artistic circles were small towards the end of the eighteenth century, many of these artists were on good terms with each other.

While the general social position of artists had moved towards professional status by the end of the century, Irish artists still struggled for recognition and remained dependent on the tightly knit social networks from which patronage emanated; the fruits of this artistic patronage would become part of the national collections. The pattern of contemporary taste in collecting Italian, Dutch, Flemish, Spanish and English pictures and the classical landscapes of Claude Lorrain, with a scattering of Irish works, would be echoed in early National Gallery collections. The late eighteenth-century collections would become dispersed by owners such as James Digues La Touche, who sold his holdings at Geminiani's Great Auction Room in Dame Street in 1764.[22] Berkeley housed his pictures in Cork: 'In the Episcopal palace of Cloyne the eye is entertained with a variety of good paintings … a Magdalene of Sir Peter Paul Rubens, some heads by Van Dyck and Keller.'[23] Another ecclesiastic, Robert Clayton, bishop of Clogher, kept his collection at his home in St Stephen's Green, Dublin; his portrait is now housed in the National Gallery.

According to the architect James Gandon, the finer collections were held by the Earl of Charlemont, the Duke of Leinster and Lord Londonderry. Leeson accumulated a prime collection of paintings and antiquities for his house at Russborough, his portrait having been painted in Rome by artists such as Anton Raphael Mengs, Hugh Douglas Hamilton and Pompeo Batoni.[24] Leeson was a keen follower of the landscapes of Claude-Joseph Vernet

Pompei Batoni (1708–87), *Joseph Leeson (1701–1783), Later Ist Earl of Milltown, 1744*
Oil on canvas, 135.5 x 98.5 cm. NGI 701.

Batoni was one of the most famous painters in Rome in the latter half of the eighteenth century. Patrons were fascinated by his ability to capture a good likeness by using an informal elegant pose combined with a fine outline and moderately bright colours to produce a polished finish. This portrait, dated 1744, is the first record of Leeson's presence in Italy. In 1763, he was awarded the title Earl of Milltown.

(1714–89), several copies of which were housed at Russborough. Other admirers of Vernet's work included Joseph Henry of Straffan, Wingfield, 2nd Viscount Powerscourt; Ralph Howard, later 1st Viscount Wicklow; Thomas Dawson, later Lord Cremorne; and Viscount Charlemont. Works from these notables' collections would later be repatriated for the national collections. Many of the Ascendancy figures were early members of the Dublin Society and the RIA and were aware of their antiquarian committees because they were equally interested in *objets d'art*. Antiquities were poorly recorded in Ireland at this time, however. A dress-fastener terminal found in the Bog of Cullen in County Tipperary (the source of much gold) ended up in the collection of John Damer, a relative of Lord Portarlington of Emo Court, County Laois.

Graduates of the Grand Tour who displayed their collections, as Thomas Conolly did at Castletown House, did so to demonstrate their knowledge of the achievements of classical antiquity.[25] Conolly, who emerged as a dominant player on the Irish political scene, used his county seat for meetings with key political figures and for hunting and entertainment. The extent of the properties of these families can be gleaned from a series of prints executed by the English engraver Thomas Milton between 1783 and 1793.[26] The fortunes of the Ascendancy fluctuated, however. One estate that has survived into the twenty-first century is that of the Cobbe family at Newbridge House in County Dublin. A cabinet of curiosities was formed around 1790 by Ann

Cobbe, daughter of Thomas Cobbe, to whom Newbridge House was presented in 1755 by his father, Charles Cobbe, archbishop of Dublin (1686–1765).[27] The Cobbes' museum of curiosities reflected the unfolding collage of family life around which its members gathered to talk about past generations and to discuss the stories behind their collection of artefacts.[28]

The significance of collections such as these lay in the part they played in educating artists and antiquarians by cultivating taste and knowledge. The body of artworks that these learned collectors brought to Ireland included some remarkably fine treasures, many of which are now in the public domain in museums and galleries. For example, Leeson's collection moved into public ownership in the nineteenth century when it was presented to the National Gallery by Lady Milltown, 'in memory of the 6th Earl of Milltown having been purchased by the 1st Earl of Milltown on the grand tour'.[29] Thanks to their foresight and generosity, these family holdings have become part of the national heritage as the basis of Ireland's national collections.

The Movement towards a National Gallery

Early proposals for an art gallery and teaching academy were put forward by the Society of Artists in Ireland, established in 1765. In 1767, having built new exhibition rooms in William Street (now South William Street), the society made an application to Parliament for assistance to complete its building project for the purpose of setting up an academy for the study of painting. Funds were voted that year to Thomas Conolly, Thomas Eyre, Redmond Morres, George Paul Monk and Colonel William Burton, 'towards the building of an academy for painting, sculpture and architecture'.[30] A further application was made in 1769, noting that the society intended to teach students in several branches of the fine arts, but it received no further grants and the building was completed through a system of bonds. The academy project was abandoned and there remains no record of the pictures (Lely and Mengs) that Burton and the painter Anthony Lee had offered towards the venture.[31]

The Society of Artists held annual exhibitions at William Street up until it disbanded in 1780. Its silver admission ticket was similar to the type used by great houses in Ireland and Britain. The society's demise was due to

A silver ticket to a Society of Artists exhibition

Society of Artists exhibitions took place at its Exhibition Room in William Street, Dublin, between 1767 and 1780. (Private Collection)

difficulties in managing its affairs. However, groups like this frequently formed and reformed, and other art associations and bodies, such as the Society of Artists of Ireland and the Royal Irish Institution, displayed work at William Street, George's Street, Allen's Printsellers, Parliament House, Ellis's Dublin Museum, Del Vecchio's, and at the Dublin Society's Hawkins Street premises between 1800 and 1819, followed by the Royal Arcade in College Green and the exhibition room in College Street. Individual artists showed at Hawkins House, number 14 New Buildings, Dame Street (Richard Hand and J.J. Barralet, 1785) and at 49 Marlborough Street (J.G. Oben, 1809) as the trend of holding one-man shows became popular.

Support for the idea of a gallery and art school was promoted by the Irish commentator Thomas Campbell in 1767.[32] In his *Essay on Perfecting the Fine Arts in Great Britain and Ireland*, Campbell gave his reasons for the need for an academy to teach painting and for the founding of a permanent collection of works by old masters. Though Campbell was positive about the Dublin Society schools, he did have reservations, which helped to provide a sense of realism:

> Ireland gave England the hint of a Drawing Academy. Some of the greatest artists have been bred here. In landscapes, we have

no competitors, Mr. West has sent out scholars of the greatest promise, now abroad … But surely to have painters from a mere Drawing School, is to reap without sowing.[33]

His proposal, namely that 'If the Society would have painters, there must be Schools for Painting', would become a reality with the foundation of the RHA in 1823. Campbell's essay was also persuasive of the need for a permanent public collection of art: 'We have no public statues, no public galleries of pictures, no academies for either painting or sculpture, nor will the great allow their pieces to be copied.'[34] He described a nation bereft of any accessible collections with which to inform the public and educate the aspirant artist, arguing determinedly for a public art collection: 'There should be, at least in the capital, one great collection of the masterpieces both of painting and

Giovanni Paolo Panini (1691–1765), *The Roman Forum*, 1742
Oil on canvas, 72.5 x 98 cm. NGI 726.

Panini was interested in antiquities, specializing in views of Rome and other famous ruins that were sought after by Grand Tourists. In 1744 Joseph Leeson went on the first of two tours of Italy, where he acquired this work, one of four landscapes by Panini dated 1742. The topographical view of the ancient Roman site was gifted to the National Gallery by Lady Milltown in 1902.

Francis Wheatley (1747–1801), *The Dublin Volunteers in College Green,*
4 November 1779, **1779–80**
Oil on canvas, 175 x 323 cm. NGI 125.

Wheatley, newly arrived from London, painted contemporary Irish events, such as this record
of the celebration of William III's birthday by the Dublin Volunteers. A lively occasion that
involved one thousand armed men, including the 2nd Duke of Leinster, their colonel (portrayed at the centre of the picture), gathered in square formation in the city. It was gifted to
the National Gallery by the 5th Duke of Leinster in 1891.

sculpture, where there might be constant access under certain regulation …
the public might view and form its eye … the student might copy and form
his hand.' This essay, which gained him the Dublin Society's first honorary
silver medal, promoted the idea of a national gallery for Ireland.

Another influential commentator was the connoisseur Joseph Cooper
Walker, a member of both the Dublin Society and the RIA. Having lived in
Italy for several years, he had absorbed neo-classical ideas on the primacy of the
fine arts and wrote about how a school could be run, 'capable of containing
three hundred boys', with a library containing books on the history of art
and art education, together with engravings 'from the designs of all the great
masters of the different schools'. His support of Irish history as a subject for
painting was similar to that of James Barry: 'venture among the works of
nature in quest of subjects for his pencil, or seek them amidst the annals of
Irish valour or Irish patriotism'. In this he anticipated the writings of Thomas
Davis.[35]

Ellis's Dublin Museum (c.1792)

The upper class may have been preoccupied with fine treasures and notions of national collections, but such concerns did not necessarily filter down the social ladder. In fact, no art exhibitions were held in Dublin for twenty years following the demise of the Society of Artists in Ireland in 1780.[36] The lack of artistic activity in Dublin at this time was evident in newspaper advertisements. In February 1792, at Mr Davis's Grand Room at number 60 George's Street, *The Eidophusikon* was displayed, comprising a series of dramatic tableaux by the landscape painter Philippe de Loutherbourg (1790–1812).[37] On 7 January an advertisement had proclaimed that at 33 Capel Street a silhouette painter named J. Thomason (*fl.*1785–1800) showed '100 animated likenesses of the principal inhabitants of Dublin', and he could take likenesses in a minute, with the finished portrait presented in a gilt frame for six guineas.[38] On the same street could be found miniatures painted for two guineas by Matthew Hunter (*fl.*1780–1812), with 'copies for rings, lockets or bracelets from procures of any size'.[39] This was all very well, but it did not constitute fine art and it seemed the impetus for creative expression was dying out. It took an enterprising person like John Ellis to embark on a new exhibiting venture.

In 1790, Ellis, a landscape and scene painter, proposed to hold exhibitions by Irish artists at his premises in number 9 Mary Street. Although this move was welcomed by fellow painters, the planned exhibitions did not materialize.[40] Ellis's other plan, dating to 1788–90, was for a permanent museum for 'Displaying and encouraging Productions in the Fine Arts, Mechanics and Manufactures of Ireland'. According to Walker, this museum would be open to the public to see 'productions in the Arts of Painting and Sculpture, Designs in Architecture, and Models of Machines for facilitating the execution of different manufactures'. Walker commended the plan for the influence it would have on sculptors and painters and the opportunity it would provide them for exhibiting and selling their works. However, 'this excellent plan wanting the lustre of an high name, failed of attracting notice, and died almost in the moment of its birth'.[41]

Ellis was not alone in believing a new museum to be a necessity. There were at that time three private museums open to the public, the Dublin Society museum, the RIA museum and the Dublin University Museum, but as products of Enlightenment Ireland, they were not places of entertainment

John Ellis's heads of a plan for an academy and museum

The advertisement promotes an idea by John Ellis (fl. 1767–1812) of forming a museum and an art academy in Dublin.

to attract young people. This was seen as a worrying deficiency because, as one Dublin magazine complained in 1790, the younger generation was behaving in an unseemly fashion, dressing casually and neglecting museums, which were described as 'improvements in wisdom and knowledge which (would make gentlemen) easy to themselves and useful to the world'.[42] So Ellis persevered, and in 1792 finally opened his Dublin Museum at the rear of his house on Mary Street for the purpose of 'the public exhibition of pictures and works of art'. The fact that the street directories of the period list him as a 'tea merchant' (1788) and as a 'printseller' (1800 and 1806) is a good indication of how he generated income, with the print-selling enterprise the key to the contents and main purpose of the museum.

Prior to the opening of Ellis's museum, an article in the *Hibernian Journal* (in 1792) gave an outline of the project:

> John Ellis … has just brought in from London an elegant and well chosen Collection of the first English Prints, plain and coloured, among which are those excellent Productions, Boydell's Shakespeare, and Macklin's Poets. He is likewise supplied with the different Materials used for Drawing, Painting, and Fancy works … those who charge him with their Commands may meet with many Advantages not usual in Houses of a similar Nature …

The article continues, '[the museum] he has erected in the rear of his House, is now nearly finished, and will in a short Time be opened for the Reception of the Works of Artists and Mechanics, free of expense to the Exhibitors. N.B. The Tea Business carried on as usual.' Following the opening of the museum later that year, the *Sentimental and Masonic Magazine* reported on 'Ellis' exhibition of Paintings, Sculptures etc. in Mary Street, Dublin July, 1792':

> It is upwards of thirty years since the Irish artists attempted first to establish an exhibition of their works in this city, in a large room constructed for the purpose in Great George's Street South; some years after, the Exhibition House, in William Street, was built by subscription, but as if that effort had exhausted the spirit or abilities of its undertakers, the design of periodical exhibitions drooped from the very day the house was opened for the purpose; it was soon after abandoned and the building has fallen into the hands of an individual who occasionally hires it for other purposes. Some feeble and abortive attempts have since been made to revive an exhibition of this kind, the best planned of these was one offered by Mr. John Ellis, about two years ago, it was approved by the artists and sanctioned by some of the first and most respectable personages in this kingdom, but whether his plan was on too extensive a scale, or from other causes that have not come to the knowledge of the writer of this account, it was given up as a public estab-lishment, and Mr. Ellis, with a praiseworthy perseverance, has, at his own expense, opened a Museum at the rear of his house in Mary Street, where every artist may freely display his work for the public inspection. Mr. Ellis' exhibition has been opened for some weeks with an excellent collection, which his taste has displayed to the greatest advantage.[43]

The article lists the works on display, including paintings by Thomas Robinson, Robert Hunter, Robert Home and Robert Woodburn jnr,[44] bas-reliefs by William Cuming,[45] and a statue of the Marquis of Buckingham by Edward Smyth.[46] It concludes: 'Besides the various productions of the pencil and chisel, are some foreign productions, particularly a number of capital engravings, which Mr. Ellis has collected.' Ellis exhibited many of the major artists of the period, including works by Solomon Williams and William Woodburn in 1792.[47] There is no reference to work by Ellis himself, although he previously showed at the Society of Artists in Ireland.[48]

Ellis's Dublin Museum marketed itself well. In 1799 the museum declared that it had 'beautiful representations of the Docklands of Chatham, most capitally painted, and so assisted by machinery as to give a surprising imitation of nature'. The advertisement in *Saunders' Newsletter* reported that this was the fifth in a series of exhibitions and that 'the public are respectfully informed, that each piece will continue no longer than a new one is preparing' – a novel way to attract the public and encourage return visits. It concluded: 'A fine collection of paintings, prints, natural curiosities and models, and as usual, the prints are for sale.'[49] The museum became a popular venue, as noted by a young woman who paid it a visit in 1801: 'visited Ellis' and spent an hour among a great collection of the finest prints, most of them different from those I had before seen, for his sales being on commission from London houses, he is enabled to have a constant change'.[50] Ellis's business-like approach to his venture was demonstrated by these efforts to change exhibitions, illustrated in a display held in 1802 of a 'collection of the arts and natural and mechanical rarities the principal attraction being a picture of *Alexandria* by himself', which 'equalled anything of the kind ever seen'.[51] He reputedly showed *Jupiter and Antiope* by Rubens, a *Portrait of Hogarth*, and works by various painters, including Dutch artists.

Ellis's enlightened concept of an exhibition of contemporary arts and manufactures, where artists could sell their works and manufacturers could see 'the frequent mechanic inventions of the English and other ingenious nations', anticipated the industrial exhibitions established by the RDS in 1834. His proposal also anticipated the future development of the RHA and the NGI.[52] In addition, the idea of educating through exhibitions and collections anticipated railway magnate, William Dargan's concept of the Dublin International Exhibition of Art-Industry in 1853 and the work of Henry Cole at the South Kensington Museum in London.[53] The Ellis museum project was a shining example of what could be achieved with innovative thinking and determination. His cabinet of curiosities of 'arts and natural and mechanical rarities' sold prints to generate a regular income and its survival for fourteen years was a source of public interest and popular appeal. He drew on his early experience as a scene painter in London to develop his print-selling business and for a while the enterprise thrived. In its time, the museum was an important part of private cultural enterprise of the city of Dublin. After its closure, the contents of Ellis's Dublin Museum (described as a Natural History Museum) were purchased by the Dublin Society in 1810.[54]

The Legacy of John Ellis

John Ellis's concept of a fine art academy and museum could not be realized when he first mooted it because the necessary parliamentary funding was not forthcoming. His ideas showed remarkable foresight, however, a fact recognized by the Duke of Rutland and viceroy of Ireland (1784–7), who absorbed Ellis's ideas into his own proposal that Dublin should have an academy and school of painting.[55]

This idea arose at a time when a broader concept of what constituted museums and public collections was beginning to develop, as a result of the royal palace of the kings of France, the Louvre, being transformed into a public museum in the wake of the French Revolution. The British Museum had opened in 1759, while the Royal Academy (founded in 1768) was in the process of mounting public exhibitions and raising the stature of the artist in British society. In America, where the independently minded new colonists were largely unaffected by older customs and traditions, there was nonetheless a European influence in the approach to early museums. When the artist and naturalist Charles Willson Peale was involved in developing a Museum of Natural History in Philadelphia (established 1786), word of its educational programmes, in addition to other American initiatives, gradually filtered back to Europe and were noted in Ireland: 'Those of them which possess directly educational functions claim an abundant harvest of good results.'[56]

The Duke of Rutland was aware of these overseas developments and they informed his proposal for an academy (with a president, keeper and lecturers) and a national gallery to house works by old masters to educate the public.[57] This academy was planned to have been run alongside the Dublin Society's

**Horace Hone (1754–1825/7), *Charles Manners,
4th Duke of Rutland* (1754–87), 1805**
Miniature, enamel on copper, 9 x 7.6 cm. NGI 2657.

Hone's miniature is based on a watercolour portrait, which he painted in 1787, the year of
the duke's death, aged thirty-three. A formal miniature, Rutland is portrayed as the lord lieutenant of Ireland, wearing the eight-pointed star of the Cross of St George.

schools and would have greatly enhanced the cultural life of the eighteenth
century. The idea was well thought out and Rutland nominated Pieter de
Gree as keeper of the new institution.[58] De Gree had arrived in Ireland from
Antwerp in 1785, his letter of introduction from Sir Joshua Reynolds, president
of the Royal Academy, declaring him to be 'a very excellent painter ... and
I promised to recommend him to your Grace's protection, which I can with
very safe conscience, not only as a very ingenious artist but as a young man
of very pleasing manners'.[59] De Gree worked for several Irish patrons, including
Conyngham, and advised Rutland on the purchase of paintings.

Following Rutland's death in 1787, his concept of a gallery combining educational functions with an academy was pursued by John Foster, supported by Lord Charlemont. Despite their best efforts the proposal came to nothing, again largely due to the lack of parliamentary support. Importantly, however, the process had revealed growing support for a fine art academy and national gallery for Ireland.[60]

As the eighteenth century reached its conclusion, it became clear that Grattan's Parliament was coming to dominate interests disposed to supporting British governance in Ireland.[61] The Dublin Society's position as the 'favourite institution' of the Irish Parliament was part of the cultural fabric of the Ascendancy in Ireland, a position shared with the RIA.[62] These factors made it an obvious target for the growing London-based imperial bureaucracy. Thus, after 1820, ironically when it was awarded its royal charter, it gradually declined in the shadow of the British Museum – 'the step-mother of the child has not certainly been as liberal as the parent'.[63] The Irish elite thought the Union would represent a return to the *status quo ante*, instead of which it witnessed its marginalization. Patronage would become the prerogative of the ascendant middle classes. The history of Irish museums, as all history, would prove to be 'an open process, never concluded, not even fully representable, and seldom agreed over by its chief interpreters'.[64]

PART III

The Nineteenth Century

The Pio-Clemente Museum, Rome

The museum was founded during the tenure of popes Clement XIV (1769–74) and Pius VI (1775–99) to expand the Vatican's collection of classical sculpture. One of many small and large Vatican Museums devoted to papal collecting and patronage from the Renaissance onwards. Opened in 1771, the Pio-Clemente houses the *Apollo Belvedere*, a Roman marble copy of the original Greek statue (AD 130–40) and the *Belvedere Torso* (*c.*150 BC).

*T*he Act of Union (1800) curtailed intellectual life in the city of Dublin as Parliament House was sold to the Bank of Ireland and the stream of polemical literature ran dry due to the paucity of parliamentary Acts and debates. Executive power devolved to London through the lord lieutenant and a civil service based in Dublin Castle, presided over by an under-secretary for Ireland. Dublin lost its attraction and overnight became a provincial city in a kingdom of which London was the capital. Great houses fell into disuse: Powerscourt House (South William Street) was sold, Aldborough House (Portland Place) was leased to a school and Ely House (Ely Place) was subdivided. The middle classes had not yet reached James Gandon's understanding of the need for patronage to 'do honour to our nation'. Irish society adapted to the new dispensation, with the lack of money causing subscriptions to decline at the Dublin Society and RIA.

The Napoleonic Wars (1799–1815) created unstable alliances in Europe and led to threats of a French attack, which in turn led to the British building Martello towers along Ireland's coast because of fears of an invasion via the 'back door' of Ireland. This uneasy period saw Irish citizens raise a monument to Horatio, Lord Nelson on the city's main thoroughfare, Sackville Street (now O'Connell Street), and cheer with great relief the Duke of Wellington's victory at Waterloo in 1815. A visitor from Paris, 'Madame Tussaud, Artist of the Grand European Cabinet of Figures', showed wax figures at the Shakespeare Theatre in Exchequer Street. Links with Europe were developed by new generations of academics, including Thomas Antisell studying with the chemist Jean-Baptiste Dumas and John Hart with the naturalist and zoologist Georges Cuvier in France. In the north of Ireland the religious geography settled into a three-way division of invisible frontiers between the Church of Ireland, Presbyterianism and Roman Catholicism. The United Irish rebellions of 1798 and 1803 had wiped out a generation of political figures – either dead or removed to England, America, France and Australia – leading to the collapse of political organizations. Into this vacuum stepped Daniel O'Connell (1775–1847), 'The Liberator', to achieve Catholic Emancipation.

The process by which Irish history became a vehicle for politics and national assertiveness has its roots in eighteenth-century antiquarianism, together with innovations in novels and history-writing, and in figures such as Mr and Mrs S.C. Hall providing records of pre-Famine Ireland (*Hall's Ireland* [1841]). The Victorian fascination with nature evolved into the scientific pursuits of naturalists' societies and field clubs, with huge enthusiasm evident for mineral collecting, plant study and birdwatching. Victorian ideology supported moral tracts such as *The Museum* by Charlotte Elizabeth Tonna (1790–1846), which used the thinly disguised British Museum natural history collection to reveal the wonders of creation. Early naturalist and astronomer

Benjamin Zix (1772–1811), *The Marriage Procession of Napoleon and Marie-Louise through the Grand Gallery of the Louvre*, 1810
Pen and ink, wash, 40 x 60 cm. Louvre.

The Louvre built up its identity as a major public monument by forming the greatest art collection the world had ever known – 'Rome is no more in Rome, it is all in Paris' – and Napoleon augmented this by using the Grand Gallery for important events, such as his second marriage to Marie-Louise of Austria.

Mary Ward (1827–69) echoed this conviction in *The World of Wonders* (1858): 'we who look through microscopes can add much to the list of things as instances of the power of God.'[1] Victorian sensibility was also evident in the schoolbooks of Belfast-born Robert Patterson (1802–72), an exponent of the moral benefits of nature study. The accumulated specimens would find their way into the Trinity College, Dublin Society, RIA and Belfast museums, to re-emerge as pedagogical teaching collections.

The revolutionary ideals that secured the opening of the first public museum in France, the Musée du Louvre, permeated Ireland in the form of a cultural nationalism that marked the careers of influential nineteenth-century figures, such as Richard Griffith, Thomas Davis, William Dargan and George Petrie. *The Nation*, a weekly Irish nationalist newspaper founded in 1842 by Charles Gavan Duffy, Thomas Davis and John Blake Dillon, seemed to promise a new and inclusive national identity, and as such became the organ of Young Ireland (*Éire Óg*), a vibrant political, cultural and social movement. The nationalism espoused by Young Ireland reflected ideals shared by Romantic intellectuals in Europe and had an impact on the momentum to recover and reclaim the past.

Alongside the political impetus, the cultural activism of Davis was immense, forming part of a broad Romantic movement sweeping Europe in the nineteenth century. Davis addressed the lack of a national museum and visual art tradition: 'we have Irish artists, but no Irish art, no national art' (*The Nation*, 2 December 1843). Although he felt that the work of Frederic William Burton (1816–1900) epitomized the Irish tradition, the artist himself understood that a school of Irish art had to emerge from a movement expressed through poetry, literature and the other creative arts. Burton designed for Davis the frontispiece of *The Spirit of the Nation* (1845), a collection of poems and ballads originally published in *The Nation*. In a later generation, Douglas Hyde and W.B. Yeats would take up the baton and provide 'heroic service worth a good man's energy'[2] in restoring culture to its central position in Irish life.

In common with the Europe-wide interest in the past, antiquarianism in Ireland gained its own significance, underscored by this growing sense of national consciousness. Bound up with this process was the issue of archaeology and the creation of collections being connected to the wider political process, demonstrated in public statements made by antiquarians and members of the RIA, and publications dealing with archaeological sites. There was also an awareness of the political role of the past, which was evident in the use of symbols (Celtic jewellery) created for one purpose (display at the Industrial Exhibition of 1853), but used to function for another purpose (as a symbol of national awareness). Contemporary political tensions meant that Irish antiquarian activity was undertaken in a more politically sensitive context than elsewhere.

The story of Ireland in the nineteenth century is, then, a story of museum foundation and collection formation. As this story takes place within a complex international setting, it is necessary to relate it as part of a wider context in order to understand the nature and impact of the broad cross-cultural influences at work in the Irish museum movement. Accordingly, Part III opens with a brief examination of museum trends in Britain and America in the nineteenth century.

While the eighteenth-century European Enlightenment was identified as the genesis of the British Museum and the Louvre in Paris, it also influenced the emergence of museum culture and institutions in Ireland and America. The nineteenth century witnessed the rise of a new impetus towards 'museum foundation and collection' alongside a fresh role for museums in the shaping of knowledge, as opportunities for learning were extended to many more men and women than ever before. These developments impacted across the Western world, helping to mould the form and function of the modern public museum. It was a 'golden age of collectors', whose activities created the necessity for custom-built spaces for storage and display of treasures. Thus, the Prado opened in Madrid in 1819, the British Parliament established the National Gallery in London in 1824, largely for the improvement of public taste, and the National Gallery of Ireland opened in 1864, while at the same time German principalities and European royal families were converting their princely collections into public institutions. It was an exciting time, when the potential of museums was beginning to be revealed and explored in a vibrant collision of old and new ideas. This energy was harnessed very effectively by the world's fairs that were held in America and the international exhibitions launched in Britain and Ireland. These cultural gatherings were crucial in the movement to found museums, focusing attention on the need to create public spaces for the benefit of all, on the need to provide educational facilities for the wider public and on the need to record and preserve heritage in all its cultural forms.

4

Cross-Cultural Influences: Museums in Britain and America

The Great Exhibition was a wonderful occasion for fusing recreation with instruction thereby improving the lot and minds of the working classes[1]

The aim of this chapter is to show the extent of the influence of British and American museum models on the Irish museum movement. At this critical juncture in museum history the interaction between Britain and Ireland, in particular, was very productive. One of the major influences came in the form of the great exhibitions and world fairs held in London, which were emulated by the Dublin International Exhibition of Art-Industry in 1853, an innovation that had a huge impact on Ireland.

The Museum in Britain

Instructing the Whole Nation: Great Exhibitions and World Fairs

The first British industrial exhibition was organized by the Society of Arts in London in 1761, from a background of medieval and post-medieval fairs.[2] By the nineteenth century the notion of the industrial exhibition had been

The Crystal Palace at Hyde Park. The 1851 Great Exhibition of the Works of Industry of all Nations, London, effectively launched the concept of world's fairs and successfully demonstrated the power of the British Empire at that time.

greatly expanded and refined, resulting in the triumph that was the Great Exhibition of 1851. It united earlier techniques of display, including landscape theatres (panoramas),[3] cabinets and Mechanics' Institute exhibitions,[4] transforming them into exhibitionary models for public inspection and for the public that inspected them. In this way it brought together disciplines that influenced the development of museums and galleries.[5]

Queen Victoria opened the Great Exhibition of the Works of Industry of All Nations on 1 May 1851, in Joseph Paxton's impressive glass structure, the Crystal Palace, in Hyde Park.[6] The manufactures came from 30 nations, colonies, dominions and dependencies, comprising 100,000 exhibits, the purpose being the promotion of industry to 'everyone not only in Britain but in the whole world'.[7] Supported by Prince Albert, organized by Henry Cole (1808–82), a maverick figure who wrote under the pseudonym 'Felix Summerly', and financed largely by private capital, the Great Exhibition identified manufactures with the 'national character', positioning Queen Victoria at its moral centre. The British nation had every reason to feel pride in this achievement: this, the first world's fair, was held over five months and welcomed six million visitors from Europe and elsewhere, all eager to see the spectacle and stimulating attendances at London's historic sites and museums.[8]

From this mammoth undertaking emerged trends that would have a bearing on modern museums. The British government had begun constructing municipal museums and these institutions would now find a public attuned to visiting exhibitions and accustomed to orderly behaviour. By century's end the new interest in art was clear in the growing visitor numbers at these museums and in the fact that exhibition centres were springing up in London and elsewhere.[9] The Royal Commission purchased land in South Kensington from the profits of the Great Exhibition (for Prince Albert's cultural centre, similar to the German museums[10]), which was invested in a national museum of design, the Museum of Manufactures (1852) which became the South Kensington Museum (1857), followed by the Science, Geological and Natural History museums, the Imperial College, Royal Albert Hall and College of Music, serving as independent institutions and a cultural quarter in the capital city. Britain was truly on the way to establishing a network of museums and galleries to teach and entertain people from all walks of life.

Cabinets, Collections, 'Instruments of Public Instruction'

The Ashmolean Museum of Art and Archaeology and the British Museum
The Ashmolean Museum, founded at Oxford University in 1683, was based on the Cabinet of Rarities and Curiosities formed by John Tradescant (*c.*1577–1638) and his son, John (1608–62), who were noted botanical travellers and gardeners. The Tradescants stored their collection in a large house in South Lambeth, known as 'The Ark', which bore the distinction of being the first museum in England to open to the public. It was in the mainstream of European collections, with a catalogue, *Musaeum Tradescantianum*,[11] recognized as a serious cabinet for research by scholars and visited by ordinary people (admission: sixpence).

The Tradescant collection was bequeathed to Elias Ashmole, who gifted it to the University of Oxford in 1677.[12] The use of the word 'museum' by the Ashmolean in its *Philosophical Transactions* (1683) is an early example of this word recorded in the *Oxford English Dictionary*.[13] By locating the museum at Oxford, the collections became available for research and teaching in the context of a university.[14]

Another seventeenth-century collector was responsible for the core collection of the British Museum. Hans Sloane created a cabinet of natural and artificial curiosities – Roman and Egyptian antiquities, ethnographic specimens, drawings and coins – that was celebrated as one of the great universal collections.[15] The Prince of Wales (who became George III in 1760), who viewed the cabinet in 1748, may have encouraged Sloane to consider his legacy: 'how great an honour will redound to Britain, to have it established for public use'.[16] In any event, Sloane's will stipulated that his collection was to be kept intact, so that the public would have access to it for 'the improvement, knowledge and information of all persons'.[17] Accepted by an Act of Parliament in 1753, the Sloane collection became Britain's national museum: 'one of the first public museums in the world'. This was the point at which, in England, the term 'cabinets of curiosities' changed meaning into a new type of institutional museum.[18]

The British Museum opened at Montagu House in January 1759. Admission was free but the official rules were strict, making it difficult to gain access; entry tickets had to be approved by the librarian. Tours were conducted by library staff but were not hugely satisfactory, as the exhibits were unlabelled. Significant acquisitions included the Elgin Marbles (1816), also known as the Parthenon Marbles, but in general progress was slow; for example, the museum had no lavatories and children under eight years of age were excluded. This changed when Robert Smirke's building (1823–52) created new galleries for collections, dominated by themes from the classical world, Egypt, Mesopotamia, Greek and Roman antiquities. In 1848 access was finally increased, with Charles Kingsley, English clergyman, historian and writer, affirming: 'It is almost the only place which is free to English citizens, the poor and the rich may meet together … the British Museum is a truly equalizing place.'[19]

Gradually, the image of the British Museum as a Victorian storehouse improved: displays were reduced, 'works of art' were acknowledged for what they were and emphasis was placed on historical, rather than aesthetic, issues. The influx of visitors for the Great Exhibition of 1851 saw 2.5 million people visit the Museum. The decline in subsequent years was due to the popularity of attractions such as the National Gallery, London Zoo, the Museum of Practical Geology, the South Kensington Museum and RA exhi-

George Scharf Snr (1788–1860), *Montagu House, the Grand Staircase,* **c.1845**
Watercolour, 24.2 x 28.8 cm. British Museum

From the 1830s, museum-going became a popular pastime as some collections became accessible to the public. People flocked to see the British Museum's influx of new antiquities. This image shows giraffes displayed on the staircase, while to one side a glimpse is provided of the early exhibition galleries at Montagu House. The Bavarian-born Scharf was known for his London scenes, including his illustrations of the British Museum, 1828–50.

bitions. Some of the British Museum's collections devolved to other institutions: paintings to the National Gallery (1824), and National Portrait Gallery (1870); natural history specimens to the Natural History Museum (1880–3); books and manuscripts to the British Library (within the museum).[20] Towards the end of the century, advancements included improved public access, a new wing, more space for the exhibits, new departments and collecting in areas like ethnography and European prehistory, as functions on a national and an international level were actively developed.[21]

During the latter part of the century the expansion of the British Empire ensured that the British Museum was the recipient of great artworks, but as the flow of cultural artefacts declined the museum, in common with other Western museums, changed its emphasis to scholarship and display. Thus, it evolved into a centre where the focus was on an aesthetic–educational experience rather than on exclusively scholarly goals. A future director's vision would emulate the founder's original purpose: 'To illuminate and explain the past of the whole world through material culture'.[22]

The Royal Academy and the National Gallery

While the British Museum was evolving, the issue of an exhibition venue in which British artists could display and sell their work was becoming critical. Prior to the establishment of the RA, European ideas about popular education had been developed in England by the Society for the Encouragement of Arts, Manufactures and Commerce ('the Society of Arts'). While public galleries did not yet exist in Britain, the improvements to Vauxhall Gardens – the exhibition space provided by the Foundling Hospital (opened 1739) in 1749 for British artists 'Reynolds, Gainsborough and Ramsay' to decorate its walls[23] – and the advent of London's first independent art exhibitions set in place the components of a modern art world. Dulwich Picture Gallery, built between 1811 and 1813 by Sir John Soane, was one of several London galleries housing an exemplary collection of old masters that became an outstanding precedent for gallery design.[24]

The RA was founded in 1768 to address this issue. It became notable among European academies in the influence it exerted over the development of art in Britain through its three foundation roles: art school, exhibition space and professional institute. The academy system, which derived from Europe, sought to foster public appreciation of the visual arts and to raise the stature of the artist in society.[25] Its first three presidents, Joshua Reynolds, Benjamin West and Thomas Lawrence, advocated the creation of a national gallery. Academy students were sent to study 'from the antique' at the British Museum – at one stage 223 artists were issued with tickets to draw. Its four successive city-centre homes, from Pall Mall to Burlington House, gradually brought it to the centre of the commercial art world.[26] The first academy exhibition was held in 1769, and when a new suite of galleries was added in 1869, it was used by the municipal art museums to purchase works of art (as in Scotland

Joseph Michael Gandy (1771–1843), *The Dulwich Picture Gallery* **c.1823**
Watercolour, 22 x 70.5 cm. Sir John Soane's Museum.

The design by Sir John Soane was built between 1811 and 1813 and amended during construction to save cost. One of many early nineteenth-century galleries in London, its shape and layout was influential on gallery design over the centuries.

Henry Jamyn Brooks (1865–1925), *Private View of 1888*
***Old Master's Exhibition at the Royal Academy, London,* 1889**
Oil on canvas, 152.4 x 406.4 cm. National Portrait Gallery.

Its triple mandate to teach, exhibit and affirm the status of the artist in society enabled the Royal Academy to assume its place in the artistic life of the nation. The canvas includes many distinguished figures in the art world. From left to right: Sir Frederic William Burton, John Ruskin, Sir John Agnew; mid-centre, Sir Richard Wallace, Countess of Jersey, Sir Frederic Leighton; in the background, Henry Doyle, Sir John Robertson and 7th Viscount Powerscourt.

and Ireland). In this way the RA, through its exhibiting and teaching roles (like the Royal Scottish Academy[27] and the RHA[28]), helped to shape taste, enhance the development of the visual arts and play a significant part in nineteenth-century British cultural life.

The ruling oligarchy in Britain had been slow to create a national gallery, feeling that their great houses and collections were evidence enough of power and cultural prestige. While there had been public discussion about the need for a gallery for public enjoyment and for the education of artists, the debate was heightened by the success of the Louvre when it became a public institution. The opening of the British Institution for Promoting the Fine Arts under the Patronage of His Majesty (1805), showing the work of contemporary British artists and exhibitions of old masters, prompted calls for government support of the arts. Following his visit to the Vatican Museums, Sir George Beaumont, one of the founders of the British Institution, determined that Britain would have the improvements that were available on the Continent. Beaumont set in motion the process of forming a gallery. In the meantime, John Julius Angerstein died in 1823. Angerstein was a wealthy patron of the fine arts and had gathered an impressive collection during his lifetime. The British government moved swiftly to acquire his collection, leasing his house at number 100 Pall Mall and installing the first keeper, William Seguier. Thus was the National Gallery established, superintended by a 'Committee of Six Gentlemen' appointed by Treasury.[29] The government founded the National Gallery for the improvement of public taste and for the education of artists – a combination of patriotism and public interest – as the institution would also provide access to works of art for a broad, democratic audience.

When the National Gallery first opened, admission was free between Monday and Thursday, and free for artists and students on Friday and Saturday; it remained closed on Sunday.[30] The gallery moved to number 105 Pall Mall in 1834, but problems of adequate space persisted, leading Sir Robert Peel, National Gallery trustee, to propose to the House of Commons (1832) that a new building be erected on the north side of Trafalgar Square. This was accomplished by 1837, in accommodation shared temporarily with the Royal Academy (1837–67).[31]

In 1838 the National Gallery opened in an elegant neo-classical building designed by William Wilkins, following the pattern of European museums.

Charles Joseph Hullmandel (1789–1850), *The Louvre or the National Gallery of France ... 100 Pall Mall or the National Gallery of England, c.1830*

The collection of John Julius Angerstein formed the basis of the National Gallery, London when it opened in 1824. The engraving expresses the contrasting situation between the gallery's modest premises and the Louvre.

(German museums had adopted a neo-classical style: the Glyptothek in Munich [1830] by Leo von Klenze; the Altes Museum in Berlin by Karl Friedrich Schinkel [1830].) The design was well conceived, with consideration given to: the functions of the newly founded gallery; the need for art education to improve the standard of British artists; the question of improving the working classes; the issue of hygiene and behaviour in the galleries; and the need to attract tourist revenue. The concept of public education was important to the gallery trustees, who wanted the public to benefit from viewing the paintings, to 'get a taste when exposed to art', just as the National Portrait Gallery, 1856, aimed to collect 'images of the heroes of the British state', which would lead to 'noble actions, and good conduct'.

Despite the comments of nineteenth-century improvers, access for working-class people to museums was contested. While a 1848 survey by the *Art Union* magazine recorded that the gallery was 'thronged by a multitude', the eminent German professor of art history and director of the Gemaldegalerie, Berlin, Gustav Friedrich Waagen, felt it was important 'for the preservation of the pictures that such persons should in future be excluded'.[32] Opinions varied: Prince Albert saw collections as valuable 'educational' resources, while the radical reformer Thomas Wyse MP defined the value of public education as being 'to improve the moral condition of the people'.[33] To this end, guides were required to explain the works of art to visitors.

A mid-century assessment of the National Gallery resulted in a new museological structure and review of the displays at Trafalgar Square. Charles Eastlake's term as director (1855–65) brought a historical approach to the collection, aided by a new hanging system that followed the pattern in Europe.[34] The public visited clean, well-lit surroundings, in which the collection was ordered in a framework of historical sequences, with distinctions between master and pupil, masterpiece and lesser work and between the schools of different nations. In the era of Victorian prosperity following the Great Exhibition, the building was further expanded as more and more people chose to visit the gallery, and the Manchester Art Treasures (1857) and the International Exhibition at South Kensington (1862). Influenced by the growing popularity of the London institutions, an attempt was made to set up a municipal museum structure.[35] This was aided by the Education Act 1870, which put in place the machinery that would make universal education possible. Thus between 1860 and 1900 the number of public museums in Britain increased from 50 to 200, numbering among them the municipal galleries in Manchester (Manchester City Art Gallery), in Liverpool (Walker Art Gallery,) in York (York City Art Gallery), in Bradford (Cartwright Hall) and in Glasgow (Glasgow Art Gallery).

The National Gallery's stature as a public art museum increased as the century wore on, its popularity illustrated by the fact that London welcomed fifteen times as many visitors as Berlin.[36] In 1854 Waagen's *Treasures of Art in Great Britain* identified a 'British' School of painting, positioning London as its cultural centre. In 1889, Henry Tate offered the National Gallery his collection of British paintings, the outcome of which saw the British School established at Millbank (now Tate Britain) in 1897.[37] The historian E.P. Thompson commented that a peculiarity of British history was the formation of the bourgeois state, and that its supporting culture evolved slowly and organically out of a complex of older forms.[38] The gallery came to rival the Louvre when political developments forced the British government to recognize the advantage of having prestigious national monuments symbolizing the nation united under universal values. Thus, the National Gallery displayed an outstanding collection of Western European artworks dating from the thirteenth to nineteenth century, setting the standard for museums in other countries, like Ireland.

The Altes Museum, Berlin, 1830

The first major purpose-built museum to absorb the space and architectural lessons of the Louvre was designed by Karl Friedrich Schinkel, who understood the importance of public institutions within the emerging political structure of the modern world. It would be followed by Leo von Klenze's Alte Pinakothek in Munich, 1836.

A Turning-Point in the Role of the State

The most significant shift in the state's attitude to museums was marked by the South Kensington Museum. First established as the Museum of Manufactures at Marlborough House (in 1852) and renamed the Museum of Ornamental Art in 1853, it emerged from a school of design (founded in 1837) with museum collections.[39] Its first home was the much-derided 'Brompton Boilers', near Cromwell Road, followed by a building designed by Captain Francis Fowke.[40] The South Kensington Museum was opened by Queen Victoria on 22 June 1857 and its contents comprised British sculpture, architectural casts, animal products, food, models and patented inventions, educational aids, the National Art Library, a circulating art library, construction and building materials,[41] and the Sheepshanks Collection of British Paintings was donated in 1856.[42]

Henry Cole, who had managed the Great Exhibition of 1851, became director of the South Kensington Museum in 1857. This role, which was to

Henry Gritton (1818–73), *View of the National Gallery, London*

This is a view of the new premises of the National Gallery before it was opened by Queen Victoria in 1838. Designed by William Wilkins and constructed between 1834 and 1838, the gallery overlooks Trafalgar Square in the heart of London.

last until his retirement in 1873, also put Cole in charge of a nationwide art education system as the instigator of new museums of art and design. He was a superb administrator, employing a pragmatic approach to the museum, which was directed towards the education of public taste, in order to promote a better understanding of the role of design in British manufactures. His first director's report stated: 'The Museum is intended to be used … not only used physically, but to be taken about and lectured upon … I venture to think that unless museums and galleries are made subservient to purposes of education, they dwindle into very sleepy and useless institutions.'[43] The issue of access was a critical success factor, as Cole viewed the museum with the public in mind: 'The working man could go and study any subject he wishes, can have a cup of tea for 2d, and if preferred, a glass of beer; it was a fact that thirteen millions of people had been admitted to the institution.'[44] Open six days a week and until 10 p.m. on three nights, two of these being free days (paying days were Tuesday, Wednesday, Thursday), with a charge of sixpence on student days, the South Kensington made museums accessible to the working class.[45] Cole's successful policies attracted 15 million visitors to the museum between 1857 and 1883; 6.5 million of those were recorded in the evening time, which was the most popular visiting time, as the brightly gas-lit interiors were a novelty in the days before electricity.

The museum was a busy, active place: circulating exhibitions (1855–63) and loans were provided to individual institutions, including the Department of Science and Art's schools, which borrowed material for two months and purchased duplicates at half cost;[46] evening events were encouraged; Cole oversaw the opening of the first museum restaurant; souvenir prints were sold by the museum's photographic studio;[47] there was an art library, a lecture series, plentiful labels[48] and catalogues of reproductions made from its own objects, including plaster casts (published 1869 onwards).[49] South Kensington Museum functioned in the manner of a school of science and art (similar to the Conservatoire des Arts et Métiers in France), with inspiration sourced from the *objets d'art* in the museum's own collections.[50] Cole worked to consolidate the museum until his retirement, having been fortunate to have the

The South Kensington Museum

A view of the loan collection in the south court; wood engraving from the *Illustrated London News*, 6 December 1862. On display was a range of medieval, Renaissance and decorative art, together with sculpture and a large collection of ceramics. The South Kensington Museum was an immensely popular and influential museum in the nineteenth century.

drive to shine under Prince Albert's patronage during a period of Victorian social stability and economic prosperity that ended with the Great Depression of 1873.

The South Kensington Museum marked an important turning point in British museum policy, articulating principles that saw museums as instruments of public education. These ideas influenced the development of the other museums in London and their impact was also felt further afield, at Dublin's Museum of Science and Art (1890) and at New York's Metropolitan Museum (1870). Now well known as the Victoria & Albert Museum, or the V&A, this venerable institution retains its central position in London's vibrant museum scene.

Britain and Ireland

Positive Influences: Industrial Exhibitions and Temporary 'Loan' Collections
The background to the evolution of industrial exhibitions in Ireland was provided by the early manufacturers' exhibitions in England (1847, 1848, 1849), which were organized by the Society of Arts in London, following similar enterprises held by the RDS,[51] and observed by Prince Albert and Henry Cole.[52] By the 1850s museums in Ireland included those of the RDS, the RIA, Dublin University and the exhibiting rooms of the RHA. France also mounted *Expositions Universelles*, to which Ireland contributed. The Irish industrial exhibitions were pioneered by the RDS and the first were held in 1834 and 1835,[53] after which they became triennial shows (1838, 1841, 1844, 1847, 1850). The purpose of the exhibitions varied from country to country: the Great Exhibition of 1851 set the standard for world fairs, establishing Britain as a world manufacturing centre and raising the level of industrial design; the French aimed to pursue enlightened, entertaining shows that affirmed universal prestige; Irish exhibitions were designed to improve the economy, while establishing an international reputation for Irish manufacturers, artists and designers.

The Irish exhibitions that capitalized on the Great Exhibition included those held in Cork (1852) and Dublin (1853, 1865). Cork's National Exhibition of Arts, Manufactures and Products of Ireland was held in the Corn Exchange, the highlight of its Fine Art section being *The Spirit of Justice* (1847–9), by

Daniel Maclise.[54] South Kensington Museum's Department of Science and Art loaned works to the Cork Exhibition to make up for the lack of public art collections. The aim of the show was ambitious:

> to induce every person who entered the walls of the Exhibition to resolve within his or her mind in doing as much as possible to give employment, diminish poverty, lessen taxes, promote happiness, and elevate the moral and physical condition of the mass of the people, by the practical encouragement of native industry.[55]

The Dublin Exhibition of Art-Industry was opened on 12 May 1853 by the lord lieutenant, the 3rd Earl of St Germans, and ran for five months, until 31 October. It was organized by the RDS and funded by William Dargan, who wished to improve the economic prospects of Ireland. It was held in a timber building, the Temple of Industry, designed by John Benson and located on the RDS grounds at Leinster Lawn. The 'Temple' comprised a grand central hall with four parallel halls, along which the stalls and exhibits were set out.[56] The *Exhibition Expositor and Advertiser* stated that the show aimed to encourage Irish industry,[57] with exhibits grouped under four categories: raw materials, machinery, manufactures, and fine art.

The most innovative aspect of the Dublin exhibition was the Fine Art Hall, which, together with the Hall of Irish Antiquities, dominated the show (in the absence of industrial exhibits) and demonstrated the country's value as a cultural centre and part of the United Kingdom. It emerged as the finest cultural display ever assembled in Ireland, combining 1,000 old master and contemporary paintings (including the work of Irish artists) with works of oriental art and 493 sculptures and carvings. The hall provided 'a great educational establishment, calculated to impress upon the minds of all classes important lessons'.[58] Its success starkly highlighted one of Ireland's failings, however – the lack of a permanent art gallery: 'A country that has given birth to Moore, McDowell, West, Maclise … cannot boast of a single national collection.'[59]

At the main entrance the display of medieval stone 'High Crosses' became adopted as symbols (along with the harp, the shamrock and the wolfhound) of a reclaimed and reinvigorated Irish identity.[60] Nearby, the Hall of Irish Antiquities displayed collections loaned by art dealers, and the RDS and RIA museums. These works reflected the pattern of dilettante collecting and amateur archaeology that was in the process of exploring Ireland's past.[61] The *Exhibition Expositor and Advertiser* drew attention to the lack of a national museum:

> This collection is still much less known than it should be, and
> we believe that it was in the hope of bringing its claims better
> before the public [that they] will thereby be enabled to form
> a correct opinion of its extent and value, and an opportunity
> will be afforded to every one to assist in the establishment of
> the Museum – the only truly *national* one in Europe.[62]

Over one million people visited the exhibition, with attendances doubling in the final month.[63] The British royal family visited in September and purchased embroidered muslin, lace and Irish Celtic jewellery; Queen Victoria offered Dargan a peerage, which he quietly declined: 'It was left for an Irishman to achieve a triumph to which either ancient or modern times affords no parallel.'[64] Three watercolours by James Mahony (1810–79) illustrated the exhibition: *The First Visit by Queen Victoria and Prince Albert to the Irish Industrial Exhibition, Dublin, ca.1853*; *The Visit by Queen Victoria and Prince Albert to the Fine Art Hall of the Irish Industrial Exhibition, Dublin*; and *The Fourth Visit by Queen Victoria and Prince Albert to the Irish Industrial Exhibition, Dublin.*[65] 'The Great Irish Industrial Exhibition stands prominently forward as one of those many proofs of the progress of Ireland.'[66]

The legacy of the exhibition's Fine Art Hall was the subsequent declaration of support for a permanent art collection. In 1853 a 'Dargan Committee' established a testimonial fund to be used to erect a 'suitable building for the reception and exhibition of works for the fine arts'.[67] In November the Irish Institution was founded to establish a 'permanent exhibition in Dublin and eventually of an Irish National Gallery'.[68] It held loan exhibitions, which generated revenue through admission charges, and invited the public to subscribe towards the enterprise with monies or artworks.[69] In 1854 the RDS discussed a site for the National Gallery on Leinster Lawn and by 10 August of that same year 'An Act to establish a National Gallery of Ireland' had been passed by Parliament.[70]

The legacy of the exhibition's Hall of Irish Antiquities was a fresh impetus to build the RDS Natural History Museum and the longer-term aim of establishing a national museum. The RDS received a grant of £5,000 in 1853 (as compensation for the building of a School of Design), representing government commitment to the establishment of its museum.[71] The National Museum archives record that Sir Richard Griffith, chairman of the Board of Works, vice-chairman of the RDS and a governor of the National Gallery, forwarded the museum plans to Captain Francis Fowke (then engaged in supervising the building of the South Kensington Museum). As a result, the final plans for the Natural History Museum (and later National Gallery) were an amalgamation of the ideas of Frederick Clarendon, Fowke and Griffith's staff at the Board of Works.[72]

The Dublin Natural History Museum opened in 1857 on Merrion Street. In the meantime, a local committee continued to pursue the issue of a national museum by establishing a Royal Irish Institute of Science and Art, to be managed by a Royal Commission of Irishmen. A government review (1868–70) of science and art teaching (under private societies like the RDS and reporting to Westminister's Department of Science) proposed that instruction be provided by public institutions.[73] The outcome of this was the passing of the Science and Art Museum Act in 1877, which provided for the establishment of a national museum in Ireland.[74]

There were other legacies of the exhibition, albeit less tangible. Dublin was not an imperial centre, like most world fair cities, but more of a colonial outpost of empire. The exhibition's success encouraged and facilitated the concept of Ireland as a political collectivity in the modern world, enabling a transformation from a devastated region of the United Kingdom into a nation with an honourable past and bright future prospects. Of course, those who supported empire but were able to imagine a nation saw contradictions at all levels in the exhibition. When the imperial representative, Queen Victoria, purchased a copy of Irish Celtic jewellery, little did she know that these self-same items of decoration would become potent symbols in a move towards national self-determination.

This brief view of the nineteenth-century links between Britain and Ireland

James Mahony (1810–79), *The Visit by Queen Victoria and Prince Albert to the Fine Art Hall of the 1853 Dublin Great Exhibition*
Watercolour on paper, 62.8 x 81 cm. NGI 7009.

The Dublin International Exhibition of Art-Industry was held on the RDS grounds on Leinster Lawn, with halls devoted to fine art and antiquities. While the purpose of the exhibition was to promote industry, the impact of the Fine Art and Irish Antiquities Halls had a major effect on the development of Irish museums. One of three watercolours by Mahony bequeathed to the gallery by Captain George Archibald Taylor in 1854.

shows how the cross-fertilization of ideas was significant for both countries. Key figures were influential in both museum movements, men like Cole and Sloane in Britain and Dargan in Ireland: 'Dargan was more significant in terms of Irish development than was his contemporary Brunel in England and Carnegie in the United States.'[75] Thus, by the mid-nineteenth century most of the main components of the Irish museum movement were in place, thanks to the impetus provided by Britain: Dublin's International Exhibition; the Act to found a national gallery; the catalyst to develop the Natural History Museum; and the drive to found a national museum. It would remain for Cole to consolidate this process by creating a cultural quarter in Dublin similar to that at South Kensington. These links ensured that as the century progressed, Ireland was ready to, and capable of, moving forward to embrace the modern public institution. So, too, were Ireland's museum directors ready to absorb the new developments that soon arrived from America, resulting in the American model also playing a significant role in shaping the parameters of the public museum.

The Museum in America

> An hour spent in the museum of Florence, or in the select society of Apollo and Co in the palace of the Vatican, would be sufficient to convert the most rude taste to something very refined and intelligent.[76]

Despite this American Grand Tourist's comment, affirmed by another – 'the European museum is the parent of museums in other countries'[77] – there were differences between American and European museums. Peale, being aware of the limitations of European museums, set out to make his museum accessible, like a school for the general public. While the term 'collection' defined the European museum, in America the museum was an institution that used collections for a specific purpose.[78] Therefore, the American museum was 'neither an abandoned European palace nor a solution for storing national wealth … [but] an American phenomenon developed by the people, for the people, and of the people'.[79]

Museums in the United States emerged in the late eighteenth and nineteenth centuries as institutions serving in the cause of legitimate knowledge – a concept drawn from the French Revolution. President Thomas Jefferson had a fossils cabinet in the presidential residence (not yet called the White House). In 1743, before independence was won, Benjamin Franklin (1706–90) wrote in *Proposals for Promoting Useful Knowledge among the British Plantations in America* that there would be time 'to cultivate the fine arts'. (Franklin visited Hans Sloane's cabinet of curiosities in London and founded the American Philosophical Society in Philadelphia in 1744.[80]) Already in America, enlightened figures were considering the formation of collections and museums as part of the pattern of educating and integrating the fresh settlers and immigrants into their new country. In common with Britain and Ireland, learning bodies and antiquarian societies in America were established as precursors to museums, but the pace of progress was much faster than that of its European counterparts. Within a short period of time a number of key figures had established libraries and museums as a method of attracting and educating the public. Irish museum directors would be drawn by the rapid pace of development in America.

Early American Museums

Charleston Museum of Natural History and Peale's Museum

The Charleston Museum of Natural History in South Carolina is considered the first and oldest museum in North America. In 1773 the Charleston Literary Society, founded in 1743, annexed a museum and appointed a committee to acquire natural history collections. Unfortunately, a fire destroyed the building and most of the collections during the American Revolution and for many years the museum remained closed. By the 1820s, there were calls for the museum to reopen, the *Charleston Courier* commenting: 'In these enlightened times, a public museum is as necessary an appendage to a city as a newspaper or a public library.' The Charleston Museum re-opened in 1824, aspiring to become 'as well known as Peale's Museum in Pennsylvania', with free admission attracting 'visitors from all parts of the country'.[81] It became a permanent collection,[82] and was commended by the Smithsonian Institution: 'the museum exerts a beneficial influence among the people'.[83]

Other museums were founded at this time, including Smibert's Gallery (1730),[84] Pine's Picture Gallery (1784),[85] and Du Simitière's Museum (1782).[86] Some were shaped by Americans who were familiar with Europe, such as Washington's Renwick Gallery (1859), which was influenced by the Louvre,[87] while others focused on both European and oriental artefacts: 'Shiploads of works of art arrived in New York, Philadelphia and Boston.'[88] The Salem East India Marine Society (founded 1799) opened its doors as the Peabody Museum in 1825, with decorative art and maritime artefacts.

While these trends were important in laying the foundations of a unique museum culture, Peale's Museum in Philadelphia was the first significant American museum. Peale started out as a painter, studying under Benjamin

Charles Willson Peale (1741–1827), *The Artist in his Museum,* **1822**
Oil on canvas, 236.5 x 202.9 cm. Pennsylvania Academy of the Fine Arts, Philadelphia.

In 1786 Peale turned his home into a cabinet of curiosities. By 1802 visitors to his museum in Philadelphia could see 760 specimens of birds from the Americas, Europe, Asia and the South Seas with the insides of the cases painted by the curator and his sons to represent appropriate habitats.

West in London, and developed a prolific practice painting portraits of historical American figures, notably George Washington. He established a picture gallery at his home in Philadelphia in 1782, and added portraits of American revolutionary figures in 1784.[89] By augmenting the gallery with art and natural history collections, he redefined it as a 'repository for natural curiosities'. The opening of this unusual museum was announced in the *Pennsylvania Packet* on 18 July 1786. By the 1790s it had grown into the first scientifically organized (Linnean classification) museum of natural history. In time Peale moved the collections (and his family) to Philosophical Hall, home of the American Philosophical Society,[90] and then, in 1802, to the Pennsylvania State House, known as Independence Hall, where his museum attracted 47,000 visitors in a peak attendance year in 1816. His repository of 'the world in miniature' gradually developed into a national museum of natural history. In 1805 he founded the Pennsylvania Academy of the Fine Arts, which opened a museum in 1807 with early American collections.[91]

Peale wanted his collections to advance 'useful knowledge', arguing that his museum's open-access policy contrasted with the exclusivity of European museums. As he was depending on a favourable review of his museum by the visitors, he provided a range of admission fees; opening hours were extended into the evenings, when oil lamps (followed by gaslight) were provided; and lectures were repeated for audiences who worked during the day.[92] Out of concern for the collections, he placed railings and glass in front of the natural history exhibits and signs to discourage disruptive behaviour. He insisted the museum was accessible and democratic, 'one of the best museums in the United States, comprising the most complete skeleton of the mammoth perhaps in the world'.[93]

Peale's Museum was the first popular museum to develop museological trends, which Charles instilled in four of his children, Raphaelle, Titian, Rembrandt and Rubens (Rembrandt and Rubens ran an art museum in Baltimore between 1814 and 1830). Following Peale's death in 1827, the museum and its satellites declined and the collections were disbursed. An Irish visitor, John Godley, described his visit to Philadelphia in 1842: 'an American kindly devoted the morning to lionizing me over all sorts of fine museums'.[94] The success of Peale's Museum, however, showed what could be achieved by well-run institutions and what benefits they could bestow on the general populace. As a result, local government began to support American museums by providing funding. One such recipient was Scudder's Museum of Curiosities in New York (founded in 1810), which was purchased by the legendary showman P.T. Barnum in 1841. Barnum sought to acquire more collections, in the process purchasing Peale's New York Museum, in 1846, for his Philadelphia branch museum (1849).[95] Barnum's museums combined entertainment with education and were described by Irish traveller Matthew Francis as 'the largest travelling exhibition in the world'. The author Theodore Dwight's advocacy of museums echoed Cole in England and Dargan in Ireland.[96]

One of the oldest museums in continuous operation was the Wadsworth Athenaeum in Hartford, Connecticut, set up by Daniel Wadsworth in 1842, opened in 1844, whose patronage sought to further cultural education.[97] The *Hartford Daily Courant* praised it as being 'unsurpassed by any in the country', with a permanent collection of European old masters and American art.[98] An Irish visitor noted: 'I have seen the objects in the museum … found them leading to profitable reflection.'[99] The wider impact on culture and learning was a natural progression. According to the noted educator Henry Barnard in 1864, 'the century was marked by a constantly increasing energy working towards educational improvement'.[100] University museums played an important role in that development. Harvard's collection (established in 1736) was incorporated into the Harvard Hall in 1766, with a 'Musaeum for Curiosities' that became a museum of natural history, together with its Fogg Art Museum, which opened in 1891. Yale's gallery (founded 1832) housed paintings by Colonel John Trumbull.[101] The founding of the Smithsonian Institution in 1846 marked a decisive move towards the museum as repository and disseminator of knowledge. These instructive collections contributed hugely to public education.[102]

The Smithsonian Institution

The Smithsonian Institution derived from the bequest of James Smithson (1765–1829), an English chemist and mineralogist. The bequest that he drew up before he died (1826) provided for the creation of a body for 'the increase and diffusion of knowledge'. It took a decade to resolve, but eventually a proposal to establish the institution was placed before the American Congress

The museum, which opened in Washington, DC, in 1881, displayed everything from mammals to geology, engineering and art. It appears to be a popular, much-visited museum.

in 1836, resulting in its foundation in 1846.[103] The first secretary, Joseph Henry, defended his use of the bequest in the journal *Scientific American*, which opposed using Smithson's funds for a museum, a library and initiatives in archaeology. Smithsonian objectives were carried out in *Reports* of the highest intellectual standard, and knowledge was shared and disseminated through a library, an art gallery and the American Natural History Museum.[104] Known as the Museum of the Smithsonian Institution until 1851, the United States National Museum originated in the merging of the National Cabinet of Curiosities and the institution.

The importance of the Smithsonian's American Natural History Museum, with its natural history, art, science, sculpture, antiquities and architectural remains, was signalled by its location in Washington, DC, at 'the seat of government to illustrate the physical geography, natural history and ethnology of the United States'.[105] Part of the museum was open by 1859, providing access for scholars and the public, as research from American and European museums was disseminated to international institutions. The Reverend Daniel Foley, first professor of Irish at the Catholic University, Dublin, stated that 'the Smithsonian Institution was much honoured there, for the diffusion of valuable information gratuitously to the public admirably fulfilling its design'.[106]

When George Brown Goode joined the Smithsonian in 1873, it was a national museum devoted to science, humanities and the arts, and he became the leading museum professional of his day.[107] Brown Goode saw the museum's educational role as a priority: 'public institutions of this kind are not intended for the few but for the enlightenment and education of the masses'. He wanted a 'people's museum', with collections displayed in exhibitions for the public and a reserve collection for research – a European arrangement referred to as 'the new museum idea' by William Henry Flower, director of the Natural History Museum, London. Brown Goode developed museological trends of records maintenance and exhibition display, while being an innovative administrator with progressive ideas. His view that the museum was a force for public good spread to Europe, as he commented in 1899: 'the degree of civilization to which any nation, city or province has attained is best shown by the character of its public museums and the liberality with which they are maintained'.[108] The Smithsonian Institution led the international growth of scientific research, becoming the parent organization for museums in the United States.

Late Nineteenth-Century Developments

The Metropolitan Museum of Art (1870) and the Art Institute of Chicago (1879)

The development of American museums in the latter half of the nineteenth century was affected by circumstances relating to public education and to unprecedented wealth held by a small minority. The progressive notion of using collections for public instruction – 'for the inspection of the learned and the great mass of the public'[109] – clashed with the displays of wealth that consolidated the position of the social elite. Nonetheless, democratic and egalitarian approaches to education continued to be promoted by American theorists, such as Franklin, Jefferson, Ralph Waldo Emerson and John Dewey, and these philosophies were echoed by cultural idealists, such as Theodore Law, Brown Goode, Paul Marshall Rea, Benjamin Ives Gilman and T.R. Adams, who developed the 'museum idea' that initiated a museological movement across America.[110] The concept of museums as instruments of education grew alongside a concern among educated Americans about the quality of the cultural life of the nation. The outcome was the construction of public museums between 1865 and 1900, and art museums between 1870 and 1929.

The catalyst for the opening of the Metropolitan Museum of Art in New York was the 1853 New York World's Fair, which highlighted the lack of a major museum in much the same way as the Dublin Exhibition of Art-Industry had done in Ireland.[111] The idea was conceived in Paris in 1868 by a group of businessmen who felt that America's first city required cultural institutions to rival European museums.[112] Following an inaugural meeting and committee in 1869, the Metropolitan Museum received its Act of Incorporation in 1870. Once that had been rubber-stamped, the trustees bought 174 works and opened the Fifth Avenue museum immediately.

The Metropolitan Museum was dependent on private funding, which meant it had to attract visitors in addition to encouraging people to support and donate to the museum.[113] Attracting an audience did not pose a problem: the museum welcomed 6,000 visitors in the first three months of 1872 alone. This success led, of course, to the need for more space, which resulted in an agreement worked out with the city of New York. The museum building in Central Park, completed in 1880, was enlarged in 1888, thanks to a grant of land from the New York City Council. In this way, the city authorities declared museums to be as important in terms of education and entertainment as other institutions, a position further backed up by the granting of land on the far side of Central Park to the American Museum of Natural History.[114] The Metropolitan's familiar façade, dominating Fifth Avenue, reopened in 1902 in a Richard Morris Hunt-designed neo-classical building that backed onto Central Park.

These new, very visible public museums were one strand of a larger civic programme that included parks, libraries and concert halls and that saw these venues as forming part of an educational enterprise to integrate new-comers.[115] The Metropolitan's Board of Management realized that public art museums were developing as important resources for learning that required works of the major European Schools, placed on display in a systematized art-historical order.[116] Just as the Museum of Fine Arts in Boston (founded 1870) was developing first-class collections, so too did the Metropolitan Museum move swiftly to acquire major works. By 1894 the Metropolitan was almost as large as the British Museum, though it had more in common with the educational approach of the South Kensington Museum.[117] By the end of the nineteenth century, the 'Met' in New York and the V&A in London

The Metropolitan Museum of Art in Central Park, early 20th century

The 'Met's' first home was on 681 Fifth Avenue in 1872. It opened in Central Park in 1880. Illustrated is Richard Morris Hunt's neo-classical façade in 1910, showing older buildings to the rear.

were advancing the social role of the museum, paving the way for a new public awareness of these institutions, thereby creating wider access opportunities.

The Art Institute of Chicago

While the foundation of the Museum of Fine Arts was a natural civic progression for Boston, the emergence of the Art Institute of Chicago in 1879 represented a museum that was built through private patronage.[118] The people who promoted the Art Institute (including wealthy women who devoted themselves to helping American museums) also backed the international World Columbian Exposition in 1893.[119] Established initially as the Chicago Academy of Fine Arts, when the name was changed in 1882 the museum element became as important as the school. The institute's impressive architecture, which was based on Boston Public Library, reflected American energy and vision, while incorporating classical Greek and Italian precedents. It was located at the centre of the city's commercial district, making it more accessible than other museums.[120] The institite soon became synonymous with public education: 'We have built this institution for the public … not for a few … we want the people to feel that this is their property.'[121]

The Art Institute had a dual function: a museum devoted to collecting and displaying fine art; and a school dedicated to the training of artists.

The Museum of Fine Arts, Boston, 1909

Founded in 1870, the museum displays an impressive monumental façade that reflects the pattern of European museum design.

Founded concurrently, the museum and school developed along parallel lines and encouraged each other's aims. The school widened public access to the museum's programmes, offering its students a course of instruction in studying the masterpieces collected and exhibited by the museum. From 1887 the museum hosted talks by figures such as the photographer Eadweard Muybridge and the architect Louis H. Sullivan. The arrival of over two million immigrants to Chicago between 1880 and the 1920s caused civic leaders to engage in social and cultural reform to help integrate and educate the 'new Americans', using the museum's free admission days (three per week, including Sundays) to draw the working classes and new citizens to the Art Institute. Large numbers came for Lorado Taft's talks on European art, 'to popularize the galleries and make collections more useful to the public'.[122] Thus the Art Institute of Chicago developed as a centre of learning, becoming in the process 'a well-arranged and well-labelled museum'.[123]

The Art Institute of Chicago on Michigan Avenue, *c*.1894

In common with European museums, the Art Institute exhibited replicas of Greek, Roman, Renaissance and modern sculpture, as well as casts of architectural elements, for instruction purposes between 1884 and the 1950s.

The closing of the nineteenth century saw educational and cultural functions in museums coalescing, with the poorer and immigrant classes encouraged to use these institutions to develop middle-class values and behaviour. The number of museums grew: 'They are starting up in all directions, untrammeled by the restrictions and traditions which envelop so many of our old institutions … the new [museum] idea has taken firm root there.'[124] The drive to educate, entertain and inform became the hallmark of the American museum and the educational practices pioneered there emerged as 'a distinctively American idea'.[125] This 'idea' found its way across the ocean to British and Irish institutions, which were also formulating their plans and visions for the future of the public institution museum in a new century.

5

The Role of Education in the Growth of Nineteenth-Century Museums

I hope [this museum] will give a powerful impulse to the study of nature and physical science fostering a taste for knowledge among all classes of our community.[1]

The nineteenth century was marked by new thinking in the museum movement, whereby the notion of museums as centres of education and learning became common currency. This was a radical departure from the previous tradition of cabinets of curiosities, scientific investigation and restricting collections to the wealthy, the educated and the 'socially desirable'. A new breed of museum director was moulded in the museums of America and latterly Britain, where education formed one of the core tenets of the museum enterprise, a principle adopted and encouraged, by degrees, in the museums in Ireland and Europe. The influence from America was significant in this regard, leading the way to the modern institutions of the twentieth century.

In Ireland, the effect of this new thinking was evident in the regional museums that were established, including the Belfast Art Gallery and Museum and the Crawford Municipal Gallery in Cork, as well as in the Government Schools of Design and the university museums that catered for knowledge-

Attributed to Strickland Lowry (1737–c.1785),
The Family of Thomas Bateson, Esq (1705–1791), **1762**
Oil on canvas, 163.7 x 264 cm. Ulster Museum UM1664.

The fine arts began to flourish in Belfast in the second half of the eighteenth century, supporting resident artists, including Strickland Lowry (then in the north of Ireland c.1762–80). Wealthy patrons included Thomas Bateson, one of three partners of the first bank (1752) in Belfast. His children are shown in the hall of the family seat at Orangefield, County Down.

hungry students. The new philosophies of education were hugely important in the founding ethos of these institutions, driving the museum movement on to seek and attain wider ambitions.

The growth of the museum movement right across the nineteenth century in Dublin, Belfast, Cork and Galway was the outcome of initiatives by individuals and groups encouraged by a yearning for culture and learning that gave rise to new universities, art schools, museums and galleries. These cultural centres came to have a particular relevance for their local communities as well as for the country. The Schools of Design were essential for the instruction they provided in fine art and design, part of which involved studying from the collections in the new museums and galleries. The introduction of the Queen's Colleges and their university museums formed part of this educational enterprise, with the main purpose of their collections being to teach students in a range of interdisciplinary subjects. Towards the end of the century, the antiquarian and fine art interest that had originated

in the science, art and learning institutions spread to a wider constituency due
to the desire of the growing Catholic middle classes to educate themselves.

Education for All: Regional Museums

Ireland's regional museums were a necessary corollary to the emergence of
field clubs and naturalists' societies, whose pursuits created an interest in
Victorian practical activities, such as birdwatching and mineral-gathering,
which in turn demanded museum space to house the specimens collected.
The increasing interest in education, natural history and science was harnessed by societies and institutions, which amassed collections that contributed to the drive to set up museums, thus becoming part of the 'museum movement' in Ireland. The rationale behind the setting up of these
museums was a desire for culture and for knowledge, a sense of local ownership, and a cultural framework that reached beyond the capital city. In
this, Belfast and Cork were the main regional museums; the development of
municipal museums and collections came later, in the twentieth century.

Belfast Museum (1831) and Belfast Art Gallery and Museum (1890)

In the opening decades of the nineteenth century Belfast was the one city on
the island whose economy was booming, which ensured that it was also rich
in antiquarian pursuits and fine art
education. It followed that the city
needed a cultural infrastructure. The
sentiments expressed in the *Northern
Whig*, on 6 November 1834, were
indicative of the cultural aspirations
of the educated people of Belfast:
'The introduction, or the improvement of the Fine Arts, is certain proof

THE BELFAST MUSEUM
Erected 1830-31

The Museum of the Belfast Natural History
Society (later the Belfast Natural History and
Philosophical Society), in College Square North,
opened in 1831. A number of local art societies
held their exhibitions in the Museum.

of the refinement and increasing wealth of a people.'[2] The regional capital of Northern Ireland post-1921 was effectively a settlement dating from the late Elizabethan period, which came vividly to life on the heightened energy of the Industrial Revolution, bringing economic success and expansion. Early nineteenth-century industrial Belfast drew economic power from its great port, fuelled by shipbuilding, engineering, the linen trade and associated manufacturing industries.[3] The city became a dominant force in the northern Irish economy, a position strengthened by the opening of its first railway, which ensured Belfast was an industrial and commercial centre by 1840.

Allowing for all the effort that went into the commercial life of the city, the professional and merchant classes nonetheless sought to develop a cultural dimension to enhance the intellectual life of the people. Numerous artists, naturalists, scientists, engineers and architects had emerged from the north-eastern counties, most of whom interacted with the members of the RDS, the RIA and Cork institutions, while others impacted on the cultural life of Britain. Among these latter were Hans Sloane from County Down, whose collection, as we have seen, formed the foundation of the British Museum, the Earl Macartney from County Antrim, who left manuscripts to the British Museum in 1806, and William Brown from Ballymena, County Antrim, who founded the Public Museum of Liverpool in 1860. The inherited collection of Sir Richard Wallace of Lisburn, County Antrim, became the Wallace Collection in the London gallery named for the collection.[4]

The establishment of Government Schools of Design in Belfast and in Derry was propelled by a nineteenth-century belief in the importance of education in public policy. James MacAdam, an industrialist and secretary of the Royal Flax Improvement Society of Ireland, adopted a commercial approach to cultural enlightenment. He understood that it was essential to educate artists in the history of art, using galleries of casts and drawings, because Belfast's modern mass-production industry was without competitive designs.[5] In addition, there was the requirement to educate public taste in the creation of high-quality goods and artworks for the gentry, to attract the 'artisan and mechanic [improving] the conditions of this class'.[6] MacAdam reputedly had one of the best private geological collections in Ireland.

The Belfast Museum's early origins can be traced to a number of sources, one being the Belfast Reading Society, which was established in 1788, and collected mineral specimens and curiosities to 'illustrate the antiquity, natural, civil, commercial and ecclesiastical history of this country', forming the genesis of the museum and library to which it would become subordinate.[7] In 1792 the Reading Society became the Belfast Society for Promoting Knowledge (today's Linen Hall Library), and in 1833 resolved to give its cabinet, comprising plants, fossils and natural science specimens and antiquities, to the Belfast Natural History and Philosophical Society. In 1804 the Society for Promoting Knowledge acquired the cabinet of the Belfast Literary Society. These collections were separated in 1830, with the antiquities going to the Belfast Academical Institution, and minerals and animals going to the Belfast Natural History Society.[8] Other bodies, such as the Belfast Academy Natural History Society (1828), also set up museums.[9]

The Belfast Academical Institution (the title 'Royal' was added in 1831) was set up in 1814 by wealthy merchants and enlightened liberals. A school and centre for higher education (the forerunner of Queen's University), it had a drawing school (1814–70) that was the foremost in Belfast. The Belfast Academical Institution planned to develp a natural history museum; eight of its former students founded the Belfast Natural History Society. Thomas Dix Hincks (1767–1857), master of the classical school at Belfast Academical Institution, had already founded the Royal Cork Institution (RCI) in 1803.[10] The Belfast Natural History Society (1821), later the Belfast Natural History and Philosophical Society, was the first body of its kind in Ireland, set up with the aim of gathering information in 'zoology, botany and mineralogy in all their branches, the investigations of natural history and antiquities of Ireland'.[11] The founders wanted a society that gave status to Belfast and a museum that would be the first in Ireland to be built by public funds, with educational programmes, public lectures and printed guidelines for amassing 'natural history specimens'.[12] The Marquess of Donegall laid the foundation stone of the museum's building at number 7 College Square North in 1830.[13]

The Belfast Museum of Natural History, displaying 'antiquities and specimens relating to the natural sciences', opened in 1831.[14] Its president, J.L. Drummond, proclaimed:

> Museums are considered on the Continent of such importance that scarcely any town of considerable size is without one. I

hope [this museum] will give a powerful impulse to the study of nature and physical science fostering a taste for knowledge among all classes of our community.[15]

In the museum's early years, from 1833, the public was admitted for three hours on Saturday and then Wednesday. In 1837 when the museum opened six days a week, admission fees were reduced and the working class was admitted under supervision. Opening on Easter Mondays from 1845, at a nominal charge of twopence per adult and one penny per child and adult, was a major bonus for the working class, who behaved with 'decorum and quietness'.[16] Easter Monday remained its most popular day. The museum demonstrated modest educational traits in publishing *Directions for Preserving Subjects in Natural History* (1835) and Smithsonian Institution recommendations for 'collecting insects', not realizing the educational dimension in its Egyptian mummy (1835) and the John Gibson bequest of Irish antiquities (1834–5).[17]

Contemporary with the growth of the museum was the desire for a fine art institution, which was advanced by the Belfast Association of Artists, founded in 1836, and local landscape painter Hugh Frazer. The drawing classes given by artists such as Gaetano Fabbrini in 1836–8 highlighted the need for an art school and art collections.[18] Museum staff included: John Cassidy, full-time curator in 1834; William Darragh, 'the best taxidermist in Ireland in respect of birds', in 1844; and botanist Samuel Alexander Stewart (1880–1907). William Thompson (1802–52), who was an amateur engaged in serious scientific work (although earning his living elsewhere), charted Ireland's natural history in his *Natural History of Ireland* (three volumes: 1849, 1850, 1852). When he left zoological and botanical specimens (plus £100 for their preservation and display) to the museum, a Thompson Room was constructed to display the collections, which were viewed by the British Association for the Advancement of Science in 1852. Robert Patterson (1802–72) published the final volume after Thompson's death in 1852.

Patterson, who was a founder member of the Belfast Natural History Society, published many texts and illustrations for educational purposes, placing strong emphasis on the study of natural history. The instructional nature of the collections arose in the 1850s, when Professor Edward Forbes, regarded at the time as a leading British naturalist, palaeontologist, chair of botany at

King's College, Cambridge, fellow of the Royal Society, spoke about 'the educational uses of museums' and the 'exhibits that the Belfast naturalists and antiquaries had produced in the Belfast Museum'.[19] The subject of art was gaining interest thanks to the opening of new art societies and the Government School of Design during the period 1849–58; meanwhile, however, the museum was in decline.[20] The Belfast Naturalists' Field Club (founded 1863) held lectures by Joseph Beete Jukes, director of the Geological Survey of Ireland, and botanist Ralph Tate. The British naturalist E.B. Carpenter promoted the idea of local collections for scientific purposes, advocating the formation of Queen's College Museum. The Field Club rearranged and catalogued the Belfast Museum collections in time for the British Association meeting in 1874. An extension built in 1879, augmented by a gift of Irish antiquities, opened in 1880. A Department of Conservation was set up as a joint venture with Queen's College in 1884, with Samuel Stewart, the scientific curator, writing the *Flora of the North-East of Ireland*, together with *A Visitor's Guide to the Museum* (both 1889). The museum's popularity further declined, however, with the opening of the Belfast Art Gallery and Museum in 1890, causing George Trobridge, head of the Government School of Art, to observe: 'The Belfast Natural History and Philosophical Society Museum has with the outside public the reputation of being the dullest of dull museums.' The society subsequently transferred the museum's collection to the city authorities in 1910, just as the Belfast Corporation adopted the Museum Act.[21]

Interest in art and education had been promoted through the opening of the first commercial galleries in 1864 and the first successful exhibiting society, the Art Union of Belfast, in 1866. In addition, the opening of the Government School of Art in 1870 provided art appreciation classes for the working-class population.[22] Although municipal museums found it difficult to assemble art collections, a 'Municipal Art Gallery' was established in 1888 in three rooms on the top floor of the Free Public Library at Royal Avenue, becoming the town's first rate-supported art gallery.[23] A municipal art collection was initiated (paintings, engravings, statues and casts) by gift and purchase from Belfast Corporation grants and South Kensington Museum loan collections (part of South Kensington Science and Art Department), on condition that the municipal authorities acquired their own holdings. Belfast Corporation provided £500 for the committee to purchase copies of antique sculptures in

Some of the antiquities, sculpture and plaster casts on display in the Belfast Art Gallery and Museum.

Paris and Naples.[24] The curator, James F. Johnson, was appointed before Belfast Art Gallery and Museum was opened.

Belfast's first municipal art gallery sought to develop its teaching role by nominating Mondays a private day for artists and students, with a fee of threepence per visitor.[25] The nature of the institution changed following the donation by Canon Grainger, Rector of Broughshane, of a collection of natural history and Irish antiquities in 1891, for which an annex to the building was added in 1892.[26] By the end of the century the north of Ireland had become a region of artistic and natural science achievement, facilitated by the alliance between science, art and education, and business and industry. This was demonstrated by the multifaceted holdings in the Belfast Municipal Art Gallery and Museum's collection, its policy of open access and the successful use of its collections as a learning resource by artists and students.

Crawford Municipal Art Gallery, Cork (1885)

Cork was a thriving cultural city in the nineteenth century with Queen's College, Cork at its heart, and antiquarian societies and fine art associations.

The local economy was built on sizeable breweries, flour-milling, an active butter market, a textile and a shipbuilding industry. These 'urban' activities were supplemented by a rich agricultural tillage hinterland, which was concentrated around Greater Cork and south Munster, while Cork Harbour was the main port for Atlantic traffic in southern Ireland.

The desire for a public art museum began with the Cork Institution, which was founded by Hincks in 1803 (chartered 1807). It was influenced by the Royal Institute in London (1799) and set up along similar lines to teach technical, scientific and art subjects, under the guidance of antiquarians. The pragmatic outlook of the Royal Cork Institution echoed that of the RDS and RIA in emphasizing practical knowledge with solid results.[27] Its holdings included a library, an observatory, a botanic garden, and a museum of natural history and mineral specimens augmented by classes in natural history, philosophy, archaeology, literature, art, agriculture, chemistry and geology, with guest lectures by Robert Kane and Edmund Davy, an English chemist, who was professor of chemistry at the Royal Cork Institution from 1813, and professor of chemistry at the RDS from 1826. A parliamentary grant

The Custom House façade of the Crawford Municipal Art Gallery, Cork, c.1960, before construction of the Opera House nearby.

of £2,000 per annum, available from 1807, was withdrawn in 1830 due to dwindling numbers that year. However, by 1835, a committee of the RCI were instrumental in founding the Cork Cuvierian Society, which adopted many of its activities.

The Cork Society for Promoting the Fine Arts, supported by local artists, architects and art patrons, was set up in 1816 following the display in Cork of 'The First Munster Exhibition of Original Pictures' the previous year.[28] Of greater significance was a gift to the society in 1818 of an 'elegant collection of casts presented by His Royal Highness the Prince Regent', approximately two hundred originating in the Vatican.[29] These important casts of works, the production of which was supervised by Antonio Canova (1757–1822), were 'the boast and ornament of the present day' and their presence provided the impetus for the RCI to initiate a programme of art education.[30] Art classes commenced in 1819, followed by lectures on painting, 'theoretical and practical

The Crawford Municipal Art Gallery, c.1900

On display in the Sculpture Gallery are some of the casts from a collection made under the supervision of Antonio Canova in Rome from works in the Vatican collection. These were presented by the Prince Regent to the Cork Society for the Promotion of the Fine Arts in 1818.

to be illustrated by drawings on the spot' (1828).[31] The society acquired the Apollo Theatre on Patrick Street in 1818 for a 'Saloon of Sculpture' and promptly held an exhibition of the Vatican antique casts. When the RCI moved to the eighteenth-century Old Custom House in 1832, it later merged with the Cork Society for Promoting the Fine Arts in 1835. As the Royal Cork Institution had purchased the Canova cast collection from the Cork Society for Promoting the Fine Arts, the casts also transferred to the old Custom House.[32]

The art classes established by the RCI were an early venture in public art education, from which, ultimately, developed an art school and art museum. It formed a valuable part of the intellectual life of Cork in its guise as a teaching body before settling into a role as a cultural society. The institution was succeeded by the Cork Cuvierian Society and the Cork Art Union, until their roles were in turn taken over by Queen's College, Cork in 1849. In 1842 William Makepeace Thackeray wrote of his visit to the Royal Cork Institution, when it was housed in the Old Custom House (now the Crawford Art Gallery):

> There is an institution, with a fair library of scientific works; a museum, and a drawing-school with a supply of casts. The place is in yet more dismal condition than the library. The plasters are spoiled incurably for want of a sixpenny feather-brush; the dust lies on the walls, and nobody seems to heed it.[33]

When the Cork School of Design opened in 1850, Headmaster William Willes set aside a 'memorial-room' to display paintings and sculpture works by Cork artists, thus forming the origins of the municipal collection.[34] The survival in the collection of works by artists who were early students of the School of Art demonstrates that an art collection with a Cork emphasis was planned from the outset; the collection included drawings by the first head-master of the school, William Willes. A major event for the city was the National Exhibition of Arts, Manufactures and Materials in 1852, with a section featuring paintings, sculpture and antiquities.[35] The exhibition's 'loan collection' highlighted the lack of a public art museum. Bertram Windle, president of Queen's College, Cork, drew attention to the need for the city to develop an

art museum in 1876, noting: 'Art can only flourish in an atmosphere of art – where true taste is spread amongst the public at large. One of the best ways of doing this is to accustom people to the sight of works of fine art in a public gallery.'[36] It took twenty years to form a committee. As a result, when the Industrial and Fine Art Exhibition was held in 1883, with a display of eight hundred works of art, including a 'loan collection of paintings' from the South Kensington Museum, the absence of a city museum was notable. During his tenure as principal of the School of Art (1860–89), James Brenan seized the initiative. He encouraged the distiller, William Horatio Crawford (1812–88), to extend the school, and purpose-built galleries were constructed in 1884 for a municipal gallery.[37] When the new Crawford School of Art and Gallery was opened by the Prince of Wales in 1885 the citizens of Munster had a ready source of art education, with teaching collections and an exhibition room for casts, in a city-centre museum in Cork.[38]

The museums of Belfast and Cork illustrate the growth of Irish museums in a regional context, while demonstrating the increasing awareness of the role of fine art, natural history and antiquities collections in the education of Irish people. That there was interaction between these two centres at opposite ends of the country is witnessed by the activities of one individual – Hincks, who founded the Cork Institution in 1803 and then became one of the key figures in establishing the Belfast Natural History Society in 1821. The museums would also develop a relationship with the new Government Schools of Design and the art academies. It is evident that Belfast and Cork went about their business effectively in setting up their own museums, galleries, art schools and university, thereby showing a sense of pride, initiative and forward-thinking by two regional cities determined to carve their own distinct place in Ireland.

Education for Industry: Government Schools of Design (1849)

The Government Schools of Design emerged at a similar time as municipal museums and galleries were being established in Britain, and later in Ireland. The branch schools set up by the Board of Trade (see below) formed part of the growth of education in the nineteenth century, with interest in the museum's teaching collections generated by the fine art and industrial exhibitions movement. The design schools understood the need to educate artists for industry, with museums and their collections forming part of this education. Irish museums attracted students from the Government Schools of Design and art academies, as well as professional and amateur artists. A relationship was formed between the art schools and the museums in the nineteenth century, with students using the fine art and cast collections for the study

The Belfast School of Design plaster casts of classical sculpture. The school purchased these casts from London for teaching purposes, illustrating the importance placed on drawing from high-quality casts in the training of artists.

and appreciation of art and antiquity in their training to become designers for commercial art and industry.

The branch Schools of Design included schools in Dublin, Cork, Limerick, Clonmel, Waterford, Derry and Belfast. The Dublin School of Design (founded 1849) became the Metropolitan School of Art in 1877 (now the National College of Art and Design, NCAD). The Cork School of Design opened in the Old Customs House in 1850, housing the collection of Vatican sculpture casts, the school's purpose being to educate designers, not mere copyists or draughtsmen; an extension was financed by Crawford in 1884. The Belfast School of Design also opened in 1850, with an industrial design-oriented curriculum, and housed a collection of casts in rooms owned by the Belfast Academical Institution. However, it was reconstituted as a Government School of Art in 1870 (run by a local board of managers) and grant-aided by the London-based Department of Science and Art to teach design for use in industrial mass production in the north of Ireland. Limerick School of Ornamental Art opened in 1852 and came under the aegis of the Corporation of Limerick in 1896, to emerge as an art school in the next century. Waterford School of Practical Art and Design opened in 1852 in a Mechanics' Institute, to become part of the Waterford Technical Institute. The Clonmel School of Art also opened in a Mechanics' Institute in 1854, but did not survive. The School of Art that opened in Derry in 1874 came under the aegis of the corporation in 1890, becoming part of the Municipal Technical School in 1899.[39] These schools formed the framework of art education in Ireland in the nineteenth century.

Henry Cole's Department of Practical Art (1852) (renamed Department of Science and Art in 1854) controlled the design schools and charged a special reduced rate for amateurs, which led to increased student numbers and generated an income at the Dublin School of Design and at the RHA. The weakness of the schools was the absence of any higher-level teaching in painting, design and theory, a deficiency that was partly remedied when the RHA began teaching painting, which ultimately led to fine art becoming the prerogative of the RHA. The South Kensington system remained *in situ* until enactment of the Agriculture and Technical Instruction (Ireland) Act 1899. The schools then reported to the Dublin-based Department of Agriculture and Technical Instruction, led by Horace Plunkett, who encouraged the schools to use their local museums and galleries: 'the beautiful and suggestive objects in the museum'.[40]

Just as the schools of art and the academies made use of their local, national and regional museums to give students an understanding and an appreciation of art, the same process was taking place in the country's university museums.

Education of the Next Generation: University Museums

The development of museums in Ireland has links with antiquarian bodies, art societies and schools and academies of art, which were involved in the pursuit of learning and associated with museums and their collections. University museums also play a part in this story, having emerged as a by-product of the growth of education in universities in Ireland, albeit with a history that is sometimes difficult to chart.

To the long-established TCD and St Patrick's College, Maynooth were added the Queen's Colleges of Cork, Belfast and Galway, established in 1845, and a Catholic University of Dublin was founded in 1854.[41] These universities acquired natural history, geology, zoology, archaeological and classical collections for the purposes of research and teaching students. The museums were teaching resources and their history is connected to particular historical and political events bound up with the lives, careers and activities of a number of key individuals who contributed to their formation – mainly collectors, donors, travellers and art and antique dealers. Many of the associated figures kept in touch with like-minded colleagues in other universities and interacted with bodies such as the RIA, the RDS and the Geological Survey of Ireland (1845), and with societies in Belfast and Cork, facilitating a wider awareness of collections and resulting, on occasion, in the exchange of specimens. These men and women made an important contribution to the wider development of Irish museums in the nineteenth century.

The Queen's Colleges were founded by the provisions of an Act that enabled Queen Victoria to endow three new colleges, at Belfast, Cork and Galway, which were incorporated on 30 December 1845. Queen's College, Belfast (now Queen's University, Belfast [QUB]) was unveiled in October 1849, a pre-opening ceremony having been performed on 11 August by Queen Victoria

Queen's University, Belfast

The Queen's College in Belfast was opened by Queen Victoria and Prince Albert in 1849. The royal party were in Belfast as part of a state visit to Ireland.

University College, Cork

Queen's College, Cork was opened in 1849 in a building designed by the architects Deane and Woodward, overseen by the college president, Sir Robert Kane. This print is taken from a nineteenth-century view of the north wing and lower grounds of the college.

and Prince Albert, who were in Belfast as part of a state visit to Ireland. The now-familiar west façade, by Charles Lanyon (1813–89), embodied Victorian virtues of confidence and continuity at a university whose plans to form a museum collection were progressed when space was allocated for a museum in 1850.[42] The college museum came under the care and management of Frederick McCoy, during his term in Belfast (1848–54) as the first professor of geology (1852), and the collections were used for teaching purposes during the nineteenth century.

Queen's College, Cork (now University College, Cork [UCC]) also opened in 1849, with early campus buildings designed by the architects Deane and Woodward. It became part of the Queen's University of Ireland (later the Royal University of Ireland, 1879–1908), later acquiring the Crawford Observatory, which was designed by Howard Grubb and set up in 1878 under the patronage of Crawford and the Duke of Devonshire. The first president was Sir Robert Kane (1809–90), during whose tenure (1845–73) a museum of natural history was established, although Kane spent most of his time at the Museum of Irish Industry in Dublin. (The Museum of Irish Industry was founded in 1845, deriving from the Museum of Economic Geology.) Correspondence on 'the stocktaking of the library and museums' is recorded, with a pattern of gifts and donations received, including: duplicate specimens from the RDS; a bequest from Sir Charles Thomas Newton, keeper of antiquities at the British Museum; an antique sundial from John Faulett, through George Boole (professor of mathematics, who invented Boolean logic and contributed to the RIA's *Transactions*); a Peruvian mummy from Francis M. Jennings; and silver ores and fossils from General Daniel O'Leary.[43] The museum was used primarily for teaching purposes.

The college acquired a rare collection of classical casts, gathered mainly from the British Museum for a Museum of Classical Art and Archaeology by Bunnell Lewis, professor of Latin. While this treasure trove comprised the earliest university collection of classical antiquities in Ireland, more than half of it was destroyed by a fire in 1862.[44] The collection included contact casts from the Parthenon frieze sculptures (Elgin Marbles) and Sir Charles Newton donated several Greek vases; Newton was made an honorary member of the RIA in 1895.[45] The surviving casts have been conserved to form a teaching collection.

Queen's College, Galway (now National University of Ireland, Galway [NUIG]) opened on 30 October 1849, becoming part of the Queen's University of Ireland in 1850. The story of its college museums is interesting because they ranked with the best teaching collections to be found in any of the universities. The collecting of geological specimens was a priority not just in Galway but in all the universities, as a result of which less fashionable subjects, such as art, were neglected.

The College Geology Museum (founded 1851) formed part of a larger complex on the first-floor, south-east corner of the main quadrangle, administered by a Museum Committee (funded partly through the chairs of Natural History and Geology), similar to the RDS Natural History Museum. The bulk of the collection was assembled by William King (1809–86), who was appointed professor of geology in 1848, and professor of natural history, geology and mineralogy in 1882.[46] The committee recommended purchasing botanical, geological, mineralogical and zoological specimens (including King's own material from the Permian fossils of north-east England) and a fossil collection from dealers such as Otto Krantz in Berlin and individuals such as Robert Ball, director of Dublin University Museum at Trinity.[47] The collection was expanded through links with the Queen's Colleges, and with the Geological Survey, which sometimes collected specimens for the colleges. Museum collections featured in King's work on the Permian fossils of north-east England (1850), many illustrated in John Dinkel's original lithographs,[48] and in his *Pleurodictyum* (1856). A copy survives of his handwritten catalogue, 'Queen's College Catalogue of Departments', with specimen labels.

The museum in Galway forms one of the best examples of the educational use of university collections, and King represents an ideal example of an academic who embraced the close links between teaching, research and museology within the university sphere.[49] He developed a teaching curriculum using the collections for contemporary advancements in science. Alexander Gordon Melville, who was appointed the first professor of natural history (1849–82), also used the museum for teaching purposes, working comfortably alongside King, but felt the facilities were inadequate. He amassed a body of botanical and zoological specimens, resulting in Galway's collection being visited frequently by professional colleagues. When Queen Victoria and her consort came to Galway in 1856, Prince Albert admired the 'completeness of

National University of Ireland, Galway

Queen's College, Galway, opened during the Famine (1845–50) in 1849. It was followed in 1851 by the opening of the College Geology Museum on the south-east first floor of the main quadrangle.

the museum collection'.[50] Another royal visitor was Prince Louis Napoleon of France, in 1857.[51] Melville's public lectures and field trips created an interest in natural history that aided the rise of amateur naturalists' field clubs, whose corpus of antiquities would devolve to Irish museums.[52]

Richard J. Anderson was appointed to the chair of natural history, geology and mineralogy in 1883, when the geology and natural history collections were amalgamated to form the Natural History Museum.[53] His contact with professional colleagues overseas enabled him to increase the botanical, geological and zoological collections. The educational role of the museum was thereby enhanced by courses for students pursuing degrees in natural history, geology, medicine and engineering, using the collections and laboratory as a resource for practical work.[54] The collections were housed in five rooms: two for 'fossils and minerals'; three for zoological specimens and apparatus, local Silurian and Carboniferous fossils; a horizontal case stretching the length of the museum held Galway minerals and fossils. Anderson ensured that the museum had modern teaching and research aids, including a lantern microscope, chemical cabinet for the mineralogical collection and lantern slide projectors.[55] He worked in the museum and adjoining laboratory, his uncompleted catalogue listing the specimens.[56] During his time glass models of marine flora and fauna were acquired (examples of phytoplankton and zooplankton, crustacean larvae and other invertebrates), hand-made to order by the Dresden-born team of Leopold Blaschka and his son, Rudolf. Anderson's published description of the workings of the museum placed it alongside the best university natural history museums of the time (1889).[57] In this way, the Geology and the Natural History Museums contributed to the instruction of the students and the research role of the Queen's University, Galway.

Dublin University Museum (1777–1857) was located in the Regent House, above the front gate of Trinity College, when Anne Plumptre visited it on her travels in Ireland in 1814–15: 'The Museum is a good room, and contains a tolerable collection of Irish minerals, with some specimens of the basaltic columns from the Giants' Causeway.'[58] The college faculty was aware of the museum and helped to expand the collection. Whitley Stokes, who lectured on geology and natural history, was responsible for the museum (1790s–1844) and published two catalogues of the collections, in 1807 and 1818.[59] A report in the *Historical Guide to the City of Dublin* (1825) referred to '1,204 specimens, with a description of the contents of twelve cases, noting the stuffed [giraffe] in the centre of the room'.[60] Irish mineral specimens of gold, silver, lead, tin, copper and iron were purchased from the Rt Hon. George Knox in 1823.[61]

Thomas Oldham, professor of geology from 1845 to 1850, looked after the geological collections and took part in the mapping of the geology of several counties. Greenland and Norwegian specimens were donated by Sir Charles Lewis Giesecke (1761–1833), RDS professor of mineralogy and geology, and incorporated into the collections by James Apjohn, professor of geology and mineralogy.[62] Apjohn compiled a catalogue (1850), adding Graydon's collection of volcanic products (1,500 items) and Richard Griffith's collection of fossils.[63] The Geological Society of Dublin (1831–90), which held meetings in Trinity College from 1848, donated its collection to the University Museum.[64] Visitors to Dublin were informed that Trinity College had its own museum (60 ft long), with its treasures described as comprising six cases, five of which contained ethnographic material while the sixth contained a miscellaneous collection of Irish antiquities.

The early university museums developed because their collections provided a ready source of instruction and learning in new subjects, such as geology, botany and physics, but also because they had a role as cultural showcases when special events took place. A highlight of the Dublin University Museum was a visit by the British Association in 1835, presided over by TCD Provost Bartholomew Lloyd (1772–1837), joined by William Rowan Hamilton (1805–65) and Professor James MacCullagh (1809–47) of TCD, all men with wide cultural interests.[65] There followed a geological house party at Florence Court, County Fermanagh, to view the fossil fish collection of the 3rd Earl of Enniskillen,[66] which was described by the Reverend William Samuel Symonds in 1857 as 'the finest collection of fossil-fishes in Great Britain'.[67]

The Dublin University Museum advanced with the appointment of its first full-time director in 1844, Robert Ball (1844–58). During the same period, Ball was treasurer of the RIA (1844–58), served on the academy's Museum Committee and advised on the arrangement of its collection in 1838 he was also secretary of the Zoological Society and president (1852) of the Geological Society of Dublin. Ball developed a pedagogical role for the University Museum by rearranging the collections in 1845 (although responsibility for the geological and mineralogical collections fell under Apjohn and, latterly, Professor Oldham), placing ornaments and tools in the hall, armour on the stairs, entomology and ethnology collections in the small room at the top of the stairs, and Irish birds, fish, reptiles and mammals in the large

Augustin Edouart (1789–1861),
Silhouette of Robert Ball (1802–58)
Naturalist, 1834
Black paper on card,
33.9 x 18.5 cm. NGI 2651.

The original Dublin University Museum was in Trinity College's Regent House above the front gate. Ball was appointed its first full-time director (1844–58) and proved to be active in organizing the collection and promoting it within college and to the public.

room. The museum acquired the Tardy Cabinet in 1847, the main authority for species published as Irish and reviewed by the distinguished entomologist, A.H. Halliday.[68] The museum was made more accessible: 'open to the Provost and fellows at all times and to persons with orders from fellows or professors, on Wednesday and Friday from 10am–3pm. Masters, scholars and students in gowns can visit and friends, if signed in the book', resulting in increased annual visitors of 14,000 by 1852.[69]

As visitor numbers for university museums are generally not large, this was an extremely well-used museum for the period. Ball used his friendship with naturalists and geologists, such as the 3rd Earl of Enniskillen, to gain donations for the museum, gifting his own zoological collection of 7,000 specimens in 1846.[70] He opened his lecture programme to the public and planned to hold classes on practical zoology as a way to promote the learning context of the museum. Ball resigned in 1856, several years after his appointment as secretary of Queen's University of Ireland. A contemporary account of the Museum in the *Dublin Penny Journal* noted 'a near perfect skeleton of an antediluvian

THE MUSEUM BUILDING.

View of the south front of TCD museum building, by Deane and Woodward (1853–7)

The building was much celebrated as a landmark of Victorian architecture. The interior hall and staircase of the museum reflected Moorish influence in the columns, arches and pillars, and it includes a banisters of Irish marble.

moose deer; a very curious collection of Irish antiquities, together with a full and detailed description of the Irish harp'.[71] A new museum building, proposed in 1833, resulted in the collections (botanical, engineering, ethnographical, geological and zoological) being scattered throughout the campus.[72] The new museum building was finally erected between 1853 and 1857, and was declared 'a great innovation in architecture'.[73] It won extravagant praise from the nineteenth century's most influential art critic, John Ruskin (1819–1900), who in 1868 described it as a landmark of Victorian architecture in Ireland.[74] The Venetian style of the building, designed by Deane and Woodward, was glowingly referred to in the *Dublin Builder* as the 'inauguration of a great revolution in public taste'. The next time the British Association visited Ireland, in 1857, the Geological Museum was housed on the top floor of the museum building. This meeting was presided over by a new body of Irish scientists, creating a positive impression of the intellectual scene and reinforcing Ireland's scholarly reputation.[75] The Geological Museum displayed its collections in floor cases and wall cabinets, under the curatorship of Apjohn (1856–81) and professor of geology, the Reverend Samuel Haughton (1856–81). Presiding over this visit was Humphrey Lloyd (1800–81), professor of natural and experimental philosophy and son of the provost, Bartholomew Lloyd, whose networking with international geomagnetism observatories provided the impetus for TCD to establish its own magnetic observatory. The nineteenth century saw these collections develop as serious pedagogical resources, and for this reason another museum building was erected to house anatomy, pathology and natural history collections. In the meantime, the zoological collection (established 1777 and today numbering 10,000 specimens) was moved to a Zoological Museum in 1876.[76] The Herbarium took up residence in the basement of house number 40, part of the School of Botany, and the Ethnographic Collection was transferred to the Museum of Science and Art in 1894. Valentine Ball, son of Robert Ball, was elected to the chair of geology and mineralogy in 1881. As curator of the Geological Museum (1881–3), he brought a collection of mammalian fossils from the Siwalik Hills in Asia, but later removed them (together with similar material) to the Museum of Science and Art.[77] Ball had long sought to manage a museum with great collections and scope and he achieved this when he became director of the Museum of Science and Art. His successor, William Johnston Sollas

(1883–7), guided the Geological Museum, providing a major teaching resource for Trinity, and developing a genuine educational role that fully reflected the new ethos of the museum as a centre for culture and learning. The university museums seemed very secure within their academic surroundings as the nineteenth century reached its conclusion. They were linked to established courses in the teaching of students and had built up followers among the faculty and staff. The museums that had earlier developed links with the RDS, the RIA, the Geological Survey and other bodies found that these associations were no longer relevant as the collections had transferred to the Museum of Science and Art. The nineteenth century had proved to be the heyday of the university museums. It provided the correct context for them to develop within a range of newer subjects (geology, natural history, zoology, etc.) and the particular teaching methods of the period that drew upon collections as a resource. These museums also had their own role to play when some of their holdings went to form the national collections of the Museum of Science and Art. All this would change in the next century, however, when a level of neglect and decline would befall these museums. That story is told in Part V, 'The Twenty-First Century'.

6

The Role of Antiquarianism in the Nineteenth Century Museum Movement

The cultivation of Irish art, Irish history,
Irish antiquities and Irish music.[1]

Antiquarian interest has its origins in the nineteenth-century science and learning institutions of Dublin (RDS, RIA, TCD, UCD), Belfast and Cork, alongside the emergence of a state-sponsored primary (1831) and intermediate (1878) education system and the collections-based learning afforded to students at St Patrick's College, Maynooth, and at the Royal University of Ireland colleges at Cork, Belfast and Galway. Initially a pursuit of the landed gentry, by century's end antiquarianism had spread to a much wider constituency. The efforts of these early collectors to advance the discovery and recording of Ireland's heritage was directed by the need to prove Ireland had an ancient past.[2] Thus, it became fashionable to form collections of antiquities, such as stone hammers, urns, beads and bronze arrowheads, although gold ornaments remained largely the prerogative of jewellers.

George Petrie, an artist and major antiquary, had a network that ensured regular contact with private collectors, such as John Bell of Dungannon, County Tyrone, and the antiquary Edwin Wyndham-Quin (1812–71), Viscount Adare,

George Petrie (1790–1866),
***The Last Circuit of Pilgrims at Clonmacnoise, Co. Offaly,* c.1843–6**
Graphite and watercolour on paper, 67.2 x 98 cm. NGI 2230.

Petrie presents an image reflecting the tradition of the 'pattern or patron's day' celebration, which took place on the feast day of St Ciarán of Clonmacnoise (9 September). The pilgrims prayed to the saint while undertaking a circuit of the sites within the enlosure. The work, which is an important record of the architecture and monuments of the Middle Ages, is suffused with a late-Romantic sense of the loss of Irish cultural heritage.

later 3rd Earl of Dunraven, who housed a cabinet at his home in Adare, County Limerick. The objects purchased by Petrie for the RIA museum (during the course of which he formed his own private cabinet) helped to identify Ireland's lost antiquity, in addition to being part of the process of assembling collections of private cultural heirlooms that subsequently transferred into public ownership.

While Dublin was the intellectual centre of antiquarian scholarship, well-documented developments also took place in Belfast and in Cork, among other places. In fact, antiquarian interest emerged countrywide as a result of the new farming methods, land reclamation and excavations for canals, roads and railways, which regularly turned up artefacts that eventually reached the RIA, via the Board of Works.[3] A fascination with science and natural history was encouraged throughout the country by the Mechanics' Institutes, the Royal Belfast Academical Institution, the Museum of Irish

Industry, the RDS, the RCI, Cork antiquarian societies, Kilkenny Archaeological Society and the Queen's Colleges. Reflecting the growing popularity of these subjects, the first professor of Irish history and archaeology was appointed to the Catholic University in 1854. Antiquarianism was also supported by the RDS industrial exhibitions, with their sections on fine art and antiquities helping to form public taste. The material lent by the RIA to the Dublin International Exhibition of Art-Industry of 1853 was deemed 'the most important collection of national antiquities for the study and examination of antiquities in this country'.[4] The exhibitions proved useful for museums because their loan collections facilitated comparison with similar artefacts in local museums, and they encouraged antiquarians to research further into Ireland's past.

In this way, antiquarianism played a specific and significant role in the creation of Irish museums. The foundation blocks of the modern museum were provided by the collections created by antiquarianism, be they art, antiquities or geological specimens, private collections or the cabinets of learned societies. There was considerable interaction between key figures in the museums of the RDS, TCD and the RIA, with regular exchanges of information and donations of important artefacts. Bodies such as the geological department of the Ordnance Survey and the Geological Survey of Ireland, whose field officers gathered finds that were used in the teaching of students, would see their collections devolve to the new Museum of Science and Art before the century's end. Most important of all was the contribution made by the RIA. Over the course of the late eighteenth and nineteenth centuries its enlightened and cultured members performed a major role in the gathering and storing of Ireland's archaeological treasures. These antiquities that were handed over to the new 'national museum' marked one of the most significant acts of patriotic altruism in the history of the academy and one for which the Irish people owe that institution much gratitude.

Collections of the Ordnance Survey (1824) and the Geological Survey of Ireland (1845)

From the 1820s onwards the flowering of Irish culture that took place was linked to the Ordnance Survey Department, then under the authority of the

James Petrie (1750–1819),
George Petrie (1790–1866)
Artist and Antiquary
Watercolour on ivory,
10.7 X 8.3 cm. NGI 2231.

George Petrie, painted here by his father, James, was a topographical artist, sometimes described as the 'father of Irish archaeology', and one of the most influential nineteenth-century antiquarians. In his early career he worked for the Ordnance Survey, running the topographical section from his home in Great Charles Street, Dublin.

Board of Ordnance (the military body responsible for mapping since 1791), and to the Geological Survey of Ireland, which was a significant player, opening up a range of field studies that included antiquities. The Ordnance Survey has a relevance to Irish museums because many of its key figures, such as George Petrie, John O'Donovan and Eugene O'Curry, were associated with collections that devolved to the Museum of Science and Art.

The Ordnance Survey was the body charged, in 1824, with mapping the boundaries and calculating the acreage of every townland in Ireland.[5] This was accomplished under Lieutenant Colonel Thomas Colby,[6] director of the Ordnance Survey (1820–37), and his deputy, Captain Thomas Larcom, the local director in Ireland in 1828. The survey was based at Mountjoy House (built in 1728) in Phoenix Park, where its head office, production site and storerooms were located (and remain so today).[7] Larcom appointed George Petrie as head of the topographical section *c.*1833–46, and he set up his offices at 'his home in Great Charles Street, Dublin', where, William Wakeman noted, 'we met daily; John O'Donovan, Eugene Curry, James Clarence Mangan, P. O'Keefe, J. O'Connor and a few more'. Petrie supported these scholars in translating and recording the geology, place names and archaeology of the island. The work they did fostered national consciousness by preserving memories of an ancient culture and creating a new Irish identity in English. While topographical maps (6 inches to 1 mile, 1:10,560) were completed county by county between 1832 and 1842, followed by other maps and a geological survey,[8] the collectors in botany and zoology who gathered the specimens (housed at the Ordnance Survey offices) were attentive to the antiquities and natural history of the countryside. Patrick Doran donated palaeontological specimens to the RDS, while James Flanagan sold 215 objects, stone (basalt, schist and serpentine) axes and some bronzes to the British Museum.[9] The scale of the activity produced geological collections, recognized for their importance when they were placed on display mid-century at the Museum of Irish Industry, and their significance continued at the Museum of Science and Art, until the eventual rise of the Irish antiquities eclipsed interest in geology, to the ongoing detriment of the geological collections.

Under the Geological Survey Act 1845 the geological department of the Ordnance Survey in Ireland was transferred to a new body, the Geological Survey of Great Britain and Ireland, to complete a centrally controlled geological survey of the British Isles. Oversight passed from the military Board of Ordnance to HM Office of Woods, Forests, Land Revenues, Works and Buildings, under the mining geologist Sir Henry De La Beche. Its Dublin offices were located at the Custom House and, like its parent body in London, it was associated with a Museum of Economic Geology, which was intended to promote the study and exploitation of the mineral riches of the country. But this museum collection was not really its own and the connections were short-lived. Indeed, the concept of the geological museum enhancing the work of the Geological Survey, and being an intrinsic part of its mission, never gained favour in Ireland.

The Geological Society of Dublin (founded 1831), a gentleman's learned society set up for 'investigating the structure of the earth, and more particularly of Ireland', had the use of rooms in the Custom House to store and display its collection from 1842 until c.1847. In this small museum, first under curator Frederick McCoy (who catalogued the holdings according to the latest scientific classification principles) and then under Thomas Oldham (who worked as a geological assistant with the Ordnance Survey in the north-east of Ireland), rock samples, together with minerals, gemstones, fossils and specimens of Irish fauna and flora and a library of books, charts and maps, were available to the 'student of geology or the investigator of its applications'. It was open to the public two days per week, with no admission charge. Requirements to house the Famine relief projects in 1847 forced the society to vacate the Custom House and its private collections were transferred, for teaching purposes, to TCD, where the society held regular meetings from 1848. While scholarly pursuits such as lectures on geology and archaeology were abandoned during the dark years of the 1840s, digging for various construction works uncovered many archaeological finds.

In 1846 the Ordnance Survey's geological collections began transferring to the Museum of Irish Industry.[10] The Geological Survey offices and laboratories were installed at the front of the house in St Stephen's Green, with the museum collections and the lecture theatre located at the rear of the building. The gathering of rocks, minerals and fossils, undertaken as a public service for educational and aesthetic value, provided evidence of crystal shapes among Ireland's rocks for fellow geologists and the public. More than 1,000 rock specimens, 11,821 Irish fossils and 5,598 British fossils were accessible to the student of Irish palaeontology at the museum of Irish Industry.[11] The position

George Victor du Noyer (1817–69), *Dunmore Castle, Co. Meath*, 1844
Watercolour on paper, 39.1 x 48.4 cm. NGI 3980.

Du Noyer was an artist, geologist and antiquary, associated with the Geological Survey of Ireland. This late-Romantic watercolour, originally in the possession of the National Museum, demonstrates the artist's interest in the layers of rock, fossils and prehistoric and ancient ruins in the Irish landscape.

of the survey within this museum was uneasy, however, and the museum discontinued analysis for the survey in 1861. (The Museum of Economic Geology was originally intended as an adjunct to the Geological Survey.)

Between 1845 and 1887, the Geological Survey employed eminent geologists to produce 1 inch to 1 mile (1:63,360) geological maps detailing the rocks of Ireland. Of these eminent geologists, none ever surpassed George Victor Du Noyer (1817–69)[12] in the construction of field sheets (landscapes, coastal scenes, rockscapes), some copies of which are housed in the NGI.[13] The industrial significance of these 205 Geological Survey map sheets and memoirs was the overview of the Irish landscape they provided for official valuations, roads, railways and engineering works.[14]

The central importance of the collections of the geological department of the Ordnance Survey and of the Geological Survey of Ireland was their use in teaching students at the Museum of Irish Industry. In 1867 the government reconstituted the Museum of Irish Industry as the Royal College of Science and the Geological Survey moved to number 14 Hume Street in 1870. In the late nineteenth century the fruits of the labours of the many geologists and scholars involved in the work of the survey would pass to the Dublin Museum of Science and Art and thus to the Irish people.

The Royal Irish Academy (1785)

The history of the RIA reflects its close association with antiquarianism in Ireland. Its modest resources in the early part of the century required that it petition Parliament in 1816 for funds, but by 1846 the city's enhanced fortunes had increased its membership. There followed the academy's 'golden age', which ended with the deaths of Sir William Rowan Hamilton (1865), George Petrie (1866), Hincks (1866) and James Henthorn Todd (1869).

From the outset the RIA's Museum of Irish Antiquities, Geology and Natural History (1790) grew mainly through donations, such as the specimens from the Danish Royal Academy of Antiquities conveyed by Giesecke in 1815. When it was based at 114 Grafton Street, some items were mislaid during the building of the library in 1834 and again during the fire in 1837. The Antiquities Committee (established in 1785) appointed two members 'to arrange and classify the Museum' in 1828. In 1836, £100 was provided to the Antiquities Committee to purchase Irish antiquities.[15] Many gifts also emerged from the growing passion for antiquarian research. Petrie's membership of the council of the RIA resulted in his arranging some of their antiquities in glass cases in the Round Room.[16] By 1841 it was accepted that 'the formation of a National Museum of Antiquities is an object which the Academy should pursue and funds were sought to this end'.[17] The reconstituted Antiquities Committee negotiated for the Dawson and Sirr collections in 1840, while Petrie drafted an address highlighting 'the advantages of a National Museum of Irish Antiquities'.[18] While there was an awareness of the educational context of the collections, there was no means for the academy to develop it. The academy's concerns were manifest over the issue of security (the board room was converted into a museum in 1844), an inventory, a catalogue and resources: 'the RIA gentry are a set of paupers who have not one shilling to spare to purchase the rarest antiquities'.[19]

A feature of the educational role of the RIA was its involvement in research and publication, which was of central importance to the work of Irish archaeological studies. For instance, the academy's exploration of a *crannóg* at Lagore, County Meath, was described by Petrie in 1840 as 'a discovery not sufficiently appreciated at the time'; the Lagore site report was provided on 27 April 1840 by Sir William Wilde.[20] The finds (mainly animal bones) described by Wilde at an academy meeting came to light by labourers' digging.[21] Other important excavations took place in 1847–8 and conservation work in 1885–6 at Dowth, County Meath (secondary only to the prehistoric tombs of Newgrange and Knowth),[22] with the assistance of the Board of Works, a pattern that continues to this day. As knowledge of Tara, Newgrange and Lagore came to light, together with ancient ruins, castles, high crosses, manuscripts and other precious finds, they were discussed within a circle of learned antiquarian and interested individuals in Dublin, who met on public occasions, at meetings or in each other's homes. From this emerged a growing sense of the connection between culture and an awareness of nationality that generated knowledge of, and respect for, the cultural achievements of ancient Ireland, linking to a similar European movement and forming a solid basis on which subsequent generations could build. This may have been part of the reason why the lack of an inventory of the academy museum to describe 'a depository for everything which may illustrate the habits and history of the Celtic tribes'[23] was critical.

The Academy and a 'National' Collection

The first real effort by the RIA to form a 'national' collection began about 1840, at a time when a wealth of antiquities was being unearthed. Many of these treasures went to the jeweller, the goldsmith and the clock-maker, who were sworn to secrecy so that the objects could not be traced by landlords or agents. This was the reason why the provenance of gold and precious metals went unrecorded, and why the hoards were split from their associated objects. Despite the initiation of the RIA *Proceedings* in the 1830s, published finds tended to appear in the *Journal of the British Archaeological Association*. Archaeologists and antiquarians gradually came to recognize the importance of tracing these hoards and finds back to their source so that they could gain some knowledge of the original setting, the position and condition of the finds and their context in the local landscape, and make systematic recordings for future use.

London-based antiquaries such as the Cork-born artist Daniel Maclise and Thomas Crofton Croker corresponded with contacts in the south of Ireland, enabling them to form cabinets that have been traced through Windele's valuable manuscript collection.[24] Other Cork collections, such as those of Robert Day and John Lindsay, devolved to the National Museum.

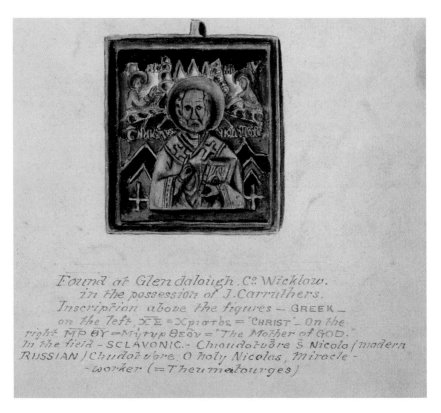

Found at Glen dalough, C? Wicklow.
in the possession of J. Carruthers.
Inscription above the figures – GREEK –
on the left, ΣΣ = Χριστός = "CHRIST". On the
right MP ΘY = Μήτηρ ΘΕΘν = "The Mother of GOD."
In the field – SCLAVONIC.– Choudotvore š Nicolo (modern
RUSSIAN) Chudotvore, O holy Nicolas, miracle –
–worker (= Theumatourges)

A watercolour of a small Russian–Greek enamelled copper alloy icon pendant of St Nicholas, found near the Seven Churches, Glendalough, County Wicklow. The enamel, which was presented by the antiquarian James Carruthers to the Kilkenny Archaeological Society Museum in 1859, may have been lost by an eighteenth- or early nineteenth-century pilgrim.

The Stephens material, 'found in different parts of Ireland', was exhibited at the Natural History and Philosophical Society's Museum for the British Association visit to Belfast in 1852.[25] The holdings of E.P. Shirley from County Monaghan also devolved to the National Museum.[26] Antiquary Robert Chambers Walker, who enjoyed the help of Petrie and access to Ordnance Survey activity in Sligo, sold gold objects to the 4th Duke of Northumberland in 1851, who in turn presented twenty-eight of them to the RIA.[27] The James Carruthers Collection, which was shown to the British Academy meeting in Belfast in 1874, was known through his articles, revealing an antiquarian network.[28] It has been dispersed between the National Museum, Ulster Museum, British Museum, Ashmolean Museum, and the Yorkshire and Doncaster museums.[29] These are just some of the known early cabinets and collections.

The ongoing development of archaeological practices began to result in a new scientific approach that was evident in advanced recording methods, including chronology, provenance, artefact typology and classification. As engravers began to disseminate images from European royal, aristocratic and institutional collections (such as the British Museum and South Kensington Museum), this helped to educate antiquarians about the context of archaeological objects.[30] Thus, by 1850, the RIA had begun to collect sufficient material towards what would become a 'national' collection, although it only received a grant for treasure trove in 1861. In the meantime, officers of the newly founded Dublin Museum of Science and Art (1877)[31] networked with collectors and monitored excavations. Their annual reports listed visits by officers such as George Coffey, who viewed collections like Sir John Leslie's prehistoric urns in Belfast, Robert Day's collection in Cork and a *crannóg* in Enniskillen in 1900.[32] In this way the private provenance of the amateur collector moved to the state-funded museum professional, just as RIA artefacts, including the primary examples listed at the end of this chapter, would transfer into the public domain.

The Growth of the RIA Museum of Irish Antiquities, Geology and Natural History

In 1852, when Navigation House became unsuitable for purpose, the academy moved to Northland House, at number 19 Dawson Street, where it resides to this day.[33] In the wake of the Great Famine the academy council negotiated an 'indemnity against loss' in order to be in a position to lend its treasures to the Dublin International Exhibition of Art-Industry.[34] There was growing recognition of the need to raise public awareness of the collection, and the exhibition presented

Northland House, number 19 Dawson Street; from 1852 it has been the home of the Royal Irish Academy.

Frederic William Burton (1816–1900), *Eugene O'Curry,*
A Peasant Woman and Sir Samuel Ferguson, 6 September 1857
Graphite on paper, 25 x 35 cm. NGI 2638.

The occasion of this drawing was the visit of the British Association for the Advancement of
Science to the Aran Islands, accompanied by Irish antiquarians, presenting an opportunity to
explore some of the archaeological monuments on Inis Mór.

the first opportunity for the treasures to go on public display. The academy
was gradually realizing that the significance of its holdings would form the
basis for a national museum that would be 'of benefit to this country, by
whom the study and preservation of our antiquities has been disgracefully
neglected'.[35] Contemporary accounts reaffirmed this aspiration: 'an opportunity
will be afforded to every one to assist in the establishment of the Museum –
the only truly *national* one'.[36]

The academy provided a new, iron-framed and top-lit museum facility,
with free-standing display cases and a library extension designed by Frederick
Clarendon of the Office of Public Works[37] (1852–4). However, the lack of a
catalogue of the collections had become a critical and embarrassing issue for
the academy,[38] which came under increasing internal pressure to get the catalogue compiled. Eventually, the scheduling of the 1857 British Association

meeting in Dublin set the target date for the long-delayed cataloguing of what was the national antiquarian collection. Wilde stepped in by facilitating 'the arrangement of the museum and in construction of a catalogue', so that volume I, 'required for the identification of these antiquities', was ready for the visit of the British Association.[39] Wilde continued with the project until the remaining volumes were printed,[40] illustrated by Du Noyer and Wakeman. Wilde's catalogue was, however, much more than a reference text to the holdings of the RIA, it was a landmark in archaeological scholarship, including items such as boots, jewellery and kitchen utensils, which connected to the public imagination in an unprecedented way. In 1863 the Prince of Wales visited the academy and it was Wilde who showed him around the museum. He was subsequently rewarded for his work by the presentation of the Cunningham Medal in 1873.

General museum enquiries were answered by Sir Samuel Ferguson's *Brief Handbook for Visitors to the Royal Irish Academy's Museum of Irish Antiquities* (1875). During the 1860s the first floor of the academy was devoted to the museum: the Long Room (front and back drawing rooms) formed the exhibition gallery, while the Council Room, being fire- and theft-proof, was reserved for the gold collection. (It is still known as the 'Gold Room' or the 'Old Strong Room'.) The crypt became a lapidary museum, displaying ogham stones and ancient canoes.

The British Museum and the Public Record Office advised on the compilation of a register of antiquities (1859). In 1861 the RIA president, Lord Talbot de Malahide (1863–83), persuaded government to increase the grant for payment of treasure trove to £100, and this was subsequently improved by a grant of £1,000 in 1866. The academy's collection had now expanded to 9,500 items, in the process producing 'the most important Celtic collection in the world'. The arrival of the Halliday Collection of pamphlets, books and manuscripts in 1867 created a crisis of space and resulted in plans for an extension to the building (1868–75).[41]

In 1870 a new committee was set up to manage the museum and its staff.[42] Complaints about its restrictive opening hours and closure during university holidays (when gold and silver objects were lodged in the bank) were met with the proposal that it 'should be opened to the public on Sundays after the hours of Divine Service'.[43] In 1873 access was improved when it started to open for three days a week, with two evening openings tried in 1879.

The Dublin Natural History Society (1838–71) transferred its collection in 1880, following its amalgamation with the RIA.[44] Modest annual visitor numbers included 1,100 in 1881–2, dropping to 500 by 1887–8. By this stage the museum, called an 'incubus' by the antiquary Lord Dunraven, was becoming extremely difficult to manage. The critical year was 1868, when Henry Cole proposed to the Kildare Commission the transfer of the collection to a new museum. Government's decision to found a museum of science and art in Dublin was conveyed to the RDS and the RIA by Lord Sandon on 6 February 1876. Despite all the problems the academy had in managing the museum and its growing collections, this was a tough decision to accept. A contemporary account reported the prevailing feelings:

> The RIA is a body devoted to the production of original papers in science and antiquities and furnished with a valuable museum and library of its own [but] has had to wage a bitter fight for its independence, and has only secured it by parting with the property and we fear with the control of its precious and unique museum of Irish antiquities.[45]

The Agreement between the RIA and the Lords of the Committee of the Council on Education was signed on 18 August 1890 by H. Samuel, RIA president, M.N. Close, RIA treasurer, A.J.R. Trendall, acting chief clerk, and Edward Belshaw, clerk of the Upper Division for the Council on Education, with the respective corporate seals affixed to it. In October of that year the Agreement to transfer the RIA museum to the Dublin Museum of Science and Art was effected and the academy's important collection of treasured Irish antiquities was removed to its new location in Kildare Street.[46] For the academy, the loss of the collection was immense, but the members resolved to remain *in situ* in order to preserve the academy library and manuscript collection and to ensure its independent status.[47]

The achievement of the RIA in the nineteenth century as a learned and cultured repository was considerable. Its general educational mandate was expended in the acquisition, care and exhibition of its collections, the museum and library, the preservation of its manuscripts and books, and scholarly publications. The advancement of Irish archaeological studies, antiquarian practice and collections was a significant aspect of its work, with donations made by naturalists' societies and field clubs and by men who saw no difference between the arts and the sciences. An important facet of this achievement was the academy's awareness of excavations and the threat of damage to ancient monuments and consequent theft of artefacts. Irish archaeology owes a great deal to the foresight exhibited by the RIA in its efforts to step into the breach and protect the country's heritage. Similarly, its publications created national and international access to Irish history and scholarship.

In terms of its contribution to the museum movement, the RIA's role was significant, but not as far-reaching as it might have been. Although museological trends were manifest in the cataloguing and the arrangement and preservation of the collections, on balance its lack of flexible opening hours, guidebooks, labels and modest displays meant that by the time it became aware of its public role, it was incapable of exercising this role. Thus, the academy's greatest achievement in the nineteenth century was undoubtedly the acquisition of the most significant Irish antiquarian collection in existence, matched by its munificence in transferring these national treasures to the public domain of the Dublin Museum of Science and Art.

It is worth detailing a selection of these treasures in order to illustrate the debt Irish archaeology, Irish museums and the Irish people owe to the RIA.

In 1837, following encouragement by Petrie, with whom he had frequent contact, James Underwood, a watch- and clock-maker of Dublin, offered an extensive collection of antiquities to the RIA.[48]

In 1839 James MacCullagh acquired for the academy the Cross of Cong, the most important ecclesiastical treasure of the late eleventh and early twelfth century, which was

The Cross Of Cong, County Mayo, early twelfth century

This County Mayo shrine, designed for processional use, was made towards the end of the early twelfth century to house a relic of the True Cross acquired in 1122 by Turlough O'Connor, high king of Ireland. It is one of the finest and last of the artistic creations of the early Christian period, presented to the Royal Irish Academy by Professor James MacCullagh.

commissioned by one of the great Viking Age dynasties, the O'Connors. The Cross of Cong was probably made in Tuam, County Galway, or in County Roscommon, rather than Cong in County Mayo, towards the end of the first quarter of the twelfth century to enshrine a relic of the True Cross that had been acquired in 1122 by Turlough O'Connor, high king of Ireland. While the form of the cross and the religious milieu in which it was produced may have been Irish, the design reflects Viking Urnes-style influence. Made for devotional display, it represents one of the finest artistic achievements of the early Christian period.

MacCullagh, who hailed from Glenelly, County Tyrone, was professor of mathematics at TCD, with a passionate interest in retrieving objects associated with Ireland's ancient past. It was he who acquired for the academy one of the finest shrines ever uncovered, the Domhnach Airgid (silver church) Book Shrine, which was made around AD 800 to contain relics given by St Patrick to St Macartan, patron saint of Clones, County Monaghan. The shrine has a history of embellishment stretching back almost a thousand years. The first container was a hollow yew-wood box covered with engraved bronze plates and with a sliding lid. An inscription along the top tells how the shrine was remade around AD 1350 by John O Barden (a goldsmith who lived in Drogheda) for John O Carbry, abbot of Clones, who died in 1353. Decorated with cast and gilt silver plaques bearing figures of the Virgin, saints and apostles, on the lower left plate, it is suggested that a clerical scribe presents a copy of the Gospels to St Macartan, founder of a church at Clogher, County Tyrone. Shrines such as this one were much used and much venerated objects, which were subject to considerable wear and therefore required regular repair. The relief casting is unusual, as most shrines are engraved or stamped on thin sheets of silver.[49]

Finally, also in 1839, MacCullagh headed a subscription for two magnificent twisted gold torcs found at the Rath of the Synods on the Hill of Tara, County Meath, where the occurrence of burial monuments suggests the hill was of ritual and political importance in the Bronze Age (*c.* 2000–*c.* 500 BC). Between them, the torcs, which date to the Middle Bronze Age (1200–1000 BC), contain over 1 kg of gold and are the finest of their class in Ireland. MacCullagh acquired them from James West: 'they narrowly escaped being sent out of the country a second time and forever'. Wilde reported that they were found 'by a peasant boy in 1810 in the side of one of the clay raths at Tara … purchased by Alderman West of Dublin [and] ending up in the Duke of Sussex's collection'.[50]

In 1840 the cabinet of Henry Richard Dawson (1792–1840), dean of St Patrick's Cathedral, was acquired:

> If a sufficient sum of money can be raised to purchase the Irish portion of the collection of the museum of the late Dean of St. Patrick's Cathedral, to be deposited in the RIA as the basis of a National Museum of Irish Antiquities, to open to students and the public.[51]

The collection comprised 1,874 Irish antiquities, gold and silver ornaments, twenty-seven fibulae and three perfect torcs, bronze pottery and substantial coins and medals. The dealer Redmond Anthony had originally sold items to Dawson, and after his death in 1840 objects from his collection went to the British Museum. Petrie had led the subscriptions and the money went to provide for Dawson's widow.[52]

In 1841 the important collection of Major Henry Charles Sirr (1764–1841) was acquired by the academy. Sirr had been a controversial figure. He joined the army in 1778, became a captain in 1791 and joined the Royal Dublin Volunteers in 1796. He was famous for his involvement in the capture of Lord Edward FitzGerald (1798) and in the arrest of Robert Emmet in 1803. He was interested in antiquities and dealt in antiques privately before selling some of his collection to Dean Dawson in 1836.[53]

In the years between 1843 and 1852 some 377 objects were recovered from rivers and lakes throughout Ireland. These were gathered by the Office of Public Works engineers and their workmen during the course of excavations and 'arterial drainage works … from places under water'.[54] In 1852 the Office of Public Works and the Shannon Navigation Commissioners presented this impressive collection, described by Petrie as 'beyond estimation', to the academy. This presentation of donations by the Office of Public Works made up for the academy's miserly grant.[55]

In 1853 a committee from the RIA (Petrie, Aquilla Smith and Rev James Henethorn Todd) inspected 'the collection of antiquities found in High

Street' before recommending the payment of £10 to the dealer, including 'specimens of work in leather, bone, wood, glass, stone etc' and possibly some ironwork.

In 1854 'an enormous hoard of gold ornaments' was found at Mooghaun North, County Clare, representing 'The greatest find of prehistoric gold ornaments ever discovered in Western Europe'.[56] The massive hoard was uncovered during construction works near Mooghaun Lake when the West Clare Railway was being built. The objects had probably been deposited there as a ritual act of appeasement. Most of the hoard was dispersed by the workmen through jewellers, who provided ready cash for the bullion value. As a result, there is no accurate figure for the hoard, which probably contained several hundred objects. (Wilde's inventory noted 5 gorgets, 2 neck torcs, 2 unwrought ingots, 137 rings and *armilliae* [dress-fasteners].) Only thirty-four original objects survived (fourteen of which are in the British Museum), although many of the objects were replicated before being melted down. The hoard contained mainly small bracelets, collars, neck-rings and ingots. The acquisition of the hoard by the academy was aided by a public subscription.[57]

In 1866 the Petrie Collection was acquired and donated to the RIA museum in 1868. A topographical artist, trained at the RDS Drawing Schools, Petrie was an art teacher and a librarian at the RHA. During his busy, diverse life he held many positions, including head of place names and antiquities at the Ordnance Survey. In 1828 he became a member of the RIA, joining the council in 1830 and becoming vice-president in 1845. He was an

extraordinary figure, central to the antiquarian movement in the nineteenth century and often called 'the father of Irish archaeology'.

The key object from this collection, the 'Petrie Crown', was a complex major

Bronze headdress known as the Petrie Crown, early Iron Age, second century AD

This complex object was expertly assembled using rivets and solder. The components, which were probably sewn to leather or textile, formed part of an elaborate horned headdress.

work of the Early Iron Age La Tène period (second century AD). It is a head-dress in the form of a crown, with circular discs mounted on a hoop or band of metal and conical horns rising from behind the decorated discs. The assembly of this decorative object would have required a highly technical craftsman using rivets and solder, with the components, which were probably sewn to leather or textile, forming part of an elaborate horned headdress. Extremely sophisticated metalworking was required to create the complex double curvature at the base of the horn. Petrie left no record of the site or circumstances of its discovery, which would have helped to place it in some sort of context, but there is similar decoration on brooches found in northern Britain.[58]

In 1868 the finest of the penannular ring brooches, the so-called 'Tara' Brooch, which dates to early eighth-century AD and had been found near the seashore at Bettystown, County Meath, in 1850, was purchased for the academy from the firm of Dublin jewellers Waterhouse & Company for £200. The association with the ancient royal site of Tara had been invented by Waterhouse in order to enhance its value and the jeweller registered his design for the 'Tara' Brooch on 9 December 1850, months after it was found, so that he could have copies made.[59] The practice of making copies of historic antiquarian jewellery was common in the nineteenth century (some of the existing copies are extremely fine) and they were actively promoted as symbols of Ireland's ancient past.[60] The 'Tara' Brooch is decorated on both sides and is made of cast and gilt silver, the front consisting of a network of recessed cells of gold filigree separated by studs of amber, enamel and glass. The guard-chain of woven silver wires ends in a swivel attachment made of cast snake and animal heads, framing two tiny glass human heads. It was created as a symbol of power and authority for the most important figures in society. The design of the brooch is superb. It measures just 2 cm from end to end but the detailing is technically exquisite and refined and the materials are of the highest quality, marking it as one of the finest treasures of early medieval Ireland.

In 1874 the Ardagh Chalice was acquired by the academy. It had been found in 1868 by a boy digging potatoes. He uncovered it from its hiding place under a stone slab at Reerasta Rath, near Ardagh, County Limerick, where it may have been placed for safe keeping. The Ardagh Hoard comprised a magnificent silver chalice, a smaller plain chalice of copper-alloy and four

The site of the Broighter Hoard find in County Derry, with, from left to right, Grenville A.J. Cole, Robert Lloyd Praeger and George Coffey. *Irish Naturalists' Journal*, vol. 11, April 1854.

Gold model boat, Broighter, County Derry. Early Iron Age, first century BC
This tiny unique model boat made of beaten sheet gold provides an indication that the Broighter Hoard was a votive deposit to the sea-god Manannán Mac Lir. It is probably a model of an ocean-going vessel, complete with seats, oars, rowlocks, steering oar and mast. 1903:323, L.19.6cm

silver brooches. The objects ranged in date from the mid-eighth century to the late ninth century AD. The latest object in the hoard is a silver thistle brooch of the type that is often found as scrap in hoards of Viking character, which leads to the suggestion that it was placed in the ground about AD 900. The Ardagh Chalice itself, dating to the eighth century AD, is a combination of a design of remarkable elegance, constraint and intricate decorative detail. As with the 'Tara' Brooch, design, technique and materials are of the highest quality. The decorative band under the rim and the circular medallions on either face may have been inspired by the jewelled metal straps of Byzantine workmanship fitted to Late Antique vessels of glass and semi-precious stone, such as those now preserved in the treasury of St Mark's Cathedral in Venice (brought there from Constantinople during the Crusades). Below the rim are accomplished geometric letter forms engraved against a stippled background illustrating the names of the apostles, James and Thaddeus.[61]

In 1896 the famous early Iron Age Broighter Hoard, dating to the first century BC, was found during ploughing in a field at Broighter, County Derry. This simple yet wonderfully refined hoard was immediately significant for the light that it shed on the technology, beliefs and international contacts with Ireland around the first century BC. The gold objects, which had been imported from the Roman world, comprised an unusual group of a gold bowl with suspension rings, two chains, a large decorated collar with buffer terminals (the design for this collar was worked by repoussé technique down the centre of two flat sheets of gold), two twisted collars and a model boat of an ocean-going vessel complete with seats, oars, rowlocks, steering oar and mast. The hoard had lain concealed for two millennia near the shore at the entrance to Lough Foyle. (Lough Foyle is traditionally associated with the sea god Manannán Mac Lir, and the location of the hoard, together with the nature of the objects found, suggest it was a votive offering to the ancient deity.) The year after it was discovered, the hoard was sold to the British Museum. The academy became aware of the Broighter Hoard through a paper published by Sir Arthur Evans in 1898, and asked the government to undertake a legal case for the return of the Irish treasure trove. The legal and related events following its discovery were significant for the RIA museum and its recognition as Ireland's national museum. The part played by Sir Edward Carson, the state's counsel and later leader of Ulster unionism, in

Royal Irish Academy museum with some gold artefacts in the Gold Room. Many of the gold objects were housed in what was known as the Old Strong Room (i.e. the Long Room). They are displayed in wall cases, desk cases and a window case – all fitted with drawers. These artefacts were listed in the Register of Objects in the Strong Room of the Museum, and in an inventory of the collection (listing 'the gold acquired up to 1881').

Royal Irish Academy museum early medieval antiquities. On display in the Long Room, in a case against the wall, is the Cross of Cong, copy of St Manchan's Shrine and the Shrine of St Patrick's Tooth. The collection was first listed in a manuscript 'Catalogue of Eccliastical Antiquities' (1856–66) by Sir William Wilde, and a 'Catalogue of Specimens in the Collection of William F. Wakeman', brought to galley stage with a preface by Director, Valentine Ball in 1894. The two-volume catalogue was prepared (unpublished) and remains part of the museum's basic register.

the return of the hoard to Ireland was considerable. In 1903 Edward VII ordered its return to the RIA.[62]

This listing represents a mere selection of some of the treasured Irish artefacts and collections that the RIA acquired in the course of the nineteenth century and early twentieth century. Taken together, these materials represent one of the finest collections of prehistoric gold and early medieval metalwork in the world. It became obvious to the antiquarians that these were masterpiece works that deserved professional standards of storage and security, availability for research and access to public display in a national museum. Their selfless generosity in collecting, recording and finally transferring these works to the Irish state is one of the high points of the nineteenth-century museum movement. Indeed, these objects continue to distinguish the National Museum of Ireland, where they are housed, from almost any other institution.

7

A 'National' Museum and a National Identity

A museum exists for the purpose of educating a community in realising the taste and artistic designs of past ages.[1]

The nineteenth century marked the establishment of a number of leading Irish cultural institutions, many of which emerged as part of a museum movement that was a facet of the RDS enterprise and that had its own links to a developing sense of national identity.[2] It was an era of scientific innovation, when figures like Edward Cooper and William Wilson set up observatories in counties Sligo and Westmeath, respectively.[3] At Birr Castle in County Offaly, William Parsons, 3rd Earl of Rosse (1800–67), constructed his 3-foot reflecting telescope in 1839 and the larger Leviathan of Parsonstown in 1845.[4] The RDS published scientific *Proceedings* and *Transactions*, grant-aided scientific research and instigated the Boyle Medal in 1899 to honour figures who had made a significant contribution to science.[5] In this way, scientific and cultural advancements became the cornerstones of modern Irish society.

This was the century when collections were formed and became of such archaeological importance in tracing Ireland's ancient history that they assumed the status of 'national' collections. This pattern of forming national

Edwin Hayes (1820–1904), *An Emigrant Ship, Dublin Bay, Sunset,* **1853**
Oil on canvas, 58 x 86 cm. NGI 1209.

Prior to the Famine Ireland was densely populated with people living in small holdings in close communities. In the wake of the Famine, families and villages disappeared, a traditional lifestyle changed, and communities were uprooted in their movement overseas to adapt to a new way of life.

museums in Europe had demonstrated the desire of society to articulate its identity through artefacts that related to its historical past. It was this same process of national consciousness, catalysed by the Dublin International Exhibition of Art-Industry of 1853, that led to the establishment of the Dublin Museum of Science and Art.

The major roles in the story of the national museums are played by the RDS and the RIA, whose collections were the critical factors in the success of the museum movement. Thus, the short-lived but impressive Museum of Irish Industry is examined here, and its connection with the Geological Survey and the RDS institutions. All of these histories are bound up with the influential RDS, as these diverse collections devolved first to Dublin's Natural History Museum and then to the Museum of Art and Science, the forerunner of the National Museum of Ireland.

Museum of Irish Industry (1845–67)

The new Museum of Economic Geology, founded in Dublin in 1845,[6] represented a government-sponsored scientific institution for the promotion of science and its practical application and was contemporary with the recent publication of the six-inches-to-one-mile maps of Ireland by the Ordnance Survey. This was the first publicly funded museum in Ireland. While set up along the lines of the Museum of Practical Geology in London (founded by Edward de la Beche in 1835), Robert Peel's Conservative government understood the need for a technical college to promote industrial development in Ireland. The Dublin museum would collect geological specimens and objects that showed the use of its various mineral substances, to become 'a national institution for the promotion of … sciences'.[7]

The new director, Robert Kane, 'an unusual distinction for one so young', highlighted the role of industrial development in his *Industrial Resources of Ireland* (1844),[8] a publication welcomed by Thomas Davis and for which Kane received the RIA Cunningham Medal in 1843.[9] From the outset, industrial education was Kane's prime objective for the museum: 'I attach the highest importance to the establishment in Dublin of a central Museum of Economic Geology … for the development of industrial resources in Ireland.'[10] Thus, while government founded the museum for the application of geology, agricultural and mining, Kane extended its remit to teach science and industrial education.[11] Contemporary with this was the emergence of the Queen's Colleges in Cork, Belfast and Galway, with Kane president of UCC (1845–73), while retaining directorship of the Museum of Economic Geology.[12]

Charles Grey (1808–92), *Sir Robert Kane (1809–1890), Scientist,* **c.1849**
(Illustration for the Dublin University Magazine, *vol. 33, 1849) pencil on paper, 23.5 x 16.9 cm. NGI 3790.*

Kane was the first director of the Museum of Irish Industry, in addition to being the first president of Queen's College, Cork.

Ireland's Famine experience (1845–50) revealed a pattern of unhelpful government policies that was not ameliorated by William Ewart Gladstone's comment: 'It is the greatest horror of modern times that in the richest ages of the world and in the richest country of that age, the people should be dying of Famine by hundreds.' The Great Famine caused a major breakdown of mid-nineteenth-century Irish society, hastened the decline of the Irish language, resulted in the acceleration of emigration and imparted a critical impulse to the imperatives of survival.[13] Pastimes such as gathering antiquities, geological specimens and works of art waned for a decade. Kane assisted the Relief Commission, working with the Central Board of Health until the crisis eased.[14]

In 1847 the Museum of Economic Geology – now renamed the Museum of Irish Industry – acquired number 51 St Stephen's Green and necessary renovations were carried out by George Papworth, influenced by Sir James Pennethorne's design for London's Museum of Practical Geology.[15] Kane set about classifying the inherited zoological, flora and fauna collections into: (a) industrial exhibits; (b) the Portlock collections; (c) geological collections representative of regions in Ireland; and (d) general collections for teaching

MUSEUM OF IRISH INDUSTRY.
STEPHENS GREEN
1857.

Exterior of the Museum of Irish Industry, 1857

This frontispiece is taken from the *General Descriptive Guide to the Museum of Irish Industry*, 1857. It shows rectangular windows in place and the exterior of the building largely unchanged from the earlier 1790s house. Joly Collection, National Library of Ireland.

Museum of Irish Industry Entrance Hall, the first part of the museum to open to the public in 1853, during the Dublin International Exhibition of Art-Industry; it was decorated with forty different types of Irish marble. The framework for displaying the marbles was made of oak-panelled wainscoting decorated with shamrocks and surmounted by honeysuckle motifs, interspersed with Doric pilasters of red and green marble.

purposes.[16] He displayed the Wilkinson Geological Collection at the rear of the building.[17]

The museum's educational function was articulated as a 'state laboratory-research institute-college with departments of mechanical arts, mining, engineering, and manufacture; the curriculum on English lines, rather than Irish conditions'.[18] The building was ready for Dublin's International Exhibition of Art-industry, the entrance hall featuring a geological cabinet of Irish stone in 1851–2, leading to 'the revival of the marble trade in Ireland, which had been all but extinct'.[19] Museum space on the staircase, ground and first floors revealed the varied nature of collections, which, despite their diverse source, formed a coherent whole.[20] Taking its role as a public institution seriously, the museum was open weekdays between 11 a.m. and 4 p.m., with late opening from 7 to 9.30 p.m. on certain evenings during class time, to make it even more accessible to the public; Sunday opening, 'after the hours of Divine Service', did not transpire.[21] In 1854 a Government School of Science Applied to Mining and the Arts was added. It was a popular exhibition centre, playing host to 23,818 visitors in 1858, followed by 22,997 day and 13,660 evening visitors (total 36,657) in 1859.[22] In 1860, its library of scientific material was used by 557 students, together with 40,000 visitors to the exhibitions and geological gallery, leading the English naturalist the Reverend Symonds to remark: 'The Museum of Irish Industry is a credit to Dublin.'[23]

In 1854 Henry Cole, head of the Department of Science and Art, reviewed the Dublin-based operations, including the lecture programme undertaken by the Museum of Irish Industry and the RDS (popular afternoon talks) since 1845 (the Museum of Irish Industry had transferred to the Department of Science and Art in 1853), his own policy on industrial instruction having enabled Kane to effect his educational objectives.[24] That year Cole's department indicated its intention to transfer the RDS professorships to the Government School of Mining at the Museum of Irish Industry. The training at the museum involved people from all backgrounds, including women, who attended systematic courses of 'advanced and technical education'. Fees were payable for the day lectures, but evening talks for artisans were free of charge. Although a popular lecture programme, the system had problems due to the staff of five professors of geology, zoology, botany, physics and chemistry being shared between the institutions (the range of courses varied each year). The provincial lecture programme was particularly significant and its importance cannot be underestimated, as its evening classes enabled science to become 'the right of all'.[25] The regional courses also promoted local scientific bodies and Mechanics' Institutes. The industrial education system was officially recognized: 'the provincial lectures are of great use in the arousing and spreading of a desire for scientific knowledge throughout Ireland'.[26] The museum, with its collections, was operating as a science and technical body.

When government set up a Select Committee in 1863 to inquire into Ireland's scientific institutions, its Committee of Council of Education recommended that science and art provision become a public, and not a private, responsibility.[27] An ancillary proposal to remove the 'Geological collections of the Museum of Irish Industry [to] the National Gallery' was rejected as 'unsuited to a gallery of art'.[28] The 'Minute of 1865' ended the link between the Museum of Irish Industry and the Geological Survey, firmly closing the museum and replacing it with a college of science.[29] Its absence was noted: 'there ought, in this technological age to be at least an economic and technical museum showing the products of agriculture and raw materials of industry'.[30] The Museum of Irish Industry's zoological collections were removed to the RDS Dublin Natural History Museum, and the industrial collections would eventually go to the Museum of Science and Art.

The Royal College of Science's 'college museum' would belong to the in-house teaching collections of science of art, such as in the less accessible museums of the RDS, TCD and Maynooth. Those with greater access would belong to a different stream of public institutions, including the NGI, Dublin Museum of Science and Art, Belfast Art Gallery and Museum and the Crawford Municipal Art Gallery. When the Royal College of Science opened in 1867, it became the first third-level institution to admit women and train science teachers, over half of whom came from England. Its college museum, containing instruments and engineering models, proved successful, with 3,063 visitors making use of it in 1878.

RDS Cultural Institutions: Repository, Drawing Schools, Museums

The role of the RDS, as noted earlier, was crucial in the move towards a national museum. It is therefore essential to appreciate the nature and impact of its various cultural institutions – Repository, School of Design, Museum of Natural History and Museum of Science and Art – in order to understand the evolution of a movement that led to the establishment of the NMI. It was the Dublin Society that fostered a process that led to the accumulation of diverse collections, which in turn laid the foundations for a national collection of treasures.

By the mid-nineteenth century the RDS had become a major educational enterprise and a successful improving society. The organization had developed substantial links with all of the bodies outlined in recent chapters, in addition to those listed above, and in the process had become a serious player in every aspect of Irish life, with a particular emphasis on developing a cultural infrastructure for Ireland. Underpinning all this development was a range of Irish societies dedicated to science, medicine, law, history, engineering, music, art, architecture and Shakespearean studies.[31] The RDS promoted its own interest in science by initiating a programme of public talks of 'enlightened education' on botany, zoology and natural philosophy, with illustrations on a 'screen for lantern projections' at its lecture theatre in Leinster House, which seated 500 people.[32] When, for example, Sir Humphrey Davy (1778–1829) gave a series of talks on electro-chemistry, chemistry and geology, he was commended 'for increasing the spirit of philosophical research in Ireland'.[33] Richard Griffith, elected RDS mining engineer and professor of geology, gave annual courses on mining and geology (1814–29), attended by men and women, which demonstrated that it was possible to engage the wider public in scientific discourse (also one of Kane's aims at the Museum of Irish Industry).[34]

Griffith had explained to a Select Committee in 1836 that the purpose of holding these programmes was to demonstrate scientific research. Thus, the 127 lectures provided in 43 locations under RDS supervision between 1838 and 1853 formed the main vehicle for conveying information on science to the Irish public.[35] The outcome saw the blossoming of all the RDS semi-state enterprises, including its museums and art schools. However, once government perceived the might of this educational operation, it swiftly took it under state control.[36]

The RDS Repository (1733)

The RDS Repository was the first home of the agricultural implements and early natural history specimens and it survived into the new century with its collections used by the Farming Society (set up by progressive landowners in 1800, many of whom were RDS members), which used Hawkins Street House for its meetings until 1820. Under pressure from Lord Downshire, the RDS set up a Committee of Agriculture in 1830, which oversaw the establishment of an agricultural museum to house the original holdings. In 1842 the RDS issued a prospectus for the Agricultural Museum (in conjunction with a museum planned by the new Agricultural Improvement Society, founded in 1841),[37] which opened in 1843 under the curatorship of James Duffus, succeeded by Andrew Corrigan in 1847.[38] A deputation from the museum viewed the RDS contribution to the Paris *Exposition Universelle* in 1855,[39] following which it was placed under the Committee of Agriculture in the same year and the Committee of Manufactures in 1857.[40] From 1871 the museum appeared in RDS records in association with agricultural shows at

Ballsbridge, and references to material lent to the Exhibition of Arts and Industries at Earlsfort Terrace in 1872. The Agricultural Museum was visited by 7,071 people in 1877,[41] after which it became associated with the RDS Spring Show.[42]

The Dublin Society Drawing Schools (1746)

The Dublin Society Drawing Schools – comprising Figure, Landscape and Ornament, Architecture, Modelling – had been accommodated at Leinster House from 1818. In 1827 a new space was provided, together with a portrait bust gallery, which comprised a top-lit gallery used for exhibitions and for students to study from the antique casts,[43] augmented by the Elgin Marble casts acquired in 1816–17 and others, from the ruins of Persepolis, donated by Colonel Stannus in 1828.[44] The RDS enlarged its collection of original drawings by seventeenth- and eighteenth-century masters, which came from a number of sources (bearing the signature of Edward Hardman, RDS assistant-secretary, 1829–50), some dated 1833, but without the original date of acquisition. This material devolved first to the Museum of Science and

The Statue Gallery, Government School of Design in Dublin, 1866

This antique sculpture collection in Kildare Street was available for the public to view and for students to use as a basis for instruction in drawing.

Art (recorded in its catalogues) and latterly to the NGI.[45]

Government identified the RDS Drawing Schools as the main art teaching institution in Dublin and thus renamed it 'a School of Design', funded by the Board of Trade from 1849.[46] It transferred to the Department of Science and Art in 1854.[47] Known as 'The Government School of Design in connection with the RDS', the school was managed by a Fine Arts Committee, which maintained free tuition until 1849, and was monitored by assistant masters until 1854.[48] Women were admitted from 1849, when the payment of fees was initiated. In 1877 it became the Dublin Metropolitan School of Art, when the state took control of RDS institutions, and by 1900 it had come under the authority of the Department of Agriculture and Technical Instruction for Ireland.

One of the significant factors that impacted on the training of students and artists during this century was the founding of the RHA, heralding annual exhibitions of living artists' work from 1826. The opening of the NGI in 1864 provided the country's first public old master and antique cast collection, together with the facility it accorded students and painters to study from the collections two days a week. The access and encouragement given to women to study at the art schools late in the century would be evident in the attendance records at the National Gallery's 'private days', and would produce highly competent women artists in the early twentieth century. The launch of the Museum of Science and Art in 1890 provided further access to collections of natural sciences, art and industries, antique casts and Irish antiquities. By century's end, within one small quarter of Dublin, students of

The Dublin Metropolitan School of Art Gallery, 1906 (M. Henderson)

The school is decorated for the distribution of prizes. B.I. Tilly, the registrar, stands by Frederick Luke, the second master, in readiness for the arrival of the students and masters.

the arts and sciences had access to all the main cultural institutions: art school and academy, university, college of science, gallery, museum and library.

The RDS Museum (1792)

The RDS Museum was the most outstanding collection in Dublin in the early nineteenth century, the only one truly meriting the term 'Irish museum'. The museum and its diverse collections were accommodated in Hawkins Street House, where they were set around a quadrangular court, with two rooms for the Leskean Cabinet and other collections, a gallery to display the busts and casts and an exhibition room. The collections housed in this 'commodious building' were open to the public, without charge, on Monday, Wednesday and Friday between midday and 3 p.m.

The antiquarian John Lee spent three-and-a-half hours visiting the Dublin Society at Hawkins Street House on 3 September 1807 and he was impressed with 'the liberality with which the whole is conducted'. He praised the lecture room, the library and the laboratory. The gallery was 'filled with busts of all the best statues' from antiquity, and a number of artists (maximum fifteen) were afforded the facility of copying from them, in silence. The 'artists are allowed every day between 7 and 9 to draw from a living figure, who is got to sit in different postures'. The exhibition spaces were well described: 'the museum for minerals is a most beautiful sight, the scientific arrangement begins with the precious stones'. He noted that the next small room contained books and a window of stained glass, and beyond was a great room with collections laid out: shells, birds, stuffed insects, butterflies, fossils, seaweeds, horns, 'a great many natural curiosities in spirit' and statues. Above the stairs was another room, which dealt with 'minerals & ore fossils' found in Ireland in the different counties and arranged accordingly. Below the stairs, a room contained 'a fine petrified fish found in a block of Portland stone and some pillars of mass work from Giant's Causeway', while a case in the second room contained Roman curiosities.

The RDS cultural educational enterprise had expanded with the addition of a course of lectures on chemistry and philosophy, delivered by William Higgins, professor of chemistry and mineralogy, the museum's first curator and a 'man of eccentric, indolent habits'.[49] The Leskean Collection of insects was damaged while it was at Hawkins Street, and when it was compared with Karsten's original catalogue, *A Description of the Minerals in the Leskean Museum* (1789), it revealed little increase since its purchase in 1792.[50] The Hawkins Street Exhibition Room was used for exhibitions of Irish art until 1820.[51] As the museum expanded, the *Proceedings* recorded references 'to gifts and purchases of zoological specimens', some of which required treatment by John Turellion, who was paid for preserving birds in 1806. Griffith gathered geological specimens and carried out a survey of simple minerals for the museum between 1809 and 1829.[52] This 'father of Irish geology' also donated his corpus of fossils: 'Their collection should be enriched by the best of everything I have been able to collect.'[53] Frederick McCoy (1823–99) documented the collection, recording 500 species of extinct animals (now in the NMI).[54]

Sir Charles Lewis Giesecke, the second curator of the museum, was nominated professor of mineralogy and geology in 1813.[55] Under his care the important natural history collections were examined by Irish scientists and influential visitors, including Robert Jameson of Edinburgh.[56] The presentation of his Greenland Collection resulted in the society awarding him its gold medal in 1817.

As the society's cultural, educational and economic activities had become of major consequence to Ireland, Parliament doubled the annual grant in 1800 and this paved the way for the society to find more spacious accommodation in the impressive quarters of Leinster House (named Kildare House until 1766).[57] The property was purchased in an agreement drawn up with Augustus Frederick (1791–1874), 3rd Duke of Leinster, in 1814, whereby RDS occupation for over a century (1815–1924) did little harm and kept the building reasonably intact. Reverend Robert Walsh commented that 'having expended vast sums to render one house unfit for any other purpose, [the Society] have purchased another which no money will render suitable'.[58]

In 1815 the museum closed for a month so that the porter could begin removing some of the collection to Leinster House and help 'Professor Giesecke in arranging the materials'.[59] *An Historical Guide to the City of Dublin* described the layout of the museum in Leinster House: the first room contained a selection of curiosities, the second room contained varieties of the animal kingdom, the third room the mineralogical collection, the fourth room the Greenland Collection, the fifth room housed the geological part of the Leskean Collection and the sixth room contained the Hibernicum, comprising mineralogical and geological specimens from the thirty-two counties of Ireland.[60] Being mindful to advance the cause of the museum, Giesecke exchanged minerals with the Imperial Museum in Vienna and the Geological Society in London in 1816. During the course of his European tour in 1818–19 (distributing mineralogical specimens), he sent materials to Goethe, who was interested in this field of study – 'the Irishman, Joy, has brought some fine mineral specimens from Giesecke' – thus furthering relations with learned circles in Europe.[61] The ambitious society resolved to add the prefix 'royal' to its name, just as it amassed 30,000 minerals to illustrate Ireland's natural history.[62]

The museum was commended by a parliamentary committee – 'in a country poor in such public repositories' – set up to inquire into the affairs of the RDS.[63] However, problems beset the museum due to the lack of funding and the expansion of the collections, which restricted space still further: it was necessary to 'enter by the door at the main staircase, to pass through the rooms in regular succession and to make an exit from the door open from the Greenland Room into the corridor'.[64] It was difficult to exhibit all the gifts, such as the 'Etruscan Vases bequeathed by George de la Touche'.[65] Proposals were put forward to have a case made for their protection, but when they were loaned to the School of Art for teaching purposes in 1861, the minutes recorded that a vase 'was broken'. It was 'not the only instance the vases have sustained injury'.[66] They were promptly returned.

Described as 'the National Museum of Ireland' when Giesecke's catalogue of entomology and ornithology specimens was completed in 1832, museum attendance was recorded as 38,000 visitors in 1831.[67] It closed in 1832 due to a cholera epidemic, and following Giesecke's death in 1833, it was closed 'for a fortnight as a mark of respect to his memory'. As an interim measure, temporary/replacement curators were appointed: the librarian Frederick Craddock was followed by the porter Thomas Wall, who proved successful at the task.[68] Concern about the museum was expressed by the 1833 RDS Committee, which felt it was inferior to 'celebrated Museums abroad and even some in this country'.[69] John Scouler, professor of natural history at the University of Glasgow, became the third curator in 1834, smartly publishing papers on Irish geology and zoology, undertaking lecture programmes, donating materials and coping with the overcrowded museum:[70] 'This valuable collection of specimens is open to students at all hours and to the public from 12.00–3.00 on Tuesdays and Fridays.'[71]

Preparations were put in place for the Dublin meeting of the British Association in 1835, and although the association's members were impressed by their visit, a German traveller noted the poverty in the city: 'here the sun must testify that Europe too has its pariahs'.[72] The society hoped the meeting would make science fashionable in Ireland, as noted by William Thompson (Irish biologist noted for his studies on the natural history of Ireland) in 1843: 'There are public collections [in Dublin], the Ordnance Museum, Phoenix Park, good in various departments of vertebrata and invertebrata … Trinity College containing the late Mr. Tardy's collection of insects, added to by Dr. Coulter … Royal Dublin Society vertebrata and invertebrata.'[73]

The need for a new museum was now critical.[74] William Elliott Hudson, a friend of Thomas Davis, articulated the desired goal: 'to form in the metropolis of Ireland a great National Museum … on a footing equivalent, for Ireland, with the station accorded to the British Museum'.[75] However, plans for a building on the Leinster House site, recommended by the architects John Papworth and Frederick Darley, were frustrated when the space was given over to the School of Design.[76] Meanwhile, the museum's educational programme continued apace, with Scouler giving talks in the lecture theatre, advertised in the *Dublin Penny Journal* as: 'Annual courses of lectures, open to the public, delivered by the professors and lecturers, for which tickets can be had.'[77] Despite the museum's limited opening hours (two days per week), 33,000 people visited in 1838, with students granted access if they applied directly to the curator.[78] As the RDS was in receipt of government funding, it was under pressure to make the museum more available to the public, particularly when visitor numbers were increasing.[79] The requirement to document the collections was also a priority: it was necessary to 'enter in a book the specimens and prices made for the museum'.[80] Fresh energy was put into plans for 'a national museum adequate to the public wants',[81] as the RDS Museum Committee monitored the operation[82] and exchanges between the museum and the British Museum continued.

As a result of Scouler's request to 'appoint an efficient curator or Director of the museum, a gentleman of education and qualifications',[83] Alexander Carte was elected director in 1851. He systematically overhauled the collection, seeking acquisitions from figures such as Sir Richard Griffith,[84] E.P. Wright, William Andrews,[85] Robert Warren, Captain Sir F. Leopold McClintock,[86] Edward Waller, J.R. Kinahan, A. Leith Adams and Sir William Wilde (as listed in the *Journal of the Royal Dublin Society*). The museum contributed to the Hall of Antiquities at the 1853 Dublin International Exhibition of Art-Industry, along with the RIA's collection of Irish antiquities.[87] The RDS decreed that during the exhibition the 'Museum would remain open daily from 12.00–3.00 during five weekdays' to facilitate visitors.[88] The organizing committee of the exhibition took the opportunity to draw attention to the lack of a national museum.[89]

Although the RDS did not have resources for a national museum, the interest shown in its natural history collections and in the Irish antiquities at the exhibition made the society sharply aware that it needed to develop its museum. Thus, an application was made to the Hon. Sydney Herbert, 1st

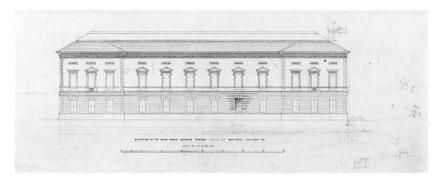

Frederick Villiers Clarendon (c.1820–1904),
***The North Elevation of the Dublin Natural History Museum*, c.1859**
Ink and graphite on paper, 34.4 x 55.6 cm. NGI 18,001.

Clarendon, a civil engineer and architect with the Office of Public Works, reveals his engineering background in the 'elegant and unfussy' design of the museum.

Baron Herbert of Lea, to lease a portion of Leinster Lawn so that a museum could be 'erected thereon'.[90] A building was proposed for the north side of Leinster Lawn, facing Merrion Square.[91] When the RDS received a grant of £2,500 in compensation for the building it had ceded to the School of Design, it moved quickly to construct the new building.[92]

In 1853 Griffith, chairman of the Office of Public Works (OPW) (1850–64), had 'Treasury approval for' new museum plans (designed by the OPW's architect, Frederick Clarendon, and also reflecting the ideas of Captain Francis Fowke (1823–65), the architect associated with the South Kensington Museum, and OPW staff).[93] The *Illustrated London News* described in detail the fashionable foundation-stone-laying ceremony with a sealed container, officiated by Lord Carlisle, lord lieutenant and general governor of Ireland, on 7 March 1856.[94] The building rose rapidly; the entrance was on the southern side, with the interior divided into two sections, one on the ground floor revealing galleries lit by side windows, and the other on the upper first floor with two galleries lit by a skylight extending the length of the roof, and a few small windows on the south side. Lighting was provided by gas. The Dublin Natural History Museum was linked to Leinster House by means of a closed curved Corinthian colonnade that was originally lit by skylights. At this stage, mid-century, the staff of the RDS Natural History Museum were attempting to manage the collections in their care while waiting for a proper building that would enable them to show the full potential of their holdings, and allow it to take its place in the future of Irish natural history.

The RDS Dublin Natural History Museum (1857)

The Dublin Natural History Museum was inaugurated in 1857, just as the British Association enjoyed its second meeting in Dublin, 'a week's repose on the neutral ground of science'.[95] The capital acquired two impressive structures that year: the Dublin Natural History Museum and Deane and Woodward's TCD Museum Building.[96]

The Natural History Museum, built of Portland stone and Dublin granite, was inaugurated with two distinguished events. The first was a *Conversazione*, held on 28 August, which comprised a discourse on the subject of the 'Atlantic Telegraph' by the Belfast-born Sir William Thomson (1824–1907), later Lord Kelvin, with 1,500 guests in attendance, including the lord lieutenant of Ireland. The second was a lecture, held on 31 August, concerning discoveries made in southern Africa, which aroused greater public interest due to the celebrated reputation of the speaker, Sir David Livingstone (1813–73). The opening exhibitions on the ground floor and first floor (with the reception on the ground floor) demonstrated the eclectic nature of the collections: the

An early view of the Dublin Natural History Museum from Merrion Street

Sited on the left flank of Leinster Lawn, with its original entrance facing on to the south side of the building. A curved corridor linked the museum to Leinster house.

The first floor of the Dublin Natural History Museum facing east c.1883

On display to the right is the bird exhibits with the Irish invertebrate exhibition on the ground floor. The display of the general invertebrate collection, together with skeletons of the Indian and African elephants placed among the table cases, would have aroused the interest and curiosity of students and the public.

TCD museum loaned Professor Harvey's South Sea Islands ethnographical material and algae and Professor Oldham's foreign insects; also on display was a range of scientific instruments, illustrations of subjects from natural history and associated library books; while the Botanic Gardens lent a heterogeneous collection of plants, arranged in cases, alongside Captain McClintock's fossils and birds from the Arctic region. The exhibition was completed by Kiltorcan fossils, edible crustaceans and molluscs, the Rev. Joseph Greene's Irish Lepidoptera and Dr Carte's birds, collected while serving in the Crimean War. Shortly after opening, the joint Committee of Fine Arts and Manufactures asked the RDS to host an exhibition from the South Kensington Museum (held in conjunction with the RDS Art Exhibition in Baggot Street).[97] On Easter Monday 1858 this 'Government Circulating Museum of Works of Decorative Art' exhibition was opened by the Earl of Eglinton and attracted 55,000 visitors over eleven weeks, thereby firmly establishing Dublin's Natural History Museum in Irish society and consciousness.[98]

The early years of the Natural History Museum were not without problems, however. When RDS buildings were placed under the responsibility of the Office of Public Works, the museum asked for space for staff and a mineralogical department, together with heating and ventilation systems that had been planned for the new building but were not installed.[99] The issue of a collection inventory remained a priority, this time for the Department of Science and Art.[100] In the meantime, it assisted its sister institution, the National Gallery, by accommodating its foundation-stone-laying ceremony and storing its growing collection.[101] In 1859 the RDS reviewed its grant in an attempt 'to maintain the Museum in a state of effective operation'.[102]

Personnel problems due to a lack of trained staff and the continuous arrival of collections grew time-consuming; full-time staff consisted of Dr Carte, the director, the taxidermist, Robert Pride, and a porter.[103] Two assistant naturalists were appointed in 1866: W.F. Kirby, an accomplished entomologist (1867–79),[104] and A.G. More, a botanist and ornithologist (keeper of the museum in 1881)[105]; R.F. Scharff developed entomology over thirty-five years; and J.E. Reynolds managed exchanges as keeper of minerals up to 1875.[106] A schedule of 'officers of the museum' gave an outline of staff duties,[107] but it was clear that more staff members were needed to manage the growing collections accumulated by the museum over a quarter of a century. Prior to this, entomology had been the preserve of both the Ascendancy and visitors from England, with their publications on science and natural history encouraged by the Great Exhibition. The newly fashionable pastime in the 1880s of gathering natural history specimens, aided by the growth of the railways and the tourist's discovery of the 'picturesque', fed into the new museums.[108]

The developing interest in antiquities, science and natural history came on foot of earlier researches into the Irish language, initiated in the eighteenth century by the Irish scholar Charles O'Conor. Field clubs and societies emerged, including the Belfast Natural History Society (1821), Belfast Academy (1828), Royal Cork Institution (1803) and Cork Cuvierian Society (1835), Kilkenny Archaeological Society (1849) and the Queen's College Natural History Museums (1850s), recording their donations in the *Proceedings of the Royal Dublin Society*.[109] Acquisitions came from donors such as Griffith, who presented his Irish Silurian and Carboniferous fossils;[110] the Irish explorers

Thomas Heazle Parke and Leopold McClintock; and from naturalists such as Valentine Ball, R.J. Ussher, J. Douglas Ogilby, William Andrews, Robert Warne and Dr Battersby. Notable acquisitions included a series of 530 superb glass models of marine animal life, created by the Blaschka family and described as 'one of the world's finest collections of intricate glass models of sea creatures'.[111] This material provided a major teaching resource for the museum, having been purchased between 1878 and 1886 from the British dealer in natural history, Robert Damon of Weymouth. As study aids, the glass models were unsurpassed at a time when microphotography was in its infancy and it was difficult for students to keep living specimens. The collection is the second largest in existence after that of Harvard University.[112] A more dramatic acquisition were two skeletons of the Giant Irish Elk, which were accorded prime position in the museum.[113] The presence of the skeletons proved to be a huge attraction for visitors, described by a biologist as 'two fully mounted magnificently antlered skeletons of the fossil deer, *Megaloceros giganteus* – informally, if incorrectly, called the Irish elk'.[114]

Public access to the museum became an issue, resulting in two evening openings a week, on Tuesday and Friday.[115] Visitor numbers increased (to 103,237 in 1870), drawn by the natural history specimens and art and industries collections in the Shelbourne Hall Annex (sometimes called 'the art museum').[116] The hall (1862–1962), originally designed for an Exhibition of Manufactures, formed an annex to the south-west of the museum, accommodating additional art and natural history collections, in addition to a Fossil Hall. The educational advancement of the collections was aided through contact with the British Museum, which regularly loaned works 'to afford the public as much instruction in natural science as they would like'.[117]

The Transition of the Museum of Science and Art

Twenty years after the opening of the Dublin Natural History Museum, the Science and Art Museum Act 1877 placed the institution under the control of the Department of Science and Art and founded the new Dublin Museum of Science and Art, of which the Dublin Natural History Museum became a department or a division. During this transitional phase (between 1857 and 1877) the character of the new museum was being formed, with the staff already viewing it as the national museum for Ireland.

Looking towards the 1880s and 1890s, Director Valentine Ball (1843–95), keeper Robert Scharff and curator George Carpenter started to develop a new vision for this museum within an Irish natural history context, which took advantage of its British status while at the same time being directed towards an Irish audience. Ball was particularly concerned with the visitor's potential to learn from the museum and he sought to make it more accessible and available to the public. As a result, the teaching context of the collections, by this date well used by students, was developed through a new display of the Geographical Distribution cases, together with five cases (each one carefully labelled) illustrating the 'History of Animals', forming a basic introduction to Charles Darwin's *The Origin of Species*.[118] The museum was increasingly a learning institution that was part of a movement to document and conserve the natural, scientific and cultural history of Ireland. The collections were used as a means to teach visitors by providing an introduction to the museum and to natural history by text in scholarly catalogues, guidebooks, simple leaflets and oral presentations. Visitors were attracted to, what was recently termed,

> one of the world's finest and fullest exhibits in the old and still-stunning cabinet style – not just a room to showcase the past, but an entire building in full integrity … it remains as capable as ever of inspiring interest (as well as awe) in any curious person.[119]

By the time it became a division of the Dublin Museum of Science and Art in 1887, the Dublin Natural History Museum was already a major centre for Irish natural history, resulting in it becoming the most significant entomological institution in Ireland by the end of the nineteenth century.[120] Thus, the RDS 'had rendered important services to husbandry and the industrial arts'.[121]

The Dublin Museum of Science and Art (1877)

The case for a national museum was determined when government stated:

> it is desirable that there should be a general industrial and fine

arts museum in Dublin. The people of Ireland would thus obtain the fullest opportunity of improvement in the cultivation of the industrial and decorative arts by the study of approved models and objects.[122]

The process whereby this came about arose from government inquiries into science and art policies in Ireland between 1868 and 1876. On 6 February 1876 Lord Sandon, vice-president of the Council on Education Committee, wrote to the RDS and RIA to ask for support to bring the Dublin institutions of science and art, administered by one director, under the Department of Science and Art.[123] The outcome saw the passing of the 1877 Act (40 & 41 Vict. Ch. CCXXXIV), which transferred the RDS buildings and collections to government.[124] In this way government acquired Leinster House (RDS retained free quarters in the building for nearly half a century), associated lands and some of the collections.[125] Government funding of the RDS ceased as it took control of the museum, library and Botanic Gardens, proposing to locate key cultural institutions in one quarter. A commentator reported: 'The Dublin press has applauded the project of a Museum, not exactly understanding what transformations will come of it, but hoping … government cash will be spent in advertising the new Museum.'[126]

William Edward Steele became the first director (1878–83) of the Science and Art Institutions, comprising the Museum of Science and Art (Art and Industries and Natural History divisions), National Library and Botanic Gardens. (Carte continued as director/keeper of the Natural History division/ museum.[127]) Under Steele's tenure, the late nineteenth-century emphasis on industrial design was pursued as the museum worked to source teaching collections of decorative arts material for use in design education. Thus, between 1878 and 1879 it purchased, through the offices of the Dublin-born Caspar Purdon Clarke (then working at its sister institution in London, the South Kensington Museum), 121 pieces of Indian and Persian high-quality textiles, ivories, seals, paintings, ceramics, enamels and metalwork, so that Irish artisans would have access to fine design.[128] In 1881 a board of visitors was established, which produced an annual report for most of the history of the museum.[129]

In 1883 Steele was succeeded by geologist Valentine Ball, a proactive figure who devoted all of his energy to progressing the museum towards its opening in 1890.[130] His observation that guides were needed 'for educational purposes' resulted in a series of handbooks being printed. The Shelbourne Hall Annex continued to attract visitors to the art and industry collections.[131] Ball's tour of Canada and the United States in 1884 had taught him about the services needed to help the public learn about the collections: 'the facilities which now exist for instruction in science and art are largely availed of in the principal cities of America'.[132] In particular, Ball had been impressed by the Agassiz Museum of Comparative Zoology in Cambridge, Massachusetts, where a section of the display was devoted to the geographical distribution of species. This encouraged him to rearrange the animal specimens, regrouping them according to the geographical distribution of species.

In 1884 Ball also introduced Sunday opening at the Natural History Museum, with an attendance of 678 on the first day and an average of 500 from then on: 'it afforded an opportunity of self improvement to persons who would not otherwise have been able to visit the museum'.[133] In common with other museums, there was 'no single instance of disorderly behaviour'.[134] He worked to develop the teaching role of the Museum by acquiring disarticulated exoskeletons of Crustacea and *Limulus*, fifteen Jacopo della Quercia (*c*.1374–1438) casts and moulds of Irish crosses, and Celtic and Scandinavian antiquities transferred from the RIA 'for educational purposes for students'.[135] R.E. Lyne, headmaster of the Dublin Metropolitan School of Art, forecast that 'a Science and Art Museum adequate to the requirements of Ireland will be shortly opened whereby a higher development of national taste may ensue'.[136]

The first step towards a new museum and library was the setting up of an architectural competition, managed by the Office of Public Works.[137] There were well-grounded objections: 'Irish architects have not been offered the chance to compete.'[138] None of the chosen designs was Irish: 'the Irish public will condemn the designs and the official obstinacy that clings to the exclusion of Irish talent'.[139] The project, referred to in London as 'Dublin's Museum of Science and Art', was beginning to be referred to in Dublin as the 'National Museum' (for example, following Giesecke's *Catalogue of Entomology and Ornithology Specimens*, 1832; by Hudson in 1842; by the RDS Natural History and Museum Committee in 1843; and by the Dublin International Exhibition Committee in 1853). In the event, objectors won the day:[140] 'The

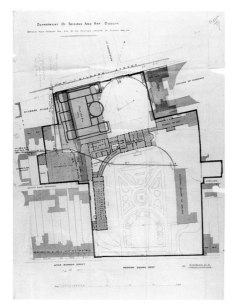

Architect's plans of the new Museum of Science and Art, Kildare Street (left)

The Cork-born architect Thomas Newenham Deane (1828–99) was a partner in his father's office, along with Benjamin Woodward. Deane later formed the practice with his son, Thomas Manley Deane, with whom he designed the museum, described as 'an accomplished exercise in Victorian Palladianism', the Rotunda having been inspired by Schinkel's Altes Museum in Berlin.

Bird's-eye view of the Leinster House Complex, c.1900 (below)

The Dublin Metropolitan School of Art was entered to the left of the National Library. The library faced directly across from the museum. The cultural complex of a school of art, library and museums was in keeping with the South Kensington model.

Government will have a new competition.'[141] The outcome saw first place being awarded to Cork-born Irish architects Thomas Newenham Deane (1828–99) and Thomas Manley Deane (1851–1933). This process highlighted the growing sense of national self-determination, manifesting itself in the desire to see Irish design and production used at all stages of the undertaking:

The building, of which the first stone is to be laid on Friday 10 April 1885, … will be in several respects the most important work that has been undertaken in Ireland for many years, causing the circulation of a large sum of money by affording employment to almost every class of tradesman in the city, giving an opportunity of exhibiting native material and workmanship in stone, marble etc.[142]

The press monitored progress closely: 'The work of excavating for the foundations of the new National Museum and Library has commenced at the Dublin Society premises in Kildare-Street.'[143] The Prince of Wales laid the foundation stone on 10 April 1885,[144] during a period of renewed effort to achieve Home Rule. (The Gladstone–Parnell alliance would produce the first Home Rule Bill, which failed in 1886.) Dr Ball anticipated displaying 'the ancient art of Ireland collected by the Royal Irish Academy'.[145]

The new museum was located on the south side of Leinster House, in Kildare Street, on the site originally occupied by the RDS Agricultural Hall.[146] The contractors, Messrs. J. & W. Beckett of Ringsend, finished the building on 2 November 1889, handing it over to the Department of Science and Art to enable the transfer of the collections.[147] The opening ceremony took place on 29 August 1890, heralding 'a new era of popular education in our country'. The lord lieutenant, the Earl of Zetland, declared: 'This National Museum may in the fullest measure fulfill the purpose for which it was raised … a source of recreation and instruction to the general public … assistance to Irish students and workers … growth of the arts and industries of the country.'[148]

This was evidence that the museum's purpose during the early Celtic Revival of the 1890s was Irish industrial education for Irish students (modelled on the South Kensington Museum). The building was entered via a rotunda and gallery that opened onto a great central court. While the rotunda first displayed field guns, followed by ceremonial carriages and copies of classical statuary, it was the presentation in the central court of casts of Irish high crosses that became significant (with some classical models gifted by the sculptor John Henry Foley) in capturing the public imagination.[149] The early Irish art, beautifully carved on the high crosses, contrasted vividly with the detailed Renaissance panels.[150] The ground-floor court and first-floor galleries

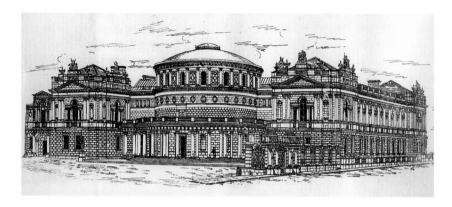

The new Science and Art Museum Building in Kildare Street
(Illustration published in the Irish Builder, *1 December 1887).*

The museum was designed by an Irish architect and built of Irish materials by Irish hands.

displayed antiquities, natural history specimens, art and industry collections, again following the pattern of South Kensington Museum in layout and design.[151]

The architects had designed a building to demonstrate Irish craftsmanship in the European museum tradition, producing one of the 'best surviving examples of Irish decorative stonework, wood carving and ceramic tiling'.[152] Irish materials were evident throughout. The exception was thirty-three 'carved foreign doors' executed by Carlo Cambi (1847–*c.*1900), who had a thriving workshop in Siena in the late nineteenth century.[153] A contemporary report compared the classical allusions in the building to St Mark's Library, Venice, and to the Pantheon in Rome. Pride was manifest that the museum was 'designed by an Irish architect and built of Irish materials by Irish hands'.[154] The *Daily Telegraph* and the *Irish Society* proclaimed: 'Mr. Deane the architect was knighted by Lord Zetland.'[155] An official notice (and first official guidebook) publicized free entrance to the museum, which was open every weekday of the year (11 a.m. to 5 p.m., March to October; 11 a.m. to dusk otherwise), with the exception of Good Friday and Christmas Day.[156] Sunday opening between 2 and 5 p.m. was alternated between the new museum and the Natural History division.[157] Any criticism of the museum was swiftly deflected.[158]

During this time the museum and the National Gallery were used regularly by students of the Dublin Metropolitan School of Art and by the RHA

The Centre Court of the museum on Kildare Street on the opening night, 1890

The museum was opened by the lord lieutenant, the Earl of Zetland, on 19 August 1890. Included in the photograph are the attendants, a policeman, a tradesman and an overseer. Thomas Newenham Deane and the director were awarded with honours on the occasion of the opening.

schools, in addition to other art schools and private classes. The museum–art school relationship was evidenced by a tour of Europe that Ball undertook with James Brenan RHA (1837–1907), headmaster of the Metropolitan School of Art in 1894, during which they visited Hamburg, Stockholm, Berlin and Vienna to study the museums and art schools together. Brenan frequently took part in the lecture-tour demonstrations at the Museum of Science and Art. During these early years of the museum, a *Conversazione* was held, loans were provided to the Belfast Art Gallery and Museum and a visit was made by the members of the British Museum Association in 1894.[159] The museum continued to acquire collections from TCD and the Royal College of Surgeons.[160] A record number of *c.* 483,010 visitors was documented in 1894. In common with early NGI directors, Ball overworked, resulting in his early death in 1895; museum registrar H. Bantry White acted as interim director until a new appointment could be made.[161]

While the collections provided an indicator of prevailing views in Irish museology (natural science, art and industry, antiquities), the focus of the museum would shift sharply within a decade of opening. The nucleus of the 'art and industrial' division (developed from 1878) was the decorative arts collections of the RDS and Museum of Irish Industry, reinforced by loans from the South Kensington Museum, purchases from private individuals, together with repatriated material acquired from Irish, English and European antique dealers. Plaster casts were acquired by loan and by purchase, resulting

Carved wooden door panels in the new museum by Carlo Cambi

These doors were carved by Carlo Cambi (1847–c.1900), who had a workshop in Siena during the late nineteenth century. His work in Ireland is associated with Thomas Manley Deane and his father, Thomas Newenham Deane, who designed the National Museum and National Library. Manley Deane later designed the National Gallery of Ireland's Milltown Wing, with many details by Cambi.

in copies of some great European art being made available to artists and students,[162] including William Orpen's 'credible studies' of the museum collections.[163] The importance of the art and industries collection was the training it provided to students in observing original sculptures and quality replicas and developing practical skills for working in industry. The system emulated the South Kensington Museum in attracting 'large numbers of visitors by day and evenings and on Sundays'.[164]

The natural science collection was the domain of the Natural History division, to which had been added an ethnographical collection from TCD and the RDS and Geological Survey collections in 1890, of interest to Ball. These accessible galleries showed minerals from the Leskean Cabinet and a relief model, in plaster (7 x 5 m), of the geological structure of Ireland, 'made by Mr. Conway a headmaster under the Board of National Education, with the assistance of pupils at Marlborough Street, Training College' in 1887. Drawings by Du Noyer and photographs from the Belfast Naturalists' Field

Club were also displayed.[165] McHenry's guide to the collection (1895) became a reference work for geologists. The *Irish Naturalists' Journal* noted the darkness of the geological spaces, which was due to the overhanging RDS lecture theatre.[166] The material in the curved gallery was praised by the new director, Lieutenant Colonel G.T. Plunkett, following his appointment in 1895, when he noted that as a result of the quality of the displays 'it would be impossible to find any collection of rock specimens exhibited better'.[167]

The final outcome of the negotiations that had taken place in 1877 resulted in the RIA's collection of treasured Irish antiquities being signed over and transferred to the newly opened Museum of Science and Art on 29 October 1890. Two weeks after their arrival they were on view in special steel cases designed by H. Bantry White. They proved an immediate attraction: 'the antiquities absorb a large portion of the attention of visitors, for whose benefit and instruction a very detailed system with printed labels has been commenced'.[168] The popularity of the display of Irish antiquities was due to their direct appeal as masterpieces of the highest quality and execution; they

The Ardagh Hoard, Reerasta, County Limerick, eighth and ninth centuries AD

Found in 1868, under a stone slab in Reerasta Rath near Ardagh, this hoard had been hidden for safe keeping. The hoard comprised a magnificent silver chalice, a smaller plain chalice of copper-alloy and four superb silver brooches.

formed a dramatic presence in the museum and revealed evidence of Ireland's ancient heritage. As a result, they became an important symbol in articulating a growing sense of national identity, causing the museum to intensify its regard for Irish antiquities. As views of history and patterns of education changed, the Irish antiquities collections gradually displaced the decorative arts collections, becoming closer to the perceived core of the museum and bound up with the development of scientific archaeology. This would later be augmented by responsive collection policies and strengthened by necessary legislation, such as the National Monuments Act 1930 and other Acts. By the end of its fourth year significant visitor figures of *c.* 483,010 represented a major start for the Museum of Science and Art.

The early success of the museum was largely due to the enlightened directorship of Plunkett, who between 1895 and 1907 saw the museum's responsibility as being to stimulate the craftsman and the manufacturer and to spread knowledge of art.[169] Learning from the South Kensington Museum, Plunkett set about promoting his institution and devising an education programme. This he did through evening openings, by publishing a series of cheap museum 'general/halfpenny guides' (chapters sold as individual guides to the collections), by printing expert catalogues on the museum's own press and by generating publicity.[170] Seeking to correct 'the aimless inspection of the interesting articles in the Museum', in 1896 he initiated 'Museum Demonstrations or personally-conducted tours through various parts of the Museum', his purpose being:

> to teach persons that in order to profit by the collections they should select the objects illustrating some particular branch of Art or of Natural History, and study them according to a definite plan. These are being given in Natural History on Tuesday (closed to the public) when only the Art and Industrial collections are open to the public, and on portions of the Art Collections on Thursday evenings (closed to the public) when the Natural History collections are open to the public; admission is by ticket only. So far the experiment has been successful.

He noted that 'the persons who have attended have been the most attentive

Central Hall, Museum of Science and Art, Dublin

The early presentation of the collections was modelled on the pattern at the South Kensington Museum, London. The casts of sculpture and the decorative arts are prominently displayed, while some replicas of Irish high crosses can be seen.

listeners and shown the greatest interest in the objects pointed out to them'.[171]

In response, press coverage was favourable.[172] In 1896 a demonstration on the theme of 'Savage Art' was given to an audience of thirty people by Professor A.C. Haddon, an assistant naturalist at the Museum. (Haddon had earlier researched the distinctions between races and sub-races and presented the findings of his work on the Aran Islanders to the RIA in 1892.[173]) The director had also developed his predecessor's initiative in regrouping the animal specimens according to their geographic distribution and by providing accompanying demonstrations or lecture tours. This pattern of lecture tours with voluntary instruction by the most eminent professionals, with tickets set aside for the press to ensure promotion of the event, was not just innovative but represented a major attempt to use the museum as a resource for learning.

Another innovation of 1896 was the casting of the first of the high crosses (the first of which was the plaster-of-Paris cast of the ninth-century Muirdeach's Cross, Monasterboice, County Louth), from which moulds were taken and casts of the crosses sent to the South Kensington Museum and to the Metropolitan Museum of Art in New York.[174]

The director's 1897 annual report drew attention to professional needs, such as the adoption of 'more improved methods of mounting specimens', in addition to public needs – 'more information about the contents of the Museum is demanded'. Plunkett attempted to address this demand with 'plans on tables to show the arrangement of the collections and assist visitors in finding the exhibits'. Teaching formed part of the role of the institution, with the curators moving easily between TCD and the Royal College of Science, demonstrating the collections as a resource for students and men of science. However, interpreting the collections for the public proved difficult to achieve due to the lack of staff, whose numbers were 'insufficient to cope with the amount of work to be done in mounting, naming, classifying and cataloguing the collections'.[175] The museum negotiated its case with government, which caused the Redmondite party to vote against the South Kensington Museum's 'extravagant expenditure on public building' because requests for 'equipment of the Dublin Science and Art Museum had been ignored'.[176]

The final decade of the nineteenth century saw the museum succeed in its education programmes, with 2,638 people attending twenty-four lecture tours in 1898, and in promoting the institution to a wider public. The director's annual report for 1899 noted that the lecture tours were proving a positive force for the museum, with visitors 'anxious to gain as much information from them as possible' by means of simple explanations of the collections that used terminology that was easily understood. There was the added involvement of outside experts, such as Brenan, from the Metropolitan School

The Burton Brooch, 1846–7

The brooch was commissioned by a group of Dublin gentlemen as a gift to the actress Helen Faucit, inspired by Faucit's performance in the Greek tragedy *Antigone* in 1845. Designed by Frederic William Burton and made of Wicklow gold, with emeralds and white enamel, by Edmond Johnson for West & Son, Dublin, this brooch was first shown in Dublin at the Exhibition of Irish Manufactures, Produce and Invention in 1847.

of Art, and Walter Armstrong, director of the National Gallery, whose talks were mini-courses in arts and crafts, and professors from the Royal College of Science, who gave lectures that formed simple courses in natural history. In addition, the casts of the high crosses, commissioned by Colonel Plunkett and placed on display in the Centre Court, were enthralling visitors.

This was also a time when figures such as Horace Curzon Plunkett[177] sought to have the museum transferred to a Dublin-based government department in order to promote greater state involvement in Irish agricultural and technical development.[178] There was another reason for the desired transfer, however: the wish to control decisions affecting Ireland from Dublin rather than from London, where Ireland was viewed as a colonial outpost of the empire. Despite a unionist, gentrified background, Plunkett had observed co-operative action in America and knew of the benefits of Irish self-help societies. He was aware that the Technical Education Act 1890 was not included in Irish legislation, although the Department of Science and Art had promoted art schools and classes throughout Ireland.[179] The enactment of the Agricultural and Technical Instruction (Ireland) Act 1899 resulted in responsibility for the museum devolving to a Dublin-based department, of which Plunkett became the first political head.[180] Horace Plunkett's vision of his department's role would see him encourage 'local freedom, aiming at distinctive national qualities having at its hand, as part of its inspiration, the beautiful and suggestive objects in the museum'.[181]

These influential figures marked a process of devolving a measure of control of Irish affairs to Dublin and of articulating the national interest in the wider issues of Irish self-determination.[182] In 1899 the Museum's annual report stated: 'The educational influence of museums is more recognized throughout Ireland and last year we aided the establishment of new museums in Cork and Waterford.' By the end of the century collections drawn from Ireland's historic and antiquarian past were part of a national museum, just as fine art collections culled from Ireland's aristocracy and Grand Tourists formed a national gallery. These emerged in cultural institutions that had become instruments of public education, with a distinct emphasis on learning. The director was clear in his outlook: 'The museum in Dublin is recognized and is a national museum, quite as much as the British Museum. It was founded in order to supply the want of a national museum in Ireland.'[183]

8

Collecting, Promoting, Exhibiting, Curating: The Broadening of the Museum Movement

We hope, and are sure, that Ireland, a nation,
will have a national gallery[1]

This chapter will explore the interim period between the calls for and the setting up of a national gallery for Ireland. Similar to the establishment of the National Museum of Ireland, the road to a national gallery was paved with good intentions, but the journey was by no means straightforward. It required the coalescing of several different forces for change to be realized.

First, the basis of a national art collection, representing works from major European art traditions and artists, had to be put in place. In Ireland, this was achieved through the formation of private collections, in particular by the Grand Tourists, who had the wealth and the knowledge to put together important collections of artworks, featuring works by Italian, Spanish, Dutch, French and English artists. These collectors were also patrons of Irish artists, who were employed in painting the portraits and estates of these wealthy landowners. In time, what had originated as a private quest for beauty and status became significant in the development of collections of Irish art. Furthermore, the generosity of these patron-collectors in donating or

Aelbert Cuyp (1620–91), *Landscape with a Portrait of a Youth and his Tutor on Horseback, c.*1650–2
Oil on canvas, 109.2 x 149.8 cm. NGI 4758.

Cuyp's work was popular with eighteenth-century British and Irish collectors. This painting formed part of Cuyp's equestrian portraits, c.1650s, and was owned by the Dukes of Leinster, probably James FitzGerald (1722–73), or his son William (1749–1804). It may have hung in Leinster House (before that property was sold to the Royal Dublin Society in 1815), later moving to the family home at Carton House, County Kildare.

bequeathing works to the institutions propelled the argument that a dedicated national gallery was needed to display these works.

Secondly, the gathering of important collections had to give way to the use of these collections by students, thus generating a public role for them. One outcome of this practice was the foundation of the Royal Hibernian Academy and a growing sense of a collective art, a network of artists. The use of these fine art and antiquarian holdings in the nineteenth century had a critical place in the move towards a national collection, thus it is necessary to examine the role of the RHA as a precursor to the National Gallery.

Thirdly, the public institutions involved in the gathering and display of artworks and artefacts had to evolve in their understanding of their role, in so far as they came to realize that their function was primarily to foster the improvement and education of the population. A far-sighted comment by the museum professional William Henry Flower, Director of London's Natural History Museum, showed how these early advocates were aware of the changes taking place and the effects they would have on the museum world in the longer term: 'museums of the future would have to aspire not alone to preserve the objects in their care, but provide for their arrangement in such a manner as to provide for the instruction of those who visit.'[2]

In essence, what had to occur to allow for the establishment of a national gallery and national art movement was the coalescing of artists, artistic ideals and new concepts of the potential public role of art; the founding of societies that formalized art links and networks; and the education of student artists, which would lead to a sense of an Irish school of art. These elements, explored here in turn, formed the key ingredients for the setting up of the National Gallery of Ireland in the mid-nineteenth century.

Private Fine Art Collections

The decline in significance of the city of Dublin following the Act of Union resulted in the dissolution of the town houses and the dispersal of many collections, as the country seats of the wealthy assumed greater importance. In spite of this, the pattern of building continued unabated with a spate of fashionable new houses, including Lord Meath's at Kilruddery, the Barrington castle at Glenstal, the Earl of Dunraven's Adare Manor in Limerick, Shelton Abbey outside Arklow and Sir Edward O'Brien's spires and folly at Dromoland Castle in County Clare.

European 'Grand Touring' to Italy and further afield resumed, with figures such as Richard White (1800–68), Viscount Berehaven and 2nd Earl of Bantry, acquiring a collection of furniture and works of art, some of which remain on display at Bantry House, County Cork, today. Not every member of the nobility followed this route, however. Many young men were privately taught a classical education at home, their training forming a preliminary to the control of the family estates. They, too, acquired major holdings, with many of the works of art that adorned their houses, farms, abbeys and castles finding their way into the national collections. This increase of interest in art saw titled professional people, wealthy businessmen and churchmen enjoying art,

Gerrit van Honthorst (1592–1656), *A Musical Party c.*1616–18
Oil on canvas, 131.5 x 182 cm. NGI 4693.

The use of candlelight and dramatic chiaroscuro in this picture to reveal facial expressions earned the artist the nickname 'Gerard of the Nights'. Following a trip to Rome, where he was influenced by Caravaggio and his followers, he became one of Utrecht's most successful artists. The painting was acquired in Rome in 1756, for James Caulfeild, viscount and future 1st Lord Charlemont, forming part of his renowned collection in Dublin, which would devolve to the gallery centuries later.

although not every donor had a country seat and not every collector was titled. For example, Mr and Mrs Alex Thom, publishers of the Dublin street and trade directories, acquired Japanese ivories and enamels.[3] In a similar fashion, there were private people with modest means, such as Mr Thomas Berry of Dublin, who gifted five pictures, not all of which were significant works or by important artists, but which they wished to donate as a contribution towards the formation of a national art collection.

The private collections that derived from many of the leading Irish families emerged from this background. The heritage of these largely eighteenth-century collections is fascinating to explore as it deals with the world of the great Irish country house and its troubled history, which would lead to the destruction of many of these houses in the early twentieth century (although many have been retrieved in the twenty-first century). A number of the key collectors will have

Studio of Peter Lely (1618–80),
James Butler, 1st Duke of Ormonde
Oil on canvas, 229 x 132 cm. NGI 136.

The Duke of Ormonde (1610-88), viceroy of Ireland, residing at the ancestral home, Kilkenny Castle, was a significant early patron of the arts. Works from the Ormonde Collection later entered the National Gallery of Ireland - this painting, however, was presented by George Howard, 7th Earl of Carlisle, in 1864.

contributed in one way or another to the formation of the National Gallery. Some of these collections, such as that of the 1st Duke of Ormonde, date from earlier periods. They have been listed to provide a broad overview of the provenance of a small portion of the collections that would devolve to the future National Gallery of Ireland.

Ormonde Collection: The 1st Duke of Ormonde (1610–88), Lord Lieutenant of Ireland, residing at Kilkenny Castle, was a significant early patron of the arts.[4] Following the sales of the contents of Kilkenny Castle, two works entered the National Gallery: after Willem van de Velde II the Younger (1633–1707), *Calm: An English Sixth-Rate Ship Firing a Salute* (NGI 1964); and after Claude Vignon (1593–1670), *A Bishop* (NGI 1912).[5] A later addition to the collection from the original Ormonde collection was Henri Gascar's (*c.*1635–1701) *Portrait of James Butler, 1st Duke of Ormonde and his Steward* (1670s) (NGI 4198). One of the early donors to the institution, George Howard, 7th Earl of Carlisle, would present a *Portrait of James Butler, 1st Duke of Ormonde (1610–88)* (NGI 136) from the studio of Peter Lely (1618–80) as a contribution towards the new gallery in 1864.

Talbot Collection: The gallery benefited from the Malahide Castle collection of James Talbot, 4th Baron Talbot of Malahide (1805–83), and indeed also gained from his energetic support when he served on the first board. The series of post-Boyne portraits that devolved to the gallery included works by Garret Morphy (*c*.1655–1715/16), 'the city of Dublin painter', such as, *William, 4th Viscount Molyneux of Maryborough (c.1655–1717)* (NGI 4151), *Richard, 5th Viscount Molyneux of Maryborough (1679–1738)* (NGI 4146); *Mary, 5th Viscountess Molyneux of Maryborough (1680–1766)* (NGI 4147); *Frances Talbot (c.1670–1718)* (NGI 4150); and the daughters of Lady O'Neill: *Anne O'Neill, later Mrs. Seagrave* (NGI 4148), and *Rose O'Neill, later Mrs. Nicholas Wogan* (NGI 4149); together with a work from the same family by an artist from the circle of Garret Morphy, *Colonel John Wogan of Rathcoffy (d.1727)* (NGI 4145). Other paintings included a double portrait by John Michael Wright (1716–94), *Ladies Catherine and Charlotte Talbot* (NGI 4184); and three works by Gaspar Smitz (*c*.1635–88) who appears to have been painting in Ireland between the mid-1660s to 1688, namely *Christopher, Lord Devlin (d.before 1680)* (NGI 4142); *General William Nugent (d.1690),* (NGI 4144); and *Margaret Countess of Westmeath (d.1700)* (NGI 4143), all of which were acquired at the Malahide Castle sale in 1976.[6]

FitzGerald Collection: Many significant pieces from the FitzGerald Collection would find their way into the future National Gallery. James FitzGerald, 1st Duke of Leinster (20th Earl of Kildare, 1722–73), had Richard Castle design Leinster House (1745), the residence of his son, William FitzGerald (1749–1804), 2nd Duke of Leinster, and his wife, Emilia Olivia St George (daughter and heir of 1st Baron St George), where her collection was displayed (gathered by her father on the Grand Tour in the 1760s).[7] Malton reported that the collection comprised paintings, sculpture and stained glass, which went to other seats of the FitzGerald family at Carton House, County Kildare, or at Kilkea Castle, County Kildare, when the 3rd Duke of Leinster, Augustus Frederick (1791–1874), sold Leinster House to the RDS in 1815.[8] *Notes on the pictures, plates, antiquities etc* (1885) gives a good idea of the collection.[9] The 3rd Duke donated Luca Giordano's (1632–1705) *St. Sebastian Tended by St. Irene* (NGI 79) in 1868, a painting remembered long after by Oscar Wilde. The 4th Duke donated a statue by François-Marie Poncet (1736–97), *Adonis* (NGI 8135), in 1878; and Hugh Douglas Hamilton (1740–1808), *Lord Edward FitzGerald (1763–98), Soldier and Revolutionary* (NGI 195), in 1884.[10] In 1891, the 5th Duke presented a work by Francis Wheatley (1747–1801), *The Dublin Volunteers on College Green, 4 November 1779* (NGI 125), in which the 2nd Duke is portrayed. Lady FitzGerald would donate several works in 1896: a portrait attributed to Angelica Kauffman; *A Mounted Cavalier* (NGI 56) by Pieter Symonsz Potter (1625–54); and two Italian views by the English painter Edward Pritchett (c.1828–64). Many other works associated with the FitzGerald family and their collection would come to the gallery in due course.

Powerscourt Collection: The 6th Viscount Powerscourt, who proved to be extremely active in aiding the formation of the National Gallery, presented an Italian sixteenth-century Venetian School painting, *The Last Supper* (NGI 4001) in 1857; Michele Tosini's (1503–77) *Venus and Cupid* (NGI 77) in 1864; attributed to Domenichino (1581–1641), *St Cecilia* (NGI 70) in 1866; and a work by Jan Marurits Quinkhard (1688–1772), *Portrait of an Old Lady* (NGI 238), in 1878.

Dawson Collection: John Dawson, Lord Carlow (later 1st Earl of Portarlington), had James Gandon design Emo Court, County Laois. Years later, Henry Dawson-Damer, 3rd Earl of Portarlington (1822–92), presented Abraham Storck (c.1630–1710), *Shipping* (NGI 228) in 1878, and Jan Wyck (c.1640–1702), *King William III at the Siege of Namur* (NGI 145) in 1884, to form part of the future national collection.[11]

Loftus Collection: The family of John Loftus, 4th Marquess of Ely at Rathfarnham Castle, was painted by Angelica Kauffman (1740–1807) when she visited Ireland in 1771. This important painting by Kauffman, *The Ely Family*, a portrait of Lord and Lady Ely and, it is thought, their nieces, Frances (seated at the harpsichord) and Dolly Monroe, 1771 (NGI 200), was presented by John Loftus in 1878.[12]

Charlemont Collection: The importance of the role and collections of Lord Charlemont has been signalled in earlier chapters. One work that was acquired for Lord Charlemont in Rome in 1756, and would be acquired by the institution, reattributed to Gerrit van Honthorst (1590–1656), is *A Musical Party* (NGI 4693), donated centuries later, in 2000, to the National Gallery

Angelica Kauffman (1741–1807), *The Ely Family,* **1771**
Oil on canvas, 243 x 287 cm. NGI 200.

Kauffman was remarkably successful for a woman of her time. She visited Ireland briefly in 1771, when she stayed with the Earl of Ely at Rathfarnham, for whom she painted this family portrait. The painting depicts the earl (d.1783), his wife and, it is thought, their nieces, Frances (at the harpsichord) and Dolly Monroe (a great beauty). The painting was presented to the gallery by the 4th Marquess of Ely in 1878.

by Lochlann and Brenda Quinn. In 1853, Francis, the 2nd Earl of Charlemont, would donate by Jules Victor Génisson (1805–60) and Florent Willems (1823–1905) *An Interior of the Church of St. Jakobskerk, Antwerp* (NGI 168).

Milltown Collection: The Earl of Milltown, who was a member of the fourth generation Dublin brewing family, would lend three pictures to the gallery for its opening in 1864; one of these was a significant work by the French artist Nicolas Poussin (1594–1665), *The Holy Family with Saints Anne, Elizabeth and John* (NGI 925). This formed part of a corpus of works by artists such as Jan Both, Rosalba Carriera, Giovanni Battista Busiri, Claude-Joseph Vernet, Giovanni Paolo Panini, Sir Joshua Reynolds, Richard Wilson, family

François-Marie Poncet (1736–97), *Adonis*, 1784
Marble, 165 cm high. NGI 8135.

The statue of *Adonis* was commissioned by Elizabeth Dominick Saint-George Usher for her daughter in Rome in 1784. Her daughter, Emilia Olivia, had married the 2nd Duke of Leinster in 1775. In 1878, the 4th Duke of Leinster, C.W. FitzGerald, donated the statue to the gallery. The statue was formerly on display in Leinster House.

portraits by Anthony Lee and Pompeo Batoni, including a superb series of sixteen paintings by George Barret, that would later form part of the important Milltown Bequest in 1902.

St Germans Collection: Edward Eliot, the 3rd Earl of St Germans, presented Ferdinand Bol (1616–80), *David's Dying Charge to Solomon* (NGI 47), and Pieter Boel (1622–74), *Noah's Ark* (NGI 42), for the gallery's initial collection in 1854.

Wallace Collection: Sir Richard Wallace of Lisburn would become a member of the gallery's board in 1879. Keen to see an Irish national gallery developed, he presented after Velazquez's (1599–1660) *A Portrait of a Gentleman* (NGI 221) and an iconic painting by Daniel Maclise (1806–70), *The Marriage of Strongbow and Aoife* (NGI 205): 'I have always felt that this masterly painting of our great Irish artist ought to find a permanent home on Irish soil.' This important work would form an appropriate donation to Ireland as his inherited collection, the Wallace Collection, would be housed in London.[13]

Lady Morgan: On a trip to Italy, the Irish writer Lady Morgan (Sydney Owenson) (1776–1859) paused in Paris about 1793 to have her portrait (NGI 133) painted by René Berthon (1776–1859), a leading French painter of portraits and historical subjects. Owenson was depicted by a number of artists during her stay in France. Lady Morgan, who regularly held literary salons at her house in Kildare Street, was one of the most vivid and discussed figures of her generation. She was the first woman to receive a pension for writing. The portrait, which hung in her boudoir in Kildare Street, Dublin, was engraved as a frontispiece to her *Passages from my Autobiography* (1859), and was bequeathed to the National Gallery in 1860.

Arthur Lee Guinness: A welcome donation by Arthur Lee Guinness (1797–1863) towards the fledgling collection arrived in 1856 in the form of Jean-Jacques Bachelier's (1724–1806) *The Death of Milo of Croton* (NGI 167), the artist's first major work with a classical theme. Arthur, who was the eldest son of Sir Benjamin Lee Guinness of the brewing family, and the brother of Edward Cecil, later 1st Earl of Iveagh, would inherit the title Sir Arthur in 1868.

This chapter has presented, and indeed commemorated, some of those who generously donated towards the formation of a national art collection. While the main body of the early donors were from a titled background or were wealthy businessmen, as noted above, there were other people of more modest means who wanted to make their own contribution towards what they percieved to be a worthy educational cause: a national gallery for Ireland. The widow, Mrs Nicolay, is an example of a person who donated two works, left to her by her husband, which were acquired specifically for a future public art institution. These large works that had once been owned by Sir Joshua Reynolds comprised copies after Raphael (1483–1520), *Saints Peter and John at the Beautiful Gate* (NGI 171) and *Elymas the Sorcerer Struck with Blindness* (NGI 172), and were presented to the gallery in 1862.

Included among these private donors is a small collection provided by 'Thomas Berry of Hume Street' who presented the gallery with five works between 1854 and 1865, the best of which is that by George Barret (1728/32–1784), *A Landscape with Fishermen* (NGI 1909) gifted in 1854.[14] Other names, like the patriot William Smith O'Brien, appear in this list, in addition to Mr W. Browne; Mr Hodder M. Westropp; Mr William Anthony; Mr John Calvert Stronge; Mr. Bartholomew Watkins and Mr Robert Clouston from Dublin, who also presented the gallery with five pictures, the most notable one by David Ryckaert III (1612–61) illustrating *Dinner at a Farmhouse* (NGI 340), which was gifted in 1855. A particularly welcome early donation came from Captain George Archibald Taylor (*d*.1854) of

Rene Berthon (1776–1859), *Portrait of Lady Morgan, Writer (1776–1859)*
Oil on canvas, 103 x 98 cm. NGI 133.

Lady Morgan (Sydney Owenson) is considered one of the first Irish professional woman writers, whose extensive literary output led her to become the first female writer to receive a pension. Owenson was conscious of the power of a good likeness, and she bequeathed this portrait, executed in her own apartment, to the gallery in 1860.

Mespil Parade in Dublin, who bequeathed to the gallery eighty British and Irish watercolours in 1855. Among these was included two views by James Mahony (1810–79) of the Dublin International Exhibition of Art-Industry, 1853 (NGI 2452 and NGI 2453), together with an extremely fine *Aerial View of Dublin from the Spire of St. George's, Hardwicke Place,* painted in 1854 (NGI 2450). This list of donors is illustrative of a broad range of people who wanted to make a personal contribution towards a national collection – a private act for the public good.

This small sample of eighteenth- and nineteenth-century private fine art collections illustrates the particular taste of the collectors who acquired works of art and antiquities for the purpose of decorating their great houses and castles, together with ordinary Irish people who wanted to contribute works of art towards a public art institution. The chequered history of the great Irish country houses demonstrates how, with the passage of time, as the collections were dispersed, some great artworks entered the national collections. Over time the collections would transfer to public ownership when individuals and groups, such as the Irish Institution (see Chapter 9), would form part of the process of setting up a permanent art gallery, helping to amass a collection through a variety of means, such as exhibitions, sales, gifts, bequests and donations. The decline of the leading families set in train a process of general disintegration of the collections, with their treasures being auctioned, 'objects of first importance, which were overlooked, unrecognized, some to reappear at a later date in the foremost public galleries and museums of the world'.[15] With the opening of the National Gallery of Ireland in 1864 a process was begun that would blossom in the late twentieth/early twenty-first century and would see repatriated significant works that historically had belonged to these famous Irish collections.

The Pattern of Artists Studying from the Collections

The requirement to gain access to high-quality collections of paintings, drawings and prints, sculpture, *objects d'art* and antique plaster casts was considered essential in the training of artists and students in the nineteenth century. To this end, art academies and design schools developed a relationship with museums and galleries whereby 'private days' were provided, when students and artists had free access to the collections, which was a prerequisite of training in the academies. Members of the public could also gain access on these days, provided they paid an entrance fee. The early Irish galleries housed collections reflecting the prevailing fashion in Italian, Dutch, Flemish, Spanish and English pictures and the classical figure studies and landscapes of Nicolas Poussin and Claude Lorrain, including some Irish works. The museums displayed natural history and decorative arts collections and, later in the century, casts of Irish high crosses, classical sculptures and Irish antiquities. Antique sculptures and plaster casts were of particular benefit to students in modelling and figure drawing, in addition to small busts, statuettes and reliefs that museums acquired from the Vatican, the Louvre and the British Museum, through agents and dealers in Rome, Paris and London.

The Dublin Society Drawing Schools recorded prizes awarded for drawings, which helped students to advance their careers. Most design school students used the museums once they had acquired a degree of competence in drawing from antique statuary and studying the figure in the round. The system encouraged the analysis of visual information and sound observational skills. Students learned the methods and styles of the Great Masters, while the practice of sketching from the antique improved drawing techniques. During the formative years of the museum, drawing from the collections was preliminary to training for a career in arts, crafts and industrial design. For instance, during the industrial revolution in Britain the South Kensington Museum supported students in the study of their collections in order to

Nicolas Poussin (1594–1665), *The Lamentation over the Dead Christ*, 1657–60
Oil on canvas, 94 x 130 cm. NGI 214.

Considered the greatest French painter of the seventeenth century, Poussin would also provide inspiration for future generations of artists. In this late work he creates a serious, thoughtful interpretation of a biblical theme. The painting was bought under Henry Doyle's astute director-ship at the Hamilton Palace sale in 1882.

promote careers in design. This pattern would be replicated in America at museums such as the Metropolitan Museum of Art, New York, and in Ireland at the National Gallery and National Museum, and at the Belfast Art Gallery and Museum. Ireland was not an industrial nation, however. As a result, interest in the decorative arts would decline as the display of Irish antiquities at the National Museum instead stimulated awareness of Ireland's ancient heritage. The presentation of awards continued with the Royal Irish Art Union and at the Government School of Design, where the ongoing practice of studying the collections was illustrated in exam pieces, samples of which would be housed in the National Gallery.

The RHA used its casts and the collections of the National Gallery and the National Museum as the basis of modelling and figure drawing, in the manner of the Royal Academy and Royal Society of Arts in London. This would change at the turn of the century when art education redirected students away from museums as the fashion for creativity drew less on collections and more on the student's imagination in a subjective approach to art. While some museums would put their cast collections in store, others destroyed them. (Today, of course, casts would have qualified, by virtue of age, as antiques in their own right.)

In the twentieth century a number of museums – though only a small minority of those who originally took pride in them – would place their casts on display again. For example, the V&A Museum had its antique cast collection and sculptures conserved and recently placed them on display to inspire a fresh generation of students and the public. While the founding principle of the museums, 'to educate public taste', was in keeping with their nineteenth-century aspirations, this can be understood today within a twenty-first century context that sees museums as stimulating, educational and enjoyable places, open to all, where every visitor feels equally welcomed. Thus, the traditional art school–museum relationship has been taken up by museums in new ways by providing fresh initiatives to encourage artists, students and the public to be inspired by the collections.

The Royal Irish Institution (1813): the beginning of modern exhibitions

Much of the impetus behind the growth of fine art institutions, leading ultimately to the establishment of an Irish fine art academy and art gallery with a permanent collection, was the contentious issue of the lack of exhibition spaces for artists to display and sell their work. Several bodies provided modest display facilities, for example the Society of Artists of Ireland exhibited at Allen's Print Sellers in 32 Dame Street in 1800 and 1804, with access to Parliament House between 1802 and 1803. The Irish Society of Artists showed at Del Vecchio's Rooms at 26 Westmoreland Street between 1812 and 1813. During the decade 1809–19 groups that formed and reformed, such as the Society of Artists of Ireland, the Society of Artists of the City of Dublin, the Hibernian Society of Artists and the Irish Artists Exhibition and the Artists of Ireland, were facilitated by the RDS Exhibition Rooms at Hawkins Street. The Artists of Ireland also showed at the Royal Arcade in College Green in 1821.

The Royal Irish Institution proved to be an important body for the

**Royal Irish Institution Exhibition of Old Masters,
held in the Exhibition Room, College Green, c.1829–32**

The institution's old master exhibitions were the earliest loan exhibitions in Ireland. This image
shows the dense nature of the presentation with visitors both looking at and executing copies
of the paintings.

future Royal Hibernian Academy and National Gallery of Ireland. It was
determined 'to assist Irish artists' by founding 'an Academy in Dublin' and
to this end held annual loan exhibitions of Old Master paintings between
1814 and 1818, which it resumed in 1829. A commentator articulated the
situation: 'the painters of this country owing to the want of patronage are
obliged to desert the higher walks of the profession for whatever employment
in the arts the moment may offer.'[16]

A significant gesture by the Royal Irish Institution was the payment of
the fee required to incorporate the RHA in 1822. The Institution availed of
the small exhibition room at College Street used by both its exhibitors and
subscribers, but had to close in the 1830s due to financial difficulties. The
importance of its 'loan exhibitions' (1829–32), drawing on works borrowed
from the Irish gentry, was that they made art available to the public and in so
doing created interest in fine art – a process that in turn drew attention to

the need for permanent collections and museums. The Institution's work in this regard was augmented by the 'loan exhibitions' held at the National Exhibition Cork (1852) and Dublin International Exhibitions of Art-Industry (1853 and 1865). It became clear that this was an unsatisfactory situation for exhibiting art and for training Irish artists.

Royal Hibernian Academy (1823)

Matters came to a head when a group of artists got together to found an academy. Granted a charter in 1823, it became established as the 'Royal Hibernian Academy of painters, sculptors, architects and engravers' (RHA) in 1823.[17] The founders took as a model the Royal Academy in London, and its membership of academicians was designated in the charter.[18] William Ashford, the short-lived first president (1823-4),[19] was followed by the architect Francis Johnston (1760-1829), who endowed the Academy with a home in Lower Abbey Street, 'a chaste and elegant edifice', at his own expense (1825-6).[20]

The first stone of the building was laid on 29 April 1824 by Francis Johnston, and contained a copper-plate bearing the date 5 August 1823 for the incorporation of the Artists of Ireland under the name of 'The Royal Hibernian Academy of Painting, Sculpture, and Architecture'. This

three-storey granite building, with carved keystones by John Smyth (c. 1773-1840) representing Palladio, Michelangelo and Raphael, was conceived of as a National Academy of Art. Its handsome premises contained a suite of exhibition rooms, a

The Royal Hibernian Academy, Lower Abbey Street, 1835

This 'chaste and elegant edifice' was a three-storey house with a recessed entrance, flagged by Doric columns topped by a head of Palladio, with Michelangelo over the right window and Raphael over the left, executed by John Smyth (c.1773-1840), an associate of the academy.

William Ashford (1746–1824), *A View of Dublin from Chapelizod*, 1795–8
Oil on canvas, 113.4 x 184.5 cm. NGI 4138.

Shortly before he died, William Ashford became the first president of the Royal Hibernian Academy. This view, which is both a topographic and idyllic landscape, is a fascinating record of Dublin and its western boundary in the late eighteenth century. A popular artist, Ashford's painting illustrates the quality of the landscapes for which he was well known.

drawing school, a council room and an apartment for the keeper. In 1830 Ann Johnston, Francis's widow, added a generous new sculpture gallery 'for antique statues and sculpture'. A feature of the Academy was its three fine exhibition spaces: one for watercolours and drawings (40 ft by 20 ft), leading via an archway to the 'great saloon', lit by a lantern, for oil paintings (50 ft by 40 ft), and to the right an octagonal gallery for sculpture. According to the *Dublin Penny Journal* (September 1835), 'The Academy is possessed of a fine collection of casts from the antique, a few pictures by the old masters, and a tolerable library of works, chiefly connected with the Fine Arts, the greater number of which were presented by the late Edward Houghton, Esq.' Academy functions involved an annual exhibition and a school, which employed skilled tutors with recourse to the collection of casts, master drawings, books and prints for drawing classes that placed the traditional emphasis on the human figure (from the antique and live model), a subject not taught in the apprenticeship system of medieval workshops.[21]

The RHA articulated its purpose as being 'the promotion of the fine arts in Ireland … by the proper management of a public annual exhibition of works of art but principally by the communication of instruction in painting, sculpture and architecture …'[22] As a professional body, it would seek to raise the status of the artist in society (partly signalled through the selection and grading of its members) in addition to its important role in fostering public appreciation of the fine arts.[23] It would lend its assistance to the formation of a national gallery and use the national collections as a learning resource for its artists and students.

The inaugural exhibition in 1826 emulated the Royal Academy in London and the official Salon in Paris by hosting seventy artists and twenty-one amateurs, contributing 371 pictures, drawings and miniatures and thirty-one pieces of sculpture for display.[24] From inception, the annual 'artist-juried' show would become central to the role of the Academy in its provision of exhibiting space and potential sales for artists, as well as in shaping public taste.[25] Its secondary role was maintaining the Academy schools, which were managed by a keeper, with tuition largely by painters and sculptors, who were Academy members. Its open admission policy was in line with the RDS Drawing Schools, necessitated by the low level of art education and the need to attract students.[26] Following the model of European art schools, the RHA acquired a collection of antique casts and held foundation classes in antique and figure drawing.[27] Students made studies from plaster casts of statues and busts, while observing shape and form in the flat from drawings and engravings that provided access to famous works of art in European collections. The student progressed to sketching the portrait head and the clothed figure before exposure to the live model and figure composition, a development that caused the RDS Schools to discontinue their life class: 'We did not think it necessary to continue an expense which could be ill-afforded after the diminution of the parliamentary grant.'[28]

Despite the RHA's official status as a national authority with a public art role and functions, it was 'private' and independent, although government awarded it an annual grant from 1832. A great asset was the establishment of the Royal Irish Art Union (1839), the first society of its type in Ireland, whose sweepstake distributed pictures as prizes at a time of reduced Academy exhibitions and income (only 30 shillings was made from sales between 1835 and 1838). As a bonus, members received 'a free engraving published exclusively for the Art Union' with their most popular print, *The Aran Fisherman's Drowned Child* (1841) by RHA artist Frederic William Burton (1816–1900).[29]

This period saw issues of national identity raised in *The Nation*, which in a review of the 1843 RHA exhibition called for an Irish school of art: 'The real object of any true lover of the fine arts in this country should be the foundation of a national school … for the genius of the Irish nation would soon make it Irish in its character.'[30] RHA exhibitions included Irish landscapes, topographical and narrative scenes, but Irish historical painting was not a major genre. Artists like Burton and Daniel Maclise epitomized the work that Davis was seeking, but did not represent a 'national' art movement: 'We have Irish artists, but no Irish, no national art.'[31]

As a result of the success of the Royal Irish Art Union, the RHA flourished, but then its fortunes began to fluctuate.[32] The lack of sales in the depressed period following the Famine resulted in the collapse of the Union, which wound up its affairs in 1859 and left its remaining funds to the National Gallery. The RHA retained its independent status, but when government established a school of design, it looked instead to the RDS Drawing School as the centre of art education.[33] A reformed RHA oversaw a government enquiry initiated at its request (1857), after which the state grant continued through the Department of Science and Art (1858).[34] Invigorated by a fresh charter (1861), its schools continued to educate future painters, many of whom had also studied at the Government School of Design.[35]

The opening of the National Gallery of Ireland in 1864 was of direct benefit to RHA students and artists, thanks to the introduction of private days when they could study from the collection of antique casts and Old Master paintings. Students also had access to displays at the International Exhibition of Arts and Manufactures (1865), 'one of the most useful, instructive and educating collections ever brought together in any country'.[36] It was a bonus when annual RHA exhibitions expanded to include a membership category for continental artists. Art training reached a high point during the presidency of Thomas Alfred Jones (1869–93), when talented painters studied under the expert guidance of Augustus Burke, professor of painting. The schools were supported by profits from the exhibitions, with the Albert Prize Fund (1871) providing awards for students: 'The Royal Hibernian Academy, where painters and sculptors exhibit their works.'[37] Sunday afternoon opening to the annual exhibition was introduced in 1877, as the only day 'at the disposal of the great majority of the citizens', in the hope that it would 'exercise a civilising influence'.[38]

The Academy schools had mixed fortunes. W.B. Yeats criticized the tuition, 'none of them were capable of teaching … we learned from each other', while George Russell commented that in the life school, 'these gentlemen, not one of whom painted figures, were put there to assist us in our work … they left us very much to ourselves'.[39] At the suggestion of the artist Walter Osborne, women were admitted in 1893 in response to a demand for equality of education, thereby increasing student numbers.[40] The appeal of the Academy was the ready availability of free tuition, with the possibility that work might be exhibited publicly. This attracted the daughters of wealthy families, resulting in the emergence of a number of first-class women painters by the turn of the century. In spite of these improvements, however, women artists still met with many obstacles that did not stand in the way of male artists.

Although the RHA produced many leading artists, including William and Walter Osborne, James Malachy Kavanagh, Joseph O'Reilly, Oliver Sheppard, Henry Allan, James Brenan and H.C. Tisdall, with attendance at the annual exhibition rising to an average of 20,000 visitors between 1875 and 1885, the Academy declined in the 1890s.[41] This downturn in the Academy's power and prestige occurred in tandem with the general demise of academies in Europe and the United States; likewise, at the National Gallery interest in student private days declined at this time. The RHA school prided itself on its instruction in the technique of painting, with the core of its academic theory based on the superiority of life drawing as a means of narrating great moral events. RHA students progressed to Antwerp, Paris and Brittany, taking in the great European museums and galleries *en route*, the outcome of which was the introduction of modernism to Ireland in the early twentieth century.

In the years prior to the founding and opening of the National Gallery, between 1826 and 1864, it was the RHA that fostered public appreciation of the fine arts when there was a singular lack of a permanent collection for public enjoyment and for the education of artists. It also developed an audience for the later museums, an audience who arrived at the national collections accustomed to visiting exhibitions and appreciating works of art. Furthermore,

Anon, *In the Sculpture Hall of the National Gallery, Dublin*, c.1880
Oil on canvas, 54.5 x 41.5 cm. (Courtesy of the Knight of Glin)

Many artists, students and amateur painters, such as this lady and her companion, would have used the 'private days' that were available in most museums. The National Gallery private days, which ceased in 1912, provided a facility to study and paint directly from the collections.

the RHA promoted solid relationships between the new museums – Natural History Museum, National Gallery of Ireland, and Museum of Science and Art – and the students of the RHA and the Metropolitan School of Art, as well as professional and amateur artists. This was an immensely important contribution, one that propelled and informed the national collection and gallery.

Although, as noted above, the RHA declined towards the end of the nineteenth century, it soldiered on remarkably well nonetheless, surviving difficulties with a determination that would see it emerge as a reinvigorated institution in the next century. Indeed, when the municipal art collections were being founded in the twentieth century, they would draw on the RHA annual exhibitions to purchase works of art. Thus, Royal Hibernian Academicians would become members of the board of the National Gallery of Ireland in a pattern that continues to this day.

9

The Development of a National Gallery for Ireland (1854–64)

George Bernard Shaw used to say, 'My university has three colleges ... Dalkey Hill, the National Gallery of Ireland and Lee's Amateur Musical Society.' [1]

It was not until the mid-nineteenth century that the NGI was finally founded, but it was eighteenth-century initiatives that started the process by demonstrating why there was a need for a permanent collection. It may seem an obvious statement today, but in the century before the foundation stone was laid, it was necessary for men and women of vision to argue passionately the reasons why it was necessary for Ireland to have a national collection, a national gallery and a national art movement. Their perseverance is what we must acknowledge for the fine building that houses a resplendent collection of artworks and one of Ireland's premier tourist attractions: the National Gallery of Ireland.

The demand for a national gallery was articulated by the Royal Irish Institution, whose old master exhibitions illustrated the unhealthy state of the fine arts in Ireland: 'there seldom gleamed a work of originality and genius'.[2] The establishment of the RHA improved matters, but created an immediate

Daniel Maclise (1806–70), *The Marriage of Strongbow and Aoife***, c.1854**
Oil on canvas, 309 x 505 cm. NGI 205.

Maclise was a successful history painter and in this picture he reveals his Romantic national-istic sympathies. It narrates an episode when the Normans, who had settled in England in 1066, were given the chance to invade Ireland. Dermot McMurrough, the King of Leinster, who had been expelled from his kingdom, sought assistance from the Norman leader, Richard de Clare (Strongbow), in return promising him his daughter Aoife's hand in marriage, together with succession to the title of King of Leinster. The canvas was presented to the gallery by Sir Richard Wallace in 1879, becoming an iconic image, along with Joseph Patrick Havery's *The Blind Piper.*

need for an old master teaching collection. While the RIAU enhanced RHA sales, its most important legacy was the profits it left to fund a permanent gallery, having understood the need for a public art collection:[3] 'Let him not be considered a true Irishman who will not, according to his means, con-tribute to the National Gallery of Ireland.'[4] Collections owned by figures such as Major Henry Sirr were offered to the RDS, sold to the RIA, devolved to the Museum of Science and Art and ultimately transferred to the new gallery.[5] Davis argued eloquently for resources in *The Nation*: 'Ireland fortunately or unfortunately has everything to do yet. We have had great artists – we have not their works'; he lamented the lack of Irish art, 'Why have we no gallery of Irishmen's or any other men's pictures in Ireland'; and he promoted the idea of a national 'public gallery', hoping that the public 'will give it their full support'. His friend, the artist Frederic William Burton, explained the need for an art gallery to the 3rd Earl of Dunraven: 'The study of art is an element of the highest moral and intellectual culture … Ireland is devoid of this instrument of education.'[6] Burton asked Dunraven if the Treasury could be approached for a grant towards a collection, having confided in Thomas Wyse (1791–1862), the Waterford-born politician, author and diplomat that 'I feel confident that his good sense and desire for the success of all Irish Art and science will lead him to act in the right ways'.[7] Other matters dominated the political agenda at that time. Nonetheless, Davis's advocacy of improved education and self-reliance for Irish people would bear fruit in the next century.

The struggle for a permanent collection continued. George Francis Mulvany (1809–69), the portrait and subject painter who was an influential figure in the RIAU, the Royal Irish Institution and keeper of the RHA in 1845,[8] outlined the requirement to provide a gallery for public education: 'As citizens of the state, we hold our places only in sacred trust for our successors … A National Gallery of paintings and a conjoined museum of sculpture is merely a matter of time.' Although the industrial exhibitions initiated by the RDS between 1834 and 1864 had played their part in showing the need for a national gallery, one of the turning points was the philanthropic gesture of Dargan to underwrite an international exhibition that he aspired would see replicated in Ireland the remarkable effect of the Great Exhibition on the British nation.[9] The Fine Art Hall of the Dublin International Exhibition of Art-Industry, held on the RDS grounds of Leinster Lawn in 1853 and boasting over one million visitors, highlighted the notable absence of 'a single national collection'.[10] Thus, the public interest generated by the exhibition's Fine Art Hall provided the momentum to harness over half a century of aspiration, effort and goodwill that was used by a group of key people to form a permanent art gallery.

Building the National Gallery

The process of forming a national gallery began in 1853 when the Dargan Testimonial Committee collected £5,000 for a 'Dargan Institute' (as a memorial to commemorate his philanthropy). The closure of the Dublin exhibition saw a separate body, the Irish Institution, constituted to promote 'the formation of a permanent exhibition in Dublin and of an Irish National

Thomas Farrell's (1827–1900) 1863 bronze statue of William Dargan (1799–1867), railway magnate and sponsor of the Dublin International Exhibition of Art-Industry, 1853. In the left background is the original entrance to the gallery; to the right, 88 Merrion Square. The ever-modest Dargan was not present for the unveiling of the statue. (From Hon. J.J. Finerty, *Ireland in Pictures*, Chicago, c.1898; courtesy Trinity College Dublin, rare books).

Gallery'.[11] The Irish Institution's intention was to 'educate public taste' through loan exhibitions and membership of the institution, accepting donations of money and artwork towards a permanent collection. Support was also provided by the RHA, which desired a teaching collection of 'ancient and modern art' from the gallery.[12] A committee of RHA artists – George Francis Mulvany, Petrie and Burton – retained works from the 1853 Exhibition for Irish Institution shows (held between 1854 and 1860) to raise funds for a gallery/collection.[13] Mulvany contacted some British institutions to find out if they provided exhibitions by gaslight (then relatively new) and other information for both the exhibitions and for the future gallery. The Liverpool Academy replied: 'we have been open to the working classes by gas for the last 5 years; found no form of complaint.'[14] Gallery committee members included: Mulvany (secretary); David R. Pigot, chief baron of the exchequer in Ireland and his eldest son, John Edward Pigot, a young lawyer (friend of Thomas Davis and Irish music collector); Maziere Brady, lord chancellor of Ireland; Richard Wingfield, 6th Viscount Powerscourt; and James Talbot, 4th Baron of Malahide (providing the critical link with the RDS). Other key committees drove the concept of the gallery forward.

Several sites were considered as the location of the new gallery: Park Street (Lincoln Place); Clonmel Square, behind St Stephen's Green; College Green (former site of the Royal Irish Institution); while 'the most convenient and appropriate for a national gallery is Leinster Lawn, part of the site of the Great Exhibition building'. The lease was held by Sir Sidney Herbert, 'who was willing to allow a portion of it to be occupied by a public building of an ornamental architectural character'.[15] Burton enthused: 'If movements of such a kind be the result of the Great Exhibition, it can never bear the reproach of having been ephemeral in character.'[16] Support came from Waagen, director of the Royal Gallery in Berlin: 'I am pleased that Ireland by this new institution will prosper in matters of the fine arts.'[17]

On 9 January 1854 the Dargan Committee announced that its funds would be put towards a building for 'the reception and exhibition of works for the fine arts'. The RDS affirmed support on 12 January, on the basis that the building would mirror the Museum of Natural History; the idea of complementary buildings had originated with Griffith and Clarendon. The proposal to include Marsh's Library as part of the National Gallery was to enable access to grants from the Department of Trade and Navigation, which at that time was taking control of the art and science institutions.[18]

The Bill to enable the National Gallery was progressed by a series of figures: John and David Pigot; John Lentaigne (legal representative on the Dargan and Irish Institution committees); Maziere Brady; and the government minister Sir John Young, chief secretary of Ireland (who divided his time between Dublin and London), and Under Secretary Colonel Thomas Larcom. Following its first reading on 20 July, it was hoped 'that the Government, which has not been niggard in its donations to London and Edinburgh, will assist us in furnishing our National Gallery'.[19] Gallery observers followed developments avidly.[20]

On 10 August 1854, Parliament passed 'An Act for the establishment of a National Gallery of painting, sculpture and the fine arts and for the care of a public library'.[21] Acts 17 and 18 Vic. Cap. 99 (1854), and 18 and 19 Vic. Cap. 44 (1855) followed, and a Board of Governors and Guardians was incorporated that included *ex officio* members from the RDS, OPW, RIA and RHA, thereby demonstrating the role of these institutions in the formation of the gallery.[22] The board met for the first time at RHA offices in Lower Abbey Street on 13 January 1855, with Griffith (chairman, OPW) presenting plans for the gallery and Natural History Museum. A Treasury grant of £6,000 enabled the RDS to acquire legal ownership of its section of Leinster Lawn from Sir Sidney Herbert by 4 August 1855. London systematically rejected funding applications, however, stating that 'museums comprising casts, prints and patterns' were adequate for Irish audiences, a concept disputed by the board, which wanted a 'real' national gallery.[23]

Forming a teaching collection was a priority. The first gallery bequest for 'the encouragement and promotion of Irish Art' was received from Captain Archibald Taylor (his gift to the RDS would result in the gallery nominating a judge for the annual Taylor Prize – a pattern that continues to this day).[24] Lord Chancellor Brady's attempts to acquire 'a large number of pictures in Rome' (assisted by British photographer and dealer Robert Macpherson (1811–72)) would form 'the nucleus of the future Gallery', comprising thirteen paintings from the collection of Alessandro Aducci in 1856.[25] Macpherson also facilitated the acquisition that year of sixteen paintings, many formerly the property of Cardinal Joseph Fesch, later adding a further twenty-three paintings to the collection. These newly acquired Italian works from the Fesch Collection[26] would prove important for the gallery. Michael Wynne, later keeper of the National Gallery of Ireland, noted that 'there was a general eagerness to avail of the Lord Chancellor's generous action, and an implicit trust in his artistic judgement'.[27] Brady commented: 'It is of great personal satisfaction to me to have been of service to the Gallery.' The Treasury refunded the gallery the cost of 'some pictures procured by the Lord Chancellor from Italy and sold by him to the Gallery'.[28] Support was sought from the Irish gentry: 'It is on the public spirit of the gentlemen of Ireland that we must depend for the attainment of so great a treasure.' The board looked for gifts of paintings 'to teach and elevate the minds of hundreds and thousands of countrymen'.[29] The unsuccessful result caused Mulvany to renew his pleas to the Treasury: 'national justice ought at least to provide for the gallery of Ireland a sum equivalent to that already expended on that of Edinburgh'.[30] London's National Gallery proved willing to lend seventeen works from a list provided by Sir Charles Eastlake.[31] Thus, the core of a national collection was presented by the disestablished Irish Institution (1863) of 115 works (13 paintings, 100 watercolours and drawings, and 2 marble sculptures).[32]

The design of the building progressed slowly. Mulvany suggested an initial outline, which was rejected. This was succeeded by plans proposed by Lanyon in 1856.[33] When the Whigs (later Liberal party) were defeated and replaced by a more positive Conservative government, gallery fortunes improved. After his meeting with twenty-six Irish MPs on 24 June 1858, Benjamin Disraeli (then chancellor of the exchequer) stated: 'You have directed your attention to the promotion of the fine arts. I shall be very happy to do what I can to

George Francis Mulvany (1809–69),
***Self-Portrait*, 1840s**
Oil on canvas, 76 x 63 cm. NGI 926.

Mulvany was a portrait and subject painter, who became the National Gallery's first director (1862–9), to which he devoted his life. The pattern for directors to be artists in the nineteenth century changed in the twentieth century to art historians and scholars.

advance your object.'[34] Events moved swiftly as Cole sent Fowke to progress Lanyon's designs. The plans produced by Fowke were approved by the board, the RDS, the Dargan Committee, Marsh's Library and the Department of Science and Art.[35] The foundation stone ceremony on 29 January 1859 (which made use of the RDS and Royal Horticultural Society marquee)[36] was officiated by the lord lieutenant: 'I trust the institution will be of the greatest benefit to the students of art in the city … and receive the liberal support from the public of which it is highly deserving.'[37] The Irish Institution provided the resources, with funds raised by the Dargan Committee, as the firm of Cockburn and Son began building.[38] This would see the gallery and Natural History Museum residing along the flanks of Leinster House, 'their skewed axes brilliantly concealed by carefully adjusted colonnaded quadrants'.[39] The board was clear in its vision of the gallery's educational purpose:

> the humbler classes want to be instructed as well as benefit by such an institution … The establishment of a National Gallery in Dublin would be of general importance not only in referring to the cultivation of public taste and in affording to all classes a source of informed enjoyment, but more immediately in regard to the aid it would give to the existing institutions for the training of artists as well as those classes of the community for whom so many elementary schools of art have of late years been established.[40]

As its new director, Mulvany attended the meeting of the board in the Gallery on 4 October 1862, while pursuing bye-laws, building issues and the unsanctioned post of registrar.[41] The board learned of a Royal Commission proposal that 'The geological collections of the Museum of Irish Industry might be removed to the Gallery', discovering that Beete Jukes, director of the Geological Survey, had already found the space inadequate. The board showed its ability to control its own destiny by determining the need for further space for 'donations or loans of works of art'.[42]

Consideration was given by the new director to the nature, display and hanging of the collection for the opening of the gallery. He had been to Paris to review the most up-to-date arrangements in the Louvre and planned to decorate the gallery rooms accordingly. Mulvany was described by Strickland as 'possessing good judgment and, for the time, no inconsiderable knowledge of art'.[43] Forming the collection had not been easy, regardless of the aspirations and priorities of a nineteenth-century director: old masters from the Italian, Netherlandish, Flemish, Spanish, French and other schools of painting. The initial collection of paintings was reserved for the upper-floor galleries, following the European model, with works hung closely together in tiers, depending on the scale and size of the galleries. Acquiring a teaching collection of antique casts and sculpture was an easier task and Mulvany allocated them to the ground floor. He knew of the RHA collection of 'antique statues and sculpture' and also of the damaged collection of casts in the RDS basement, of the Cork collection housed at the School of Design and that Belfast had 'casts and examples of art on their way from London by steamer'.[44]

The board was informed by Mulvany of the need to provide casts of antique and classical sculpture for the training of artists.[45] The Treasury approved a grant, understanding its function to 'educate and ... illustrate the history and progress of sculptural art'.[46] Wyse, British minister at Athens, whom Burton had contacted regarding casts in 1844, offered to obtain some examples in Greece.[47] His niece would later present a marble bust of Wyse (NGI 8185) by the Greek sculptors Cossos and Brontos in 1907. In learned circles it was felt that sculpture provided a morally improving effect and the physical presence of statues could even inspire 'glorious deeds in the beholder'.[48] Thus, the board acquired '16 cases of casts from the British Museum and frames were ordered for the Metopes and Frieze of the Parthenon in the

"Sculpture Hall"'.[49] Gifts arrived from Lord Cloncurry, some damaged and requiring attention.[50] In this way, the board demonstrated awareness of the importance of antique statuary in the education of young artists, by acquiring casts during a period when authenticity was not a key issue and the display of antique sculpture was felt to be an integral part of the collection. This presented a practical solution for a small country such as Ireland, incapable of purchasing originals, where a modest collection of casts of sculptures from the classical period of art, displayed on scientific principles, was useful for the appreciation of art.

Sunday Opening

Another matter, that of access, also highlighted the board's awareness of its duty towards the public. A petition was received from James Haughton and Nugent Robinson concerning the rights of Dublin citizens to Sunday access: 'the opening of Glasnevin Gardens on Sunday proved that our fellow-citizens are pre-eminently entitled to the boon sought from your hands'.[51] Regulations governing opening hours to public galleries and museums had been noted and sometimes it was left to the discretion of the person in charge. In the context of the fledgling art gallery, John Pigot proposed that the bye-laws be deployed to resolve the issue, due to the letters of support received from Irish MPs, and eminent and ordinary citizens. The gallery would be open 'to the public in the afternoon of all Sundays in the year except during vacation'.

Why was Sunday opening a contentious issue? Early in the nineteenth century Dublin's citizens had demanded their right to have St Stephen's Green open on Sundays, having originally been a municipal park but enclosed for the residents in 1814.[52] An Act of Parliament and the generosity of Lord Ardilaun, Arthur Guinness – Irish businessman, politician and phi-lanthropist – resulted in its opening to the public in 1880. Dublin's Royal Zoological Gardens opened on Sunday afternoons (one penny entrance fee) from 1844, with 'not one instance of mischief since the gardens fully opened'.[53] The Botanic Gardens waited until 1861 to open the gates on Sundays, only to find visitors increasing in a manner that was 'orderly and decorous'.[54] The RHA opened on Sundays for its annual exhibition in 1877. The Natural History Museum opened in 1884,[55] alternating Sunday afternoon openings with the Museum of Science and Art from 1890.[56] And although there is no record of Sunday opening at the Museum of Irish Industry (1845–67) or the RIA museum,[57] there is ample evidence that, in Catholic Ireland, public bodies opened their doors to the public after 'the hours of Divine service'.

This was a contested issue overseas, too. For instance, in Britain, where Sunday was a religious day of prayer, it took a resolution of Parliament in 1895 for Sunday opening to become everyday practice at London's museums. Following this, the British Museum obeyed 'the Trustees [who] have ordered that the Museum shall be open daily'.[58] The National Gallery and Portrait Gallery followed suit in 1896.[59] In Scotland, the National Gallery and Portrait Gallery did not open on Sundays until 1907.[60] The Louvre opened on Sundays from 1806, and opened six days a week (closed Mondays) from 1855.[61] The pattern of opening in Rome and elsewhere in Italy varied, with admission more often by means of a small fee to the *custodes*.[62] The Prado in Madrid opened on Sundays, with free admission, from 1876.[63] The Royal Museums in Germany opened on Sunday from 1859, the remaining museums from 1871.[64] Sunday opening became a standard practice at the Rijksmuseum in Amsterdam in 1885.[65] In the United States it varied: while some museums feared an influx of 'the labouring class and immigrants', the Boston Museum of Fine Arts opened on Sundays in 1876, the Art Institute of Chicago in 1893, the Metropolitan Museum, New York, in 1891 'as an experiment', happily finding the visitors to be 'respectable, law abiding and intelligent', followed by the American Museum of Natural History in 1892.[66]

The issue revolved around the working population (so-called operative class), who worked six days a week. As Sunday was their only free day, how that time was spent was of critical importance to them. They needed access to public facilities, outside of religious service – hence the battle to gain entry to public parks, museums, gardens and zoos. Thus, if the NGI believed that 'the purpose of the collection was the great advantages secured to the public by such opportunity for study as it supplied', then access on Sunday was an imperative. The conservative gallery hesitated,[67] however, before Mulvany told Haughton and Robinson: 'I have much pleasure in announcing that at the last Board meeting on 14 January 1864 the Governors resolved the Gallery will be open all Sundays in the year, except during vacation, after 2pm.'[68] The director was instructed to put the rules and regulations 'on a board placed inside the entrance gate' and in the entrance vestibule.[69]

By opening half-day on Sunday, the board demonstrated its heightened awareness of the needs of the local community, particularly the working class, and by implication acknowledged its responsibility 'to teach and elevate the minds' of its countrymen on the only day available to them. By making this established policy from the outset, it set a pattern that other institutions would emulate. This innovation took place in Ireland nearly thirty years ahead of museums in the United Kingdom and many in America and Europe. Mulvany gave evidence on its success to the 1864 Select Committee: 'Sunday opening has worked admirably. I have been pleased to see the interest taken … by the working classes and people at large, all orderly and well-behaved.'[70] Lady Gregory visited with Sir William Gregory, 'that I might see the people coming in … working men with their wives and children', pleased that Sunday opening had occurred 'long before London museums and galleries had unlocked their Sabbath door'.[71] Sunday became, and remains, the most popular day for the Irish public to visit their National Gallery.

The New Gallery

On 30 January 1864 the lord lieutenant unveiled the statue of William Dargan by Thomas Farrell RHA, accorded a prominent place in front of the gallery to honour that most 'significant of Irishmen'.[72] The ever-modest Dargan, described as 'the great apostle of Irish industry and self reliance', was absent from the celebrations, having made 'an anonymous' donation of £2,000 to help the gallery acquire a collection.[73] The official opening was held on the first-floor Queen's Gallery in the presence of 1,500 nobility and gentry, and the board stated that 'It now lies with the Irish public to improve and extend [the gallery] to the requirements of the nation'. The lord lieutenant's response, however, was underwhelming:

> The previous course of Irish history has scarcely been smooth enough to foster the growth of galleries or museums of the fine arts … It is my earnest wish that the institution which we now inaugurate may by the display of foreign excellence supply a fresh incentive and starting point to your own.[74]

HIS EXCELLENCY THE EARL OF CARLISLE OPENING THE NATIONAL GALLERY OF IRELAND.—SEE PAGE 157.

**The Lord Lieutenant of Ireland, 7th Earl of Carlisle,
opening the National Gallery on 30 January 1864**
Published: Illustrated London News, *13 February 1864. Wood engraving, 21.6 x 28.3 cm. NGI 11595.*

Following the unveiling of the statue of William Dargan, the opening took place in the first-floor gallery (then known as the Queen's Gallery). While filled to capacity for the opening event, the paintings shown here are just an impression of what was on display.

The new catalogue, *Descriptive and Historical of the Works of Art in the National Gallery of Ireland with descriptive notes by George F. Mulvany, RHA, (Director)* (1864), listed 130 paintings, 4 sculptures and 106 casts, with the painters listed alphabetically in the manner of the Louvre. As Ireland's National Gallery had no royal collection to draw upon, its modest display was similar to that of the National Gallery in London and in Edinburgh.

Visitors entered the gallery via a small Nineveh and Egyptian vestibule containing Assyrian and Egyptian casts. The main Sculpture Hall displayed Greek and Roman antique casts and busts, 'life-sized statues and colossal groupings' mounted on movable pedestals and judiciously placed, 'lighted from one side by four large windows'.[75] The great double staircase led to the first floor, 'princely in its dimensions and its decorations are gorgeous', where galleries displayed paintings from the different national schools.[76] The majority of the works were Italian, emphasizing the importance placed on classical art: 'examples of the highest classes of art, worthy of the able means for the education of public taste'.[77] This pattern of display was common in nineteenth-century European museums, influenced by the systematic reorganization of the Louvre in 1793 under Dominique-Vivant Denon (1747–1825), its rationale based on the great civilizations, of which classical and Renaissance art were considered the most important. The purpose of the arrangement was to illustrate the history of Western art, based on humanist ideals, depending on what was available to the institution at that time. Modern advancements were a feature of the building: columns on the ground floor concealed a ventilation system; the Sculptural Hall was lit by six gas burners of sixty lights; pre-cast concrete (an early fire-proof form) was used on the floors; and natural overhead lighting in the upper floors.

The public gained entry in March (due to a delay caused by problems with the Sculpture Hall gas system) and at first the lighting proved to be the gallery's greatest attraction, being one of the first museums to open after the hours of darkness.[78] It exceeded expectations: 'a structure worthy of the country … showing what care, attention and refined taste can accomplish'.[79] Favourable comparisons were made: 'Ireland, like England and Scotland, has now its National Gallery which will become the nursery of Irish art.'[80]

Jeremy Williams (20th century), *The National Gallery as it appeared in 1864*
Ink on paper, 29.8 x 42 cm. NGI 7945.

This image is a contemporary reconstruction of the 1864 exterior of the gallery with the entrance vestibule. It was purchased from the artist in 1981.

Accordingly, the public came in great numbers: 'On Sunday last between 2 p.m. and 5 p.m. the visitors numbered 3,845, proving what a great benefit the National Gallery will be to the community.'[81] The collection was greatly admired: Jacob Jordaens' *Church Triumphant* 'must have cost the artists who produced it much labour and deep thought';[82] 'Pictures that strike us forcibly include *Adoration of the Shepherds* by Francesco Pascucci (*fl.*1787–1803) and *Christ on the Cross* by Antonio Panico (*c.*1575–1620).'[83] Criticism focused on the nature of the collection, 'many of the pictures are not of that class suited to instruct', with recommendations that future purchases 'serve not only to please and interest the visitor, but also instruct the student'.[84] Over ten months in 1864, 167,698 people visited to appreciate the building, the artworks and the vision of its founders.

The Gallery's Educational Role

The director's opening speech drew attention to the educational context of the collections and the innovation of classical statuary, 'which forms an important feature of the Irish National Gallery, distinct from either that of London or Edinburgh'. The Society of Ancient Art had tried to form a cast collection 'to supply young artists with models and to educate the mind of the people', so that the 'opportunity of seeing a large and well arranged series of sculptures' would be instructive.[85] Mulvany stressed the teaching role of the casts: 'true *fac similes* of the great originals and though in plaster their fidelity makes them of the greatest value to the art student whose eye they are intended to educate'.[86] Forming over half of the display, they represented copies of original sculptures held in the Vatican, the British Museum and the Louvre, which would be enhanced by the later addition of Lord Talbot de Malahide's casts of female busts, 'lately discovered in excavations' in Rome (1875).[87]

The plaster cast, or plaster sculpture, originally formed the cornerstone of most cultural institutional displays. For over 150 years museums and colleges across Europe and America amassed collections of casts from the antique so as to better study the classical world.[88] From the early nineteenth century the British Museum admitted artists to draw in the sculpture galleries as an important part of the museum's function. Instruction by means of observation

The Principal old master gallery on the first floor, with Italian paintings on one side (unseen), and Flemish, Dutch and Spanish paintings on the opposite wall, c.1900

The upper rooms, originally for small cabinet pictures and works on paper, show some French, British and Irish paintings. The paintings are hung in two and three tiers, according to the fashion of the time. Gaslights can be seen just below the glazed roof. The slide was taken by Ephraim McDowell, a friend of the registrar, Walter Strickland. (Slide courtesy of the Royal Society of Antiquaries of Ireland).

and study of classical sculpture by academies of art was encouraged not just by students from the RA schools but by professional and amateur artists.[89] Friday was originally reserved for artists and supervised students from the RA (a practice discontinued in 1855), with a successful drawing undertaken in the museum forming a condition for admission to the academy. London's National Gallery set aside Thursday and Friday as private days up to 1880, allowing no more than fifty persons per day.[90] The South Kensington Museum opened six days a week, and three nights until 10 p.m., with open access to students and artists throughout. Scotland's National Gallery set aside Thursday and Friday 'for artists and others copying the pictures'.[91] The Altes Museum in Berlin kept Tuesday and Friday for artists and students up to 1871. Access for

The ground floor Sculpture Hall looking towards the stairs, *c.*1900

Oscar Wilde saw his first classical art at the age of ten when the National Gallery opened to the public. On display was a collection of Greek and Roman antique casts and sculptures in the ground floor sculpture gallery. The room under the stairs was designated for Marsh's Library, but became the National Historical and Portrait Gallery in 1884.

students and artists was provided when the Belfast Art Gallery and Museum opened in 1890.[92] The Crawford Art Gallery in Cork was housed in the same building as the art school, its cast collection available to students and the public, demonstrating the extraordinary importance of casts in general education.

Irish students eagerly took to their National Gallery, including the young Oscar Wilde, who saw his 'first classical art at the age of ten' when he observed the 'casts of Greek and Roman originals' in the Sculpture Hall.[93] Students and artists from the RHA and the Schools of Design availed of the system of private days on Friday and Saturday (10 a.m. to 4 p.m.), registering their names in an attendance book, providing their own easels, drawing boards, stools and mats, and obeying the bell that rang out fifteen minutes before closure. Professional artists were free to copy; amateur artists had to produce a work executed by them and approved by the director; RHA students produced a certificate from the keeper; and School of Design students provided one from the headmaster. The system encouraged students to observe the styles of the great masters and improve drawing techniques, demonstrated in a self-portrait by Richard Thomas Moynan (1856–1906), sketching on the ground floor of the gallery where the casts were displayed: *Taking Measurements: The Artist Copying a Cast in the Hall of the National Gallery of Ireland* (1887).[94] Private days were changed to Thursday and Friday in 1888, and finally abolished in 1912.[95] The tradition of providing cast collections continued to the end of the nineteenth century, by which time they had lost their appeal in the teaching of art. As the fashion declined, the 123 plaster casts were removed to facilitate the building of the Milltown Wing.

The attendance books used by students between 1864 and 1916 reveal an interest in sculpture, casts and Italian painting. The private days were used over nine months, occasionally eleven (the gallery closed for a month in the autumn for cleaning), and some years five months or less (1873, 1882, 1894, 1895, 1907, 1913 and 1916). Significant artists using this teaching facility included Stephen Catterson Smith, Nathaniel Hill, Susan Mary Yeats and Elizabeth Corbet Yeats, Lady Butler, Rose Barton, William Orpen, Sarah Purser, Mary Swanzy, Patrick Tuohy, Leo Whelan and Evie Hone.[96] Students came singly, in a private group with a teacher (the young Swanzy visited with May Manning in 1900) or in groups from the RHA, the Slade School of Art in London or the Metropolitan School of Art (twenty-seven women students came with William Orpen in 1894).

The pattern of attendance varied: Mulvany's 1869 *Annual Report* noted '35 students admitted during the year'; Henry E. Doyle's 1885 *Annual Report* noted '25 new students', fifteen ladies and ten gentlemen. Although an image from the 1880s shows a lady with her companion drawing from the casts in an empty Sculpture Hall, 1,535 students used the facility that year.[97] Walter Armstrong's 1899 *Annual Report* noted that 'tickets to copy were issued to 30 students (20 ladies and 10 gentlemen) and the number of student attendances was 1,417'. Disruption was caused on occasion by closure 'for repairs and repainting', for example, as happened over seven months in 1874–5, for 'refurbishment of' the National Historical and Portrait Gallery in 1884, for building of 'the Milltown Wing' between 1899 and 1903 and for arranging of the Milltown Collection in 1906.

To summarize: private days were mainly used between 1864 and 1916, largely over nine months of the year, for the study of sculpture, casts and Italian painting. Of those students who attended, 99 per cent had Dublin addresses, with almost 90 per cent made up of women students, amateurs and professional artists (Walter Osborne, Swanzy, Purser and Hone). Use of the facility averaged a daily attendance of four students in 1869 to an annual figure of 1,535 in 1885 and 1,471 in 1899. The collection ceased to be a major learning resource when art teachers stopped drawing on classical sculpture, attention being diverted by the decorative arts and contemporary fashion, as new methods of teaching were employed in the art colleges. At times like this the gallery could be a lonely place, with 'an enthusiastic lady here and there sketching in the solitary Hall'.[98]

The Collections

Collections formed the heart of the museum, with the policy throughout its history being to display 'examples of the highest classes of art' to form and educate public taste. Mulvany had amassed a corpus of seventy works representing the main European schools, not all major masters but useful for study by 'the imperfect means of copying'. The definition of fine art included paintings (oils and panels), watercolours, drawings and prints (works on paper), sculpture and cast collections, miniatures, silhouettes, stained glass and *objets d'art*, the hierarchy depending on fashion and taste.

Irish art was not a priority for Mulvany. Of twelve Irish works acquired for the opening, the first was *A Landscape with Fishermen* by George Barret, the patriot William Smith O'Brien offered *Creeping to School* (NGI 384) by George Sharp (1802–77), a portrait and figure painter better known for his teaching skills, and *The Blind Piper* (*c*.1844) (NGI 166) by Joseph Patrick Haverty (1794–1864), a portrait and subject painter whose appealing picture became second only in popularity to the later donation of Maclise's *The Marriage of Strongbow and Aoife*.[99] Originally left to the RDS, O'Brien's gift to 'the Irish nation' devolved to the gallery.[100]

The learning context of the collections was understood by the board as follows:

> It is desirable to place before students for their instruction and education carefully selected examples of the best productions of contemporary art, which in the present state of the market

Francesco Granacci (1469–1543), *Rest on the Flight into Egypt with the Infant St John the Baptist*, c.1494

Egg tempera and oil on wood, 100 x 71 cm. NGI 98.

Granacci was a pupil in Ghirlandaio's workshop at the same time as Michelangelo and the two became friends. The sculptural quality of the Virgin, the Child and St John reflects Michelangelo's influence. This Italian Renaissance painting, acquired by George Mulvany in 1866, made a strong impression on early visitors to the gallery.

are ever more difficult to obtain than specimens of the old masters. Under this heading would come a fair representation of our own mature artists eg, Mulready, Maclise, Danby.

The foundation of a National Portrait Gallery of distinguished personages either Irish by birth or connected with the public transactions of Ireland.

The extension of our Sculpture Gallery especially with a view of forming a collection of casts from the best works of our native artists, a branch of art for which our countrymen have shown a special aptitude eg Hogan, McDowell, Foley.

Although [the Gallery is] not strictly a teaching department in the sense of providing practical instruction in art within its walls, yet their arrangements are made as to afford the greatest possible facility to students who may be sufficiently advanced by the art schools already in Dublin, to take advantage of the opportunity for copying and studying excellent models in the various branches of ancient and modern art, which it is the chief object of the institution to afford them.[101]

An open competition for a new director resulted in the appointment of Henry E. Doyle (1827–92) in 1869,[102] his 23-year term marked by the acquisition of 170 oils (46 of Irish origin), including works by Poussin, Fra Angelico and Rembrandt, and the growth of the Irish collection.[103] His re-hang of the gallery followed a pattern established by the Louvre, with Italian art taking precedence, followed by Flanders, the Netherlands, Spain, France and England. It was during his tenure that the young George Bernard Shaw could be seen prowling 'for hours through Dublin's deserted National Gallery dragging McNulty with him – two schoolboys … going from picture to picture … until they knew every work there and could recognize at sight the style of many Flemish and Italian painters'.[104]

Doyle's directorship addressed the issue of Irish art and a national portrait collection. He set aside a small room as an Irish gallery in 1872 and then tackled the issue of a portrait collection that would celebrate Irish men and women, the idea for which arose from a section of the 1872 Dublin Exhibition of Arts, Industries and Manufactures and a loan exhibition featuring an

The National and Historical Portrait Gallery c.1921

This rare keyhole view shows the 'National and Historial Portrait Gallery', established by second director, Henry Doyle, in 1884, and then relocated from the ground floor of the Dargan Wing to the lower Milltown rooms. Writers Lady Morgan and Julia Kavanagh can be seen on the left with William Carleton on the right, above a small portrait of George Petrie and a silhouette of Richard Robert Madden.

'Irish National Portrait Gallery'. The Treasury would not sanction resources because it did not approve of a separate enterprise for Ireland, feeling that London's National Portrait Gallery adequately celebrated Irishmen who were important to the United Kingdom, men such as MP reformers like Joseph Hume, William Ewart and Irishman Thomas Wyse, who was a member of the 1836 Select Committee. This concept was based on Noel Desenfans's plan[105] 'to preserve among us, and transmit to posterity, the portraits of the most distinguished characters of England, Scotland and Ireland'.[106] Sir Charles Eastlake supported portraits 'as a not unimportant element of education'.[107] Doyle knew of the display of Scottish portraits at Edinburgh's National Gallery (between 1850 and 1889) prior to the advent of a portrait gallery in 1882.[108] While London's Portrait Gallery commemorated Irishmen who had given service to England, Doyle patiently explained to the Treasury that Irish people wanted to celebrate native figures who formed part of an Irish identity in their own country. It would not 'lessen the importance of an essentially national collection if a separate and competing gallery was established in Dublin confined to portraits of Irish celebrities'.[109]

Unhappy with this precedence, government left the gallery to find the resources, the outcome of which saw Doyle dedicate a space for modern Irish artists, such as Maclise, Francis Danby and James Arthur O'Connor, and set aside a temporary gallery devoted to Irish portrait busts, paintings and drawings in 1875.[110] The *Daily Express* noted its value to 'the student and

**Richard Thomas Moynan
(1856–1906),** *Taking
Measurements: The Artist
Copying a Cast in the hall of the
National Gallery of Ireland,* **1887**
*Oil on canvas, 99.5 x 62 cm.
NGI 4562.*

This is a typical image of an artist
sketching from the cast collection on
the ground floor of the gallery in
1887. He is observed by two children
as their guardian reads from the
catalogue. Moynan measures up the
cast of a lion from the Mausoleum at
Halicarnassus. In the background
is a carayatid from the Erechtheum,
together with *bas-reliefs* from the
Parthenon, Xanthos and Eleucis.

the public', with its 'collection of
portraits of eminent Irish men
and women'.[111] Doyle sourced 'a
large room on the ground floor',
where the 'National Historical
and Portrait Gallery' finally
opened in 1884, featuring 144 portraits of 'eminent Irish men and women as
well as others though not of Irish birth, have been politically or socially
connected with Ireland or with her historical, literary or artistic records'.[112]
The public was receptive: 'one of the most interesting places … with most
pleasure to the portraits of our noble men and women'. Its popularity was
due to the broad sweep of Irish society that was represented: poets, writers,
musicians, actors, artists, well-known political and aristocratic figures.[113]
When Doyle met Burton, then director of the National Gallery, London, who
had donated some portrait drawings to Dublin, the latter gave his countryman
first selection of works available under the National Gallery Loan Act.[114]
Doyle's death in 1892 saw the passing of a director who actively fostered a
sense of national identity through the introduction of Irish art and a
National Portrait Collection.

During the tenure of Walter Armstrong (1892–1914), Doyle's successor,
the young William Orpen, a student at the Metropolitan School of Art (1891–7),

frequented the gallery, recording in his sketchbooks the Greek and Roman sculptures and casts.[115] Also absorbing the strong light contrasts in Luca Giordano's *St Sebastian Tended by St. Irene* (NGI 79) (much admired by Wilde), he acknowledged his 'technical debt' to Ribera's *St. Onuphrius* ((NGI 219) acquired from the 4th Duke of Leinster in 1879).[116] Orpen became friendly with Armstrong, a prolific writer on art who was close to Walter Osborne.[117] While the new director made important acquisitions and expanded the figures from Irish cultural life in the portrait collection, he could not persuade the owners of the great Irish houses to donate works to the gallery.[118] His revised catalogue was critical of resources: 'no separate fund is at the disposal of the Gallery for the acquisition of works'.[119]

The gallery's growing awareness of tourists was denoted by the decision, in 1896, to open on St Patrick's Day and other public holidays, 'despite the absence of American visitors during the summer season'.[120] Attendance figures

Rembrandt van Rijn (1606–69),
***Landscape with the Rest on the Flight into Egypt*, 1647**
Oil on wood, 34 x 48 cm. NGI 215.

This panel is Rembrandt's only painted night landscape, acquired by Henry Doyle in 1883. The subject was inspired by Adam Elsheimer's *Flight into Egypt,* and was later identified and copied by J.M.W. Turner at Stourhead, Wiltshire.

dwindled towards the end of the century: 90,413 visitors in 1892 had declined to 72,117 by 1900. This pattern was in marked contrast to the buoyant figures at the Museum of Science and Art, although the museum's success was due to its newness and the increasing interest in the Irish antiquities. Meanwhile, the gallery was facing an issue over space for the growing collection, as the pictures were being hung in overcrowded rooms. In addition, the pattern of hanging paintings in tiers, as favoured in Berlin and other European museums, was now changing to facilitate intervals between each of the works, and this required more wall space. The building was crying out for expansion.[121] Fate intervened in a timely fashion when a missive arrived from the Countess of Milltown proposing to donate works of art and antique furniture from Russborough to the National Gallery. Lady Milltown wished the works of art to be exhibited as the Milltown Collection in memory of her husband, Edward Nugent (Leeson), the 6th Earl of Milltown.[122] The fresh impetus provided by this benevolence would spur the National Gallery on to a new chapter in its history as it faced into the twentieth century.

Century's End: A Culture in Transition

So, where stood Ireland as the winds of change fanned the flames of nationalist fervour and pushed the century to its end? The museums that emerged under British rule, including the Museum of Irish Industry, the Natural History Museum, the National Gallery, the Museum of Science and Art, the Crawford Municipal Art Gallery, Belfast Art Gallery and Museum and the university museums, all represented an extraordinary achievement. *Ambitieux* was the word used by one visitor to Dublin: '*A cette époque, au terme d'une exposition universelle de l'industrie et des arts qui s'était tenue à Dublin, un reunion de riches particuliers, d'artistes et d'amateurs Irlandais decida la foundation d'un museé de tableaux.*'[123]

The cumulative contents of the museums, formed from private and public collections, acquired through gift, purchase and donation, represented a century of museological development from amateur cabinet to professional museum. The artefacts that comprised the late eighteenth- and early nineteenth-century cabinets, amassed by both private and philanthropic means, became symbolic of the changed nature of Irish society as they became absorbed into national museums. They represented the critical transition from private collections to the rationalized public institution in the form of the National Gallery and National Museum. Pride in the institutions was denoted by employing native architects, using Irish craftworkers and materials and by the prominent display of Irish antiquities at the museum. It was also demonstrated in the creation of an Irish school of painting and a portrait gallery of distinguished Irish men and women at the National Gallery. The making of these national cultural institutions, with their emphasis on 'Irish collections', offered a reminder of how a shared vision of permanence and inclusion could help to hold a country together. Self-esteem was evident in the growing sense of national consciousness for Irish people.

The design of the buildings, some of which had architectural references to earlier periods, contributed a visual representation that was in keeping with the status of the city at that time. The Museum of Science and Art represented current ideas in Irish industrial education until interest in Irish antiquities drew attention instead to Ireland's historic past. These cultural institutions were clear in their aspiration to conserve the artefacts in their care and arrange the displays to provide for the instruction of the public. The transfer of the Irish cultural institutions from London to the Dublin-based Department of Agriculture and Technical Instruction was a further step in Irish self-determination. The nineteenth century had witnessed the emergence of public collections originating in the RIA museum (1790), Dublin Society museum (1792), Belfast Natural History Museum (1831) and the Museum of Irish Industry (1845–67), just as their instructional role progressed at the Dublin Natural History Museum (1857), National Gallery (1864), Crawford Municipal Art Gallery, Cork (1885), Belfast Art Gallery and Museum (1890) and Dublin Museum of Science and Art (1890).

There was another agenda at work in all these developments – a growing sense of national consciousness. For some considerable time Irish territory had been part of the United Kingdom of Great Britain and Ireland, with the law enforced by the Royal Irish Constabulary (1814–1921) and the Dublin Metropolitan Police (1836–1925), together with a British army presence to quell rebellions.[124] Now there emerged a cultural movement, unifying enthusiasts from diverse backgrounds, which sought a nationalism beyond Charles Stewart Parnell's constitutional campaign. The closest thing to a unified

movement, it existed within branch organizations and self-help societies and
owed much to the efforts of Douglas Hyde,[125] Lady Gregory, Thomas Finlay,[126]
George Russell, W.B. Yeats,[127] James Stephens, Arthur Griffith and Horace
Plunkett, who all sought to improve the lot of the nation: 'We aim at a self-
reliant, self-controlled, self-sufficient Ireland.' Many of these figures, including
Gregory, Yeats, Stephens and Plunkett, were associated with the newly created
museums, about which their views and opinions were sought, considered
and acted upon.

The wider context of Irish life at the end of the nineteenth century saw the
sports of hurling and football gain countrywide support for the newly formed
Gaelic Athletic Association (GAA) in 1884.[128] The Congested Districts Board
(1891–1923) reorganized the pattern of landholding to give farmers bigger
plots and move them to areas where there was untenanted land, thereby
leaving more land for distribution. Davis's promotion of educational structures
to help people to 'plan for their own and their children's education' grew to
form part of the movement to establish individual self-reliance as the foundation upon which the character of the people would be built.[129] Hyde's Gaelic
League (established in 1893) also promoted self-respect through awareness of
Irish ancestry and traditions.[130] Nationalist papers enabled the 'imagining' of
the Irish nation,[131] just as literary magazines emerged to a golden era rooted
in the Irish Literary Revival and Irish nationalism of the 1890s. The Irish
Co-operative Movement, which was also founded in 1893 by Plunkett to
improve the state of the powerless members of Irish society,[132] witnessed
Plunkett becoming the first head of the Dublin branch of the Department
of Agriculture and Technical Instruction and emerging as a genuine advocate
of Irish museums.

The individuals involved in the museums and cultural institutions listed
in these chapters – the Ordnance Survey Geological Department and the

Geological Survey of Ireland, the RDS enterprises, the RIA, the RHA, the university museums, schools and academies of art, national and regional museums – were all involved at some time or another with the question of identity. Identity had a different meaning in the nineteenth century in Ireland because the country was under British rule, an outpost of empire. As the century progressed, however, many people began to explore what it meant to be Irish, inculcating in Irish people a new pride in their history while demonstrating how 'Irishness' might appear in the future. The Irish Revival was significant in the evolution of modern Ireland because its key figures recognized that cultural self-belief was fundamental not only to economic prosperity but to national independence. The catchphrase 'educate so that you will be free' was echoed by Shaw, who stated his debt to the National Gallery, 'to which I owe much of the only real education I ever got as a boy'.[133] This legacy of Revivalist initiative, characterized by a complex ferment of rich political and cultural thought, placed Ireland in a tantalizing position.[134] The outlook must have seemed very positive for Irish museums as they faced into the new century, and saw within their sights the potential of new acquisitions, extensions and the opportunity to develop the collections in their care for the education and enjoyment of the wider public.

PART IV

The Twentieth Century

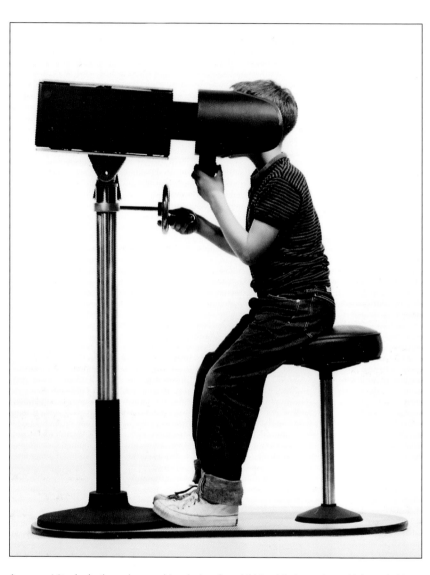

A young visitor looks through a machine during the exhibition *Mathematica*, which used objects and ideas to explain the abstraction of measurement, quantity and mathematical concepts in 1961. The early exhibition experiments of the 1920s and 30s were explored by American museums, which drew on educational psychologists to help provide more exciting interactive exhibitions.

*F*ollowing a century of museum foundation, we now reach 'the museum age', the point at which the modern museum emerged. In order to tell this story in full, it is necessary to first return to the role played by museum movements in Britain and America, which influenced curators and directors in Ireland. Taking these cultures as a starting point, we can trace the exchange of ideas across the ocean and between institutions that were striving to meet the demands and expectations of a fast-changing world.

For those visiting Dublin during the early decades of the twentieth century, enjoyment was sought from the Irish antiquities at the National Museum of Science and Art; from the Milltown Collection in the National Gallery's new wing; from UCD's Museum of Ancient Art at Earlsfort Terrace; from TCD's Zoology Museum, Herbarium and Geology Museum; and from Dublin's new cultural institution, the Municipal Art Gallery (now Dublin City Gallery The Hugh Lane), one of the first public galleries of modern art in the world.[1] Unfortunately, the world in which the late nineteenth-century natural historians, archaeologists and antiquarians had grown up disappeared forever with the outbreak of the First World War (1914–18). In Ireland the Easter Rising of 1916 was followed by the War of Independence (1919–21) and then the Civil War (1922–3), making it impossible for groups of geologists and naturalists to pursue their interests in natural history in the countryside. Following the destruction of the RHA's building in 1916, the schools struggled to survive up to 1942; meanwhile the design schools, under the remit of the Departments of Education from 1924 (in the North and the South),[2] became absorbed into Institutes of Technology.

The achievement of independent statehood in 1922 saw the Irish government place the the cultural institutions under the Department of Education in 1924. There ensued one of the most challenging periods for the government, politically, economically and socially, which partly explains the inconsistent resourcing of the cultural institutions during this era. Research in all areas suffered in the 1920s and 1930s because the new government had no funds to divert to such activities. The relative unimportance of the arts and culture under the Department of Education reflected the prevailing political and cultural context of the age, which was dictated by the restrictive policies of the Department of Finance. In the case of the cultural institutions, appeals to their parent department for assistance went largely unheard.

The devastation of the Second World War (1939–45) was followed by the post-war depression of the 1950s. Thus it was that it was not until the 1960s that the government began to make funds available to survey Ireland's heritage, in order to demonstrate the potential value of geology, natural history, floral and faunal studies, and the importance of associated fieldwork. In Ireland, as in many parts of Europe, the twentieth century was mostly one of lost opportunity for researchers, with the level of activity and investment only catching up in the latter part of the century, the outcome of which would feed into institutions such as the National Museum of Ireland, the Ulster Museum and the changing context of the university collections.

The gradual development by the state of a coherent policy for educational expansion in the latter half of the century mirrored the growth of living standards and public interest in the arts, as the country experienced accelerated economic development. These cultural institutions became integrated into the fabric of a society and an economy that would grow and expand as the century advanced. The outcome of the establishment of trusts, such as the Gibson Bequest (1919), Friends of the National Collections (1924), Haverty Trust (1930) and the Contemporary Irish Art Society (1962),[3] was their ability to draw on the RHA exhibitions as a resource to acquire works of art that would be donated to national, regional or municipal art collections.[4] The culture of the museum and the art gallery gradually moved to the fore, with museums opening in Dublin, Belfast, Cork and Limerick, followed by municipal, local authority and independent museums. These museums benefited from a wealthier Irish nation and a developing taste for consumerism, with many sectors of the population enjoying high disposable incomes.

The *fin-de-siècle* evidence of achievement that occurred nationally and internationally bestowed a fresh sense of self-confidence on the country. Irish museum professionals could be confident of the services they were providing within the cultural sphere, in partnership with competencies in collecting, conserving, displaying, studying and interpreting objects, which were contributing to the quality of individual lives and enhancing the community's well-being.

10

The Public Role of the Museum: Patterns and Trends in the UK and the USA in the Twentieth Century

Museums of the 1920s onwards owe more to the developments of the 1870s than any other period in the history of the American art world.[1]

The mission of most major museums is to collect, study, preserve and exhibit objects of significance, either aesthetic or historical, for public enjoyment and enlightenment. While the nineteenth century had been a 'century of museum foundation and collection',[2] the early twentieth century began with institutions grappling with concepts of education and engagement, while trying to develop their social role in the context of a new public awareness. Thus did America enter its 'museum age'. Within a short period, however, the threat of war loomed large. In the United Kingdom the impact of the war would be felt right across the nation as people left their jobs to join the war effort and museums struggled to survive. Irish museums were similarly depleted of staff, as many Irishmen opted to enlist in the British army.

In Europe, the progress made by museums was diminished by the advent of the First and Second World Wars, the economic consequences of which left institutions struggling to survive, expand and develop, while coping with the new realities of post-war recession. This impacted on museums in Europe and the United States as they faced into a phase of reconstruction and redevelopment. The silver lining was that the intoxication of peace sparked intense cultural activity from which American museums benefited later in the century, when new museums proliferated and major exhibitions and designer extensions in the 1980s and 1990s became part of late twentieth-century museum life. These twentieth-century trends in British and American museums are explored here, with a particular focus on the public role and its increasing importance as the century progressed.

Britain and America up to the First World War

In Britain and Ireland in the early twentieth century the emphasis was on the role of the museum as a place of learning, informed by the views of men such as Frederic G. Kenyon, director of the British Museum (1909–31): 'The history of museums as an educational force operating on the general public is part of the history of educational progress in the nineteenth century, and of the response of museum officials to the opportunity created by that progress.'[3]

The growing professionalism of curatorship gave rise to publications, such as the *Museums Journal* (1901), that promoted museums as centres of learning.[4] The Museums Association declared that 'a museum would appear to be a collection of specimens arranged on educational lines and with educational purpose'.[5] New improvements included a systematic arrangement of the collections that would facilitate a better understanding of them, together with education services that would help to make the collections more relevant to the public.

A British report, *Museums in Relation to Education*,[6] drew on American practice in encouraging museums to be effective tools of public education. British efforts were modest when compared to their American counterparts, where education was considered a primary function. Nonetheless, successful loan services to schools were developed in Britain following the precedence of a service set up at Liverpool Museum that was based on the child-centred principles of Johann H. Pestalozzi (1746–1827), the Swiss pedagogue and educational reformer:

> The object of the circulating museums is not so much teaching as training; not so much the inculcation of facts as the illustration of the happiness to be obtained through the habits of observation … In every possible case the interest of the specimen should be associated with man.[7]

These duplicate specimens (historical, archaeological, natural history material) encouraged children to form their own collections. They promoted 'object-centred' teaching that supported the child by advancing his or her faculties of acquiring knowledge (rather than passing on facts) and by developing his

A group of children on a tour of the Metropolitan Museum of Art, New York

The Metropolitan Museum of Art appointed Henry Watson Kent supervisor of museum instruction in 1907, following which he developed a range of influential educational programmes and initiatives.

or her sense-perceptions in relation to activities. These educational ideas were being explored in America, principally in the child-centred theories of education espoused by John Dewey (1859–1952). As object-lessons could be taught in relation to many subjects, loan collections, therefore, offered ways to learn and acquire skills, including training the senses and developing thinking, language and verbal skills.

The provision of a guide-lecturer service was a significant step forward for British museums. It was a move that was first debated in the House of Lords in the early twentieth century, with official reports noting the need for the interpretation of the collections for visitors.[8] From the beginning, the British Museum had combined elements of an eighteenth-century learned society/academic institution with the public role of collections, display and education, but it was nonetheless an example of a national museum that took the step, in 1911, of introducing a guide-lecture service.[9] The demand was immediate: by 1924, 35,000 people were attending talks; the same year that visitor numbers reached one million.

Meanwhile, the ongoing co-operation between the British Museum and the National Museum of Ireland resulted in Irish staff studying at the British Museum.[10] During the war years, E.C.R. Armstrong, keeper of antiquities at the National Museum, would be seconded to assist at the British Museum. In addition, Dublin's Natural History division would report stranded whales, porpoises and dolphins on the coast and the British Museum's Research Laboratory would conserve valuable Irish finds.[11] This pattern of provision of guides and lectures at the national museums continued at the National History Museum in 1912, the V&A Museum in 1913, the Tate Gallery and the Wallace Collection in 1914.

The reputation of the National Gallery, London, as an art museum for the nation was enhanced by its free admission policy: 'people run in for half-an-hour … and it is precisely those half-hours that are the most precious, for people confine their attention to one or two things and study them well'.[12] The gallery also appointed its first guide-lecturer in 1914. By 1917 its links with the Tate Gallery had ended, following which the Tate formed its own board.[13] During the First World War, the National Gallery's collections were stored in the Strand underground station. In 1922, it began holding concerts, which would later be emulated by the V&A Museum.[14] A loan of

A copyist working in the National Gallery, London, in the 1920s. The gallery's original regulations specified that two days per week were to be set aside for art students to study the paintings. While a study of classical statuary and paintings was considered an essential part of the education of artists and the public, copying from the collection had become increasingly popular during the nineteenth century.

paintings was returned from the National Gallery of Ireland.[15] During the inter-war years the National Gallery in London held a programme of lectures, several of which (1935–7) were given by Irish-born George Furlong and Thomas MacGreevy (future directors of the National Gallery of Ireland).[16] Also during the First World War, as many teachers enlisted, museums stepped in to play a role in providing schools programming for children[17] and to mount exhibitions on subjects like childcare, health and hygiene (at the Natural History Museum), which helped to improve people's lives.[18]

A number of reports (1920–50s) looked at access opportunities in museums, with H.A. Miers's *Report on the Public Museums of the British Isles* (1928), commenting that museums were for 'storing, exhibiting and utilizing objects of cultural and educational value', but noting that few of the 530 regional museums addressed their educational role.[19] While a distinction in Britain began to emerge between the museum functions, resulting in the acquisition and conservation of collections emerging as primary roles, E.E. Lowe's report, *American Museum Work*, nonetheless advocated the more pro-active museum practices in the United States.[20] The Board of Education, meanwhile, listed good practices in Britain and overseas.[21] In 1932 the Museum Association began museum training courses, and a UK Carnegie Trust Survey recommended a ministry to oversee museums.[22] Despite these reports, British museums were still felt to be centres of research rather than public learning.

America: New Movements in Pedagogy

In America the desire for self-improvement continued from the previous century, partly stemming from the need to educate new immigrants and integrate them into society. Just as there was a motivation for learning to promote human welfare, the more progressive influence of German thinking about education, museum management and design was beginning to impact on museum directors. The shift from museums having a utilitarian purpose in favour of a high art, civilizing and aesthetic pursuit was noticeable. The larger museums began to equate fine art with 'European painting and sculpture', elevating it above folk art, mechanical arts and non-Western and pre-Columbian art, thus impacting on the early collections of American arts institutions. There was a fresh commitment to public education as the founding documents of most museums espoused goals of public instruction together with functions of collecting, preserving and exhibiting objects.

Wealth was another feature of modern American life, producing men of colossal fortunes. The establishment of museums, driven by rich, civic-minded people (many of whom were women) in a private/public partnership,[23] to some degree helped to promote the educational and community role of the museum. Some aspired to the European notion of the art museum as 'a temple-treasure house' because it brought social status and recognition (for example, J. Pierpont Morgan, Isabella Stewart Gardner, Henry Clay Frick and Albert Barnes[24]), while others did not wish to be 'cultural appendages to Europe'. Thus, the museum emerged as one of the symbols of civic pride in the great American cities.

The new movement in pedagogy that underpinned the educational role of American museums was promoted by John Dewey and complemented by

The practice of using guides and lectures was introduced to British museums in the early twentieth century. Public lectures were introduced to the National Gallery in 1919. This photograph shows A. Tyndall, giving a talk to a group of visitors in front of Uccello's *The Battle of San Romano*.

innovative curators such as Benjamin Ives Gilman (Boston Museum of Fine Arts), John Cotton Dana (Newark Museum) and Henry Watson Kent (Metropolitan Museum of Art, New York). Dewey, 'America's greatest philosopher', believed that experience was the basis for learning and that this should influence museums, which he felt were central to public education.[25]

The Boston Museum of Fine Arts illustrated some of these developments as it tried to make the museum more effective as a tool of public education. Under Gilman, secondary objects were relegated to the study collections on the lower floor and the finest art was displayed in spacious galleries on the main upper floor. Gilman made visitor response a priority, which led to improvements in lighting, hanging, seating and signage. He also created a range of education programmes, even though he did not see museums as instruments of self-improvement, instead wanting visitors to make discoveries for themselves. In 1907 Gilman invented the principle of gallery instruction, coining the term 'docent' (from the Latin *docere*, 'to teach') to describe new volunteer guides, whose tours reflected his aesthetic-type approach to art (1907).[26] By 1916, 30 trained docents guided 4,300 visitors through the collections during a year that saw 5,600 schoolchildren and teachers visit the museum, as well as 2,380 students who visited of their own accord. During the summer of that year, 6,800 underprivileged children were brought to the museum and 850 children attended Saturday storytelling sessions. Sunday drew increased numbers; as Gilman put it: 'The Sunday visitors especially represent the American visitor at its best.'[27] By 1918, admission charges were abolished, and in 1924 attendance figures rose to over 400,000, with 9,000 opting to take docent tours. A similar pattern of educational achievement and use of docents was evident at other museums, including the Metropolitan Museum under Kent, the Newark Museum under Dana, and the Art Institute of Chicago.

As director of the Newark Museum, Dana was effective in promoting museums as 'instruments of popular education and recreation'. Considered 'America's most original thinker about museums', Dana commissioned Louise Connolly, on behalf of the Newark Museum Association, to review American museums. In 1914 Connolly reported 'a great unanimity of sentiment in favor of the conscious educational mission of all museums'.[28] Dana, along with Philip N. Youtz of the Brooklyn Museum of Art, sought to make the collections understandable to the average person.[29] Dana's innovations included establishing a lending department at Newark Museum, setting up a museum apprenticeship course, organizing concerts, sketching clubs and a junior museum.[30] He viewed George Brown Goode of the Smithsonian Institution as a pioneering figure because he preached a democratic doctrine of museums, a view that reached audiences beyond America.[31] Laura Bragg (the first woman director of Charleston Museum[32]) and Dana both viewed museums as places of discovery and learning, a philosophy that coincided with Dewey's pedagogical approach.

The Acquisition, Development and Display of Collections in America

The Metropolitan Museum of Art[33] is an example of a museum that faced into the new century determined to acquire the highest quality works of art, arranged historically and systematically by professionals. 'The Museum was, in short, going to be great,' wrote Henry James in *The American Scene* (1907).

George Caleb Bingham (1811–79), *Fur Traders Descending the Missouri*, **1845.**
Oil on canvas, 73.7 x 92.7 cm. Metropolitan Museum of Art, New York.

This emblematic image refers to trade, settlement, the nation's north–south axis – the Missouri and Mississippi Rivers – and the issue of race. The artist called it 'French-Trader – Half Breed Son' to emphasize its racial theme. It is one of many masterpieces reflecting the history of American painting on display in the Metropolitan Museum's American Wing, which opened in 1924.

Incoming president Pierpont Morgan (1904–13)[34] hired professional museum staff, such as Roger Fry and Dublin-born Sir Caspar Purdon Clarke. (Clarke's directorship of the museum, in 1905, saw him draw on his background at the South Kensington Museum.[35]). Kent, who trained as a librarian, was appointed supervisor of museum instruction in 1907 and he expanded the museum's education services in all directions (influenced by Boston's Museum of Fine Arts): 'The main idea developed by Mr. Kent of the Metropolitan Museum was to discover in what way museums might be made more serviceable to those teaching art', an idea that gained the attention of the director of Dublin's Museum of Science and Art.[36]

By 1923 *The New York Times* stated that the Metropolitan Museum and American Museum of Natural History had 'become some of the city's greatest educational forces'. The Metropolitan Museum opened its American Wing in 1924, becoming the first major museum to initiate collections in American decorative arts and providing a resource for the public to learn about early Americans and their historic houses.[37] In 1921 visitor numbers passed the one million mark (second only to the Louvre in Paris). The museum was open freely to members, schoolchildren and teachers (a 35 cent charge was imposed on Mondays and Fridays), while free concerts (started as a wartime experiment) attracted crowds on Saturday evenings:

> It is not a private gallery for the use of our Trustees and members. It is a public gallery for the use of all the people, high and low, and even more for the low than for the high, for the high can find artistic inspiration in their own homes.[38]

The Inter-War Period and the American Museum

During the First World War, as museums in America began to develop training to ensure the professionalism of museum staff, curatorial responsibilities for acquiring and arranging works of art, together with the role of conservation, were separated from the task of public interpretation (a pattern that was replicated in Britain). A priority during this period was the determination of American institutions to match the holdings of some of the major European museums. They set about this in a business-like fashion, drawing on their highly qualified curators, scholars and directors to seek out the finest works available. This created an imbalance between the goals of collecting and interpretation due to the structure of the museum, whereby directors and curators were following a European model with academic standards, while educators were left dealing with a public audience seeking knowledge. Thus educators and docents worked with the growing numbers of visitors, while curators, who had trained at the universities, focused on the collections.

There followed a changing pattern in the presentation and display of works of art. Paintings were reduced to hang in a single row, under controlled electric lighting and in more spacious galleries, so the works of art could be appreciated more easily. This pattern was confirmed by a series of visitor behaviour study patterns in the 1920s and 1930s, which revealed that the denser two- and three-tier hanging systems in the older museums caused distraction and visitor fatigue.

After the First World War, museums in America began to be seen as an educational force that could make a distinct contribution to the cultural life of the community. Museums were viewed as places that might provide greater access to learning for the wider public. Issues that impacted on this process included the introduction of free, compulsory, universal education, together with extending the school age and increasing the subject range available in schools. Another aspect was the development of new teaching methods that required a psychological understanding of the child and his/her learning abilities together with these new educational methods requiring a philosophy.[39] While museum professionals had set up the American Association of Museums (AAM) in 1905, they began to look at the area of training programmes, such as curatorial courses at Pennsylvania in 1908, together with new museum studies programmes provided by figures like Paul Sachs, Dana and Brown Goode, until formal training began in the 1970s.[40]

America's Specialized Museums and Modernism

During the 1920s and 1930s, more specialized art museums began to appear, such as the Museum of Modern Art (MoMA), New York in 1929 and the National Gallery of Art, Washington, DC in 1937. The origins of the National Gallery of Art lay with a collection of paintings provided by Andrew Mellon, who paid for and directed the creation of a museum that became a symbol

Changing patterns in the display of collections

An illustration of the traditional hanging system at the Louvre, followed by a reorganization in the 1930s, resulting in a reduced number of works hung at eye level on a plain background.

of the nation's cultural wealth.[41] The more influential MoMA is an example of a modern museum, whose importance lay in focusing attention for the first time on American and modern art.[42] The Armory Show in 1913 provided the catalyst, whereby modern European art, which dominated, was displayed alongside American avant-garde art (to audiences ignorant of European culture and American art).[43] The Armory Show heralded the arrival of the new collector of modern art, starting America's massive institutionalization of modernism after 1950, as MoMA began to create awareness of contemporary artistic expression through displays, major exhibitions, modern design and technological developments.[44]

The United States started to become the front-runner in museum development, as the number of museums rose from 600 in 1914 to 2,500 in 1939, with fifty million people visiting museums in 1944 and availing of 'conducted tours, lectures and museum clubs'.[45] New 'period rooms' that placed paintings in the context of furniture, fittings, glassware, etc. included the Japanese Court and Decorative Arts Wing at Boston Museum of Fine Arts;

the American Wing of the Metropolitan Museum; and the English and American period rooms at the Pennsylvania Museum of Art in Philadelphia. The open-air Museum of Colonial Williamsburg in

Alfred Barr, photographed by Jay Leyda (1910–88)

Alfred Barr spent nearly his entire professional career with the Museum of Modern Art (MoMA), in New York. Considered an inspirational figure, he developed a pivotal role in acquainting American audiences with the modernist movement in art in the early twentieth century.

Virginia (founded in 1934) enabled visitors to re-create early eighteenth-century American life, emulated at Ford's Museum of Industrial and Domestic Arts and at the Edison Institute at Greenfield Village.[46]

The 1930s saw the expansion of programmes as museums became aware that they needed to make contact with people outside the building (a practice known as 'outreach'), motivated in large part by social pressures arising from the Great Depression in 1929 and subsequent years. During the Chicago Century of Progress International Exposition (1933–4), the Art Institute of Chicago held a major exhibition, 'the finest art exhibition ever held in America',[47] which was attended by three million visitors.[48] When Daniel Catton Rich became director of the Art Institute in 1938,[49] he made education one of his priorities and called on the architect Ludwig Mies van der Rohe to help redesign the children's museum into a Gallery of Art Interpretation in 1940, 'to give children and adults a clearer understanding of different artists and their various means of artistic expression'.[50] This centre revolutionized education at the Art Institute, served as a national model of progressive programming and became the first interpretive space for adults established by an American museum. In 1943 Katharine Kuh organized its exhibitions in a modern, minimalist design, hung asymmetrically, juxtaposing media and objects, photography, 3D designs and new typeface – using simple labels asking the public to consider how artists came to make their decisions.[51]

Britain: The Second World War and its Aftermath

By the time the Second World War broke out, museum provision in Britain was generally understood to mean guides for adults in the national museums and school tours and school loan services in provincial museums. Most museums had reduced the number of their collections on display through use of a simpler form of hanging and presentation (as outlined above). They were beginning to take account of the public's need to understand and appreciate the collections. Pioneering developments that took place during wartime included the Glasgow Schools Museum Service (1941), whose innovative range of services had a long-term value.[52]

During wartime, the British Museum closed and the collections were

Georges Seurat (1859–91), *A Sunday on La Grande Jatte*, 1884–6.
Oil on canvas, 207.5 x 308 cm. Art Institute of Chicago.

This enormous canvas depicts city dwellers gathered at a park on *La Grande Jatte*, an island on the River Seine, where people stroll, lounge, sail and fish. A popular work, often considered to reflect the growing middle classes at leisure, it was acquired in 1926, since when it has become one of the Art Institute of Chicago's most iconic images.

placed in storage for the duration of the conflict. The building was more bomb-scarred than most other museums and did not physically recover until the 1960s/1970s. Some confusion developed as to the differences between the collections of the British Museum and those of the V&A: the distinction between 'art' (for the education of artists and craftsmen) and 'archaeology' or 'history' (the resort of collectors, connoisseurs and antiquaries) was still current in 1927.[53] John Pope Hennessy (director of the V&A, then of the British Museum) described the V&A as a museum that 'concentrated on works of art'.[54] However, the British Museum's Department of British and Medieval Antiquities was later subdivided as an historical collection in 1969, and a modern collection established in 1979 (overlapping with V&A decorative arts collections),[55] resulting in the two museum collections complementing one another.[56]

The National Gallery evacuated its collections during the war years to a slate quarry in Wales,[57] which made painfully evident the lack of cultural

War damage at the British Museum, 1941

The dark days of the blitz in the 1940s were of enormous concern to British museums. Many museums were damaged – for example, the Central Saloon of the British Museum was completely destroyed during a bombing raid in 1941. Due to the major effects of the Second World War, the museum did not physically recover until the 1960s/1970s.

facilities in London at that time. Thus, when the trustees announced the acquisition of Rembrandt's *Portrait of Margaretha de Geer, Wife of Jacob Trip* (*c*.1661), a letter appeared in *The Times* in 1942 asking for the picture to be shown to the public.[58] The gallery launched a 'Picture of the Month' display, allowing the public 'the delight and refreshment which the sight of a great picture would give'.[59] This initiative was complemented by concerts performed by the pianist Dame Myra Hess, making the gallery a popular haven throughout the war period. The return of the collection after the war raised the issue of environmental conditions, the outcome of which was the establishment of a Conservation Department in 1946 (a scientific adviser had been appointed in 1934). A 'controversy' that arose over the 'newly restored' paintings was featured in *The Times* and the *Burlington Magazine*.[60]

In 1946 the *Visual Arts Report* recorded that museum attendances had dropped by 25 per cent over twenty years in Britain, and recommended that attendance figures could be improved if the directors and staff paid more attention to attracting and educating the public and less attention to 'the specialist needs of students and connoisseurs'.[61] Museums became aware of the need to provide services for the public, especially young people, although by the 1950s only a small number of specialist education staff were employed by museums. Loan services were set up in many parts of England, and in 1948 the National Museum of Wales set up a schools service, through which staff learned how to teach children (as in other museums). In another example, Clarke Hall Educational Museum in Wakefield, a restored period house, used teachers to act the role of seventeenth-century people in order to bring the past to life for schoolchildren and children with special needs.[62]

America: The Second World War and its Aftermath

During the Second World War the Metropolitan Museum of Art, under the directorship of Francis Henry Taylor (1940–55), placed its 1,500 major art treasures in storage.[63] In their absence exhibitions were held, such as *The Art of Rembrandt*, the plaster casts were reinstalled to provide a natural drawing academy and a Junior Museum was created in 1941. In 1944 the museum initiated a series of major shows facilitated by European museums, which loaned their treasures for exhibitions that travelled to the National Gallery in Washington, the Metropolitan in New York and other museums.[64] This attracted visitors who would not have set foot in an art museum before the war, causing *Life* magazine to begin reporting 'fine art' news (1947) – creating a new public for art in America and establishing Taylor as the leading museum director. The Metropolitan set up a Department of American Art that held exhibitions, including *American Painting Today*, at precisely the time New York artists were forging a native abstract expressionism style that gained an international influence.[65] Taylor set up links outside America, too, and was received by the director of the National Gallery of Ireland on a visit to Dublin in 1956.[66]

After the war American museums looked to Theodore Law's report, *The Museum as a Social Instrument*, for new ways to engage the community.[67] (A similar British report had encouraged museums to better serve their visitors.[68])

During the war the National Gallery in London wanted to play a part in the cultural life of the capital and placed one painting a month on display, the first featuring Pieter de Hooch (1660-1), *Courtyard of a House in Delft*, with over 15,000 members of the public viewing the work in June 1942.

While museums were involved in gathering, preserving, displaying and studying their collections, some declared a prime responsibility to their collections, not to their visitors. Despite this, there was an increasing emphasis on the learning context of the collections. Enthusiasm in this direction, however, got lost as the Cold War period of the late 1940s intervened and America swung towards the civil rights movement of the 1950s.

In 1949 Alma Wittlin's survey, *The Museum: Its History and its Tasks in Education*, suggested that learning in museums might be explored by using exhibitions more proactively, by finding new ways of conveying information and of explaining the context of original objects to people within the museum environment. While art museums continued collecting the finest original masterpieces they could afford, there emerged an awareness of the need to try to understand the mindset of the visitor, to train museum professionals and to explore outreach projects with a wider community.[69] The concepts of Jean Piaget (1896–1980) and his followers, 'play is the work of the child', began to influence American museum practitioners, encouraging teachers to move towards 'discovery learning'. The reality, though, was that art museums tended to be monopolized by educated people and a new approach would have to be found to attract wider audiences.[70]

British Museums in the Modern Era

In the 1960s museums in Britain started to become more specialized, drawing on different kinds of staff, including designers, press officers and marketing people. Various reports charted the development of services in museums.[71] The establishment of the Arts Council of Great Britain[72] coincided with the debate about modern art that led to the opening of contemporary art galleries and Tate Britain satellites at St Ives and Liverpool.[73] While the Rosse Report, *Provincial Museums and Galleries* (1963), pointed out the need for curatorial work, conservation and education services, there was an uneven growth of services, with exhibition and education officers appointed only to the national museums. The Wright Report (1973) suggested the involvement of education officers in exhibitions, publications and communications, placed on an equal footing to other museum departments.[74] A number of figures carrying out innovative work included Molly Harrison at the Geffrye Museum in London,[75] Rene Marcouse at the V&A,[76] and Barbara Winstanley in museums in Derbyshire.[77]

During the directorship of Elizabeth Esteve-Coll, the V&A resumed its associations with art and design education, the Design Museum, the Design Council and the Crafts Council. Coll pointed out that curatorial roles had been separated from their educational purpose and she called for an action plan to return learning as a core museum function.[78] Considered a landmark document in Britain, *A Commonwealth: Museums in the Learning Age* (first edition 1997, reprinted 1999), by David Anderson, reviewed the activities of 2,500 national, local and independent voluntary museums in the United Kingdom and identified ways in which formal and informal learning could be developed.[79] Its implications in the wider field of lifelong learning became evident. Quoting Kierkegaard, 'Life can only be understood backwards, but be lived forwards', Anderson pointed out that museums were places where people could enjoy themselves through learning.

There followed a government Green Paper, *The Learning Age*, that pulled together the strands of formal and informal learning.[80] Museums began to reach out to wider communities by using experienced staff and expanding their range of services, informed by audience surveys, market research and evaluations.[81] *Opening Doors: Learning in the Historic Environment* (2004) identified formal and informal learning opportunities at historic sites in the United Kingdom and Ireland.[82] The Department of Culture, Media and Sport developed a code of practice on access to museums, funded the Area Museum

The Guggenheim Museum, New York, 1959

Designed by American architect Frank Lloyd Wright (1867–1959), this museum became one of the twentieth century's most important architectural landmarks. Lloyd Wright developed his design for the museum as far as it could go, and this view shows the interior skylight with the curving staircase and walls.

Councils, an International Technology Challenge fund and the 24-hour museum.[83] *Culture, Creativity and the Young: Developing Public Policy* (1999) focused on the creative development of young people within Europe.[84] Government investment in regional English museums emerged as an integrated system of hubs called 'Renaissance in the Regions' (including national museums). In addition to focusing on public services, care of the collection came under attention. An example of a museum that used the collections to create an awareness about science is the National Gallery, which devised exhibitions called *Art in the Making*, which investigated pictures so that audiences could find out about the physical nature of a work, its technique, function, and history.[85] *Making & Meaning* focused on the Wilton Diptych, 'the greatest painting to survive from fourteenth-century England', by promoting different ways of looking at and understanding pictures.[86] The two years' work to clean and study the diptych (including analysing the paint structure) revealed a combination of northern European and Italian methods of panel painting.[87] Exhibitions such as *Making & Meaning* were accompanied by catalogues and videos and promoted by educators skilled at explaining the wider context of works of art.[88]

A key development of the 1990s was the opening of the Sainsbury Wing at the National Gallery (which aroused controversy over the designs for the building), incorporating major exhibition galleries, retail and associated facilities.[89] By this time the building of extensions had changed from the provision of space for the permanent collection to the creation of areas for temporary exhibitions, catering and retail. It raised the issue of whether museums could remain popular without shifting the approach from art to commerce and spectacle. (Many of the techniques employed in the temporary-loan exhibitions drew their example from developments in retail.)

Attendances at the National Gallery increased, aided by a series of publications,[90] videos of its exhibitions and collaboration with the BBC in programmes presented by the director. Visitors also had the opportunity of seeing the recently discovered Caravaggio, *The Taking of Christ*, on loan from the National Gallery of Ireland. It was a time of prosperity for the museum institutions: the National Gallery was thriving; the British Museum was eagerly awaiting delivery of its new Great Court; and other innovative building programmes, such as the impressive Tate Modern at Bankside, were moving towards their much-publicized openings.

American Museums in the Modern Era

During the politically radical and socially conscious 1960s and 1970s, concerns were raised regarding the function and philosophy of American museums, with accusations that museums did not cater for the wider community (for example, ethnic minorities, immigrants, people with disabilities and special needs, and the educationally disadvantaged).

The primary issue of public access caused protest and agitation both in the United States and in Europe, as articulated by sociologist Pierre Bourdeau, who, with Alain Darbel, wrote *The Love of Art*, in which they produced empirical data demonstrating that art museum visitors were consistently of the 'cultivated classes', due to education and upbringing. Bourdeau's critique resulted in protests against museums during the Paris uprisings in 1968, many of which were addressed by the opening of the popular Centre Pompidou in 1977. This period of protest and demonstration impacted on other areas of the museum, when groups queried the lack of democratization of museum personnel at all levels of museum life. This in turn provoked museums to look at the effectiveness of their exhibitions and interpretative services, and to call on education departments to restructure their activities. As museums grappled with managing public programmes and 'blockbuster' exhibitions, while maintaining standard functions of collecting and conserving, scholars started to query accepted artistic hierarchies, such as the preference for Western over non-Western art, painting over the decorative arts, that a 'masterpiece' could educate and transform viewers through its presence, and the social and cultural context in which art is made and understood. These organizing principles needed to be reassessed. It became increasingly clear that the role of the museum was both a repository of treasures and a public institution. Museums were entering an era of accountability, when visitors would matter as much as the permanent collection.

In America, the 1980s saw the exploration of visitor studies and surveys to see if greater insights could be gained into what impacted on visitor curiosity and learning; this emphasis on audience research and evaluation continues to this day. Demographic studies revealed that the social backgrounds of adult visitors reflected the educated, higher-level occupations and they were more likely to be engaged in local community and cultural activities than the general population, causing researchers to deduce that museum-visiting was a pattern of learned behaviour. Other researchers pointed out that poorly educated visitors required more effort to achieve 'museum literacy'. They were not programmed to seek it from youth, differed in the way in which they understood information and benefited from explanatory material. Research revealed that museum visitors were consumers, people who guarded their decreasing free time carefully, but who were prepared to spend time and money on leisure activities. C.G. Screven, a University of Wisconsin psychologist, looked at strategies to increase visitor interaction and feed-back.[91] Howard Gardner's multiple intelligence theory (1983) suggested seven ways people engage in thinking, each of which described a unique

The Wilton Diptych (*c.*1395-9) was the centre of a *Making & Meaning* exhibition that explored the technical and conservation aspects of works of art. The aim of these exhibitions was to demonstrate how understanding and appreciating a picture could be helped by knowledge of how it was made.

cognitive style for understanding the world.[92] Gardner advocated the museum's informal environment and apprenticeship method of learning as more relevant to modern children than the formal models of school.[93] An outcome of the surveying process was a new awareness that the public was increasingly viewing museums and their collections as part of the modern search for authenticity.[94]

The economic boom of the 1990s and the desire to be at the forefront of architectural innovation encouraged museums to erect new, multimillion-dollar structures.⁹⁵ It also focused attention on the museum's role in the provision of entertainment, leisure and commerce, as well as being places of aesthetic experience and learning.⁹⁶ A series of reports identified museum practices and associated learning functions, providing educators with professional recognition in a field where the curator had traditionally been the dominant 'professional'.⁹⁷ The AAM's publication *Excellence and Equity: Education and the Public Dimension of Museums* (1992) argued for a stronger public role for museums, explaining that learning was a 'museum-wide endeavour' involving all members of staff.⁹⁸ This resulted in museum curators and educators working together to create exhibitions that would be better understood by the public.

   Museums: Places of Learning (1998), by George Hein and Mary Alexander, provided a comprehensive survey of the educational contribution of museums within society.⁹⁹ Dewey suggested that museum education required a

Crowds queue to view the *Mona Lisa* at the National Gallery of Art, Washington, DC. In 1963 the Louvre loaned the *Mona Lisa* to the United States. When it was shown at the National Gallery of Art in Washington it drew two million people. This phenomenon, together with Thomas Hoving's major shows at the Metropolitan Museum of Art, New York, in the late 1960s, were the first of the blockbuster exhibitions.

well-considered philosophy, in the belief that while all genuine education comes from experience, that does not mean that 'all experiences are genuinely or equally educative'.[100] Hein and Alexander stated that an educational theory required a theory of knowledge (an epistemology), a theory of learning, and a theory of teaching (a pedagogy), all based on questions critical to the purpose and practice of museum learning. They concluded that museums could excel in object-based, experiential, thought-provoking, problem-solving types of learning, could offer visitors profound, even life-changing experiences and were capable of making a substantial contribution to the broad enterprise of lifelong learning.[101]

One of the legacies of the 1970s was the blockbuster exhibition – a temporary exhibition that had become a way of life for most museums, as it brought in both visitors and money. The problem with these exhibitions was that they required substantial ongoing work by a range of staff to provide a steady stream of special shows, in addition to which these events required ancillary services, such as exhibition desks, sales outlets, cafés, cloakrooms and toilets. As a further extension of this, museums embarked on major building programmes to house all these services. In the process, the buildings became star architectural attractions in their own right. While this produced the desired outcome, that is increased numbers, what has become less clear is whether these swelling numbers continue to come from an educated and affluent class, leaving museums with the same problem of reaching the disadvantaged.

Overview: Patterns in the Public Role of Museums

Museums and galleries in Britain and the United States have a particular role in the political and social life of their communities. Their disposition to access and learning developments is the outcome of the educational function appearing as a major aspiration in British museums and in the constitution of American museums. However, the pattern of development in museums worldwide is broader than just learning and access.

Emerging trends in the latter part of the century took into account new methods of display of the collections, which involve a more specifically historical and cultural context, together with the presentation of works of art in a contextual environment of period galleries and rooms. Architecture

Treasures from Tutankhamun, Metroplitan Museum of Art, 1976-9. This type of major touring exhibition, which was viewed by 8.25 million people in the United States, involved very careful design and labelling of the exhibits, security and directional signage for visitors, and it introduced new practices, such as advanced sales and timed tickets.

has become significant in the concept of new museums, a trend that began with the Guggenheim Museum in New York, which opened in 1959. Some of the designs of the new museums, such as I.M. Pei's reconfiguration of the Louvre (opened in 1989), have taken into account the major role of retail and catering facilities in the modern institution. Museum visitors today expect special exhibitions and associated amenities because visits should involve pleasure as well as enlightenment. The opening of the Guggenheim Museum, Bilbao, in 1997 reflected a growing sophistication not just of architectural conception but of the place of the museum in the life of the city. Major exhibitions are now part of a planning exercise that employs skilled designers and the careful selection and presentation of works of art. This process includes publications, education programmes, audio guides and information technology, in association with retail, promotion and catering opportunities. The growing sophistication of planning requires museum services to be capable of catering for visitors of all ages. Museums are continuing to enjoy public and private support due to the priority given to tourism in the economy of major cities, where frequently it is the largest single industry.

Information is another growth area of the modern era. Visitors to museums on both sides of the Atlantic expect the extensive range of services that are now a standard part of the operation, including information/welcome desks, websites listing activities, posters and brochures, programmes including lectures, tours and audio guides, advertisements and promotions on television and radio, cafés and shops. The new digital world of multimedia, mobile phones and social networking has made significant inroads into the way museums view access to the physical and the virtual museum.

The issue in the United States is that Americans as a people are more accustomed to paying attention to the developing nature of society, which is decentralizing, with immigrants no longer congregating in cities but in small communities (one million people emigrate to the United States every year), although it is notably the museums of science and technology that are increasing their immigrant visitor numbers. The museum, which is like a small multicultural world, tends to be a city institution and as people build new communities, they build new museums. Thus, museums are adept at outreach programmes that engage new communities in the collections, with every effort made to encourage inreach towards a museum visit. It is in their observation of the changing nature of communities that American museums have become aware of the huge multiplicity of cultures residing in the United States and the need to devise programmes to meet the needs of this growing sector. American museums are good at reviewing and examining the service they provide to the public. They are aware that museums are part of a society with 'rising expectations': popular, because there is a universal human need for a personal experience with something higher than everyday life, which for many people is provided by the museum; attractive, because it is the focus of social occasions, providing an experience that can be shared with families, friends and other visitors; educational, because it appeals to visitors seeking to make sense of their world, providing them with the freedom of movement to interpret the objects in their own way and enabling a personal dimension through learning opportunities in the museum.

As museums approached the new millennium it became clear that a new definition of the 'museum' would be required due to the worldwide proliferation of new forms of the institution – technical, ecological, ethnographical, scientific, image-based, sound-based, etc. The current ICOM

I.M.Pei's pyramid design for the Louvre, Paris, which was unveiled in 1989

The reconfiguration of the Louvre in the 1980s, centred on E.M. Pei's glass and steel Pyramid (housing retail, catering and museum services), which captured the public imagination and has since become synonymous with the Louvre

definition is under review,[102] just as the term 'living museum' needs to include a wider definition of 'object', involving more bodies, such as botanical gardens, zoos or aquaria, if a living plant, fish or an animal is to be described as an 'object' in a museum.[103] A museum is essentially an institution in which objects are the principal means of communication, and museum practitioners have tried to make this understandable: 'Establishments in which objects are not used at all, or are not used as main carriers of messages, are not museums, whatever their qualities may be otherwise ... objects remain the stars of the cast.'[104] Thus the concept of what a museum was in 1706 – 'A study or library; also a college or public place for the resort of learned men'[105] – has undergone radical change globally:

> The American museum was and is an idea. The European museum was a fact. Almost without exception the European museum was first a collection. With few exceptions most American museums were first an ideal ... Almost without exception the larger American museums began with a deliberate appeal to the public. Most of the earlier European museums remained semi-exclusive cabinets of curiosities visible only to a few. The American museum began, and has remained, wide open.[106]

Stephen Jay Gould, Harvard's noted palaeontologist, was clear in his understanding: 'Museums exist to display authentic objects of nature and culture – yes they must teach and include all manner of computer graphics to aid in this worthy effort; but they must remain wed to authenticity … authenticity stirs the human soul.'[107]

The goal of the National Gallery, London, 'to show the finest art made anywhere in the world', uses scholarship to make the collection accessible, while remaining faithful to its nineteenth-century ethos of looking at works of art as being instructive as well as enjoyable.[108] These observations form part of a growing commentary on the critical function of art museums.[109] Eilean Hooper-Greenhill, Leicester University's well-known educator, advocated the 'disciplinary museum', feeling that the art museum served a well-informed audience but could provide for a wider public.[110] The Metropolitan Museum of Art aspires for an intuitive, aesthetic appreciation of works of art, so that visitors know that the objects they have come to see are authentic. In the meantime, its retail outlets sell the finest of reproductions of its masterpiece works. The British Museum aims to illuminate and explain the past of the whole world through its material culture: 'When Sir Hans Sloane set up the Museum he gathered the objects to help one think, as tools for a philosopher.'[111]

Colin Trodd, an art historian at the University of Manchester, summarized the discussion, 'identifying the processes that generate a sense of value from the experience of being in the art museum', by drawing on Michel Foucault's notion of competing interests and forces producing contradictory meanings, which he suggests 'reveals the heterotopic nature of the art museum', as it absorbs past traditions and makes provision for new ways of using the museum.[112]

Museums often refer to visitors, their experiences within the museum environment and the needs of the public as though it was a generalised abstract concept, whereas in reality every person's experience of the museum is different.

> There is no such thing as 'the typical visitor', and there is no single level which can be expected and then addressed. The museum has to cater for increasingly fragmented publics who

want to learn and do different things at different speeds. Further, the body of knowledge that could be imparted in museum displays is continuing to grow, and in certain instances it can be very complicated and even contradictory. For museum specialists who attempt to address the issue of imparting knowledge, their methods will be continually undermined by frustrating compromises which will rarely, if ever, be satisfactorily resolved. It is like trying to reach the horizon: however far one goes, the ultimate goal will always be beyond one's grasp.[113]

An Irish advocate of museums, Jeanne Sheehy, suggested that museums are flexible and that by their nature and diverse collections they have an ability to provide a broad range of experiences to the widest audience. American museum practitioner Danielle Rice formed a simple description of visitor interaction as 'pleasure through enlightenment', which is accomplished by treating learning in museums 'as a creative endeavor in its own right'.[114] Rice

The Guggenheim Museum, Bilbao, Spain, which opened in 1997. Urban planners often speak of the 'Bilbao effect' as an engine of urban renewal, economic expansion and local pride. They are referring to the success of Frank Gehry's innovative museum at Bilbao in northern Spain.

Exploring ancient ceramics from South America at the Art Institute of Chicago

A project 'Art Museums and Communities' (1980s) looked at visitors' needs and programmes for multicultural audiences. Labels were printed more clearly and the permanent collections were rearranged, which encouraged families to visit the ceramics galleries.

felt that this opened up many ways of 'thinking about art and the role of the museum as an educator' because it is a concept that is alive and ongoing.[115] The next generation of museum professionals will pose questions in new ways: 'if learning can be accidental and suffuses every moment of our lives, then all aspects of an experience can contribute to learning'.[116] Irish museum practitioners view ideas about access, engagement, learning and creativity as being the outcome of the visitor's own interaction with artefacts in the museum, having the possibility of being shared, exchanged and developed, thereby providing a fulfilling museum experience.[117] The idea that a number of ideologies, even contradictory ones, can exist at the same time fits in with the view that there is no neat definition of museums because their nature, role and collections are flexible and organic. Looking towards the next decades, the collections, as a source of pleasure and enlightenment, will continue to be an ever-changing part of the role of the public institution museum.

11

New Ideas and Fresh Initiatives: An Overview of Museum Development in the Twentieth Century

*Schools and school curricula have been described as instruments
for the creation of minds. We might also describe cultural institutions
such as museums, theatres and galleries as instruments for the
creation of experiences.*[1]

The twentieth century proved to be one of mixed fortunes in Irish cultural
life. Irish museums entered a challenging period in the early part of the century,
facing diminished economic circumstances with a growing determination to
survive and succeed as the century progressed. This determination characterizes
Irish museums across the board; it has given rise to new ideas and fresh
initiatives that have had an impact on the national and international stage.
In order to appreciate these trends, this chapter will take a look at a broad
representative spectrum of Irish institutions: national museums, a city art
gallery and regional museums. A number have shared links – for instance, the
Ulster Museum in Belfast and the Crawford Municipal Art Gallery in Cork are
historic institutions that devolved from nineteenth-century initiatives and drew

John Hogan (1800–58), *Hibernia with the Bust of Lord Cloncurry*, 1844
Marble, 148 cm high. UCD Art Collection.

This sculpture depicts Hibernia (Ireland) with a coronet and laurel leaves, seated on a chair of antique design, with a harp by her side, and at her feet an Irish wolfhound, some books, a scroll and an inverted crown decorated with shamrock. She has her arms around a bust of Valentine Lawless, Lord Cloncurry, a patron of the arts and Irish patriot.

their sustenance from the local community. Others have similar origins, such as the Chester Beatty Library in Dublin (a museum in the fullest sense of the word) and the Hunt Museum in Limerick, both of which owe their existence to private benefaction. In the case of the two Dublin modern art galleries, the Hugh Lane Municipal Gallery of Modern Art opened at the beginning of the twentieth century, while the Irish Museum of Modern Art emerged at the century's end. These six diverse museums, each with its own distinctive character, represent the best cross-section of the Irish museum world, which is why they have been chosen here to provide an overview of Irish museum developments in the twentieth century.

Ireland's heritage institutions provide a range of experiences, both historical and contemporary, that are recognized today as being of immense cultural, educational and economic value. However, the realities that shaped decision-makers in the 1960s, 1970s and up to the 1980s came from a view that saw visiting museums, galleries and historical sites as a minority pursuit, marginal to public policy and Irish life. This was set to alter in the 1990s, along with wholesale changes across Irish society in general.

In 1990 Ireland elected its first woman president, Mary Robinson, for a seven-year term, and she quickly became an effective instrument for change, introducing a cultural sphere into her work and in the process identifying and embracing, for the first time, Ireland's diaspora. Robinson was associated with a fresh new spirit in Irish life that had been diminished for half a century.

She engendered a sense of self-confidence that heralded a more positive out-look, and in so doing enabled ordinary citizens to feel that their participation in society was a real resource. The 1990s also witnessed a 'Heritage Boom' that coincided with a period of growth in the United States and Europe, resulting in the setting up of a number of new museums and galleries in Ireland. Many of these received financial aid from the EU, with grants totalling €185 million made available from the European Regional Development Fund (ERDF) and European Social Funds from 1989, with '40% of the ERDF funding allocated to historical and cultural tourism products', which impacted significantly on cultural heritage venues.[2] The establishment of an arts department (Department of Arts, Heritage and the Gaeltacht) with a dedicated cabinet minister helped to bring culture and the arts in from the margins of public policy. These factors, combined with the strategic planning, work and ambition of the cultural institutions, delivered a genuine return on the investment. Thus the decade that included the Robinson era (1990–7) progressed from economic difficulty to prosperity within a process of secu-larization that witnessed a decline in the authority of the Catholic Church. Alongside this, a muted peace in Northern Ireland led to the long-awaited outcome of the Good Friday Agreement (1998).

Mary McAleese's succession as president in 1997 witnessed her popular championing of many causes, including heritage, local communities and young entrepreneurial initiatives, which served to articulate the upbeat mood of the time. As the country strode towards the new millennium, the arrival of large numbers of immigrants would raise the issue of national identity leading towards a concept of identities that could aspire to reflect a broader view of who we are, 'in relations of persons to one another'. Robinson and McAleese travelled overseas promoting Ireland's heritage and connecting with the Irish diaspora, while at home they drew the nation's attention to the wider concerns of society. Thus, the latter half of the century witnessed a reversal of earlier attitudes, due not only to social and economic changes, but also to education and an increased awareness of the importance of the cultural sector in Irish society. While the situation in Northern Ireland was more complex, due to patterns of community division and conflict that have had a long-lasting effect on social cohesion and integration, the process of readjustment following peace did result in investment and regrowth.

Belfast Municipal Museum and Art Gallery, 1929

This image of the new museum shows an impressive building, viewed facing on to Stranmillis Road. The entrance is on the north side facing out on to the Botanic Gardens. The photograph is reproduced in *Belfast Municipal Museum and Art Gallery Souvenir of the Opening by His Grace the Governor of Northern Ireland, the Duke of Abercorn, on 22 October 1929.*

The Ulster Museum, Belfast (1961)

The story of Belfast's first Municipal Art Gallery and Museum was addressed in Chapter 5, but here the story is taken up in the twentieth century as the museum goes through several reconfigurations to become Belfast Museum and Art Gallery in 1929, then the Ulster Museum in 1961, before finally coming under the aegis of the umbrella organization Museums and Galleries of Northern Ireland (MAGNI) in 1998. The story takes place in challenging times.

When Arthur Deane served as curator of the Belfast Municipal Art Gallery and Museum between 1905 and 1942, it was located at Royal Avenue and opened six days a week (closed Sundays), with free admission.[3] Like his predecessors, Deane was keen to develop the pedagogical role of the collections. In 1910 the scientific and antiquarian holdings, geology, zoology and botany collections of the Belfast Natural History Museum, 'Ireland's first museum built by voluntary subscription' (1831),[4] were brought under the care of Belfast Corporation, as part of a plan to have one museum to house all of the collections.[5]

In 1912, a site was acquired to this end, but due to the intervention of the First World War the foundation stone was not laid until 1924.[6] In 1919 the museum held a touring exhibition of children's art organized by Franz Cizek of Children's Art, Austria.[7] The Art Gallery and Museum Committee, having developed an acquisition policy in 1910, acquired a collection that was transferred to the new museum building in 1928. In 1929 the Belfast Municipal Museum and Art Gallery at Botanic Gardens, on Stranmillis Road, was officially opened by the governor general, the Duke of Abercorn. A local newspaper prophesied that 'this Museum will be an Ulster Museum and as such will be the mother of many smaller ones throughout the province'.[8]

Deane drew attention to the pedagogical context of the collections by providing staff to act as guides/lecturers (following the pattern at the British Museum), catering not just for the public but for specialist groups, such as students of art and geology as well as 'parties of Ministry of Labour juvenile trainees'.[9] Museum events included educational films, an excavation programme (1933), weekly winter lecture schedules and concerts held in conjunction with the BBC up to 1934. As a result of the threat posed by the Second World War, staff evacuated parts of the collection to strong rooms and stores outside the city, in areas considered safe from bombing. Despite the blackout forcing a reduction of winter opening hours (Sunday opening was not agreed until 1948), afternoon public talks and film shows were held and extra-mural lectures were provided for armed services personnel in Belfast and some provincial areas.[10] During the war, the museum organized exhibitions, used Ministry of Information touring shows and drew on Irish art exhibitions provided by the Council for the Encouragement of Music and the Arts (CEMA) in 1943.[11]

Deane's successor, Sidney Stendall (1942–53), devised a strategy for the museum in 1943 that included a schools organizer, guide lecturer and student library.[12] A *Children's Art* exhibition organized by the Ulster Academy of Arts encouraged large numbers of children to attend the Christmas talks and film shows.[13] The adoption of Stendall's 1947 report resulted in Elizabeth Fulton's appointment as the first schools organizer and guide lecturer (the first woman appointed to a professional post at the museum).[14] Hundreds of tours of the collections were provided, relieving 'other members of staff who were previously called upon to carry out this important work'.[15] Clare MacMahon took over in 1948, organizing courses and regular visits by classes from intermediate schools in the city.[16] The 'Schools Service' noted that 10,694 children had visited from the city's intermediate schools, with 9,147 receiving tuition on 362 lesson-tours in 1951.[17] Loan collections in portable cases were also circulated.[18]

In 1958, following the establishment of the Ulster Folk Museum,[19] an Ulster Transport Museum was set up in 1962, and in 1973 the two museums

John Luke (1906–75), *The Three Dancers,* **1945**
Oil, tempera on canvas on board, 30.7 x 43 cm. No. UM 1919

This work is an example of Luke's highly stylized and precise technique. The Belfast-born artist became absorbed in experimenting with a variety of techniques in the 1940s. He described *The Three Dancers* to the keeper of art in the Belfast Municipal Museum and Art Gallery as a piece of craftsmanship in which he practically reached 'the limits of his knowledge'.

merged as the Ulster Folk and Transport Museum.[20] In the meantime, the early development of fine art at the Belfast Municipal Museum and Art Gallery can be dated to John Hewitt, who was succeeded as keeper of art in 1957 by Anne Crookshank: these two figures were pivotal in laying down the foundations of the fine art collection. In 1959 the museum acquired an assistant keeper of natural history and a schools organizer.

Ownership of the institution changed when the Museum Act (Northern Ireland) 1961 was enacted, establishing the museum as a national institution called the Ulster Museum, with its own Board of Trustees.[21] The museum had, in effect, been a 'national museum' since inception, having had the same status as the natural history museums of England, Scotland and Wales.[22] The museum continued to acquire and display new acquisitions and staff encouraged schools to study its local collections.[23] In 1963 the Ulster Museum bye-laws came into effect. In 1966 a foundation stone was laid for a gallery that its founders hoped would place Northern Ireland on a truly national level.[24]

Then in 1968, other events conspired against progress. Protests and violence broke out in Northern Ireland, escalating into civil strife in the 1970s. During this turbulent period the new director, Alan Warhurst (1970–7), oversaw the opening of the new Ulster Museum extension in 1972,[25] reaffirming that 'the museum should be used … particularly by the young'.[26] A highlight of the new display was an exhibition of the museum's fine collection of superb jewellery, gold and silver coins, navigational instruments and a cannon that had been acquired from the *Girona*, one of the ships in the ill-fated Spanish Armada fleet.[27] The following year the Ulster Museum undertook responsibility for Armagh County Museum.[28] In 1976, Ian Vincent was appointed the first education officer (following the pattern in Britain and at the National Gallery and National Museum in Dublin). Vincent sought to demonstrate how the collections could be used as a resource inside and outside the museum, for student teachers and teachers on in-service courses.

Alan McCutcheon's term as director (1977–83) was marked by deepening unrest in the North that continued into the tenure of his successor, John Nolan,[29] when the Hunger Strikes and other events conspired to create an unstable environment that threatened to transform the northern problem into an all-Ireland one. It became increasingly obvious that the situation in the North would have to become a preoccupation of the political class in Ireland. This eventually led to the political interventions of the late 1990s. The political unrest had its own impact on cultural sites and presented a challenge for the museum to keep above the fray and provide alternatives to civic strife.

Nolan's educational background formed the catalyst to support new approaches to the area of learning in museums. It motivated him to find ways to engage the public and he used every opportunity to promote the collections. He encouraged interaction by young people, 'demonstrating not only successful teaching and learning, but most of all, joyous creativity'.[30] Facing similar recessionary challenges as Dublin's National Gallery, he realized that the museum would have to create much-needed resources.[31] A particular interest for him was the development of an education service. In 1980 the museum's new education officer, Sheela Speers, devised an Education Policy and Service that encouraged museum educators to act as advocates for new audiences by 'actively promoting public understanding of the work of the institution: collection, conservation, scholarship, presentation and interpretation'.[32] This was developed by a Learning and Access Policy that was underpinned by a series of values that placed education at the heart of the Museum.[33]

The wide-ranging collections of the Ulster Museum included: Irish archaeology and historical material, artefacts from Egyptian and classical cultures, the Armada artefacts, natural science and ethnographic specimens, and significant holdings of fine and applied art from the seventeenth century to the contemporary. (The fine art collections warranted an art gallery of their own.) The art curators provided a regular programme of temporary and permanent displays that drew on the work of major Northern Irish artists, such as Paul Henry (1877–1958), Sir John Lavery (1856–1941) and Gerard Dillon (1916–71). Exhibitions were also rotated among other areas, such as natural sciences, archaeological material, costumes and ethnography, and curators regularly gave talks and met with the public. The Conservation Department was augmented by five conservators, who covered the natural sciences, organic materials, paintings and paper disciplines, as well as caring for the museum's other collections.

In the 1990s, changes led to the establishment of the Northern Ireland Museums Council (1993), which provided advisory and training services, grant aid and information.[34] In 1998 MAGNI was created as the body responsible for Northern Ireland's national collections, under new chief executive, Mike Houlihan.[35] In 1999 all of the cultural institutions were transferred to the Department of Culture, Arts and Leisure, strengthening the position of the museums and galleries in Northern Ireland.

The museum's head of education developed an innovative Science Discovery Bus Project that involved conversion of a coach into a mobile science education facility, which was made for use with children in socially disadvantaged areas of Belfast. Its sophisticated, hands-on design appealed to young people: 'it's like going into a spaceship'.[36] Careful thought went into devising projects that involved ways of learning that young people perceived as fun and that encouraged them to think of themselves as scientists. Schools selected themes that related to the science curriculum and then each theme was explored through projects that combined the use of museum specimens and scientific equipment. The fact that the project was mobile meant that the museum was in a position to access the targeted audience of particularly disadvantaged children. The Science Discovery Bus provided science education programmes for about 10,000 children and teachers in 1994. This achievement went some way towards making 'children feel valued' and encouraged visits to the museums.[37] It was one of many projects that won awards for the museum.

Activities for all ages as curators and educators interact with the Ulster Museums collections

This frieze of images shows museum staff engaging young people with the natural history, costume, geology and earth science collections.

For some time the Ulster Museum had been proactive in engaging the public with its collections within the context of a 'divided society', where museums were seen to offer a place of trust and reconciliation. When the Good Friday Agreement was signed by the British and Irish governments and key political northern parties, museum staff began to consider fresh ideas for exhibitions that might engage the public. Museum educators found themselves facing real challenges because separate education for Catholics and Protestant children was provided,[38] within a system of private and state-controlled public education that was non-discriminating but 'most certainly divisive'.[39]

The museum's fine art curators continued to mount temporary and permanent displays, some of which toured to the United States to bring awareness of the collections to American audiences. Two shows were mounted in collaboration with the Smithsonian Institution's Traveling Exhibition Service: *Portraits and Prospects: British and Irish Watercolours and Drawings* (1989); and *Dreams and Traditions: 300 Years of British and Irish Paintings from the Collections of the Ulster Museum* (1997).[40] Other exhibitions engaged the public in historical events, including: *Kings in Conflict* (1990);[41] *Up in Arms! The 1798 Rebellion in Ireland, a Bicentenary Exhibition* (1998);[42] and *War and Conflict in Twentieth Century Ireland* (a touring exhibition 1998). In 1998 curators worked with educators, who used the outreach programme and touring exhibition to communicate the message of *Up in Arms!* out to a wider audience and to make it an effective learning resource. The outreach officer devised a series of community-based projects and linked activities involving large numbers of community groups, which helped to relate the history exhibition to their lives.[43] The peace process helped in this regard and the community groups found the museum a safe haven in which to explore the historical exhibition. The learning context provided a 'common ground for the community in their own area to explore the continuing significance of the event',[44] assisting people, through discussion and workshops, to exchange ideas and experiences towards understanding something of their shared yet diverse past.[45]

Northern Ireland has been struggling to construct a cohesive identity in recent times. Exhibitions like these help in the process of defining 'identity', expecially in an area where there is no easy or agreed sense of what it means to be a citizen.[46] The Ulster Museum provides reminiscence boxes containing everyday objects as another way for groups to use to recall personal past experiences. The museum's outreach programme (including touring exhibitions, lectures, workshops and handling sessions) assist in keeping existing visitors engaged, while also developing new audiences.[47] These are just a few of the methods the museum is employing, while it sets about organizing a refurbishment programme, that will see the transer of over 800,000 objects to new offsite stores. With a hard-won peace, investment and renewed hope, the Ulster Museum is in a prime position to play its part in changing the potential of museums in Northern Ireland to engage with wider constituencies, and to increase understanding of the region's complex heritage.

The Crawford Municipal Art Gallery, Cork (1885)

The Crawford Municipal Art Gallery is a nineteenth-century city art museum that was the result of initiatives by Cork art societies, imbued with a sense of educational zeal. During most of the century, when the School of Art coexisted with the gallery, its major attraction was a collection of 150 Greco-Roman and neo-classical sculpture casts, which were important both for their educational significance and as images in their own right.[48] Complementing this collection was Cork Public Museum founded in 1910, which re-opened in 1945 to tell the story of Cork's social, economic and municipal history, thus providing the city with another significant cultural resource.[49]

The Crawford Municipal Art Gallery, Cork

The Crawford Art Gallery, which is located in the heart of the city beside the Opera House, offers free admission for all. A popular art museum, it plays an important role in the contemporary life and culture of Cork.

The early development of the *de facto* municipal collection was guided by the headmaster of the School of Art, who was also keeper of the collection until the 1960s (which explains the presence of a number of the headmaster's own paintings in the collection). The gallery's holdings grew to include works by major Cork-born painters, such as James Barry, Daniel Maclise and the sculptor John Hogan, together with some leading twentieth-century and contemporary artists. Due to the lack of a purchase grant, however, it was marked by the absence of international works. That changed, though, with the acquisition of the Joseph Stafford Gibson Bequest in 1919.[50] When the Gibson Committee was formed in 1922, it enabled the museum to start acquiring a strong interwar, academic collection and also facilitated the advent of student scholarships.[51]

In 1979 the School of Art moved to Sharman Crawford Street, thus freeing up the gallery building and enabling the old north-facing studios to be incorporated into exhibition spaces.[52] While the antique casts that remained in the gallery continued to be a source of inspiration to artists and students, they also formed the dramatic first impression of visitors to the Municipal Art Gallery in Cork.[53]

For most of the twentieth century accommodation was shared
with Cork Education Centre.
In addition, as the Crawford
Municipal Art Gallery came
under the Cork Vocational Education Committee, resources had to be
deployed in many other areas as well as the museum, as a result of which
there was a lack of funding to support more than a few key posts. Events in
the gallery were frequently organized by outside bodies, including the Cork
Literary and Scientific Body and Cork Archaeological and Historical Society.
This was augmented by the foundation of the Friends of the Crawford in
1987, a useful body that organized lectures and guided trips overseas, together
with acquiring works for the collection.

The final decades of the twentieth century have seen this museum make
remarkable efforts to capitalize on its modest resources. Director Peter Murray
manages the gallery with a small team of committed staff.[54] The permanent
collection has grown to over 2,500 works, including paintings, sculptures,
prints and other works of art, its strength lying in twentieth-century and
contemporary Irish art. The collection was augmented by the Arts Council's
joint-purchase scheme in the 1960s, which enabled the acquisition of contemporary artworks. It was further enriched by the donation of the Seamus
Murphy sculpture collection, added to by donations from the Contemporary
Irish Art Society and the Friends of the National Collections. In 1995 the
Crawford mounted a touring exhibition, *Irish Art 1770–1995: History and*

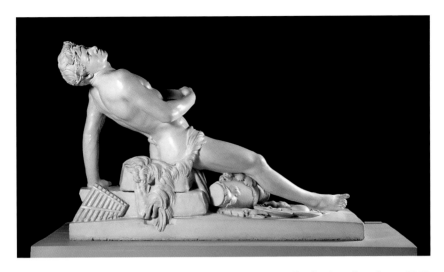

John Hogan (1800–58), *The Drunken Faun*, 1826
Plaster original, 98 x 155 x 70 cm. signed J. Hogan. Crawford Municipal Art Gallery.

Hogan's finest work, *The Drunken Faun*, was executed in 1826 when the artist was in Rome. It responded to a challenge by Gibson, a fellow sculptor, that no new original pose was possible. While Hogan drew inspiration from the Barberini Faun, he demonstrated that it was possible to create a fresh presentation of the subject. Hogan became Ireland's most distinguished neo-classical sculptor, with many of his works in the Crawford collection.

Society from the Collection of the Crawford Municipal Art Gallery,[55] to bring the collections – and knowledge of the gallery – to a number of venues in the United States. The exhibition programme has included thematic exhibitions, such as *Onlookers in France*,[56] with the facility to bring together group shows and retrospectives on individual artists, such as Rose Barton, Mildred Anne Butler, Alicia Boyle and Joan Jameson, managed by the part-time exhibitions officer. This ambitious institution has become a major centre of art in the south of Ireland.

The Chester Beatty Library (1953)

In 1953 the Chester Beatty Library opened to researchers and a limited public audience in the Dublin suburb of Ballsbridge (followed in 1957 by the addition of a small exhibition gallery). Chester Beatty (1875–1968) was a successful American mining engineer, industrialist and art collector, who became disillusioned with Britain and so moved to Dublin in 1950. Senior Irish officials

assisted Beatty in the transfer arrangements of his collection and encouraged him to settle in Ireland and establish his library at Shrewsbury Road, Ballsbridge.[57] He amassed his collection quietly over sixty years by relying on professional advice and acquiring only the finest material. Like many American collectors of his generation, he set up his library on the basis that it would be kept intact following his death. In this way his patronage was secured not just for the Chester Beatty Library but also for the NGI and for the Military Museum at the Curragh, County Kildare, together with his donations to hospitals and medical charities (mainly in Britain). When he died, the Irish government granted him a state funeral in recognition of his benefaction to his adopted country.

Beatty's library has been a public charitable trust since 1969, grant-aided by the state and governed by a board of trustees.[58] It first opened under the librarian Richard Hayes, was expanded under directors Patrick Henchy and Wilfred Lockwood and augmented by initiatives undertaken by curators, such as overseas exhibitions. The library was little used in Ballsbridge, given that it had limited display and conservation facilities. An acting-director stepped in during the interim while a new director was being sought, the post being filled by Michael Ryan. In 1992 Ryan took steps towards finding a new home for the library, the outcome of which saw a proposal made to government in 1993 for use of the Clock Tower Building in Dublin Castle, itself an historic city-centre location dating back to the early thirteenth century. The

The Chester Beatty Library, Dublin Castle

In 2000, the first major cultural development of the millennium year saw the opening of the Chester Beatty Library at its new home in the Clock Tower Building, Dublin Castle. Both an art museum and a library, it houses rich collections of manuscripts, miniature paintings, prints, drawings, rare books and the decorative arts.

library transferred to the Clock Tower Building as part of Dublin Castle's complex, where the collection was based in a restored eighteenth-century building with a modern, purpose-built block.[59] The collections are now housed in modern galleries with state-of-the-art display and environmental conditions, augmented by a reference library and reading room for study and research. The first major cultural development of the millennium year saw the opening of the Chester Beatty Library at Dublin Castle, on the 125th anniversary of its benefactor's birth.

This national cultural institution is, in effect, a library and art museum. Its holdings encompass manuscripts, prints, miniature paintings, drawings, *objets d'art*, and early and rare printed books that demonstrate the evolution of the book from ancient times to the present. It has become a centre for study in the Old and New Testaments due to its rare Islamic and Far Eastern material. The wider collections come from north Africa and Europe, across Asia and the Middle East, some of which date from the third millennium BC to the present day.

The director has worked with a small team to build up the essential services and facilities that underpin a museum.[60] While the collection is displayed around two themes – 'Sacred Traditions' and 'Artistic Traditions' – this is augmented by rotated exhibitions, scholarly conferences and a public programme of music and events as an effective way of conveying the encyclopaedic nature of the library's holdings. An education officer was appointed to deliver an ambitious programme of education and outreach, using modest resources and the help of a volunteer programme: 'Education is centred on people and most outreach work is rooted in the community. It is, therefore, essential to maintain links with the various community groups.'[61] The library is in the process of developing wide-ranging activities that includes inter-cultural education and a children's Silk Worm Club.[62] A conservation laboratory also forms part of its plans and is considered an essential service for the preservation of the library's collection, demanding the treatment of diverse artworks, ranging from the most fragile objects to delicate works on paper, some of which are its famous *objects d'art*.

The Silk Road Project illustrates the library's intercultural educational mandate, which is geared towards improving understanding of the European,

Middle Eastern, Asian and East Asian holdings. This intercultural approach, involving activities for all ages, including family days, children's workshops, tours, films and lunchtime talks, has become the hallmark of Chester Beatty Library work. Children are guided through the collections on the Silk Road Project

The permanent collections: the new presentation of Islamic Art at the Chester Beatty Library

The Chester Beatty Library's Islamic collections are internationally renowned, with over 4,000 manuscripts, single-page paintings and calligraphies, augmented by an assortment of precious objects that are the source of ongoing scholarly research.

by travellers who narrate tales of great adventures, firing their imaginations through storytelling and role play and showing how museums can engage successfully with multicultural groups. The library also participated in the Pegasus Foundation's Schools Adopt a Monument project, where schools created their 'own impression of the collections'.[63]

Exhibitions are important for the library, both those managed by its own curators and those mounted in partnership with other museums.[64] They provide fresh displays with which to attract the public, but also the chance to showcase the famous treasures in the library's holdings, which are undoubtedly among the finest in the world. Certainly, the Chester Beatty Library has the world's finest collection of Islamic manuscripts. It also possesses an incredible collection of Egyptian papyrus texts, illuminated copies of the Qur'an, the Bible, European medieval and Renaissance manuscripts, Turkish, Mughal Indian and Persian manuscripts and miniatures, Buddhist paintings, Chinese dragon robes and rare Japanese woodblock prints and literary scrolls. Guided by its director, the Chester Beatty Library is assuming an international significance by showcasing pre-eminent collections in scholarly exhibitions, while in a national context it will have an equally important role in highlighting its multi-faceted collections and their relevance to Ireland's new multicultural society.

The Hunt Museum, Limerick (1997)

Limerick was fortunate to benefit from the benevolence of John and Gertrude Hunt, a couple who had an interest in art and antiquities. John, a cultured man, was a dealer in medieval art in London during and after the Second World War, while his father-in-law was curator of Mannheim Castle in Germany. In 1939 the Hunts purchased a farm in County Limerick, later moving to Howth, County Dublin, in 1956. They devoted their lives to the study and collection of Irish antiquities, which they had been amassing between the 1930s and the 1970s.[65]

In 1974 the Hunt Museums Trust was established (a company limited by guarantee), to which the Hunt Collection was given through a series of deeds of gift between 1974 and 1999. The collection was initially housed and available for public viewing from 1978, when the Hunt Museum at Plassey

The Hunt Museum, Limerick

The Hunt Museum is housed in the Old Custom House, on the banks of the River Shannon, situated in the heart of Limerick city. This more unusual view of the museum is taken from the perspective of the river. The museum, which opened in 1997, forms a major cultural resource for Limerick.

opened at the University of Limerick (formerly the National Institute for Higher Education), designed by architect Arthur Gibney.[66] A permanent home was found for the museum in Limerick city at the Davis Ducart-designed Custom House, on the banks of the River Shannon. It was refurbished by the OPW, the funding aided by private individuals and their children John and Trudy Hunt.[67] The Hunt Museum is managed by the Hunt Museum Limited, operating as a trading company and one of the Irish museums required to charge admission to support its sustainability.

In 1997 the museum was opened at the Custom House, the remainder of the collection having been donated by John and Trudy Hunt.[68] The collection comprises antiquities and fine and decorative art, including artefacts from Greece, Rome, Egypt and the Olmec civilization. Irish archaeological material ranges from the Neolithic to the Bronze Age, with an important corpus of medieval artefacts (crucifixes, ivories, crystal, enamels, jewellery, ceramic painted panels and statues in stone and wood). The eighteenth- and nine-teenth-century decorative arts feature examples of ceramics, glass and silver. The fine art collection includes works by Picasso, Renoir, Roderic O'Conor, Jack B. Yeats, and Henry Moore. The collections are displayed in a manner desired by the Hunt children, to echo the life of a private home.[69] The Study Collection Rooms present objects in the form of a 'cabinet of curiosity', with glass cases displaying the decorative arts materials and drawers that can be opened to view the contents closely.[70]

The Hunt Museum devised educational programmes to engage primary, post-primary and third-level students from the local universities and art colleges, with children's activities delivered by volunteers from the museum's docent programme. In addition to events such as talks, tours and seminars in the Education Wing, the workshops use discovery-based learning techniques,[71]

Maiolica drug jar, *Italian, Venice workshop or style of Domenico da Venezia, c.*1550–80
Tin-glazed earthenware, height 29 x base 13 cm. NCM 290.

This painted oviform jar may be one of a group made for a pharmacy, attached to a monastery and school, built by the Jesuits at Novella, Reggio Emilia, at the invitation of Camillo I Gonzaga in 1570. It is inscribed with the emblem of the Society of Jesus.

Pegasus brooch, Western European, late sixteenth century
Enamelled gold set with cabochon ruby and cut diamonds, H 3.5 x W 5 cm. T 021. Hunt Museum.

Pegasus, the winged horse, offspring of Poseidon and Medusa and tamed by the hero Bellerophon, was one of the themes from classical mythology that was the design source of much Western European jewellery. The Pegasus brooch would have been the main part of a pendant jewel, worn on a ribbon or chain, or as a brooch.

which emphasize the role of discovery as part of the learning process. A portrait workshop, for example, is followed by a practical session drawing self-portraits, focusing on the artistic qualities of the exhibits: 'learning is actively created by the learners for themselves … students learn from what they do, not from what the teacher does'. The museum produces resource packs to accompany exhibitions and the permanent collection.[72]

From the outset the museum provided a programme of temporary exhibitions in its 1,400 sq. ft. exhibition space, which attracted the local community and introduced new approaches to its collections, enhanced by a shop and riverside restaurant. An annual show by students from Limerick School of Art and Design presents works inspired by the Hunt Collection.

The museum's ethos is working for its visitors of all ages and it regularly attracts tours by schools in the mid-west region to explore and sketch the works of art and artefacts. The Hunt Museum has become an essential part of the cultural infrastructure of Limerick.

Hugh Lane Municipal Gallery of Modern Art, Dublin (1908)

'There is not in Ireland one single accessible collection of masterpieces of modern or contemporary art,'[73] thus spoke Hugh Lane, an art connoisseur with a singular ambition: to provide for Ireland a national institution of modern and contemporary art. As a result, Dublin city's modern art gallery was the outcome of an initiative by a pioneering and very determined individual, who founded the Municipal Gallery of Modern Art in 1908: 'to create a museum … give this treasure … to a town that one loves – is the ultimate gesture of this ingenious man'.[74]

Lane was aware of the need to foster a visual arts culture that would train students and support them in the development of 'a school of Irish painting'.[75] However, difficulties with sourcing an appropriate building saw him remove his paintings to London's National Gallery in 1913. In 1915, following his death, his will and an unwitnessed codicil sparked a dispute between Britain and

John Butler Yeats (1839–1957),
Sir Hugh Lane (1875–1915),
Later Director of the National
Gallery of Ireland, **1905**
Graphite on paper, 17.5 x 12.7 cm.
NGI 2866.

Lane was a Cork-born, London-based art dealer whose ambition was to establish a gallery of modern art (now Dublin City Gallery The Hugh Lane), which he realized in 1908. This astute portrait captures the elegance and drive of the sitter. It was presented to the National Gallery by the Yeats sisters, in 1919.

The Hugh Lane Municipal Gallery of Modern Art

This city art museum (now Dublin City Gallery The Hugh Lane) is based in Charlemont House, Parnell Square, in the heart of Dublin. In addition to its well-known nineteenth-century French and Impressionist paintings, it houses a collection of modern art, which together with its exhibitions, educational activities and concerts, has made it a popular attraction for Dubliners and visitors to the capital.

Ireland that lasted many years, finally leading to an agreement, reached in 1959, to share the Lane paintings between London and Dublin. Since 1979 the majority of the Lane pictures have been in Dublin, with eight paintings (four in each gallery) rotated every six years.[76]

In 1933 a permanent home for Lane's 'modern collection of fine art' opened at Charlemont House on Dublin's Parnell Square.[77] The institution's mixed fortunes over the course of the century saw it emerge in a revitalized form at the latter end of the century, with a renegotiated Lane Pictures Agreement in 1993.[78] That year the gallery hosted an exhibition of young people's art, organized by the Departments of Education in Dublin and Belfast, together with a programme of lectures, tours and concerts and a publication, *Picture This!*, which comprised an art book, children's video and teacher's aid.[79] Under director Barbara Dawson this is a gallery noted for its innovative programme of events, including popular Sunday concerts of classical music.

The gallery's collection forms a chronology of Irish and international art from the late nineteenth century to the present day. A major initiative for the institution was the staging of a touring exhibition, *A Centenary of Irish Painting*, which travelled to three venues in Japan in 1997. In 1998 the gallery

**The donation of the Francis Bacon Studio, 1998,
Collection Dublin City Gallery The Hugh Lane**

In 1998 the gallery received the donation of the Francis Bacon studio. This image of his studio at 7 Reece Mews, London, was photographed by Perry Ogden. The studio has since become a major attraction for visitors to the gallery.

acquired a prime curatorial, archaeological and educational resource with the donation of the complete London studio of the Irish-born artist Francis Bacon (1909–92).[80] This was celebrated with an exhibition of the artist's work, *Francis Bacon in Dublin*, curated by David Sylvester. The Francis Bacon studio archive at the renamed Hugh Lane Municipal Gallery of Modern art (1975) represents original material owned by Bacon that forms a critical component in any discussion or research about the artist. It is a substantial holding that is an essential point of reference for scholarship on Bacon, in addition to providing a source of interest for visitors. The gallery continues to pursue works by this artist, while also lending items from the studio to all the major Bacon exhibitions.

The Irish Museum of Modern Art

The Irish Museum of Modern Art opened in 1991, in the Royal Hospital, Kilmainham. Finding a home for the museum had proved difficult; however, the former hospital, considered the finest seventeenth-century building in Ireland, incorporating gardens, a meadow and medieval burial ground, was cleverly adapted to house the modern collections.

The Irish Museum of Modern Art (1991)

In 1991 the Irish Museum of Modern Art (IMMA) was opened by Taoiseach Charles J. Haughey, who had long championed the cause for a modern art gallery.[81] The background to the museum's genesis came from a legacy of international contemporary art exhibitions entitled *Rosc* (1967–88), which were hugely influential in Ireland and prepared audiences for the cultural and social changes that would be reflected in a modern art museum.[82]

It was not an easy journey to the opening of IMMA, however. The location of the new museum proved a controversial decision. The first proposal was to use the site of the Dublin Docklands Financial Centre, which would have seen the museum open in a newly configured gallery, with purpose-built facilities, centred in the heart of Dublin city. Instead, the final decision was to locate in the Royal Hospital, Military Road, Kilmainham, which was originally designed by William Robinson (1645–1712) as an army pensioners' retirement home. Built between 1680 and 1684 and based on Les Invalides in Paris, it comprised a complex of buildings with a formal, classical façade centred around a large, elegant courtyard.[83] The chapel is the climax of the building, with a sumptuously decorated ceiling, finely carved woodwork and stunning east window and side windows featuring heraldic stained glass.

The Royal Hospital was considered the finest seventeenth-century building in Ireland, with grounds incorporating a formal garden, meadow and medieval burial ground.[84] This location represented an unusual choice for a modern art museum, not only because of the historical nature of the buildings but also because of the limitations of the buildings in terms of hosting international exhibitions and facilitating the display of works of a certain scale. While its peripheral location marginalized the museum in its early days, it has since made a virtue of its unusual setting, with many popular shows and events making innovative use of the spaces and the gardens.

Incoming director Declan McGonagle (1991–2001) grappled with the issues presented by the unusual location as he set about putting structure on the new museum. The museum used its late Renaissance building as part of a process of reflecting contemporary changes in society, manifest through the pace of economic growth, information technology, immigration, the decline in influence of the Catholic Church and the emergence of a confident, ambitious and impatient young nation. A critical success factor was the 'inaugural collection' of over two hundred Irish and international works gifted by the Gordon Lambert Charitable Trust for Modern Art in 1992, specifically designated for the 'first national institution of modern and contemporary art in the country'.[85] This was complemented by an old master print collection donated in 1988 by Claire Madden in memory of her daughter Étaín, and son-in-law Friedrich Arnholz, called the Madden Arnholz Collection. Another substantial gift of 150 prints by mainly Latin American artists was donated in 2000 from the Smurfit: Cartón y Papel de México Collection.[86]

McGonagle saw the museum as a vehicle 'to bring people into contact with art and art ideas' and he sought to mount exhibitions with 'public and private collections on a European scale, with younger, lesser-known artists in Ireland and elsewhere'.[87] From the outset, the institution expressed a strong community education-based ethos. The Education and Community Department developed formal and informal educational structures, while also making links with living artists. The programmes flowed from the input of local community groups, which had a hand in shows like *Inheritance and Transformation*.[88] The head of collections felt that as the nature of contemporary art was experimental, there was a need to involve the public in that experimentation, so that IMMA would become a democratic and discursive museum.[89] In tandem with the growth of the museum's collections and exhibitions was the addition of artists' studio blocks, which created the busy atmosphere of a working art space. The museum often aroused debate and commentary, as contemporary art often does, in addition to which it won awards, at a time when its visitor numbers were steadily growing to approximately 200,000 in the early 1990s.

In its early years IMMA was helped by access to a series of loans from private and corporate, Irish and international collections as it set about developing its own permanent collection.[90] These loans included the Weltkunst Foundation Collection of British sculpture and sculptors' drawings and works on paper, lent in 1994 for a decade. In 1998 the Musgrave-Kinley Outsider Art Collection was acquired on indefinite loan, to be shown alongside IMMA's permanent collection. Since then, IMMA's artworks have been displayed at a number of curated exhibitions abroad, including *Irish Art Now: From the Poetic to the Political*, which was shown at the McMullan Museum of Art, Boston College, the Art Gallery of Newfoundland and Labrador, the Pittsburg Centre for the Arts, and the Chicago Cultural Centre. On a national level, the museum's National Programme facilitates widespread access to the collection in Ireland through its involvement in 150 projects in towns and villages, arts centres, libraries and even churches, with access programmes co-funded with the Department of Education and Science. The Artists' Works Programme involves education in monitoring a residency scheme that can cater for about twenty artists a year, drawing upon the new studio spaces.

What differentiates IMMA from other museums in Ireland is the nature of its approach to education and community work, together with its facilities: three studios for practical work, a lecture room and spaces where people can engage in ongoing work and where outside groups associated with the museum can display their art. This focus, from inception, on community education is partly to do with its remit as a museum of modern art and partly the fact that it is a very young institution. While its spaces prohibit it from mounting or hosting major international shows, an associated exhibition facility is planned for the Kilmainham site. As a young institution, it also has the added value of being able to plan and host new programmes without the constraints of institutional practice or tradition.

James Coleman (b.1941), *Lapus Exposure***, 1992–4. IMMA Collection**

This slide work by James Coleman is one of a trilogy of the artist's most significant works, in which he experimented with pictorial media to convey his thoughts on the meaning of the image and how it moves or freezes. The presentation of the work of modern artists like Coleman reflects contemporary culture and here illustrates one of Ireland's most eminent avant-garde artists working in the international scene today.

The museum's aim 'to explore artworks, artistic and aesthetic expression, creative thinking and making' has been espoused in collaborative work and lifelong learning programmes involving teachers, artists, educators and children. The quality of educational work is innovative, reflected in an art project like *Unspoken Truths*, which involved group visits that were described as providing 'excellence of learning process and of experience as well as excellence of product'.[91] The publication *A Space to Grow* (1999) was important in providing guidelines for creative work with young people involving modern art.[92] Fuelling the project was 'child-centred research' undertaken with the Touchstone Centre, New York.[93] The book's accessible approach fostered primary school programmes and teacher training.[94] Another publication, *Yours and Mine* (2000), demystified the concept of collecting for children (ages 6–12), parents, teachers and guardians.[95]

The museum has a policy of encouraging understanding and participation

Children take part in a tour mediated by Joakim Gleisner focusing on
***St Francis Street Boys*, 1994, by John Ahearn (b.1951). IMMA**

The Irish Museum of Modern Art has developed wide-ranging community education and out-reach programmes that focus on engaging audiences with contemporary art through exhibitions and mediated activites. Created by the American sculptor John Ahearn, *St Francis Street Boys* (plaster and acrylic paint) is an example of the importance of engaging young people with contemporary art collections.

in the visual arts through programmes that cater for a variety of audiences by means of lectures, tours, artists' talks and seminars.[96] Events for primary schools include a tour schedule together with in-career teacher training courses. Second- and third-level students have access to the collections through tours and 'museum modules'. Family programmes include Explorer 1, a gallery-based activity that draws 500–1,000 adults and children who participate in small groups. Youth programmes explore the development of artists through various projects, while Focus-on introduces the museum to community groups (for example after-school groups, people with learning disabilities, new communities and community development groups).[97] Evaluation and liaison with overseas partners is a standard part of IMMA's work.[98]

One of its early activities was the Older People's Programme, which involved studio-based interaction with artists and artworks illustrated in work by older people from St Michael's Parish, Inchicore. In 1999 the United

Nations International Year of Older Persons was marked by the hosting of an exhibition of work by the St Michael's Parish Active Retirement Association Art Group and the Bluebell Painting Group, informed by the policies of the national agency, Age and Opportunity.[99] Critical to the project was the group's involvement with contemporary art and artists, which enabled them to develop new forms of expression. The role adopted by the St Michael's group as participants, exhibitors, hosts and mediators is important in encouraging other museums to view older people as playing 'an active role in contemporary culture'.[100] IMMA's influence on learning in the contemporary visual arts field has placed it centre stage in Irish community education and outreach work.

Conclusion

The importance and significance of this grouping of national, regional and city museums and galleries is the contribution they have made to society through their educational role, their development of the potential of the museum ideal, and the public role of the museum. Each institution has its own individual collections that form the heart of the enterprise – art and installations, books and manuscripts, sculpture and antique casts, natural science and ethnographic specimens, history and the decorative arts – all of which help to make its collection distinctive for the local community. A number of the museums show that they have the potential to lead international trends. What all of these museums demonstrate, each in their own unique way, is that museums matter to society, that the collections, exhibitions, cultural programmes and publications they provide engage and interact with audiences of all ages, and in so doing make a significant educational, cultural and economic contribution to the community.

12

The National Museum of Ireland: 'Promoting the Widest Understanding and Appreciation of Ireland's Distinctive Culture and Natural History'

The collection of Irish antiquities is so important to Ireland and central to the raison d'être of the National Museum. [1]

The twentieth century was a time of radical change for both the NMI and the NGI. The National Museum displayed the same sense of optimism and potential at the outset of the century as did the National Gallery: the gallery was about to embark on an extension while awaiting receipt of the Milltown Bequest; the museum was benefiting from major interest in the Irish antiquities as it developed new programmes to cater for rising visitor numbers, while at the same time forming part of the South Kensington project. At that point the country was still under British rule, but political circumstances intervened early in the century and changed the *status quo*. Following the Easter Rising of 1916 and the War of Independence, the Irish Free State was set up in 1922.

For the next sixty years the cultural institutions came under the aegis of the Department of Education, which was bound by the restrictive policies

Jacques Émile Blanche (1861–1942), *James Joyce author (1882–1941),* **1934**
Oil on canvas, 82 x 65 cm.
NGI 1051.

When James Joyce published *Ulysses* in Paris in 1922, his novel chronicled the passage of Leopold Bloom through Dublin during an ordinary day (16 June 1904). He walks along Molesworth Street towards the National Museum, 'the handsome building Sir Thomas Deane designed'. Joyce was keen to have Émile Blanche paint his portrait but was careful to tilt his head to one side so as not to accentuate his thick lenses.

of the Department of Finance. Senior officials regarded Education as a junior department, under-resourced and unable to take on any additional responsibilities: 'it was very tight where money was concerned'. Similarly, the constraints imposed by the Department of Finance reinforced the prevailing official policies: 'We were completely under the thumb of Finance.'[2] The inconsistent support of the cultural institutions was a state issue, not helped by the fact that under the previous jurisdiction there had been a clearer understanding of the contribution of museums to society in the form of public education. Had the country not been so divided and so under-resourced following the creation of the Free State, the public might have demanded greater support for their cultural institutions.

This situation changed, however, when the far-sighted First Programme for Economic Expansion, drawn up by the economist and public servant T.K. Whitaker, was adopted by government in 1958. Seán Lemass became Taoiseach (1959–66) and his strategy for industrial development in the 1960s was undertaken in the belief that the state should develop cultural institutions that would offer evidence of economic prosperity and show its concern for, and support of, the arts. By 1968 the state had devised a comprehensive educational programme that echoed the improved living standards, and public interest in the arts, as the country experienced the beginnings of economic progress. As part of this programme modest funding was allocated to the cultural institutions towards staffing, building projects, public lectures and school tour programmes.

When the cultural institutions were placed under the Department of the Taoiseach in 1984, and then under a newly created Department of Arts, Culture and the Gaeltacht in 1993, a new era began of resourcing the cultural institutions and supporting the development of a positive appreciation of the wide-ranging benefits of the arts and culture in Irish life.

The National Museum of Ireland in the Twentieth Century

The new century started on a promising note at the Dublin Museum of Science and Art. The positive mood of the Irish Revival was reflected in the popularity of the halfpenny-guide, which entered its fifteenth edition, together with the rising visitor numbers: in 1900, the museum had *c.* 425,844 visitors over twelve months, although this level of visitor numbers gradually declined from 1914.[3] The museum's place as an architectural landmark was noted by James Joyce (1882–1941) in *Ulysses*: 'Making for the museum gate … he lifted his eyes. Handsome building.'[4]

The display of the casts of famous Irish high crosses and other architectural ornaments on show in the Centre Court fascinated visitors and became a familiar part of the museum's identity, until they were removed and placed in store in the 1970s. Between 1895 and 1907 G.T. Plunkett had commissioned the reproduction of a number of Irish artefacts, including a select series of high crosses, to make Irish people aware of the significance of their archae-ological heritage and to illustrate the crosses' exemplary sculpture and stylized motifs.[5] The high crosses would form part of a growing awareness of national identity. The museum was further enriched by the arrival of the cabinet of the Royal Society of Antiquaries of Ireland, which the society had begun to form in 1849 (as the Kilkenny Archaeological Society).[6] The fourth series of museum lecture-tours, in the winter of 1900, attracted 755 people, increasing to an average attendance of 73 people per lecture by 1914; the series ended when the lecture theatre was taken over as a heating plant area in 1916.[7] The controversy over the Broighter hoard had drawn further attention to Irish antiquities, making the hoard an attraction when it went on show early in the new century.

Meanwhile, the decorative arts and industrial collections continued to be promoted, following the pattern of the South Kensington Museum, with material for teaching purposes loaned to the Metropolitan School of Art. Support for home industries was illustrated in commissions for lace, tapestries and enamel work for a gallery called Applications of Art and Industry. This was designed to be used by artists, designers and Irish, English, European and American manufacturers to 'disseminate instruction and information on the collections'.[8] Loan exhibitions of silver and furniture were mounted, with lectures for people involved in local industries, so that craftworkers could 'regain the high standard they enjoyed in former times'.[9] These exhibition galleries would be used by future directors, such as George Noble, Count Plunkett (1906–16), for displays reflecting Irish history and heritage. Despite the emphasis on the decorative arts, a gradual decline in their importance was observed as interest in the Irish antiquities increased. The proactive outlook of the institution at this point exuded promise 'for the purpose of educating a community in realising the taste and artistic designs of past ages'.[10]

The Circulation Collection

A major initiative at the museum was the inauguration of the Circulation Collection by Plunkett in 1903. Plunkett believed in exploring every avenue to engage the public in the collections, in what is now called the public role of the museum. The loan collection forms an ideal example of the way he went about this. Consisting of reproductions, mounted in cases, of museum materials in botany, zoology, industrial crafts, metals and minerals, archaeology, and art and crafts, these collections were sent for specified periods to local industrial exhibitions, shows, festivals, technical and art schools, agricultural classes and national schools.[11] The instructive nature of the loan collections was in keeping with the South Kensington origins of the museum. Cole had circulated the South Kensington Museum's loan collections to art schools in 1864,[12] a system that was further developed when Liverpool Museum set up a 'schools loan service' in 1884: 'The object of the circulating museums … is the happiness to be obtained through the habits of observation.'[13]

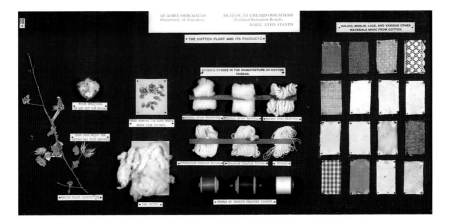

Flax and its Products: A Circulation Collection Loan Case

This is an example of one of the cases in the National Museum of Ireland's circulation collection, available during the period 1903–17, modelled on the V&A's system. The cases covered the full range of the museum's collections – botany, zoology, industrial crafts, metals, minerals, archaeology, art and crafts – and could be booked and transported by train throughout Ireland, north and south. It represented one of the most significant Irish museum initiatives ever, in making information on its collections accessible throughout the island.

While Plunkett was aware of school services that were promoted by the Museums Association, he also knew about the American loan services.[14] Following his establishment of the loan service in Dublin, curatorial and educational concerns of the highest order were manifest in the content and design of the cases, with the primary aim that information would be imparted correctly, regardless of whether it was as basic as crafting 'girders and riveted joints' or the more refined skills of 'illuminated manuscripts'. The loan collections were exemplary, used both as an aid in the teaching of art, crafts and technical skills, as well as reading, history, geography, writing and mathematics, on the basis that both young and old should be exposed to the finest examples available. A schedule of one year illustrates the lengths to which staff went to provide the most comprehensive range of materials to teach and to demonstrate the practical application of the museum's collections.[15] These loan collections were significant when used together with the revised Programme of Education for Primary Schools (1900), which promoted object-centred teaching 'to illustrate object lessons to the pupils'.[16] They were just as important at secondary level, helping teachers to make their lessons 'interesting and instructive', and were used also to teach 'students at technical school'.[17]

The initial fifty-six cases were increased in number annually, accompanied by instructive notes to help people explain the contents.[18] The service was promoted by 'school committees and organizers of exhibitions'. The senior keeper of South Kensington Museum visited in 1905 to monitor progress and oversee the dispatch of cases to twenty-eight Irish centres.[19] This much-used service required production of several cases of each subject for maximum application. A high point was reached in 1915, when 339 cases (a minimum of 2 to 6 duplicate sets of each case: for example, woodcarving, bookbinding, illuminated manuscripts or brass repouseé work) were in circulation, with 6 new subjects having been added that year. Records reveal that sets of these cases were issued some 667 times in 1915.[20]

As problems over storage grew more pressing, the loan service was suspended 'for the duration of the war' and the cases, left in damp conditions, began to deteriorate.[21] The gradual decline of this service after 1916 was an 'educational loss to the country'. Following a Board of Visitors' statement of concern – 'In no other civilised country would so valuable an assistance to the education of its rural inhabitants be thus neglected' – it was reported that the cases had been 'definitely removed from the museum' by 1930.[22] The Art and Industrial Circulation Collection had been a great asset to the museum, forming one of its most successful operations ever, through Plunkett's creation of a countrywide dissemination of knowledge about the collections and the provision of genuine pedagogical material to all levels of Irish society.

The Question of National Identity

The gathering momentum of the quest for national identity was beginning to have an impact as interest in the Irish collections increased, witnessed by a *conversazione* held for a visit of the Royal Archaeological Institute of Great Britain and Ireland in 1900 to inspect 'the famous collection of Antiquities'.[23] A change of direction took place in 1907, when the director retired and was replaced by George Noble, Count Plunkett (1851–1948).[24] His decision to open the museum in the evenings between August and October in 1907 to facilitate visitors to the Irish International Exhibition gained it a reputation that 'no contemporary success in commerce or science or war can confer'.[25] The lecture-tours extolled the collections:

The native exhibits include models of Irish Romanesque architecture and of the greater Irish crosses; of statuary by modern Irish artists; also some interesting examples of craftsmanship from Dublin interiors of the seventeenth and eighteenth centuries. Here also is deposited the great treasury of Celtic arts, the collection of the Royal Irish Academy.[26]

Early evidence of Irish self-determination began to crystallize with the change of the museum's title to the National Museum of Science and Art in 1908. The emphasis moved to 'the collection of things distinctively Irish, ancient and modern', due to the fact that visitors were less interested in 'the foreign objects than the historical series of Irish Antiquities and the Irish arts and industries'.[27] As a security measure a fireproof Strong Room was introduced, with steel shutters for the 'National Gold Objects', to ensure the antiquities were protected. The Strong Room was provided by Bantry White, the long-serving museum secretary, whose skills included designing display cases.[28] The decision taken 'to devote the whole of the lower floor to objects of Irish interest and bring them more prominently before the public' was understandable in the light of the growing awareness of their historical significance, during a time when there was increasing civil unrest in the country.[29] In 1910 progress was recorded somewhat

**The 'Tara' Brooch, early eighth century AD,
National Museum of Ireland,
Archaeology, Kildare Street**

The brooch was found at Bettystown, County Meath, in 1850. The association with the ancient royal site of Tara was an invention of a Dublin firm of jewellers to enhance its value. The brooch (decorated on both sides) is made of cast and gilt silver, the front consisting of a network of recessed cells of gold filigree, separated by studs of amber, enamel and glass. The guard chain ends in a swivel attachment of snake and animal heads framing two glass human heads. The design, exquisite technical detailing and materials are of the highest quality.

The 'Fossil Hall' of the Museum Annex, c.1910

When the art and industrial collections were removed to the museum in Kildare Street, the temporary annex housed most of the palaeontological specimens.

cautiously: 'The Museum is steadily advancing in usefulness. The number of students making constant use has increased during the past year.'[30]

Museum initiatives continued as Count Plunkett reported on a meeting of 'Museum co-operation in art teaching' that formed part of the International Art Congress in London in 1908, which was addressed by Kent, the American educator of the Metropolitan Museum: 'The people to be concerned with are those who go to learn. We should have docents for art as they have in American museums ... I am anxious to enlist the art schools in the service of the museum and the museum in the service of art schools.'[31] Improvements included an eastern entrance to the Natural History Museum, and a Students' Room for university students of science and veterinarian studies to handle 'material relevant to their courses'.[32] Schools were provided with a loan collection of lantern slides and a projector, and a *Bulletin* was published to disseminate information on the museum.[33] Following on from talks in the museum, art students were offered prizes for the 'best sets of drawings illustrating objects in the Collection'.[34] A proposal to introduce guides to provide conducted tours was mooted as a new idea. The lecture theatre in the annex was fitted out for talks by the staff and these were attended by about one hundred people, drawing 'public attention to the advantages which may be obtained from a study of the collections'.[35] Women were part of the National Museum staff during this period.[36] The museum was being thoroughly availed of by the public.

The threat of conflict became a reality in 1914, with the outbreak of the First World War. The loss of visitors was minor in comparison to the number of people at universities and schools, including staff from the museums who joined up for military service. It was difficult to develop on any essential area, be it conservation, documentation and curatorial, or to make the collections 'an instrument for the advancement of learning'.[37] When the 'Irish revolutionary experience' began to be felt, Plunkett retired as director, due to his son's involvement in the Easter Rising.[38] From that point until the 1930s, the institution was managed by a sequence of acting-directors.

When the keeper of natural history, R.F. Scharff, took over as acting-director in 1916, he found himself having to oversee suspension of the publications programme and the Circulation Division.[39] The decline of visitors to a low of 229,515 in 1916–17 was due to people being engaged in war work at home, together with the 'absence of so many of the Irish male population'.[40] The museum closed from 24 April to 8 May 1916 owing to the 'disturbed

state of Dublin due to the Rebellion at Easter'.[41] Nonetheless, 2,882 students were recorded using the Students' Room in 1916. Scharff noted that despite exemplary work with schools by American and English museums, almost no attempt was being made in

Seán Ó Sullivan (1906–64), *George Noble, Count Plunkett (1851–1948),* **1940**
Graphite on paper, 51 x 44.5 cm. NGI 3039.

This portrait of Count Plunkett depicts an elderly person, who, following his directorship of the National Museum, became minister for foreign affairs, then minister for fine arts, all forming a part of a busy active career.

Ireland 'by the educational authorities to bring the school and the Museum into closer contact'.[42]

The Easter Rising created an atmosphere of uncertainty and unease as people were forced to consider their feelings about the national question. Since 1908, when Irish history had been introduced into the curriculum, teachers had begun to foster an awareness in their pupils of 'Irishness', as distinct from 'Englishness', a trend influenced by the late nineteenth-century Cultural Revival. While many people would have remained with Home Rule tactics and constitutional means, the group who initiated the Easter Rising believed that armed struggle was the only way to obtain Ireland's desired freedom. The Rising had its own dynamic and the 'willingness to fight' was based on a set of ideas about 'Ireland's place in the world'.[43] These ideas were not universally shared, however. The public was largely divided in opinion on the rights and wrongs of the Rising and what it could have and did achieve. But there followed a catalyst that served to unify public sentiment: the summary executions of the leaders of the Rising at Kilmainham Jail. This bloodshed horrified the Irish people, and when it was followed by the threat of conscription to the very army that had executed prisoners, a radical shift occurred in Irish public opinion, which had been pacifist up until then. These events reverberated through every level in Irish society. For example, Eoin MacNeill, professor of early Irish history at UCD (and a future minister for education in the Free State government), was expelled from the RIA following his court-martial for involvement in the Rising. Professor Timothy Corcoran of UCD worked successfully to overturn the academy's ruling and reinstate Professor MacNeill in 1922.[44]

Scharff was particularly anxious about the lack of use of the museum during this troubled period:

> In England and in America, the great advantages offered by the
> Museum as a source of general education have long been rec-
> ognized ... The authorities controlling the education of the
> country might take more advantage of the facilities for education
> offered by this Museum ... I need scarcely say that would be
> most welcome and meet with the support of the Museum staff.[45]

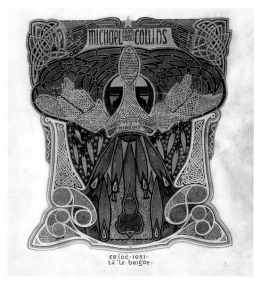

Leabhar na hAiséirí,
(Book of the Resurrection)
1931–1951,
by Art O'Murnaghan
(1872–1954), 1923
The Michael Collins (1890–1922)
and Kevin O'Higgins
(1892–1927) Page.

This book consists of twenty-six vellum pages made up of traceries and a series of quotations that commemorate the Republican leaders and their ideals.

He mounted a series of displays to attract the public back into the museum: an exhibition of Greek vases purchased at the 'Hope heirlooms' sale in 1917,[46] a wartime display of 'explosives … used in trench warfare'; photographs of women involved in war work lent by the Ministry of Munitions of War; and a scientific display of wartime parasites to assist doctors and the Army Medical Corps.[47] There were criticisms of this approach: 'Due to the way Irish national culture was constructed in conscious opposition to Enlightenment values, science came to be identified with all that Ireland in its own nationalist tradition was not: Protestant, modernizing, foreign, and thereby associated with the Ascendancy.'[48] But others, like the naturalist and historian Robert Lloyd Praeger (who, as a child, had taken part in the activities of the Belfast Naturalists' Field Club), spearheaded the growth of field clubs while making notable antiquarian, linguistic and folkloric inquiries into the 'national heritage'. The period between 1916–24 and during the War of Independence was one of ongoing upheaval with a restrictive regime in place. Funding was limited to essential services. The Armistice of 1918 would have meant the return of Irish men, many wounded.[49] Nonetheless, Scharff pursued his improving agenda, making a proposal to introduce guides: 'Such lecturers have been appointed in London and Edinburgh and have given great satisfaction to Museum visitors.'[50]

The problematic Government of Ireland Act 1920, which introduced partition, dividing Ireland into two separate states, was followed by the controversial Anglo-Irish Treaty in 1921. Irish independence was celebrated in the renaming of the institution that year, when it became the National Museum of Ireland.[51] The celebration was short-lived, however. In 1922, Michael Collins requisitioned Leinster House, on behalf of the Provisional Irish Government, to be used as an assembly chamber in which to hold the Dáil. (The use of a traditional seat of power like the building then occupied by the Bank of Ireland (earlier employed for Grattan's Parliament) was excluded by virtue of the treaty with Britain.) With the requisitioning of Leinster House, the final separation of the institutions of science and art from the Dublin society that had given birth to them took place.[52] On government instructions, the museum closed from 28 June 1922 to 2 June 1924, with the Seanad expressing concern over 'the safety of the national collections'.[53] The museum ceased its link with the V&A Museum and progress was extinguished, albeit temporarily.

Politics and the Public Institutions

Change came about when legislation enacted in 1924 brought the museum under the care of the Department of Education.[54] Two years later it was welcoming 262,034 visitors.[55] The new minister, Eoin MacNeill, commissioned a report (1927) on the role of the museum so that an appropriate policy could be devised in the context of the new nation. Headed by Professor Nils Lithberg, director of Stockholm's Northern Museum, the committee produced a well-rounded, progressive report with a set of recommendations. The committee was clear in its vision and definition (even if it omitted any reference to museum visitors):

> The main purpose of the National Museum of Ireland should be to accumulate, preserve, study and display such objects as may serve to increase and diffuse the knowledge of Irish civilisation, of the Natural History of Ireland and of the relations of Ireland in these respects with other countries.[56]

This was a key statement in the wake of a divisive civil war, when the country needed to mark the arrival of nationhood and celebrate its heritage, and importantly it reinforced the reason why the RIA antiquities had devolved to the museum. As a result, the Irish antiquities were given much greater prominence on the ground floor, while the museum continued to receive objects acquired by the RIA through treasure trove. The museum was closely involved in the drafting of a National Monuments Bill. Adolf Mahr (1887–1951), keeper of antiquities, was a key driver of the legislation, which dealt with monuments as well as antiquities.[57] The committee recommended expanding 'the educational scope of the Museum', to include a lecture hall and a room for children, through circulating exhibits and by opening the museum certain evenings each week, with lectures to be given by members of the staff.[58]

The committee's promotion of Irish antiquities saw a consequent decline in support for Irish entomology, while the Art and Industry division was allocated responsibility for documenting Irish political and military history.[59] Another recommendation was implemented: to make the museum's 'non-Irish cast collection' available for loan. The casts were deployed to the Metropolitan School of Art, to UCD and to the RDS. Unfortunately, the meagre storage facilities available meant that the remaining pieces in Kildare Street were destroyed.[60] In due course the Department of Education would transfer further works to the National Gallery.

Minister for Education John Marcus O'Sullivan responded positively to the committee's report in a memorandum to government, which was rejected by the Department of Finance, with only three recommendations approved because they 'involved no cost to the Exchequer'.[61] Despite government approval of some of the Department of Education's recommendations, it was a cursory way to treat a serious report and aroused the ire of opposition deputies, to which O'Sullivan retorted that the problem was 'a financial one', thereby concluding the debate.[62] Although Thomas Bodkin (a lawyer, art historian and collector, who was director of the NGI from 1927 to 1935) pursued William T. Cosgrave, president of the Executive Council of the Irish Free State from 1922 to 1932, on the wider issue of the arts, this sector was not a priority for government because of the state's precarious financial situation, which partly explained the position of the Department of Education.

These were difficult times for the National Museum. The committee recommended reissuing some of the 'circulating exhibits', but unfortunately the museum had overseen the demise of the loan collections (1903–17) due to an inability to maintain the service. The Museum Board of Visitors regretted the loss: 'In a country whose prosperity depends so largely on a higher standard of education … the Circulation cases, which should be so valuable an assistance to education in the rural districts, have been withdrawn from circulation and are not available to the student.'[63] Nonetheless, Bolton Street Technical School, Dublin, was facilitated with some loan collections for use with its own scientific material.[64] The upheavals of the Second World War and its aftermath caused the collections to be forgotten and they were put in storage, although the issue was raised in the Seanad: 'There was a travelling collection of the National Museum which … disappeared from public view.'[65] The loan collections were stored in the attic of the Bolton Street school, until their discovery sixty years later.[66]

In 1928 the *Carnegie Report* reaffirmed the *Lithberg Report*, noting that 'while the present situation is excellent, the Museum should be of a thoroughly national character. New sections on ethnology and folklore should be introduced and the exhibits should represent the development of the country from age to age.' Its conclusion, that Irish museums were not of the same standard as those in England and Scotland, was put down to the disturbances that had affected the 'cultural services of the country'.[67]

The museum participated in overseas exhibitions,[68] and the *Saorstát Éireann Official Handbook* (1932) portrayed an exemplary image of the collection:

> The finest examples are found in the wonderful collection in the National Museum which owes its existence to the Royal Irish Academy … The marvellous workmanship of these relics … unite to prove that this island, small and remotely placed in the western sea, played a decisive part in laying the foundations of European civilization.[69]

While this publication gave a positive impression of Ireland in order to promote an image of a country that was progressive, in reality morale was fairly low. Nonetheless, this impression was reaffirmed by Mahr at a Eucharistic Congress meeting in 1932, when he stated that Ireland's heritage dated to the early Christian period.[70] The museum's assertion of a national character in the context of the early Christian period was an inspiration for a new Ireland and would be reflected in fresh presentations of the collections as each new generation reinvented what it meant to be the 'National' Museum of Ireland.

The Arhat Upsaka Dharmatala

Detail of a Thangka painting, illustrating the Arhat Upsaka Dharmatala. On cotton, eighteenth-century Tibetan-Buddist, probably Gansu Province, China, donated by Albert Maurice Bender, collector and friend of writers and artists. Works from this collection that went on display in the original Augusta Bender Memorial Room (1934) were redisplayed in 2008.

In the 1930s the display of the masterpiece artefacts from Ireland's golden age on show in the main galleries, including the Broighter Hoard, the 'Tara' Brooch, early Bronze Age lunulae, reliquaries and shrines, was described in the museum's *Short General Guide to the National Collections* (1932). A gift of Far Eastern art and oriental objects was received from the Dublin-born Jewish businessman and collector, Albert Maurice Bender.[71] The aspiration was that this fine collection would go on permanent display to provide a wider view of world history. Taoiseach Éamon de Valera (1937–48) opened the Augusta Bender Memorial Room on 25 June 1934 (Bodkin of the National Gallery having helped in the arrangement) in honour of the mother of the museum's generous donor Albert Bender.

The Second World War

There was little change at the National Museum from the time of the *Lithberg Report* up to the Second World War. This stasis was the direct result of staff shortages, a lack of funding and the museum being under the care of a series of acting directors. In 1934, however, Mahr was appointed to the top post of museum director by de Valera's cabinet. An Austrian archaeologist who had joined the staff of the museum in 1927, Mahr, set about putting a shape and structure on many of the museum's activities, while continuing to scour the country seeking artefacts. The range of his work included involvement in Irish and overseas exhibitions, publication of catalogues, the display of new finds and the provision of lectures 'given to metropolitan and provincial bodies interested in Irish archaeology'.[72] He worked assiduously to promote and develop the museum within the constraints of the inter-war limitations, while simultaneously working on his own political agenda which we will hear about later.

In an attempt to make students aware of their heritage, the Department of Education sent a circular to school principals encouraging them to organize 'visits of school-children to the National Museum'.[73] Mahr was keen to introduce young people to the collections and reported that 'school classes of elementary and secondary schools are conducted round the Museum by their teachers, but occasionally also by the staff'.[74] The museum responded to the *Lithberg Report* by opening up one evening a week, in addition to providing a hall for 'day-time and evening lectures', and this resulted in a series of organized visits by university students from Dublin and Galway. A series of courses was held on 'Irish Archaeology' for 'professors in the Irish-speaking Training Colleges of Dublin'.[75]

Despite the changed political situation, the National Museum continued to co-operate with, and receive co-operation from, the British Museum (and museums in Bristol, Cardiff and Cambridge), an indication that the collegiate spirit of the nineteenth-century still prevailed. An instance of this was the help of the British Museum Research Laboratory in conserving 'valuable finds' from two Viking graves in Dublin's Islandbridge Cemetery, which were excavated in 1933.[76]

Mahr emerged as a key figure in modern Irish archaeology. He advanced the museum during straitened times, and his decision in 1932 to support the Harvard Archaeological Expedition in setting up scientific excavations in Ireland brought a significant body of new material to the museum, and proved of long-term value to Irish archaeology.[77] His legacy is an important one, but it has been somewhat overshadowed by his well-known Nazi background. He knew of the plan to evacuate the national treasures during wartime and attended a meeting convened by the Department of Education on 23 March 1939 to discuss evacuation arrangements.[78] At this meeting he revealed an unusually 'detailed knowledge of the geography of the country' and also a familiarity with the 'ARP [air-raid precautions] proposal'.[79] This level of knowledge of such information would have been highly unusual for a museum director, but it transpired that Mahr was head of the Nazi Party in Ireland. At the outset of the war he returned to Germany and was imprisoned at war's end, so was unable to resume his position at the museum. Privately, he had been feeling pressure from senior Irish officials, who were aware of his role in the Nazi Party, and he was conscious of being monitored by the army's military intelligence arm. Mahr was retired with a pension and never returned to Ireland.[80]

The impact of the war was felt in every Irish cultural institution. The museum reported that reduced staffing and funding made it difficult to maintain services under the 'adverse conditions [with] which the members of the staff have had to perform their duties during the emergency period'. The baton of acting director (in Mahr's absence) was taken up by Patrick O'Connor (1940–7), who oversaw 'the removal to a safe place of the chief treasures of the Museum'.[81] The major antiquities were crated and stored safely, with a series of replicas made of the key treasures and placed on display, so that the collections appeared unchanged during wartime.[82] Less fragile material was transported to a storage facility owned by the Department of Education in Athlone.[83] Contemporary accounts noted their absence, however: 'such treasures have been housed elsewhere for the emergency period',[84] and their eventual return to the museum was welcomed.

The reality of the situation in Ireland at that time was that the government was preoccupied with surviving, establishing the state and demonstrating its sovereignty and independence from Britain. Ó Riordáin's observation that 'In the United States … the development of museums has in recent times outdistanced that of any other country' took account of the fact that despite lacking in cultural policy, the Irish government viewed its National Museum as an expression both of the ancient and the 'modern nation'.[85] The wartime period and its aftermath left the museum with many difficulties,[86] not least a notable lack of space: 'the National Museum cannot at present surrender any further accommodation'.[87]

The Mid-Century Years

On his appointment as museum administrator (1947–54), Michael Quane (of the Department of Education) wrote a report wisely suggesting that the museum's mission should be to serve the country and the education of its people.[88] His proposal of five separate departments was practical: archaeology, folklife, history, industry, and natural science. During this brief interlude the economy experienced some growth and there was a phase of increased cultural activity. In 1949 this was manifest when Bodkin was commissioned by Taoiseach John A. Costello (1948–51) to report on Irish arts institutions. Bodkin singled out the complacent policies of the museum, which he felt were inappropriate to a cultural establishment of its calibre. His list of recommendations included an inventory of the collection and a conservation programme, storage facilities, an exhibition programme, redeployment of the collections, publications and staff training (in line with the *Lithberg Report* of 1927). He also suggested the idea of evening openings with refreshment rooms. And he declared:

> It is desirable that a Department or sub-Department of Fine Arts should be established as a branch of some Ministry or preferably under the control of the Taoiseach … charged with direct responsibility for the administration of the present National Gallery, National Museum and National College of Art.[89]

This would become a reality when the national cultural institutions were transferred to the Department of the Taoiseach in 1984.

In common with other cultural institutions, the National Museum saw its numbers dwindle mid-century, with an average attendance that hovered between 200,000 and 300,000 visitors a year.[90] The Dáil, meanwhile, noted the absurdity of starving the cultural institutions of resources.[91]

A.T. Lucas was an ethnologist for whom the development of the collections was paramount. His directorship of twenty-two years (1954–76) was largely focused on the museum's main aim of collecting and preserving 'the documentation of the land and people of Ireland in objects'.[92] His interests lay in research and recording the collections, which were described as 'relating to the antiquities, history, arts, crafts, fauna, flora and geology of the country'.[93] His focus was therefore less on the public role of the museum, despite which activities still took place. School tours continued, supported by the Department of Education and organized and facilitated by Coras Iompair Éireann (CIÉ),

The National Museum of Ireland – Natural History

A unique Victorian museum, this photograph shows a display of many of the fragile natural history collections, which are arranged on three floors of the Natural History Museum.

which transported 28,000 pupils to the museum in 1959, and in 1960 conveyed 511 schoolchildren to receive guided tours.[94] This practice was encouraged by the ICOM: 'Your duty is not so much to tell as to ask; not so much to fix facts as to invite hypotheses.'[95] Talks were given to archaeological and cultural societies by the antiquities staff. In 1960 the museum worked with the Department of Education to produce a filmstrip on ancient Ireland, which would be circulated to cultural bodies and schools because it had been noted that 'our people do not seem to be fully aware of these institutions'.[96]

There was a new sense of optimism following the government's Second Programme for Economic Expansion in 1963, when the leadership of Lemass, together with Whitaker, secretary of the Department of Finance, encouraged an atmosphere of self-confidence that supported businesses and industry. The positive mood was affirmed by journals such as *Studies*, which presented these figures as being pivotal in the changing economic climate of Ireland.[97] The National Museum Board of Visitors, which had ceased meeting between 1952 and 1960 (due to a lack of action by the Department of Education), welcomed Bodkin's exposé of the museum situation in Ireland. And the Seanad noted that 'material expansion without education will do us no good'.[98]

The museum put its meagre resources into excavating Viking and medieval sites in Dublin, acknowledging the support of the OPW, which had 'no official responsibility for the preservation of movable antiquities; but its services to the nation in excess of its official duty have earned it the gratitude of past, present and future generations of archaeologists'.[99] A Dáil debate recorded the potential of textbooks to provide 'knowledge of the treasures of our National Museum … then our children could speak with lawful pride of the achievements of the past'.[100] There was a further deployment of the collections to the National Gallery and botanical material to the National Botanic Gardens in Glasnevin.[101] A short-term Natural History Museum Club availed of the National Gallery's lecture theatre.[102]

The Board of Visitors painted a bleak picture in 1965:

> We feel that the Museum's place in our State is as a public institution of the greatest cultural and educational importance and that it should be of increasing international renown. We would urge that this period of lull in its growth be made use of to initiate a sound and far-sighted policy for development.[103]

Unfavourable comparisons were made with the National Gallery, which seemed to be making good progress: 'There is a quiet revolution going on in the World's national galleries and museums – it has yet (alas) to reach our National Museum.'[104]

Two reports on the National Museum were compiled by civil servants.[105] The first was produced in 1969 for internal circulation to academic institutions, the Department of Education, the Museum Board of Visitors and the Oireachtas. The second report, in 1973, was significant in pointing out that public service was the duty of the Museum, not just the ownership and care of the collections – which was understood – but to make efforts to create access by means of programmes and activities. It argued that as the museum was maintained from public funds, the community was entitled to a return on its investment. This was a market-driven view that many scholars would find inimical to the welfare of a civic institution. The report revisited the public role of the institution, which it envisaged as providing a service to attract the widest audience. Its chart of visitor figures from 270,233 in 1919–20 to 178,486 in 1970–1 demonstrated the need for change. While the Dáil listened to a submission that 'the Department of Education had behaved abominably towards the National Museum', the Minister for Education stated that he was largely satisfied with the situation.[106] In the summer of 1970, the National Herbarium, which had been housed in the National Museum for over eighty years, was transferred to the National Botanic Gardens.[107]

The Late Twentieth Century

The 1970s was a period when contemporary discussions might have given cause for optimism, with commentators anticipating Ireland's accession to the EEC in 1973.[108] Meanwhile, the closing of the Augusta Bender Memorial Room in 1971 provoked the ire of some politicians, who saw the need to make every possible use of the 'educational purposes of the material available'.[109]

In 1974 a welcome initiative, which acted on earlier reports, was the creation of a Folklife Division in the museum. A subsequent report raised serious issues, however: 'the museum has long been the subject of strong criticism for its conservative policies, boring display and general inadequacy of the service it provides. Such criticisms are undoubtedly justified, as a visit to the Museum immediately makes clear.' The report recommended the establishment of an independent Board of Trustees, similar to the National Gallery.[110] The frustrations of the period were discussed in the Seanad: 'It reflects poorly on us as a nation that our National Collections, which are a priceless cultural asset, fared far better at the hands of the former alien governments.'[111] It was unusual for commentators to speak in support of the previous political situation in the country, but it could not be avoided, as substantial cultural and educational development had taken place in the

Shrine of St Lachtin's Arm, **early twelfth century**

The early Christian Shrine of St Lachtin's Arm with its late Hiberno-Norse *Urnes*-style plates (illustrating a dense network of interlaced, ribbon-like animals, separated by a cast copper-alloy openwork band of beasts) is just one of many significant Viking artefacts in the National Museum's collection.

nineteenth century under British rule. In a progressive move in the 1970s, James White, director of the National Gallery, approached the Department of Education seeking sanction for the post of education officers in order that the cultural institutions could establish education services that would engage the public in their collections.

During Joseph Raftery's tenure as director (1976–9), the first education officer was appointed by the museum. The officer, Patrick F. Wallace (1976), who had produced an archaeological exhibition for the education centres at Trim and Castlebar, hoped that funds would be 'available to develop an education service'.[112] The Board of Visitors supported this post: 'Considerable work in this field is necessary within the Museum to cater for school visits and other groups and to encourage the public to take an interest in the collections.'[113] The museum commemorated a century of its foundation with a show highlighting its four divisions: Natural History (1857), Art and Industry (1877), Irish Antiquities (1890) and Irish Folk Life (1974). The Dáil was made aware that the Natural History Museum's important Leskean and Giesecke collections were being stored in unsuitable conditions in the chapel of the Royal Hospital at Kilmainham.

In 1977, the museum collaborated on an international touring exhibition that would be significant in enhancing the image of Ireland and of its cultural

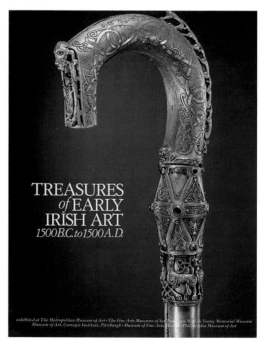

Catalogue cover of
Treasures of Early Irish Art,
1500 BC to 1500 AD

This touring exhibition, from the collections of the National Musem of Ireland, the Royal Irish Academy and Trinity College, Dublin, was significant in displaying the most important masterpiece works of early Irish art to leading American museums in New York, San Francisco, Pittsburgh, Boston and Philadelphia.

TREASURES
of EARLY
IRISH ART
1500 B.C. to 1500 A.D.

exhibited at The Metropolitan Museum of Art • The Fine Arts Museums of San Francisco, M.H. de Young Memorial Museum Museum of Art, Carnegie Institute, Pittsburgh • Museum of Fine Arts, Boston • Philadelphia Museum of Art resources. *Treasures of Early Irish Art, 1500 BC to 1500 AD* was drawn from the collections of the National Museum, TCD and RIA, opening in October 1977 at the Metropolitan Museum of Art, New York, and thereafter touring other cities in the United States.[114] Thomas Hoving, director of the Metropolitan Museum, enthused that 'The patrimony of the extraordinary Irish civilization has been made available almost in its entirety for this exhibition ... lending these precious possessions to us is an exceedingly generous act.'[115] Professor Frank Mitchell, one of the organisers of the exhibition, stated: 'In committing her most treasured possessions to an extended tour of American museums, Ireland is paying tribute to the American people for the generous help she has received throughout the past two hundred years.'[116] Although this exhibition enabled the museum to makes its presence felt on an international stage, the poverty of the situation at home was evident as the museum evacuated the geological and folk life collections to Daingean, County Offaly, in 1979. Mitchell, who knew the museum intimately, expressed his deeply felt concern:

> There must be a complete re-animation of the Museum, giving to it the staff, premises and facilities it so desperately needs ... Government Ministers should be made to realise how rich our countryside is in records of the past and how rapidly this record is disappearing ... this material should be computerised so that it can become immediately available to scholars all over the world.[117]

Mitchell's words fell on deaf ears. The Department of Education seemed impervious to reports about the museum; Dáil Debates recorded the sequence of reports that had been undertaken between 1927 and 1949 and asked why no constructive use was being made of this material.[118] In the meantime, the high crosses, having been displayed in the Rotunda of the museum, were removed to create space for temporary exhibitions. Shortly after Breandán Ó Riordáin's appointment as director (1979–88), a report was published, *The Place of the Arts in Irish Education,* that reaffirmed a proposal for the Department of Education to create branch museums so that the public could access artefacts from the national collections, which could be related to the local communities and to the lives of the people.[119] The museum librarian was appointed to the post of education officer, just as a process for dealing with the cultural institutions finally began to take shape.[120] In 1981 a Ministry for State for Arts and Culture was created by the coalition government in a move that would pave the way for further change.[121]

The 1981 report of the Board of Visitors, marking one hundred years of its existence, catalogued a half-century of neglect by successive governments through the lack of a museum policy and the serious inadequacies of staff, accommodation and technical resources. It highlighted the absence of services for the public and expressed dissatisfaction with the decisions of former directors to dispense with non-Irish cast collections: 'What would the reaction be if our National Gallery should dispose of its famous collections of works by artists unconnected with Ireland?' The successful tour of *Treasures of Early Irish Art* in the United States resulted in a showing of the exhibition in Dublin before a revised version began touring European cities between 1982 and 1984.[122] At the same time the museum generated travelling exhibitions or participated in major international exhibitions. Some shows were held in Kildare Street and the museum made a policy of loaning material to regional exhibitions.[123]

A major cause for celebration was the newly discovered Derrynaflan Hoard, which was placed on show in 1980 alongside the Ardagh Chalice, for comparative purposes. A suite of galleries would be planned for the display of these key Irish antiquities, while a gold exhibition scheduled for the Centre Court would be installed in the 1990s. In the meantime, the head conservator of the Museum of Mankind in London observed: 'it is imperative that urgent steps are taken to see [the ethnographic materials in Dublin] are properly stored and conserved'.[124] An inter-departmental committee suggested relocating some of the museum's collection to the Royal Hospital, Kilmainham. At this time the museum was trying to win support for an independent board and several branch museums.

When Taoiseach Garret FitzGerald made the welcome announcement that the cultural institutions were being transferred to the Department of the Taoiseach, the initiative was seen as one that could potentially awaken the government to the importance of cultural heritage to the nation.[125] The view may have been that within the Department of Education the cultural institutions were competing unsuccessfully with schools, colleges and other bodies for resources, whereas under the remit of the Taoiseach's Department they might have a better chance of receiving attention. The transfer took effect in 1984 during a decade of economic recession, so the portents for change were not auspicious, although there was a feeling of optimism when the Curriculum and Examination Board published a discussion paper in 1985, *The Arts in Education*. It was endorsed by the Arts Council, but ignored by the Department of Education. However, Minister of State Ted Nealon reported that the government intended to publish a White Paper on cultural policy that would set down, for the first time since independence, its objectives for the cultural development of the country. Nealon subsequently commissioned a report on the museum from G.A. Meagher, which noted, among other things, the absence of any services, pointing to the lack of action on a 1980 Memorandum to Government for two assistants for the Education section. It stated: 'One Education Officer in the National Museum was but a drop in the ocean when one considered the necessity to provide nationwide coverage.'[126] The Board of Visitors reaffirmed the report's findings, aware that an adequately staffed service would improve the potential of 'the public's understanding and use of the national collections'.[127]

In the meantime, the museum continued to provide exhibitions and accompanying lectures by staff, as a succession of shows – *Irish Gold and Silver*,[128] *The Work of Angels*,[129] *Vikings and Christians*,[130] and *Gods and Heroes of the Bronze Age*[131] – toured to international venues. The fact that the museum was taking part in, and initiating, these shows is noteworthy, as they must have provided an excellent forum with which to showcase Ireland's heritage. They also represented a shift in the policies of the museums that received them towards a new interest in loan exhibitions. The fact that the museum itself hosted relatively few such exhibitions was also notable when compared to Irish and international norms. The issue of whether museums should participate in these shows aroused controversy in some quarters. The return of *Treasures of Early Irish Art* from its international touring programme drew attention to the need to create special display and conservation cases in which to show the treasures in Kildare Street.

Patrick F. Wallace was appointed director in 1989, and his stated aim was to develop the full range of services required by a national museum. The museum's plans continued to be frustrated by the lack of investment, however, due to the severe fiscal rectitude of the 1980s, causing one commentator to point out that cultural institutions required support that did not 'stress cost effectiveness but the contribution made to the quality of life'.[132]

The 1990s opened on a more positive note, with an air of optimism generated by economic growth, assisted by EU investment. In 1993, after sixty years of cultural inactivity, a major development took place when government announced the creation of a Department of Arts, Culture and the Gaeltacht, under Michael D. Higgins, TD. For the first time in over half a century the director and the National Museum were imbued with a sense of optimism. The emergence of the Heritage Council expressing interest in the development of the Irish museum sector was another positive signal.[133] While the Heritage Council's remit was wide, it expressed a commitment to collections care through its aspiration to create a Museum Standards Programme for Ireland. The National Museum was becoming more aware of the need to develop a commercial approach to its operation. In light of this, the display cases in the Rotunda were removed to make way for the museum shop, followed by the opening of a gallery café/restaurant in the mid-1990s. Further developments would see audio-visual rooms installed to help explain the background to some of the major works on display.

The shift to a new era in the life of the museum was consolidated in 1993 when a complex of refurbished eighteenth- and nineteenth-century buildings in Dublin, formerly known as the Royal Barracks and then Collins Barracks, were acquired. During the eighteenth century the need to house William III's standing army had resulted in the construction of a network of barracks across the country, the most noteworthy building being Captain Thomas Burgh's (1670–1730) Royal Barracks, built in the early decades of the century. Over the intervening centuries the Royal Barracks had been pivotal to many milestones in Ireland's national development and also in those international wars in which Britain played a part. The site was suffused with history. When the Anglo-Irish Treaty was signed in 1921, Michael Collins, commander-in-chief of the Irish Free State army, took control of all the barracks, of which the oldest, the Royal Barracks, was the last to be handed over. In 1988 government decided to close (the then) Collins Barracks as a military

installation, and in 1993 it was agreed the site would be developed for use by the NMI.[134]

The programme of development and refurbishment undertaken by the director took place over three years, managed by the OPW. Spurred on by this important gesture of support and expansion, the museum began to look at new attitudes to visitor access that would govern how Collins Barracks would be used by the public. This examination took account of ideas on the nature and content of displays, text panels, labelling and ancillary information, in conjunction with the selection and display of the choicest works to illustrate aspects of history and Irish life. This process emerged as the outcome of a strategic plan for the museum that addressed its purpose and mission, structure and revenue generation, together with a marketing plan that would link its three sites and a promotional campaign to convey the message.[135]

The Museum of Decorative Arts and History at Collins Barracks opened to widespread acclaim and extensive press coverage in 1997. This major series of buildings, designated as the new headquarters of the museum, would provide the main portion of the space needed for displaying collections that had

been in store for decades. It would enable delivery of the director's aim of providing new galleries to mount exhibitions, together with spaces for education rooms and a lecture theatre for public events, and a restaurant.

Welcome progress was witnessed on other fronts, too, with the purchase of new acquisitions for Irish antiquities, decorative arts, folk life and the natural science collections. The enlarged museum was developing a greater need for enhanced press services and the creation of a range of new exhibitions.[136] Documentation and conservation departments were established, followed by the opening of a new conservation laboratory.[137] The first year of the Museum of Decorative Arts and History saw the arrival of 200,000 visitors, who were attracted by the inaugural exhibitions of Irish period and country furniture and Irish silver, as well as the novel 'out of storage' and 'curator's choice' displays, together with new multimedia facilities. It was salutary to find the decorative arts collections, out of fashion for over a century, returned to public display to become the main focus at Collins Barracks.

The museum began unveiling some of its longer-term displays with the launch of the exhibition *The Way We Wore: 250 Years of Irish Clothing and Jewellery*, which illustrated the clothing, accessories and jewellery worn in Ireland over the previous 250 years. This display, mounted by the keeper of decorative arts, was particularly successful due to its innovative interpretative approach and use of materials to make the information easily accessible. A range of smaller, temporary exhibitions also proved a popular way to introduce the public to the diversity of the collections in the new museum. No sooner was this exhibition opened than the museum acquired the Eileen Gray (1878–1976) Collection, followed by the purchase of the Eileen Gray Archive, representing a significant body of material associated with this pre-eminent Irish-born furniture designer and architect, who was a pioneer of the modern movement and one of the most influential women in these fields. Plans were put in place immediately for an exhibition devoted to Eileen Gray that would be augmented by a conference exploring the designer's international sphere of influence.

The Department of Arts, Culture and the Gaeltacht, having devised a staffing strategy with the director and the museum, began making a series of administrative and curatorial appointments, including education and community outreach officers, supported by a core of education assistants, to help improve the existing public service. This enabled the setting up of an education department and service that would allow the museum to provide programmes for all ages, drawing on the learning resources of the collections.[138] Across the city in Merrion Street, the keeper of the Natural History Museum drew on these resources as he devised new ways to promote the 'ten thousand specimens' in his care in an ongoing effort to draw the attention of new generations to the fascination of natural history specimens.[139]

Members of the public viewing the Decorative Arts collections

The facilities at the National Museum of Ireland – Decorative Arts and History in Collins Barracks are very extensive, enabling the staff to mount displays covering virtually every aspect of its collections.

The museum has acquired an extensive body of work by the internationally renowned Eileen Gray, which has made it a major resource for research on this modern Irish designer.

The Natural History Museum contained the early natural history specimens that formed the original core of the National Museum, up to the introduction of the decorative arts collections. It had been a very popular educational institution from 1857 until the opening of the larger National Museum in 1890, under which it became a division. Interest in natural history and the geological collections declined in the twentieth century, and this neglect meant that it was left intact as an original Victorian Natural History Museum. It suffered from the contemporary lack of interest in classes of works, such as trays of natural history specimens, the public being more attracted to the presentation of individual objects, aided by improved standards in lighting and temperature control. The aspiration to refurbish this venerable institution takes into account the desire to return it to its original state.

The opening of the Museum of Decorative Arts and History was of particular benefit to the curators, because it provided them with a range of galleries in which to display the varied collections, enabling them to work with designers in the creation of a host of displays highlighting the decorative arts and history, resulting in a regular programme of new shows. In the background the growing team of conservators were treating the collections, just as the registrar and documentation team were recording the holdings of this vast museum. The new awareness of the public role of the museum was seized upon by both curators and other professional staff, who worked together to devise curatorial practices and education services that would engage the public in the collections. Thus the National Museum's public programming was advanced by its education staff through the creation of innovative programmes, drawing on well-equipped Resource Rooms that facilitated practical activities. Education throughout the 'whole museum' was a policy devised by staff seeking to emphasize the central position of learning in the institution with a clear mission statement:

> The National Museum of Ireland endeavours to provide a welcome environment in which to enable diverse audiences to explore the national collections for inspiration, learning and enjoyment. The Museum collects, safeguards and makes accessible artifacts and specimens, which it holds in trust for the nation. The national collections include the portable and cultural material heritage of Ireland and other cultures.[140]

Underpinning this work was the concept of lifelong learning, which identified all aspects of learning as forming part of a process that took place throughout a person's lifetime, rather than being confined to young people or college students.[141] It acknowledged that different strategies for learning were acquired as part of a person's everyday life experience. The programmes were divided into categories of 'Formal Sector' (primary, second and third level), 'Adult and Non-formal Sectors' (adult learners/community groups, family groups, children and young people) and identified 'People with Special Needs' (adults with learning disabilities) as an audience sector requiring particular attention. The museum organized activities such as exhibition lectures and worksheets to ensure the collections were accessible. Regular events included My Museum Sunday Family Programme and Sunday Family Tours, which encouraged families to explore the collections together at all the sites.[142] The schools programme included guided tours of the collections and the induction of third-level and transition-year students on work experience in museum departments, while primary-level teachers could take part in In-Career Development Courses. The museum's popular Saturday Club for young people was augmented by a summer school that involved arts- and crafts-based activities that drew on the collections.

The wider implications of this work have seen the museum move away from a traditional ideological framework to explore the intercultural context of its extensive collections, drawing particularly on the What's in Store display,

A century old: the replica Irish high cross

In the 1890s, Director G.T. Plunkett began commissioning replicas of the most famous Irish high crosses. Over a century later the National Museum of Ireland placed these antique plaster casts on display to illustrate to contemporary audiences the significance of their archaeological heritage and to illustrate the exemplary sculpture and stylized motifs on the high crosses.

which revealed some of the reserve collections, including non-Irish, oriental materials.[143] The success of the museum's work has been acknowledged by the many awards garnered by the institution and by the numbers of visitors responding to its exhibitions. It is worth looking briefly at two exhibitions, to see what was achieved and what is the benefit of the museum's innovative approach.

Muse99 was a project that demonstrated the use of the collections as a learning resource, based on research undertaken by second-level students, from which works of art were created on the theme of Irish history and culture.[144] This led to regional displays and a national exhibition, which was accompanied by a programme of practical activities that enabled children and the public to become involved in creative art and craftwork at the museum; it was attended by 35,000 people. A key element in the success of the project was the museum's collaboration with the Association of Secondary Teachers of Ireland.[145] The Association highlighted the visual arts in secondary schools and drew on the contribution of post-primary art teachers, who took pride in the achievements of their students at the national and regional exhibitions.

A young person interacting with the collections at the National Museum of Ireland – Decorative Arts and History, Collins Barracks. The range of exhibitions and educational programmes have increased to cater for the growing audiences that visit the National Museum's Dublin sites.

Star attraction: a replica Viking ship, the *Sea Stallion*

The *Sea Stallion*, Dublin's Viking warship, was displayed in pride of place in the Central Court of Collins Barracks, where visitors were not just able to explore the Viking ship, but to experience a range of crafts and techniques, programmes and activities, that highlighted Viking Ireland.

The project also promoted the National Museum as a major cultural resource, demonstrating the close links between the institution and the schools featured in the catalogue.[146] A different type of initiative was the exhibition *A Few of Our Favourite Things*, involving the work of adults with intellectual disabilities. This project addressed a specific museum objective: 'to maximize access, both physical and intellectual, for all categories of visitor'. This exhibition would represent the outcome of the experience of a group of adults from St John of God Carmona Services, Sunbeam House Services and St Michael's House, who researched the collections and devised every aspect of the exhibition, including acting as guides for the public.[147] Writer Brian Keenan launched the project: 'History is what we do now. If history has this dynamic, it is not only about the great moments or the great persons – it is about the small magical moments and things that engage us with life and make it so important, so insightful.'[148]

Award-winning ventures such as these also won column inches and accolades for the museum, but the real benefit of undertaking these initiatives was the experience of the participants: 'With projects such as this, no-one need be marginalized, differentiated or invisible.'[149] These projects teach museum staff new ways of working with people with different levels of ability, which in turn improves the profile and perceived value of people with intellectual disabilities in society. The long-term benefits of these collaborative processes continue to inform the work at the museum's sites in Collins Barracks, Kildare Street and Merrion Street.

The Millennium Era

The National Museum ended the twentieth century as it had started it, on a positive note. Turlough Park House in Castlebar, County Mayo, was designated as the museum's first regional branch, to form a repository for the Folklife Collections, which were amassed by the museum from the 1930s, with the collections themselves dating from the 1850s to 1950s. The director had witnessed a turnaround in the institution's fortunes, leaving the Museum facing into the new millennium with a new impetus and a fresh vision of its resources and their potential.

The pace of development overseen by the director at the NMI over the period 1990–2000, when it had within its grasp the potential of four separate museums, was remarkable. This progress was accompanied by a commensurate increase in funding and staffing levels to enable the museum to assume a position of strength in the new century. It also began to explore the multi-cultural nature of its holdings, enabling the 'imagining' of historical Irish material placed within the context of wider cultures.[150] The primary purpose of the National Museum to collect, preserve, research and exhibit examples of Ireland's portable material heritage and natural history, positioned it to greet the new millennium as: 'A first class institution that promotes the widest understanding and appreciation of Ireland's distinctive culture and natural history, and their place in the wider world.'[151]

13

The National Gallery of Ireland: 'Supporting, Understanding, Appreciation and Enjoyment of the National Collections'

When the National Gallery of Ireland was established, it gave public expression to what had long been a private passion, namely the collection of works of art.[1]

The National Gallery entered the twentieth century with a positive outlook that mirrored that of the National Museum. Neither institution could have foreseen the political turmoil that lay ahead, when a new government would strive to create employment in an economically challenging environment. The changed situation left the two museums struggling to cope, a struggle that was not helped by the discontinuing of the National Museum's link with the South Kensington Museum in the new state, and the ending of the National Gallery's relationship with the Treasury. However, the National Gallery had the advantage that its Act (1854) and independent board saved it some of the difficulties that the museum would later experience.

Michelangelo Merisi da Caravaggio (1571–1610) *The Taking of Christ,* **1602**
Oil on canvas, 133.5 x 169.5 cm. NGI 14,702.

On indefinite loan to the National Gallery of Ireland from the Jesuit community of Leeson Street, Dublin, who acknowledge the generosity of the late Marie Lea-Wilson, 1992. The painting, first shown to the public in 1993 at an exhibition entitled *Caravaggio: The Master Revealed,* is a major attraction for visitors to Dublin.

While the RHA was not as buoyant as its fellow institutions in the first half of the century, its links with the National Gallery proved beneficial when the gallery stepped in to help with a venue for RHA annual exhibitions. It has already been noted that the RHA suffered a decline during the twentieth century, but it nonetheless retained its own place in the story of the National Gallery during this period, and the two were intertwined to a certain degree. That is why the story of the gallery in the twentieth century begins with an update on the fortunes of the RHA.

The RHA: A Precursor of the NGI

The RHA experienced a decline in popularity from the end of the 1890s. As a result, the academy–museum relationship waned in the early twentieth

The ruins of the Royal Hibernian Academy house on Abbey Street, destroyed during the Easter Rising, 1916

When Academy House was destroyed during the Easter Rising, 1916, along with the building went the collection, archives and the annual exhibition (1916). The keeper, James Malachy Kavanagh, escaped with the academy's charter.

century as the emphasis focused on the original work of art – the authentic artefact – and students were attracted by modernism and abstraction. Sir William de Abney's report in 1901 on the arts in Ireland noted a lack of development and suggested electing women as members of the RHA because many of the best Irish artists were women.[2] Despite this, Sarah Purser, twenty-nine years a member of the NGI board, fifty-three years exhibiting with the RHA, had to wait until 1924 for full membership of the RHA.

An official inquiry into the work of the RHA and the Metropolitan School of Art heard a recommendation from William Orpen (who revived life classes at the School of Art in 1902–15) that the RHA should emulate the practices of the Slade School of Fine Art in London.[3] Orpen, an ex-student and visiting teacher at the School of Art who knew the Slade intimately, pointed out that it was practising artists who taught at the Slade, 'a painter is the only one who can teach painting', and that fine art teaching included the life class.

The real catastrophe for the RHA came in 1916 when both its premises and collections in Lower Abbey Street were destroyed during the Easter Rising. The academy's school struggled to survive, first holding classes at number 6 St Stephen's Green (1916–39) and then at 15 Ely Place (1939–42). Ireland's young art practitioners, who were influenced by European avant-garde ideas, formed their own groups,[4] and a new generation of artists exhibited at shows that reflected new identities: 'Who would have ventured to predict ten years ago that such a festival would be held in Dublin having as an accompaniment a collection of works by Irish artists.'[5] While Bodkin gave a positive review of the RHA exhibitions at the College of Art (over the period 1917–69), the fact was that practising artists had little time for academies.[6]

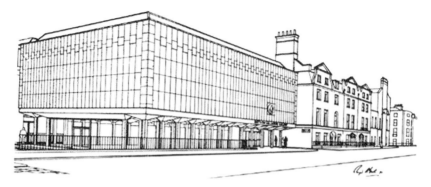

Raymond McGrath's design for the new Royal Hibernian Academy Gallagher Gallery

Raymond McGrath (1903–77), an Australian-born architect and interior designer, was professor of architecture at the Royal Hibernian Academy, where he worked on a design for a new building. The RHA has since been remodeled and extended, enabling it to assume traditional and innovative roles within the art world.

The decline evident at the RHA from the 1940s[7] had escalated by the 1960s, when the academic style of teaching employed by RHA tutors at the College of Art caused student rioting. After 1969, RHA staff ceased to dominate fine art teaching at the college.[8]

The National Gallery took up the mantle of displaying RHA annual exhibitions from 1971 to 1984 and this encouraged student interaction with the collections. The acquisition of new premises at Ely Place in 1938 opened the academy up, not just to painters, sculptors and architects, but also to artists working in new media.[9] Late in the century, in a remarkable reversal of fortune, the RHA turned itself around as a reinvigorated restructured institution (director Patrick T. Murphy), by affirming its traditional roles of promoting the status of the artist, providing exhibitions and activities, and developing its studios/master-classes, prior to the re-opening of its schools.[10]

The National Gallery of Ireland

The twentieth century opened with good news for the National Gallery when bequests were received from Henry Barron and Henry Vaughan, including a series of watercolours by Joseph Mallord William Turner (1775–1851), which could be shown only in January, when the sunlight was at its weakest.[11] The death of Sir Frederic William Burton in 1900 was a blow to the gallery because, despite being in charge of London's National Gallery, Burton had

J.M.W. Turner (1775–1851), *Fishing Boats on Folkestone Beach,* **c.1828**
Graphite and watercolour on paper, 18 x 26 cm. NGI 2415.

Turner was one of the most important British painters of the nineteenth century. When Henry Vaughan died, he left his Turner watercolours to be divided between the National Gallery of Scotland (38), the National Gallery of Ireland (31), and the National Gallery, London (23) – and they later devolved to the Tate Gallery. To this day, Dublin's share of the watercolours are exhibited only in January, spending the remainder of the year in a special wooden cabinet. **Inset:** The special cabinet housing the Turner watercolours.

assisted Ireland's gallery through support and donations, while also acting as one of the first guarantors of the Irish Literary Theatre.[12] The board demonstrated its regard by holding a retrospective exhibition devoted to Burton, which was attended by 8,000 people and sold 'eight hundred' catalogues.[13] This paved the way to mount a Turner show, which proved so popular it led some Dubliners 'to visit the Gallery for the first time'.[14]

The negotiations of the pending Milltown gift by Lady Milltown, through her intermediary, the solicitor W.A. Lanphier of Naas, County Kildare, tested all of the business skills of the director, Walter Armstrong, and his patient board. The new extension to house the donation was much progressed before Lady

Milltown finally signed the Deed of Gift for the Collection in 1902, making over the pictures, sculpture, decorative furniture, silver, books and other works of art to the gallery. The extension opened on 16 March 1903, with the Milltown Collection notably absent.[15] Designed by Thomas Manley Deane, the building took three years to complete[16] and was reported by *The Irish Times* to be 'One of the best-equipped neatly designed and elegantly fitted Public Galleries in the Kingdom', its enfilade of doorcases by Cambi being particularly fine. The *Freeman's Journal* declared it to be a gallery 'any city in Europe might well be proud of', with twenty-three rooms displaying seven hundred 'Old Masters and Irish portraits', enhanced by the loan of Vermeer's *The Soldier and the Laughing Girl* (*c.* 1655–60), which would enter New York's Frick Collection in 1911.[17] Lady Milltown's prolific correspondence regarding the bequest resulted in the need for an Act of Indenture to clarify the donation.[18] The outcome saw one of the most important private Irish Grand Tour collections devolving to a public art museum, where it would be housed in its own wing, commemorated as the Milltown Wing.[19]

In 1907 Lady Butler assumed her place as the first woman to join the board, only to be succeeded by Purser in 1914, whose long tenure highlighted the rise of women artists in the early twentieth century. The scholar Françoise Henry served for twenty years from 1962, and her tenure in turn highlighted the growing significance of the role of women in Irish society.

In 1914 Armstrong retired as director after just under a quarter-century's service. He had watched the decline of art students at the gallery, resulting in his recommendation to the board to abolish the 'private days' and instead increase public opening hours to 10 a.m. to 5 p.m. weekdays. This marked a more democratic approach for Ireland's National Gallery.[20] The new director, Hugh Lane (1914–15), had a connoisseur's eye for old master paintings.[21] His interest in Irish art had been encouraged by his aunt, Lady Augusta Gregory, and reinforced by an exhibition of Irish paintings by Nathaniel Hone (1831–1917) and John Butler Yeats (1839–1922). When his commission to John Butler Yeats to paint portraits 'of outstanding Irishmen' halted, he approached Orpen to complete the project. Orpen described Lane as 'a force one could not with-stand'.[22] As Lane's support for contemporary Irish art grew, he mounted exhibitions including one at the Guildhall in London, to which the NGI lent several works.

In 1908, Lane founded the Municipal Gallery of Modern Art, but the task of finding a home for this gallery would prove to be one of the greatest challenges of his life.[23] He had already gifted the NGI with pictures during his term on the board (1903–14), and now he donated a further twenty-four paintings. When Lane took over as director, he requested that the post be made part-time to facilitate continuation of his art business in London and to demonstrate that he was a man of independent means. Although he donated his salary to the gallery, the fact that the director's post was now part-time was a burden that subsequent directors would carry until the 1950s. Lane's awareness that the country needed a good international collection to attract visitors to its National Gallery was articulated in a letter to the Treasury: 'The ordinary visitor and student can gather from [the National Gallery] a fair idea of the course of European painting ... The presence of some more famous pictures would make a great difference to the reputation of the Dublin Gallery and attract visitors from all over Europe.'[24]

The threat of war resulted in staff from the National Gallery and the

Frans Snyders (1579–1657), *A Banquet Piece*, late 1620s
Oil on canvas, 92.3 x 156.1 cm. NGI 811.

In 1915, Hugh Lane acquired this still life painting, which later formed part of the Lane Bequest (1918). It is most likely the table of a nobleman, or a merchant with a country estate, the focus of which is a porcelain bowl overfilled with sumptuous fruit. During his lifetime, Sir Hugh Lane gifted the National Gallery twenty-four works. Following his death in 1915, the Lane Fund (1917) has provided assistance to acquire over fifty-four works.

museum leaving to enlist in the British army. When war broke out, the board took the decision, as a cautionary measure, to remove its furniture from Dublin Castle, which was being used as a hospital for British troops. When the Treasury cut the gallery's funding, on the grounds that it was unjustifiable to use public money to purchase pictures 'in a national emergency', the board retaliated immediately: 'This institution, unlike the Galleries of England and Scotland, is wholly dependent on the grants made by Government.'[25]

The director, who was constantly on the move, made a trip to New York in 1915 with an unfortunate outcome: he was sailing on the ill-fated *Lusitania*, which was sunk by a German U-boat near Cork. Lane lost his life in the tragedy. His will and unwitnessed codicil would form a major dispute between Britain and Ireland for years to come.[26] The board was shocked by the sudden death of Lane. It was equally surprised when it discovered that, despite his complicated legacy, he had left the majority of his estate to the NGI. In 1918 the board marked its appreciation by mounting an exhibition of sixty-two pictures devoted to the Hugh Lane legacy.[27]

Walter Strickland, the gallery's elderly registrar, was drafted in to act as director (having compiled his *Dictionary of Irish Artists* in 1913), along with his clerk, the writer James Stephens. Despite the Treasury's wartime caution to close the doors, the gallery remained open in order to provide 'inspiration, education and enjoyment of the public'. However, while Strickland was in London on business in 1916, the Easter rising erupted on Easter Monday, 24 April. The gallery was slow to hear about the upheavals in the city, and it was left to Stephens to have 'the public excluded', the gallery being reputedly the last institution in Dublin to close its doors that day.[28] Stephens reasoned and remonstrated over the Rising: 'The fault lies with England – we are a little country and you, a huge country, have persistently beaten us – no nation has forgiven its enemies as we have forgiven you.'[29] The board, largely unaware of the implications of 'one of the most romantic rebellions in European history', commiserated with the RHA over the 'destruction of its Academy House during the late Rebellion'.[30] Despite this series of events, 232 artists and students visited the gallery and copied from the collections during 1916.[31]

Incoming part-time director Robert Langton Douglas (1916–23), having enlisted in the war effort, continued his war duties in London (the board granted him leave in 1915). Although he relinquished his commission in July

1917, he continued to work at the War Office.[32] In the meantime, an exhibition comprising the recently acquired Nathaniel Hone Bequest was mounted by Dermod O'Brien and Thomas Bodkin.[33] The passing into law of the Government of Ireland Act 1920 resulted in the gallery's board having to produce its Act of Parliament to prove that 'the collection should remain in Dublin in its entirety'.[34]

During the War of Independence and subsequent treaty, Purser's friendship with Arthur Griffith (first president of the government of the Irish Free State) kept the gallery updated on events, until the death of Griffith on 12 August 1922, followed by the death of Michael Collins ten days later. Purser

Walter Osborne (1859–1903), *Nathaniel Hone, Artist (1831–1917)*, 1894
Oil on canvas, 86 x 94 cm. NGI 987.

Nathaniel Hone and his friend Walter Osborne liked to paint the landscape of north County Dublin together. The Hone Bequest formed the largest gift to the gallery, comprising oils and watercolours that reflected all aspects of the artist's career.

Edgar Degas (1834–1917), *Two Ballet Dancers in a Dressing Room,* **c.1880**
Pastel on paper, 48.5 x 64 cm. NGI 2740.

Degas was a founder member of the Impressionists. Edward Martyn, an Irish cultural figure associated with the Celtic Revival, bought this work from Degas's dealer, Paul Durand-Ruel, in 1886, when he was in Paris with the writer George Moore. Martyn bequeathed seven works to the gallery in 1924, including a Monet, two Degas pastels and a Corot.

kept the board informed of the political situation through contact with the third president, William T. Cosgrave.[35]

As it turned out, 1922 was to be an auspicious year. On the international front, it marked the publication of Joyce's *Ulysses*, a book that would profoundly change twentieth-century literature. Ireland continued to be dominated by political events, however, which saw the Civil War lead once again to the closure of the gallery. During this period, the OPW repaired damage to the building that had been sustained during the hostilities.[36] In the course of a Dáil Debate, it was proposed that the Gallery provide art lectures for the public.[37] Within the gallery, the board had begun to find the director's absences annoying and it raised concerns over the management of the institution. In addition, there were issues over his handling of Lane's affairs and his picture-selling activities. These concerns led Douglas to resign on 4 July 1923. (Despite this, he would later offer paintings to the gallery.[38]) Meanwhile, the Department of Home Affairs (Justice from 1923) monitored the closure of the gallery between October 1922 and February 1924. During this interim 'permits for students' continued to be provided, resulting in 225 artists and students drawing on the gallery collections between 1921 and 1924.[39] The seventy-year relationship with the British Treasury ended as the gallery was moved first under the Department of Finance, in 1922, and then under the Department of Education.[40]

In 1923, the board appointed the architect Lucius O'Callaghan as the next part-time director.[41] In 1924 one of his first tasks was to re-open the gallery and to announce details of the Edward Martyn (1859–1923) Bequest. It also marked the year that Sarah Purser founded the Society of the Friends of the National Collections of Ireland, which would provide important works for many museums, including the gallery.[42] The new government had the power to appoint members to the gallery board, outside of *ex officio* members, and there were celebrations when incoming board member W.B. Yeats was awarded the Nobel Prize for Literature in 1923,[43] his achievement being followed by that of Shaw in 1925. The role of the gallery in facilitating the public was noted as the director recorded his first request for a guide in 1926, 'for the use of persons conducting school-children over the gallery'.[44]

When Bodkin assumed the directorship in 1927, he briskly encouraged the cultural institutions to make much better use of their collections.[45] He studied a report by Sir Henry Miers for the Carnegie Trust, which stated that although the gallery was a 'typical art gallery containing examples of many of the old masters', museums had a role to provide instruction to the public.[46] Bodkin took up Miers' suggestion of promoting the collection through talks, speaking himself at the Hermione series at Alexandra College; he also spoke at UCD courses and at the universities of Leiden and Berlin. An Act effected on 25 July 1928 allowed the gallery to start lending pictures overseas.[47] In 1929, when the centenary of Catholic Emancipation was celebrated, an Academy of Christian Art (1929–46) was set up to foster Christian concepts in art, spearheaded by Count Plunkett, former director of the National Museum, and minister for fine arts (1921–2).[48] Both the director and George Atkinson, headmaster of the Metropolitan School of Art, made themselves available during Dublin Civic Week in 1929 to show visitors around the gallery.[49] Bodkin provoked the ire of Atkinson, however, when he commented on the decline in the use of the gallery by students: 'Professional students of art show a depressing apathy to the lessons to be learned from the achievements of the Great Masters.' To which Atkinson retorted that they 'used it extensively for the purpose of their studies'.[50] The gallery opened late during the Eucharistic Congress in 1932, resulting in over 4,000 visitors.[51]

In 1932 Bodkin wrote: 'Every modern town of importance devotes attention and revenue to maintaining a gallery of pictures for the education and enjoyment of its citizens. A National gallery is a prime part of the response.'[52] Desiring to see this aspiration a reality, Bodkin met with the minister for education in 1931 to put forward a case for the 'provision of at least £100 a year to enable lectures on the collection to be given'. The director's subsequent report outlining the need for critical resources resulted in two board deputations to meet government in 1931 and 1934. The gallery was made aware of the difficulty of finding even 'sufficient money for absolutely necessary services'.[53] Bodkin nonetheless supported the minister's idea of encouraging 'schoolchildren to visit the Gallery'.[54] The problems with acquiring resources for the institution left Bodkin feeling unsuccessful in his efforts and that his position was untenable: 'no concessions would be granted to the Gallery while he remained as Director'. He concluded: 'I heard last night that the Minister for Education is prepared to recommend a full-time post … if my resignation has really produced this happy result I have done something for the cause of art in Ireland.'[55]

In the interim Registrar Brinsley MacNamara (playwright and novelist) stepped in as acting director. Bodkin's departure was noted in the Dáil, where the chamber was told about the 'services which Dr Bodkin rendered to this country and to the National Gallery in particular'. A parliamentary debate discussed the need to hold lectures to attract visitors to the gallery; however, it was acknowledged that there were no funds to facilitate this.[56]

In 1935 the Department of Education sent a circular to schools advocating 'organized visits of school-children to Dublin-based educational institutions including the National Gallery'. It pointed out that the European Paintings and National Portrait sections were of 'interest to pupils in connection with their study of Irish history'.[57] When George Furlong was subsequently

The MacEgan (1856–1939), *The Main Gallery*, 1932

John Darius Joseph MacEgan studied in Dublin and London and exhibited at the RHA. His work is to be found in several public collections. This painting represents an everyday image of the Dargan Wing, main gallery in the early part of the twentieth century, the double hang of the Italian paintings being the custom of the period. (Courtesy of the Burns Collection, Boston College, @ The artist's estate).

appointed director (1935–50), he examined the collection to see if it could be restored, consulting with the conservator at the Kunsthistorisches Museum in Vienna (where Furlong had worked as a guide). In the meantime, the Milltown silver was provided on loan to the National Museum, where there was a decorative arts context for the display of this material. Furlong, who was interested in publicizing the collection, gave a number of broadcasts on 'pictures in the collection' and submitted a request to the board for lectures to be given to groups in the gallery.

It was Furlong's wish to lay an oak floor in the Sculpture Hall in 1937 that heralded the demise of the cast collection. 'It was agreed that the plaster casts could be stored downstairs in a room not open to the public but which students or those wishing to draw from them could have access.'[58] For decades the antique cast collections had served as a source of inspiration for artists and students, at a time when museums were seen as centres of instruction. While the art colleges had originally been embedded in museums, art teaching had changed, as a result of which students were no longer required to draw from antique casts. As the emphasis shifted to studying original works of art, students were encouraged instead to focus on modernism and the growing impact of abstraction. The disappearance of the antique casts was inevitable as more room was sought for the collections.

Furlong also set about decorating the galleries and re-hanging the collection. He followed contemporary practice in Europe and for the first time hung the works on the line, so that the paintings could be viewed at eye level, with sufficient space surrounding each work to allow it to be properly seen and appreciated. Evie Hone, the stained-glass artist, joined the gallery's board following the first Irish Exhibition of *Living Art* in 1943.[59]

The repercussions of the Second World War were felt in Ireland, requiring de Valera's renowned diplomatic skills to steer the country on a safe passage by pursuing a policy of neutrality. In common with all of the cultural institutions, the gallery witnessed a decline in attendance to an average of 38,500 visitors per year. Concern was expressed in the Dáil about the safety of the national collections.[60] In March 1939, Furlong attended a meeting, convened by the Department of Education, to establish an Air-Raid Protection Plan for the treasures in the cultural institutions.[61] Following this discussion, the Department of Education arranged for the storage of the pictures in the

The Preparatory College, Tourmakeady, County Mayo

As events in Germany deteriorated during the 1930s, the Irish government drew up plans to protect the national collections. The gallery received instructions from the Department of Education to remove its collections to store. They were transported to the Preparatory College at Tourmakeady in Mayo, where they remained for the duration of the Second World War.

'vaults of the Bank of Ireland', with the remaining works secured in 'safe parts' of the building.[62] Furlong set up a shelter for fire fighters in the basement and made air-raid precaution arrangements with the staff of numbers 88 and 89 Merrion Square. The government's reduction of the gallery's grant was accepted due to the critical state of 'the economy' and came as concern was being expressed over the condition of the paintings in storage.[63] The Department of Education agreed to provide alternative accommodation at the Preparatory College, Tourmakeady, County Mayo.[64] Furlong told the story of the evacuation of the collection to County Mayo:

> I visited the College and found the building in which it was proposed to house the pictures. It met the Board's requirements as regards light, air, heating and protection from fire or outside interference. Arrangements were made and on 2 June the transfer of 224 selected pictures, which had been packed in 132 cases, was begun. The transfer was carried out by the Great Southern Railway Company and three Attendants were sent to open the cases and arrange the pictures in the selected portions of the building, which took ten days to complete. One Attendant was left in charge at Tourmakeady where he has since remained.[65]

As a result of this transfer, visitors soon discovered that key works were missing from the gallery, having been 'moved to places of greater safety, owing to emergency conditions'.[66] In 1944 the Friends of the National Collections borrowed a number of works for an exhibition of modern French paintings held at the College of Art in 1944. The gallery's collection returned to Dublin in 1945: 'A few were found to have suffered minor damage, mainly through blistering.'[67] This concluded a major episode in gallery history, echoed in war evacuation of collections by London's National Gallery to Wales,[68] by the Louvre to Brittany, and by New York's Metropolitan Museum of Art to Philadelphia.[69]

Bodkin's *Report on the Arts in Ireland* was published in 1949 and was critical of the institution: 'So far as the education of the public and the prestige of the State are concerned the National Gallery is, as it functions at present, of little utility.'[70] A request was made for the provision of guides, 'to make the

Gallery better known to the public', and classes on 'drawing, painting, modelling'.[71] Furlong oversaw the installation of electric light (1946–51), while keeping an eye on developments in 'the galleries in America'. He had developed an astute eye for acquisitions, and received the Mrs Magawley Bannon Trust in 1947 before his resignation in 1950.[72]

In 1950 Shaw died at his home at Ayot St Lawrence, Hertfordshire, having previously corresponded with the board regarding the gallery's Prince Paul Troubetzkoy statue of Shaw. Brinsley MacNamara, again acting as temporary director, noted: 'Although most of Mr. Shaw's remarks were phrased in his usual light-hearted manner, he paid tribute to the Gallery for a priceless part of his education in recognition of which he had left it a third part of his residual estate.'[73] It was reported in the Dáil that Shaw had stood by Ireland when the 'country had few friends'. In time it emerged that the most sharp-witted, astute and good-humoured of Irishmen would become the gallery's major financial benefactor.[74] While his legacy is calculated in millions, its true value can be judged by the unparalleled enjoyment visitors gain from the paintings that it provides.

When Thomas MacGreevy was appointed director (1950–63), he informed the board of Sir Alfred Chester Beatty's exceptional gift of 'nineteenth-century French paintings'.[75] MacGreevy's experiences in London and Paris made him alert to the deficiencies of the gallery and he wasted no time in

Jules Breton (1827–1906), *The Gleaners,* **1854**
Oil on canvas, 93 x 138 cm. NGI 4213.

Breton painted scenes of contemporary provincial life, demonstrating the dignity of the labourers in the quiet way that they went about their work. In the background is the village of Courrières, Breton's birth place in north-east France. Sir Alfred Chester Beatty bequeathed over ninety nineteenth-century paintings to the gallery in 1950, of which this is one.

outlining the backward state of the institution, using Bodkin's *Report on the Arts in Ireland* to justify his argument that 'as a nation we are woefully ill-equipped to judge of the visual arts'.[76] MacGreevy was aware of the Purser–Griffith lectures on European painting begun at UCD in 1935, and the history of art talks at the College of Art in 1943, several of which he had given;[77] nonetheless, he determined that there would be a series of public lectures to develop knowledge and appreciation of the national collections.

MacGreevy's commitment and devotion to the gallery was evident, demonstrated in a memo to the president in 1950: ' the collection is not being utilized as it should be for the public good … little interest is taken by ordinary citizens in our great pictures which, if they were appreciated could not fail to have a highly beneficial effect, directly on education and good taste.' He further pointed out that 'changes in the present antiquated method of working the Gallery must be effected'.[78] In support of his position he cited previous unsuccessful requests to the Department of Education concerning staff, his own 'half-time post', the inadequacy of the premises, the lack of postcard reproductions and the absence of public lectures: 'A public demand for lectures has long existed, the Board have been anxious to meet the demand but have not the means of meeting it.' Echoing these comments, the Dáil noted that 'Our National Gallery has been crippled and hampered for want of money'. MacGreevy concluded: 'if sanction is withheld and the estimate for lectures rejected, the responsibility must rest with the Department'.[79] The response was immediate:

> A sum of £250 has been included in the Estimates to meet the cost. The Minister for Education would be obliged if consideration is given to having some lectures in Irish. [While the Government was promoting the Irish language, the collection had not yet grown to form the major School of Irish Painting that it would later in the century.] A sum of £1,250 is included for the purpose of having post-card size reproductions in colour of some pictures in the Gallery.[80]

A Dáil debate subsequently noted that thirty-eight colour postcards were available by 1955.[81]

In 1952 the director began developing a wider role for the gallery, starting with his free public lecture series, for which he encouraged 'young Irish artists and art historians' to make suggestions, including Donal Murphy (sculptor) and James White (art historian).[82] MacGreevy's programme was popular and in demand, 'lectures on alternative Sundays and Wednesdays', although one member of the public wished 'children under twelve years should not be allowed in the Gallery during the lectures'.[83] Funding was provided for the programme: 'The sum allocated to lectures in the National Gallery is £250 ... with enough over to allow lectures to schools and educational institutions.'[84] MacGreevy was a good communicator: 'Your way of showing the boys how to look at pictures has caught their imagination and opened up a new world for them.'[85] He gave his support to schools: 'I showed it to the great artist, Mr. Yeats ... He was delighted and wishes the boys the best of luck.'[86] His friend, Samuel Beckett, wrote about a painting by Jack B. Yeats that had captured his imagination and that would later enter the collection: 'One small picture especially, *Morning* ... Do you think he would be amenable to instalments. It's a long time since I saw a picture I wanted so much.'[87] Beckett acquired the painting and treasured it throughout his life. The lecture programme would help to develop a public appreciation of art in Ireland.

In 1956 a Government Bill finally returned the director's post to 'full-time'.[88] In 1957 the impact of the death of his friend, Jack B. Yeats, together with a heavy workload – 'I know how much you are doing for the Gallery'[89] – took its toll on MacGreevy, contributing to his failing health. The director regularly entertained international figures, including Sir Kenneth Clarke (former director of London's National Gallery), Professor Magnani of the University of Rome, Francis H. Taylor of Worcester Art Museum and James J. Rorimer, incoming director of the Metropolitan Museum of Art, New York.[90] MacGreevy's aim of raising standards at the gallery and making it an accessible institution was evidenced by his many far-sighted initiatives: public lectures; the sale of reproductions; approval to have a lift installed; recording of visitor numbers; sanction for staff; a catalogue of the paintings; the Shaw and Lane Funds used to buy artworks; the restoration of the building; and plans for a conservation studio.[91]

The condition of the collection had been a cause for concern, even though works had been restored in Dublin and in London. MacGreevy sought sanction from the board to consult Cesare Brandi of the Istituto Centrale del Restauro in Rome, who advised on a future conservation laboratory for Dublin. In the meantime, a new wing that MacGreevy had proposed, which would be designed by Frank Du Berry of the OPW, received approval from the board. In explaining why this wing was needed, the chairman told the Dáil that 'Pictures were made to be seen and not to be hidden away'.[92] Due to MacGreevy's ill health, William O'Sullivan, keeper of Art and Industry at the NMI, was seconded to assist the director between 1958 and 1963.[93]

MacGreevy received many honours and served twice on the new Arts Council. The board noted with appreciation that as a result of his efforts on behalf of the institution, MacGreevy had raised visitor numbers to the gallery from 40,664 in 1950 to 55,125 in 1963. When he retired in 1963, 'having performed his duties with diligence and fidelity',[94] he took pleasure in seeing art history departments set up at UCD in 1965, followed by TCD in 1966.

While the 1960s was a time of optimism in the country, the 1970s was marked by financial instability, rising unemployment and by the beginning of an oil crisis, as Ireland marked the start of the transition from being rooted in a rural way of life to becoming increasingly urbanized. This era saw the first ground-breaking *Rosc* exhibition of modern art in 1967, and the introduction of an innovative tax-free status for creative artists in 1969.[95] Across the River Liffey in Parnell Square, James White had begun to revitalize the city's Municipal Gallery of Modern Art (1960–4). In 1964 he moved across to the NGI to become one of its most successful directors (1964–80).[96]

White's immediate proposal to hold an exhibition in 1964 to mark the centenary of the institution and to commemorate MacGreevy's directorship is an example of the way in which his own directorship would evolve.[97] The catalogue stated some of his aims, such as 'extending the service and making the Gallery more attractive to the public', listing opening hours with talks on Sunday and Wednesday and tours on Sunday, to promote the gallery.[98] White's first report to the board showed the type of results he would achieve: '6,000 files installed for the cataloguing of the works in our possession … lecturers increased to five'.[99] The National Gallery of Ireland Act 1963, which facilitated loans to approved institutions, including international exhibitions and provincial museums, would promote the collections further. The Lane and Shaw Funds were used to expand the collections, just as White desired to 'strengthen the Irish school of painting' and acquire icons.[100]

In 1962, White had initiated a Children's Art Holiday at the Municipal gallery, in response to the lack of art education available to most children. In 1964 he introduced the concept of a Children's Christmas Art Holiday at the National Gallery: 'To make children feel that the Gallery was a friendly place where they could enjoy themselves by permitting them to paint pictures under the guidance of well-known artists.'[101] Like most successful events, it was based on a simple idea – an art class hosted by a painter for young people to observe and take part in. Gerard Dillon explained how it worked:

> about 500 from 12–18 year olds and 900 from age 7–12 … lovely children from all classes – good schools to back street kids. They loved it so it made me love it – mums patiently waiting down the stairs. When it was over they asked me about

George Campbell, who they had the day before, 'he must be over one hundred years old' and I replied yes, but lots of old men and women have hearts of children.[102]

It is remarkable that over 4,000 parents and children attended the Art Holiday in 1965.[103] A journalist described how 'The children went about their work with a unique degree of single mindedness while their parents were kept at bay in the entrance hall', and this was noted by the director to the board.[104] This was a significant educational development that proved innovative for Dublin in the 1960s and it changed the public perception of the gallery, which for the first time became a welcoming place to children and parents. The fact that it was free made it accessible to everyone, and for many it was their only introduction to art, despite all the aspirations articulated in the Dáil. White's first year as director saw gallery attendance figures rise to 68,127.[105]

There was progress and growth on other fronts, too. In 1964 the director reviewed the issue of restoring the collection by visiting the Istituto Centrale del Restauro in Rome, where he discussed the provision of conservation treatments by the Roman institution in Dublin. On the advice of Professor Bruno Malojoli, a new studio was designed for the gallery by Professor Selim Augusti of the Istituto Centrale del Restauro. Teams of Roman restorers came to Dublin over several summers, working on the reserve collections, rediscovering pictures, and assisting on exhibitions.

White was aware that museums worldwide were developing a stronger

President Cearbhall Ó'Dálaigh (1911–78) visiting the Children's Christmas Art Holiday in 1966.

Since 1964 this annual event (now a family art holiday) has taken place on the last days of December, the longest running museum activity in the country. In 1966 President O'Dalaigh visited to see for himself the huge numbers of young people enjoying the art classes.

public role through exhibitions and education services, and a commercial role through publications, catering and retail facilities. Drawing on limited resources, he mounted temporary exhibitions such as *W.B. Yeats (1865–1965): A Centenary Exhibition* (Yeats had served on the board from 1924 until his death in 1939), and *Swift & His Age 1667–1967: A Tercentenary Exhibition*, which drew on the services of the gallery staff, the works having been treated by the Istituto's conservators.

The ongoing conservation programme included some paintings chosen from those purchased in Rome in 1856, from Alessandro Aducci. This included two great works by Giovanni Lanfranco (1582–1647), *The Last Supper* and *The Multiplication of the Loaves and Fishes*, painted for the Blessed Sacrament Chapel of the Basilica of St Paul's-without-Walls in Rome, which were a revelation when they emerged from the layers of dirt and discoloured varnish. In 1968 Michael Wynne organized a display of Lanfranco's works, together with the canvases that formed the decorative scheme of the chapel.[106] Another exciting discovery emerged with a small panel, *Madonna and Child*, by Paolo Uccello (1397–1475). When tests revealed a false dark blue veil over-painted to cover the head and face, the offending cloak was removed (a tempera painting on panel) to reveal the Madonna's rounded face, beautiful hair and delicate ears. Many works in the collection were uncovered and restored as a result of this programme. Irish graduates of the Istituto began to join the gallery staff, while continuing their links with their Roman colleagues. They also worked on gallery pictures at the British Museum. The Gallery's Conservation Department dealt with these oil paintings and works of art on paper, in a manner that continues today.[107]

The RDS collection of drawings that had been passed to the National Museum c.1877 were transferred to the gallery in the 1960s.[108] A picture clinic was established that enabled the public, for the first time, to have works of art examined by the staff, a practice that still continues.[109] The opening on 25 September 1968 of what would become known as the Beit Wing was the cause of celebration (Alfred Beit, a British art collector, connoisseur, philanthropist and honorary Irish citizen, who purchased Russborough, in Blessington, County Wicklow, in 1950, had become a board member in 1967), producing a record 196,102 visitors that year.[110] New facilities included twelve galleries, a library, a lecture theatre, storage in the basement, the first restaurant and a shop sales desk. In 1973 a room adjacent to the entrance was fitted out as a shop to generate income and provide souvenirs. The director used the vehicle of the media to create awareness of the gallery's new initiatives, which included lectures and a Painting of the Month event, comprising a talk and a dinner; a series of temporary exhibitions, such as *William Orpen: A Centenary Exhibition* (1978); and international touring shows, with accompanying catalogues.[111] At this time Sir Alec Martin, after nearly sixty years, the longest-serving board member, together with the Hon. Justice Murnaghan, departed from the board.[112]

Comments in the Dáil saw the gallery acknowledged as a 'place for extending the education of our children'.[113] White's recognition of the need 'to educate people about the collections' led him to seek education staff to set up structured services that would make the gallery even more accessible to the public. He was well aware of the services in American museums and had heard about education posts being created at the British Museum and the National Gallery in London, publicized by the Museums Association.[114] Following systematic approaches by White to the Department of Education, the post of education officer was sanctioned.[115] In 1974 the first education officer, Frances Ruane, was appointed at the gallery,[116] followed by the appointment of education officers at the National Museum, National Library and the Ulster Museum in 1976. Positive reports of the post emerged: '[Ruane] has been highly successful in making contact with schools and educational bodies. Lectures and tours have increased and new features for children and others have been introduced due to her enterprise.'[117] The education officer restructured the public lectures, with Tuesday coffee morning talks, followed by Wednesday afternoon talks in 1977, and had these initiatives advertised by means of a poster, in addition to which she started teachers' seminars. A 'Children's Saturday lunch and treasure hunt' was rewarded by 'a book token'.

In 1977 a new education officer, Niamh O'Sullivan, put in place a booking system that illustrated the growing importance of school visits to the gallery (308 provided in 1978).[118] Her fact-finding trip to the United States in 1979 resulted in new ideas, including Saturday Leaving Certificate art seminars, which were held for '700 pupils from schools outside Dublin'.[119] She encouraged children to interpret a painting, in the form of a play, which involved the children making props and costumes and enacting the play for parents and teachers.[120] Of greater significance was her collaboration with the National

Museum, National Library and Public Records Office on the touring exhibition *The Year of the Child*, illustrating aspects of childhood in Ireland in earlier times.[121] Her attempt to initiate a *News Review* was short-lived due to a lack of funding.

Having increased the staff, White worked with them to make the gallery a welcoming place, leading the artist Louis le Brocquy to comment that the museum had 'entered the life of the Nation'.[122] Like his predecessor, MacGreevy, White's prominence in the Irish museum world was followed by a series of public roles following his retirement in 1980.[123]

In 1980 the appointment of the new director, Homan Potterton (1980–8), coincided with a steep economic recession,[124] in spite of which the Irish Film Board was established (1982) and the Arts Council set up *Aosdána* (1982), a body honouring the achievement of creative individuals. It was during this decade that responsibility for the cultural institutions transferred from the Department of Education to the Department of the Taoiseach, where, in 1984, it came under the wing of the newly created minister of state for arts and culture, Ted Nealon.

Prior to taking up his post as director, Potterton had been an assistant keeper at the National Gallery, London, with responsibility for the seventeenth- and eighteenth-century Italian schools. His directorship of the NGI came at a difficult time, when resources were limited. Admission to the gallery was still free and in 1981 Potterton placed donation boxes in the entrance hall as a fund-raising measure (successful and in place to this day). He also introduced a sponsorship programme, which would form a part of the institution's resourcing henceforth. His initiative in publishing calendars, prints and postcards and a series of books illustrating *50 Pictures* from the collection proved successful, aided by developing the gallery bookshop.[125] Potterton placed a short-term moratorium on loans and exhibitions in order to facilitate the task of examining the collection, prior to publishing the first series of illustrated summary catalogues of the collection (1981–8). He followed this with a series of volumes on individual schools of painting, his own appearing in 1986: *Dutch Seventeenth and Eighteenth Century Paintings in the National Gallery of Ireland*, 'the most noteworthy school of any we possess'.[126] In 1981 the trustees of the British Museum presented a plaster cast of the *Death Mask of George Bernard Shaw (1856–1950)*, by Charles Smith.

The director's initiative of a poster competition for secondary schools in 1981 and 1982 coincided with links that were being forged with the media to create greater awareness of the gallery. The incoming education officer reviewed the type of educational services that were appropriate to a national art gallery, from experience gained at European and American museums. As resources were limited, volunteers were recruited who had an interest in art, together with graduates on work placements. An interim Kids' Corner for young children was based on linking theory (a discussion in front of the painting) with practice (practical activities exploring the work of art).[127] The American psychologist Jerome Bruner noted that children seemed to grasp ideas and retain information better when it involved an interactive process, 'looking and responding', which produced a beneficial type of learning.[128] The dynamic between the learner and the process of learning was fundamental to the experience of the museum (echoed by contemporary philosophers).[129] The director reported: 'The idea is that children together with their parents will find a visit to the Gallery more enjoyable.'[130] There followed a series of programmes for young people designed to develop aesthetic awareness and critical thinking, underpinned by Gardner's multiple intelligence theory that expanded the ways in which children thought about and conceived of art. Summer events would be developed, some linked to European Heritage Classes,[131] while others included portfolio courses for teenagers, supplemented by activity sheets and drawing books.[132] Research revealed a lack of materials and creative projects for young people.[133]

The public tour programme was expanded to wider audiences, drawing on the services of art history graduates.[134] The type of tour offered was based on age profile, pre-school, first- and second-level, with third-level students and specialized groups facilitated by staff. Worksheets based on the collections were provided as a learning tool for use with groups in the galleries, although in practice were adopted by teachers in the classroom. An annual schools mailing was initiated, with the assistance of the Department of Education, providing a mutually beneficial partnership that created a greater awareness of the visual arts and the national collections.[135] Services for teachers included seminars demonstrating the links between the collections and the curriculum, in-service courses (supported by the Department of Education) and teacher training programmes. The director responded to the *Arts in Education Report*

A woman with impaired sight using a tactile picture set

The National Gallery provides a range of facilities, including special tours, audio guides and tactile picture sets, to make the collections accessible. The image shows a visitor using a tactile picture set with an outline of *St Francis in Ecstasy* from the circle of El Greco (1541–1614) to gain a sense of the painting.

(1985) by recommending integration of the arts into the school curriculum and advocating art training for teachers and inspectors.

The issue of creating awareness of the National Gallery was a major preoccupation of the director, leading him to draw on the skills of the staff in developing new areas in press, exhibitions, rights and reproductions, as well as expanding curatorial experience. A series of popular exhibitions with associated catalogues was mounted, including: *Walter Osborne* (1983); *Irish Impressionists* (1984), with an attendance of 60,000; *James Arthur O'Connor* (1985); *Masterpieces from the National Gallery of Ireland* (shown at the National Gallery in London, 1985); *Roderic O'Conor* (1986); *Irish Women Artists* (1987) (held jointly with the Douglas Hyde Gallery, TCD); a series of four *Recent Acquisitions* exhibitions (1980–1; 1981–2; 1982–3; 1986–8); and a *Best of the Cellar* (1982) show. The institution acquired a Georgian townhouse on Merrion Square, to be used by the Friends of the National Gallery (set up in 1989 and operating from 1990) for hosting illuminating and entertaining cultural programmes for a body of people who would lend their support to the gallery. At a more modest level, the gallery mounted small touring exhibitions, including *Painting in Focus* displays, facilitated by the Committee for National Touring Exhibition Services.[136]

The task of promoting the gallery involved the director in discussing aspects of the collections on radio and television programmes, together with the publication of a *Calendar of Events*, which would in the 1990s be developed into the quarterly *Gallery News*. As a result of a sustained programme of activities, the director, assistant director, curators, conservators and educators mounted exhibitions, published articles and wrote Painting of the Month leaflets, all to encourage interest in the gallery.[137]

Potterton's resignation in 1988 came after an eight-year tenure. His achievements were acknowledged: visitor numbers had risen from 426,426 in 1980 to 506,023 in 1988; major gifts were acquired, including the donation of seventeen masterpieces by Sir Alfred and Lady Beit and the Máire MacNeill Sweeney Bequest;[138] an astute acquisition policy;[139] the collection had been documented with scholarly publications; and the hope that future refurbishment might take place.[140]

The newly appointed director, Raymond Keaveney, took up his post in 1988, his tenure coinciding with the country's slow recovery from a decade of recession and a sense of Irish society opening up to new possibilities, at home and abroad. He discussed with the board a phased approach to refurbishing part of the gallery and the re-hanging of the collection, in time for Ireland's presidency of the European Union (1990). From the outset he was concerned about the fabric of the historic buildings and the need for new spaces to display and store the growing collections. He was equally aware that spaces were needed for ancillary gallery services. This development of the institution's buildings, to be developed as a Master Development Plan, was of primary importance to him.[141] Dublin's successful term as Cultural Capital of Europe in 1991 coincided with the rapidly emerging profile of its National Gallery.[142] The concluding event of 1991 saw a dramatic enactment of Maclise's painting *The Marriage of Strongbow and Aoife* before an audience of 1,000 visitors.[143]

The 1990s was a busy decade in the life of the gallery as the profile of the institution was developed by means of services to the public through exhibitions (including one by the Irish poet Paul Durcan, entitled *Crazy about Women,* which was emulated by the National Gallery, London),[144] education and cultural events, plus a range of new publications, press and promotional opportunities. In the midst of this the planning of the refurbishment of the Beit Wing was taking place in conjunction with a touring exhibition programme.[145] Meanwhile, research was undertaken to ascertain visitor needs,[146] and an internship programme for Irish and overseas graduates was set up, followed by a volunteer programme that would later be developed under a new Visitor Services operation.

Engagement with the public was developed by means of an Exhibitions Department (underpinned by the Registrar's Office), which worked to provide a range of temporary and longer-term displays, augmented by catalogues, in addition to loans to museums in Ireland and overseas. The Conservation Department, whose primary role was caring for the collections, worked on the collection during the Beit Wing refurbishment programme (1992–6), managed by the OPW, and prepared paintings for overseas loans. An education service would be structured to include: public programmes; adult lifelong learning; teacher, schools and youth programmes; children's and family events; community outreach; resources and publications, which had regular access to visitor research. In 1992 an exhibition was devoted to the work of young people, entitled *Children's Art: A Celebration*.[147] It drew on children's interaction with the collections, informed by the child-centred education ideals of the Italian educator Maria Montessori and the Swiss educationalist Friedrich Froebel, and proved a huge success: more than 36,000 people attended the exhibition.

One of a number of visitor surveys in 1992 drew attention to the need for adult lifelong learning (research had shown that adults formed the highest percentage of visitors to museums). The gallery began an art studies course on Thursday evenings (focusing on aspects of the history of art), in association with weekend drawing studies courses (to facilitate working people) that aimed to highlight the importance of drawing as a disciplined practice within the gallery environment and as a way of using the collections as a creative resource.

As part of the gallery's aim of furthering interest and awareness of the collections, an outreach programme was started in the mid-1990s. The programme (which is ongoing) included illustrated talks and workshops provided by freelance experienced tutors organised in partnership with a variety of bodies, including Age and Opportunity, local museums, arts centres, heritage organizations, education centres, healthcare settings and the Public

Library system. A review of this work recommended the appointment of an outreach officer.[148] Allied to this was the development of services for people with disabilities.[149] The gallery's new Saturday Family Programme enabled adults and children to enjoy themselves as they worked together under the guidance of an artist.[150] Family packs provided another resource for families to engage with the collections.

By far the most major event of the decade, however, was the announcement of the discovery of a lost masterpiece. *The Taking of Christ* was painted in 1602 by Michelangelo Merisi da Caravaggio (1571–1610) for the Roman nobleman Ciriaco Mattei. By 1802, when Scotsman William Hamilton Nisbet bought it, it had been misattributed to the Dutch painter Gerrit van Honthorst. The painting was purchased in Scotland years later by Marie Lea-Wilson, the widow of a Royal Irish Constabulary officer who had been shot dead by the IRA in 1920, and during this difficult time in her life she was supported by the Jesuit fathers. In gratitude, she presented the painting, still misattributed, to the Jesuit fathers and it hung in the order's Leeson Street residence until 1990, when Sergio Benedetti, then a senior conservator and art historian at the gallery, caught sight of it. Over three years he worked on restoring and researching the painting in order to authenticate it, while liaising with researchers in Italy. In 1992, the exhibition *Caravaggio and his Followers* was launched, drawing on *The Supper at Emmaus*, on loan from the National Gallery, London (also painted for Ciriaco Mattei in Rome in 1602). In the meantime, the Jesuit community generously agreed to place its painting on indefinite loan to the gallery in memory of Marie Lea-Wilson (NGI 14702).

In 1993 there was great excitement when *The Taking of Christ* was unveiled at an exhibition entitled *Caravaggio: The Master Revealed*. The painting and the story of its 'loss' and recovery created an immediate stir, attracting national and international press coverage and drawing a huge audience of 120,000 admiring visitors.[151] Officiating at the launch of the exhibition was the scholar, art historian, connoisseur and collector Sir Denis Mahon (b.1910), who was familiar with the gallery's collection. Mahon had known of Benedetti's interest in seventeenth-century Italian art and had given him assistance in authenticating the painting. As a result of the attention the gallery received, visitor figures soared to nearly one million in 1993 (since then averaging

700,000–800,000 visitors per year). Mahon has since endowed the National Gallery with eight seventeenth-century Italian paintings from his prestigious collection (together with a library). In 1997 these paintings were displayed in an exhibition entitled *The Scholar's Eye*.[152]

Meanwhile, as the refurbishment of the Beit Wing was ongoing,[153] the director, assistant director and curators worked on a schedule of important international touring exhibitions.[154] This included the successful *Master European Paintings from the National Gallery of Ireland: Mantegna to Goya*, which, following its tour to the United States, returned home to be shown as *The Masters' Return*. Exhibitions also travelled to Australia and Japan.[155] In May 1996, the gallery held a series of receptions, attended by 6,000 guests, in the run-up to the launch of the Beit Wing. The refurbishment programme included much-needed new facilities: modern lighting, security and environmental systems; remodelled galleries and storage; an atrium to improve circulation spaces; a gallery to display works on paper; plus the building was rendered accessible to all. As a consequence of the director's initiatives, the gallery received acclaim, widespread media coverage and many awards over the years.

The focus on the condition and environment of the gallery during the refurbishment was a feature of a scientific approach to the care of the collections, following the pattern of international trends and models of good practice in museums. Attention was paid to displaying works of art in conditions that contrasted with the situation earlier in the century. Following consultation with the curatorial and conservation staff, the galleries were remodelled with louvres in the rooflights to provide subtle indirect natural light, technologically programmed to alter, depending on the strength of the daylight, and transferring to sophisticated lighting systems as the light declined. This lighting, graded to protect the paintings, provided sufficient light to observe the works of art clearly. Paintings were hung well spaced with discrete labels, text panels appropriately positioned to explain the sequence of hanging of schools (for example, Italian) or themes (for example, Baroque paintings or modern Irish art), and sculpture was placed in the context of the paintings.

The director turned his attention to the production of high-quality publications underpinned by research on the collections (catalogues, guides, books, diaries, calendars), and sponsored symposia.[156] As the need for learning materials for teachers became evident, resource packs were created, which were disseminated throughout Ireland by the Department of Education and Science. The Exploring Art Project (1997–9) is an example of a cross-border initiative that formed part of this process, consisting of a handbook and set of Irish art posters, and a touring exhibition that set out to demystify the subject of art and make learning about the visual arts and museums an enjoyable experience.[157] Staff also worked on concise and detailed guides and floor plans, and audio guides which provided the public with fascinating information on the collections.[158]

The Beit Collection had come to public attention in the mid-1990s when a number of paintings were stolen in a daring robbery at Russborough House in County Wicklow. Indeed, it was not the first such unpleasant incident endured by the Beits. The Beit Collection had been installed at Russborough in 1953, and in 1976 Sir Alfred and Lady Beit gifted the house and art collection to the Irish people by establishing the Beit Foundation. In 1987, seventeen masterpieces were presented to the National Gallery, with the freedom to exhibit them on occasion at Russborough, together with other works from the collection.[159] However, in 1986, when preparations were being made to donate the masterpieces, part of the collection was stolen from Russborough for the second time. In this instance, four of the seventeen paintings were taken, including a Vermeer, a Goya and two works by Gabriel Metsu. Fortunately, these latter four works were

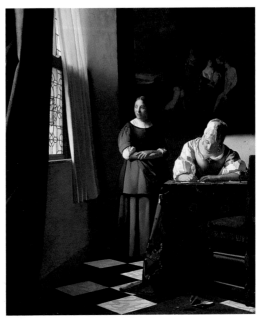

Johannes Vermeer (1632–75), *Woman Writing a Letter, with Her Maid,* **c.1670** *Oil on canvas, 71.1 x 60.5 cm. NGI 4535.*

In his native Delft, Vermeer specialized in interior domestic scenes, of which this is a superb example. The painting is only one of about thirty-five known works by Vermeer. It was gifted to the gallery as part of a major benefaction comprising seventeen masterpieces of Dutch, Spanish and British art, by Sir Alfred and Lady Beit in 1987.

subsequently recovered and returned
to the gallery.

When the returned master-
pieces were checked and treated by
the gallery's Conservation Department, it raised awareness of a subject that
fascinates the public. It was in this context that the gallery's Head of
Conservation and conservators mounted an exhibition, *The Deeper Picture*, to
reveal to the public many of the techniques and treatments involved in the
care and preservation of paintings and works on paper.[160] The importance of
caring for the latter highlighted how these works (prints, watercolours,
miniatures and drawings) were stored in the Prints and Drawings Room and
cared for by specialist curators. The incident also raised questions about
researching precious collections, a role that is facilitated by the Library,
Research Services and Archive departments of the gallery.

Exhibitions, traditionally the cornerstone of every museum, were enriched
by partnerships with new centres, which produced a series of wide-ranging,
innovative shows. *Art into Art: A Living Response to Past Masters* was one of
a number of exhibitions organized by the curator (later head of exhibitions)
held in association with Graphic Studio Dublin to explore the relevance of
old master works for contemporary art practice.[161] When *Kroyer and the
Artists' Colony at Skagen* was held, it represented the first Danish exhibition to
come to the gallery and would be followed in time by other shows, including

Jack B. Yeats (1871–1957), *A Morning,* **1935–6**
Oil on panel, 23 x 36 cm. NGI 4628.

Jack B. Yeats and Samuel Beckett first met in 1931 when, with an introduction by Thomas MacGreevy, Beckett visited the artist in his studio. Beckett was immediately struck by this painting and he acquired it directly from the artist, paying for it in instalments. Beckett: 'always morning, and a setting out without the coming home'.

German, Polish, Finnish and Norwegian exhibitions. An important acquisition of this period was Canova's *Amorino*, commissioned by La Touche during his stay in Rome in 1789.[162] The sculpture was presented to the gallery by the Bank of Ireland (with connections to the original La Touche bank), through Section 1003 of the Consolidated Taxes Act 1997.

A process of seeking out works of art to develop the Irish collection had been taking place for some time, just as the gallery had been acquiring works by the early twentieth-century Irish artist Jack B. Yeats. This was augmented in 1996 by the generous gift of the Yeats Archive by his niece, Anne Yeats. In 1999 the Yeats Museum was opened by Taoiseach Bertie Ahern in the presence of Anne Yeats and her brother, former senator Michael Yeats. While the initial display focused on works by the Yeats family, more recently it has been devoted to the paintings of Jack B. Yeats. The Yeats Collection became immediately popular, as new books were published on both the Yeats family[163] and highlights of the Irish collection.[164] This process coincided with an increasing

A sculptor conservator

A conservator is in the process of treating the marble sculpture, *A Girl Reading*, by Patrick MacDowell (1799–1870). This work formed part of the National Gallery's sculpture conservation project.

interest in the late 1990s in the subject of Irish art at a time when contemporary issues of 'Irishness' and 'identity' surfaced as Irish society was positioning itself to face into the new millennium.

Concern over the conservation of the sculpture collection emerged in the late 1990s. The gallery's original collection of antique casts, which had been useful for the appreciation of art, had long since been augmented by a sculpture collection. In 1999, the director initiated a sculpture conservation programme that prioritized the treatment of 40 of the 392 works in the gallery's collection. The conserved works drew attention to the gallery's collection of sculpture, forming an attractive display that proved very popular with the public.[165]

By the late 1990s the attention of the director was focused on the development of a new Millennium Wing that was needed for essential services, including temporary exhibitions, rooms to house the growing twentieth-century Irish collections, space for a Centre for the Study of Irish Art, a Yeats Archive, retail and catering facilities, together with recruitment of staff needed to manage these operations.[166] This major project would demonstrate the gallery's awareness of the importance of the public to the institution and the need to provide critical services and facilities. Having previously acquired the Clare Street site (which had been considered as a potential location for the original building in the 1850s[167]), number 5 South Leinster Street was procured in 1995. A long process ensued, involving an international architectural competition (won by the firm of Benson + Forsyth), planning permissions and fund-raising towards the new wing.

Thus, by the end of the century, the National Gallery had proved itself to be at the forefront of museum development in Ireland, having overseen an immense phase of sustained development and about to unveil its fourth wing. The director had monitored a decade of achievement that was recognized and appreciated, as evidenced by new gifts and acquisitions, popular exhibitions, publications and programmes, increased visitors numbers (c. 750,000 per annum), leading towards the commencement of the Millennium Wing. Under his stewardship, the public role of the institution was everywhere visible, in the display of the permanent collections and temporary exhibitions, the education and outreach activities, the library, website, press and visitor services, the friends, retail and catering facilities. In parallel, new research on individual schools would lead to the publication of the first major volume on the Irish collection: *Irish Paintings in the National Gallery of Ireland*.[168] Thus, the National Gallery faced into the new millennium with a powerful vision of its place in Irish society 'to enrich the cultural, artistic and intellectual life of present and future generations'.

PART V

The Twenty-First Century

The opening of the National Gallery of Ireland's Millennium Wing, 2002

Designed by the London-Scottish firm of Benson + Forsyth, the unveiling of the much-acclaimed Millennium Wing in 2002 was accompanied by an Impressionist exhibition that attracted 130,000 visitors. This new wing has become a very popular facility within walking distance of Dublin's fashionable Grafton Street.

*T*he primary subject of this book is the history of Irish museums in terms of culture, identity and the educating principle that underpins the purpose of these institutions. It is a story that has been particularly compelling in the last three hundred years, when museums have moved from the notion of collection and display to include the concept of an interactive public space. Although the book's remit was an examination of this phenomenon between 1733 and 2000, it would be difficult to end at the millennium year because the achievements of the late twentieth century have taken root and assumed a new significance in the first decade of the twenty-first century. The central thesis of this study is that museums matter to people, a role that emerged as being essential in the second half of the twentieth century, when museums became concerned with access, engagement and outreach, in a pattern that has become even more significant and well-defined in the 2000s. Chapter 14 will provide a general overview of new developments in Ireland, and internationally, in the 2000s.

The museum's public role has to do with how the institution provides access to the collections because these artworks are the core of the enterprise. One of the main reasons the collections are so important is because most of their contents were made by humans. These artefacts, therefore, speak to people across the ages and encourage them to reflect on their place in the world. For instance, a Neolithic flint axehead is not just a product of the hand that made it, but also of the mind and the developing brain power and inventiveness of humans. The part of the human brain that enables a person to create such a tool is the same part responsible for forming speech sounds, so the mind that can shape an axe can shape a sentence. The ability to convey this message so that it becomes immediate, personal and relevant to each person is where museum staff come into play. It is they who make the collections and the museum meaningful to the public. To quote the Nobel Prize-winning economist Amartya Sen: 'I like to think of the history of the world as a history of civilizations evolving in often similar, often diverse ways, always intersecting with each other.'[1] Thus, the ripples of chipped flint and the smooth texture of the stone axehead on display in the NMI reflect the intent of the maker as well as the beauty of primitive craft. This juxtaposition of the micro and macro meanings of human life is what museums can do.

This final chapter will look at the new museological trends that are emerging in the twenty-first century. These innovations are based on the challenges being presented to museum practitioners in the new millennium – 'in such a world, educators are forced to consider with renewed urgency their purposes and their methods'.[2] The digital world forms part of this challenge because it holds out a tantalizing future for both the physical and the virtual museum. It will prove a huge boon to museums that are striving to become dynamic centres of learning, creativity and enjoyment, with their aims of strengthening communities, nourishing minds and spirits, and of enriching people's lives. Irish museums are answering these challenges by leading, inspiring and educating. The circumstances of life today, including technology, leisure, tourism, wider educational provision and relatively flexible personal resources, allow greater numbers of people to realize their aspirations. A point has been reached where museum professionals are even more aware of the significance of their role in engaging the public through exposure to the cultural capital that lies in the holdings of the great Irish heritage institutions.

14

Combining the Virtual and the Physical: Key Developments in the Twenty-First-Century Museum

With the digital image, we're seeing the body of the paintings. What we don't see is the soul. The soul will always only be seen by contemplating the original.[1]

Since 2000 the growth and expansion of Irish museums has kept pace with the global pattern of development. It is an uneven story, as the Irish situation is resource-dependent and it does not take into account remarkable local initiatives, such as Waterford Museum of Treasures, the Butler Gallery, Kilkenny, the Tower Museum in Derry/Londonderry, the Highlanes Municipal Art Gallery in Drogheda and The Model contemporary arts centre in Sligo, which re-opened in 2010 featuring works by Jack B. Yeats from its permanent collection. Nonetheless, a brief outline of the major achievements demonstrates the pace and success of developments during this period.

A series of new branches, wings and extensions opened in the 2000s to enhance the capacity of the Irish cultural institutions to display their growing collections and to provide improved programmes and services, temporary

A presentation of old master paintings, 1900s

The hanging pattern of the principal gallery on the first floor of the National Gallery of Ireland's Dargan wing shows paintings hung in tiers, close together, with Flemish, Dutch and Spanish paintings on one side, the opposite wall given to Italian masters. Top lighting was supplemented by gas lighting after dark; electricity came later to the National Gallery.

A modern presentation of the collection, 2000s

The hanging pattern of the National Gallery of Ireland Millennium Wing is at eye level, in a single line, with works well spaced apart and aided by discrete labels. The modern galleries are flooded with daylight, directly from top lights (on the top floor) and through the ground level wall openings, providing as much natural light as possible, supplemented by lighting systems when daylight declines.

and permanent exhibitions, and retail outlets. A common feature of the museums listed below is the increase in their exhibition and education services due to their desire to engage more fully with the public and to cater for the increasing visitor numbers. The range of new developments demonstrates the level of priority that Irish museums have attached to catering for visitors of all ages and interests, and their increased awareness of the importance of the public to twenty-first-century museums.

Following its opening in the Clock Tower Building in Dublin Castle in 2000, the Chester Beatty Library acquired the coveted designation of European Museum of the Year in 2002. It set about cementing its role in Irish cultural life by hosting a series of permanent exhibitions, *Sacred Traditions* and *Arts of the Book*,[2] alternating with shows, such as *Leonardo: The Codex Leicester* and exhibitions inspired by the collections, such as *Artist's Proof*.

That same year IMMA acquired the restored Deputy Master's House at its Kilmainham site, resulting in a series of new exhibitions – *Contemporary Art from China*; *Miquel Barcelo: The African Work*; *Lucian Freud*; *Alexander Calder and Juan Miro*; *James Coleman*; and *Hughie O'Donoghue* – bringing visitor numbers to approximately 400,000 in 2008.

In 2001 the NMI unveiled its fourth site, and first regional branch: the Museum of Country Life at Turlough Park House, in County Mayo, which displays the 'renowned Irish folk-life collections'.[3]

The opening of the NGI's critically acclaimed Millennium Wing was celebrated with a special exhibition that attracted 130,000 visitors: *Monet, Renoir and the Impressionist Landscape* (Museum of Fine Arts, Boston).[4] The ensuing years of popular shows, one highlighting a decade of acquisitions (2000–2010), included *Impressionist Interiors; Gabriel Metsu: Rediscovered Master of the Dutch Golden Age; Hugh Douglas Hamilton: A Life in Pictures; Thomas Roberts 1748–1777*; and *Samuel Beckett: A Passion for Paintings*, marking the centenary of the birth of the Nobel laureate and illustrating the writer's passion for the visual arts and his engagement with the gallery.[5] Meantime, a series of newly commissioned portraits enriched the Portrait Gallery with a contemporary presence.

In 2003 the Crawford Municipal Art Gallery revealed its new extension,[6] showing to best advantage a series of popular shows, including *James Barry 1741–1806; Rembrandt to Mondrian; Realism and Modernism in Irish Art (1900–1990)*; and *Daniel Maclise 1806–1870*.

In 2005 the NMI: Decorative Arts and History unveiled the refurbished Riding School, which has since played host to a series of popular shows, along with the permanent exhibition: *Soldiers and Chiefs – The Irish at War at Home and Abroad since 1550*. This has contributed to attracting over one million visitors to the museum's four sites in 2007.

The trend continued when Dublin City Gallery The Hugh Lane revealed its modern wing in 2006, a highlight of which was the Sean Scully Room, showcasing paintings the artist had donated to the gallery.[7] The gallery's centenary in 2008 was marked with a display of the thirty-nine Lane Bequest

The National Museum of Ireland – Museum of Country Life at Turlough Park, County Mayo

The original Victorian building, Turlough Park House, had been designed by Thomas Newenham Deane between 1865 and 1867 for a member of the Fitzgerald family. The new purpose-built stone-clad building, designed by the Architectural Services of the Office of Public Works, has integrated the old and the newer buildings to present a modern museum for the folk-life collections. Its opening in 2001 attracted large visitor numbers.

paintings, followed by a major Francis Bacon show. The country's rapid phase of development started to slow down with the early signs of a global downturn in that year.

In 2009 the eagerly anticipated re-opening of the Ulster Museum took place, marking its eightieth anniversary (1929–2009). The new chief executive officer of National Museums Northern Ireland (NMNI), Tim Cooke (2003), oversaw the transformation of the museum building, which revealed an atrium leading to four floors with sixteen galleries, from history (prehistoric Ireland to the present) to natural science (from the Ice Age to evolution), each with its own discovery area.[8] The permanent art collection is displayed in spacious galleries on the top floor, adjacent to the Gallery of Applied Art.

Other developments during this decade witnessed the NMI achieving its much-desired independent status as a government agency in 2005, together with its own board. Similarly, in 2006 the Crawford Art Gallery moved under the Department of Arts, Sport and Tourism to be designated a 'national' cultural institution as responsibility for its building transferred to the OPW. The range of senior staff and other key posts was increased at museums such as the National Gallery and the National Museum to meet the needs of the rapidly expanding operations.

A welcome initiative was the increased number of overseas touring

The Great Court of the British Museum

The Great Court, designed by Norman Foster, was unveiled in 2000. Comprising a glass dome of over 3,000 triangular-shaped panels, it covers the museum's former open courtyard and original British Library Reading Room. The court provides a central meeting point for the museum with generous circulation spaces.

exhibitions mounted by Irish museums, following the example set by the NMI and NGI, which enhanced Ireland's visual arts reputation abroad. IMMA, under a new director, Enrique Juncosa (2003), extended its international presence through touring shows to Holland, Belgium, the United States, Beijing and Shanghai, and collaborating with Rome's National Museum of 21st-Century Art and the Pinacoteca do Estado, Brazil. The Chester Beatty Library provided touring shows to China in addition to the impressive exhibition, *Muraqqa': Imperial Mughal Albums*, which toured to the United States, prior to its showing in Dublin.

It is clear from even this cursory listing of the changes and improvements in the museum sphere that the developments in the first ten years of the new century demonstrate the sustained growth and visibility of the Irish museum

The Muraqqa: Imperial Mughal Albums from the Chester Beatty Library

These superb Mughal paintings comprising six albums (*muraqqa's*), compiled in India between about 1600 and 1658 for the Mughal emperors Jahangir and Shah Jahan, returned to Dublin for exhibition from a tour of four museums in America between 2008 and 2009.

sector, which is largely the result of increased and consistent state funding. The Department of Arts, Culture and the Gaeltacht provided the resources to fund, staff and develop the arts and the cultural institutions, augmented by the Heritage Fund (established in 2001).[9] The major national museums are funded by this department, while other museums receive support from local authorities and through financial aid for development and one-off projects, with many benefiting from state-funded agencies like the Heritage Council.

The nature of the Department of Arts changed in 2002, when it was reconfigured to include Sport and Tourism, which meant that by implication, state sponsorship of the arts could have been interpreted as the promotion of economic growth through cultural tourism. As Ireland is a small country with competing demands for limited funding, the link with tourism proved to be a positive step that encouraged greater engagement between the tourism agencies (for example, Fáilte Ireland), the cultural agencies (for example, Culture Ireland) and the cultural institutions. It has created an enhanced awareness of their ability to share resources, particularly in terms of advertising and promotion, towards a mutually beneficial outcome.

A problem arose in 2008–9, however, during the severe economic downturn, when the question of resourcing the arts came under attack. In response, business leaders and economic thinkers spoke out at the Global Irish Economic

Forum in defence and support of Ireland's world-renowned cultural legacy and talent.[10] A countrywide movement of artists and arts practitioners lobbied government to resource adequately the arts and Irish culture, the force of which had the desired outcome. In the meantime, the Department returned to dealing with the Arts, Heritage and the Gaeltacht. Nonetheless, it provided a salutary lesson that the Irish contribution to an internationally renowned arts and heritage legacy cannot be taken for granted and must be resourced effectively so that it can protect its place in the culture and well-being of the nation. The ideal solution would be a government department devoted exclusively to the arts, culture and heritage, which would take all Irish museums under its wing.

While the period to the end of the twenty-first century's first decade has proved a difficult time for Irish society and the economy, improvements are everywhere evident: the Museum Standards Programme for Ireland, introduced by the Heritage Council, has increased the capacity of museums to achieve the highest professional standards and to improve the processes that underpin their operations. In 2010 the NGI and Muckross House, Farm & Research Library were the first museums to achieve accreditation-maintenance of accreditation, under the Heritage Council's commitment to collections care. The Museum Awards, run biennially by the Heritage Council in partnership with the Northern Ireland Museums Council (NIMC, 1993), encourage best practice and publicly acknowledge and celebrate all the work undertaken to make museums more accessible, more people-centred and more enjoyable for all visitors:

> The museums and galleries that win these awards clearly have the drive and commitment to make a contribution, reach into society and provide real public value. They are the ones engaging communities of interest and enhancing local and national social space. This commitment to public value has to be applauded.[11]

A much-improved service for the public is the goal of a number of organizations. The Irish Museums Association (IMA) is an all-island museum association that organizes conferences, lectures, training, publications and a touring exhibition, *Museums Matter*, which showcases links between Ireland's larger and smaller collections and supports co-operation between museums.

Attributed to Meleager Painter (an ancient Greek vase painter of the Attic red-figure tradition), *Red-Figured Attic Column-Krater*
Terracotta, 43.3 x 42.2 cm. NMI.

Produced in Athens in the last quarter of the fifth century BC, the paintings on the vase feature a banquet scene. The vase was acquired by John David La Touche and later donated by George La Touche to the RDS, then transferred to the National Museum and is now on long-term loan to the Classical Museum, University College, Dublin.

The IMA advocates on issues of museum ethics, jobs and training in order to improve and extend the role of museums in Ireland. NIMC also supports museums in maintaining and improving standards of collections care and service to the public. The Arts Council of Ireland works in partnership with arts organizations, artists, public policy-makers and others to build a central place for the arts in Irish life. The Arts Council of Northern Ireland operates in a similar fashion, while also offering a broad range of funding opportunities through the UK Exchequer and National Lottery funds.

The care and treatment of collections is advanced by the Irish Professional Conservators' and Restorers' Association and by the Institute for the Conservation of Historic and Artistic Works in Ireland. Other bodies involved in the preservation of historic architecture and collections include the Centre for Historic Irish Houses and Estates (NUI, Maynooth), the Irish Georgian Society, the Irish Architectural Archive, the Irish Heritage Trust, An Taisce/National Trust (Ireland) and the National Trust (UK and Northern Ireland). There is now a language and a system of best practice that is discussed, debated and updated regularly. As a result, there is a fresh emphasis on access to cultural heritage, and the holding of international lectures and symposia, plus a growing literature on museums and museum practice that continually pushes the boundaries further and demands the highest standards of practitioners.

Alongside these changes in museum practice, there have also been key developments in how museums recruit and train new generations of practitioners. The idea put forward by the curator of the Louvre that 'the museum of the future will more and more resemble an academy of learning' has proved prophetic in more ways than one.[12] The Council of National Cultural Institutions (CNCI, 1997) – a statutory body that pools the knowledge and experience of the directors of the cultural institutions for culturally beneficial purposes – produced *A Policy Framework for Education, Community, Outreach*, underlining the importance of integrating learning into the ethos of the cultural institutions.[13] New centres created to pursue research included the Centre for the Study of Irish Art (based in NGI), the National Visual Arts Library (based in NCAD) and the Trinity Irish Art Research Centre (based in TCD). Complementing these centres is a range of postgraduate courses involving third-level professional development courses (full-time, part-time and distance learning) in cultural studies/policy, heritage management and arts administration. The longest running of these, at UCD,[14] has produced 502 graduates (1987–2007), many of whom have progressed into museum careers and breathed new life into some of the older institutions.

The picture is not all 'sunshine and roses', however, and there are significant issues that have yet to be addressed and overcome. These include: the need for sustained funding to provide a secure base for present and future developments; the lack of sufficient conservation, education and outreach staff in many museums; the need for a much wider application of technology in museums; and concerns relating to limiting the growth of heritage in Ireland.[15] Nonetheless, the research presented here should contribute towards building a base of scholarship that will establish an intellectual foundation for Irish museological studies, because the subject of museum studies has its own role to play in the shaping of the modern museum. It is hoped that a reasonable attempt has been made to address the concerns of Irish museums in this book as a preliminary to opening up the area of research on individual institutions, municipal, local authority and voluntary museums. This cross-fertilization of scholarship and practice should ensure that informed, innovative and intelligent discussion and decision-making will further the role and ambitions of the modern Irish museum.

Ireland's University Museums

The university museums provide a different chapter in the story of the twenty-first-century Irish institutions. Their nineteenth-century origins afforded them a particular niche in the early part of the museum story, but it is true to say that they have since found it increasingly difficult to justify their existence in a twenty-first-century world.

The original function of the university museums was the genuinely important role they played in the instruction of generations of students through use of their collections as a teaching resource in conjunction with a range of interdisciplinary subjects. They also developed links with the RIA

The Douglas Hyde Gallery, Trinity College, Dublin

The gallery opened in 1978 as a leading avant-garde forum to present exhibitions of contemporary art, attracting an audience interested in modern and contemporary works. Illustrated is a shot of the interior of the gallery, which functions on two floors in a series of unfolding spaces.

and the RDS, in addition to feeding into the collections of the NMI and the Ulster Museum. This changed in the twentieth century, however, when their decline, neglect and, in many cases, demise was the result of changing patterns in teaching, the cost of maintaining collections, and the difficulties presented by wartime economic downturn and the newly competitive environment of third-level education. When such museums eventually declined, their collections typically devolved to appropriate departments, such as archaeology, anatomy, natural history and entymology, geology, chemistry, physics and geography, where they remain to this day as teaching and research collections. In this discussion of twenty-first-century museum culture, it is worth observing the pattern of the university museums before selecting from their number a few examples of those that have managed to survive intact, and with a solid purpose, in the modern era.

At the Queen's University Museum of Classical Archaeology (founded in 1911–12), Oliver Davies (Classics Department) and E. Estyn Evans (Geography Department) collaborated on excavations in 1932, under the auspices of the Belfast Naturalists' Field Club, which were documented in the revived *Ulster Journal of Archaeology*. The outcome witnessed the creation of a lectureship in archaeology in 1948,[16] which inaugurated the pattern of modern Irish fieldwork, in conjunction with the 1932 Harvard Archaeological Expedition to Ireland. The university collections have since been housed in the relevant departments and when the Geology Department closed in 2001 its collection of minerals, rocks and materials devolved to the Ulster Museum.

UCC's university museums experienced difficult times in the twentieth century, becoming a subject of debate between 1920 and the 1940s, as many of the exhibits were languishing in packing cases, with classification that was inadequate.[17] As in the case of other universities, its holdings, including natural history and geology specimens, became departmental collections, used for research and retaining a value as part of the university's history.[18] In 1995, however, UCC took the step of setting up a Heritage Committee and in 1999, appointing a curator to provide curatorial and advisory services to the university and its teaching departments. It is currently integrating its collections of art, archival records and the Boole Library into the history of the institution.

As mentioned above, not all of the university museums have devolved into departmental collections. There are examples of those that have forged a working identity as museums, finding a place within the university's teaching role that holds promise for their future. A brief examination of three examples follows: the James Mitchell Geology Museum, the TCD Geological Museum and UCD's Classical Museum.

Established in 1977, the James Mitchell Geology Museum at NUI Galway was based on a museum collection that had been well used in the nineteenth century, but which had virtually disintegrated in the early twentieth century when the college, like the rest of the country, was affected by nationwide political unrest. (During this period, the main body of the geological collections were kept intact.) From the time Professor James Mitchell was appointed to the chair of geology and mineralogy in 1921 up to his retirement in 1966, he kept the geological collections under his 'protective wing', a dedication recognized in the designation 'James Mitchell' in the new museum's name.

M.D. Fewtrell commented that 'The decline of interest in museums not only in Galway but elsewhere in Ireland (and abroad) led to the disbanding of similar collections in the other University Colleges.'[19] It transpired that neglect and inattention had, in fact, helped this particular museum to survive, as a result of which the refurbished James Mitchell Geology Museum, under the auspices of the Earth and Ocean Sciences Department, opened in 1992.[20] (The collections of the university's former Natural History Museum have been relocated to the Martin Ryan Marine Science Institute.) The custodians of the Mitchell Museum now make the collection of rocks, minerals and fossils available for teaching and as a resource, not just for students and staff but also for second-level students. 'Galway's hidden Museum', with its unique history, is the only such museum in the west of Ireland.

TCD's Geological Museum was one of several college museums gifted by significant donors, such as 'Fitton, Griffith, Jukes, Oldham, Portlock and the Balls'. Since its inauguration (1777) the Geological Museum in the School of Natural Sciences has been served by fifteen directors/curators, many of whom gave assistance to the collections of the NMI. The emergence of the institution in modern times (1956) took place under the curatorship of Professor Dan Gill,[21] aided by postgraduate development programmes in the 1960s and furthered by redesign of the displays and the introduction of school tours by Veronica Burns (from the 1960s to 1980), when she was an attendant responsible for the museum.

The current curator, Patrick Wyse Jackson, has found a valid context for the museum in the twenty-first century and has been proactive in communicating the educational importance of the collections: 'if you find a new fossil you have to describe it because they are the unique items that describe a species'.[22] Wyse Jackson utilizes the university's role as a research institution with teaching collections to involve students, schoolchildren and the public in the museum.[23] TCD, in common with many long-established universities, has a large number of other collections of varying sizes and importance, including the Anatomy Museum and the Zoological Museum. The Dublin University Museum originally included anatomy and natural history collections (such as the geological and zoological collections); its history, however, has been traced through the Geology Museum. The Anatomy Museum, Zoological Museum and Weingreen Museum of Biblical Antiquities (founded in 1977),[24] together with academic and artistic holdings, are held in departmental and other collections.[25]

UCD's Museum of Ancient History, founded in 1908, was influenced by the Ashmolean in Oxford.[26] The collections that were acquired through contact with figures like Arthur Smith at the British Museum and Sir Charles Newton's excavations at Knidos, in Turkey, were housed in the two-roomed museum at Earlsfort Terrace[27] and used for exhibition and teaching purposes. Henry Browne, professor of Greek (1900–23) at UCD and the founder of the original museum, visited America in 1916 and what he observed there led him to write about the provision of loan collections for schools.[28] He collaborated with the National Museum on a number of occasions, including the acquisition of the Hope vases, originally owned by Sir William Hamilton.[29]

In 1971, UCD and its museum relocated to a new campus at Belfield in Donnybrook. Since then the Classical Museum, as it is now known, has elaborated and capitalized on its research, exhibiting and teaching role, bringing in undergraduates for tutorials and to work on exhibitions, as well as encouraging use of the collection by staff, second-level students and teachers and groups from societies. The role of the Classical Museum in the twenty-first century is to facilitate the study of original objects from classical antiquity and ancient Greek and Roman culture, so that students can observe authentic artefacts from classical civilization and learn how to use such collections.[30]

What, then, is the place of university museums and collections in the twenty-first century, when many of them have become unfashionable and outdated in the context of teaching? The diverse holdings of the natural history museums are difficult to place with their geology collections, which seem to be of decreasing interest to the public and, in some cases, to earth scientists. While they declined in importance in the twentieth century as museums moved away from the traditional display of specimens, this proved not to be the case in Ireland, where the university museums that survived remained independent of international developments. The American Museum of Natural History in New York illustrated this by moving well beyond dioramas in the 1920s to introduce new types of display and technology.

Despite these museums' stated purpose as learning resources, the majority suffer from a distinct lack of visitors. For those who do make the effort to visit and use the collections, they enjoy the sense that university museums are microcosms of the larger museums and this bestows a sense of old-world charm on them. Students also describe the privilege of direct access to the collections and the personalized treatment they have experienced from the curators. This is the quality that university museums can build on. Their future lies in strengthening their role as teaching resources and underlining their ability to serve students, schoolchildren and the general public. The harder they work to extend this role, the more they safeguard their position as being integral to the university because that will demonstrate their value in providing a service to the local community.

University Galleries and Art Collections

Change came swiftly to the universities in the form of galleries (*kunsthalle*) that do not have holdings but have recourse to college collections, and are empowered to provide exhibitions and programmes that demonstrate they serve the student population and the wider public. Some university galleries are run through a studio art programme, and many receive outside support.

The purpose of UCD's art collection is to bring art into the everyday experience of students and improve their understanding and appreciation of the visual arts.[31] The university does not yet have a gallery, but it does have a cultural resource in Newman House.[32] However, plans are in place to build a cultural facility that will expand its remit beyond the college and into the community.

When the Douglas Hyde Gallery opened in 1978 it was the earliest of the university galleries, showing great foresight on the part of TCD.[33] It derived from a College Gallery (1959) and History of Art Department, followed by a series of exhibitions held in the Exhibition Hall in 1967–76. The gallery was named after Douglas Hyde (1860–1949), a TCD graduate, UCD professor of Irish, and the first president of Ireland (1938–45). It was designed in a 1970s style, forming a purpose-built art space on the south side of the campus. The TCD art collection, begun as early as 1710, gradually came to form a record of the evolving taste and political attitudes in Irish painting. In the latter part of the twentieth century the university acquired and commissioned works in order to put together a modern collection, which is independent of, and has no formal links to, the gallery.[34]

The Douglas Hyde Gallery initially focused on exhibitions (with accompanying catalogues) of individual contemporary Irish and European artists, with educational programmes for second- and third-level students held in conjunction with the Education Department of the National College of Art and Design.[35] Under director John Hutchinson (1991), the gallery has become a leading avant-garde forum, hosting unusual and thought-provoking exhibitions by contemporary artists, including Louise Bourgeois, Peter Doig, Luc Tuymans, Dorothy Cross, Willie Doherty and Kathy Prendergast, attracting a broad audience in the process.[36] Like the QUB Naughton Gallery and UCC's Lewis Glucksman Gallery, the Douglas Hyde Gallery is professionally run, with its own budget.

University College, Galway's Art Gallery was opened by James White in 1981 with an exhibition entitled *The Delighted Eye*.[37] The gallery serves the college and the city, notably during Galway Arts Week, when it hosts national and international exhibitions. The gallery has access to the UCG art collection, which includes paintings, works on paper and sculpture.[38] The role of the gallery and collection is to encourage students to look at and respond to works of art in an everyday situation and to support aesthetic awareness and appreciation of the visual arts in Galway.

In 2002, QUB opened the Naughton Gallery in the Lanyon Building at the centre of the main campus, under the care of curator Shan McAnena.[39]

It was the initiative of Professor Sir George Bain, vice-chancellor of the university, subsequent to the appointment of a part-time curator of the university's art collection in 1988. The collection dates from 1847 and includes works by Irish sculptors, painters and British portraits, providing a valuable resource for the Naughton Gallery. It was showcased at an exhibition mounted

The Lewis Glucksman Gallery, University College, Cork, 2000s

In 2004, this modern river side gallery, which was designed by O'Donnell Twomey, opened at University College, Cork. It has become a major attraction for Cork citizens and visitors.

by the Ulster Museum: *A Sesquicentennial Celebration: Art from the Queen's Collection Belfast.*[40] The purpose of the Naughton Gallery is to provide a facility that enhances the university experience for staff, students and the wider community. It is doing this by means of a rolling programme of works from the collection, touring exhibitions and shows by local and international artists.

In 2004 a significant addition to the university and gallery scene was the opening of the Lewis Glucksman Gallery on the UCC campus, which quickly came to be regarded as one of the finest modern public buildings in Ireland.[41] The gallery explores visual culture through stimulating and challenging shows that are considered innovative, such as a print show, curated by Professor James Elkins, that examined how Albrecht Dürer was caught between two styles: the Northern Renaissance and the Italian Renaissance. The gallery has recourse to the university art collection, initiated in 1975 by a House Advisory Committee, which in turn led to the setting up of a Visual Arts Committee.[42] This collection of Irish art and contemporary art from Cork provides public art on the campus for the purpose of 'helping to inform the eyes of the students'. The Lewis Glucksman Gallery under director Fiona Kearney places learning at the heart of its activities and hosts programmes by artists and educators that enable it to play a significant role in the academic and cultural life of Cork.

In terms of forging a future position for themselves in the wider context of the university, the same holds true for the university galleries as for the museums: to survive and succeed in the twenty-first century they must continue to develop exhibitions and educational programmes that engage the public and thereby demonstrate to the university their importance to the community. This should not prove difficult, as the gallery management teams have shown themselves to be adept at linking their programmes to the local community, creating an identity that is at once part of, and yet distinct from, the university itself. The role these museums and galleries play in illustrating the visible form of the university's respect for cultural traditions cannot be underestimated.

International Museological Trends in the Twenty-First Century

The trends emerging overseas at museums in Europe and in the United States reflect similar experiences to Ireland, as the 'boom' years provided the ideal opportunity for museums to reassess, re-evaluate and, in some cases,

The Miosach, Clonmany, County Donegal, late eleventh century (redecorated 1534)
National Museum of Ireland, Archaeology, Kildare Street

This medieval book shrine dates from the eleventh century (repaired in the sixteenth century). The reliquary was originally associated with St Cairneach of Dulane, County Meath, and with St Colmcille's monastery at Derry. The main face bears a series of repeating stamped silver foil panels showing the Virgin and Child and three saints (perhaps Sts Patrick, Columba and Brigid). This Christian shrine is mentioned in historical records from the twelfth century onwards.

reinvent themselves. The period leading up to and directly following the millennium has been a critical time in the development of museums. Across the world, museums have embraced their own potential as public spaces, offering education and enlightenment in equal measure, seeking out new ways to involve their audiences, displaying their collections and stimulating debate about, and interest in, the visual arts. It has been an exciting time for practitioners, as the ideals and the realities have collided in a heady combination of spectacular exhibits, escalating audience numbers and increased support through corporate, as well as government, funding.

It has been estimated that in Europe there are at least 38,000 museums drawing over 500,000 visitors a year and that over 50 per cent of these institutions did not exist before the Second World War.[43] That is an impressive statistic and it reflects the pattern evident across Europe of creating greater access to culture and the collections. A good example of this new ethos is the 'long night of museums', an idea that originated in Berlin in the late 1990s, and that involves dedicating a night in mid-winter when a city's museums remain open, with a host of special events to mark the occasion. Known as Nuits Blanches in France, as La Notte Bianca in Rome, as White Nights in southern Europe, Canada and South America and as Late Nights in England, the idea has spread to numerous other countries and sometimes takes place at other times of the year, such as May or September or December. In Ireland there is a focus on cultural events during a week in May, followed by a heritage week in August, and the popular Culture Night in September. It is a simple but very effective way to engage audiences and create a buzz around the museums and their collections.

The story in Britain is also positive, where increasing visitor numbers have seen museums boosted by technological advances and renewed 'public enthusiasm for history and culture'. Britain's museums are playing a key role in that nation's expanding tourist industry, alongside their critical role in community development – access to the benefits of learning formed the main arguments for creating education centres, such as those at the National Museum of Scotland and the National Gallery of Scotland. The National Gallery, London, opened an education centre to make its collections more accessible to students and further enhanced public access to the institution by means of a pedestrian zone facing onto Trafalgar Square.[44] The V&A's refurbished galleries were accompanied by a series of innovative interactive exhibits, and the unveiling of its Sackler Centre for Arts Education in 2008 demonstrated the institution's determination to provide a focus for public learning through creative design and the arts, where visitors can make practical use of the knowledge and inspiration gained from the museum and its collections.[45] Britain's oldest museum, the Ashmolean in Oxford, reopened in 2009 in a refurbished building, housing an education centre and conservation studios and twice as much space for the collections.

The British Museum celebrated the new millennium as 'a museum of the world' represented by seven million objects, and within a decade marked the

250th anniversary of its opening to the public in 1759 as the first national museum in the world. Director Neil MacGregor is working towards a new conservation and exhibition centre so that 'the Museum can meet its present and future obligations to the collections and to its visitors'.

The innovative Tate outposts – Tate Britain (1897), Tate Liverpool (1988), Tate St Ives (1993) and Tate Modern (2000) – have blossomed under the directorship of Sir Nicholas Serota (1988–).[46] Tate Modern is the best known of the group as Britain's national museum of British and international modern and contemporary art, 'a public institution owned by, and existing for, the public'. Its mission is to increase knowledge, understanding and enjoyment of art through its collection and inspiring programmes, which reach five million visitors each year. Learning informs the critical thinking behind the enterprise, with Tate giving huge consideration to its collections, their management and display, and to a public programme that is constantly under review in a process designed to ensure that the art museum remains at the cutting edge of learning and creativity. This ethos has been given a seal of approval by the museum directors conference representing all the major museums in the UK, which in its *Manifesto for Museums* stated that 'the educational role of museums lies at the core of our service to the public'.[47] It is hoped that the new aspiration in Britain that all young people will be included in a quality cultural programme will not be diminished by the downturn in the economy. Certainly, until now

The fourth of the Tate outposts, Tate Modern, at Bankside

Tate Modern, Britain's national museum of international modern art, caters for five million visitors each year. The building was converted by architects Herzog and de Meuron and opened in 2000.

public enthusiasm has been at a tremendously high level, with queues of people waiting patiently to visit the Natural History Museum's Darwin Centre, for example, and the 2009 announcement that the country's national museums now make up eight of the ten top British visitor attractions.

The story is repeated in the United States, where in one year alone (2006) sixty arts institutions underwent renovation.[48] The snapshot given here of developments in America is necessarily limited, but in a decade of outstanding achievements one of the highlights was the reopening of MoMA, New York, in 2004. The eagerly anticipated relaunch of the museum revealed a top-floor chronological survey of its collections, which continued down to contemporary art on the ground floor, drawing attention to MoMA's role as a civic centre with a mission to educate the American nation towards 'continual enquiry into the evolving nature of modern art'.[49]

The Metropolitan Museum of Art – Henry James's 'museum of museums'[50] – finalized its master-plan, which placed order on its vast buildings, housing two million works of art, which range in date from classical antiquity to modern American design.[51] It unveiled the Ruth and Harold D. Uris Education Centre in 2007, warmly welcomed by director Philippe de Montebello (1977–2008): 'education has been fundamental to the Museum's mission since its founding in 1870, and the re-designed and re-equipped facilities of the Uris Centre will bring 137 illustrious years of education into the 21st century'. In 2009 its transformed American Wing, including twelve refurbished period rooms, opened with an unparalleled collection of American art.[52]

Elsewhere, the Art Institute of Chicago completed its largest ever expansion with the opening of a Modern Wing in 2009 that increased spaces by one-third, providing light-filled galleries to showcase its extensive collections and the Patrick and Shirley Ryan Education Centre.[53] Director James Cuno described the meaning of this progress for the future of the Art Institute: 'with an entire new building devoted to the museum's collection of twentieth- and twenty-first century art and design ... and free and open access to the Ryan Education Centre ... we can take our place as one of the leading encyclopaedic collections in the country'.[54]

What the Metropolitan Museum and Art Institute education centres have in common is their awareness of the need to pay attention to the changing needs of visitors by providing state-of-the-art electronic media infrastructure

The modern wing of the Art Institute of Chicago, 2009

View of the Modern Wing of the Art Institute of Chicago from the Nicholas Bridgeway. Opened in 2009 and designed by Pritzker Prize-winning architect Renzo Piano, the new wing is the centre for the museum's collection of twentieth/twenty-first-century art, sculpture, architecture, design and photography.

in every room, reflecting the radical change that new technology has brought to education. The digital age has truly arrived in the museum world, with curators and staff eager to explore the new avenues opened up by global technology. This is where the future lies in terms of visitor interaction and accessibility. While nothing can surpass the original artefact, which will always be the primary draw of any museum or gallery, there is much that can be gained from joining the digital community and exploring the myriad ways in which museums can connect directly with people, without any borders. Thus it is here we must look to see the future museological trends that will dominate the story of museums.

The Virtual Museum and the Physical Museum

As we have seen, new technology is a significant factor in museums' closer engagement with the public. Through the use of digital technologies and the Internet, museums are fostering a greater sense of community with their online audience by going beyond offering information and images to encouraging new audiences and creating and sustaining online communities, including social networking sites (SNS). Museums employ these formats, including comments, tagging, rating an object, tweeting and blogging, to seek user-generated content from experts and from the general public. In the world of today, museum experiences are now just as likely to take place around online collections, databases and archives of images. A good example of this development is the Prado Museum's partnership with Google Earth in 2009, which allows viewers who download the free Google software to 'visit' four of the museum's masterpieces in high definition, along with a 3D tour of the museum. Prado director Javier Rodríguez Zapatero sees the technology as a means of letting a worldwide audience enjoy 'these magnificent works as never before'.[55]

It might be tempting, given all this novelty and freedom of access, to think that the physical museum is now the poor cousin to the virtual world. This is not the case, however. While museums are investing much time and money in their virtual services, they also know that the physical museum is the core of the entire enterprise and must be treated as such in order to continue successfully. Mihaly Csikszentmihalyi, who has described learning in the museum environment as involving a prior expectation, need or desire, points out that the experience can go beyond people's expectations and achieve something that is surprising, perhaps even unimagined.[56] The challenge is to recognize the different types of museum experience available and to find a way to offer these to diverse audiences, but not at the expense of any one experience. There is often more information on the website than inside the museum, where the visitor can be left to enjoy the collection unmediated or to find the level of information that suits his or her purpose. The aspiration is to have information-rich experiences in the galleries, without interfering with the personal interaction with the work of art.

Museums will try to balance the virtual and the physical by employing technology to reduce the sense of distance and to improve their ability to share information quickly and efficiently. No matter how innovative a museum is on the web, the artefacts and services of most museums are still based in the physical building. Museum practitioners can align their experiments to the museum's core mission and demonstrate that their successes can be translated into the physical galleries, exhibitions and programmes.[57]

New Museum of the Acropolis, Athens

This new museum has provided a home for classical antiquity, bringing it into the twenty-first century. The Acropolis Museum opened in 2009 following the installation of 4,500 important antiquities. Designed by Bernard Tshmi, the building is mounted on roller bearings so that the structure and contents are protected from earth movements.

Visitors in the museum are presented with a range of multimedia tools (interactive kiosks, computers, mobile phone tours, audio guides, podcasts, videos, guided tours, text panels, activity sheets, brochures and catalogues). Online museum experiences, however, are different. A new generation of museum curators and practitioners will have to think through all these challenges so that the museum reaches more people meaningfully. As Zapatero eloquently observed: 'With the digital image, we're seeing the body of the paintings with almost scientific detail. What we don't see is the soul. The soul will always only be seen by contemplating the original.'[58]

One of the main reasons why the original artefact is so compelling is because it portrays this profound impulse, 'the soul', that helps people to be at home in the world. The growing world of the online museum is a wonderfully versatile, absorbing place – hugely attractive to young people – that can be observed from any PC. Within the walls of the museum, however, are the original works, created and crafted by people: in these are found poignant stories of being human as well as being works of art. Good museum staff and tutors can really bring these pictures to life, so that they become at once vivid, meaningful and personal, particularly to young people.

This is a key factor in the future of the museum: the ability to continue to attract a young audience through its doors and keep them interested and stimulated for the duration of their visit. The next generations are tech-savvy and therefore prone to putting all things technological first, but it is essential that they are encouraged continually to seek out the experience of the physical museum as well, to deepen their understanding and appreciation of history, art and humanity. A child's perception of the world is different from an adult's, motivated as it is by curiosity, wonder and the joy of understanding and creating. Take, for example, this appreciation of a Jack B. Yeats painting by nine-year-old Conor Maguire: 'In *The Liffey Swim* the artist Jack B. Yeats put thick sploshes of coloured paint onto the canvas. This is called impasto. I really like Jack's paintings and he gives lots of inspiration, but whenever I try at home my painting turns into a disaster! I would love to get a few tips from Jack but he's dead.'[59] This is where museums can cater so well for their younger audience members. As a reminder of how young people experience art and artefacts in the physical museum, Nobel Prize-winning writer Isaac Bashevis Singer captures the essence of the museum experience for children:

> we forget that children do not see pictures as critics and reviewers, they hate sociology and psychology, they do not try to 'under-stand' either Van Gogh or Picasso, they love a good story rather than a guide, they still believe in God, the family, angels, devils, witches, logic, clarity and other old fashioned nonsense, and if a picture is boring they will happily move on.[60]

Thus, the purpose of the lovingly observed portrait of the painter's son Camillus in *The Piping Boy* by Nathaniel Hone the Elder (1718–84), with its fine individual brush strokes and polished finish, is what makes this eighteenth-century painting, on display in the NGI, one of the defining characteristics of being human, as well as of portraying an image of the son by the proud father. This is what art museums are about.

The public role of the museum – that of making museums accessible, which includes intellectual, visual and contextual access, so that the collections become meaningful for the public – is being addressed by various trends informing the physical museum experience. One of these is the better techniques of display of artworks, an area that has become a key focus of curators. In the nineteenth and early twentieth centuries it was the practice to hang paintings in several tiers, enabling most of the collection to be on display rather than in storage. Similarly, museums tended to crowd galleries with classes of works (trays of specimens), or cases of artefacts (for example, Bronze Age pottery) and rooms of objects. All this changed in Europe (notably Germany) and in the United States in the twentieth century, when display patterns were altered. The result saw the hanging of works of art at eye level, on the line, with a sequence of single paintings spaced apart so that the visitor could concentrate on one work at a time.

In museum displays, the focus moved from trays and cases to individual objects and artefacts, resulting in fewer objects on show, which were easier to view and understand, as exemplified by the selective displays at the Chester Beatty Library. Another change of emphasis was the move from the copy to the original – the authentic artefact – which saw many antique casts and sculptures removed from display. Of the few that remain in museums, those at the Crawford Art Gallery create a dramatic first impression to the museum. Another example is the transfer of Francis Bacon's London studio and its integration into the displays at Dublin City Gallery The Hugh Lane. A contextual arrangement of displaying furniture, glassware, decorative fittings, etc., alongside works of art, as in the case of the decorative arts collection at the National Museum in Collins Barracks, has enabled a much broader understanding of the collections.

The virtual museum and the physical museum complement one another but are also separate entities offering different museum experiences. The benefits of this dual approach are clear: the ability to reach a much wider audience, the ability to cater for diverse audience types, the ability to disseminate as much or as little information as the visitor wants, and the ability to augment physical exhibits with online collections, databases, libraries and archives. The digital tools now available to museums are allowing them to dig deeper than ever into their own roles, ideals and aspirations, as well as into the minds, desires and experiences of their audience. Thus far, it has been an exciting journey into a new world and it will no doubt continue to be so, as museums push the boundaries further between the physical and the virtual.

Future Decades

Taken altogether across a broad landscape, the portents in this book promise a period of modest growth and consolidation in the Irish museum sector in the coming decades, with less capital-intensive 'grand projects' and a more careful use of existing resources, which is no bad policy. It is safe to conclude

Gerard Dillon (1916–71), *Yellow Bungalow*, 1954
Oil on canvas, 76.8 x 81.2 cm. No UM 283.

This image by the immensley popular Belfast-born painter Gerard Dillon, who worked in London, Dublin and the west of Ireland, is synonomous with the Ulster Museum. It was donated by the Haverty Trust in 1956.

that museums are moving into a new era, with accessibility, exhibition, learning and interpretation being the keys to ensuring that the collections, and the ideas they embody, provide the catalyst for development in the modern world. The museum experience is characterized by a person's encounter with the original work of art or artefact, and therefore the twenty-first-century view of museums as part of one's understanding of life, and as part of a person's lifestyle, heralds the greater integration of museums into society.

A major facet of this greater integration is the population flux that has seen millions of people crossing borders every year. While the debate today encompasses the ability of a people to present their cultural heritage in their own territory, many public museums emerged from countries affected by the French Revolution and similar revolutionary upheaval,[61] just as others emerged from an overthrow of foreign control, or in the wake of Bolshevist and Maoist revolutions and, more recently, in the context of changing political boundaries. Globalization is a defining feature of modern society, in which a universal space for the transfer of labour has been created. The nature of Irish population change is a case in point.

In 2006 the population of approximately 4,172,013 in the Republic (1,742,000 in Northern Ireland) included 420,000, approximately 10 per cent, of people classified as non-Irish nationals, from 188 countries. While some have left, due to the economic downturn, a significant proportion of the current and future population, such as the Polish and Chinese, are and will be immigrants who will remain a feature of Irish society and education provision into the future. Population trends show Ireland having 1,056,947 children under the age of eighteen years, with the highest proportion of population aged 0–19 years in the EU. The number of immigrants are also increasing in the post-primary sector.[62] More people are now choosing to reside in urban areas, and the number of people aged over sixty-five years is set to double by 2050. These are significant changes for a small island, unprecedented in scale. As a result, Ireland has become a multicultural society in which the make-up of the population is more culturally diverse than ever before.

Traditionally, museums play a formative role in the shaping of the nation, but the powers of the nation-state become limited with the arrival of new communities, whose presence makes the need for a post-cultural-nationalist politic ever more compelling. This involves ideas and initiatives from one country picked up and applied elsewhere in a swirl of cross-border intellectual traffic that requires moving beyond narrow concepts of national identity to embrace a wider view of a multi-ethnic society that enables 'identities' to be formed by all the citizens of the state.

> Whence a paradox: on the one hand, the nation has to root itself in the soil of its past and forge a national spirit in the face of colonial censure and disparagement. But in order to become modern, it is necessary at the same time to take part in scientific, technical and political rationality, something that may require a reinterpretation of the past. Not every culture can sustain and absorb the shock of modern civilization. There is the dilemma: how to become modern and to return to sources, how to revive an old, dormant civilization and take part in universal civilization.[63]

At this juncture in modern history, Irish museums can respond to the challenge of globalization by encouraging new citizens to invigorate Irish culture, a policy the writer Eavan Boland describes as the gain that society can achieve from adopting an inclusive outlook.[64] Ireland can embrace an inclusive approach that celebrates diversity and multi-ethnicity, inspires inclusivity and creativity and better serves the public. Critically, this is what this book has shown: the immense potential of museums to devise creative opportunities for the public they wish to serve, striving beyond the vision of Henry Flower when he spoke of future museums having 'to aspire not alone to preserve the objects in their care, but provide for their arrangement in such a manner as to provide for the instruction of those who visit'.[65]

Museums are grasping the promise of creative philosophies that work between theory and practice to focus on a visitor-centred approach that views 'pleasure through enlightenment' as the goal of the institution. They are employing active learning to help realize the multifaceted possibilities of the collections and to support a process of self-directed education that enables the visitor to adjust learning to his or her own pace. This vision includes the simple desire of museums to contribute to a person's development as a cultured and confident individual. The vision embraces collaboration on issues

Vincent Van Gogh (1853–90), *Rooftops of Paris*, 1886
Oil on canvas, 45.6 x 38.5 cm. NGI 2007.2.

One of several views of rooftops created by Van Gogh following his arrival in Paris in 1886. The cityscape was painted from the Butte, Montmartre, where the artist was staying with his brother Theo, at his apartment on Rue Lepic. The painting is transitional as Van Gogh leaves behind the dark tonality of his early work, before he begins to paint in the now-familiar colourful palette of his later career. A popular recent acquisition to the modern collections of the National Gallery of Ireland.

concerning technology, social networking sites and linked Internet provision; on ethical matters of child welfare, protection and special educational needs; on points of professional museum registration and training; on the subject of resourcing the arts in education; and on the importance of documenting the story of communities. These issues are relevant to Irish society, as multiculturalism, gender equity and reconciliation are revealing museums to be inclusive institutions, an essential part of a country that is seeking to accommodate shared futures together.

Conclusion

The original impetus for this book was the wish to better understand the historical context of Irish museums and to identify the public role of the museum within that story. It has been shown that the history of Irish museums follows a route devolving from European museums that was similar to the pattern of British, and latterly American, museums. In one key area the Irish story is unique, however, in that the outcome points up a difference from the typical pattern of the emergence of museums that came with the consolidation of the nation-state.

Irish museums emerged out of late eighteenth-/early nineteenth-century collecting practices by Ascendancy and other figures, which occurred at a time when Britain's influence on Ireland was particularly formative. Under British colonial rule Irish museums grew and advanced in the nineteenth century, even if that relationship was uneasy, and the growth took place during a time of rising national consciousness. This constitutes a major episode in the history of Irish museums, one that is awaiting further interdisciplinary research and study.

The advent of Irish independence in the early twentieth century slowed down this progress because the new state did not see cultural institutions as being important to an independent Ireland. The irony of this situation is

Francois Boucher (1703–70), *A Female Nude Reclining on a Chaise-Longue*, c.1752
Graphite, red and white chalk on brown paper, 22.2 x 36.2 cm. NGI 2007.3.

This is a study for Boucher's painting, *The Blonde Odalisque*, 1752, in the Alte Pinakothek, Munich. Traditionally, the model has been identified as the fourteen-year-old Marie-Louise O'Murphy (1737–1814), one of four sisters of Irish descent who became mistress to Louis XV. A superb drawing, it is a reminder of the works on paper that are held in the prints and drawings collections of most major museums.

that the collections, in particular the antiquities of the NMI, supplied most of the imagery of the Celtic Revival, which in itself formed a bridge between the Ascendancy and the key figures of the new Free State. For nearly sixty years the arts and the cultural institutions were placed low on the list of government priorities, as the struggle to establish the independent state was impacted by two world wars, internal strife and recurrent periods of economic recession. Only in the last decades of the twentieth century did the state recognize that the cultural institutions had an important role to play in the well-being of the country. This role was enhanced by the worldwide growth of cultural tourism, which had a positive effect on Ireland and which drew on the resources of the cultural heritage institutions, notably museums and galleries.

There are a number of major themes covered in this study, some of which involve the manner in which individual museums and galleries developed, while others include the underlying historical, political and social situations that underpinned this development. A number of institutions emerged independently without being influenced in this way. The major themes, however, concern those that influenced the development of Irish museums from the eighteenth century onwards, following the advent of the first public museum, the Louvre, which was ushered into being by the French Revolution. The modern public museum emerged during this critical phase in French history, providing the catalyst for change elsewhere in Europe and in the United States.

As we have seen, Irish, British and American museums did not devolve from princely collections but were government-sponsored or independently funded institutions. In Ireland the associated development of antiquarian and fine art collections that formed these museums and galleries largely came from the town houses and country estates of eighteenth- and nineteenth-century Ascendancy figures. They amassed these private collections or cabinets for their own enjoyment, to demonstrate their knowledge and sense of taste, and to share their enthusiasm with like-minded individuals and societies. The RDS and the RIA had a formative role in this story. In addition, the Dublin International Exhibition of Art-Industry in 1853 provided the stage upon which the aspiration for museums crystallized. In time, these Irish collections transferred from private ownership to the public domain in a pattern that was replicated throughout Europe and further afield.

During the course of the nineteenth century, the British government investigated aspects of the management and output of the institutions that it was partly funding. The Department of Science and Art in South Kensington saw itself as the centre of a multifaceted enterprise, whose duty was to provide science and art instruction in Ireland through the various bodies it funded, for example the Schools of Design, RDS, RIA and Museum of Irish Industry. When Henry Cole, director of the Department of Science and Art (also director of the South Kensington Museum), indicated that he was conscious that 'Great Britain owes every possible compensation of Ireland for the years of tyranny and injustice to which Ireland has been subjected',[1] he viewed the provision of science and art facilities and a museum as a form of political compensation. He also understood the importance of the Irish antiquities collections held by the RIA, which he recognized were being stored in an overcrowded space and in need of a more secure environment in a public institution. He believed that the state needed to intervene to set up a museum and take control of the collections, under his department in London.

MADONNA IRLANDA

Michael Farrell (1940–2000), *Madonna Irlanda or*
The Very First Real Irish Political Picture, 1977
Acrylic on canvas, 174 x 185.5 cm. Dublin City Gallery The Hugh Lane, No. 1436.

Farrell used *Madame O'Murphy* or *Madonna Irlanda*, also known as *The Very First Real Irish Political Picture*, to develop a series of visual references to politics, religion and sex in Ireland. The artist transposed Boucher's image of Marie-Louise O'Murphy (previously illustrated) together with many other visual and literary allusions, as a commentary on the political situation then prevalent in Ireland in the 1970s. Both IMMA and the National Gallery of Ireland hold works relating to this painting.

Lord Sandon wrote independently to both the RDS and the RIA in 1876, requesting that the Dublin institutions of science and art be brought under the Department of Science and Art and be administered by one director. The outcome of this intervention saw the passing of the Dublin Science and Art Museum Act 1877, which transferred the RDS buildings and collections into government control. Government funding of the RDS ceased when it took control of the Museum, Library and Botanic Gardens. In 1890, when

Taking part in a 'nationwide' Drawing Day provides an ideal opportunity for visitors to gain an understanding of works of art, by observing the collections as a preliminary to sketching under the guidance of professional tutors.

the agreement between the RIA and the Lords of the Committee of the Council on Education was signed, the Irish antiquities were transferred from the private domain of the RIA museum to the public arena of the Dublin Museum of Science and Art. This transfer took place just when there was a growing sense of Irish national consciousness and a developing awareness of Irish culture. A measure of this self-determination was evident when the cultural institutions came under the aegis of the newly founded Dublin branch of the Department of Agriculture and Technical Instruction in 1900.

The museums that emerged under British rule – including the Museum of Irish Industry, the Dublin Natural History Museum, the National Gallery of Ireland, the Museum of Science and Art, the Crawford Municipal Art Gallery, the Belfast Art Gallery and Museum and the university museums – formed a cultural and educational infrastructure for the country. The cumulative contents of these museums, including amateur cabinets and professional collections from private and public sources, represented a century of museological development. They became symbolic of the changed nature of Irish society as they were absorbed into the national museums. The Irish Revival was significant in the evolution of modern Ireland because its key figures recognized that cultural self-belief was fundamental not only to economic prosperity but to national independence. The Revival advanced on the energy of a wave of writers, poets and artists, as the Municipal Art Gallery in Dublin opened to become one of the first public galleries of modern art in the world.

The outbreak of the First World War saw the depletion of staff in all Irish

museums. The Easter Rising, followed by the War of Independence, the Anglo-Irish Treaty and the Civil War, began a period of decline, as with the achievement of independent statehood the funding of museums changed and the new government placed the cultural institutions under the Irish Department of Education. Adversely affected by both the prevailing circumstances and the restrictive policies of the Department of Finance, the cultural institutions became relatively unimportant, underlining the widespread political attitudes of the time. In Northern Ireland, on the other hand, the Belfast Municipal Museum and Art Gallery, with its cumulative art and antiquarian collections, opened in a new museum at Botanic Avenue in 1929.

The gradual development by the state of a coherent policy for educational expansion in the latter half of the century mirrored the improvement in living standards and increased public interest in the arts as the country experienced positive economic development, which was consolidated by Ireland's accession to the EEC (now EU) in 1973. In 1984 the cultural institutions were transferred to the Department of the Taoiseach, leading to the beginning of a process of regrowth as the country moved towards financial stability in the 1990s. While Irish museums and galleries lagged behind developments in Britain and in the United States in their early history, this altered in the later twentieth century when there was a greater knowledge of museum developments internationally, in particular in America, resulting in Irish museum directors and curators becoming more aware of the public and conscious of the need to effect change. When the cultural institutions were placed under their own Department of the Arts, with a minister to argue their case at cabinet, it marked a phase of fresh new growth and development for Irish museums.

The articulation of the public role of the museum has been a key motivation of this book. It is a role that has seen museums move away from being *about* something to being *for* somebody, as Stephen Weil put it.[2] The purpose of the book is to demonstrate that museums matter to society, to people, and that the relationship between the museum and the public, which was always a contested issue, had become in the latter part of the twentieth century *the* critical issue as the changing nature of society redirected museums towards placing the public role – in the form of access, engagement and outreach – as a key function (for some museums, the main function). The benefit of this situation is that it increases the importance of the role of the collections, insofar as there is a stronger requirement to convey their meaning and significance to the public. While it is the public that has sought more flexibility in the opening hours of the museum, so that it caters for the working population, and a greater range of services and facilities to meet the diverse needs of changing lifestyles, it is the state that has argued for increased access

Children: fun and creativity. Young people have a way of finding the most interesting collections in museums and they have no inhibitions in using them as a resource for fun and entertainment.

to museums, much greater inclusivity, versatility in programming and a demonstration of the fact that the museum is aware that its commercial role can contribute towards the operation. Some museums have been attentive, shifting the emphasis so that their programming and commercial services show awareness of the need to address the public and the state. This presents a dilemma for other museums, however, some of which are not equipped to develop a commercial role or to understand the requirement to justify state funding and have yet to develop the skills and acquire the staff to carry this out.

The major shift in the emphasis of the museum in the twenty-first century will be on adjusting and realigning its operations and services to fit with a person's lifestyle, so that the museum becomes a much more instinctive choice of place for people to visit and enjoy 'pleasure through enlightenment'. This requires careful thinking about the nature and focus of the institution. For example, if Irish museums emphasize what is distinctive, individual and special about their collections and services, presenting different views of Irish heritage and its interaction with other cultures, and if they ensure that this is conveyed by staff who enjoy engaging and interacting with the public, then it follows that the museum will attract Irish visitors, who will perceive that a conversation is taking place with them about their own culture. How much more powerful will be the effect on overseas tourists, who will realize that they are gaining a genuine insight into Irish life and society and who will take from the museum an experience that is both personal and unique. Focusing on what is distinctive about a museum and its collections will place fresh challenges on the museum to be both intelligent and creative in setting about reshaping its vision and purpose in relation to the local community. The museums that succeed will encourage their staff to work together in a flexible manner, to explore the potential of the collections in many different ways, both physical and virtual, while ensuring that there is a sound commercial basis to the operation and that the mission of the institution is kept intact. By being particularly attentive to interaction with local audiences, museums can ensure their own integrity, because it is the repeat visitor, in addition to overseas visitors, who matter in the Irish context. Thus, meeting and anticipating the needs of the public will be a priority. This is the reality of the evolving nature of the museum in the twenty-first century.

This modern configuration of the museum's original guiding principle is a significant development. It is important to recall that museums matter to society because they offer real objects in a primary place for *aesthetic* pleasure and for *enlightenment* (to educate people visually, socially and historically), in venues that are accessible to people of all ages and backgrounds. The new millennium has seen museums become increasingly important as places where people feel secure and at ease, where a quality of experience is provided from superbly presented collections, popular exhibitions, first-class interpretative material and programmes, excellent visitor information services, including research, study and conservation, underpinned by efficient administration.

Possibly the greatest advancement within the museum world in the last fifty years, and what differentiates it from earlier centuries, is this new commercial role, evidenced in ticketed exhibitions and cultural events, concerts, corporate sponsorship and functions, shops, cafés and restaurants, marketing and fund-raising. Supporting and enhancing this role are the members or friends organizations and the patrons of the museum. Despite all these changes, the traditional role of the museum remains intact, and many would argue that the outcome of these new services is the ability of the museum to cater more successfully for increasing numbers of visitors of all ages. Museums do matter and simple things explain the good that they do – they are accessible, demonstrate excellence, affirm tolerance, enable appreciation of personal expression and provide spaces in which to pursue individual peace and happiness. People flocked to museums in the wake of the terrorist attack

The Eileen Gray Circular Table

This circular glass and chrome side table was made in the late 1920s for the house E-1027 (E for Eileen, 10 Jean, 2 Badovici, 7 Gray) that Gray and Jean Badovici designed, in Roquebrune-Cap-Menton in southern France. The Gray Archive and items from her furniture collection have been acquired for permanent display at the National Museum of Ireland.

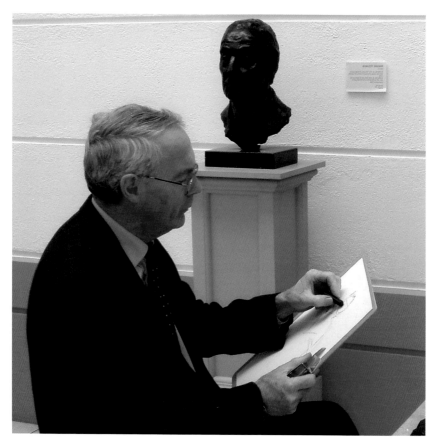

Museums provide many different ways to open up the collections to all ages: audio-guides, tours and talks, courses, activities, family packs and creative spaces. Adult lifelong learning is assuming an important place in these museum programmes.

on the World Trade Center, New York on 11 September 2001 because of their need for the affirmative, regenerative power of authentic artefacts and to be restored in trustworthy places of peace and reflection.

Museums and galleries are important to Irish people because they contain unique, precious and significant objects that tell the story of this island. Irish museums matter because of their ability to use their artefacts and impressive buildings, their research, exhibiting and interpreting endeavours – when managed creatively – to engage the public, celebrate human achievement and enrich people's lives. It is the collections that draw this reaction. The impact of the Celtic artefacts and Bronze Age gold at the National Museum and the welcome extended to different communities in the multicultural galleries at the Chester Beatty Library demonstrate how these collections matter. Visitors who find themselves marvelling at works of art by Caravaggio, Vermeer or Jack B. Yeats at the National Gallery, and paintings by northern artists like Paul Henry and John Lavery at the Ulster Museum, also appreciate museum facilities, such as the café and shop. Innovative educational programming helps to encourage interaction with works by contemporary artists such as Dorothy Cross at IMMA and historical paintings by James Barry at the Crawford Art Gallery in Cork. Museums such as the Hunt Museum matter to the quality of life in Limerick because they have links to the city, within which they play an economic, educational and social role.

William Scott (1913–89), *Frying Pan, Eggs and Napkin,* **1950**
Oil on canvas, 74 x 91 cm. NGI 2010.5.

Born in Scotland of Scottish-Irish parents, the artist was brought up in Enniskillen, County Fermanagh, attending Belfast College of Art and the Royal Academy Schools. One of the National Gallery's recent acquisitions, this work displays all of Scott's skill at analysing the shapes, textures and contours of everyday objects, to produce a strong abstracted composition, in which the eye is drawn by the vibrant yellow-lemons.

The Lewis Glucksman Gallery is as relevant to the staff and students of UCC as it is to its visitors. University museums, such as the James Mitchell Geology Museum, whose geological collections are used by students in Galway, and contemporary exhibitions, such as those at the Naughton Gallery in Belfast, are intrinsically bound up with both the student population and the local community. Small museums are also important because of how they look after their public, making the visitor feel welcome and wanted. In a similar way to their overseas counterparts, Irish museums emphasize the significance of culture to people's lives.

2010 was a year that saw the world shaken by an economic downturn, with few sections of society escaping its effects. A behavioural and attitudinal survey revealed that the majority of Irish people intended to work their way through the situation by trying to maintain their level of education and entertainment activity.[3] As government reviews the cultural institutions with a view to improving their economic viability within a cultural tourism environment, the critical issue of the significance of these historical collections to the nation remains. It is hard to think of any cultural project by a national cultural institution that has had such a successful impact on society as the online 1901 Census and 1911 Census provided by the National Archives of Ireland.

Furthermore, the figures support the economic viability of the arts and cultural sector. The level of state investment in museums demonstrates the importance of arts and culture to the status of Ireland as a nation, and to the economic and social progress of the country. Reports show that the arts sector is worth around €782 million in Gross Value Added (GVA), employs more than 26,000 people and generates around €382 million in tax revenue (2009). Economist Alan Gray states that 'The numbers employed are higher than would be expected by the economic profession', concluding that the analysis demonstrated the cultural sector's economic impact: 'While I do not believe that arts and culture should be evaluated solely on economic grounds, it is clear that the sector is important, labour intensive, and makes a significant contribution to Exchequer revenues.'[4]

Reviewing the development of museums in Ireland over the past three centuries (and cabinets and collections in earlier periods), it is clear that the desire by Irish people to establish museums that articulate forms of national identities at various times in the country's history is similar to the pattern in

The refurbished Ulster Museum by night

In 2009, the Ulster Museum re-opened to much acclaim after a three-year refurbishment programme, following which it was the winner of the Art Fund Prize for an outstanding refurbished museum.

Europe and elsewhere. The issue of collections that reflect 'identities', so that a wider context can be represented than one that is purely national, is a theme that is likely to arise in museums and galleries in the future. Research devoted purely to collection foundation and acquisition in Ireland would be most useful in this regard. Among the many museums that developed in the mid-nineteenth century, very little is known, for example, about the Museum of Irish Industry due to the short term of its existence. It was, however, a very influential institution. The role of this museum and its collections and their place in training and industrial education in Ireland is significant and deserving of in-depth study.

The nineteenth century, which was mainly one of museum foundation and collection development in Ireland – 'the golden age of collectors' – owed much to the ruling authorities who did what they could within the political and economic constraints to develop museums, galleries and associated cultural institutions as a standard part of the colonial enterprise of the empire. Herein lies ground for fruitful research and comparative findings. Like their counterparts in other countries, Irish museums reacted to the prevailing circumstances, influenced by Britain, Europe and latterly the United States. These influences are worthy of study, as is the period in Ireland between 1924 and 1984. Much remains to be written on the changed circumstances of the cultural institutions during the sixty-year interval following independence, in order to pinpoint the root cause of their neglect and to trace the full extent of the damaging effects of this inattention. Does this sixty-year hiatus differentiate Irish museums from their counterparts elsewhere? In other words, is this case particular to Ireland? To date there has been a lack of institutional histories, but it is hoped that with the advent of fresh anniversaries and centenaries, this might be remedied. An in-depth study of even a single museum or gallery casts light on prevailing collecting and museum practices, in addition to its context within the social and political circumstances of the time.

Museums have a very real and significant contribution to make to society and to individuals. They are also a source of creativity for generations of Irish artists – as Paul Durcan described it, the collections 'lit up the gloom of life and turned my eyesight inside out'.[5] In a century of innovation, advanced technological development and new concepts of 'nation' and 'identity', the museum's role can be extended to incorporate a fascinatingly wide remit in terms of both principle and policy. There is nothing to limit this development if museums, like the first collectors, are guided by passion, intelligence, curiosity and an inclusive sense of 'story'. The 'curiosities' made by people provide an object lesson in human living, consciousness and aspiration. As Zapatero remarked, they are repositories of the soul. This philosophy has been echoed by Professor Declan Kiberd, who argues that if museums can reconnect us with 'some unexpected, long-lost but immensely healing element of our own buried selves', then they are essential, they deserve our support and they should have our recognition.[6] In Ireland, the museums and galleries have recognized this role, are engaging with it and are striving to meet its challenge head on. Irish museums have found their place in the social history of this island and continue to be an ongoing source of inspiration to its people. Seamus Heaney's poetic project – linked to objects in several Irish museums – gives voice to the dead and enables his excavation of his own depths as a person:

To an imaginative person, an inherited object ... is not just an object, an antique, an item on an inventory; rather it becomes a point of entry into a common emotional ground of memory and belonging. It can transmit the climate of a lost world and keep alive in us a domestic intimacy with realities that otherwise might have vanished. The more we are surrounded by such objects and are attentive to them, the more richly and contentedly we dwell in our own lives.[7]

This, then, is the aim of the book: to tell the story of the evolution of Irish museums, to examine the circumstances that shaped their development, to focus on their public role, to provide a multifaceted context within which future informed debate could facilitate the realization of their potential in the new millennium and, ultimately, to show that museums matter to society. They matter not only because they provide 'windows to the past' but because they help the country to develop a fresh sense of identity. The story of Irish museums in the early twenty-first century demonstrates how much museums matter, how they make their own contribution to the Irish economy and how the role that they play in engaging the public in their diverse collections makes a real and significant contribution to individuals' and the community's well-being.

Pablo Ruíz Picasso (1881–1973), *Still LIfe with a Mandolin*, 1924
Oil on canvas, 101 x 158 cm, NGI 4522

Notes and References

Introduction

1. International Council of Museums, *Code of Ethics for Museums* (ICOM, 2006), p. 14.
2. 'For myself, I always write about Dublin because if I can get to the heart of Dublin I can get to the heart of all the cities of the world. In the particular is contained the universal.' R. Ellmann, *James Joyce* (Oxford: Oxford University Press, 1982), p. 505.
3. Alongside the list of abbreviations provided herein, the principal Irish figures are covered in J. McGuire and J. Quinn (eds), *Dictionary of Irish Biography* (Cambridge: Cambridge University Press, 2009). Re the use of terms in Irish: Saorstát is the Free State (1922); Taoiseach is the Irish prime minister; Tániste, the deputy prime minister; Éire, the name given to Ireland in the 1937 Constitution, was used outside the country to denote the southern Irish state; Uachtarán na hÉireann is the office of the president (1937) and An tUachtarán is the president (elected for a seven-year term); An (the) Dáil is the Lower House of the Parliament, Seanad Éireann is the Upper House, Oireachtas means 'parliament'; An Garda Síochána or Gardaí is the Irish police force; the Gaeltacht denotes an Irish-speaking area; political parties: Fianna Fáil (Soldiers of Destiny), founded 1926; Fine Gael (Tribe of the Gael), founded 1933 (evolved from its parent party, founded 1923); and Sinn Féin (We, ourselves or Ourselves Alone), founded 1905.
4. N. Nesbit, *A Museum in Belfast* (Belfast: Ulster Museum, 1979); P. Murray, *The Crawford Municipal Art Gallery* (Cork: Cork Vocational Education Committee, 1991); J. Turpin, *A School of Art in Dublin Since the Eighteenth Century: A History of the National College of Art and Design* (Dublin: Gill & Macmillan, 1995); E. Black (ed.), *Catalogue of Drawings, Paintings and Sculptures* (Belfast: MAGNI, 2000); E. Crooke, *Politics, Archaeology and the Creation of a National Museum of Ireland* (Dublin: Irish Academic Press, 2000); M. Ryan, et al., *Chester Beatty Library: Essential Guide* (London: Scala, 2001); C. Marshall and H. O'Donoghue, *The Collection 1999–2001, Irish Museum of Modern Art: Celebrating a Decade* (Dublin: IMMA, 2001); J. Hunt, et al. (eds), *The Hunt Museum: Essential Guide* (London: Scala, 2002); P.F. Wallace and R. Ó Floinn, *Treasures of the National Museum of Ireland: Irish Antiquities* (Dublin: Gill & Macmillan, 2002); P. Somerville-Large, *1854–2004: The Story of the National Gallery of Ireland* (Dublin: NGI, 2004); B. Dawson (ed.), *Hugh Lane, Founder of a Gallery of Modern Art for Ireland* (London: Scala, 2008).
5. G. Smyth, 'In the War Memorial Museum', in *The Fullness of Time* (Dublin: Dedalus Press, 2010), p. 152.
6. W.B. Yeats to Ezra Pound, 15 July 1918, cited in R.F. Foster, *W.B. Yeats: A Life, Volume II: The Arch Poet 1915–1939* (Oxford: Oxford University Press, 2003), p. xxii.

Chapter 1

1. A.S. Wittlin, *The Museum: its History and Its Tasks in Education* (London: Routledge & Kegan Paul, 1949), p. xiv.

2. A.C. Kors, *Encyclopedia of the Enlightenment* (Oxford: Oxford University Press, 2003), pp. 445–56.

3. J. Milton, *Paradise Regained* (London, 1671), p. 253.

4. References to the Alexandrian project as the key source of the Latin term *musaeum* and its German, French and Italian derivatives *museum, muséum, museo* are in eighteenth-century editions of *Encyclopaedia Britannica* and Diderot's and d'Alembert's *Encyclopédie* of 1751–65.

5. M. Fabianski, 'Musea in Written Sources of the Fifteenth to Eighteenth Centuries', *Opuscula Musealia*, vol. 4, no. 948, 1990, pp. 7–40; P. Findlen, 'The Museum: Its Classical Etymology and Renaissance Geneaology', *Journal of the History of Collections*, vol. 1, no. 1, 1989, pp. 59–78.

6. P. Young Lee, 'Museum of Alexandria and the Formation of the Museum in Eighteenth-Century France', *Art Bulletin*, vol. 79, no. 3, 1997, pp. 379–442.

7. The word *pinakothekai* derives from *pinas*, meaning 'plank'; paintings called *pinakes* were executed on wood. The term *pinacotheca* in ancient Greece implied a collection of paintings or sculpture, or a room in which they were exhibited (alternatively, a gallery). Vitruvius, *De Architectura* (Lugd, 1586), pp. 14, 228, 236.

8. J. Travlos, *Pictorial Dictionary of Ancient Athens* (New York: Praeger, 1971), pp. 482–93.

9. E. Pommier (ed. and trans.), *Lettres a Miranda sur les Deplacements des Monuments de L'Art de L'Italie par Antoine Quatremère de Quincy* (Paris: Editions Marcula, 1989).

10. Quoted in H. Seling, 'The Genesis of the Museum', *Architectural Review*, vol. 141, no. 840, 1967, p. 114.

11. Quoted in G. Bazin, *The Museum Age* (Brussels: Desoer, 1967), p. 129.

12. F.H. Taylor, *The Taste of Angels: A History of Art Collecting from Rameses to Napoleon* (Boston: Little Brown, 1948), p. 69; E.P. Alexander, *Museums in Motion* (Nashville: American Association for State and Local History, 1979), p. 20.

13. F.H. Anderson, *Francis Bacon: His Career and Thought* (Los Angeles, USC Press, 1962), p. 247.

14. Bazin, *The Museum Age*, p. 159.

15. Ibid., pp. 123–6.

16. C. Duncan and A. Wallach, 'Universal Survey Museum', *Art History*, no. III, 1980, pp. 448–69.

17. Young Lee, 'Museum of Alexandria', p. 403.

18. Ibid., pp. 379–442. The Louvre was renamed Muséum Français in 1793, Musée de la Republique in 1793, Muséum des Arts in 1793, Musée Central des Arts in 1797 and Musée Napoléon in 1803. Seling, 'The Genesis of the Museum', p. 109.

19. Seling, 'The Genesis of the Museum', p. 109.

20. G. Bazin, *The Louvre* (New York: Harry N. Abrams, 1959), p. 51.

21. I. Pears, *The Discovery of Painting: The Growth of Interest in the Arts in England 1680–1789* (New Haven, and London: Yale University Press, 1988).

22. C. Duncan, 'From the Princely Gallery to the Public Art Museum', in D. Boswell and J. Evans (eds), *Representing the Nation: A Reader, Histories, Heritage, and Museums* (London and New York: Routledge, 1999), pp. 304–32.

23. Wittlin, *The Museum*, p. xiv.

24. D.R. Brigham, *Public Culture in the Early Republic: Peale's Museum and its Audience* (Washington and London: Smithsonian Institute Press, 1995), p. 2. Charles Willson Peale (1741–1827), artist, inventor, naturalist, key figure in the American Enlightenment, studied painting with Benjamin West in London.

25. L.V. Coleman, *Mousion* (Paris, 1927), p. 268.

26. E.A. Talbot, *Five Years' Residence in the Canadas* (London: Longman, Hurst, Rees, Orme, Brown & Green, 1824), pp. 147–8.

27. W. J. Rhees, *Manual of Public Libraries, Institutions and Societies in the United States and British Provinces of North America* (Philadelphia: 1859), p. 450.

28. See E.P. Alexander, 'Early American Museums, from Collection of Curiosities to Popular Education', *International Journal of Museum Management and Curatorship*, vol. 6, 1987, pp. 337–51; Brigham, *Public Culture in the Early Republic*.

29. R.J. Godley, *Letters from America* (London: 1844), vol. 2, p. 168. The view of an Irish visitor impressed by the USA.

30. Quote from her book, reprinted for an American audience: C. E. Tonna, *The Museum* (Dublin: Religious Tract and Book Society for Ireland, 1832; New York: 1847), p. 123.

31. T. Dwight, *The Northern Traveller and the Northern Tour* (New York: Goodrich & Wiley, 1834), p. 216.

Part II Preamble

1. Archbishop Charles Cobbe built Newbridge House in Donabate in 1736, inherited by his son Thomas Cobbe in 1769, remaining the home of the Cobbe family until 1985. The Cobbe family were benevolent landowners in the nineteenth century assisting the poor during the Famine.

2. W.B. Sarsfield Taylor, *The Fine Arts in Great Britain and Ireland*, 2 vols (London: Whittaker & Co., 1841), vol. 2, p. 253.

3. V. Pakenham, *The Big House in Ireland* (London: Cassell, 2000; repr. 2005), p. 56.

4. This idea was set out in Benedict Anderson's *Imagined Communities* (London: Verso, 1991).

Chapter 2

1. Quote from A. Young, *A Tour in Ireland* (London, 1780), p. 67.

2. From a poem inscribed to the Dublin Society, by Mr. Arbuckle. Printed by R. Reilly for George Ewing at the Angel and Bible in Dame Street, 1737.

3. H.T. Berry, *A History of the Royal Dublin Society* (London: Longmans, 1915); also T. de Vere White, *The Story of the Royal Dublin Society* (Dublin: RDS, 1955); J. Meenan and D. Clarke (eds), *The Royal Dublin Society 1731–1981* (Dublin: Gill & Macmillan, 1981); K. Bright, *The Royal Dublin Society 1815–45* (Dublin: Four Courts Press, 2004); M. Kelleher, *The Founders of the Royal Dublin Society and Their Houses* (Dublin: RDS, 2004).

4. 'The Dublin Society in its early formation relied heavily on the advice and assistance of the Royal Society of which many were to become members.' See Foreword in K.T. Hoppen, *The Common Scientist in the Seventeenth Century* (London: Routledge & Paul Kegan, 1970); also K.T. Hoppen, 'The Royal Society and Ireland', *Notes and Records of the Royal Society*, vol. 20, 1965, pp. 78–99.

5. Statement of the Council, 25 February 1841, in *Proceedings of the Royal Dublin Society* (hereafter, *PRDS*), vol. 1, no. 27 (1841).

6. 'That every member of this society, at his admission, be desired to choose some particular subject in natural history or in husbandry, agriculture or gardening, or some species of manufacture, or other branch of improvement, and make it his business … and to report in writing the best account they can get by experiment or enquiry relating thereunto.' Berry, *Royal Dublin Society*, pp. 16–17. Dublin Society rules were approved 18 December 1731, published 1787, with a Preface by Rev. Robert Burrowes.

7. B.B. Kelham and D. McMillan, 'Experimental Science in Ireland and the Scientific Societies' in N. McMillan (ed.), *Prometheus's Fire: A History of Scientific Technological Education in Ireland* (Kilkenny: Tyndall Publications, 1999), p. 106.

8. George III (1791), cp. xxviii: An Act to grant the Dublin Society £5,000 for the improvement of husbandry and other useful arts was passed in the Irish Parliament; £3,000 provided to furnish the Repository and for implements of husbandry, £300 to provide/maintain a

Botanic Garden, £800 for salaries of officers of the DS and School of Drawing. Berry, *Royal Dublin Society*, p. 86.

9. A letter from Lord Sidmouth to Lord Oriel, read at Dublin Society general meeting (29 June 1820) affirmed the agreement of George IV to become patron of the society. Government did not officially recognize the royal prefix until the first supplementary charter was issued in 1865 and from 1866 it was officially deemed the 'Royal Dublin Society'. *The Charters and Statutes of the Royal Dublin Society* (Dublin: RDS, repr. 1989).

10. M. Dunlevy, 'Samuel Madden and the Scheme for the Encouragement of Useful Manufactures', in A. Bernelle (ed.), *Decantations: A Tribute to Maurice Craig* (Dublin: Lilliput Press, 1992), p. 25.

11. C. Smith, *The Ancient and Present State of the County and City of Cork, vol. 1* (Cork: John Connor, 1750), pp. 146–7; see also R. Day and W.A. Copinger (eds), *Journal of Cork History and Archaeology Society* (1893–4).

12. W.G. Strickland, *A Dictionary of Irish Artists*, 2 vols (Dublin: Irish University Press, 1969, repr. of original 1913 edn), vol. 1, p. 304: 'These annual premiums continued and the Society held exhibitions of the works of the competitors for some years in a room in the Parliament House. Of these exhibitions, however, no catalogues exist, the names of the prizewinners only being given in the Society's records. James Barry, it is said, was awarded a premium of 10 guineas in 1763 for his picture *The Baptism of the King of Cashel by St. Patrick*, 1763 (NGI 4623). Barry would become one of Britain's greatest history painters.

13. Dunlevy, 'Samuel Madden', p. 25.

14. P.C. Webb, MS, 'An Account of the Dublin Society, Royal Society of Arts', GBI, no. 120; dated only 1756. Minute, 16 June 1756. Meeting between William Shipley (founder of the Society of Arts) and Dr Stephen Hales in 1753, re the Dublin Society. The RSA directly imitated the Dublin Society in many of its premiums. See D. Allen and R.E. Scholfield, *Stephen Hales: Scientist and Philanthropist* (London: Solar Press, 1980), pp. 100, 164.

15. *PRDS*, 18 October 1764, p. 74: 'any place set apart as a repository for things that have immediate relation to the sciences'; *Encyclopedia Perthensis*, 2nd edn, vol. 15 (Edinburgh: John Brown, 1816), p. 432.

16. J.A. Bennett, *Church, State and Astronomy in Ireland* (Belfast: Institute of Irish Studies/ Queen's University and Armagh Observatory, 1990), p. 18.

17. Berry, *Royal Dublin Society*, p. 22.

18. *PRDS* Minute Book 1731–3, p. 62.

19. Berry, *Royal Dublin Society*, p. 22.

20. G. Wright, *Historical Guide to the City of Dublin* (London: Baldwin, Craddock & Joy, 1825); H.O. Bruskill, *Short History of the Irish Parliament House* (Dublin: Bank of Ireland, 1934).

21. Kors, *Encyclopedia of the Enlightenment*, p. 6.

22. *PRDS*, 8 May 1735.

23. *PRDS*, 24 April 1735.

24. *PRDS*, 13 February 1734.

25. *PRDS*, 13 July 1935.

26. *PRDS*, 10 July 1735; *PRDS*, 13 February 1736.

27. *PRDS*, 14 April 1736; *PRDS*, 1 May 1740.

28. *Faulkner's Dublin Journal*, 17 October 1752.

29. RDS Minute Book, September 1732, records an instruction to 'look out a piece of ground, about an acre, proper for a nursery'; E.C. Nelson and E.M. McCracken, *The Brightest Jewel: A History of the National Botanic Gardens* (Kilkenny: Boethius Press, 1987), p. 15.

30. M. Craig, *Dublin 1660–1860* (Dublin: Allen Figgis, 1969), p. 121.

31. *The Gentleman's Magazine* (1786), p. 217.

32. Royal Irish Academy (RIA), Dublin, MS 24K14, 23 July 1802, p. 242.
33. Strickland, *Dictionary of Irish Artists*, vol. 2, pp. 587–8.
34. *Irish Magazine*, June 1811, pp. 275–6.
35. *Dublin Chronicle*, 16–18 September 1788.
36. *Transactions*, vol. 1, no. 2 (Dublin: RDS, 1800), pp. 1–142.
37. C.E. O'Riordan, *The Natural History Museum* (Dublin: Stationery Office, 1983), p. 7.
38. D.L.G. Karsten, *A Description of the Minerals in the Leskean Museum*, 2 vols, trans. G. Mitchell (Dublin: Mercier, 1798). Volume 1 contains the characteristic and systematic collections; Volume 2 contains the geological, geographical and economical collections. No. 85A, RDS Library.
39. Strickland, *Dictionary*, vol. 2, p. 641.
40. Irish scholars were aware of the systematic arrangement of collections: 'the most complete system of natural history yet given to the public' advocated by Carl Linnaeus; *Encyclopaedia Perthensis*, vol. 15, p. 597; P. Somerville-Large, *Irish Eccentrics* (Dublin: Lilliput Press, 1990), pp. 176–7.
41. J.M. Sweet, 'Robert Jameson's Irish Journal, 1797', *Annals of Science*, vol. 23, 1967, pp. 97–126.
42. P.N. Wyse Jackson and E. Vaccari, 'The Rev. George Graydon (c. 1753–1803): Cleric and Geological Traveller', in *Royal Irish Academy 4th Annual Lecture* (Dublin: RIA, 1997), pp. 8–9.
43. *PRDS*, 18 June 1795.
44. Berry, *Royal Dublin Society*, p. 355.
45. RIA, MS 24K15, 23 July 1802, p. 242.
46. B. O'Reilly, *A Catalogue of the Subjects of Natural History in the Museum of The Dublin Society, Systematically Arranged, also of the Antiquities* (Dublin: Graisberry & Campbell, 1813).
47. RIA, MS24K15, 23 July 1802, p. 242.
48. Strickland, vol. 2, p. 515.
49. J. Coolahan, 'The Fortunes of Education as a Subject of Study and Research in Ireland', *Irish Education Studies*, vol. 4, no. 1, 1985, p. 3.
50. In 1772 W. Flynn of Cork advertised Newbery's books. John Newbery's *A Little Pretty Pocket Book*, 1744, was one of the first books produced for the amusement of children. His successors, the London booksellers Francis and Elizabeth Newbery, produced children's books in the second half of the eighteenth century.
51. C. Maxwell, *Dublin under the Georges* (Dublin: Lambay Books, 1936).
52. P.J. Dowling, *The Hedge Schools of Ireland* (Cork: Mercier Press, 1968). The children received basic reading and writing skills, with few attending for more than a few years.
53. *RDS Minute Book*, 18 May 1746.
54. J.F. Maguire, *The Industrial Movement in Ireland* (Cork: J. O'Brien, 1853); see also Isaac Weld, 'The First Public Distribution of Prizes at the Drawing Schools', RDS Minute Book, 18 May 1746.
55. *Faulkner's Dublin Journal*, 27–30 October 1750; see Turpin, *A School of Art in Dublin since the Eighteenth Century*, pp. 7–8.
56. M. Clarke and R. Rafussé, *Dictionary of Dublin City Guilds* (Dublin: Dublin Public Libraries, 1993).
57. A. Crookshank and the Knight of Glin, *Ireland's Painters 1600–1940* (New Haven, and London: Yale University Press, 2002), pp. 83.
58. Strickland, *Dictionary*, vol. 1, p. xv.
59. *Faulkner's Dublin Journal*, 20–21 November 1739.
60. Strickland, *Dictionary*, vol. 1, p. 60.

61. *Old Dublin Intelligencer*, 1730. Strickland, *Dictionary*, vol. 2, p. 18.

62. Possibly the French artist Pierre Mondale Lesat, promoted in *Dublin Daily Advertiser*, 25 November 1736. See Crookshank and Glin, *Ireland's Painters,* p. 87.

63. T. Campbell, *An Essay on Perfecting the Fine Arts in Great Britain and in Ireland* (Dublin: s.n., 1767); J. Fenn, *Instructions Given in the Drawing Schools Established by the Dublin Society*, 2 vols (Dublin: Alexander McCulloch, 1769–72); J. Robinson, *Plan for the Improvements of the Fine Arts in Ireland* (Dublin, 1792).

64. A. Pasquin, *An Authentic History of the Professors of Painting, Sculpture and Architecture who have Practised in Ireland* (London: Symonds, Queen & Bellamy, 1796), p. 5 [original emphasis]. Anthony Pasquin was the alias of John Williams, an itinerant painter and the principal source on the subject of art in eighteenth-century Ireland.

65. L. Courajod, *L'École Royale des Elévès Protégés* (Paris and London: Librairie de l'Art, Rouam Gilbert Wood, 1874).

66. J. Turpin, 'Irish Art and Design Education', *Irish Arts Review*, vol. 10, 1994, pp. 209–16.

67. E. McParland, 'Thomas Ivory: Architect', *Gatherum*, no. 4, August 1973, p. 7.

68. J. O'Keeffe, *The Recollections of John O'Keeffe* (London: Henry Colburn, 1826) pp3–4.

69. J. Turpin, 'Introduction', in G. Willemson, *The Dublin Society Drawing Schools* (Dublin: RDS, 2000), pp. vii–xiv.

70. Crookshank and Glin, *Ireland's Painters*, p. 70.

71. Turpin, *A School of Art in Dublin Since the Eighteenth Century*, pp. 124–5.

72. PRDS, Minute Book, 13 January 1757.

73. PRDS, Minute Book, 4 November 1770: 'During the late Recess, David La Touche, junior, Esq. had presented them with an excellent cast of the *Laocoön*, which he had procured from the original figures in Rome.' In 1506 the famous *Laocoön* group had been excavated from the Baths of Titus. The statue arrived in pieces from Rome and was put together in Dublin by Philip Adam, who was paid 'for his trouble and expense' on 10 February 1791.

74. Turpin, *A School of Art in Dublin Since the Eighteenth Century*, pp. 124–5.

75. The collection included the following casts: *Antinous, Flora, Dancing Faun, Sancta Susanna, Bacchus, Venus aux Belle Fesses, Venus de Milo, Venus of the Campidoglio*, casts of the sculptures of Persepolis, cast of J.H. Foley's *Youth at a Stream*; the Royal Irish Art Union donated Patrick McDowell's *Girl at Prayer*. The collection had twenty busts including *Marcus Aurelius, Alexander, Brutus, Homer, Desmonsthenes, Cicero, Ariadne, The Listener, The Boxers, Head of Laocoon, River God, Commodus, Venus de Medici*. The finest cast, the *Laocoön*, was awarded pride of place in the Hawkins Street premises.

76. A committee under Thomas Burgh and Andrew Caldwell supervised the collection. Edward Smyth and William Waldron restored the statues and busts. Society of Artists of Ireland held three exhibitions in the RDS gallery in the 1800s. See RDS Minutes, 8 December 1796. Description of displays in *Saunders' Newsletter*, 2 July 1799. Also used by RDS students. PRDS, 46, 6 September 1810.

77. RIA, MS 24K15, 23 July 1802, p. 242.

78. See Act of Parliament 1791; see note 11 for details.

79. The name National Botanic Gardens, Glasnevin derived directly from Royal Botanic Gardens, Glasnevin, which was officially decreed in July 1885. See Nelson and McCracken, *Brightest Jewel*, pp. 46–53.

80. W. Wade, *Catalogues Systematicus Plantarum Indigenarum in Comitatu Dublinensi* (Dublin: RDS, 1794).

81. A systematic arrangement of collections advocated by Carl Linnaeus. *Encyclopaedia Perthensis*, vol. 15, p. 597.

82. Daily tickets from Wade and others. Thomas Sherrard's 1800 map illustrates the grounds.

83. Nelson and McCracken, *Brightest Jewel*, pp. 68–9.

84. W.B.S. Taylor, *History of the University of Dublin* (London: T. Cadell, 1845), p. 296.

85. J. Dunton, *The Dublin Scuffle: Being a Challenge, Sent by John Dunton, Citizen of London to Patrick Campbell, Bookseller in Dublin* 1699 (Dublin: RIA Minute Books, 1785).

86. F. O'Dwyer, 'Building Empires: Architecture, Politics and the Board of Works 1760–1860', *Journal of the Irish Georgian Society*, vol. 5, 2002, p. 122.

87. Ludwig Wittgenstein (1889–1951) came to Dublin 1948–9 to visit a friend studying medicine at Trinity College, and ended up spending a decade, on and off, in Ireland. He was familiar with the museum. M.C. O'Drury, 'Some Notes of Conversations with Wittgenstein', in R. Rhees (ed.), *Recollections of Wittgenstein* (Oxford: Oxford University Press, 1984), p. 137.

88. P.N. Wyse Jackson, 'The Geological Collections of Trinity College, Dublin', *The Geological Curator*, vol. 5, no. 7, 1992, pp. 263–74.

89. R.L. Praeger, *Some Irish Naturalists* (Dundalk: Dundalgan Press, 1949).

90. E. Vaccari and P.N. Wyse Jackson, 'The Fossil Fishes of Bloca and the Travels in Italy of the Irish Cleric George Graydon in 1791', *Museological Scientifica*, vol. 12, no. 4, 1995, pp. 57–81.

91. RIA Minute Book, Antiquities, vol. 1, 28 February 1785.

92. P.N. Wyse Jackson, 'Fluctuations in Fortune: Three Hundred Years of Irish Geology', in J. Wilson Foster and H. Chesney (eds), *Nature in Ireland: A Scientific and Cultural History* (Dublin: Lilliput Press, 1997), p. 94.

93. RIA Minute Book, Antiquities, vol. 1 (listed 1806).

94. P.N. Wyse Jackson, *In Marble Halls: Geology in Trinity College Dublin* (Dublin: Trinity College, Dublin, 1994), p. 55.

95. W.B. Taylor, *History of the University of Dublin* (London: R. Jennings, 1819).

96. G. Long, 'The Foundation of the National Library of Ireland 1836–1877', *Long Room*, no. 36, 1991, p. 41.

97. Bennett, *Church, State and Astronomy*, pp. 17, 21.

98. J.W. Foster, 'Encountering Traditions', in Foster and Chesney (eds), *Nature in Ireland*.

99. *The Book of Trinity College Dublin 1591–1891* (Belfast: Hodges & Figgis, 1920), pp. xxi, 316.

100. Rev. Robert Burrowes (1762–1841) wrote the Preface to the first volume of the RIA *Transactions*. R.B. McDowell, 'The Main Narrative', in T. Ó Raifeartaigh (ed.), *The Royal Irish Academy: A Bicentennial History 1785–1985* (Dublin: RIA, 1985), p. 18.

101. Ó Raifeartaigh (ed.), *The Royal Irish Academy*.

102. The Dublin Society committee was formed between 1772 and 1774 under the chairmanship of Sir Lucius O'Brien with General Charles Vallancey and Dr Thomas Leland as joint secretaries; 1,877 books and manuscript material collected by the committee went to the National Library, some remaining with the RDS library. W.D. Love, 'The Hibernian Antiquarian Society', *Studies*, vol. 51, 1962, pp. 419–31.

103. McDowell, 'Main Narrative', p. 9.

104. Members: General Charles Vallancey, Burton Conyngham, Earl of Moira, Rev. William Hamilton, James Gandon, bishops Barnard of Killaloe, Percy of Dromore.

105. Aims set out in *Transactions*, published 1787, the title page carrying the RIA motif and motto 'We will endeavour'. See Ó Raifeartaigh (ed.), *Royal Irish Academy*, p. 12.

106. Timothy Cunningham, a barrister, left the RIA £1,000, to be spent on premiums to be awarded for 'the improvement of natural knowledge and other subjects'. McDowell, 'Main Narrative', pp. 26–7.

107. Charles O'Conor, antiquarian, grandson of Charles O'Conor the elder, and later librarian at Stowe, was commissioned by the RIA in 1786 (the year it founded its library) to copy Irish manuscripts in the Vatican Library. C. O'Conor, 'The Origins of the RIA', *Studies*, vol. 38, 1986, pp. 325–7.

108. The first meeting was held at Charlemont House (Lord Charlemont being the first president), the second at the treasurer's house in Harcourt Street, the third at Charlemont House.

From then on they met at Navigation House which they had acquired in 1788.

109. Ó Raifeartaigh (ed.), *Royal Irish Academy*, p. 18.
110. G.F. Mitchell, 'Antiquities', in Ó Raifeartaigh (ed.), *Royal Irish Academy*, p. 106; RIA, Council Minutes, vol. 1, p. 179.
111. RIA, Council Minutes, vol. 1, pp. 184, 190.
112. Mitchell, 'Antiquities', p. 102.

Chapter 3

1. J. O'Keeffe, *Recollections of the Life of John O'Keeffe, Written by Himself* (London: Henry Colburn, 1826), vol. 2, p. 16. There are 2 volumes.
2. Frederick Hervey offered to purchase the Temple of Vesta and ship it to Downhill.
3. Quinn, a physician and landowner, collaborated with James Tassie to invent the glass used to make Tassie gems.
4. J. Soane, *Memoirs of the Professional Life of an Architect* (Privately printed, 1835), p. 15.
5. Between 1791 and 1799 James Malton produced a series of twenty-five views of Dublin that complemented Hugh Douglas Hamilton's earlier *The Cries of Dublin* (1760).
6. M. Bourke and S. Bhreathnach-Lynch, 'Introduction', in *Discover Irish Art* (Dublin: NGI, 1999).
7. *Frederick Augustus Hervey (1730–1803), Bishop of Derry and Fourth Earl of Bristol with his Grand-daughter Lady Caroline Crichton*, c.1790–91, NGI 4350. Hugh Douglas Hamilton worked with John Rocque on Kildare Estate Maps (1755–60) for Lord Kildare (later 1st Duke of Leinster) executing *The Cries of Dublin* (1760), an album of sixty-six drawings and a frontispiece depicting eighteenth-century Dublin genre life. W. Laffan, *The Cries of Dublin, drawn from the life by Hugh Douglas Hamilton* (Dublin: The Georgian Society, 2003).
8. A. Plumptre, *Narrative of a Residence in Ireland during the Summer of 1814 and that of 1815* (London: Colburn, 1817).
9. Somerville-Large, *Irish Eccentrics*, pp. 84, 88.
10. B. Fothergill, *The Mitred Earl* (London: Faber & Faber, 1974), p. 177.
11. *London-Derry Journal*, 13 May 1783.
12. La Touche's portrait (coloured pastels over pastel on paper), signed 'H. Hamilton / Rome 1790'. Private Collection. A. Hodge, *Hugh Douglas Hamilton: A Life in Pictures* (Dublin: NGI, 2008).
13. *The Amorino* (NGI 8358) by Antonio Canova (1757–1822). The statue followed the fate of the La Touche family; inherited by a descendant who moved to England. Recovered in the garden of a house in Britain's West Country, 1966. The Bank of Ireland (founded by the La Touche family) donated the statue to the National Gallery in 1997.
14. C.S. King and H. Weir, *Henry's Upper Lough Erne* (Dublin: 1892; repr. Co. Clare: Ballinakella Press, 1987), p. 40.
15. Irish painters in Rome included: Thomas Hickey from 1762–7; Matthew William Peters 1762–4; James Barry 1766–70; Solomon Delane 1764–70s; Robert Crone 1755–67; James Forrester 1755–76; and sculptors Christopher Hewetson 1765; John Crawley 1750–9; and antiquarian Matthew Nulty from 1758 to 78.
16. Cited in Crookshank and Glin, *Ireland's Painters*, p. 51.
17. Jonathan Fisher's *View of the Lower Lake, Killarney* (NGI 1797) and *View of the Eagle's Nest, Killarney* (NGI 1813); J.W. Foster, 'The Topographical Tradition in Anglo-Irish Poetry', *Irish University Review*, vol. 4, 1974, pp. 169–87.
18. Edmund Burke was active in TCD, RDS and RIA circles and was well acquainted with the Earl of Powerscourt. With an interest in art he would have seen the potential in the estate for subjects for Barret and for patronage.

19.   J. Walton, 'Classicism and Civility', *Irish Arts Review*, vol. 21, no. 1, 2004, pp. 102–7.

20.   W. Laffan and B. Rooney, *Thomas Roberts 1748–1777: Landscape and Patronage in Eighteenth-Century Ireland* (Tralee: Churchill House Press for the National Gallery of Ireland, 2009). Roberts died in Lisbon in 1777, aged twenty-eight.

21.   William Ashford (*c.*1746–1824), though born in Birmingham, moved to Dublin to work for the Ordnance Survey, which required him to travel the length and breadth of Ireland. He showed landscapes from 1772 and for the remainder of his career, ending his life as the first president of the RHA. The listed works are in the NGI collections.

22.   Son of David Digues La Touche, the first La Touche to come to Ireland, his collection was sold at auction: *A Catalogue of the Genuine Collection of Italian, Flemish and Other Pictures of the late James Digges La Touche, 16 May 1764* (Dublin, 1764).

23.   Smith, *Cork, vol. 1*, pp. 146–7. Some of these attributions were inflated and inaccurate.

24.   Joseph Leeson, later 1st Earl of Milltown, was painted by Pompeo Batoni on his first visit to Italy. S. Benedetti, *The Milltowns: A Family Reunion* (Dublin: NGI, 1997), pp. 20–1. He used his inherited wealth to buy land in County Wicklow, where he built Russborough House. He married three times: Celia Leigh (1729), Anne Preston (1739), and Elizabeth French (1768). Robert Wood was his advisor on the first Italian trip (1744–5; second trip 1750–1); Leeson amassed £60,000 of statues and pictures, seized by the French in transit to Ireland. A set of pastels of the four seasons by Rosabla Carriera, purchased for Leeson by Wood, is in the National Gallery's Collection. See S.R. Drumm, 'The Irish Patrons of Rosalba Carriera', *Irish Architectural and Decorative Studies*, vol. 6, 2003, pp. 202–26.

25.   J. Mack, *The Museum of the Mind* (London: British Museum Press, 2003), pp. 138–43.

26.   T. Milton, *The Seats and Demesnes of the Nobility and Gentry of Ireland in a collection of the most Interesting and Picturesque Views, engraved by Thomas Milton* (Dublin: Irish Georgian Society, 1963).

27.   J. Peill, 'Heirlooms of Newbridge House', *Irish Arts Review*, vol. 20, no. 2, 2003, pp. 98–103.

28.   *Newbridge House* (Dublin: Association of Fingal Historical Societies), pp. 7–8.

29.   H. Potterton 'Introduction', in *The Illustrated Summary Catalogue of Paintings* (Dublin: National Gallery of Ireland, 1981), p. xxiv. The Milltown gift of 1902 arrived between 1906 and 1914.

30.   Parliament voted £500 in 1767 (George III). Colonel William Burton (1733–96) of Buncraggy, County Clare, assumed the name of Conyngham on succeeding to the family estates on the death of his uncle, the Earl of Conyngham. Became MP for Ennis and Killybegs, teller of the exchequer in Ireland and a privy councillor. A member of the Dublin Society, he was involved in antiquarian, artistic and architectural activities. On the collapse of the Antiquities Committee, he replaced it with his own in 1780. Craig, *Dublin*, p. 199n.

31.   *Freeman's Journal*, 9–12 May 1767.

32.   T. Campbell, 1767. *An Essay on Perfecting the Fine Arts in Great Britain and Ireland* (Dublin: William Sleator, 1767), p. 35. In the Halliday Collection, RIA.

33.   Campbell, pp. 35–40.

34.   Ibid.

35.   J.C. Walker, *Outlines of a Plan for Promoting the Art of Painting in Ireland: With a List of Subjects for Painters Drawn from the Romantic and Genuine Histories of Ireland* (Dublin: Bonham, 1790), pp. 7–20.

36.   The Society of Artists did not exhibit for twenty years after 1750. G. Breeze, *Society of Artists in Ireland* (Dublin: Criterion, 1985).

37.   *Dublin Evening News*, 2 February 1792.

38.   *Dublin Evening News*, 7 January 1792.

39.   *Dublin Evening News*, 4 June 1792.

40.   Strickland, *Dictionary*, vol. 1, pp. 319–21; Breeze, *Society of Artists*, p. 34.

41. Walker, *Outlines of a Plan*, pp. 26–7.
42. S. Crowder, *A Museum for Young Gentlemen and Ladies, or Private Tutor and Pocket Library* (Dublin: James Hoey, 1790).
43. *Sentimental and Masonic Magazine*, July 1792, p. 74.
44. Strickland, *Dictionary*, vol. 1, pp. 289–92, 536–9; vol. 2, 500–8, 553–4.
45. William Cuming (1769–1852), president of the RHA 1829–32, exhibited 'bas reliefs in the style of De Gree' at Ellis's museum in 1792.
46. A statue of this title is listed under RDS Drawing School collections. Strickland suggests it may have been owned by Lord Tyrawley in 1809 before being presented to St Patrick's Cathedral, Dublin, where it now is. Strickland, *Dictionary*, vol. 2, p. 389.
47. Strickland, *Dictionary*, vol. 2, pp. 536–7, and for Woodburn, p. 554.
48. Breeze, *Society of Artists*; listed in the Index of Exhibits under 'Ellis, Mr., 1767 and 1768' are five paintings, with an address at 'Mary-Street', p. 34.
49. *Saunders' Newsletter*, 2 July 1799.
50. RIA, MS 24K14, 24 March 1801, p. 83.
51. *Saunders' Newsletter*, 15 July 1799.
52. Turpin, *A School of Art in Dublin Since the Eighteenth Century*, pp. 67–8.
53. Walker, *Outlines of a Plan*; Henry Cole's theories in E. Bonython and A. Burton, *The Great Exhibitor: The Life and Work of Henry Cole* (London: V&A Publications, 2003).
54. Resolved at Extraordinary Meeting of the Dublin Society at Hawkins Street, 6 September 1810, 'That the sum of £200 be paid to Mr. Ellis, for the purchase of his Museum of Natural History, formerly exhibited in Mary Street; that £100 be paid to the said Mr. Ellis on his delivering to the Society, the several Articles specified in his printed Catalogue, and £100 on the 25th of March next'. *PRDS*, September 1810. The museum may have included Hawaiian figures, a Hawaiian feather helmet, a Tongan headrest (listed in K.H. Digby's 'Naturalist Companion', the manuscript held in the Mitchell Library, New South Wales).
55. The Duke of Rutland, Charles Manners, was described by James Gandon as 'the only Chief Governor who could find leisure to pay the least attention to the Fine Arts'.
56. V. Ball, *Museum of Science and Art Director's Report for 1884*, p. 310. NMIA.
57. His proposal was an extension of one earlier suggested by the Society of Artists of Ireland.
58. C.E. Moore, *The Life and Career in Ireland of Pieter De Gree* (Dublin: Trinity College, Dublin, 1989).
59. Reynolds' letter to Rutland on 10 September 1785. Strickland, *Dictionary*, vol. 1, p. 269.
60. Strickland, *Dictionary*, vol. 2, p. 644.
61. J. Kelly, *Prelude to the Union: Anglo-Irish Politics in the 1780s* (Cork: Cork University Press, 1992), pp. 245–7.
62. *PRDS*, Minute Book, 56, 27 January 1820.
63. *Freeman's Journal*, 22 April 1835. Quote by John Boyd, RDS vice-president, in the company of the lord lieutenant.
64. D. Kiberd, 'Learning in Museums', in *Proceedings of the National Gallery of Ireland Museum Education Symposium*, 2003, p. 8.

Part III Preamble

1. H.M.M., Ward, *The World of Wonders as Revealed by the Microscope* (London: Groomsbridge, 1858), p. 78.
2. 'Davis could show forth the service of Ireland as heroic service worth a good man's energy, because he had in his words and in his actions a moral quality akin to that quality of style which can alone make permanent a picture and a book.' W.B. Yeats made this statement at a public meeting to celebrate the Thomas Davis Centenary held in the Ancient Concert

Rooms, Dublin on 20 November 1914. R. McHugh, *Davis, Mangan, Ferguson* (Dublin: Dolmen Press, 1970), p. 19.

Chapter 4

1. Quote from J.M.S. Golby, *The Great Exhibition and Re-Reading 'Hard Times'* (Milton Keynes: Open University, 1986), p. 19.
2. Established by William Shipley in 1754, the Society for the Encouragement of Arts, Manufactures and Commerce took as its model the Dublin Society. It became the Royal Society of Arts in 1908.
3. See R.D. Altick, *The Shows of London* (Cambridge, MA and London: Harvard University Press, 1978), p. 227 for these developments.
4. T. Kusamitsu, 'Great Exhibitions before 1851', *History Workshop Journal*, vol. 9, spring 1980, p. 77.
5. T. Bennett, 'The Exhibitionary Complex', in his *The Birth of the Museum* (London: Routledge, 1995), pp. 59–86.
6. Thackeray's description in his 'May Day Ode to the Great Exhibition'; C. Hobhouse, *1851 and the Crystal Palace* (London: John Murray, 1950), p. 169. The term 'Crystal Palace' first appeared in *Punch* on 2 November 1850; it was made of iron and glass by Joseph Paxton; J. Alwood, *The Great Exhibitions* (London: Studio Vista, 1977) and K.W. Luckhurst, *The Story of Exhibitions* (London and New York: The Studio, 1951).
7. S. Johansen, 'The Great Exhibition of 1851: A Precipice in Time?', in L. Purbrick (ed.), *The Great Exhibition of 1851* (Manchester: Manchester University Press, 2001), p. 3.
8. British Museum visits increased from 720,643 in 1850 to 2, 230,242 in 1851.
9. *The Art Journal Illustrated Catalogue of the International Exhibition*, 1862 (London, 1863), xii, p. 110.
10. K. Hudson, *Museums of Influence* (Cambridge: Cambridge University Press, 1987) pp. 43–9.
11. *The Catalogue of the Musaeum Tradescantianum, or A Collection of Rarities Preserved at South Lambeth near London*, written by John Tradescant the younger, was published in 1656.
12. A. McGregor, 'The Cabinet of Curiosities of Seventeenth-Century Britain', in his *The Origins of Museums* (London: Strauss Holdings, 1985), p. 206.
13. An earlier mention in the Epistle Dedicatory to Grew's *Museum Regalis Societatis* (1681). The use of the word 'museum' only slowly established itself in English usage. The Ashmolean was almost invariably referred to as 'the repository' in the accounts of the vice-chancellor of Oxford.
14. Opening in 1683, the character of the museum was established as a centre for natural science until the natural history specimens were moved to a new Natural Science Museum (today the Oxford Museum of Natural History), opening in 1860. The survival of the Ashmolean hung in the balance, as new influxes of antiquarian material in the 1800s created a crisis, resolved by building an extension to the University Galleries (1845) to which they were moved in 1894. The two institutions merged to form the Ashmolean Museum of Art and Archaeology in 1908, and the 1894 extension was replaced by a new suite of galleries in 2009.
15. M. Mulvihill, *Ingenious Ireland* (Dublin: Townhouse & Countryhouse, 2002), pp. 144–5; Mack, *The Museum of the Mind,* pp. 11–12; D.M. Wilson, *The British Museum: A History* (London: British Museum Press, 2002), pp. 11–21.
16. 'An Account of the Prince and Princess of Wales Visiting Sir Hans Sloane', *Gentleman's Magazine*, vol.18, July 1748, pp. 301–2.
17. Ibid; See Wilson, *British Museum*, pp. 18–21, for Sloane's complicated legacy.
18. Sloane's collection was augmented by the rare libraries of Sir Robert Bruce Cotton and of Robert and Edward Harley, forming the nucleus of the British Museum and the British Library.

19. Quoted in Wilson, *British Museum*; see 'Access and Accessions 1759–99'.
20. E. Hooper-Greenhill, 'The First Museum in Europe', in *Museums and the Shaping of Knowledge* (London and New York: Routledge, 1992), p. 99.
21. Links would be formed with Irish museums. C.E. O'Riordan, *The Natural History Museum, Dublin* (Dublin: Stationery Office, 1983), p. 25.
22. Wilson, *British Museum*, p. 8.
23. A. Borg, 'Theodore Jacobsen: A Gentleman'; C. Hourihane (ed.), *Irish Art Historical Studies in honour of Peter Harbison* (Dublin: Four Courts Press, 2004) pp. 276–94.
24. G. Waterfield, *Collection for a King: Old Master Paintings from the Dulwich Picture Gallery* (Washington, DC, and Los Angeles: National Gallery of Art and Los Angeles County Museum of Art, 1985); G. Waterfield, *Soane and After: The Architecture of Dulwich Picture Gallery* (London: Dulwich Picture Gallery, 1987).
25. G. Perry and G. Cunningham, *Academies, Museums and Canons of Art* (New Haven, and London: Yale University Press, 1999), pp. 72–9.
26. 1769–79 exhibitions were held at Pall Mall; 1780 moved to purpose-built rooms at Somerset House; 1837 moved to Trafalgar Square, sharing a building with the National Gallery. In 1867 the academy took out a lease on Burlington House, Piccadilly.
27. The Royal Scottish Academy was established in 1826.
28. S. McKenna, *Academies: Royal Hibernian Academy, One Hundred and Twenty-Third Exhibition* (Dublin: RHA, 2003), pp. 15–19.
29. The committee members were the trustees of the British Museum, who recorded some of their meetings in the museum minute books. At first the National Gallery functioned as part of the British Museum, to which the trustees transferred their most important pictures (not portraits), handing over control to the gallery in 1868 (formalized by an Act of Parliament 1856 establishing it as an independent body). See Wilson, *British Museum*, p. 253 n. 149.
30. See G. Martin, 'The National Gallery in London', *Connoisseur*, vol. 185, 1974, pp. 280–7; and vol. 187, 1974, pp. 124–8; J. Conlin, *The Nation's Mantlepiece: A History of the National Gallery* (London: Pallas Athene, 2006); C. Saumarez Smith, *The National Gallery: A Short History* (London: National Gallery, 2009); A. Crookham, *The National Gallery, London* (London: National Gallery, 2009).
31. M.H. Beard, 'The Historicality of Art: Royal Academy (1780–1836) and Courtauld Galleries (1990–) at Somerset House', in S. Pearce (ed.), *Art in Museums* (London: Athlone Press, 1990), p. 236.
32. Gustav Friedrich Waagen, 'Thoughts on a New Building to be Erected for the National Gallery of England', *Art Journal* (1849), p. 123.
33. Prince Albert, *The Principal Speeches of H.R.H. the Prince Consort* (London, 1862), p. 110; T. Wyse, *Educational Reform or the Necessity of a National System of Education* (London: 1836) p. 41; O. Boneparte Wyse, *The Issue of Bonaparte Wyse, Waterford's Immperial Relations* (Waterford: Waterford Museum of Treasures, 2004); 'Report on a Meeting', *Spectator*, vol. 46, 1837, p. 517.
34. Devised by the keeper, Thomas Uwins, RA, 'to class the pictures as far as space and circumstances would permit according to the different schools'.
35. The Museums Act 1845 resulted in regional museums at Sunderland (1846), Warrington (1848), Leicester and Salford (1849), Ipswich and Winchester took over local society museums in 1850s, Liverpool Museum was founded through a gift by the Earl of Derby, Maidstone (1858), Birmingham and the Royal Albert Memorial Museum Exeter were founded in the 1860s. Wilson, *British Museum*, p. 123.
36. Lord Seymour's figures dated 1850 comprised 200 visitors per day for Berlin (a smaller city), 3,000 per day for London: *Select Committee National Gallery, Q7094*.

37. B. Taylor, 'From Penitentiary to Temple of Art: Early Metaphors of Improvement at the Millbank Tate', in M. Pointon (ed.), *Art Apart: Art Institutions and Ideology across England and North America* (Manchester and New York: Manchester University Press, 1994), p. 11; Taylor, *Art for the Nation* (Manchester: Manchester University Press, 1999), pp. 100–32; and G. Waterfield (ed.), *Palaces of Art: Art Galleries in Britain 1790–1990* (London: Dulwich Picture Gallery 1991), pp. 113–16.

38. E.P. Thompson, 'The Peculiarities of the English', in *The Poverty of Theory and Other Essays* (London, Merlin Press, 1978), note 46, passim.

39. L. Pubrick, 'South Kensington Museum: The Building of the House of Henry Cole', in Pointon (ed.), *Art Apart*, pp. 82–3.

40. E. Horne, *The Great Museum: The Re-Presentation of History* (London: Pluto Press, 1984), pp. 121–2.

41. See J. Physick, *The Victoria & Albert Museum: The History of the Building* (Oxford: Phaidon, 1982), for an account of the architecture and its decoration.

42. C. Samurez Smith, 'Museums, Artefacts and Meanings', in P. Vergo (ed.), *The New Museology* (London: Reatkin Books, 1989), p. 8.

43. Speech made at the opening of the Spitalfields School of Art, 20 November 1873, reported in the *Standard*, 21 November 1873.

44. 'Out for a Holiday', *Leisure Hour*, 1 April 1870, p. 248.

45. M. Conway, *Travels in South Kensington, with Notes on Decorative Art and Architecture in England* (New York: Trubner, 1882), p. 56.

46. Hudson, *Museums of Influence*, p. 49.

47. See J. Physick, 'Photography and the South Kensington Museum', in V&A brochure (1975).

48. For Henry Cole, see A. Burton, *Vision and Accident: The Story of the Victoria and Albert Museum* (London: V&A Publications, 1999), p. 84.

49. B. Robertson, 'The South Kensington Museum in Context: An Alternative History', *Museum and Society, University of Leicester*, vol. 2, no. 1, 2004, pp. 1–14.

50. Quoted as 'his own words' in 'South Kensington Museum', *Building News*, 21 September 1860, p. 739.

51. A.C. Davies, 'Ireland's Crystal Palace 1853', in J.M. Goldstrom, and L.A. Clarkson, (eds), *Irish Population, Economy and Society* (Oxford: Clarendon Press, 1981), pp. 249–70.

52. E. Bonython and A. Burton, *The Great Exhibitor: The Life and Work of Henry Cole* (London: V&A, 2003), p. 136; Berry, *Royal Dublin Society*, p.252.

53. *PRDS*, 23 February 1837.

54. *The Spirit of Justice* was designed as a companion piece to Maclise's *The Spirit of Chivalry* (1845–7) for the English House of Lords. J.F. Maguire, *The Industrial Movement in Ireland, as Illustrated by the National Exhibition of 1852* (Cork: J. O'Brien, 1853).

55. Organizers: J. Francis Maguire and Daniel Corbett. Maguire, *The Industrial Movement in Ireland*, p. 17.

56. *Freeman's Journal*, 30 May 1853.

57. The *Exhibition Expositor and Advertiser*, edited by John Sproule, was the main voice. *Illustrated London News*, 21 May 1853, and *Freeman's Journal*, 13 May 1853.

58. *Exhibition Expositor and Advertiser*, no. 5, 1853, p. 1.

59. *Atheneum*, 14 May 1853.

60. *Illustrated London News*, 14 May 1853.

61. This antiquarian domain of Irish society emerged from educated conservative Protestants and ambitious committed Catholics. See H.A. Wheeler, *Ornamental Irish Antiquities*, 2nd edn (Dublin: Waterhouse & Co., 1853), pp. 9–10.

62. *Exhibition Expositor and Advertiser*, no. 11, 1853, p. 5.

63. There were 1,149,365 visits in six months: season tickets were sold (3 guineas for men, 2

guineas for women), admission dropped to a shilling on weekdays, and at the end of September admission was lowered to sixpence a day.

64. A.J. Saris, 'Imagining Ireland in the Great Exhibition of 1853', in L. Litvack and G. Hooper (eds), *Ireland in the Nineteenth Century: Regional Identity* (Dublin: Four Courts Press, 2000), p. 73.

65. National Gallery of Ireland collections: Watercolour on paper, 62.8 x 81 cm. NGI 7009; watercolour on paper, 60.1 x 73.3 cm. NGI 2453; watercolour on paper, 72.8 x 65.6 cm. NGI 2452. N. Netzer, 'Picturing an Exhibition: James Mahony's Watercolours of the Irish Industrial Exhibition of 1853', in A. Dalsimer (ed.), *Visualising Ireland: National Identity and the Pictorial Tradition* (Boston and London: Faber & Faber, 1993), pp. 89–98.

66. 'The Opening of the Dublin Great Industrial Exhibition', 4 June 1853, in *Illustrated London News*; M. Cappock, 'Pageantry or Propaganda?', *Irish Arts Review*, vol. 16, 2000, pp. 89–91.

67. *Exhibition Expositor and Advertiser*, no. 2, 1853, p. 1.

68. 'The Great Industrial Exhibition of Ireland', *Illustrated London News*, vol. 22, January–June 1853, p. 390.

69. Donation of Trust by Robert Henry Kinahan and others and the Rt Hon. the Earl of Charlemont and others, 29 March 1859, NGIA; re the background to the formation of the Dargan Institute and Irish Institution meeting of June 1854.

70. NGI, minute books 1853–60, and associated archival material (correspondence, statements, Irish Institution catalogues), NGIA.

71. Subject to a further £2,500 being raised by public subscription.

72. Plans were provided by Frederick Clarendon; Captain Francis Fowke is also credited with the design of the Natural History Museum, having been sent the plans by Sir Richard Griffith, chairman of the Office of Public Works.

73. J. White and K. Bright, *Treasures of the Royal Dublin Society* (Dublin: RDS, 1998), p. 10.

74. Parliamentary Report 1868/9, XX1V, p. xxii, cited in E. Crooke, *Politics, Archaeology and the Creation of a National Museum of Ireland* (Dublin: Irish Academic Press, 2000), p. 80.

75. N. McMillan and J.M. Feeney, *The Tyndall and Dargan Science and Engineering Exhibition* (Tullow, 1985), pp. 3–4.

76. T. Dwight, *The Northern Traveller and the Northern Tour* (New York: Goodrich & Wiley, 5th edn, 1834), p. 216.

77. Wittlin, Preface in *The Museum*, p. xiv.

78. L.V. Coleman, *The Museum in America* (Washington, DC: American Association of Museums, 1939).

79. Coleman, *Mousion*, p. 268.

80. Boston Philosophical Society was founded in 1683 (by Increase Mather who had studied at Trinity College, Dublin in the 1650s); 1780: American Academy of Arts and Sciences set up in Boston; 1791: Massachusetts Historical Society; 1804: New York Historical Society; 1805: Pennsylvania Academy of the Fine Arts; 1822: Maryland Academy of Sciences in Baltimore.

81. Rhees, *Manual*, p. 450.

82. L.M. Bragg, 'The Birth of the Museum Idea in America', *Charleston Museum Quarterly*, vol. 1, 1923, pp. 3–13.

83. Rhees, *Manual*, p. 450.

84. H.W. Foote, 'Mr. Smibert Shows His Pictures, March, 1870', *New England Quarterly*, vol. 8, March 1935, pp. 14–18.

85. Robert Edge Pine (1730–88) was an English artist who opened a picture gallery in 1784, displaying pictures of the American Revolution.

86. The Swiss Du Simitière's collection was sold in 1785, acquired by the American Library Society in Philadelphia.

87. N. Burt, *Palaces for the People: A Social History of the American Museum* (Boston, 1977), pp. 58–9.

88. C. Mackay, *Life and Liberty in America* (New York: Harper & Brothers, 1859), pp. 101–2.

89. Kors, *Enlightenment*, p. 259.

90. E.P. Alexander, 'Early Museums: From Collection of Curiosities to Popular Education', *International Journal of Museum Management and Curatorship*, vol. 6, 1987, pp. 346–9.

91. The academy was founded by Peale, the sculptor William Rush and other artists and businessmen; it held art classes in 1810 and its first exhibition in 1811.

92. E.P. Alexander, *Museum Masters: Their Museums and their Influences (*Tennessee: American Association for State and Local History, 1983), p. 53.

93. Brigham, 'Contemporary Institutions of Education and Entertainment and their Audiences', in *Public Culture*, pp. 27–33.

94. Godley, *Letters from America*, p. 168.

95. P.T. Barnum, *Struggles and Triumphs* (Buffalo: Courier & Co., 1889), p. 107.

96. Dwight, *Northern Traveller*, p. 216.

97. L. Ayres (ed.), *'The Spirit of Genius': Art at the Wadsworth Athenaeum* (New York: Hudson Hills Press, 1992), pp. 11–24.

98. *Hartford Daily Courant*, 31 July 1844.

99. Tonna, *The Museum*, p. 123; Godley, *Letters from America*, p. 168.

100. C.B. Hayes, *The American Lyceum* (Washington, DC: Hudson Hills Press, 1932), p. vii. The quotation dates to 1864 and is attributed to Henry Barnard, an important American educator.

101. Colonel John Trumbull (1756–1843), aide-de-camp to General George Washington, is considered one of America's key history painters. R. Hughes, *American Visions: The Epic History of Art in America* (London: Harvill Press, 1997), pp. 75–7.

102. F.G. Taylor, *Babel's Tower: The Dilemma of the Modern Museum* (New York: Columba University Press, 1945), p. 18.

103. James Smithson was the illegitimate son of an English duke, whose status prevented him from inheriting his father's title. Bazin, *Museum Age*, p. 259; Alexander, *Museum Masters*, p. 284.

104. Report of the secretary for the year 1856 in the *Annual Report of the Board of Regents of the Smithsonian Institution*, pp. 7–8.

105. Ibid.

106. D. Foley, *The People and Institutions of the United States of America* (Dublin: 1858), p. 38. Foley visited the Smithsonian Institution during his summer holidays in Washington.

107. The museum moved to a new building in 1881.

108. Alexander, 'Memorial of George Brown Goode', in *Museum Masters*, pp. 237–40, 288.

109. A. Jamieson, *A Dictionary of Mechanical Science, Arts, Manufactures, and Miscellaneous Knowledge* (London: H. Fisher, Son & Co., 1829), p. 700.

110. P.M. Rea, 'One Hundred and Fifty Years of Museum History', *Science*, vol. 57, no. 1485, 1923, p. 680; and Rea, 'Educational Work of American Museums', *Museums Journal*, vol. 14, no. 11, 1915, p. 351.

111. The NGI was advanced by the Dublin International Exhibition 1853; the Philadelphia Museum of Art from the 1876 Centennial Exhibition; the De Young Memorial Museum of Art San Francisco found its first home in a pavilion of the California Midwinter Exposition of 1893–4.

112. John Jay, a prominent New Yorker, United States minister to Germany and president of the Union League Club, was the key spirit behind the Metropolitan Museum of Art.

113. The Metropolitan's earliest home was number 681 Fifth Avenue (Dodsworth building between 53rd Street and 54th Street); in 1873 it moved to number 128 West 14th Street.

114. Albert Smith Bickmore was the force behind the American Museum of Natural History, as well as director of the first wing of its 1877 building.
115. Bazin, *Museum Age*, pp. 247–9.
116. Hudson, *Museums of Influence*, pp. 54–8.
117. *Metropolitan Museum of Art Bulletin*, vol. 12, 1917, pp. 126–9.
118. Robertson, 'The South Kensington Museum in context', pp. 1–14.
119. The educational aspect of the world's fairs was important for national displays of art, but the real function of the shows was trade. J. Allwood, *The Great Exhibitions* (London: Studio Vista, 1977), pp. 206–8.
120. The Art Institute moved to its Michigan Avenue building in 1893, where the museum function was larger than the school function.
121. D.L. Miller, *City of the Century: The Epic of Chicago and the Making of America* (New York: Simon & Schuster 1996), p. 387.
122. Miller, *City of the Century*, pp. 387 and 391.
123. W.H. Flower, *Essays on Museums and other subjects connected with Natural History* (London: Macmillan, 1898), p. 57.
124 Ibid.
125. J. Orosz cited in G. Hein, *Learning in the Museum* (London: Routledge, 1998), p. 6.

Chapter 5

1. Quote by J.L. Drummond, *Address of the President of the Belfast Natural History Society on the Opening of Belfast Natural History Museum, 1 November 1831* (Belfast: R. Hunter, 1831).
2. Cited in E. Black, *Art in Belfast 1760–1888: Art Lovers or Philistines?* (Dublin and Portland: Irish Academic Press, 2006), p. 15.
3. Mulvihill, *Ingenious Ireland*, pp. 154–5.
4. A. Deane, *Belfast Municipal Museum and Art Gallery. Souvenir of the Opening by His Grace the Governor of Northern Ireland, 22 October 1929* (Belfast: Belfast Municipal Museum and Art Gallery, 1929), p. 15; J. Ingamells, *The Wallace Collection* (London: Scala, 1990), p. 7.
5. J. Bardon, *Belfast: An Illustrated History* (Belfast: Blackstaff Press, 1983).
6. J. MacAdam, *On Schools of Design in Ireland* (Dublin: Hodges & Smith, 1849).
7. J. Anderson, *History of Belfast Library and Society for Promoting Knowledge, Commonly Known as the Linen Hall Library* (Belfast: Linen Hall Library, 1888).
8. A.G. Malcolm, *The History of the General Hospital, Belfast and Other Medical Institutions of the Town* (Belfast: Agnew, 1851).
9. J. Bryce, *Tables of Simple Minerals, Rocks and Shells with Local Catalogues of Species for the Use of Students of Natural History in the Belfast Academy* (Belfast: Sims & McIntyre, 1831).
10. N. Nesbitt, *A Museum in Belfast* (Belfast: Ulster Museum, 1979); Black, *Art in Belfast*.
11. R. Bayles, 'Understanding Local Science: The Belfast Natural History Society in the Mid-Nineteenth Century', in D. Attis and C. Mollan (eds), *Science and Irish Culture* (Dublin: RDS, 2004), pp. 139–69.
12. Belfast Natural History Society Minutes, 28 May 1828: PRONI D/3263/AB/1.
13. Nesbitt, *Museum in Belfast*, p. 10.
14. E. Black (ed.), *Catalogue of Drawings, Paintings and Sculptures* (Belfast: Museums and Galleries of Northern Ireland, 2000), p. ix.
15. J.L. Drummond, *Address of the President*.
16. Black (ed.), *Catalogue*, p. ix.
17. H.C.G. Chesney, 'Enlightenment and Education', in J.W. Foster (ed.), *Science in Ireland: A Scientific and Cultural History* (Dublin: Lilliput Press, 1997), p. 379.
18. M. Catto, 'A Normal School?', in *Art & Design Matters* (Belfast: University of Ulster, 1994), p. 32.

19. Deane, *Belfast Museum and Art Gallery*, p.18.
20. Ibid., p. 20. Belfast School of Design opened in 1849, the official opening in April 1850; Catto, 'A Normal School?', p. 33.
21. The Museums and Gymnasiums Act 1891.
22. Catto, 'A Normal School?', pp. 31–51.
23. This was enabled through the Public Libraries Act in 1882.
24. Black (ed.), *Catalogue*, p. ix.
25. Nesbitt, *Museum in Belfast*, p. 35.
26. Other donors providing collections for a museum included: George Benn, James MacAdam, George E. Thomson and William Thompson.
27. RIA, MS 12 L 5, f.132.
28. Strickland, *Dictionary*, vol. 2, p. 655.
29. *Southern Reporter*, 7 November; 22 December 1818.
30. The casts were made in Rome, under Canova's supervision, from works in the Vatican collections. Ordered by Pope Pius VII for presentation to the Prince Regent of England (later George IV) in recognition of British help to Antonio Canova, the pope's envoy, in retrieving works of art in 1816, which had been looted by Napoleon from the Vatican. In 1818, through the intercession of Viscount Ennismore, president of the Cork Society of Arts and later Lord Listowel, the Prince Regent was encouraged to give the 150 casts to Cork. P. Murray, *The Crawford Municipal Gallery of Art: Illustrated Summary Catalogue* (Cork: VEC, 1992), pp. 196–9.
31. *Cork Constitution*, 21 October 1828.
32. Murray, *Crawford Municipal Gallery*, p. 210.
33. W.M. Thackeray, *An Irish Sketchbook* (London: Chapman Hall, 1842), p. 83.
34. Nathaniel Grogan, James Barry, Samuel Ford, Godfrey Kneller, sculpture by James Heffernan.
35. William Dargan was a contributor to the exhibition (11 June–11 September 1852).
36. Bertram Windle, 'Science and Art Prospects in Cork', *Irish Builder*, vol. 18, no. 391, 1 April 1876, p. 85.
37. V. Ryan, 'The Crawford Municipal Gallery, Cork', *Irish Arts Review*, vol. 8, 1991–2, pp. 181–4.
38. *Cork Examiner*, 16 April 1885.
39. Turpin, 'Irish Art and Design Education', *Irish Arts Review*, pp. 109–16.
40. P.F. Wallace and R. Ó Floinn, *Treasures of the National Museum of Ireland: Irish Antiquities* (Dublin: Gill & Macmillan, 2002), p. 9.
41. G. Ó Tuathaigh, 'The Establishment of the Queen's Colleges: Ideological and Political Background', in T. Foley (ed.), *From Queen's College to National University* (Dublin: Four Courts Press, 1999), pp. 1–39.
42. Queen's College Belfast, calendar for the year 1850, p. 34; T.W. Moody and J.C. Beckett, *Queen's, Belfast 1848–1949: The History of a University* (London: Faber & Faber, 1959), pp. 129–32.
43. J.A. Murphy, *The College: A History of Queen's University College Cork 1845–1995* (Cork: Cork University Press, 1995), pp. 55–6.
44. A. Johnston and C. Souyoudzglou-Haywood, *Corpus Vasorum Antiquorum: Ireland 1* (Dublin: University College, Dublin, 2001); the Introduction notes it was listed in the UCC president's report for 1860–1, p. 9.
45. C. Haywood, *The Making of the Classical Museum: Antiquarians, Collectors and Archaeologists* (Dublin: University College, Dublin, 2003), p. 23.
46. G.L. Herries Davies, 'William King and the Irish Geological Community', in D. Harper (ed.), *William King D.Sc. – A Palaeontological Tribute* (Galway: Galway University Press, 1988), pp. 25–32; T. Pettigrew, 'William King (1809–86) – A Biographical Note', in

Newsletter of the Geological Curators Group, vol. 3, 1980, pp. 327–9; S. Turner, 'Collections and Collectors of Note: 26. William King (1809–86)', *Newsletter of the Geological Curators Group*, vol. 3, 1980, pp. 323–6.

47. *Report of the Museum Committee to the Council of Queen's College Galway* (1852).

48. W. *King*, 'Monograph of the Permian fossils of England', *Palaeontographical Society (Monogr.)*, 1850, pp. xxxviii, 258; Dinkel's prints were restored in the1990s by Maighread McParland, then head of conservation at the NGI. W. King, 'On Pleurodictyum Problematicum', *Annual Magazine of Natural History*, vol. 17, 1856, pp. 11–14.

49. D. Harper, 'Professor William King and the Establishment of the Geological Sciences in Queen's College Galway', in Foley (ed.), *From Queen's College to National University*, pp. 242–65.

50. T. Collins, 'Early Teachers of Natural History', in Foley (ed.), *From Queen's College to National University*, p. 272.

51. *The Queen's Colleges Commission: Report* (Galway: University College, Galway, 1858). King sought a full-time curator, with no success.

52. Belfast Naturalists' Field Club was the first, in 1863, followed in 1886 by the Dublin Naturalists' Field Club; 1892 Cork Naturalists' Field Club; 1892 Limerick Naturalists' Field Club; 1900 Galway Archaeological and Historical Society.

53. R.J. Anderson, 'The Natural History Museum, Queen's College, Galway', *Irish Naturalists' Journal*, vol. 8, 1899, pp. 125–31.

54. D. Harper and M.A. Parkes, 'Geological Survey Donations to the Geological Museum in Queen's College Galway: 19th Century Inter-Institutional Collaboration in Ireland', *Geological Curator*, vol. 6, no. 6, 1996, pp. 233–6.

55. Anderson, 'The Natural History Museum', pp.125–31.

56. R.J. Anderson, *A Catalogue of Specimens in the Zoological, Botanical, Geological, Mineralogical, Ethnological and Art Collections Contained in the Museum of the University College Galway: Part 1* (Galway: Express Printing, 1911); Part 2 of this catalogue was published 1912.

57. T. Collins, 'Rhymes and Races: A Note on the Life and Published Work of R.J. Anderson, Professor of Natural History, Geology and Mineralogy 1883–1914', *Journal of the Galway Archaeological and Historical Society*, vol. 56, 2004, pp. 190–212.

58. Plumptre, *Narrative of a Residence*.

59. W. Stokes, *A Catalogue of the Minerals in the Museum of Trinity College Dublin* (Dublin: W. Watson, 1807); W. Stokes, *A Descriptive Catalogue of the Minerals in the Systematic Collection of the Museum of Trinity College Dublin* (Dublin: Dublin University Press, 1818).

60. G.N. Wright, *An Historical Guide to the History of Dublin* (London: Baldwin, Cradock & Joy, 1825).

61. P.N. Wyse Jackson, 'The Honorable George Knox (1765–1827), Parliamentarian and Mineral Collector', *Mineralogical Record*, vol. 37, no. 6, 2006, pp. 543–51.

62. P.N. Wyse Jackson, 'Sir Charles Lewis Giesecke (1761–1833) and Greenland: A Recently Discovered Mineral Collection in Trinity College, Dublin', *Irish Journal of Earth Sciences*, vol. 15, 1996, pp. 161–8.

63. P.N. Wyse Jackson, 'The Geological Museum', in his *In Marble Halls*, pp. 55–63. The museum also housed costumes, weapons, domestic items, East Indian corals, natural history objects, stuffed birds, coins and Irish antiquities.

64. G.L. Herries Davies, 'Geology in Ireland before 1912: A Biographical Outline', *Western Naturalist*, vol. 7, 1978, pp. 79–99.

65. C. Mollan (ed.), Introduction in *Science and Ireland: Value for Society* (Dublin: RDS, 2005), pp. xxv.

66. K.W. James, *'Damned Nonsense!' The Geological Career of the third Earl of Enniskillen* (Belfast: Ulster Museum, 1986), p. 4.

67. G.L. Herries Davies, 'Before a Blood-Stained Tapestry: Irish Political Violence and Irish Science', in Attis and Mollan (eds), *Science and Irish Culture*, pp. 33–50.

68. J.A. Good and M. Linnie, 'The History of the Early Nineteenth Century Coleoptera Collection of James Tardy at Trinity College Dublin, and the Validity of Records Based on this Collection', *Irish Naturalists' Journal*, vol. 23, no. 8, 1990, pp. 298–305; R. Ball, *Second Report on the Progress of the Dublin University Museum, January 1847* (Dublin: Dublin University Press, 1847).

69. R. Ball, *First Report on the Progress of the Dublin University Museum, January 1846* (Dublin: Dublin University Press, 1846).

70. G.L. Herries Davies, 'The Palaeontological Collection of Lord Cole, Third Earl of Enniskillen (1807–86) at Florence Court, Co. Fermanagh', *Irish Naturalists' Journal*, vol. 16, no. 12, 1907, pp. 379–81; S. Lysaght, 'Themes in the Irish History of Science', *Irish Review*, vol. 19, 1996, p. 92; Ball, *First Report on Progress of Dublin University Museum*.

71. *Dublin Penny Journal* (Dublin: Dublin University, 1885), pp. 114–15.

72. For competition details: TCD Register and Board Minutes 1830–1834 and MUN/P/261; E. Blau, *Ruskinian Gothic* (Princeton, NJ: Princeton University Press, 1982), pp. 138–9; Craig, *Dublin*, pp. 304–5.

73. E. McParland, *The College Building: Trinity College Dublin and the Idea of a University* (Dublin: Townhouse, 1991), pp. 153, 160.

74. TCD MUN, MS, P/2/354 & P/2/353/B; P.N. Wyse Jackson, 'A Victorian Landmark, Trinity College's Museum Building', *Irish Arts Review*, vol. 11, 1995, pp. 149–54.

75. G.L. Herries Davies, 'Irish Thought in Science', in R. Kearney (ed.), *The Irish Mind: Exploring Intellectual Traditions* (Dublin: Wolfhound Press, 1985), pp. 294–310.

76. The Zoological Museum was set up in 1857, in the building housing Zoology, Pharmacology and Physiology, designed by college architect, John McCurdy. The museum continues to thrive as part of the departments of Pharmacology, Physiology and Zoology.

77. Wyse Jackson, 'The Geological Museum', pp. 55–9.

Chapter 6

1. Quote by George Petrie in M. Dillon, 'George Petrie (1789–1866)', *Studies*, vol. 56, 1967, pp. 266–76.

2. R. Sweet, *Antiquaries: The Discovery of the Past in Eighteenth-Century Britain* (London: Hambledon & London, 2004), p. xxi.

3. The old Civil Building Commissioners was casually referred to as the Board of Works in 1790s. From 1831 it was officially known as the Office of Public Works (it was also the Commissioners of Public Works and Fisheries between *c*.1842 and 1868).

4. *PRIA* 5, 1853, p. 395.

5. J.H. Andrews, *A Paper Landscape: The Ordnance Survey in Nineteenth-Century Ireland* (Oxford: Oxford University Press, 1975); J.H. Andrews, *Shapes of Ireland: Maps and Their Makers 1564–1839* (Dublin: Geography Publications, 1997).

6. Larcom's published memoir (encyclopaedic local survey); R.E. Colby, *Memoir of the City and Northwestern Liberties of Londonderry, parish of Templemore*; (Dublin: Hodges & Smith, 1837). P. Dixon Hardy, *Proceedings of the fifth meeting of the British Association for the Advancement of Science* (Dublin: 1835), vol. 4, p. 131.

7. G.M. Doherty, *The Irish Ordnance Survey: History, Culture and Memory* (Dublin: Four Courts Press, 2004), pp. 13–32.

8. Larcom Papers, NLI, MS, 7555, 1826.

9. Mitchell, 'Antiquities', p. 102.

10. *Report on Scientific Institutions (Dublin) together with the Proceedings of the Committee,*

Minutes of Evidence, Appendix and Index, 15 July 1864, (London: HMSO, 1864), p. ix.

11. G.L. Herries Davies, *North of the Hook: 150 Years of the Geological Survey of Ireland* (Dublin: Geological Survey, 1995), pp. 255–6.

12. A.M. Stewart, *Royal Hibernian Academy of Arts, Index of Exhibitors* (Dublin: Manton Publishing, 1986), pp. 237–8; P. Coffey, *George Victor Du Noyer (1817–69): Hidden Landscapes* (Dublin: NGI, 1993); P. Coffey, 'George Victor Du Noyer (1817–69)', *Sheetlines* (The Charles Close Society), vol. 35, 1993, pp. 14–26.

13. G.H. Kinahan, 'Obituary: George Victor Du Noyer (1817–69)', *Geological Magazine*, vol. 6, no. 2, 1869, pp. 93–5; J.B. Archer, 'Geological Artistry: The Drawings and Watercolours of George Victor Du Noyer in the Archives of the Geological Survey of Ireland', in A. Dalsimer (ed.), *Visualising Ireland* (Boston: Faber & Faber, 1993).

14. On 1 April the Geological Survey of Ireland was transferred to the Department of Agriculture and Technical Instruction for Ireland. The Irish section thus became autonomous, under the directorship of Grenville Cole (professor of geology at the Royal College of Science). In 1894 the Royal Geological Society of Ireland (which published the *Geological Journal*) wound up its affairs in 1894. Following this, geological material was published by the RDS, RIA and the *Irish Naturalists' Journal*.

15. Mitchell, 'Antiquities', p. 107.

16. Petrie Papers, RIA, 12, N.22.

17. G. Coffey, *The Royal Irish Academy Collection, Guide to the Celtic Antiquities of the Christian Period Preserved in the National Museum* (Dublin: Hodges & Figgis, 1909); RIA Minute Book, 1785–1870, Antiquities, 1, 6, 6 December 1841.

18. Mitchell, 'Antiquities', pp. 109–12.

19. RIA Minute Book, 1785–1870, Antiquities, 1, 2 April 1844; RIA Minute Book, 1785–1870, Antiquities, 1, 18 February 1845; Redmond Anthony in RIA, MS, 4B6, 1847, p.1030.

20. *PRIA* 1, 1836–40, pp. 420–6.

21. The major excavation took place in 1934–6. *PRIA* 53C, 1950–1, pp. 1–247.

22. RIA Minute Book, Antiquities, 1 (1785–1870), p. 269. These sites came into state care.

23. RIA, MS, 12L10, p. 59; RIA Minute Book, Antiquities 1, 1785–1870, 20 April 1848, p. 279; NLI, MS, 795. Letter from Petrie to Adare.

24. J. Rockley, 'Towards an Understanding of the Development of Antiquarianism and Archaeological Thought and Practice in Cork up to 1870', unpublished PhD thesis, University College, Cork, 2000.

25. Listed in the Catalogue of the Collection of Antiquities noted in the *Journal of the British Archaeological Association*, vol. 8, 1853, p. 143.

26. *JRSAI*, vol. 98, 1968, p. 93.

27. A. Ireland, 'Robert Chambers Walker: A Sligo Antiquarian', *Journal of Irish Archaeology*, vol. 11, 2002, pp. 147–87. Most are in the National Museum.

28. M. Cahill, A.M. Ireland and R. Ó Floinn, 'James Carruthers: A Belfast Antiquarian Collector', in C. Houricane (ed.), *Irish Art Historical Studies in Honour of Peter Harbison* (Dublin: Four Courts Press, 2004), pp. 219–60.

29. W.G. Strickland, 'The Carruthers Collection, 1 January 1857', *JRSAI*, vol. 12, 1922.

30. G. Fyfe, 'Reproductions, Cultural Capital and Museums: Aspects of the Culture of Copies', *Museum and Society*, vol. 2, no. 1, 2004, p. 57.

31. 1877 is when an Act of Parliament was passed to establish a National Museum and a National Library – this often causes confusion in the text because, as the Natural History Museum was already open (under RDS, 1857), its collections had begun to expand and from 1877 they began to include decorative arts – so between 1877–90 collections were being amassed and the Natural History Museum added an annex (Shelbourne hall with a fossil hall) to enable this material to be displayed.

32. G.T. Plunkett, *Report of the Director of the Museum of Science and Art, Dublin (1901)*, p. 2, NMIA.

33. F. O'Dwyer, 'Building Empires: Architecture, Politics and the Board of Works', *Journal of the Irish Georgian Society*, vol. 5, 2002, pp. 108–75; R. Lohan, *Guide to the Archives of the Office of Public Works* (Dublin: OPW, 1994); S. Lincoln, *Mansions, Museums and Commissioners* (Dublin: Irish Architectural Archive and OPW, 2002).

34. *PRIA*, 5, 1853, p. 359; RIA, MS, 4B13, p. 447.

35. *PRIA*, 2, 1842, pp. 278, 291.

36. *Exhibition Expositor and Advertiser*, vol. 11, 1853, p. 5.

37. Barrack Board/Board of Works/Board of Public Works/Office of Public Works are all stages in the formation of the OPW in 1831.

38. McDowell, 'Main Narrative', p. 40.

39. *PRIA*, 7, 1859, p. 134.

40. Museum curator Edward Clibborn may have helped with the volumes: stone, earthen and vegetable material (1857); antiquities of animal materials and bronze (1861); catalogue of antiquities of gold (1862). W.R. Wilde, *A Descriptive Catalogue of the Antiquities of the Museum of the Royal Irish Academy (class I–V)* (Dublin: RIA, 1857; repr. 1863); W.R. Wilde, *A Descriptive Catalogue of Antiquities in Gold of the Museum of the Royal Irish Academy (class V continued)* (Dublin: RIA, 1862); *PRIA*, 7, 1859, p. 138.

41. *Report on the Scientific Institutions (Dublin)*, p. xxi; Mitchell, 'Antiquities', p. 128.

42. Edward Clibborn, 1839, assistant secretary and librarian at RIA; in 1872, resigned as museum curator out of concern for the valuable objects. He bought antiquities for the RIA (*PRIA* 5, 1852, Appendix, p. xxv). Major Robert McEniry appointed resident curator, was replaced by George Coffey. In 1872 museum committee duties taken over by Polite Literature & Antiquities Committee.

43. *Report on the Scientific Institutions (Dublin)*, p. xxiii.

44. Bayles, 'Understanding Local Science' p. 147 n. 20.

45. Anon, 'A New Museum in Dublin', in *Industrial Art* (Dublin, 1877), pp. 35–7.

46. McDowell, 'Main Narrative', pp. 56–68.

47. Crooke, *Politics, Archaeology and the Creation of a National Museum of Ireland*, ch. 4.

48. Underwood to Petrie, 8 March 1856, RIA.

49. Wallace and Ó Floinn, *Treasures of the National Museum of Ireland: Antiquities*, pp. 217–18, 232, 262, 270.

50. *Dublin Penny Journal*, vol. 1, 1832–3, pp. 156–7; also *PRIA*, 1, 1862, p. 72; Wallace and Ó Floinn, *Treasures of the National Museum*, pp. 52, 64.

51. Canon Dawson Correspondence, RIA, MS, 4, B, 36, 1830–40; *Saunders' Newsletter*, 4 December 1840.

52. Dean Dawson Cabinet, RIA, MS, 12, n22, pp. 13–14; *General Advertiser*, 9 April 1842; N. Herity, 'Irish Antiquarian Find and Collections of the Early Nineteenth Century', *JRSAI*, vol. 99, no. 1, 1969, pp. 21–37. The collection was sold at Sotheby's.

53. RDS Minute Book, 9 September 1841; *PRDS*, 28 April 1842; RDS Minute Book, 12 May 1842; J.W. Hammond, 'Town Major Henry Charles Sirr', *Dublin Historical Record*, vol. 4, 1941–2, p. 95; Mitchell, 'Antiquities', p. 112; RIA, MS, 12111, p. 397.

54. PRIA, 5, 1852, Appenidx 5, pp. 239, 243, 244; p. 377 notes the presentation of the artefacts.

55. *PRIA*, 5, 1852, Appendix 5, pp. 239, 243, 244; P. Murray, *George Petrie (1790–1866): The Rediscovery of Ireland's Past* (Cork: Crawford Municipal Art Gallery/Gandon Editions, 2004), p. 82; RIA, MS, 12, n12 (notes by William Stokes), p. 17.

56. Wallace and Ó Floinn, *Treasures of the National Museum*, pp. 89–90, 99, 114.

57. P. Harbison, 'The Bronze Age', in P. Cone (ed.), *Treasures of Irish Art 1500 BC to 1500 AD* (New York: Metropolitan Museum of Art, 1977), pp. 22–3; *PRIA*, 6, 1855, p. 204;

Wallace and Ó Floinn, *Treasures of the National Museum*, p. 99.

58. Murray, *George Petrie*, pp. 82–90; Wallace and Ó Floinn, *Treasures of the National Museum*, pp. 130, 140.

59. E. McCrum, 'Irish Victorian Jewellery', *Irish Arts Review*, vol. 2, no. 1, 1985, pp. 18–25. Registered as design No. 74210; *Saunders' Newsletter and Daily Advertiser*, 10 December 1850; N. Whitfield, 'The Finding of the Tara Broach', *JRSAI*, vol. 104, 1974, pp. 120–42.

60. Wallace and Ó Floinn, *Treasures of the National Museum*, pp. 176–8, 183–4.

61. Mitchell, 'Antiquities', pp. 128, 138–9; Wallace and Ó Floinn, *Treasures of the National Museum*, pp. 178–9, 184–5.

62. Mitchell, 'Antiquities', pp. 128, 139–40.

Chapter 7

1. Lieut. Col. G.T. Plunkett, *Report of the Board of Visitors of the Science and Art Museum for 1904–1905*, NMIA.

2. J. Coolahan, *Irish Education: Its History and Structure* (Dublin: Institute of Public Administration, 1981).

3. N. Whyte, 'Digging Up the Past: A Visit to Markree Castle', *Stardust*, vol. 25, no. 4, 1992, pp. 27–30.

4. Herries Davies, 'Irish Thought in Science', pp. 303–4; J.A. Bennett, 'Lord Rosse and the Giant Reflector', in J. Nudds, et al. (eds), *Science in Ireland, 1800–1930: Tradition and Reform* (Dublin: Trinity College, Dublin, 1888; D.L. Weaire, 1988), pp. 105–13.

5. N. Whyte, 'The Ascendancy Scientists', in his *Science, Colonialism and Ireland* (Cork: Cork University Press, 1999), pp. 58–9.

6. 27 December 1844: Treasury approval for the Museum of Economic Geology. *Report on Scientific Institutions (Dublin)*, p. 354.

7. Museum of Irish Industry, *General Descriptive Guide to the Museum of Irish Industry* (Dublin: A. Thom, 1857), p. 1.

8. *PRIA*, 1, 6, 1857, p. 496; Mulvihill, *Ingenious Ireland*, p. 50.

9. D.J. O'Donoghue (ed.), *Essays Literary and Historical by Thomas Davis* (Dundalk: Dundalgan Press, 1914); *PRIA*, 1, 11, 1840–1, p. 419.

10. *Report of the Commissioners on the Ordnance Memoir, Minutes of Evidence, Appendices and Index* (London: HMSO, 1844), p. 78.

11. *Report on Scientific Institutions (Dublin)*, p. 66.

12. T.S. Wheeler, 'Sir Robert Kane: Life and Work', *Studies*, vol. 33, no. 1, June–September 1944, p. 318.

13. C. Ó Grada, *The Great Irish Famine* (Dublin: Gill & Macmillan, 1989), p. 2; M. Daly, *The Famine in Ireland* (Dundalk: Dublin Historical Association, 1986), pp. 113–24.

14. E. O'Brien, et al. (eds), *A Portrait of Irish Medicine* (Dublin: Ward River Press, 1984), p. 138.

15. *Report on Scientific Institutions (Dublin)*, p. 66. Built by George Paul Monck *c.*1760 on the site of a house built by his great grandfather. Owners: Baron Castlecoote (1798), Lord Manners (1807–27), lord chancellor of Ireland, known as Lord Chancellor's House. George Papworth (1781–1855), an English architect, made alterations loosely based on the Museum of Economic Geology in London. *Dublin Builder*, vol. 1, no. 11, November 1859, p. 140.

16. *Report of the Royal Dublin Society, 1863* (Dublin: Royal Dublin Society, 1863), pp. 13–15.

17. C. Casey, *The Buildings of Ireland: Dublin* (New Haven, CT and London: Yale University Press, 2005), pp. 541–2.

18. Mulvihill, *Ingenious Ireland*, p. 50.

19. Lincoln, *Mansions, Museums and Commissioners*, pp. 123–34; *Dublin University Magazine*, vol. 24, no. 248, August 1853, p. 234; R. Kane, *General Descriptive Guide to the Museum*

of Irish Industry (Dublin: Her Majesty's Stationery Office, 1857), p. 3; *Exhibition Expositor and Advertiser*, 1853, p. 7.

20. The lower hall showed building materials and stones of England and Ireland; the south gallery showed specimens of rock salt and Kilkenny coal; the north gallery showed the history of the manufacture of pottery, glass, fuels, mineral chemical and iron manufacture. The staircases displayed maps and plans of industrial interest. *Irish Builder*, 1 February 1840, pp.189–90. The left first-floor gallery showed industrial applications to animal and vegetable substances; the right gallery held Geological Survey palaeontological collections; the cross gallery revealed models, nets, boats and tools for fishing. 'The Great Industrial Exhibition of 1853', *Dublin University Magazine*, vol. 41, 1833–1882, p. 246.

21. *Report on Scientific Institutions (Dublin) together with the Proceedings of the Committee, Minutes of Evidence, Appendix and Index*, 15 July 1864, p. xxiii.

22. Herries Davies, *North of the Hook*, p. 258.

23. 'Museum of Irish Industry Report for 1860', *Dublin Builder*, vol. 111, nos. 37 and 39, 1 July and 1 August 1861, pp. 563, 581–2.

24. Conflicting views on the role of the RDS and the museum were addressed at a committee of inquiry: *PRDS*, 90, 17 April 1854; *PRDS*, 90, 25 May 1854; *Report on Scientific Institutions (Dublin)*, pp. xiv–xv.

25. W.K. Sullivan, 'On Societies for the Promotion and Encouragement of Industrial Arts', *Journal of Industrial Progress*, vol. 6, June 1854, p. 40; *Report on Scientific Institutions (Dublin)*, p. xxvi.

26. *Report on Scientific Institutions (Dublin)*, p. xxvi.

27. *Report of the Royal Dublin Society*, 1863; *Report on Scientific Institutions (Dublin)*; Herries Davies, *North of the Hook*, p. 263.

28. *Report on Scientific Institutions (Dublin)*; NGI Foundation Minutes, 16 July 1863.

29. *18th Report of the Science and Art Department*, 1871, pp. 189–94.

30. A. Marsh, 'Dublin's Museums', *The Bell*, vol. 4, no. 1, 1943, pp. 52–8.

31. Whyte, 'The Ascendancy Scientists', p. 21.

32. *Freeman's Journal*, 24 February 1838. The lecture theatre, added to the south end of Leinster House in 1893, was designed by the Deanes.

33. Berry, *A History of the RDS*, p. 161.

34. Herries Davies, 'Irish Thought in Science'; *Report of the Select Committee on Irish Miscellaneous Estimates,* 1829, 342, 1X.

35. E. Leaney, 'Missionaries of Science: Provincial Lectures in Nineteenth-Century Ireland', *Irish Historical Studies*, vol. 34, no. 135, 2005, pp. 266–88.

36. Bright, *Royal Dublin Society 1815–45*.

37. *PRDS*, Minute Book, 20 October 1842.

38. It was open daily from 11 a.m. to 4 p.m.

39. *PRDS*, 25 May 1855.

40. *PRDS*, 11 June 1857. This year the museum curator visited Edinburgh.

41. W.E. Steele, *Museum of Science and Art Director's Report for 1877–1878*, p. 528, NMIA.

42. The Spring Shows held in Leinster House stables in 1831 had moved to Ballsbridge by 1871.

43. *PRDS*, 1 March 1827.

44. Twenty-four casts from Persepolis arrived from Persia via Bombay and London in April 1833. *PRDS*, 21 March 1833.

45. Turpin, *A School of Art in Dublin Since the Eighteenth Century*, pp. 126–30; A. McGoogan, *Catalogue of Watercolours and Oil Paintings, Chalk and Pencil Drawings* (Dublin: Department of Agriculture and Technical Instruction, 1920). The Preface is dated 1915.

46. Strickland, *Dictionary*, vol. 2, p. 616.

47. Turpin, *A School of Art in Dublin Since the Eighteenth Century*, pp. 134–45.

48. Ibid., pp. vii–xiv.
49. T.S. Wheeler, 'William Higgins Chemist (1763–1835)', *Studies*, vol. 43, 1954, pp. 78–91, 207–28, 327–38.
50. B. O'Reilly, *Catalogue of the Subjects of Natural History in the Museum of the Rt. Hon. the Dublin Society* (Dublin: Graisberry & Campbell, 1813); RDS, 1039, No. 2; J.P. O'Connor, 'Insects and Entomology', in J.W. Foster (ed.), *Nature in Ireland: A Scientific and Cultural History* (Dublin: Lilliput Press, 1997).
51. That the exhibition was used is evidenced by a letter from William Ashford (19 January 1819, Sandymount): 'an exhibition of my own paintings and drawings [was held] in the Board Room of the Dublin Society's House, Hawkins Street', noted in *PRDS*, 21 January 1819. Approval was also granted to 'the Artists of Ireland' for an exhibition in April, May and June. *PRDS*, 23 February 1819.
52. *Report of the Select Committee of the Royal Dublin Society* (London: HMSO) 445, XII, 1836, p. 204.
53. Quotation, 18 March 1844, in letter to John Scouler. Valuation Office Letter Books, NAI.
54. N.T. Monaghan, et al. (eds), *Irish Innovators in Science and Technology* (Dublin: RIA, 2002), p. 133.
55. G.F. Mitchell, 'Mineral and Geology', in J. Meenan and D. Clarke (eds), *The Royal Dublin Society* (Dublin: Gill & Macmillan, 1998), p. 161.
56. N.T. Monaghan, 'Sir Karl Ludwig Metzler-Geisecke (1761–1833), Royal Mineralogist, Greenland Explorer and Museum Curator', in E. Hoch and A.K. Bransten (eds), *Centenary of the Geological Museum, Copenhagen University, Deciphering the Natural World and the Role of Collections and Museums* (Copenhagen: Geological Museum, 1993), pp. 83–6.
57. Kildare House was built in 1745 by James FitzGerald, 20th Earl of Kildare, designed by Richard Castle on land known as Molesworth Fields. When he was created Duke of Leinster, it became known as Leinster House. It is illustrated in Thomas Milton, *The Seats and Demesnes of the Nobility and Gentry of Ireland: in a collection of the Most Interesting and Picturesque Views* (1783). Today it is the seat of the Irish Parliament.
58. J. Warburton, et al., *A History of the City of Dublin* (London, 1818), p. 958.
59. RDS Minute Book, 2 February 1815.
60. Wright, *An Historical Guide to the History of Dublin*, pp. 4–5.
61. G. Waterhouse, 'Goethe, Giesecke, and Dublin', in *PRIA*, 41C, 1933, pp. 210–18.
62. George IV agreed in a letter dated 16 June 1820 to become patron. The prefix was not officially recognized until the1860s. *PRDS*, 29 June 1820.
63. '… besides the Mineral Cabinet it contains a collection in Zoology, as well as in the other departments of Natural History, and an interesting collection of antiquities and works of art': *The Report on the Select Parliamentary Committee on the Royal Dublin Society* (London: HMSO, 1819).
64. *PRDS*, 24 March 1835.
65. *PRDS*, 61, 12 May 1825.
66. *PRDS*, 64–5, 16 July 1829; *PRDS*, 18 December 1861; *PRDS*, 5 November 1875.
67. Bright, *Royal Dublin Society 1815–45*, pp. 64–5; *PRDS*, 16 July 1829. *Descriptive Catalogue of a New Collection of Minerals in the Museum of the Royal Dublin Society to which is added an Irish Mineralogy* (Dublin: Graisberry, 1832).
68. *PRDS*, 9 May 1833; PRDS, 31 May 1832; *PRDS*, 21 November 1833.
69. *PRDS*, 61, 8 June 1825.
70. *PRDS*, 13 February 1834; *PRDS*, 24 July 1835.
71. J. Morrell and A. Thackray, *Gentlemen of Science* (Oxford: Clarendon Press, 1981), pp. xxiv, 175–86, 592; PRDS, 21 May 1835; *Dublin Penny Journal*, no. 174, 31 October 1835.
72. F.L.G. Von Raumer, *England in 1835: Being a Series of Letters Written to Friends in German,*

vol. 3 trans. H.E. Lloyd (London: John Murray, 1836), vol. 3, p. 203.

73. W. Thompson, *Report on the Fauna of Ireland: Div. Invertebrata. Reports drawn up at the request of the British Association* (London: Jon Ado, 1843), pp. 245–91.

74. *PRDS*, 26 January 1836; M. Craig, 'The Society's Buildings', in Meenan and Clarke (eds), *The Royal Dublin Society 1781–1981*, p. 63.

75. *PRDS*, 24 November 1842.

76. RDS Council Minute Book, 30 May 1839; RDS Minute Book, 28 May 1840; RDS Council Minute Book, 10 March 1842.

77. *PRDS*, 90, December 1853. Scouler's lectures were attended by 2,199 people. *Dublin Penny Journal*, no. 174, 31 October 1835, lists the lecture schedules.

78. RDS Committee of Natural History and Museum Minute Book, 1831–54, 12 March 1839.

79. *PRDS*, 3 June 1845.

80. *PRDS*, 24 January 1840.

81. *PRDS, Natural History and Museum Committee Report on the state of the Museum, 1 June 1843*.

82. *PRDS*, 9 February 1848.

83. *PRDS*, 19 March 1851.

84. RDS Minute Book, 2 April 1840; *PRDS*, 14 June 1838.

85. Andrews presented Irish fish over a number of years.

86. P. Hackney, 'Out of Ireland: Naturalists Abroad', in Foster (ed.), *Nature in Ireland*, pp. 342–9.

87. *An Illustrated Catalogue of the Exhibition of Art-Industry in Dublin, 1853* (London: Virtue, 1853) p. vii.

88. *PRDS*, 11 March 1853; *PRDS*, 8 November 1854.

89. *Exhibition Expositor and Advertiser*, vol. 11, 1853, p. 5.

90. *PRDS*, 26 April 1850; *PRDS*, 90, 13 October 1853.

91. *PRDS*, 21 January 1851.

92. *PRDS*, 91, 8 December 1853.

93. RDS MS Minute Book, 31 May 1854.

94. *JRDS*, vol. 1, 1856, pp. 50–6; *Illustrated London News*, 15 March 1856. The items in the sealed container are all listed.

95. *Athenaeum*, 15 August 1857.

96. The Armagh Natural History and Philosophical Society also founded a museum in 1856, which opened in 1857 and became Armagh County Museum in 1931. R.M. Weatherup, 'Armagh County Museum, Archaeological Acquisitions: The Collection of Armagh Natural History and Philosophical Society', *JRSAI*, vol. 112, 1982, pp. 51–71.

97. Stewart, *Royal Hibernian Academy of Arts, Index of Exhibitors*, p. xvi; *PRDS*, 9 February 1858.

98. *PRDS*, 11 May 1858.

99. *PRDS*, 18 November 1858; *PRDS*, 6 September–1859.

100. *PRDS*, 17 June 1859.

101. *PRDS*, 21 April 1859.

102. *PRDS*, 15 March 1859.

103. *PRDS*, 16 April 1862; *PRDS*, 1 February 1867; *PRDS*, 17 August 1866; J. Hutchinson, 'Bird Study in Ireland', in Foster (ed.), *Nature in Ireland*, p. 165.

104. B.P. Beirne, 'Supplement: Irish Entomology: The First Hundred Years', *Irish Naturalists' Journal*, vol. 28, 1985, pp. 21–2.

105. D.E. Allen, *The Naturalist in Britain* (Princeton, NJ: Princeton University Press, 1994), pp. 195–217.

106. The recommendation was made on 2 March 1867; authority to undertake exchanges on 16 June 1867.

107. The director's duties involved charge of the museum, directing and superintending the assistants in the preparation, arranging and cataloguing the specimens. The keeper of minerals cared for, arranged labels and catalogued the specimens belonging to the Mineral Department. The assistants performed duties in naming, arranging and cataloguing the specimens as prescribed by the director, while the taxidermist prepared and arranged specimens as prescribed by the director. Instructions regarding annual leave were prescribed on 19 May 1871.
108. Beirne, 'Supplement: Irish Entomology', p. 6.
109. Allen, *Naturalist in Britain*, pp. 46–7.
110. *PRDS*, 15 November 1873.
111. Leopold (1822–95) and his son Rudolph (1857–1939) Blaschka, known internationally for glass flowers produced for the Ware Collection of glass models, or plants at Harvard University (1887–1936). N.T. Monaghan, 'Modelling Nature', *Irish Arts Review*, vol. 20, no. 4, 2003, pp. 120–3.
112. Other Blaschka collections in Ireland are held by University Colleges Galway, Cork, and Queen's University, Belfast.
113. M. Viney, *Ireland: A Smithsonian Natural History* (Belfast: Blackstaff Press, 2003), p. 37.
114. S.J. Gould, 'Cabinet Museums Revisited', *Natural History*, vol. 103, 1994, pp. 12–20; M. Viney, 'The Giant Elk Mystery', *The Irish Times*, 13 September 2003.
115. *PRDS*, 30 June 1867.
116. The Shelbourne Hall annex was attached to the south western end of the museum. *PRDS*, 28 October 1870.
117. *PRDS*, 17 June 1870.
118. J. Aldeman, 'Evolution on Display: Promoting Irish Natural History and Darwinism at the Dublin Science and Art Museum', *British Journal for the History of Science*, vol. 38, 2005, pp. 411–36.
119. Gould, 'Cabinet Museums Revisited', p. 18.
120. R.B. Sharpe (1874–98), *Sharpe Catalogues: A Catalogue of the Birds in the British Museum* (London: British Museum).
121. Anon, 'A New Museum in Dublin', *Industrial Art*, vol. 1, 1877, p. 36.
122. House of Commons, *Report from the Committee on the Science and Art Department in Ireland together with Minutes of Evidence 1868–9*, xxiv (4103).
123. Letter from W.H. Smith, secretary to the Treasury, to RDS (in response to RDS enquiry: RDS, MS Minute Book, 11 March 1875) confirmed the need for an Act to give the state 'requisite control over property and buildings upon which a large amount of public monies is to be expended', dated 18 November 1876.
124. Chapter CCXXXIV, 'An Act to authorise the Commissioners of Public Works in Ireland to acquire from the Royal Dublin Society and others Lands for the Erection of a Science and Art Museum in Dublin and to establish a National Library in Dublin; and for other purposes (14 August 1877).'
125. This did not include the RDS art collections in Leinster House, which are still in the care of the RDS.
126. Anon, 'New Museum in Dublin', p. 37.
127. *Royal Dublin Society Report of the Delegates to the Council as to Information required by the Science and Art Department*, 6 May 1879. NMIA.
128. A. Whitty, 'The Caspar Purdon Clarke Indian and Personal Collection of the National Museum of Ireland, 1878–79', *Museum Ireland*, vol. 14, 2004, pp. 68–75.
129. *Report of the Board of Visitors* from 1880–1 onwards. NMIA.
130. Wyse Jackson, *In Marble Halls*, pp. 29–30.
131. V. Ball, *Museum of Science and Art Director's Report for 1884*, NMIA, Appendix H. 'Art

and industry' collections included pottery, enamels, lacquers, wooden objects, medals, Egyptian antiquities, embroidery, copies of British Museum engravings, reproductions of English, Italian, German, Russian and Spanish art.

132. V. Ball, 'Report on the Museums of America and Canada', in *Report of the Science and Art Department* (Dublin, 1884), p. 310. Ball was on a trip to observe twenty-five museums in the United States and Canada.

133. Ball, *Museum of Science and Art Director's Report for the year 1885*, NMIA.

134. Ibid.

135. Ball, *Museum of Science and Art Director's Report for 1886*; Ball, *Museum of Science and Art Director's Report for 1887*; Ball, *Museum of Science and Art Director's Report for 1888*, NMIA.

136. Ball, *Museum of Science and Art Director's Report for the year 1885*, NMIA.

137. 1880s: Files relating to the Architectural Competition for the Dublin Museum of Science and Art, NMIA.

138. RDS, MS Minute Book, 20 December 1880.

139. *Daily Express*, 14 November 1882.

140. *Irish Times*, 26 February 1885.

141. RDS, MS Minute Book, 1 March 1883.

142. *Freeman's Journal*, 7 April 1884.

143. *Irish Times*, 19 December 1884; *Building News*, 31 October and 14 November 1884.

144. A. MacLochlainn and C.E. O'Riordan, et al., *Science and Art 1877–1977* (Dublin: National Museum of Ireland, 1977), pp. 1–8; see also Deane newspaper cuttings 1881–1901, NGIA.

145. Newspaper cuttings on the opening of the Science and Art Museum, NMIA, 1885.

146. RDS, MS Minute Book, 1 March 1888; *Daily Express*, 19 October 1888.

147. William Beckett was the grandfather of Samuel Beckett, playwright and novelist. V. Ball, *Museum of Science and Art Director's Report for 1890*, NMIA. For accounts of the official opening, see: *Daily Express*, 21 August 1890; *Irish Times*, 27 August 1890; *Freeman's Journal*, 28 August 1890.

148. *Irish Times*, 30 August 1890; *Freeman's Journal*, 30 August 1890; Newspaper cuttings on the opening of the Science and Art Museum, NMIA, 1885.

149. *General Guide to the Science and Art Museum* (Dublin: HMSO, 1892), pp. 28–33; Deane newspaper cuttings 1881–1901, NGIA. Following a request by the director to the Council of the RIA, a collection of old moulds of Irish high crosses and miscellaneous sculptures together with casts made for the 1853 Dublin International Exhibition of Art-Industry had been delivered to the museum in 1887.

150. The National Museum's original casts were conserved and exhibited at the Irish pavilion at Expo 2005 in Aichi, Japan: see R. Ó Floinn (ed.), *Celtic Art: High Crosses and Treasures of Ireland* (published in Japanese, Tokyo). They were subsequently displayed at the museum's Decorative Arts and History branch at Collins Barracks in 2007, in an exhibition entitled *The Irish High Cross*. (In 2003 Raghnall Ó Floinn was made Head of Collections.)

151. *Evening Telegraph*, 10 October 1889. It was reported in the *Daily Express*, on 15 and 31 March 1890; N.T. Monaghan, 'The National Museum of Ireland', in N. Buttimer, C. Rynne and H. Guerin (eds), *The Heritage of Ireland* (Cork: The Collins Press, 2000), p. 404.

152. Casey, *Buildings of Ireland: Dublin*, pp. 7–8.

153. P. McCarthy, 'From Torpedo Boat to Temples of Culture: Carlo Cambi's Route to Ireland', *Irish Arts Review*, vol. 18, 2002, pp. 71–9; Sir Thomas Manley Deane Sketchbooks, NGIA.

154. *Daily Telegraph*, 11 April 1895; Deane newspaper cuttings 1881–1901, NGIA; A. Le Harivel, *National Gallery of Ireland Illustrated Summary Catalogue of Drawings,*

Watercolours and Miniatures (Dublin: NGI, 1983).

155. *Daily Telegraph*, 1 September 1890; *Irish Society*, 6 September 1890.

156. V. Ball, *Official General Guide to the Science and Art Museum, Dublin* (Dublin: Alex Thom & Co., 1890). There were two parts: 'Natural History Department in the Old Museum Building', and 'Art and Industrial Department in the New Museum Building'.

157. *Report of the Director of the Museum of Science and Art, Dublin for 1891*, NMAI.

158. Correspondence commenting on the new museum, such as letters in *The Irish Times*, were responded to promptly by the Rt Hon. Sir William Gregory of Coole Park, Galway, writer, politician, governor general of Ceylon, privy councillor (Ireland).

159. *Report of the Director of the Museum of Science and Art, Dublin for 1892*, NMAI.

160. *Report of the Director of the Museum of Science and Art, Dublin for 1895*, NMAI.

161. H.B. White, 'History of the Science and Art Institutions, Dublin', *Bulletin of the National Museum of Science and Art, Dublin*, part 4, vol. 8, 1911, pp. 7–34.

162. 'Art and Industry' was used from 1840 to 1900 for industrial and mass-manufactured objects given aesthetic values. The term 'applied art' was first used in *Burlington Magazine*, 2 April 1933, p. xvi. The term 'decorative arts', used since mid-century, is the preferred term.

163. R.E. Lyne in *Report of the Director of the Museum of Science and Art for 1888*, NMAI.

164. *Report of the Department of Science and Art, XXXII*, 1890, p. 315, NMI.

165. *Report of the Director of the Museum of Science and Art, for 1891*, NMAI.

166. *Irish Naturalists' Journal*, November 1895. This monthly journal was published 1892–1924. A. McHenry and W.W. Watts, *Guide to the Collections of Rocks and Fossils*, 1898 (8p) one of a series of penny guides produced by the museum in the late nineteenth century.

167. Herries Davies, *North of the Hook*, pp. 269–70.

168. Wallace and Ó Floinn, *Treasures of the National Museum of Ireland*, p. 7.

169. White, 'History of the Science and Art Institutions', pp. 7–34. In 1907, Count George Noble Plunkett became director.

170. Monaghan, *Heritage of Ireland*, p. 404.

171. *Irish Daily Independent*, 4 December 1896; Plunkett, *Museum of Science and Art Director's Report for the year 1896*, NMIA.

172. G.T. Plunkett, *Museum of Science and Art, Director's Report for 1897*, NMIA.

173. Ó Raifeartaigh (ed.), *Royal Irish Academy*, pp. 72, 147, 194, 303.

174. See n. 145. Requests in the 1890s for casts of Muirdeach's Cross were received from the Museum of Fine Arts, Boston; the Irish Industrial Exposition New York (1905); and the London Franco–British Exhibition (1908).

175. G.T. Plunkett, *Museum of Science and Art, Director's Report for 1899–1900*, NMIA.

176. *Freeman's Journal*, 30 March 1898.

177. Sir Horace Curzon Plunkett was an agricultural reformer and pioneer of the agricultural co-operative movement setting up the Irish agricultural organisation in 1894. A politician and author, he was the first head of the department of agricultural and technical instruction for Ireland from 1899.

178. H.C. Plunkett, *Ireland in the New Century* (London: John Murray, 1904).

179. Turpin, *A School of Art in Dublin since the Eighteenth Century*, pp. 184–5.

180. *Irish Times*, 9 February 1900.

181. Wallace and Ó Floinn, *Treasures of the National Museum*, p. 9.

182. Crooke, *Politics, Archaeology and Creation of the National Museum of Ireland*, Ch.5.

183. *Report of a Committee Appointed by the Lords Commissioners of Her Majesty's Treasury to inquire into the circumstances under which certain Celtic Ornaments found in Ireland were recently offered for sale to the British Museum, and to consider the relation between the British*

*Museum and the Museums of Edinburgh and Dublin with regard to the acquisition and reten-
tion of objects of Antiquarian and Historic interest.* LXXVII, London, Parliamentary Report,
1899, p. 35, NMIA.

Chapter 8

1. Thomas Davis, 1843, in O'Donoghue (ed.), *Essays Literary and Historical by Thomas Davis*,
   pp. 119–23.
2. W.H. Flower, *Essays on Museums and Other Subjects Connected with Natural History* (London:
   Macmillan, 1898), p. 47.
3. M. Dunlevy, 'God Bless Collectors', in *35th Irish Antique Dealers' Fair Catalogue*, 2000, pp.
   10–11.
4. J. Fenlon, *The Ormonde Picture Collection* (Ireland: Kilkenny Castle and Duchas, 2001).
5. The Vignon was bought at the Ormonde Sale. The Van de Velde was acquired through the
   Sherlock Bequest, 1904.
6. The collection was purchased from the Hon. Rose Talbot, 1976.
7. In 1747 FitzGerald married Emily Mary Lennox. In 1766, when created Duke of Leinster,
   the house became known as Leinster House, due to its origin as an eighteenth-century seat
   of the FitzGeralds (Earls of Kildare) and later ownership by RDS, 1815–1924. D.J.
   Griffin and C. Pegum, *Leinster House 1744–2000: An Architectural History* (Dublin: Irish
   Architectural Archive/OPW, 2000), pp. 2–4; D.J. Griffin and S. Lincoln, *Drawings from
   the Irish Architectural Archive* (Dublin: Irish Architectural Archive, 1993), p. 35.
8. Political upheaval during the 1790s encouraged Ascendancy parents to educate their children
   at Eton. The image of Augustus by James Northcote *c.*1809 is one of twenty portraits left by
   Irishmen on leaving Eton. M. Davis, 'Irish Portraits in the Eton College Leaving Collection',
   Irish Arts Review, vol. 12, 1996, pp. 61–5.
9. J. Malton, *A Picturesque and Descriptive View of the City of Dublin 1792–99 displayed in a
   series of Most Interesting Scenes Taken in the Year 1791 by James Malton. With a Brief Authentic
   History from the Earliest Accounts to the Present Time* (London: W. Faden, 1799); Crookshank
   and Glin, *Ireland's Painters*, p. 61; *Notes on the Pictures, Plates, Antiquities,* etc. added in
   1855.
10. *Adonis*, 1874 by François-Marie Poncet, French School, NGI 8135, derived from the classical
    marble of Apollo, signed F.M. PONCET.INV.F. Commissioned in Rome by the mother
    of Emily Olivia Lennox in 1784.
11. The Dawson-Damers were clients of Kauffman in London. She did several versions of family
    pictures for their Irish seat at Emo Park.
12. Kauffman stayed with the wife of the bishop of Clogher, the Townshends and other leading
    Irish families in 1771, painting portraits in the fashionable neo-classical style.
13. NGI Minutes, 24 July 1879, NGIA; K. McConkey, *Memory and Desire: Painting in Britain
    and Ireland at the Turn of the Twentieth Century* (Aldershot: Ashgate, 2002), pp. 258 n. 27,
    276 n. 15.
14. The second picture to be donated to the early National Gallery. Irish Institution Minutes, 20
    June 1854, NGIA.
15. C. O'Connor, 'The Dispersal of the Country House Collections of Ireland', *Bulletin of the
    Irish Georgian Society*, vol. 35, 1992–3, pp. 38–47.
16. W. Grattan, *Patronage Analysed* (Dublin: 1818).
17. Strickland, *Dictionary*, pp. 608–39; C. de Courcy, 'The History of the Royal Hibernian
    Academy of Arts', vol. 2, in *Royal Hibernian Academy of Arts, Index of Exhibitors 1826–1979*
    (3 volumes) (Dublin: Manton, 1986), vol. 1, A–G, pp. xi–xxii; J. Turpin, 'The RHA Schools
    1826–1906', *Irish Arts Review*, vol. 8, 1991–2, pp. 198–209.

18. T. Ryan, 'The Vicissitudes of the Royal Hibernian Academy', *Irish Arts Review*, vol. 2, no. 3, 1985, pp. 26–8; G. Walsh and K. Bouchier, 'The Royal Hibernian Society, Its Forerunners and Establishment', in G. Walsh and K. Bouchier (eds), *Royal Hibernian Academy of Arts* (Dublin: Martello, 1991), pp. 1–14.

19. P. Harbison, 'Our first President, William Ashford, as Antiquarian Artist', in J. Hanley (ed.), *Royal Hibernian Academy Exhibition 2003* (Dublin: RHA, 2003), pp. 24–6.

20. P. Dixon Hardy, 'Royal Hibernian Academy', *Dublin Penny Journal*, vol. 3, no. 173, 1835, p. 136; E. McParland, 'Francis Johnston, Architect, 1760–1829', *Quarterly Bulletin of the Irish Georgian Society*, vol. 12, 1986, pp. 61–139.

21. C. Fallon, 'The Royal Hibernian Academy and What It Is About', *Art Bulletin/ebulletin*, December, 2000, www.artistsireland.com, pp. 1–3; S. McKenna, 'Academies', in Hanley (ed.), *Royal Hibernian Academy Exhibition 2003*, pp. 15–20.

22. D'Alembert listed the fine arts as painting, sculpture, architecture, poetry and music in Diderot's *Encyclopedie* (1750–80); H. Osborne (ed.), *The Oxford Companion to Art* (Oxford: Oxford University Press, 1989), pp. 406–7. Painting was elevated to an intellectual discipline in the sixteenth century rather than manual craft, with a state academy founded in Rome in 1793. The RA taught students to work from life without idealization, emulated by the RHA until Cole's design schools used the South Kensington system.

23. G. Fyfe, 'Reproductions, Cultural Capital and Museums: Aspects of the Culture of Copies', *Museum and Society, University of Leicester*, vol. 2, no. 1, 2004, pp. 47–67.

24. E. Wilkinson, 'A Short History of the Annual Exhibition', in Hanley (ed.), *Royal Hibernian Academy Exhibition 2003*, p. 31.

25. M. O'Dea, 'The Annual Exhibition: A Perspective', in Hanley (ed.), *Royal Hibernian Academy Exhibition 2003*, p. 20.

26. J. Turpin, 'The Royal Hibernian Schools and State Art Educational Policy from 1826 to National Independence', in Walsh and Bouchier (eds), *Royal Hibernian Academy of Arts*, pp. 23–9.

27. The *Laocoön*, casts of the *Apollo Belvedere, Dying Gladiator, Discobolus, Meleager, Antiocus* of the Vatican, *Venus Andyomene*, busts by Canova, Thorvaldsen and others.

28. *Report of the Select Parliamentary Committee on the Royal Dublin Society (evidence of Isaac Weld)* (London: HMSO, 1836).

29. E. Black, 'Practical Patriots and True Irishmen: The Royal Irish Art Union 1839–59', *Irish Arts Review*, vol. 14, 1998, pp. 140–7; M. Bourke, The Aran Fisherman's Drowned Child *by Frederic William Burton, RHA* (Dublin: National Touring Exhibition Services, 1987), p. 14.

30. *The Nation*, 27 May 1843.

31. Thomas Davis, 'Hints for Irish Historical Paintings', *The Nation*, 29 July 1843.

32. *Evening Mail*, 2 January 1857.

33. Strickland, *Dictionary*, vol. 2, pp. 588–90, 613–21.

34. NLI MS 793, pp. 541–8 (RHA draft reports); *Evening Mail*, 2 January 1857.

35. *Report on the Affairs and Past Management of the Royal Hibernian Academy, by Norman Macleod, and Any Correspondence that has Taken Place between the Department of Science and Art, the Irish Government and the President and Secretary of the Royal Hibernian Academy* (London: HMSO, 23 May 1858).

36. *Freeman's Journal*, 25 July 1854; *Freeman's Journal*, 9 May 1865.

37. Anon, 'A New Museum in Dublin', pp. 35–7.

38. Steele, *Museum of Science and Art Director's Report for 1877–1878*, p. 664, NMIA.

39. J. Turpin, 'The RHA Schools 1826–1906', pp. 198–209.

40. The Watercolour Society of Ireland, founded by six women in 1871, was a forum for amateur artists.

41.   RIA MS 4B 30 (Thomas Larcom file: correspondence, notes and newspaper cuttings); *Report by the Committee of Enquiry into the Work of the Royal Hibernian Academy and the Metropolitan School of Art* (Dublin: HMSO, 1906).

Chapter 9

1.   M. Holroyd, *Bernard Shaw, Volume 1: The Search for Love* (London: Chatto & Windus, 1988), p. 42.
2.   *Saunders' Newsletter*, 30 March 1839.
3.   Black, 'Royal Irish Art Union', pp. 140–6.
4.   *Report of the Royal Irish Art Union*, 1843, Appendix, pp. 56–68.
5.   Turpin, *A School of Art in Dublin Since the Eighteenth Century*, p. 130; J.W. Hammond, 'Town Major Henry Charles Sirr', *Dublin Historical Record*, vol. 4, 1941–2; Bright, *Royal Dublin Society*, p. 195.
6.   F. Cullen, *Sources in Irish Art: A Reader* (Cork: Cork University Press, 2000), pp. 65–74.
7.   Letters from Frederic William Burton to the Earl of Dunraven. Dunraven Papers, University of Limerick, 184, D3 196/1/11/1–4.
8.   G. Mulvany, *Thoughts and Facts Concerning the Fine Arts in Ireland, and Schools of Design* (Dublin: Cumming & Ferguson, 1847).
9.   *PRDS,* 29 June, 15 July, 21 October 1852, and 3 February 1853.
10.   *Illustrated London News*, 14 May 1853, p. 390.
11.   Minutes of the Irish Institution, 1 November 1853, NGIA.
12.   Minutes of the Irish Institution, 10 November 1853, NGIA.
13.   Stewart, *Irish Art Loan Exhibitions,* pp. xv–xvi.
14.   Minutes of the Irish Institution, 15 December 1853, NGIA; Letter from J.W. Bates of Liverpool Academy to Mulvany, 6 December 1853.
15.   Minutes of the Irish Institution, 17 November 1853, NGIA.
16.   Minutes of the Irish Institution, 1 December 1853, NGIA; Frederic Burton to Robert Callwell, Munich, 22 November 1853.
17.   *Journal of the British Archaeological Association*, NGIA, vol. 8; Dr Waagen to Mulvany, 24 January 1854.
18.   Minutes of the Irish Institution, 4 July 1853, NGIA. In 1701 Archbishop Narcissus Marsh established the library to the design of William Robinson beside St Patrick's Cathedral. The building was in a dismal state mid-nineteenth-century, so it was proposed moving it to the National Gallery. Marsh's Library in its original setting was restored by Benjamin Lee Guinness in conjunction with St Patrick's Cathedral in 1862.
19.   *Freeman's Journal*, 25 July 1854; 'The Irish National Gallery', *The Packet*, 27 July 1854.
20.   'The National Gallery and Public Library', *Saunders' Newsletter*, 9 August 1854; 'National Gallery for Dublin', *The Advocate*, 9 August 1854; Minutes of the Irish Institution, 1 August 1854, NGIA.
21.   Marsh's Library was vested in the OPW by a clause of a supplementary Act 1865, renouncing any move to the gallery.
22.   The board of seventeen members to be made up of *ex officio* members: president of the RHA, president RIA, chairman OPW, president and vice-president of the RDS, two RHA members, and the remaining members appointed by government on five-year terms. The board remains the same today; elected members, ten government appointees, appoints its own chairman and amends its own bye-laws.
23.   NGI Foundation Minutes, 31 July 1856, NGIA; correspondence from Lansdowne to Lord Meath, 8 November (watermarked 1856), NGIA.
24.   NGI Foundation Minutes, 3 September 1855, NGIA; Minutes of the Irish Institution, 31

July 1855, NGIA; NGI Foundation Minutes, 16 October 1860, NGIA.

25. NGI Foundation Minutes, 3 December 1855, NGIA; National Gallery of Ireland Foundation Minutes, 15 September 1856, NGIA.

26. NGI Foundation Minutes, 3 November 1856, NGIA. Joseph Fesch (1763–1839), a French cardinal and uncle of Napoleon Bonaparte, was a very significant art collector.

27. M. Wynne, 'Fesch Paintings in the NGI', *Gazette des Beaux-Arts*, vol. 89, January 1977, p. 6.

28. NGI Foundation Minutes, 25 July 1862, NGIA.

29. Larcom Letter Box No 1, 6 October 1856, NGIA. Mulvany's draft (September 1857) and paltry sums from Irish nobility noted: NGIA, Administration/1/Folder 1.

30. Correspondence, Memorial from Mulvany to Treasury dated 18 December 1860, NGIA.

31. NGI Foundation Minutes, 2 February 1857, NGIA.

32. The Irish Institution was disestablished in 1860, leaving its collection to the gallery.

33. NGI Foundation Minutes, 5 November 1855, NGIA; NGI Foundation Minutes, 24 July 1856, NGIA; NGI Foundation Minutes, 5 December 1857, NGIA.

34. C. de Courcy, *The Foundation of the National Gallery of Ireland* (Dublin: NGI, 1985), p. 43.

35. NGI Foundation Minutes, 2 October 1858, NGIA. Fowke's design (1861–4) placed the gallery and Natural History Museum corresponding, lengthening aspects so the differences would be imperceptible.

36. *PRDS*, 21 April 1859; NGI Foundation Minutes, 17 January 1859, NGIA; *PRDS*, 21 April 1859.

37. NGI Foundation Minutes, 29 January 1859, NGIA.

38. NGI Foundation Minutes, 4 December 1862, NGIA.

39. Casey, *Buildings of Ireland: Dublin*, p. 499.

40. NGI Foundation Minutes, 10 November 1857, NGIA.

41. NGI Foundation Minutes, 6 September 1862, NGIA. 'The office of salaried Director and that of Hon. Secretary and Governor should not be held by the same person': this ruling continues to apply to the post of director.

42. *Report on Scientific Institutions (Dublin)*

43. Strickland, *Dictionary*, vol. 2, p. 153.

44. *Northern Whig*, 1 December 1849.

45. National Gallery of Ireland Foundation Minutes, 2 July 1860, NGIA.

46. National Gallery of Ireland Foundation Minutes, 4 August 1860, NGIA.

47. National Gallery of Ireland Foundation Minutes, 3 November 1860, NGIA.

48. G. Waterfield, 'Anticipating the Enlightenment: Museums and Galleries in Britain before the British Museum', in R.G.W. Anderson, et al. (eds), *Enlightening the British* (London: British Museum Press, 2003), p. 9.

49. National Gallery of Ireland Foundation Minutes, 7 December 1861, NGIA.

50. National Gallery of Ireland Foundation Minutes, 4 December 1862, NGIA.

51. National Gallery of Ireland Foundation Minutes, 7 March 1863, NGIA.

52. Craig, *Dublin 1660–1860*, p. 324.

53. Chesney, 'Enlightenment and Education', pp. 367–86; *Report on Scientific Institutions (Dublin)*, p. xvii–iii.

54. J. McEvoy, *The Royal Dublin Society and the Citizens of Dublin: Why Should Exclusiveness and Sabbatarianism be the Rule at the Glasnevin Botanic Garden, whilst under Her Majesty at Kew, Free Admission is the Rule on All Days of the week and on Sunday* (Dublin: Markay, 1860), p. 6; Nelson and McCracken, *Brightest Jewel*, pp. 129–31.

55. Steele, *Museum of Science and Art Director's Report for 1877–1878*, p. 664, NMIA.

56. O'Riordan, *Natural History Museum*, pp. 23, 269.

57. Herries Davies, *North of the Hook*, p. 258; *Report on Scientific Institutions (Dublin)*, p. vii.

58. Wilson, *The British Museum: A History*, pp. 186–7; E. Miller, *That Noble Cabinet: A History*

of the British Museum (London: British Museum, 1973), p. 256.

59. Taylor, *Art for the Nation*, pp. 96–7.

60. *The Scotsman*, 4 May 1907.

61. J. Galard, *Visiteurs du Louvre* (Paris: Reunion des Musées Nationaux, 1993), p. 31; C.G. Berkheim, *Lettres sur Paris (1806–1807)* (Heidelberg and Paris: Moet et Zimmer, 1809), pp. 351–3; E. Chesneau, *La Vérité sur le Louvre, le Musée Napoléon III et les artistes industriels* (Paris: E. Dentu, Libraire-Editeur, 1862), p. 2.

62. *Handbook of Travellers in Central Italy* (London: John Murray, 1865), p. 11.

63. S.A. Blanch, *Peintres de Prado* (Barcelona: Ediciones Polígrafa, S.A., 2002).

64. Personal Communication, Petra Winter, archivist, Staatlichen Museum, Berlin.

65. Personal Communication, Dr. Ellinoor Bergvelt, University of Amsterdam.

66. C. Tomkins, *Merchants and Masterpieces: The Story of the Metropolitan Museum of Art* (London: Longman, 1970), pp. 75–9.

67. NGI Foundation Minutes, 14 January 1864, NGIA.

68. Larcom Letter Box 1855–76, NGIA.

69. NGI Catalogue, NGIA; NGI Foundation Minutes, 28 January 1864, NGIA.

70. *Report on Scientific Institutions (Dublin)*, p. xxxi.

71. A. Gregory, *Hugh Lane's Life and Achievement, with Some Account of the Dublin Galleries* (London: John Murray, 1921), p. 196.

72. NGI Foundation Minute*s*, 2 April 1863, NGIA.

73. *Irish Times*, 27 January 1864; NGI Foundation Minutes, 14 February 1867, NGIA; *Daily Express*, 11 February 1867.

74. NGI Foundation Minutes, 14 January 1864, NGIA.

75. *Irish Times*, 27 January 1864.

76. *Daily Express*, 1 February 1864; T. Bodkin, 'Modern Irish Art', in B. Hobson, *Saorstát Éireann: Irish Free State Official Handbook* (Dublin: Talbot Press, 1932), pp. 233–9.

77. *Northern Whig*, 1 December 1849.

78. *Freeman's Journal*, 17 February 1864.

79. *Irish Times*, 27 January 1864; *The Irishman*, 21 January 1865.

80. *Daily Express*, 1 February 1864.

81. *Freeman's Journal*, 17 February 1864.

82. *Freeman's Journal*, 19 February 1864.

83. *Irish Times*, 19 February 1864.

84. *The Post*, 30 January 1864; *Irish Times*, 23 March 1864.

85. Dunraven Papers, University of Limerick, 1844, D3 196/1/11/1–4.

86. *Freeman's Journal*, 17 February 1864.

87. NGI Minutes*,* 12 March 1875, NGIA.

88. The term 'plaster' refers to plaster of Paris, a gypsum-based hemihydrate of calcium sulphate in its powder form, which becomes fully hydrated and solid with the addition of water. The name was adopted in the fifteenth century, when Paris gypsum became valued for its consistent quality.

89. Wilson, *The British Museum*, p. 67.

90. Taylor, *Art for the Nation*, p. 36.

91. *Catalogue of the National Gallery of Scotland*, 34th edn, vol. 11 (Edinburgh: Stationery Office, 1894).

92. Nesbitt, *Museum in Belfast*, p. 35.

93. B. Belford, *A Certain Genius* (London: Bloomsbury, 2000), p. 31.

94. NGI No. 4562, oil on canvas, 99.5 x 62 cm. It was purchased in 1989.

95. NGI Minutes, 7 August 1912, NGIA.

96. Gallery Student Attendance Books: Stephen Catterson Smith 1866; Miss Rose Orpen

1873; Miss May Manning 1874; Miss McCausland 1877; Nathaniel Hill 1878; Joseph O'Reilly 1883; Henry Allen 1884; W.B. Yeats and Miss E. Yeats 1885, Miss Lily Yeats 1886; Lady Butler (Elizabeth Thompson) Dublin Castle, and Major McEnry, RIA 1887; 11 female students from the Dublin Metropolitan School of Art (DMSA) 1889, 21 female students and 1 male student, Miss Rose Barton 1890; 20 students mainly women from DMSA 1891; 14 female students DMSA 1893; 27 female students with William Orpen DMSA, Percy French 1894, Miss Trevor 1895; 26 DMSA students and 1 registered as RHA pupil 1896; 16 female DMSA students, Miss Purser, Miss L. Davidson 1887; 8 female students, 2 students from Slade School of Art in London, 2 RHA, 3 under Mr. Brenan, Beatrice Moss Elvery, Miss G.P. Gifford, Miss Shackleton 1898; 4 students listed under Miss Stephens (this occurs frequently and is a reference to their teacher), 11 DMSA, Mr. W.L. Whelan, Mr. Burrell, a pupil of H. Allen 1899; Miss Swanzy under Miss Manning 1900; students from DMSA and RHA, Miss Manning, Miss Bell under Miss Underwood, Miss Solomons DMSA, Miss Barclay under Miss Manning 1901, Miss K. Pierce under Miss Trevor, DMSA and RHA students 1903; W. Crampton Gore, Miss Butler under Miss Stephens 1904; Miss Olivia Burton, Miss Kathleen Fox DMSA 1906; DMSA students 1907 and 1908; Patrick Tuohy, Leo Whelan, Miss Evie Hone, Dennis Gwynn 1910; DMSA students, Kathleen Quigley 1911; DMSA students, Miss O'Brien 1912, DMSA and RHA students 1914 and 1915; Miss Blackburn, Miss Kathleen Fox, May Manning 1916.

97. W. Laffan (ed.), *Painting Ireland: Topographical Views from Glin Castle* (Tralee: Churchill House Press, 2006), pp. 204–5.

98. *Freeman's Journal*, 13 March 1868.

99. Stewart, *Royal Hibernian Academy of Arts, Index of Exhibitors*, vol. 3.

100. NGI Minutes, 3 March 1864, NGIA. O'Brien refers to Sharp's *Going to School* as his choice for a prize of £10 'for the formation of a collection of pictures which is to form the National Gallery'. William Smith O'Brien, Cahirmoyle, Newcastle West, 10 June 1863, NGIA. Bequest accepted by the RDS at their meeting (*PRDS*, 21 September 1864) following which they devolved to the National Gallery; Bright, *Royal Dublin Society*, p. 233.

101. NGI Minutes, 2 March 1875, NGIA.

102. NGI Minutes, 25 June 1862, NGIA; NGI Minutes, 22 March 1869, NGIA.

103. Doyle acquired a range of key paintings, watercolours and drawings, notably works for the Irish and the portrait collections.

104. Holroyd, *Bernard Shaw, Volume 1*, pp. 37, 140–3. His boyhood friend was Matthew Edward McNulty.

105. Noel Desenfans (1744–1807), French art dealer and collector, who along with Sir Peter Francis Bourgeois was commissioned in 1790 by the king of Poland to form a Royal Collection for Poland. In 1795, when the king abdicated, they were left with the collection. In 1799 Desenfans suggested the establishment of a national gallery; however, following his death in 1807, Bourgeous bequeathed the collection with funding to Dulwich College to establish a gallery. Dulwich Gallery was designed by Sir John Soane 1811–14 (with a mausoleum for Desenfans, his wife and Bourgeois), opening in 1817 as England's first public art gallery.

106. Hansard's Parliamentary Debates, 27 June 1845, cols. 1,329–31; Taylor, *Art for the Nation*, pp. 92–9; N. Desenfans, *A Plan, Preceded by a Short Review of the Fine Arts, to Preserve Among Us, and Transmit to Posterity, the Portrait of the Most Distinguished Characters of England, Scotland and Ireland, since His Majesty's Accession to the Throne* (London: Sampson Low, 1799).

107. Philip Stanhope, 5th Earl of Stanhope, was a British politician and historian whose main achievements were in the field of literature and antiquities. He proposed the establishment

of the National Portrait Gallery in 1856. He quoted Eastlake in Hansard's Parliamentary Debates, 4 March 1856, col. 1,774.

108. N. Prior, *Museums and Modernity: Art Galleries and the Makings of Modern Culture* (Oxford: Berg, 2002), pp. 188–90.
109. NGI, 30 December 1872 (letter), NGIA.
110. H. Doyle, *National Gallery of Ireland Director's Report for 1875–76*, NGIA.
111. *Daily Express*, 19 March 1875.
112. H. Doyle, *National Gallery of Ireland Director's Report for 1884*, p. 4, NGIA; W. Armstrong, *Catalogue of Pictures and Other Works of Art in the National Gallery and the National Portrait Gallery, Ireland* (Dublin: Alex Thom, 1898), p. 215.
113. *Freeman's Journal*, 3 October 1896.
114. NGI Minutes, 31 July 1884, NGIA.
115. P.G. Knody and S. Dart, *Sir William Orpen: Artist and Man* (London: Seeley Service, 1932), p. 133.
116. Belford, *Certain Genius*, p. 278; NGI No. 219, 90 x 70 cm, *St. Onuphrius*, signed Jusepe de Ribera Espanol f. 1630; T. MacGreevy, 'Fifty Years of Irish Painting 1900–1950', *Capuchin Annual*, vol. 19, 1949, pp. 497–512.
117. J. Campbell, *Walter Osborne in the West of Ireland* (Dublin: James Adams Salesrooms, 2004).
118. *Irish Times*, 10 April 1897. Fintan Murphy presented an 1890 catalogue owned by Armstrong, interleaved with annotated notes about Carton, Gosford Castle in Armagh, Kilcooley Abbey, Castletown, Bellvue in Wicklow. NGI Minutes, 5 June 1935, NGIA.
119. Armstrong, *Catalogue of Pictures and Other Works of Art*.
120. NGI, 12 March 1896, NGIA; Armstrong, *National Gallery of Ireland Director's Report for 1898*, NGIA.
121. NGI Minutes, 6 August 1896, NGIA.
122. Milltown Correspondence, 16 October 1897, NGIA. The Countess of Milltown wished the material to be exhibited 'as one separate collection, to be known as the Collection of Edward Nugent Leeson, sixth Earl of Milltown'. A. Kelly, 'The Milltown Collection', *Irish Arts Review*, vol. 22, no. 3, 2005, pp.114–17.
123. 'At this period, during the holding of an exhibition of art and industry in Dublin, a gathering of artists and Irish figures have decided to found a picture museum.' T. Duret, 'Une Visite aux Galleries Nationales D'Irlande et D'Ecosse', *Gazette des Beaux-Arts*, vol. 25, 1882, pp. 180–3.
124. T. Grey, *Ireland this Century* (London: Little Brown, 1994), pp. 1–4.
125. T. Ó Fiaich, 'The Great Controversy', *The Gaelic League Idea*, ed. S. Ó Tuama, (Cork: Mercier Press, 1970), cp. 67.
126. The *New Ireland Review* associated with UCD started out in 1898 and was edited by Father Thomas A. Finlay.
127. Yeats set up the Irish Literary Society of London in 1891 and the National Literary Society of Dublin in 1892.
128. E. Hobsbawm, 'Mass Producing Traditions: Europe, 1870–1914', in E. Hobsbawm and T. Ranger (eds), *The Invention of Tradition* (Cambridge: Cambridge University Press, 2003), pp. 263–307; W.F. Mandle, 'Sport as Politics: The Gaelic Athletic Association 1884–1916', in R. Cashman and E. McKernan (eds), *Sport in History* (St Lucia: Queensland University Press, 1979).
129. F. Moore, '"Young Ireland" and Liberal Ideas', *Dana – An Irish Magazine of Independent Thought*, vol. 2, 1904, pp. 62–4.
130. G.W. Dunleavy, *Douglas Hyde* (London: Buckness University Press, 1974).
131. B. Anderson, *Imagined Communities: Reflections on the Origins and Spread of Nationalism* (London: Verso, 1991), pp. 34–5.

132. T. West, *Horace Plunkett: Co-operation and Politics, an Irish Biography* (Gerrards Cross: Colin Smythe, 1986), p. 63; T. Clyde, *Irish Literary Magazines* (Dublin: Irish Academic Press, 2003), pp. 140–1.

133. Michael Holroyd, *George Bernard Shaw* (London: Chatto & Windus), vol. 2, p. 500. (vol. 1, *The Search for Love* (1856–98), 1988; vol. 2, *The Pursuit of Power* (1898–1918), 1989; vol. 3, *The lure of fantasy* (1918–1950), *1991;* vol. 4, *The Last Laugh* (1950–1991), 1992).

134. R.V. Comerford, 'Introduction: Ireland, 1870–1921', in W.E. Vaughan (ed.), *A New History of Ireland VI: Ireland under the Union, II, 1870–1921* (Oxford: Clarendon Press, 1996).

Part IV Preamble

1. The Folkwang, then in Hagen, Germany, now in Essen, is widely acknowledged in Germany to be the oldest modern art gallery in the world, having opened in 1902.

2. Dublin, Limerick and Cork survived, Clonmel did not. Belfast became a faculty of Ulster Polytechnic, latterly University of Ulster. Waterford and Derry were absorbed into technology institutes. Dun Laoghaire became an institute of art, design and technology. Regional Technical Colleges Act 1992 (amended 1997, 1998, 1999).

3. The Haverty Trust, bequeathed under the will of Thomas Haverty (son of painter Joseph Haverty), is the largest endowment devoted to contemporary painting in Ireland. The Contemporary Irish Art Society uses members' funds to acquire works for about forty public institutions.

4. Some newly founded municipal art collections: Waterford (1939), Limerick (1937), Kilkenny (1943), Drogheda (1946), Clonmel (1948), Sligo (1950s). For information on forming municipal art collections, see P. Jordan, *Waterford Municipal Art Collection* (Cork: Gandon Editions, 2006).

Chapter 10

1. Quote from J.M. Mancini, *Pre-Modern: Art-World Change and American Culture from the Civil War to the Armory Show* (Princeton, NJ: Princeton University Press, 2005), p. 120.

2. Quoted c.1889. K. Thomas (2003), 'Afterword', *Enlightening the British,* R.G.W. Anderson, M.L. Caygill, A.G.MacGregor and L. Syson (London: British Museum Press), p. 185.

3. Comments by Sir Frederick Keynon, director of the British Museum, 'Museums and National Life' (Romanes Lecture, 1927) showed increased attention by public museums in their duties to the community.

4. H. Plantnauer, 'What is a Museum?', *Museums Journal*, vol. 11, no. 1, 1911, p. 5.

5. Earl of Rosse, *Survey of Provincial Museums and Galleries, London, Standing Commission on Museums and Galleries* (London: HMSO, 1963), p. 288.

6. *Final Report on Museums in relation to Education* (London: British Association for the Advancement of Science, 1920); reference was made to practices in the United States and Australia.

7. E. Howarth (ed.), *Educational Value of Museums and the Formation of Local War Museums: Report of Museums Association Conference* (Sheffield: Museums Association, 1918), p. 8.

8. This service was in place at New York's Metropolitan Museum of Art and Boston's Museum of Fine Art in 1907, and the Art Institute of Chicago in 1909.

9. Two officers, C.W.C. Hallett and W.W. Skeat, were paid £315 per annum, plus relief lecturers. Informal lectures were held from the 1880s.

10. Miss M.C. Knowles studied cryptogamic botany (lichens) under Lorraine Smith at the British Museum.

11. A. Mahr, *Report of the Director of the National Museum of Ireland for 1934–5*, NMIA.

12. William Burges, Art Applied to Industry: A Series of Lectures (1865), in Burton, *Vision and Accident: The Story of the Victoria and Albert Museum*, p. 47.

13. While a separation took place in 1917, the National Gallery and Tate Gallery Act 1954 finally established the Tate as a legally independent institution, with British art and European modern paintings (after 1900) and a board of trustees responsible for its management and trust funds. The Act was repealed by the Museums and Galleries Act 1992, creating a board of trustees to operate the Tate.

14. 'Art and Artists, Music at the National Gallery', *Morning Post*, 18 July 1922.

15. L. O'Callaghan, *National Gallery Director's Report for 1925*, NGIA. During the nineteenth century the National Gallery of Ireland obtained a loan of works from the National Gallery, London (as did the National Museum from, for example, the South Kensington Museum). At intervals in the twentieth century these loans were recalled.

16. Directors of the NGI: George Furlong (1935), Thomas MacGreevy (1950).

17. *Final Report of the Committee on Museums in relation to Education*, pp. 267–80.

18. G. Kavanagh, 'The First World War and its Implication for Education in British Museums', *History of Education*, vol. 17, no. 2, 1988, pp. 163–76.

19. H.A. Miers, *Report on the Public Museums of the British Isles* (Edinburgh: Carnegie United Kingdom Trustees, covering England, Scotland, Wales, Northern Ireland, Isle of Man, Channel Isles, 1928).

20. E.E. Lowe, *Report on American Museum Work* (Edinburgh: Carnegie United Kingdom Trustees, 1928), p. 31.

21. *Museums and the Schools: Memorandum on the Possibility of Increased Co-operation between Public Museums and Public Educational Institutions*, Educational Pamphlet No. 87 (London: HMSO, 1931).

22. S.F. Markham, *Report of the Museums and Galleries of the British Isles* (Dunfermline: Carnegie United Kingdom Trustees, 1938).

23. J. Pierpont Morgan made major donations to the Metropolitan Museum (together with Benjamin Altman, American businessman, art collector and philanthropist), also founding the Pierpont Morgan Library in New York.

24. Hughes, *American Visions: The Epic History of Art in America*, pp. 214–15.

25. J. Dewey, *Art as Experience* (New York: Minton, Balch & Co., 1934), p. 9; D. Hawkins, 'Teacher of Teachers', *New York Review of Books*, vol. 10, no. 4, 1968, pp. 25–9.

26. M. Bronson Hartt, 'Docentry: A New Profession', *Outlook* (1910).

27. B. Ives Gilman, *Museum Ideals of Purpose and Method* (Cambridge: Boston Museum of Fine Arts, 1923).

28. L. Connolly, *The Educational Value of Museums* (New Jersey: Newark Museum Association, 1914), pp. vii–xvx, with an introduction by J.C. Dana.

29. Others included Theodore Low, Paul Rea, Charles Richards (president of the American Association of Museums [AAM]), and Thomas Adam.

30. J.C. Dana, *The New Museum* (Woodstock, VT: Elm Tree Press, 1917).

31. G. Browne Goode, 'Principles of Museum Administration', *Museums Journal* (1895).

32. C. Malt, 'Museology and Museum Studies Programs in the United States: Part One', *International Journal of Museum Management and Curatorship*, vol. 6, 1987, pp. 165–72.

33. The Metropolitan Museum moved to Central Park in 1880, first wing 1888, the neo-classical façade 1910, designed by the architects McKim, Mead and White, and new South Fifth Avenue 'American' wing 1924 by Richard Morris Hunt.

34. *Metropolitan Museum of Art Annual Report*, 1905, p. 11 (Metropolitan Museum archive).

35. Whitty, 'The Caspar Purdon Clarke Indian and Persian Collection at the National Museum of Ireland', pp. 68–75. Burton, *Vision and Accident: The Story of the Victoria and Albert Museum*, pp. 118–20.

36. Count G.N. Plunkett, *National Museum of Science and Art Director's Report for 1908–1909*, NMIA.

37. R.W. de Forest, 'Museum Extension', *Bulletin of the Metropolitan Museum of Art*, vol. 14, no. 9, 1919, p. 189.

38. R.W. de Forest, 'The 150th Anniversary of the Museum', *Bulletin of the Metropolitan Museum of Art*, vol. 15, 1920, p. 124.

39. L.V. Coleman, *The Museum in Society: A Critical Study* (Washington, DC: AAM, 1939), pp. 419–21.

40. F.H. Taylor, *Babel's Tower: The Dilemma of the Modern Museum* (New York: Columbia Press, 1945), p. 18; F.H. Taylor, 'Museums in a Changing World', *Atlantic Monthly*, vol. 164, no. 6, 1939, pp. 789–92.

41. In 1936, in a letter to President Franklin D. Roosevelt, the 81-year-old Andrew W. Mellon (1855–1937) offered his paintings to the nation as the nucleus of a national collection, to be followed by an endowment and a building.

42. The origins of MoMA derived from people like the lawyer-collector John Quinn (friend of Lady Gregory and patron of Irish art, notably John Butler Yeats), Walter Arensberg and Agnes Meyer. Prompted by Quinn, Louisa Havemeyer, Lizzie P. Bliss and others, the Metropolitan Museum organized a French Impressionist and post-Impressionist exhibition in 1921, which was denounced in newspapers for its 'degenerate', 'Bolshevik' art. Although the Met had accepted the Havemeyer Impressionists in 1928, Quinn's offer to lend Impressionist paintings was rebuffed. Following Quinn's death in 1927, the sale of his modern collection encouraged the foundation of the Museum of Modern Art in New York.

43. The Armory Show in 1913 was organized by the painters Walt Kuhn and Arthur B. Davis, based on the Sonerbund Exhibition held in Cologne in 1912 (the precursor of contemporary *Biennales* and *Dokumentas*). It was held in the Armory (home of the 'fighting Irish', the New York 69th Regiment) on Lexington Avenue, between 24th Street and 25th Street. Marcel Duchamp's *Nude Descending a Staircase, No. 2* (1912) was the celebrated work of the show and beneficiaries were European artists Matisse, Picasso, Brancusi and Duchamp.

44. Alfred Barr (1902–81), MoMA's founder, was at heart a pedagogue. Through MoMA, Barr (director 1929–67) made modern art mandatory in America by collecting it, showing it, moving big money behind it, evangelizing for it, and by moving the function of the museum from acquisition to teaching and advocacy.

45. Wittlin, *The Museum, its History and its Tastes in Education*, pp. 62–7.

46. W.A. Simonds, *Henry Ford and Greenfield Village* (New York: F.A. Stokes, 1938).

47. M. Vaughan, 'The Significance of the Century of Progress Art Exhibition', *Bulletin of the Art Institute of Chicago*, vol. 27, no. 5, 1933, pp. 82–3.

48. Among the exhibitors at the Chicago exhibition was the National Museum of Ireland, facilitated by the Department of Industry and Commerce in Dublin. *National Museum of Ireland Acting Director's Report for 1932–33*, NMIA.

49. J. Smith, 'The Nervous Profession: Daniel Catton Rich and the Art Institute of Chicago 1927–1958', *Art Institute of Chicago Museum Studies*, vol. 19, no. 1, p. 65.

50. Catton Rich held symposia, lectures related to major exhibitions and a High School Extension Art project. 'The Gallery of Art Interpretation', *Bulletin of the Art Institute of Chicago*, 1940, vol. 34, no. 2, p. 24.

51. Katharine Kuh, 'Seeing is Believing', *Bulletin of the Art Institute of Chicago*, vol. 39, 1956, p. 54.

52. Glasgow Art Galleries and Museums Committee, *Educational Experiment 1941–51* (Glasgow: Corporation of the City of Glasgow, 1951).

53. R. Strong, *The Victoria and Albert Museum Souvenir Guide* (London: Thames & Hudson, 1997), p. 4.

54. 'Art, archaeology or history could not be pigeon-holed into the collections of the British Museum and the V & A or of any of the nation's museums.' J. Pope-Hennessy, *Learning to Look* (London: Heinemann, 1991), p. 165.

55. J. Rudoe, *Decorative Arts 1850–1950: A Catalogue of the British Museum Collection* (London: British Museum Press, 1991).

56. The British Museum is divided into nine departments dealing with antiquities, prints and drawings, and ethnography. John Wolfenden's departure in 1973 coincided with the separation of the British Library from the British Museum. He was succeeded by the short-directorship of Sir John Pope-Hennessy (then director of the V&A Museum), 1974–6, followed by David Wilson, 1977–91.

57. MacGreevy assisted in the dispatch of the paintings to a slate quarry at Manod in Wales.

58. C. Baker and T. Henry, *The National Gallery: Complete Illustrated Catalogue* (London: National Gallery Publications, 1995), p. xvi.

59. *Illustrated London News*, 24 January 1942, p. 101.

60. *Burlington Magazine*, vol. 91, 1949, pp. 183–8; vol. 92, 1950, pp. 189–92; vol. 104, 1962, pp. 51–62, 452–77; vol. 105, 1963, pp. 90–7; see also *British Journal of Aesthetics*, vol. 1, 1961, pp. 231–7; vol. 2, 1962, pp. 170–9.

61. *The Visual Arts: A Report Sponsored by the Darlington Hall Trustees; Published on Behalf of the Arts Enquiry by PEP (Political and Economic Planning)* (Oxford: Oxford University Press, 1946), p. 145.

62. Set up by Alec Clegg and including libraries, works of art, advisers and in-service courses for teachers.

63. This caused him to curtail building and renovating projects and put in store its major art treasures, at Whitemarsh Hall (12 miles north-west of Philadelphia), a 150-room mansion constructed of fireproof steel and concrete with air conditioning and humidity control throughout, its own electrical system and water supply, and a natural security of a fenced park. The staff moved 90 vanloads containing 1,500 works, decorative and fine arts. Other museums availing of this facility (leased by the Metropolitan Museum for two years) included the American Philosophical Society, the Brooklyn Museum, Cooper Union and some private collectors.

64. In 1944, when the museum's 1,500 art treasures returned from storage, a series of post-war loan shows were mounted establishing Taylor as the leading museum director of the day. The shows were facilitated by European museums, which, in the aftermath of war, agreed to loan their treasures for exhibitions held at the Metropolitan Museum and other American museums. The shows included: Dutch Paintings (1945); English Paintings (1947); French Tapestries, Paintings from Berlin Museums; A Survey of Van Gogh; and Art Treasures from Vienna (1949).

65. The Metropolitan had also been involved in museum training: the Metropolitan Museum and Columbia University; the Metropolitan and New York University; the Metropolitan and the Brooklyn Museum.

66. Taylor visited Ireland in February 1956 where, according to Thomas MacGreevy, director of the National Gallery of Ireland, 'it will be a pleasure and privilege to hear your lecture in Dublin': MacGreevy to Taylor, 29 October 1955, NGIA.

67. T. Low, *The Museum as a Social Instrument* (New York: Metropolitan Museum of Art, 1942), p. 7.

68. *The Visual Arts: A Report*, pp. 148–9.

69. M.G. Hood, 'Staying Away: Why People Choose not to Visit Museums', *Museum News*, vol. 61, April 1983, pp. 50–7.

70. Low, *The Museum as a Social Instrument*, pp. 24–30.

71. J. Bateman, 'The Control and Financing of Museum Education Services in Britain', *Museums*

Journal, vol. 84, no. 2, 1984, pp. 51–6.

72.   Announced by the chancellor as a successor to the Council for the Encouragement of Music and the Arts (CEMA) in 1945, it was established by a royal charter in 1946. The Irish Arts Council was established in 1951. The Arts Council of Northern Ireland was established in 1962.

73.   For a good description of 'modern foreign art', see chapters 5 and 6 of Taylor, *Art for the Nation*. The V&A Museum had exhibited the controversial, successful *Picasso–Matisse* exhibition in 1946; the Tate and the Institute of Contemporary Art had been displaying modern art; only the Royal Academy of Arts lagged behind.

74.   *Pterodactyls and Old Lace: Museums in Education* (London: Schools Council, 1972), pamphlet no. 34; C.W. Wright, *Provincial Museums and Galleries, Department of Education and Science* (London: HMSO, 1973); A. Drew, *Framework for a System for Museums, Standing Commission on Museums and Galleries* (London: HMSO, 1979).

75.   M. Harrison, *Learning Out of School: A Teacher's Guide to the Educational Use of Museums* (London: Ward Lock Educational, 1970). Her work was carried out between 1940 and 1970.

76.   R. Marcouse, *The Listening Eye: Teaching in an Art Museum* (London: HMSO, 1961).

77.   B. Winstanley, *Children and Museums* (London: Blackwell, 1967).

78.   E. Esteve-Coll, 'A Yearning for Learning', *Museums Journal*, vol. 93, no. 5, 1993, pp. 23–6.

79.   Written by David Anderson, director of Visitor Services and Learning at the V&A Museum, (first edition 1997, revised and reprinted 1999).

80.   *The Learning Age: A Renaissance for a New Britain* (London: Department of Education and Employment, 1998).

81.   Handling sessions involved original objects (that could not be damaged, e.g. fossils, chain mail, pottery) or good replicas being made available for students to handle. Sometimes these were provided as loan boxes with instructions. More often they were provided in the museum to use with classes.

82.   G. Waterfield (ed.), *Opening Doors: Learning in the Historic Environment* (London: Attingham Trust, 2004).

83.   Following on from the Department of National Heritage, the Department of Culture, Media and Sport replaced the Museums and Galleries Commission and Library and Information System with Re:SOURCE – a strategic national council for museums, galleries and archives. It also established a joint scheme with the Department for Education and Employment for museum and gallery education projects. Re:SOURCE was renamed the Council for Museums, Archives and Libraries in 2003 (www.culture24.co.uk).

84.   K. Robinson, *Culture, Creativity and the Young: Developing Public Policy* (Belgium: Council of Europe Publishing, 1999).

85.   The work of the Scientific and Conservation department is featured in videos and films such as the BBC series *Making Masterpieces* (1997).

86.   D. Gordon, et al., *Making & Meaning: The Wilton Diptych* (London: National Gallery Publications, 1993).

87.   Other exhibitions included: *The Young Michelangelo* (1994–5), *Rubens Landscapes* (1996–7), Hans Holbein's *The Ambassadors* (1997–8).

88.   E. Barker and A. Thomas, 'The Sainsbury Wing and Beyond: The National Gallery Today', in E. Barker (ed.), *Contemporary Cultures of Display* (New Haven and London: Open University Press, 1999), pp. 94–8.

89.   Built through the endowment of three Sainsbury brothers (John, Simon, Timothy), located west of the main building and designed by Venturi, Scott Brown and Assoc., the extension was opened in 1991. It provided new galleries for display of the collection, a lecture theatre, a micro gallery, a shop, restaurant and conference room.

90.   *Landscape* (1997); *Frames* (1997); *Faces, Flowers and Fruit* (1998); *Impressionism* (1999),

printed by National Gallery Publications and distributed by Yale University Press.

91. C.G. Screven, 'Exhibitions and Information Centres: Some Principles and Approaches', *Curator*, vol. 29, 1986, pp. 109–37.

92. These seven human intelligences; linguistic, logical-mathematical, spatial, musical, bodily kinaesthetic, inter-personal and intra-personal, are knowing processes, ways of perceiving, interpreting and organizing phenomena. H. Gardner, *Frames of Mind: The Theory of Multiple Intelligences* (New York: Basic Books, 1983).

93. H. Gardner, *The Unschooled Mind: How Children Think and How Schools should Teach* (New York: Basic Books, 1991).

94. N.H.H. Graburn, *Tourism, Leisure and Museums*, Annual Meeting of the Canadian Museums Association, 1982.

95. Building programmes in the United States in the 2000s: Los Angeles Museum of Contemporary Art, its County Museum of Art, and UCLA Hammer Museum Texas's Dallas Museum of Fine Arts, Houston's Museum of Fine Arts, and the Austin Museum of Art; New York's Neue Galerie, Asia Society HQ, American Folk Art Museum, Brooklyn Museum of Art, Bronx Museum of the Arts, Queen's Museum of Art, Whitney Museum of American Art, and the American Museum of Natural History; Mississippi's Ohr Museum in Biloxi; Milwaukee Art Museum; Cleveland Museum of Art; Boston's Institute for Contemporary Art; Minneapolis's Walker Art Centre; Denver's Art Museum, Wadsworth Atheneum Museum of Art in Haitford, Connecticut; Corcoran Gallery in Washington, DC, Cincinnati Contemporary Arts Centre; UCLA Hammer Museum, Kansas City's Nelson-Atkins Museum of Art; and San Francisco's Fine Art Museums.

96. *Report of the Commission on Museums for a New Century* (Washington, DC: AAM, 1984), p. 28.

97. K.A. Yellis, 'Museum Education', in S. Shapiro and L.W. Kemp (eds), *The Museum: A Reference Guide* (New York: Greenwood Press, 1990), p. 170; *Art Museums and Educators, Partners in Excellence, Proceedings of a National Conference for Museum Education Professionals* (Washington, DC: AAM, 1992), p. 40.

98. *Excellence and Equity: Education and the Public Dimension of Museums: Report from the American Association of Museums* (Washington, DC: AAM, 1992); H.M. Williams, *Public Policy and the Arts* (Ohio: Getty Centre for Education in the Arts, 1993).

99. G.E. Hein and M. Alexander, *Museums: Places of Learning* (Washington, DC: AAM, 1998).

100. J. Dewey, *Experience and Education* (New York: Macmillan, 1938), pp. 13–14.

101. G.E. Hein, 'Educational Theory', in his *Learning in the Museum* (London: Routledge, 1998), pp. 14–41.

102. 'A museum is a non-profit making permanent institution in the service of society and of its development, open to the public, which acquires, conserves, researches, communicates and exhibits, for purposes of study, education and enjoyment, the tangible and intangible evidence of people and their environment', from *ICOM Code of Ethics for Museums* (Paris: International Council of Museums, 2002), p. 14; for institutions that qualify as museums under the definition, see *ICOM Code of Ethics for Museums*, p. 26.

103. ICOM Statutes, article 2, paragraph 1, 2001, from *ICOM Code of Ethics for Museums*, p. 26.

104. A.S. Wittlin, *Museums in Search of a Usable Future* (Cambridge, MA: MIT Press, 1970), pp. 203–4.

105. E. Phillips, *The New World of Words; or, Universal English Dictionary* (London: R. Bentley, J. Phillips, H. Rhodes & J. Taylor, 1706).

106. N. Burt, *Palaces for the People: A Social History of the American Art Museum* (Boston: Little Brown, 1977), p. 14.

107. S.J. Gould, 'Dinomania', *New York Review of Books*, vol. 40, no. 14, 1993, pp. 51–6.

108. 'Saving Art for the Nation', *Art Newspaper*, no. 146, December 2003, p. 25.

109. Waterfield, *Palaces of Art: Art Galleries in Britain 1790–1990*; C. Duncan, *Civilizing Rituals* (London and New York: Routledge, 1995); T. Bennett, *The Birth of the Museum: History, Theory, Politics* (London and New York: Routledge, 1995).

110. E. Hooper-Greenhill, *Museums and the Shaping of Knowledge* (London: Routledge, 1992), p. 189.

111. *Art Newspaper*, no. 136, May 2003, p. 25.

112. C. Trodd, 'The Discipline of Pleasure; or, How Art History Looks at the Art Museum', *Museum and Society*, vol. 1, no. 1, 2004, pp.17–29.

113. G. Wright, 'The Quality of Visitors' Experiences in Art Museums', in P. Vergo (ed.), *The New Museology* (London: Reaktion Books, 1989), p. 119.

114. D. Rice, 'On the Ethics of Museum Education', *Museum News: Washington*, vol. 65, no. 5, 1987, pp. 13–19.

115. D. Rice, 'Museum Education Embracing Uncertainty', *Art Bulletin*, vol. 77, no. 1, pp. 15–20.

116. Hein and Alexander, *Museums: Places of Learning*, p. 11.

117. 'Conclusion', in *A Policy Framework for Education, Community, Outreach* (Dublin, Council of National Cultural Institutions, 2004), developed by the CNCI Education, Community, Outreach Working Party, p. 27.

Chapter 11

1. C. Benson (ed.), *Art and the Ordinary: The ACE Report* (Dublin: Arts Council, 1989), p. 16.

2. G. Ó Donnachadha and B. O'Connor, 'Cultural Tourism in Ireland', in G. Richards (ed.), *Cultural Tourism in Europe* (Wallingford: CAB International, 1996), p. 202.

3. The gallery and museum became a sub-department of the library, becoming a department in its own right on foot of a report, 'The Best Means for Utilizing the Materials and Exhibits at the Dispersal of the Committee in its Museum and Art Gallery', by an art sub-committee, submitted to Library and Technical Instruction Committee, 1905. Address listed as Public Library, Royal Avenue, Belfast. R. Patterson (ed.), *Ulster Nature Notes* (Belfast: W. Mullan, 1908).

4. A. Deane, 'Ireland's First Museum', *Belfast Municipal Art Gallery and Museum: Quarterly Notes*, vol. 25, March 1914, pp. 11–14.

5. Deane, 'Ireland's First Museum'; *Guide to Belfast and the Counties of Down and Antrim by the Belfast Naturalists' Field Club* (Belfast: Linen Hall Press, 1902), p. 31.

6. James Cummings Weynnes was the architect. Accompanying the foundation stone was a body of material including a letter from the Duke of York (later George VI), the seal of Belfast Corporation, and the list of committees and museum staff.

7. W. Viola, *Child Art and Franz Cizek* (New York: Reynal & Hitchkock, 1936). Frank Cizek (1865–1946) was a pioneering Austrian art teacher whose new ideas contrasted with the formal approach of Irish educationalists, such as Henry Lewis Vere Foster (1819–1900), who created copybooks for schools and these remained in use in Ireland up to the 1920s. The books gave instruction in handwriting (printed by Ward and Sons, Belfast), drawing (written by John Vinycomb, illustrated by Harrison Weir) and watercolour painting. His fortune was spent on philanthropy for Irish people.

8. Quoted in Nesbit, *A Museum in Belfast*, p. 35, n. 6.

9. Ibid., p. 37.

10. Between 1940 and 1945, 316 films together with Ministry of Information films were screened; 78 lectures were attended by 12,227 people.

11. *Belfast Museums and Art Gallery Report of the Committee for 1940–1945*, UMA.

12. Stendall advocated branch museums and an open-air museum, which was developed by

Wilfred Seaby, via the Ulster Folk Museum Act 1958, which founded the Ulster Folk Museum under George Thompson. A transport museum (collection amassed in 1954 and given to Belfast Corporation in 1955) was developed in 1960.

13. Four hundred children attended the Christmas talks.

14. *Belfast Museums and Art Gallery Report of the Committee for 1946–1947*, UMA.

15. *Belfast Museums and Art Gallery Report of the Committee for 1947–1948*, UMA.

16. *Belfast Museums and Art Gallery Report of the Committee for 1948–1949*, UMA.

17. *Belfast Museums and Art Gallery Report of the Committee for 1950–1951*, UMA.

18. The loans in cases were provided by the Education Authority and included groups of specimens, maps, charts, posters, press cuttings and slides. Forty loans were made of natural history and archaeological material. *Belfast Museums and Art Gallery Report of the Committee for 1951–1952*, UMA.

19. The director at the time was Wilfred Seaby.

20. Ulster Folk Museum (Northern Ireland) Acts 1958, 1964, 1967 and The Museums (Northern Ireland) Order 1973, No. 416, N.I.7. In 1961, the trustees of the Ulster Folk Museum purchased the Cultra Manor Estate in north County Down. This provided the necessary space for the merger of the Ulster Folk and the Ulster Transport Museums in 1973. A. Gailey, 'The Ulster Folk and Transport Museum and Historic Buildings Conservation in Northern Ireland', *Ulster Folk and Transport Yearbook*, 1976–7, pp. 13–14.

21. Funded by annual grants from the Exchequer and the Ulster Land Fund. *Belfast Museum and Art Gallery Report for Ten Years ended 1962*, UMA.

22. C. Moriarity, et al., *The Natural History Museum: Present Status and Future Needs* (Dublin: Royal Irish Academy, 2005).

23. *Ulster Museum Belfast Report of the Trustees for the Year 1968–1969*, UMA.

24. *Ulster Museum Belfast Report of the Trustees 1963–1964*, UMA.

25. The museum's five curatorial departments: Art; Antiquities; Botany and Zoology; Geology; Technology and Local History.

26. *Opening of the New Extension to the Ulster Museum, 30 October 1972* (Belfast: Ulster Museum, 1972), p. 8.

27. Discovered off the north Antrim coast by Belgian underwater archaeologist, Robert Steniut.

28. Armagh Natural History and Philosophical Society founded a museum in 1856, which opened in 1857, and became Armagh County Museum in 1931. R.M. Weatherup, 'Armagh County Museum, Archaeological Acquisitions: The Collection of Armagh Natural History and Philosophical Society', *JRSAI*, vol. 112, 1982, pp. 51–71.

29. John Nolan: assistant director (1983–8) and director (1988–96) of the Ulster Museum.

30. J.C. Nolan, 'A Message from John C. Nolan, Director, Ulster Museum, Belfast', in *A Festival of Young People's Art* (Dublin: Department of Education, 1993), p. 9.

31. J.C. Nolan, 'Income Generation for Museums: Problems and Prospects', *Museum Ireland*, vol. 1, 1991, pp. 20–5.

32. Sheela Speers, head of education, sought 'to realise the educational potential of the Museum's collections and information resources by all means which will encourage and facilitate their use and enjoyment by people of all ages, interests, capabilities and backgrounds'. She set out the education department's aims and objectives: the role and function of the museum education service and its plans to meet new challenges, including the Northern Ireland curriculum; gallery development; on-site education services; outreach services; staffing and resourcing: 'Ulster Museum Education Policy' (unpublished, 1991), p. 1.

33. J. Williams, 'MAGNI Learning and Access Policy' (unpublished, 2003). It is based on a mission with values implemented by a series of objectives via audiences: people: providing effective learning opportunities; places: creating accessible and inspiring learning environments; partnerships: building creative partnerships; placing learning at the heart of the museum, policy, plans, performance.

34. *Mapping Trends in Northern Ireland's Museums* (Belfast: Northern Ireland Museum Council, 2003). Thirty-eight museums were surveyed, of which twenty-seven were registered and twenty-six with education officers.

35. M. Houlihan, 'Opening Horizons: A New Vision for Northern Ireland's National Museums and Galleries', *Museum Ireland*, 2000, vol. 10, pp. 10–15.

36. The Science Discovery Bus received the Museum of the Year Education Award (1992). S. Montgomery, 'Learning can be Fun: Interactives at W5 Science and Discovery Centre', in M. Bourke (ed.), *Proceedings of the National Gallery of Ireland Museum Education Symposium*, 2003, pp. 54–5.

37. 'What we are doing may have one small impact on the troubled society in which we live': S. Speers, et al., 'Towards Reconciliation: A Role for Museums in Divided Society', in L. Silverman and J. Hirsch (eds), *Transforming Practice: Sections from the Journal of Museum Education 1992–1999* (Washington, DC: Museum Education Roundtable, 2000), pp. 135–7. The Residential Centre for Education for Mutual Understanding at the Ulster Folk and Transport Museum comprises a series of self-contained units in terraced houses. The accommodation and space provide recreation for teachers and children from schools in both communities, catering for 8,000 'bed nights' a year with access to a 160-acre estate. Co-Operation Ireland uses this facility to promote contact between groups in the North and southern Ireland.

38. The All Children Together movement provided schools for Catholic and Protestant children to be educated together by staff from both communities. 'The Timescapes Project', *Journal of Museum Education*, vol. 19, no. 1, 1994, pp. 10–13.

39. Quoted in Speers, et al., 'Towards Reconciliation', pp.133–42 at 139.

40. M. Anglesea, *Portraits and Prospects: British and Irish Watercolours and Drawings* (Belfast: Ulster Museum in association with the Smithsonian Institution Traveling Exhibition Service [SITES], 1989); E. Black (ed.), *Dreams and Traditions: 300 Years of British and Irish Paintings from the Collection of the Ulster Museum* (essays by E. Black, S.B. Kennedy, W.A. Maguire) (Belfast: Ulster Museum in association with SITES, 1997).

41. Commemorating the tercentenary of the Battle of the Boyne, 1 July (Julian calendar), now 12 July 1690. E. Black (ed.), *Kings in Conflict: Ireland in the 1690s* (Belfast: Ulster Museum, 1990); A.T.Q. Stewart, 'Kings in Conflict', *Irish Arts Review*, vol. 8, 1991–1992, pp. 152–3.

42. It opened eight days before the Good Friday Agreement of 10 April 1998. B. Ó Seaghdha, 'Conflict' (Belfast: Ulster Museum, 2004); *Museum Ireland*, vol. 14, pp.120–2.

43. T. Parkhill, 'Outreach or Over-reach? A Consideration of the Ulster Museum/MAGNI History Outreach Initiative 1997–2002', a paper presented at the 2002 INTERCOM Conference, *Leadership in Museums: Are Our Core Values Shifting?* (Dublin: NMI, 2003); K. Jeffery, 'Culture, Place and Identity', in N. Garnham and K. Jeffery (eds), *Culture, Place and Identity* (Dublin: University College Dublin Press, 2005), pp. 1–22.

44. Anderson, *A Common Wealth: Museums in the Learning Age*, p. 71.

45. The exhibition received visitors from areas of higher than normal levels of violence (for example Garvaghy Road Residents' Association), and attracted 1,500 members of community groups (5 per cent of the total visitor figure of 22,500). The activities and community-based projects involved 7,000 members of community groups.

46. The Northern Ireland Citizenship Curriculum pilot programme and the Ulster Folk and Transport Museum 'Education for Mutual Understanding' experience led to the MAGNI Citizenship project.

47. G. Reid, 'Defining the Nation: Memory, Identity and Tradition in Ireland's National Museums', *Museum Ireland*, vol. 13, 2003, pp. 22–31.

48. *Cork Examiner*, 16 April 1885.

49. The local authority museums do not fall within the scope of this book.

50.   *Cork Art Galleries* (Cork: City of Cork Vocational Education Committee, 1954), pp. 11–19; S.B. Kennedy, *Irish Art and Modernism 1880–1950* (Belfast: Queen's University, Institute of Irish Studies, 1991), pp. 84–5.

51.   At least fifty scholarships per year were provided up to the mid-1940s. V. Ryan, 'The Crawford Municipal Gallery, Cork', *Irish Arts Review*, vol. 8, 1991–92, pp. 181–4.

52.   P. Murray, 'The Visual Arts in Ireland', in N. Buttimer, C. Rynne and H. Guerin (eds), *The Heritage of Ireland* (Cork: The Collins Press, 2000), pp. 233–59.

53.   P. Murray, *The Crawford Municipal Gallery of Art: Illustrated Summary Catalogue* (Cork: Cork VEC, 1992).

54.   Previous headmasters of the School of Art were also directors of the gallery, including W. Mulligan (1901–18); Hugh Charde (1918–39); Soirle MacCana (1939–68); and Diarmuid O'Donovan (1968–84). Peter Murray was appointed curator in 1984.

55.   P. Murray, *Irish Art 1770–1995: History and Society from the Collection of the Crawford Municipal Art Gallery* (Cork: Crawford Municipal Art Gallery, 1995).

56.   J. Campbell, *Onlookers in France: Irish Realist and Impressionist Painters* (Cork: Crawford Municipal Art Gallery, 1993).

57.   Chester Beatty was born in New York of Ulster-Scots, English and Irish descent: J. McGuire and J. Quinn (eds), *Dictionary of Irish Biography* (Cambridge: Cambridge University Press, 2009), vol. 1, pp. 390–2. He employed a librarian from 1919, who worked on his collection until the official opening of the library. He developed mining enterprises in the United States, Central America, Europe, Africa and Asia, his wealth enabling him to become a major figure. C. Horton, *Alfred Chester Beatty: From Miner to Bibliophile* (Dublin: Townhouse, 2003).

58.   Chester Beatty left London for Dublin in 1950 when he was aged seventy-five, becoming the first honorary citizen of Ireland in 1957 and the only private citizen to be accorded a state funeral. M. Ryan, et al., *The Chester Beatty Library* (London: Scala, 2001). Only 5,000 visited the library in Shrewsbury Road each year. P. Donlon, 'Purring with Pleasure: The New Chester Beatty Library', *Irish Arts Review*, vol. 17, 2001, pp. 28–33.

59.   The Clock Tower Building in the garden of Dublin Castle was constructed *c.*1752, serving as military and revenue offices, and remodelled in the early nineteenth century by the eminent architect Francis Johnson. The older part of the building houses the temporary exhibition gallery, reference library, offices and services, with the newer block containing exhibition galleries, public services and a roof garden. The library is situated on the site of the Dubh Linn ('Black Pool'), which gave the city of Dublin its name.

60.   The library has twenty-five members of staff, twelve employed for security purposes.

61.   The education mission is to 'develop an education programme that encompasses cultural, religious, historical and aesthetic aspects of the collection to an Irish and international audience as well as highlighting the significance of Sir Alfred Chester Beatty's gift to the nation'. J. Siung, 'Workshop 4: Touring Exhibitions and Outreach Residencies', in *Proceedings of the National Gallery of Ireland Museum Education Symposium*, 2000, pp. 57–9.

62.   M. Ryan, 'Divine Interventions', *Irish Arts Review* (special edition), 2004, pp. 42–7; J. Siung, 'Setting Up an Education Service in the Chester Beatty Library', *Museum Ireland*, vol. 11, 2001, pp. 30–1.

63.   Funded by the Heritage Council, Gulbenkian and Paul Hamlyn Foundations, in partnership with the National Gallery, the National Museum, Chester Beatty Library, Dublin City Gallery, The Hugh Lane and Dublinia. Charles Duggan managed the project and edited *I Have a Museum* (Dublin: Dublin Civic Trust, 2001).

64.   M. Ryan, 'Displaying Sacred Manuscripts: The Experience of the Chester Beatty Library', in *Cathedral Workshops on Religious Arts and Crafts Proceedings* (Rome: Pontifical Commission for the Cultural Heritage of the Church, 2003), pp. 317–21.

65. There are 2,062 items on the museum's register: V. Teehan, 'Big Brother and Country Cousins: Relations between Regional and National Museums, A Response', *Museum Ireland*, vol. 14, 2004, pp. 107–9. The collection was acquired according to the quality of design, craftsmanship and artistic merit. It includes a variety of material ranging from the decorative arts to Irish archaeological and medieval antiquities, comprising jewellery, porcelain, sculpture, reliquaries, paintings, table silver and glass.

66. This was effected through Professor Patrick Doran of the National Institute of Higher Education (now University of Limerick) and Edward Walsh, the institute's president.

67. A public–private partnership involving the University of Limerick, Shannon Development, Limerick Corporation, the Department of Arts, Heritage, Gaeltacht and the Islands and local businesses secured the buildings.

68. The Old Custom House is an eighteenth-century Palladian-style building designed by the Franco-Italian architect Davis Ducart in 1765. J. Hunt, et al. (eds) *The Hunt Museum: Essential Guide* (London: Scala, 2002). Hunt directors: Mairead Dunlevy (on secondment from the National Museum); John Hunt (acting director); Ciaran MacGonigal; Philip McNamara (acting director); Virginia Teehan; Dr Hugh Maguire (2009).

69. M. Bourke, 'John Hunt (1957–2004): An Appreciation', *Museum Ireland*, vol. 14, pp. 110–11.

70. John Hunt jnr. organized several rooms without labels to encourage visitors to look closely and respond to each object itself on the basis that early museums had no labels.

71. N. Hickey, 'Discovery as a Vehicle for Learning', in *Proceedings of the National Gallery of Ireland Museum Education Symposium*, 2003, pp. 64–7.

72. N. Hickey, *Reading 20th Century Irish Art: Resource Pack* (Limerick: Hunt Museum, 2004); R. Mulhern (ed.), *Shades of Light, Evocations of Summer: Teacher's Resource Pack* (Limerick: Hunt Museum, 2005).

73. Quote from H. Lane, 'Introduction', in *Catalogue of the Exhibition of Works by Irish Painters, Art Gallery of the Corporation of London* (London: Art Gallery of the Corporation of London, 1904).

74. *Le Figaro*, 20 March 1908; T. MacGreevy, 'Fifty Years of Irish Painting 1900–1950', *Capuchin Annual*, vol. 19, 1949, p. 499.

75. H. Lane, *Catalogue of Pictures Presented to the City of Dublin to Form the Nucleus of a Gallery of Modern Art* (Dublin: RHA, 1904); J. O' Donnell, 'Hugh Lane's Vision', in B. Dawson (ed.), *Hugh Lane: Founder of a Gallery of Modern Art for Ireland* (Dublin and London: Scala, 2008), pp. 49–57.

76. A. Gregory, *Case for the Return of Sir Hugh Lane's Pictures to Dublin* (Dublin, 1926); T. Bodkin, *Hugh Lane and His Pictures* (Dublin: Arts Council, 1956).

77. Sarah Purser suggested Charlemont House in Parnell Square to Taoiseach William T. Cosgrave: S. O'Reilly, 'Charlemont House: A Critical History', in E. Mayes and P. Murphy (eds), *Images and Insights: Hugh Lane Municipal Gallery of Modern Art* (Dublin: Hugh Lane Municipal Gallery of Modern Art, 1993), pp. 43–54; N. Gordon Bowe, 'Art and the Public: The Friends of the National Collections of Ireland', in H. Clarke and A. O'Flanagan (eds), *75 Years of Giving: The Friends of the National Collections of Ireland* (Dublin: Friends of the National Collections of Ireland, 1999), pp. 11–30.

78. The 1993 agreement enables thirty-five Lane pictures to remain in Dublin for twelve years: D. Walker, 'Dublin's Hidden Treasure', *Irish Arts Review*, vol. 4, no. 3, 1987, pp. 28–36; B. Fallon, 'Reflecting on Ireland in the 1950s', in D. Keogh, F. O'Shea and C. Quinlan (eds), *Ireland: The Lost Decades in the 1950s* (Cork: Mercier Press, 2004), pp. 31–47.

79. *A Festival of Young People's Art: Works of Art by Pupils from Primary and Post-Primary Schools in the Republic of Ireland and Northern Ireland* (Dublin: Department of Education, 1993); D. O'Connell, *Picture This! Looking at Art in the Hugh Lane Municipal Gallery of Modern Art* (Dublin: Hugh Lane Municipal Gallery of Modern Art, 1997), accompanied by a Graflinks Production video.

80. Francis Bacon lived at his studio, 7 Reece Mews, South Kensington, London, from 1961 to 1992. On his death, John Edwards presented the Bacon Studio to Dublin on the proviso that it would be reconstructed *in situ* and placed on permanent display: B. Dawson (ed.), *Francis Bacon: A Terrible Beauty* (Gottingen: Steidl, 2009); J. O'Donnell, *Kids Guide to Francis Bacon's Studio* (Dublin: Hugh Lane Gallery, 2001). Curators, Hugh Lane: Ellen Duncan, Patrick O'Connor, James White, Eithne Waldron.

81. Announced in the Dáil, 17 November 1989. Opened by Taoiseach Charles J. Haughey in 1991: Dáil Debates: The Taoiseach to Deputy J. Bruton, vol. 405, 19 February 1991. Originally to be in the Docklands Stack 'B' Financial Centre: J. Hutchinson, 'From the Edge to the Centre', in J. Hutchinson, *Inheritance and Transformation: The Irish Museum of Modern Art* (Dublin: IMMA, 1991), pp. 7–11.

82. *Rosc* is an old Irish word meaning 'the poetry of vision'. Six exhibitions were held between 1967 and 1988, initially the idea of the architect Michael Scott, helped by James Johnson Sweeney, Dorothy Walker, Cecil King and Anne Crookshank, latterly Patrick Murphy and Gordon Lambert. Moore from B. McCann, '"A Poetry of Vision": The Rosc Exhibitions', *Irish Arts Review*, vol. 18, 2002, pp. 124–32.

83. The hospital was built on a 60-acre site granted by Charles II at the instigation of James Butler, 1st Duke of Ormonde. It was erected on the ruins of a medieval hospital and monastery of the Knights of Saint John of Jerusalem (Knights Hospitallers) founded by Strongbow in 1174, replacing the seventh-century early Christian settlement of Cill Maighneann, from which Kilmainham derives its name. In 1922, it was formally handed over to the Irish Free State army. Plans to turn it into the seat of the Dáil and Senate were revoked and for twenty years it was the headquarters of the Garda Síochána, the Irish police force. The process of change came about when it was restored and opened in 1985 as the National Centre for Culture and the Arts.

84. Designed in 1684 and used for this purpose for 250 years. E. McParland, 'The Royal Hospital, Kilmainham, Co. Dublin', *Country Life*, 9 and 16 May 1985; V. Igoe and F. Dwyer, 'Early Views of the Royal Hospital, Kilmainham', *Irish Arts Review*, vol. 5, 1988, pp. 78–88; J. Olley, 'Sustaining the Narrative at Kilmainham', *Irish Arts Review*, vol. 8, 1991–2, pp. 65–72.

85. C. Marshall, '"A Quiet National Treasure": Gordon Lambert and the Making of a Collection', *Irish Arts Review*, vol. 15, 1999, pp. 71–9.

86. Donated to mark the incorporation of Cartón y Papel de México with the Dublin-based Smurfit Group.

87. D. McGonagle, 'The Necessary Museum', *Irish Arts Review*, vol. 8, 1992, pp. 61–4.

88. Personal communication. Helen O'Donoghue, senior curator, Education and Community Department.

89. C. Marshall, 'Sustaining and Raiding the Larder: The Development of a Collection at IMMA in its First Thirteen Years', *Museum Ireland*, vol. 14, 2004, pp. 11–16.

90. M. Herrero, *Irish Intellectuals and Aesthetics: The Making of a Modern Art Collection* (Dublin: Irish Academic Press, 2006), pp. 103–41.

91. Anderson, *A Common Wealth*, p. 71.

92. H. O'Donoghue and A. Davoren (eds), *A Space to Grow: New Approaches to Working with Children, Primary School Teachers and Contemporary Art in the Context of a Museum* (Dublin: IMMA, 1999).

93. The Touchstone Centre, concerned with developing the imagination of children and adults, held workshops with primary teachers, artists and staff from IMMA, the Ark and the Abbey Theatre.

94. R. Lynch, M. Maguire, H. O'Donoghue, 'Evaluation and Review: IMMA In-Career Development Courses 2002' (unpublished, IMMA); M. Maguire, 'Review of the Primary

School Programme: Classroom-Based Project 2001/2002' (unpublished, IMMA).

95. A. McArdle, *Yours and Mine: Thoughts on Collecting and Collections* (Dublin: IMMA, 2000).

96. G. Stoeger and A. Stannett (eds), *Museums, Key Workers and Lifelong Learning: Shared Practice in Five Countries* (Dublin: IMMA, 2001).

97. *Intersections: Testing a World View*, an exhibition reviewing education and community exhibitions 1991–6. Education exhibitions listed in *Irish Museum of Modern Art: Celebrating a Decade* (Dublin: IMMA, 2001), pp. 91–2.

98. Evaluations dating 1992–9 and internal reports 1994–9 available in-house.

99. H. O'Donoghue, ' ... *and start to wear purple*' (Dublin: IMMA, 1999). Age and Opportunity encourages older people to use skills to exchange ideas and confront issues that concern them.

100. The Socrates project was undertaken with: V&A; University of Surrey Educational Studies School; Swedish Museum of Architecture; Forum d'Art Contemporain, Luxembourg; Buro fur Kulturvermittlung, Vienna; Museu Municipal de Vila Franca de Xira, Portugal.

Chapter 12

1. P.F. Wallace in Wallace and Ó Floinn (eds), *Treasures of the National Museum of Ireland*, p. 12.

2. Both quotations are taken from James Dukes' interview with John Walsh, who served as private secretary to the ministers of education, General Richard Mulcahy, Jack Lynch and Patrick Hillary; see J. Walsh, *The Politics of Expansion: The Transformation of Educational Policy in the Republic of Ireland, 1957–72*. (Manchester: Manchester University Press, 2009) pp. 1–6, 8–27.

3. The total visitor numbers were 425,884 for the year as listed in the director's report for 1900.

4. J. Joyce, *Ulysses* (London: Penguin, 2000), p. 183.

5. Of all the reproductions manufactured, the most impressive were the plaster of Paris casts of the high crosses, copies of which were exhibited in England, America and Australia. They were originally displayed in the Centre Court of the National Museum, Kildare Street, before being moved to the entrance hall Rotunda, and removed to storage in the 1970s. They were exhibited in the Museum of Decorative Arts and History, Collins Barracks in 2007 and 2010.

6. *Report of the Board of Visitors of the Science and Art Museum for 1901*, p. 3, NMIA. The RSAI's collection of historic Irish material was transferred to the museum in 1901.

7. *Report of the Board of Visitors of the National Museum of Science and Art for 1915–1916*, NMIA.

8. *Report of the Board of Visitors of the Science and Art Museum for 1904–1905*, NMIA.

9. *Freeman's Journal*, 20 July 1898.

10. *Report of the Board of Visitors of the Science and Art Museum for 1904–1905*, NMIA.

11. *Freeman's Journal*, 31 January 1903; G.T. Plunkett, *Museum of Science and Art, Director's Report for 1903–1904* (Dublin: NMIA, 1904). Circulation cases were ordered from R. Strahan and Co. on 4 January 1905.

12. In 1876 Cole said that in twenty years the museum had circulated 26,907 art objects and 23,911 pictures among art schools, the exhibits seen by six million people. 'The South Kensington Museum', *Chambers Journal,* 31 October 1873, p. 629; Burton, *Vision and Accident: The Story of the Victoria and Albert Museum*, p. 104.

13. G. Lewis, *For Instruction and Recreation: A Centenary History of the Museums Association* (London: Museums Association, 1989), p. 5.

14. J. Chard, 'On Circulating Museum Cabinets for Schools and Other Educational Purposes', *Report of the Proceedings of the First Museums Association Meeting* (Liverpool, 1890), pp. 54–63; Lewis, *For Instruction and Recreation: A Centenary History of the Museums Association*, p. 5.

15. Application forms for loans were applied at first on South Kensington Museum forms, which stated that the material had to be approved before dispatch (signed by the Dublin Museum of Science and Art), countersigned by the school on receipt of the cases (National Museum letter file 3, part 2, NMIA, 1905). Forms for loans from the Dublin Museum were later issued by the Department of Agriculture and Technical Instruction for Ireland, as the 'Dublin Museum, Circulation Division', listing cases: i) botany; ii) zoology; iii) metals and minerals; iv) industrial crafts; v) artistic crafts; vi) archaeology, with each type of case (up to fifty-six cases) listed under the appropriate section (National Museum letter file 3, part 2, NMIA, 1905).

16. By 1904–5 the list of cases was encyclopaedic. Each case was available in up to two to six duplicates, and some venues were lent several cases.

17. By the year 1904–5, the list of cases was becoming encyclopaedic. Each case was provided in editions of 4–6 for maximum distribution, some venues were lent numbers of cases. It was quite a project for Dudley Westropp to manage. G.T. Plunkett, *Museum of Science and Art, Director's Report for 1904–05*, NMIA.

18. There were 123 cases in 1904; 114 cases in 1905; 161 cases in 1906; 214 in 1907. Dudley Westropp, assistant keeper in the Art Division, managed the service. G.T. Plunkett, *Museum of Science and Art, Director's Report for 1904–1905*, NMIA.

19. Correspondence from S. Wood, senior keeper, Science Division, Board of Education, V&A, South Kensington, to the Dublin Museum of Science and Art, dated 11 May 1905. Letter file 3, part 2, 1905, NMIA.

20. In 1910–11, 326 cases, including the duplicates, were issued 472 times. In 1913–14, 333 cases were issued 601 times. In 1914–15, 339 cases were issued 667 times. Count G.N. Plunkett, *National Museum of Science and Art, Director's Report for 1914–1915*, NMIA.

21. There is no mention of the Circulation Division in the 1915–17 reports. In 1917–18, twenty-three cases were issued to Kingstown Technical School, thirty to Waterford, several to the Metropolitan School of Art, all remaining at the venues. The acting director's report shows eight cases issued in 1919 and three in 1920, twenty in 1921, five in 1922. 'The circulation collection has not been added to nor have any issue of cases been made to schools during the war.' R. Scharff, *National Museum of Science and Art Acting-Director's Report for 1918–1919*, NMIA. It is possible cases were not returned and some went to education centres in Trim and Castlebar.

22. *Report of the Board of Visitors of the National Museum of Science and Art for 1926–1927*, NMIA; *Report of the Board of Visitors of the National Museum of Science and Art for 1930–1931*, NMIA.

23. *Report of the Board of Visitors of the Science and Art Museum for 1900–1901*, p. 3, NMIA.

24. George Noble Plunkett, count in the papal nobility (1851–1948), art historian and Irish republican, was born in Dublin, attended school at Nice and in Dublin, followed by Clongowes Wood and TCD. Entered politics in 1900 before his appointment as director of the Museum of Science and Art, 1907.

25. Editorial article, 'The Purpose and Policy of National Museums', *The Burlington Magazine*, vol. 9, no. 37, April 1906. Editors: Charles Holmes and Robert Dell (January 1904–October 1906).

26. Lecture tours continued until the lecture theatre was taken over by the OPW, *c.*1915. O'Riordan, *The Natural History Museum*, p. 37; *Handbook to the City of Dublin and the Surrounding District* (Dublin: University Press, 1908), pp. 317, 355–60.

27. Count G.N. Plunkett, *National Museum of Science and Art, Director's Report for 1908*, p. 1, NMIA.

28. H.B. White, 'History of the Science and Art Institutions, Dublin', *Bulletin of the National Museum of Science and Art, Dublin*, 1911, p. 34.

29. *Irish Times*, 13 January 1912.

30. Count G.N. Plunkett, *National Museum of Science and Art, Director's Report for 1909–1910*, p. 1, NMIA.

31. Plunkett acted as vice-president of the International Art Congress at the London meeting. Count Plunkett, *National Museum of Science and Art, Director's Report for 1908*, p. 2, NMIA.

32. The date of the change to the entrance is unclear. It may have been modified by Thomas Drew (see Casey, *Buildings of Ireland*, p. 561) or by the Deanes. By March 1911, 676 students used the Students Room. Between 1911 and 1918, over 2,000 students used it each year. In 1918–19, 3,310 students used it; 5,071 in 1919–20; and 5,089 in 1920–1. The annex was closed in 1922 and soon the practice of allowing students use of the collections and library was discontinued, with a short revival in the 1960s. O'Riordan, *Natural History Museum*, p. 37.

33. Department of Agriculture and Technical Instruction, File 460–12, Museum Committee Meetings, 27 October 1910, 1 November 1910, NAI. Four volumes of the *Museum Bulletin* had appeared by 1914, when the series ceased due to the First World War.

34. Report of the Board of Visitors of the *National Museum of Science and Art for 1910–1911*. NMIA.

35. Department of Agriculture and Technical Instruction, File G 3721–13, 7 October 1910, NAI.

36. *Report of the Board of Visitors of the National Museum of Science and Art for 1910–1911*, NMIA. The Department of Agriculture and Technical Instruction gave permission for Knowles to study cryptogamic botany under Lorraine Smith at the British Museum. A commentary on the role of women in the early century was the board's opinion that Miss Knowles' salary should be raised due to the fact that 'the responsibility of her position and the character of her work have not, so far, received proper recognition, as pointed out in previous Reports'. A temporary assistant in 1902, and a non-pensionable assistant in 1907, she took charge of the botanical collections; as a specialist in phanerogams and lichens, producing *The Lichens of Ireland* (1929) detailing 800 species. She was granted work extension until her death in 1933.

37. Count G.N. Plunkett, *National Museum of Science and Art, Director's Report for 1914–1915*, p. 3, NMIA.

38. Plunkett's son, Joseph Mary Plunkett, was executed for his part in the 1916 Rising.

39. *Report of the Board of Visitors of the National Museum of Science and Art for 1915–1916*, NMIA.

40. R.F. Scharff, *National Museum of Science and Art, Acting-Director's Report for 1915–1916*, NMIA.

41. *Report of the Board of Visitors of the National Museum of Science and Art for 1916–1917*, NMIA.

42. R.F. Scharff, *National Museum of Science and Art, Acting-Director's Report for 1916–1917*, NMIA.

43. J. Augusteijn, 'The Importance of Being Irish: Ideas and the Volunteers in Mayo and Tipperary', in D. Fitzpatrick (ed.), *Revolution? Ireland 1917–1923* (Dublin: TCD, 1990), pp. 25–42.

44. Most academicians did not react to his expulsion, but nationalist members did so and campaigned to restore his position. The authority of the RIA was challenged when a group of members led by UCD professors sought to found a rival 'National Academy of Ireland', holding a foundation meeting in March 1922. When MacNeill was reinstated at the RIA, joined by Robert Macalister (1922), he formed a committee overseeing the academy's antiquities collections. Nothing more was heard of the 'National Academy'. T. Bourke, 'Nationalism and the Royal Irish Academy', *Studies*, vol. 75, 1986, pp. 196–208.

45. Scharff, *National Museum of Science and Art, Acting-Director's Report for 1916–1917*, NMIA.

46. Professor Henry Browne of UCD helped the National Museum curatorially in the acquisition of classical material.

47. Scharff, *National Museum of Science and Art, Acting-Director's Report for 1915–1916*, NMIA. A total of 2,000 visitors viewed the wartime arms exhibition.

48. D. Outram, 'Heavenly Bodies and Logical Minds', *Graph*, no. 4, 1988, pp. 9–11.

49. R.F. Scharff, *National Museum of Science and Art, Acting-Director's Report for 1919–1920*, NMIA.

50. R.F. Scharff, *National Museum of Science and Art, Acting-Director's Report for 1920–1921*, NMIA.

51. O'Riordan, *Natural History Museum*, p. 61. The title changed about 1921 with Eoin MacNeill encouraging the museum to assert its national status.

52. The RDS agreed to accept a grant for Leinster House and move to its Ballsbridge site, acquired in 1880: *PRDS*, 13 November 1924.

53. *Freeman's Journal*, 24 May 1923. The Dáil took over nine curatorial offices, the Watercolour Room, Bridge Room, Curved Geological Gallery, Annex and Art and Industrial exhibition galleries in Kildare Street; Seanad Debates: Mrs Stopford Green, vol. 3, 4 June 1924.

54. Ministers and Secretaries Act 1924, no. 16.

55. *Irish Times*, 8 January 1925; *Second Report of the AGM of the Friends of the National Collections of Ireland*, NIVAL (NCAD) 1926. Figures for April 1925–March 1926.

56. Lithberg, et al., *Report of the Committee of Enquiry into the Working of the National Museum* (Dublin: Department of Education, 1927).

57. The Bill, passed in 1930, ensured the protection of national monuments under law and introduced fines for anyone who damaged them. The National Monuments Advisory Council was set up and discoveries of a find or a national monument had by law to be reported to the Gárda Síochána or keeper of Irish antiquities at the National Museum.

58. *Committee of Enquiry Report*, 1927, ix.

59. Beirne, 'Supplement – Irish Entomology: The First Hundred Years', in *Irish Naturalists' Journal*, pp. 3–40.

60. J.J. Buckley, *National Museum of Ireland Acting-Director's Report for 1927–1928*, NMIA. The issue would resurface at the museum in 1981.

61. The minister's memo was circulated at a government meeting on 4 June 1928, approved on 3 July 1928: Department of Finance file S 2/28/29. NIA. Recommendations: a redefinition of the purpose of the museum; the removal of the cast collections; the transfer of the museum's engravings and watercolours to the National Gallery and, in exchange, 'the Gallery transfer its collection of topographical prints and maps to the Museum'; B.P. Kennedy, *Dreams and Responsibilities: The State of the Arts in Independent Ireland* (Dublin: Arts Council, 1990), pp. 20–2.

62. Dáil Debates: Deputy Earnán Altún, vol. 29, 15 May 1929, and vol. 32, 13 November 1929; Deputy Seoirse de Bhulbh, vol. 30, 10 June 1929; Deputy Bryan Cooper, vol. 32, 30 October 1929.

63. *Report of the Board of Visitors of the National Museum of Science and Art for 1926–1927*, NMIA.

64. An extension of the loan is noted in the director's report for 1936 and also *National Museum of Ireland Report for 1937–1938*, NMIA.

65. Seanad Debates: Mr. Horgan, vol. 68, 11 June 1970.

66. The movement of some of the cases is listed in a Circulation Division logbook, File A1/156/2002, NMIA. The return of 303 cases from Bolton Street to the National Museum in two lots took place on 20 September and 15 October 2002. There are currently 312 cases in the museum store. See also File A1/03/043, NMIA.

67. Miers, *Report on the Public Museums of the British Isles*, pp. 212–13. 'The National Museum of Ireland in Dublin is a fine building containing collections illustrating every

side of Irish national life. The Irish antiquities comprise relics of the Stone and Bronze Age, which include the well-known series of gold ornaments of early Christian times, such as the Tara Brooch, Ardagh Chalice, Cross of Cong, St Patrick's Bell and Shrine. Irish industries (porcelain, glass, silver, furniture etc) are well represented, well displayed and labelled, and there are also oriental collections. In the Natural History division the collection of Irish birds, fossil Irish elks, and the Irish minerals are notable. There are also store collections which are not usually accessible.'

68. The museum participated in the *Centenary of Progress Exhibition* at the Art Institute of Chicago, with the RIA, RSAI, County Louth Archaeological Society, the Irish Folklore Society and the Monument Service of the OPW. *National Museum of Ireland Acting Director's Report for 1932–1933*, NMIA.

69. C.P. Curran, 'Archaeology', in B. Hobson (ed.), *Saorstát Éireann: Ireland Free State Official Handbook* (Dublin: Talbot Press, 1932), pp. 212–32.

70. Crooke, *Politics, Archaeology and the Creation of the National Museum of Ireland*, p. 154–5.

71. The gift of 260 objects of Far Eastern art was donated between 1932 and 1938. According to Department of Education files, it was gifted 'to the State for permanent display' at the museum. Albert Maurice Bender (1866–1941), son of Rabbi Philip Bender, was born in Dublin, emigrated to America and became a wealthy insurance broker in San Francisco, was a patron of artists and a trustee of Mills College, Stanford University. See: Files A1/108/009–012, marked Bender Collection, in NMIA. The Bender Collection was re-displayed at the National Museum, Collins Barracks, in 2008. A. Whitty, *A Dubliner's Collection of Asian Art: The Albert Bender Exhibition* (Dublin: NMI, 2008).

72. A. Mahr, *Report of the Director of the National Museum of Ireland for 1932–1933*, NMIA.

73. *Organised Visits to Public Institutions in Dublin* (S. Ó Neill, Rúnaí, Department of Education, February 1935). The official circular was entitled: 'Visits of School Children to the Botanic Gardens, National Museum, National Gallery and Municipal Gallery of Modern Art', NGIA.

74. *Report of the Director of the National Museum of Ireland for 1937–1938*, NMIA.

75. *Report of the Director of the National Museum of Ireland for 1932–1933*, NMIA; O'Riordan, *Natural History Museum*, p. 66.

76. *Report of the Director of the National Museum of Ireland for 1934–1935*, NMIA.

77. P.F. Wallace, 'Adolf Mahr and the Making of Sean P. Ó Riordáin', in H. Roche, et al. (eds), *From Megaliths to Metal: Essays in Honour of George Eogan* (Oxford: Oxbow Books, 2004), pp. 254–63; M. Herity and G. Eoghan, *Ireland in Prehistory* (London: Routledge Kegan Paul, 1977), pp. 13–15; *Minutes of Meeting in Department of Education, 23 March 1939*, Irish Military Archives, G2/0130; Dáil Debates: Minister for Education: Deputy Derrig to Deputy Dillon, vol. 98, 6 December 1945.

78. D. Keogh, *Jews in Twentieth-Century Ireland* (Cork: Cork University Press, 1998), p. 150; G. Mullins, *Dublin Nazi No. 1: The Life of Adolf Mahr* (Dublin: Liberties Press, 2009).

79. Cabinet Minutes, 5 November 1945, Item 6, G.C. 5/45. Copy on D.T S6631B, NAI; D. O'Donoghue, 'State within a State: The Nazis in Neutral Ireland', *History Ireland*, vol. 6, November/December 2006, pp. 35–9.

80. Issues concerning national collections were dealt with by the 1938 'war' cabinet meeting under Frank Aiken.

81. *Report of the Board of Visitors of the National Museum of Science and Art for 1944–45*, NMIA. According to Joe Murray, an attendant at the museum who joined the army on 8 September 1938, some of the Art and Industry collections, such as glass, silver and less valuable antiquities, were placed in 4-foot wide crates, each case numbered, accompanied by a list of contents, stored in the crypt in Kildare Street.

82. The young Etienne Rynne, later professor of archaeology at UCG, recollected visiting the

museum during the war and seeing what he thought were the treasures on display, whereas they were in fact replicas.

83. Basil Clancy, *Irish Art Handbook* (Dublin: Cahill & Company, 1993). The return of the collections was noted: Dáil Debates: General Debate, vol. 110, 25 February 1948.

84. Ibid.

85. S. Ó Riordáin, 'Museums', in *Cork Public Museum Souvenir Guide to the First Exhibition* (Cork: Cork Public Museum, 1945).

86. *Report of the Board of Visitors of the National Museum of Science and Art for 1947–48*, NMIA.

87. T. Bodkin, *Report on the Arts in Ireland* (Dublin: Stationery Office, 1949), pp. 58–9. Thomas Bodkin was professor of fine arts and director of the Barber Institute of Fine Arts, University of Birmingham, and a member of the 1927 Committee of Enquiry.

88. M. Quane, 'Report on the National Museum of Ireland for the Department of Education' (unpublished, 1947).

89. Bodkin, *Report on the Arts in Ireland*, pp. 11–17.

90. The declining visitor numbers was also evident at the National Gallery, where attendance in 1950 was 40,664. T. MacGreevy, *National Gallery of Ireland Director's Report for 1950*, NGIA.

91. Dáil Debates: General Debate, vol. 125, 24 April 1951.

92. A.T. Lucas, 'The National Museum of Ireland', *Éire: Bulletin of the Department of Foreign Affairs*, vol. 198, 1969, pp. 6–10. Quoted in A.T. Lucas, 'The National Museum: Its Place in the Cultural Life of the Nation', *Oideas: Iris na Roinne Oideachais*, vol. 1, 1968, p. 1.

93. Description by J. Meehan and D.A. Webb (eds), *A View of Ireland: Twelve Essays on Different Aspects of Irish Life and the Irish Countryside* (Dublin: British Association for the Advancement of Science, 1957), p. 250.

94. *Report of the Director of the National Museum of Ireland for 1959–1960*, NMIA. The following year, 1960–1, 335 guided tours were provided for the public and 21,500 children.

95. International Council of Museums, *Museums and Teachers* (Paris: ICOM, 1956). The museum also encouraged third-level students; see UCD Summer School Programme in MacGreevy correspondence file 1955, NGIA.

96. Text for the filmstrip was compiled by the director, with photographs supplied by the museum. Part one (*Prehistoric Material*) was published by the National Film Institute of Ireland in 1960. Dáil Debates: General Debate, vol. 152, 6 July 1955.

97. G. FitzGerald, 'Mr. Whitaker and Industry', *Studies*, vol. 48, 1959, pp. 138–50; R. Burke Savage, 'Seán F. Lemass TD', *Studies*, vol. 6, 1966, pp. 337–8.

98. Seanad Debates: Professor Stanford, vol. 50, 10 December 1958; Dáil Debates: Deputy O'Malley, vol. 202, 15 May 1963.

99. Between 1960 and 1982 the museum conducted excavations, first under Breandán Ó Ríordáin and later under Patrick Wallace, at High Street, Christchurch Place and Winetavern Street, on the site of the Dublin Civic Offices at Wood Quay. P.F. Wallace, *The Viking Age Buildings of Dublin* (Dublin: Medieval Dublin Excavations 1962–81, 1992), Series A, no. 1; quote by J. Raftery, 'Drainage and the Past', *Oibre*, no. 4, 1966, p. 13.

100. Dáil Debates: General Debate, vol. 195, 6 June 1962.

101. A. Le Harivel, *National Gallery of Ireland, Illustrated Summary Catalogue of Drawings, Watercolours and Miniatures*, pp. xxii–xxiv, pp. 823–6. About 346 drawings, together with watercolours and miniatures, a total of 377 works, were transferred between the 1960s and 1980s. Books were transferred to the National Library. See: NAI, Box: S.5392.

102. *National Gallery of Ireland Director's Report for 1974*, NGIA. Six classes in 1974, and seven in 1975.

103. *Report of the Board of Visitors of the National Museum of Science and Art for 1964–65*, NMIA. Seven isolated and mostly unsuitable buildings (none under the control of the

museum) held portions of the collection: geology and folk life: Royal Hospital, Kilmainham; coaches and canoes: Dublin Castle; casts, etc: the Four Courts; zoology spirit stores: Industry and Commerce Building, Kildare Street; zoology dry stores: Institute of Advanced Studies, OPW, Schoolhouse Lane; and coaches in Kilkenny Barracks.

104. S. Leslie, 'Our National Gallery: A Personal History', *Irish Tatler & Sketch*, 1969, December, p. 6–7.

105. *Report on Conditions in the National Museum of Ireland compiled by the Museum Branch of the Institute of Professional Civil Servants* (Dublin: Stationery Office, 1969); Fóntas Músaem Éireann, *Museum Service for Ireland* (Dublin: Institute of Professional Civil Servants, 1973).

106. Dáil Debates: Minister for Education Deputy Faulkner, vol. 245, 9 April 1970; Dáil Debates: Deputy Dr. Byrne, vol. 247, 16 June 1970.

107. Maura Scannell and Donal Synnott of the National Botanic Gardens removed the collection.

108. J. Teahan, 'Museums for the People', *Public Affairs, Journal of the Institute of Public Administration*, vol. 5, no. 10, 1973, pp. 2–3.

109. The Bender Room was open between 1934 and 1972 (closed 1972). Bender Collection files A1/108/009-012, NMIA. There were questions about it several times. Dáil Debates: General Debate, vol. 168, 23 October 1973 and Dáil Debates: Deputy Enright asked the Taoiseach where was the Bender Memorial Room, vol. 383, 26 October 1988.

110. J.M. Richards, *Provision for the Arts* (Dublin: Arts Council and the Gulbenkian Foundation, 1976).

111. Seanad Debates: Professor Murphy and Mrs. Robinson, vol. 80, 16 April 1975.

112. Dáil Debates: Deputy Wilson to the Minister for Education, Deputy Bruton, vol. 274, 24 July 1974. Education officer, P.F. Wallace. *Report of the Board of Visitors of the National Museum of Science and Art for 1975–76*, NMIA.

113. A. MacLochlainn, et al., *Science and Art 1877–1977*; Dáil Debates: Deputy Horgan to Minister for Education, Deputy Wilson, vol. 310, 14 December 1978.

114. It opened at the Metropolitan Museum and toured to four museums: Fine Arts Museums of San Francisco, Museum of Art Carnegie Institute, Pittsburg, Boston Museum of Fine Arts, and the Philadelphia Museum of Art between October 1977 and May 1979. P. Cone (ed.), *Treasures of Early Irish Art 1500BC to 1300AD from the Collection of the National Museum of Ireland, Trinity College, Dublin, Royal Irish Academy* (New York: Metropolitan Museum, 1977).

115. T. Hoving, Foreword, and G.F. Mitchell, Preface to the exhibition catalogue, ibid., pp. viii, ix.

116. *Report of the Board of Visitors of the National Museum of Science and Art for 1977–78*, pp. 14–15, NMIA. A 1980 British Museum touring exhibition, *The Vikings*, with Irish material, was held in London, New York, Minneapolis, and Stockholm.

117. Mitchell's presidential address to the RIA: 'Planning for Irish Archaeology in the Eighties'; *Report of the Board of Visitors of the National Museum of Science and Art for 1977–78*, p. 3, NMIA

118. Dáil Debates: Deputy B. Desmond to Minister for Education Deputy Wilson, vol. 317, 13 December 1978; Dáil Debates: General Debate, vol. 268, 8 November 1973.

119. C. Benson, *The Place of the Arts in Irish Education* (Dublin: The Arts Council, 1979).

120. Education officer, Felicity Devlin. The board had drawn attention to the need for improvements at the museum. *Report of the Board of Visitors of the National Museum of Science and Art for 1980*, NMIA.

121. *Report of the Board of Visitors of the National Museum of Science and Art for 1981*, pp. 5–7, NMIA.

122. *Report of the Board of Visitors of the National Museum of Science and Art for 1979*, NMIA. The exhibition was re-titled *Treasures of Ireland 3000 BC to 1500 AD*, touring to Paris, Cologne, Berlin, Amsterdam and Copenhagen from 1982 to 1984; M. Ryan (ed.), *Treasures*

of Ireland 3000 BC to 1500 AD (Dublin: NMI, 1983). An Irish silver exhibition organized by the Smithsonian Institution Traveling Exhibition Service visited ten museums in the US from 1982 to 1984; J. Teahan, *Irish Silver from the Seventeenth to the Nineteenth Century* (Washington, DC: Smithsonian Institution, 1982). The 1980 exhibition *Gold and Silver from Ireland* opened at Maison du Roi, Brussels, followed by Frankfurt, Munich and Linz in Austria; M. Cahill and M. Ryan, *Gold aus Irland* (Frankfurt: Museum für Vor-und Frühgeschichte, 1981). The exhibitions *A Sense of Ireland* and *Pipes and Piping* were shown in London 1980.

123. In 1980, as an example of the ongoing practice of lending artefacts, material was loaned to 'Treasures of Thomond' at Limerick City Museum; *Childhood* at Castlebar, Trim and Youghal; *1798* at Nenagh, Mullingar and Wexford; *Pearse* at Castlebar, Kildare and Newbridge; *Land War* in Cork; *Markievicz* in Castlebar; *Irish Heritage* at Sherkin Island, County Cork; *Bicentennial Exhibition* in Prosperous, County Kildare; *Coopering* at the Bank of Ireland Exhibition Hall as part of the Dublin Arts Festival. *Report of the Board of Visitors of the National Museum of Science and Art for 1980*, NMIA. Other exhibitions such as one on folk life attracted 16,000 visitors, while a GAA exhibition in 1984 gained 20,000 visitors; both succeeded because they had a particular resonance for Irish visitors.

124. *Report of the Board of Visitors of the National Museum of Science and Art for 1983*, p. 5, NMIA.

125. Cultural institutions under the Taoiseach's Department included National Museum, National Gallery, Chester Beatty Library, Marsh's Library, State Paper and Record Office, and the Irish Manuscripts Commission. A ministerial commitment to establish a governing body for the museum dates from this time.

126. G.A. Meagher, 'Report on the Administration and Development of the National Museum' (unpublished, 1985), p. 46. This report also summarized the functions of the museum: (a) public exhibition of the national collections; (b) care and conservation of collections in storage; (c) acquisition (by purchase, donation or loan) of appropriate material; (d) the investigation of discoveries of archaeological objects of interest and investigation of relevant sites; (e) the recording of collections and the provision of education and information services for the public, for research workers and for schools.

127. *Report of the Board of Visitors of the National Museum of Science and Art for 1985*, NMIA.

128. This exhibition toured the Australian cities of Melbourne, Hobart, Perth, Brisbane, Sydney and Canberra in 1988 and 1989.

129. This exhibition, in collaboration with the British Museum and National Museums of Scotland, toured to London, Dublin and Edinburgh between 1989 and 1991.

130. This exhibition was shown in Paris, Berlin, Copenhagen, 1992–3.

131. This Council of Europe international loan exhibition toured to Paris, Berlin and Copenhagen, 1992–3. Both exhibitions were mounted in association with the National Museum of Denmark and toured to Copenhagen, Bonn, Paris and Athens, 1998–9.

132. The National Lottery provided some assistance. B.P. Kennedy, 'Towards a National Cultural Policy', *Séirbhís Phóiblí*, vol. 9, no. 2, 1988, pp. 35–40.

133. The National Heritage Council, established in 1988, became a statutory body in 1995, creating the post of museums officer in 1996. *A Training Strategy for the Irish Museum Sector* (Kilkenny: Heritage Council, 2000); E. Verling, *A Policy Framework for the Irish Museum Sector* (Kilkenny: Heritage Council, 2003).

134. The complex started out as 'The Barracks', 1720, changed to the 'Royal Barracks' in the early nineteenth century and was named Collins Barracks in 1922, after Michael Collins, the first commander-in-chief of the Irish Free State. The early buildings designed by Captain Thomas Burgh (1670–1730) were refurbished by the OPW. M. Dunlevy, *Dublin Barracks: A Brief History of Collins Barracks, Dublin* (Dublin: NMI, 2002).

135. An interim board, set up by the Department of Arts, Culture and the Gaeltacht in 1994,

reviewed the museum's operation. The resulting *Report of the Interim Board of the National Museum of Ireland* was presented to the Minister for Arts, Culture and the Gaeltacht in 1995, Appendix 11 forming the Strategic Plan (prepared by Lord Cultural Resources, Planning & Management Ltd, 1994).

136. Exhibitions in the late 1990s at Kildare Street included: *Viking Age Ireland* and *Medieval Ireland (1150–1550)* in 2001, and *The Spice Islands Voyage* (temporary exhibition of a voyage by Tim Severin). Exhibitions at Collins Barracks: *Fellowship of Freedom: The United Irishmen and the Rebellion of 1798* (produced with NLI); *Peacekeepers: Forty Years of the Irish Defence Forces within the United Nations* (temporary exhibition); *Muse99*, together with temporary exhibitions at other National Museum branches. Following the death of John Teehan, in due course Mairead Dunlevy became the keeper of the decorative arts.

137. A new conservation department was set up 1997 (followed by a purpose-built conservation laboratory in 2002) under a head of conservation appointed at keeper level. Conservation had previously been undertaken in the separate divisions by technical staff under the direction of curatorial staff.

138. Dáil Debates: Deputy Carey to Deputy Síle de Valera, vol. 477, 8 April 1997. Helen Beaumont was appointed education and outreach officer in Collins Barracks. Nigel Monaghan was keeper of Natural History.

139. Education work continued at the Kildare Street and Merrion Street sites during this time, with a display entitled *Children's Art Exhibition*, 'The Natural World of Europe'. N.T. Monaghan, *Guide to the National Museum of Ireland: Natural History* (Dublin: NMI, 2005).

140. National Museum of Ireland Education and Outreach Policy 2007, NMIA.

141. UNESCO, *50 Years for Education* (Paris: UNESCO, 2006), National Museum Education and Outreach Policy.

142. Family programmes include talks, tours, art workshops, storytelling workshops and craft demonstrations.

143. What's in Store is an accessible storage facility displaying 16,000 objects from the museums reserve collections (glass, ceramics, scientific instruments, metalwork and silver, oriental collections) in a suite of glass-fronted cabinets to represent a working museum collection.

144. The students studied the collections for their artwork during a museum 'open week'.

145. Public workshops were given by contemporary artists, craftspeople and designers.

146. I. O'Doherty, 'Muse99', *ASTIR*, May 1999, pp. 16–17; *Muse99 Catalogue* (Dublin: NMI, 1999). Ninety-one students created paintings, sculptures, ceramics, embroidered wall hangings, all inspired by the collections and displayed at Collins Barracks.

147. *National Museum of Ireland Report for 2000–2002*, NMIA, p. 46; Quote by Patrick Wallace, *A Few of Our Favourite Things*, Education and Outreach Department (Dublin: NMI, 2002).

148. From the speech by the Northern Ireland writer, Brian Keenan, for the opening of show: 'Museums are traditionally mausoleum-like receptories of the past … their displays are inadvertently delivered to a specific mindset; they cater for the able, the literate and the interested. But questions of who we are, or what we are, are not solely defined by the classified clutter of the past. History is what we do now. If history has this dynamic … Here is a real hands-on approach to a two way learning experience.'

149. The fifteen adults with intellectual disabilities planned to meet weekly to work with arts facilitators, education staff and curators to explore the collections. H. Beaumont and A. Carroll, '"A Few of Our Favourite Things … "', *Museum Ireland*, no. 12, 2002, pp. 27–32.

150. Egyptology is displayed in Kildare Street. The reserve collections are displayed in What's in Store, illustrating treasures from Tibet, Japan, China, Pakistan, India, Burma, Middle East, Europe, Britain and Ireland. The recommendation to expand the context of the

museum's collections was made in the board's Interim Report 1995.

151.   *National Museum of Ireland Statement of Strategy* (Dublin, 2000).

Chapter 13

1.   R. Keaveney, Foreword, in *The Milltowns: A Family Reunion* (Dublin: NGI, 1997), p. vi.
2.   Closure of the RHA was a recommendation of W. de Abney's report (1910). M. Anglesea, *The Royal Ulster Academy of Arts* (Belfast: Royal Ulster Academy of Arts, 1981); C. Frayling, 'Nourishing the Academy', *Drawing Fire: Journal of the National Association for Fine Art Education*, vol. 1, no. 3, 1996, pp. 16–22.
3.   An official inquiry held by Lord Plymouth in 1906 proposed closing the schools.
4.   J.P. Boland, 'The Future of Irish Art', *New Ireland Review*, vol. 26, no. 1, 1906–7, pp. 295–301; Society of Dublin Painters 1920, Ulster Society of Painters 1921, Irish Exhibition of Living Art, 1943; R. Coulter, 'Hibernian Salon des Refuses', *Irish Arts Review*, vol. 20, no. 3, 2003, pp. 80–5.
5.   E. Curran, 'World War II Revived Our Art', *Irish Digest*, 1947, pp. 74–7.
6.   R. Greacen, 'Five Arts in Ireland', *Irish Digest*, November 1949, pp. 12–15.
7.   K.M.K., 'This Year's Academy: Achievement, Failure and Promise,' *National Student* (Dublin: UCD), vol. 111, May 1932, pp. 42–4.
8.   The Metropolitan School of Art was renamed the National College of Art in 1936. Following reconstitution by statute it became the National College of Art and Design (NCAD) in 1971, and a constituent of the National University of Ireland in 1996. There are sixty-one works in the NCAD collection.
9.   Matt Gallagher's donation in 1970, together with compensation from the loss of its premises, enabled recovery. P. Murphy, in *Exhibitions*, J. Hanley (ed.), *Royal Hibernian Academy: One Hundred and Seventy-Fifth Exhibition* (Dublin: RHA, 2005). In 1970 the RHA held its annual exhibition in Dublin Castle. Patrick Murphy is director of the RHA Gallery.
10.   S. McKenna, 'The Philosophy and Structure of the Proposal School', in Hanley (ed.), *Royal Hibernian Academy*, pp. 19–23. There are 280 works in the RHA collection.
11.   National Gallery of Ireland Minutes, 29 November 1900, NGIA. Henry Barron (1824–1900), wealthy landowner from Waterford. NGI Minutes, 23 January 1900, NGIA. Henry Vaughan (1809–1900) left Turner watercolours equally divided between the V&A, the British Museum, and the National Galleries of Scotland and Ireland. B. Dawson, *Turner in the National Gallery of Ireland* (Dublin: NGI, 1988).
12.   M. Bourke, 'Romantic Journey: New Research on Frederic William Burton's *The Blind Girl at the Holy Well*', *Irish Arts Review*, vol. 20, no. 4, 2003, pp. 128–33; A. Gregory, *Seventy Years 1852–1922* (New York: Macmillan, 1974), p. 140: 'At Christie's sales [Burton] resented questions as to the authenticity or value of pictures from even so gentle a rival as Henry Doyle'; A. Gregory, 'Sir Frederic Burton', *The Leader*, vol. 1, no. 15, 1900, pp. 231–3.
13.   *Loan Collection of Works by Sir Frederic William Burton RHA* (Dublin: Hely's Ltd, 1900), comprising 104 works.
14.   NGI Minutes, 21 February 1901, NGIA.
15.   Benedetti, *The Milltowns*; M. Wynne, 'The Milltowns as Patrons, Particularly Concerning the Picture-Collecting of the First Two Earls', *Apollo*, vol. 99, February 1979, pp. 104–11. The vicissitudes of the Milltown Bequest are described in gallery minutes.
16.   Thomas Newenham Deane's original 1892 plans were amended by his son Thomas Manley in *Irish Builder*, 9 April 1903.
17.   *Handbook to the City of Dublin and the Surrounding District* (Dublin: University Press, 1908), p. 317. In 1910 Mrs Joseph lent a 'Vermeer': see W. Armstrong, *National Gallery of Ireland Director's Report for 1910,* NGIA.

18. The Deed of Gift was signed on 30 June 1902: NGI Minutes, 21 July 1902, NGIA. The collection comprised over 2,000 items, including: pictures, sculptures, prints, pieces of silver, items of furniture, library, miscellaneous objects, including the Star of St Patrick, listed in correspondence from Armstrong to the Under-Secretary, Dublin Castle, 2 January 1905, NGIA.

19. The viceroy under-secretary arranged transfer following her death. Most of the collection arrived on 16 March 1914, with other material having been added since the original bequest of 1899. The Milltown silver was loaned to the National Museum, 1935, and books transferred to the National Library, 1936. NGI Minutes, 19 March 1906, NGIA.

20. *National Gallery of Ireland Director's Report for 1905,* NGIA.

21. NGI Minutes, 25 February 1914, NGIA.

22. MacGreevy, 'Fifty Years of Irish Painting 1900–1950', pp. 497–9; B. Arnold, *Orpen: Mirror to an Age* (London: Jonathan Cape, 1981), p. 49.

23. Lane held an *Exhibition of Old Masters from Irish Country Houses* at the RHA, Abbey Street in 1902–3. His 'Prefatory Notice' to the Guildhall Art Gallery, London catalogue promoted 'A gallery of Irish and modern art in Dublin'. *Catalogue of the Exhibition of Works by Irish Painters* (London: Art Gallery of the Corporation of London, 1904).

24. NGI Minutes, 1 April 1914, NGIA; NGI Minutes, 2 June 1914, NGIA. The NGI collection comprised: 923 portraits, 1,203 oils, 501 engraved portraits, 185 miniatures and drawings, 36 busts and autographs.

25. NGI Minutes, 20 January 1915, NGIA.

26. The codicil to his will, forming the basis of the dispute, was written on 3 February 1915, locked in his desk at the National Gallery and was found after his death on the suggestion of Lane's sister.

27. NGI Minutes, 18 May 1915, NGIA. Following legalities (1918), it comprised forty-two paintings with the remainder of his estate sold to provide a fund for the gallery. R. O'Byrne, *Hugh Lane's Legacy to the National Gallery of Ireland* (Dublin: NGI, 2000).

28. The decision to call on Strickland was taken on 18 May 1915 and Stephens on 21 July 1915. NGI Minutes, 5 January 1916, NGIA. Gallery closure: (1916) TCD Bodkin MS, 6961–53, TCDA.

29. J. Stephens, *The Insurrection of Dublin* (Dublin: Maunsel & Co., 1916), p. 77.

30. S. Ó Faoláin, 'The New Criticism', *The Bell*, vol. 18, no. 3, p. 133.

31. Annual reports noted attendances – 1900: 929; 1908: 1,154 (the highest figure); 1918: 284; and 1920: 585. Letter from James Stephens, Registrar, to Miss M.B. Sparrow, 2 July 1918, NGIA.

32. R.L. Douglas, *National Gallery of Ireland Director's Report for 1916*, NGIA. Douglas, a former clergyman and scholar, pursued the field of art dealing. He lied about his age to enlist, had an ex-wife, a mistress and fifteen children.

33. NGI Minutes, 2 August 1919, NGIA. Hone's Bequest: 211 oils, 336 watercolours. T. Bodkin, *Four Irish Landscape Painters (1920)* (Dublin: Irish Academic Press, 1987); J. Campbell, *Nathaniel Hone the Younger* (Dublin: NGI, 1991).

34. The under-secretary queried the collection in relation to the Government of Ireland Act 1920. The board sent a copy of NGI Statues and Act indicating it would remain in Dublin. NGI Minutes, 6 April 1921, NGIA.

35. NGI Minutes, 7 December 1921, NGIA; J. O'Grady, *The Life and Death of Sarah Purser* (Dublin: Four Courts Press, 1996), pp. 129–30.

36. NGI Minutes, 1 February 1922, NGIA; NGI Minutes, 4 October 1922, NGIA; NGI Minutes, 6 December 1922, NGIA.

37. Dáil Debates: Deputy T. Johnson, vol. 1, 16 November 1922.

38. *National Gallery of Ireland Director's Report for 1922*, NGIA.

39. NGI Minutes, 1 July 1925, NGIA.
40. The Ministers and Secretaries Act, 1924 constituted and defined the ministers and departments of state in Saorstát Éireann pursuant to the Constitution and declaring the functions and powers of the attorney-general and enabling the appointment of parliamentary secretaries and for purposes incidental thereto. Dated 21 April 1924. The Department of Education was also responsible for the Geological Survey, Metrological Services, National Museum, National Library, National Gallery and Metropolitan School of Art.
41. NGI Minutes, 5 December 1923, NGIA. O'Callaghan retained his architectural practice during directorship. NGI Minutes, 6 February 1924, NGIA.
42. The Society of the Friends of the National Collections of Ireland was founded by Purser on 14 February 1924 for Irish citizens 'who have a care for our public collections and value the prestige which they confer upon our country'. Clarke and O'Flanagan (eds), *75 Years of Giving: The Friends of the National Collections of Ireland: Works of Art Donated by the Friends of the Public Collections of Ireland*.
43. In 1924 the taoiseach appointed new board members W.B. Yeats and John Lavery.
44. NGI Minutes, 2 June 1926, NGIA.
45. *National Gallery of Ireland Director's Report for 1927*, NGIA.
46. 'The only purely museum exhibits are a few cabinets containing silver ware.' Miers, *Report on the Public Museums of the British Isles*, pp. 212–13.
47. *National Gallery of Ireland Director's Report for 1928*, NGIA.
48. S. Bhreathnach-Lynch, 'The Academy of Christian Art (1929–46): An Aspect of Catholic Cultural Life in Newly Independent Ireland', *Éire-Ireland,* autumn/winter 1996, vol. 3, nos. 3 and 4, pp. 102–16; *Irish Art Handbook* (Dublin: Cahill & Company, 1943), p. 121; B.P. Kennedy, 'Seventy-Five Years of Studies', *Studies*, winter 1990, pp. 361–73.
49. *National Gallery of Ireland Director's Report for 1929*, NGIA; E.M. Stephens (ed.), *Dublin Civic Week Official Handbook* (Dublin: Civic Week Council, Mansion House, 1929), p. 66.
50. *National Gallery of Ireland Director's Report for 1929*, NGIA; NGI Minutes, 6 June 1934, NGIA.
51. The 6th Roman Catholic World Eucharistic Congress of ecclesiastics and laymen took place in Dublin in 1932.
52. T. Bodkin, 'Modern Irish', pp. 240–1.
53. NGI Minutes, 10 December 1929, NGIA; NGI Minutes, 21 October 1931, NGIA; *NGI Director's Report for 1934*, NGIA.
54. Correspondence from the Director to the Minister for Education, 24 November 1934, NGIA.
55. Quoted in A. Kelly, 'Thomas Bodkin and the NGI', *Irish Arts Review*, vol. 8, 1991–2, pp. 171–80.
56. Dáil Debates: Deputy T. Costello, vol. 55, 4 April 1935; Dáil Debates: Minister for Education, Deputy Derrig, vol. 59, 6 December 1935.
57. *Organised Visits to Public Institutions in Dublin* (S. Ó Neill, Rúnaí, Department of Education, February 1935); see also correspondence from the Department of Education to the Registrar, 7 May 1935, NGIA.
58. NGI Minutes, 7 April 1937, NGIA: 'The room in which it is proposed to show the casts has a top light and its size will permit of the arrangement in chronological order of all the pieces of Greek sculpture from those of Greco-Roman origin.' *NGI Director's Report for 1937*, NGIA.
59. NGI Minutes, 1 December 1943, NGIA; J. White, 'The Visual Arts in Ireland', vol. 44, spring 1955, pp. 107–17.
60. Dáil Debates: Deputy Sir John Keane to Deputy Aiken, vol. 23, 13 July 1939; Dáil Debates: Deputy McMenamin to Minister for Education, Deputy Derrig, vol. 83, 28 May 1941.

61. Keogh, D., *Twentieth-Century Ireland*, (Dublin, Gill & Macmillan, 1994, revised 2005), ch.3.

62. NGI Minutes, 15 February 1939, NGIA: 'Minister of Education's authority only that under Ministers and Secretaries Act (1924) Section 9 (3). Willing to use it to authorize removal of paintings for safe keeping in times of an Emergency'. *NGI Director's Report for 1939*, NGIA; NGI Minutes, 2 October 1940, NGIA archive: 'Forty-five pictures were sent to the Bank of Ireland and 175 removed to approved positions in the Gallery cellars.' *National Gallery of Ireland Director's Report for 1940*, NGIA.

63. NGI Minutes, 4 June 1941, NGIA. Alternative accommodation suggested: Lord Granard's Castle Forbes, County Longford; Lord Dunraven's Adare Manor, County Limerick; Lord Longford's Pakenham Hall, County Westmeath. NGI Minutes, 2 July 1941, NGIA.

64. Correspondence from Furlong to the Secretary of the Department of Education, 10 April 1942, NGIA.

65. *National Gallery of Ireland Director's Report for 1942*, NGIA.

66. *Irish Art Handbook*, p. 137.

67. G. Furlong, *National Gallery of Ireland Director's Report for 1945*, NGIA.

68. During the war Thomas MacGreevy helped in the dispatch of London's paintings to Wales. Baker and Henry, *The National Gallery: Complete Illustrated Catalogue*, p. xiv.

69. The director had 1,500 works moved to a secure mansion at Whitemarsh Hall. See Tomkins, *Merchants and Masterpieces: The Story of the Metropolitan Museum of Art*.

70. T. Bodkin, *Report on the Arts in Ireland* (Dublin: Stationery Office, 1949), pp. 18–22.

71. NGI Minutes, 4 October 1944, NGIA; S. Atkinson, 'Give Your Children Art!', *Irish Digest*, 1946, pp. 48–50.

72. NGI Minutes, 5 June 1946, NGIA; *National Gallery of Ireland Director's Report for 1950*, NGIA.

73. The gallery received a third of royalties accruing from Shaw's published works (renegotiated in 1997). 'Drafting the will has been more trouble than ten plays,' said Shaw (1950). NGI Minutes, 5 April 1950, NGIA.

74. Dáil Debates: General Debate, vol. 159, 19 July 1956. See Paul Troubetzkoy's 1927 statue of Shaw, 'modelled by him from the life, when I was still respectable. I am now 88 and externally out of the question.' Shaw to George Furlong, 6 July 1944, NGIA.

75. Chester Beatty gave ninety-three French works to the National Gallery in 1950: NGI Minutes, 5 July 1950, NGIA. This was gifted in addition to 48 paintings, 253 drawings and miniatures and 6 sculptures.

76. Bodkin's report was sent to MacGreevy at the direction of the taoiseach. *National Gallery of Ireland Director's Report for 1950*, NGIA. MacGreevy alluded to the strain of a full-time post being carried out part-time, correspondence dealt with at night, and the urgent need for public lectures with slides. J.O.P. Heuston, 'Book of the Month: Irish Art Handbook', in *The Irish Rosary*, 1943, quote by Mairin Allen.

77. Sarah Purser and Sir John Purser endowed a scholarship in the history of art, with lectures given by Professor Françoise Henry at UCD from 1935, alternating between TCD and UCD thereafter.

78. Memo re the NGI submitted by direction of the Board for the President's consideration (1950), NGIA.

79. Dáil Debates: Arts Bill, 1951 – Second Stage, The Taoiseach, vol. 125, 24 April 1951. 'In 1935, with a view of drawing attention to the demand, the Board had introduced a clause into the terms of Dr. Furlong's appointment to the effect that the Director might be requested to lecture up to 15 times a year. The pressure of work was so considerable that Dr. Furlong was never asked to lecture.' MacGreevy to Secretary of Department of Education, 15 January 1952, NGIA.

80. Correspondence from the Department Secretary to MacGreevy, 9 February 1952, NGIA;

NGI Minutes, 4 June 1952, NGIA.

81. Dáil Debates: Deputy General Mulcahy, vol. 153, 16 November 1955.

82. Talks were given by: Ruth Dromgoole (lecturer at the gallery) and Donal Murphy (National College of Art). Correspondence from Donal Murphy to MacGreevy mid-1950s, NGIA, annotated by MacGreevy, enclosing 24 lectures on the history of European painting; correspondence from James White to MacGreevy mid-1950s, NGIA; NGI Minutes, 3 October 1951, NGIA.

83. Judith Monaghan, Glenageary, to MacGreevy, 3 January 1953, NGIA; Mrs. Mary Toomey, Mercer's Hospital Pharmacist, to MacGreevy, 13 January 1956, NGIA; D.J. O'Shaughnessy, to MacGreevy, 12 January 1953, NGIA.

84. MacGreevy to the Clerk of the Council, City Hall, Dublin, 26 January 1952, NGIA.

85. Joyce Padbury, Acting Secretary of UCD Summer School, to MacGreevy, 7 July 1955, NGIA; Estelle de B. Williams to MacGreevy, 4 February 1957, NGIA.

86. MacGreevy to John Hicks, Head Boy, High School, Harcourt Street, 1 March 1957, NGIA.

87. 29 January 1936: Beckett material: TCD, MS 10402. Beckett purchased it for £30 in instalments, the first down payment of £10 in spring 1936. *A Morning* 1935–36 (NGI 4628) is signed Jack B. Yeats, inscribed in another hand, 'Aut 1935, April 1936'. Beckett later gifted it to actor Jack MacGowran. It entered a private English collection in 1972. The gallery purchased it, with the aid of the Bryan Guinness Charitable Trust, in 1996.

88. The post was pursued by the Board from 1950, and returned full-time in 1956. *The Departments of State Bill: Section 30,* 'Appointment of Civil Servants' 1949: 'The board very much appreciated and strongly approves the decision of the Minister for Education to return to recognition the office of Director of the National Gallery as the full-time post.' MacGreevy Correspondence files, 1 July 1956, NGIA.

89. Evie Hone to MacGreevy, 31 March 1952, NGIA.

90. Rorimer to MacGreevy, 28 November 1955, NGIA; MacGreevy to Francis Taylor, Worcester Art Museum, 29 October 1955, NGIA. Taylor gave a talk in Dublin in 1956.

91. *National Gallery of Ireland Director's Report for 1952*, NGIA; 'Public Lectures on the History of Art begun on 16 October 1952': Correspondence File 1950s, NGIA. Reproductions of the collection began 1952. *National Gallery of Ireland Director's Report for 1952*, NGIA; Report by Brandi, director of Rome's Central Institute for Restoration, 1960, in NGIA; NGI Minutes, 5 July 1963, NGIA; A. O'Connor and N. McGuinne, *The Deeper Picture: Conservation at the NGI* (Dublin: NGI, 1998).

92. NGI Minutes, 6 October 1961, NGIA: Funding by Department of Education approved on 4 December 1962. Board thanked OPW, notably Frank Du Berry. NGI Minutes, 2 October 1964, NGIA; Dáil Debates: Deputy McGuire, vol. 56, 20 February 1963.

93. William O'Sullivan of the National Museum, Art and Industrial Division, was seconded as secretary to the new Arts Council between 1951 and 1957. NGI Minutes, 20 August 1958, NGIA.

94. MacGreevy retired on 30 September 1963: NGI Minutes, 6 December 1963, NGIA. Appointed consultant to the gallery from 1 October 1963.

95. D. Walker, *Modern Art in Ireland* (Dublin: Lilliput Press, 1997), p. 115.

96. James White (1913–2003), Dublin-born art critic, lecturer and museum director. Honoured by France, Italy and Germany, received an honorary doctorate from the National University of Ireland.

97. White, elected at the board meeting on 10 April, took up office on 1 June 1964. The *Centenary Exhibition* (October–December 1964) commemorating MacGreevy's directorship comprised 205 works, including loans from Munich, Venice, Stockholm, Rome, Montreal, Oslo, New York, Milan, The Hague, Florence, Brussels, Berlin, Amsterdam. NGI Minutes, 5 June 1964, NGIA.

98. 'Introduction' in J. White, *Centenary Exhibition 1864–1964* (Dublin: NGI, 1964).

99. Lecturers included Donal Murphy, Mairin Allen, John Creagh, Ruth Dromgoole and Michael McManus.
100. M. Wynne, 'Acquiring Irish Paintings', in B.P. Kennedy (ed.), *Art is My Life: A Tribute to James White* (Dublin: NGI, 1991), pp. 196–205. The gallery purchased twenty-three icons from W.E.D. Allen in 1971.
101. NGI Minutes, 4 December 1964, NGIA. Participating artists Maurice MacGonigal, Anne Yeats, Blaithín Nic Ciobhain and John Skelton, with costs covered by the Arts Council.
102. J. White, *Gerard Dillon: An Illustrated Biography* (Dublin: Wolfhound Press, 1994): an account is given in a letter from Dillon to a friend in London. George Campbell was an artist from Northern Ireland; M. Bourke (ed.), *Artists' Profile: A Children's Workbook* (Dublin: NGI, 1993), pp. 5–8.
103. *Irish Press*, 23 December 1964; *Irish Times*, 29 December 1964.
104. *National Gallery of Ireland Director's Report for 1965*, NGIA.
105. 'School children should pay a brief visit to the National Gallery': Dáil Debates: Deputy Jones to the Minister for Education, Deputy Hillery, vol. 199, 6 February 1963.
106. NGI Minutes, 5 November 1965, NGIA. Matthew Moss was appointed temporary assistant restorer and worked on gallery pictures at the British Museum. *National Gallery of Ireland Director's Report for 1967*, NGIA. In 1965 Michael Wynne was appointed temporary cataloguer, then assistant in 1966, became assistant director, then keeper, retiring in 1997. Three restorers were engaged.
107. *National Gallery of Ireland Director's Report for 1966*, NGIA. Conservation Department (paintings) opened in 1966; paper conservation in 1971, followed by photography. *Catalogue of Paintings Restored in the NGI to December 1971*, 2nd edn. (Dublin: NGI, 1972).
108. Works by John Butler Yeats (NGI 1963), Sean O'Sullivan (NGI 1863) and Martin Quadal (NGI 1899). Turpin, *A School of Art in Dublin Since the Eighteenth Century*, pp. 126–30.
109. *National Gallery of Ireland Director's report for 1967*, NGIA.
110. NGI Minutes, 7 April 1967, NGIA. In 1987, the Beits donated seventeen paintings to the NGI. A. Le Harivel, *NGI: Acquisitions 1986–88* (Dublin: NGI, 1988).
111. Lectures on Wednesdays, Thursdays, Sundays (one a month in Irish), 11 a.m. tours July–September: Correspondence file 1969, NGIA. 1966 Bye-Laws (30) changed to permit concerts. *National Gallery of Ireland Director's Report for 1973*, NGIA.
112. NGI Minutes, 4 June 1971, NGIA. Murnaghan departed after fifty years. Dáil Debates: General Debate, vol. 268, 8 November 1973.
113. *National Gallery of Ireland Director's Report for 1968*, NGIA.
114. *Museums in Education, No. 1* (London: Museums Association, 1970); C.W. Wright, *Provincial Museums and Galleries* (London: Department of Education and Science, HMSO, 1973).
115. NGI Minutes, 19 April 1974, NGIA: for 'an officer in charge of education'; NGI Minutes, 11 October 1974, NGIA. Frances Ruane, education officer (October 1974 to July 1977).
116. *National Gallery of Ireland Director's Report for 1974*, NGIA.
117. Copies of entries for treasure hunts named 'Search & Discovery', June 1976–7. Gallery files, NGIA.
118. NGI Minutes, 14 October 1977, NGIA. Niamh O'Sullivan, education officer (1977–80). NGI Minutes, 9 December 1977, NGIA; *NGI Director's Report for 1978*, NGIA; Correspondence to Pádraig Thornton, Catholic Youth Council, Dublin, 12 February 1979, NGIA.
119. Correspondence to Olive Holbrook, Institute of Internal Education, Washington, DC, 14 February 1979, NGIA.
120. The play based on Maclise's *The Marriage of Strongbow and Aoife* was commissioned from Gordon Snell, and involved 120 children aged 10 to 14. *Education Officer's Annual Report for 1979*, NGIA.

121. *NGI Director's Report for 1979*, NGIA.

122. Louis le Brocquy, 'James White', in Kennedy (ed.), *Art Is My Life*, pp. 127–9.

123. H. Potterton, 'Obituary: James White (1913–2003), *Burlington Magazine*, vol. 145, 2003, pp. 652–3.

124. Homan Potterton (1946–), born County Meath. Educated at TCD, won Purser–Griffith Diploma and Prize. Post graduate studies in Edinburgh, two years as temporary cataloguer in Dublin at National Gallery. Became assistant keeper responsible for seventeenth- and eighteenth-century Italian Schools at London's National Gallery, mounting a 'Painting in-Focus' exhibition on Caravaggio's *Supper at Emmaus* (1975), and an exhibition of Venetian seventeenth-century painting (1979). Author of *London National Gallery Essential Guide Book* (London: Thames & Hudson, 1977). Active researcher and writer on art.

125. *Fifty Pictures* (1981); *Fifty Irish Painters* (1983); *Fifty Irish Portraits* (1984); *Fifty French Pictures* (1984); *Fifty Views of Ireland* (1985); *Fifty Irish Drawings and Watercolours* (1986); V. Barrow, 'The National Gallery of Ireland', *Dublin Historical Record,* xxxvi, 1983, pp. 132–9.

126. M. Wynne, *Later Italian Paintings* (1986); D. Oldfield, *German Paintings* (1987); C. Vogelaar, *Netherlandish Fifteenth and Sixteenth Century Paintings* (1987); R. Mulcahy, *Spanish Paintings* (1988); David Oldfield, *Later Flemish Paintings* (1992).

127. The education officer drew on her experience at the Metropolitan Museum of Art in New York to create the Kids' Corner.

128. J. Bruner, *Acts of Meaning* (Cambridge, MA: Harvard University Press, 1990).

129. G.B. Matthews, *The Philosophy of Childhood* (Cambridge, MA: Harvard University Press, 1994); K. Egan, *The Educated Mind* (Chicago: University of Chicago Press, 1997).

130. Director to Leslie Victor Warren, 20 August 1980, NGIA: the director noted there was a need for a workshop/seminar room; R. Keaveney, *NGI Director's Report for 1988*; NGIA.

131. The education officer was a member of the Council of Europe Committee of Specialists on Heritage Education and drew on this experience for gallery events, and to judge the 'City beneath a City' project at Waterford Heritage Centre.

132. N. Harte (illustrations), *NGI Drawing Book* (age 3–6) (Dublin: NGI, 1996); C. Bates (illustrations), *NGI Colouring Book* (age 7–12 (Dublin: NGI, 1996).

133. Unpublished research undertaken by students (1990s) from Arts Administration, UCD; DIT College of Marketing & Design; Statistics Department, TCD; Loughborough University and NCAD.

134. Director to John Wilson, TD, Minister for Education, 11 August 1980, NGIA.

135. *National Gallery of Ireland Director's Report for 1980–1982*, NGIA; *NGI Director's Report for 1980–1982*, NGIA. The courses were promoted by the Irish National Teachers' Organisation, the Association of Secondary Teachers of Ireland, the Art Teachers' Association of Ireland, the IMA, and the Irish Heritage Education Network.

136. Dáil Debates: Deputy Bruton, Minister for Education, vol. 282, 19 June 1975; H. Potterton, *National Gallery of Ireland Director's Report for 1985*, NGIA. The first *Painting in Focus* show was produced by Anne Miller, followed by a show on *The Aran Fisherman's Drowned Child* by Frederic William Burton, RHA, that toured a number of venues between 1987 and 1988.

137. Key Potterton exhibitions: *Walter Osborne*, curated by Jeanne Sheehy (1983); *Irish Impressionists*, curated by Julian Campbell (1984); *Masterpieces of the NGI*, shown at the National Gallery, London (1985); *James Arthur O'Connor*, curated by John Hutchinson (1986).

138. H. Potterton, 'The Beit Collection' and 'The Máire MacNeill Sweeney Bequest', *Acquisitions 1986–1988* (Dublin: NGI, 1988), pp. 2–84.

139. Potterton acquired thirteen important paintings, watercolours by Mildred Anne Butler and some sculpture.

140. NGI Minutes, 11 December 1987, NGIA.
141. 'The Clare Street Project Strategy Document' (unpublished, 1991) marks the first report seeking a reconfiguration of the National Gallery that ultimately became the Master Development Plan, NGIA.
142. A. Crookshank, 'In My View … The National Gallery of Ireland', *Apollo*, September 1992, pp. 166–8.
143. The production involved fifty actors, musicians, dancers and students.
144. P. Durcan, *Crazy about Women*, a volume of poetry inspired by the collection (Dublin: NGI, 1991). with foreword by B.P. Kennedy.
145. *National Gallery of Ireland Director's Report for 1991*, NGIA.
146. Unpublished research: Fiona McWilliams, 'Visitor Report' (Loughborough University Business School, 1993).
147. *National Gallery of Ireland Director's Report for 1992*, NGIA; M. Bourke (ed.), *Children's Art: A Celebration* (Dublin: NGI, 1992), with commentaries by Louise Masterson;
148. S. Delaney, 'Report (Evaluation with Recommendations) of the Outreach Programme', unpublished 2001, NGIA.
149. *National Gallery of Ireland Director's Report for 1996*, NGIA.
150. P. McManus, 'Families in Museums', in R. Miles and L. Zavala (eds), *Towards the Museum of the Future: New European Perspectives* (London: Routledge, 1994).
151. The first old master show in twenty-five years was opened by Sir Denis Mahon in 1993, with an associated seminar: 'Florence in the Age of Lorenzo de' Medici'. S. Benedetti, *Caravaggio: The Master Revealed* (Dublin: NGI, 1993; rev. edn, 1999). Sergio Benedetti became keeper and head curator in 1999.
152. S. Benedetti, *The Scholar's Eye: Paintings from the collection of Sir Denis Mahon* (Dublin: NGI, 1997) with a foreword by R. Keaveney.
153. 'The Architectural Brief' (unpublished, 1996) formed the basis of the plans for the Millennium Wing (2002).
154. *Irish Watercolours and Drawings* to Boston College Museum, the accompanying catalogue with contributions by R. Keaveney, Dr B.P. Kennedy, Dr M. Wynne, F. Croke, A. Le Harivel: 1991; *French Nineteenth- and Twentieth-Ccentury Paintings from the NGI* to Japan (Yokohama, Chiba, Yamaguchi, Kobe, Tokyo 1996–7), with accompanying catalogue by F. Croke and an introduction by R. Keaveney.
155. *From Titian to Delacroix: Masterpieces from the NGI* toured to Yokohama Sogo Museum of Art; Chiba Sogo Museum of Art; Yamaguchi Prefectural Museum of Art; Kobe City Museum; and Isetan Museum of Art, Tokyo, the accompanying catalogue with contributions by R. Keaveney, B.P. Kennedy, Professor Nobuyuki Senzoku: 1993–4; *European Masterpieces from the NGI* toured to Australia (Canberra and Adelaide) the accompanying catalogue with contributions by R. Keaveney, B.P. Kennedy, M. Wynne, A. Le Harivel, F. Croke: 1994–5.
156. A. Fitzgerald, *The National Gallery of Ireland Guide* (Dublin: National Gallery of Ireland, 1996), edited by A. Le Harivel and an introduction by R. Keaveney.
157. *National Gallery of Ireland Annual Report for 1997*, NGIA; K. Fogarty, and J. O'Donnell, 'Evaluation and Assessment of the Exploring Art Project 1997–98' (unpublished, 1998), NGIA, recommended the appointment of a schools officer (assistance from Myra O'Regan, Statistics Department, TCD); M. Bourke, *Exploring Art at the National Gallery of Ireland* (Dublin: NGI, 1997).
158. In 1997, Brian P. Kennedy, assistant director (1989), became director of the National Gallery of Australia. Marie Bourke was appointed keeper, head of education, in 1998.
159. A Le Harivel (ed.), *Acquisitions 1986–1988* with contributions by F. Croke, R. Mulcahy, H. Potterton, M. Wynne.

160. O'Connor and McGuinne, *The Deeper Picture*: Andrew O'Connor was keeper and head of the Conservation Department, Maighread McParland, head of paper conservation.
161. F. Croke (ed.), *Art into Art: A Living Response to Past Masters* (Dublin: NGI, 1998). Exhibition and catalogue by artist printmakers. Fionnuala Croke, head of exhibitions, would be appointed keeper and head of collections in 2008.
162. S. Benedetti, *The La Touche Amorino: Canova and His Fashionable Irish Patrons* (Dublin: NGI, 1998).
163. H. Pyle, *Yeats: Portrait of an Artistic Family* (Dublin: NGI, 1997). Hilary Pyle, Yeats curator (1996).
164. Síghle Bhreathnach-Lynch, Irish Art curator (1998); M. Bourke and S. Bhreathnach-Lynch, *Discover Irish Art* (Dublin: NGI, 1999), preface by Micheál Martin TD, Minister for Education and Science.
165. S. Bhreathnach-Lynch , 'Highlights of the Sculpture Conservation Project' (Dublin: NGI, 2003); J. Ellis, 'Plaster Cast Collections and their Conservation,' *Museum Ireland*, vol. 14, 2004, pp. 95–102; S. Corr, *Caring for Collections: A Manual of Conservation* (Kilkenny: Heritage Council, 2000).
166. 'The Architectural Brief' for the Millennium Wing 2002 Project (unpublished, 1996, rev. 1998), formed part of the *Master Development Plan* which drew together requirements for the historic buildings and new building plans.
167. Clare Street site numbers (27–29) acquired 1990. Viewed by the 1853 committee as a possible location for the first gallery building; considered by the architects of the Milltown Wing (1903); Bodkin recommended the purchase of buildings on Clare Street/South Leinster Street as early as 1929. From the top floor windows can be seen the building of the former Finn's Hotel, where Nora Barnacle worked when she first met James Joyce; the attic of number 6 Clare Street where Beckett wrote the novel *Murphy*; 1 Merrion Square, where Oscar Wilde lived. *National Gallery of Ireland Annual Report for 2002*, NGIA.
168. N. Figgis and B. Rooney, *Irish Paintings in the National Gallery of Ireland, Volume 1* (Dublin: NGI, 2001) with a foreword by R. Keaveney.

Part V Preamble

1. Quote from 'Humanity's Great Works', *Art Newspaper*, vol. 210, February 2010, p. 36.
2. S. Heaney, 'Foreword', in J. Dunne and J. Kelly, *Childhood and its Discontents* (Dublin: Liffey Press, 2002), pp. xiii–xvi.

Chapter 14

1. Quote by director of the Prado Museum, Javier Rodríguez Zapatero, Prado Museum Press Release, 13 March 2009.
2. C. Horton, 'The Chester Beatty Library: Ireland's Museum of the Book', *Leabharlann–The Irish Library*, vol. 18, no. 1, 2008, pp. 18–25.
3. P. Doyle, 'National Museum of Ireland: Country Life', *Property Valuer, Irish Auctioneers & Valuers Institute*, Autumn 2002, pp. 12–14.
4. The Millennium Wing, where the Impressionist exhibition was held, added 4,000 sq.m. to the gallery.
5. J. McLean (ed.), *Impressionist Interiors* (Dublin: NGI, 2008) with contributions also by Professor Hollis Clayson, Professor S. Singletary; A. Waiboer (ed.), *Gabriel Metsu: Rediscovered Master of the Dutch Golden Age* (NGI in association with Yale University Press, 2010), with contributions also by W.E. Franits, Professor L. Stone-Ferrier, P. Roelofs, B.M. du Mortier, M. Schapelhouman, E.M. Gifford. The exhibition was shown at the National Gallery of Ireland, the Rijksmuseum, Amsterdam and the National Gallery of

Art, Washington; A. Hodge (ed.), *Hugh Douglas Hamilton: A Life in Pictures* (Dublin: NGI, 2008) with contributions also by R. Kenny, N. Figgis, A. Le Harivel, L. O'Connor, B. Rooney; W. Laffan and B. Rooney, *Thomas Roberts: Landscape and Patronage in Eighteenth-Century Ireland*; F. Croke (ed.), *Samuel Beckett: A Passion for Paintings* (including proceedings of the round table 'Samuel Beckett and the Visual Arts') comprising a series of essays with an introduction by R. Keaveney (Dublin: NGI, 2006).

6. Designed by Dutch architect Erick van Egeraat, adding 1,000 sq. m. to the gallery.

7. Designed by the Dublin firm of Gilroy McMahon. It was renamed in 2002. Sean Scully (b.1945–) is the Irish-born internally renowned contemporary artist.

8. In 2006 NMNI took over from MAGNI in overseeing the Ulster Museum, the Ulster Folk and Transport Museum, the Ulster American Folk Park, the Armagh County Museum, and W5 Science Centre which opened in Belfast in 2001.

9. The Heritage Fund was established by government in 2001 to enable national cultural institutions (National Archives, Gallery, Library, Museum and IMMA) with national collections to acquire outstanding heritage objects from a limited fund.

10. The Global Economic Forum, organized by the Irish government, was held at the Farmleigh Estate near Dublin in 2009.

11. Professor Declan McGonagle, director of the National College of Art and Design, speech given at the presentation of the Museum Awards Scheme at Iveagh House, 18 May 2009.

12. Bazin, *The Museum Age*, pp. 260–1.

13. Council of National Cultural Institutions, *A Policy Framework for Education, Community, Outreach*.

14. In 1977 the Irish Museums Trust developed educational programmes that evolved into a full-time postgraduate diploma in arts administration, offered by University College Dublin in 1986. In 2002 UCD redesigned its courses offering an MA and MLitt. in cultural policy and arts management, and doctoral programmes. The University of Ulster offers postgraduate training programmes online in partnership with the Heritage Council. Waterford Institute of Technology offers an MA in arts and heritage management.

15. P. Cooke, *The Containment of Heritage: Setting Limits to the Growth of Heritage in Ireland* (Dublin: Policy Institute, TCD, 2003).

16. Herity and Eoghan, *Ireland in Prehistory*, pp. 13–15.

17. Seán Ó Ríordáin, professor of archaeology (1936–43), proposed a public museum (Cork Public Museum had been founded in 1910. Fitzgerald Park House, the designated site, was handed over to the trustees of the museum in 1943 and, following restoration, was opened in 1945); the curator, Michael J. O'Kelly, Professor of Archaeology (1946–81) at UCC, managed the museum until it was handed over to Cork Corporation in 1965.

18. Mulvihill, *Ingenious Ireland*, p. 367. UCC collections: furniture, paintings, sculpture, university memorabilia, historic scientific instruments and geological specimens.

19. M.D. Fewtrell, 'The James Mitchell Geology Museum, University College, Galway', *Irish Naturalists' Journal*, vol. 19, 1979, pp. 309–15.

20. D.A.T. Harper (ed.), *An Irish Geological Time Capsule: The James Mitchell Museum, University College Galway* (Galway: James Mitchell Museum, 1996).

21. G.L. Herries Davies, 'A Forty-Year Retrospect', in Wyse Jackson (ed.), *In Marble Halls*, pp. 93–7.

22. The collection: 70,000 palaeontological, 7,000 mineralogical and 15,000 petrological specimens.

23. Wyse Jackson, 'The Geological Museum', in *In Marble Halls,* pp. 55–61.

24. Zuleika Rodgers is curator of the Weingreen Museum.

25. Martin Linnie is curator of the Zoological Museum, the collection of 20,000 specimens is available as a teaching research facility for students, staff and visitors. For information see TCD website: C. Giltrap. Trinity College Dublin. The Academic and Artistic

Collections. (TCD, 2010).

26. C. Haywood, *The Making of the Classical Museum: Antiquarians, Collectors and Archaeologists* (Dublin: Department of Classics, UCD, 2003), p. 12.

27. H. Browne, *Museum of Ancient History: Report* (Dublin: University College, Dublin, 1913), p. 8.

28. These ideas were published in H. Browne. *Our Renaissance: Essays on the Reform and Revival of Classical Studies* (New York: Longmans, Green & Co. 1917).

29. NMI registers document the transfer of antiquities between the UCD museum and the National Museum in 1912. The museums also collaborated on the purchase of twenty Hope vases at Christie's on 23 July 1917, and *The Hope Heirlooms* exhibition.

30. C. Haywood, *Classical Civilisation in the Classical Museum: Teacher's Pack* (Dublin: University College, Dublin, 2002).

31. The collection: portrait busts, copies of old masters of unknown provenance, sculptural groups, a stained-glass window, original oil paintings from the late seventeenth to the twentieth century, and 1,000 works (mainly on paper). A. Rowan, 'Art for an Institution', in *University Collage: Catalogue of the Art Collection of University College Dublin* (Dublin: AnCO/Irish Museums Trust Arts Administration Course, 1983), pp. 5–7.

32. Newman House, the original home of UCD in 1854, comprises two Georgian town houses (numbers 85 and 86 St Stephen's Green, notable for their fine interiors and splendid plasterwork) and a Victorian hall. Ruth Ferguson is curator of Newman House.

33. An independent charitable organization supported by TCD and the Arts Council.

34. A. Crookshank and D. Webb, *Paintings and Sculptures in Trinity College Dublin* (Dublin: Trinity College Dublin Press, 1990). Catherine Giltrap is the curator of TCD art collections.

35. G. Dawson, 'The Douglas Hyde Gallery', *Irish Arts Review*, vol. 4, no. 4, 1997, pp. 39–42. Early directors: Sean McCrum, Patrick Murphy, Medb Ruane.

36. Hutchinson in conversation with A. Smith, 'The New Directors', *Irish Arts Review*, vol. 10, 1994, p. 79.

37. It was hosted by C. Ó hEocha, UCG president, and Gerry Lee, UCG buildings officer, who began constructing the gallery in the basement of the quadrangle buildings in 1976. Walker, *Modern Art in Ireland*, pp. 141–3.

38. G. O'Brien, 'Between a Thing and a Thought: A Brief History of the Collection', in S. Pierce and G. O'Brien (eds) *Imagining Ireland: Selected Works from the Collection of the National University of Ireland, Galway* (Galway: NUIG, 2004), pp. 79–80.

39. Martin and Carmel Naughton gave a substantial donation towards the gallery.

40. The collection: paintings, prints, works on paper, sculpture, furniture, metalwork and silver and contemporary works by Northern Ireland artists. E. Black, *A Sesquicentennial Celebration: Art from the Queen's University Collection* (Belfast: QUB, 1995).

41. G. Tipton, 'The Lewis Glucksman Gallery, Cork', *Museum Ireland*, vol. 15, 2005, pp. 121–3. The gallery, designed by O'Donnell + Tuomey, is named after Lewis Glucksman.

42. James White provided advice in 1975. In 1985 the committee was endorsed by the UCC Governing Authority. The collection: 350 Irish art and Cork-based contemporary art works. James Elkins of the School of the Art Institute of Chicago was head of UCC Art History Department 2003–6.

43. *Newsletter of the Network of European Museum Organisations*, German Museums Association, vol. 2, 2009, p. 1.

44. Charles Saumarez Smith was director of the National Gallery in London in 2002–7; Nicholas Penny was appointed director in 2008.

45. Mark Jones was appointed director of the V&A in 2001.

46. Tate Modern was converted by architects Herzog and de Meuron, who are designing the new extension to open in time for the 2012 Olympic Games.

47. *National Museum Directors' Conference* (London: National Museum Directors' Conference, 2004), p. 6.

48. For a listing of some of these institutions, see note 90, Chapter 10. M. Rich, 'Build Your Dream, Hold Your Breath', *New York Times*, 6 August 2006, sec. 2, p. 22.

49. R. Hughes, 'Thoroughly Modern MoMA', *Guardian*, 4 November 2004. Yoshio Taniguchi designed the refurbished MoMA.

50. H. James, *The Golden Bowl* (New York: Charles Scribner's Sons, 1909), p. 146. The museum occupies about 2 million sq. ft. Thomas Campbell was appointed director in 2009.

51. Plan devised by Irish architect Kevin Roche of Roche Dinkerloo and Associates.

52. Metropolitan Museum of Art Press Release, 6 June 2007: 'The Ruth and Harold D. Uris Centre for Education'.

53. The Art Institute's one million sq. m. makes it the second largest art museum in the United States.

54. Art Institute of Chicago Press Release, 13 May 2009: 'The Art Institute of Chicago inaugurates Modern Wing designed by Renzo Piano with weeklong free open hours 11–16 May, 2009'.

55. Prado Museum Press Release, 13 March 2009. The project was initiated by Google Earth Spain. A video of the three-month process showing 8,200 photographs of a number of masterpieces is on YouTube.

56. M. Csikszentmihalyi, *Flow: The Psychology of Optimal Experience* (New York: HarperCollins, 1990).

57. N. Simone, *The Participatory Museum* (Santa Cruz, California: Museum 2.0, 2010).

58. Quote by director of the Prado Museum, Javier Rodriguez Zapatero, Prado Museum Press Release, 13 March 2009.

59. Quoted in S. Quinn (ed.), *Learning from Art* (catalogue with essays) (Dublin: NGI, 2004), p. 22.

60. Nobel Prize winner, Isaac Bashevis Singer devised ten commandments on children and literature, as a personal guide. Adapted by E. Cederstrom, 'Look, Here's a Butterfly', in *The Royal Museum of Fine Arts* (Copenhagen: Royal Museum of Fine Arts, 1995), pp. 50–3.

61. G. Lewis, 'The Universal Museum: A Special Case?', *ICOM News*, vol. 57, no. 1, p. 3.

62. Executive summary, 'Intercultural Education Strategy 2010–2015', Department of Education and Skills and Office of the Minister for Integration (2010), pp. 1–5.

63. P. Ricouer, 'Universal Civilization and National Cultures', quoted in J. Cleary and C. Connolly (eds), *The Cambridge Companion to Modern Irish Culture* (Cambridge: Cambridge University Press, 2005), p. 293.

64. Eavan Boland, RTÉ Radio, 18 August 2003.

65. W.H. Flower, *Essays on Museums*, p.47.

Conclusion

1. H. Cole, Parliamentary Report on the Science and Art Department 1868/9, vol. xxiv, p. 206. See Crooke, *Politics, Archaeology and the Creation of the National Museum of Ireland*, p. 110.

2. S.Weil, *Making Museums Matter* (Washington, DC: Smithsonian Institution Press, 2002), pp. 28–52.

3. 'Ireland Today Behaviour & Attitudes Survey in the Republic of Ireland': 1,004 adults surveyed in October 2009, *Irish Times*, 21 November 2009.

4. A. Gray, 'Assessment of Economic Impact of the Arts in Ireland', *Arts and Culture Scoping Research Project, submitted by Indecon International Economic Consultants* (Dublin: Arts Council Press Release, 4 November, 2009).

5. Durcan, *Crazy About Women*, pp. x–xi.

6. D. Kiberd, 'Learning in Museums', in *Proceedings of the National Gallery of Ireland Museum Education Symposium*, 2003, pp. 3–5.

7. S. Heaney, 'A Sense of the Past', *History Ireland*, vol. 1, no. 4, winter 1993, pp. 33–7.

Bibliography

PRIMARY SOURCES

Manuscripts

National Gallery of Ireland

Architectural Brief (1996), forming the basis of the plans for the Millennium Wing Project (2002) and *Master Development Plan*
Armstrong, W., *National Gallery of Ireland Director's Reports 1898–1910*
Bodkin, T., *National Gallery of Ireland Director's Reports 1927–1935*
Clare Street Project Strategy Document 1991
Deane, Thomas Manley, newspaper cuttings 1881–1901
Deane, Thomas Manley, Sketchbooks
Douglas, R.L., *National Gallery of Ireland Director's Report 1916*
Doyle, H., *National Gallery of Ireland Director's Reports 1875–1884*
Furlong, G., *National Gallery of Ireland Director's Reports 1936–1945*
Keaveney, R., *National Gallery of Ireland Director's Reports 1988–2008*
Larcom Letter Book 1855–1876
MacGreevy, T., *National Gallery of Ireland Director's Reports 1950–1963*
Minutes of the Irish Institution 1853–1860
National Gallery of Ireland Extension and Refurbishment of Historic Wings
    Heneghan Peng Architects (2008)
National Gallery of Ireland Foundation Minutes 1855–1864
National Gallery of Ireland Minutes 1864–2008
National Gallery of Ireland, Strategy Statements 2000–2010
O'Callaghan, L., *National Gallery of Ireland Director's Report 1925*
Potterton, H., *National Gallery of Ireland Director's Reports 1980–1987*
White, J., *National Gallery of Ireland Director's Reports 1964–1979*

National Museum of Ireland

Architectural competition for the Dublin Museum of Science and Art, 1880s
Ball, V., *Museum of Science and Art Director's Reports 1883–1895*
Circulation Division logbook, A1/156/2002 (2002)
Lucas, A.T., *National Museum of Ireland Director's Reports 1959–1960*
Mahr, A., *National Museum of Ireland Director's Reports 1932–1936*
Meagher, G.A., *Report on the Administration and Development of the National Museum (1985)*
National Museum of Ireland, Acting Director's Reports 1927–1933
National Museum of Ireland, Art and Industry correspondence, File 580, 166 (1904)
National Museum of Ireland, Bender Collection, A1/108/009-012

National Museum of Ireland, 'Circulating loan collections', A1/03/043 (2003)
National Museum of Ireland, *Director and Acting-Director's Reports* [missing years noted]: 1900–1921, 1922–1926; 1927–1945; 1945–1952; 1953–1954; 1955–1957; 1958–1959; 1965–2007
National Museum of Ireland, Interim Board Report 1995
National Museum of Ireland Reports 1952–2002
National Museum of Ireland Strategy Statement 2008–2012
National Museum of Science and Art/National Museum of Ireland, Board of Visitors Reports [missing years noted]: 1881–1953; 1954–1959; 1960–1977; 1978–1979; 1981; 1982–1985; 1986–1988; 1990–1992; 1993–1997
Newspaper cuttings on the opening of the Science and Art Museum, 1885
O'Connor, P., *National Museum of Ireland Acting-Director's Reports 1941–1942*
Plunkett, Count G.N., *Museum of Science and Art, Director's Reports 1897–1915*
Scharff, R.F., *National Museum of Science and Art Acting-Director's Reports 1915–1921*
Steele, W.E., *National Museum of Science and Art Director's Report 1877–1878*

Ulster Museum

Belfast Museum and Art Gallery Reports 1940–1952
Belfast Museum and Art Gallery Report for decade ending 1962
Ulster Museum, Belfast, Report of the Trustees 1963–1969

Trinity College Dublin

Ball, R., *First Report on the Progress of the Dublin University Museum (1846)*
Ball, R., *Second Report on the Progress of the Dublin University Museum (1847)*
Beckett Papers, Ms 10402
Bodkin Papers, Ms 6961-53, 1916
Trinity Muniments, Ms P/2/354 and P/2/353/B

Royal Dublin Society

Charters and Statutes of the Royal Dublin Society (reprinted 1989)
Natural History and Museum Committee Report 1843
Proceedings of the Royal Dublin Society 1734–1924
Proceedings of the Royal Dublin Society Minute Books 1731–1741

Royal Irish Academy

Antiquities, Minute Book (1806)
Dawson Correspondence (1830–40), Ms 4 B 36
Dawson Papers, Ms 12 N 22, ff 13–14
Insurance of Antiquities collection for International Exhibition, Ms 4 B 13
Larcom Papers, Ms 4 B 30
Minute Book, Antiquities, 1784–1870
Minute Book, Museum Committee, 1870–1955
O'Donovan Papers, Ms 12 L 10
Petrie Papers, Ms 12 N 22
Redmond Papers, Ms 4 B 6, f. 184
Stokes Papers, Ms 12 N 12

National Library of Ireland

Customs Accounts, Ms 353–376
Heads of Inquiry (1832), Larcom Papers, Ms 7550
Larcom Papers, Ms 7555
Petrie to Adare, Ms 795
RHA draft reports, Ms 793, ff 541–8

National Archives of Ireland

Cabinet Minutes, 5 November 1945, Item 6, G. C. 5/45
Department of Agriculture and Technical Instruction. National Museum committee meetings, 27 October 1910, 1 November 1910. File 460–12
Department of Agriculture and Technical Instruction. National Museum committee meetings, 7 October 1910. File G 3721–13
Department of Education, Minutes of meeting 23 March 1939, Irish Military Archives. G 2/0130
Department of Finance file S 2/28/29 (1929)
Irish Heritage Education Network files (1998)

University of Limerick

Dunraven Papers, University of Limerick Library, D 3196/1/11/1–4

Public Record Office of Northern Ireland

D/3263/AB/1 (1844)

Royal Society of Arts

Royal Society of Arts, London, Minutes of Committee 1852
Webb, P.C., *An Account of the Dublin Society*, GBI, No. 120 (Minute, 16 June 1756)

Parliamentary Papers

Dáil Debates, 1922–2009
Hansard's Parliamentary Debates, 1845–1856

Published Reports

American Association of Museums, *Excellence and Equity: Education and the Public Dimension of Museums* (Washington, DC, 1992)
Arts Council, *Guidelines for the Protection and Welfare of Children and Young People in the Arts Sector* (Dublin, 2006)
Benson, C., *The Place of the Arts in Irish Education* (Dublin, 1979)
Benson, C. (ed.), *Art and the Ordinary: The ACE Report* (Dublin, 1989)
Bodkin, T., *Report on the Arts in Ireland* (Dublin, 1949)
Brown Goode, G., 'The Museums of the Future', in *Annual Report of the United States National Museum: Year Ending 30 June 1897* (Washington, 1898)
Chard, J., 'On Circulating Museum Cabinets for Schools and Other Educational Purposes', in *Report of the Proceedings of the First Museums Association Meeting* (Liverpool, 1890)
CHL Consulting, *A Training Strategy for the Irish Museum Sector* (Kilkenny, 2000)
Combat Poverty/Arts Council, *Poverty: Access and Participation in the Arts* (Dublin, 1997)

Council of National Cultural Institutions, *A Policy Framework for Education Community Outreach (ECO)* (Dublin, 2004)

Curriculum and Examinations Board, *The Arts in Education Discussion Paper* (Dublin, 1985)

Department of Culture and Media, *Understanding the Future: Museums and 21st Century Life. The Value of Museums* (London, 2005)

Department of Education and Employment, *The Learning Age: A Renaissance for a New Britain* (London, 1998)

Duggan, C., *Irish Museums Association Survey of Museums in Ireland 2005* (Dublin, 2006)

Eighteenth Report of the Science and Art Department (London, 1871)

Further Report of the Committee on the Provincial Museums of the United Kingdom, in *Report of the British Association for the Advancement of Science* (London, 1888)

Gray, A., *Assessment of the Economic Impact of the Arts in Ireland* (Dublin, 2009)

Howarth, E. (ed.), *Educational Value of Museums and the Formation of Local War Museums, Report of Museums Association Conference* (Sheffield, 1918)

Institute of Professional Civil Servants, *Museum Service for Ireland* (Dublin, 1973)

Lithberg, N., et al., *Report of the Committee of Enquiry into the Workings of the National Museum* (Dublin, 1927)

Lowe, E.E., *Report on American Museum Work for the Carnegie United Kingdom Trustees* (Edinburgh, 1928)

Markham, S.F., *Report on the Museums and Galleries of the British Isles (Other than National Museums) to the Carnegie United Kingdom Trustees* (Edinburgh, 1938)

Miers, H.A., *Report on the Public Museums of the British Isles for the Carnegie United Kingdom Trustees* (Edinburgh, 1928)

Museums and Social Inclusion: The GLLAM Report (Leicester, 2000)

National Economic and Social Forum, *Equality Policies for Older People: Implementation Issues* (Dublin, 2003)

Our Children – Their Lives: The National Children's Strategy (Dublin, 2000)

Portlock, J.E., *Report of the Geology of the County of Londonderry and Parts of Tyrone and Fermanagh* (London, 1843)

Ready, Steady, Play! A National Play Policy (Dublin, 2004)

Renaissance in the Regions: A New Vision for England's Museums (London, 2001)

Report by the Committee of Enquiry into the work of the Royal Hibernian Academy and the Metropolitan School of Art (Dublin, 1906)

Report from the Committee on the Science and Art Department in Ireland together with minutes of evidence 1868–9, House of Commons, xxiv (4103)

Report from the Select Committee on Irish Miscellaneous Estimates (London, 1829)

Report of a Committee Appointed by the Lords Commissioners of Her Majesty's Treasury to inquire into the circumstances under which certain Celtic Ornaments found in Ireland were recently offered for sale to the British Museum, and to consider the relation between the British Museum and the Museums of Edinburgh and Dublin with regard to the acquisition and retention of objects of Antiquarian and Historic interest (London, 1899)

Report from the Select Committee of the Royal Dublin Society (London, 1836)

Report of the British Association of the Advancement of Science (Dublin, 1835)

Report of the Commission on Museums for a New Century: American Association of Museums (Washington, DC, 1984)

Report of the Commissioners on the Ordnance Memoir: Minutes of Evidence, Appendices and Index (London, 1844)

Report of the Department of Science and Art (London, 1890)

Report of the Museum Committee to the Council of Queen's College Galway. Antiquarian and Historic Interest (London, 1852)

Report of the Royal Dublin Society (Dublin, 1863)

Report of the Royal Irish Art Union (Dublin, 1843)

Report of the Select Parliamentary Committee on the Royal Dublin Society (London, 1836)

Report on Conditions in the National Museum of Ireland compiled by the Museum Branch of the Institute of Professional Civil Servants (Dublin, 1969)

Report on Scientific Institutions (Dublin) together with the Proceedings of the Committee, Minutes of Evidence, Appendix and Index, 15 July 1864 (London, 1864)

Report on the Affairs and Past Management of the Royal Hibernian Academy (London, 1858)

Richards, J.M., *Provision for the Arts* (London, 1976)

Robins, M.W., *America's Museums: The Belmont Report* (Washington, DC, 1969)

Robinson, K., *Culture, Creativity and the Young: Developing Public Policy* (Brussels, 1999)

Roe, S., *The Report of the Public Consultation for the National Recreation Policy for Young People* (Dublin, 2006)

Royal Dublin Society, *Report of the Delegates to the Council, as to Information Required by the Science and Art Department, 6 May 1879* (Dublin, 1879)

Second Report of the AGM of the Friends of the National Collections of Ireland (Dublin, 1926)

Securing the Potential of Cultural Tourism for Ireland. Report of the Cultural Tourism Task Force, Department of Arts, Sport and Tourism (2006)

Stierle, K. and H. Lanigan Wood, *A Survey of Museums in Ireland for the Irish Museums Association* (Dublin, 1994)

Survey of Provincial Museums and Galleries, London: Standing Commission on Museums and Galleries (London, 1963)

The Great Industrial Exhibition of Ireland (Dublin, 1853)

The Queen's Colleges Commission: Report. Galway, University College (London, 1858)

Thompson, W., 'The Fauna of Ireland: Division Invertebrata', in *Report of the British Association* (London, 1843)

Trustees of the Victoria and Albert Museum, *Education for All* (London, 1992)

Verling, E., *A Policy Framework for the Irish Museum Sector* (Kilkenny, 2003)

Waterfield, G. (ed.), *Opening Doors: Learning in the Historic Environment* (London, 2004)

Williams, H.M., *Public Policy and Arts Education* (Ohio, 1993)

Windle, B., *President's Report, Queen's College Cork 1904–5* (Cork, 1905)

Newspapers Prior to 1900

Advocate
Athenaeum
Cork Constitution
Cork Examiner
Daily Express
Dublin Builder
Dublin Chronicle
Dublin Daily Advertiser
Dublin Penny Journal
Evening Mail
Evening Telegraph
Exhibition Expositor and Advertiser
Faulkner's Dublin Journal
Freeman's Journal
General Advertiser
Illustrated London News
Irish Builder
Irish Daily Independent
Irish Times

Irishman
Nation
Northern Whig
Old Dublin Intelligencer
Packet
Patriot and Farmer's Monitor
Saunders' Newsletter
Southern Reporter
The Times

Newspapers since 1900

Art Newspaper
Cork Examiner
Cork Free Press
Freeman's Journal
Guardian
Irish Builder
Irish Examiner
Irish Independent
Irish Press
Irish Times
Le Figaro
New Statesman
Scotsman
Sunday Times
Western People
Westminster Gazetteer

Articles in Journals and Periodicals Prior to 1900

'A New Museum in Dublin', *Industrial Art, Dublin*, vol. 1, 1877, pp. 35–7

'An Account of the Prince and Princess of Wales Visiting Sir Hans Sloane', *Gentleman's Magazine*, vol. 18, July 1748, pp. 301–2

'The Great Industrial Exhibition of 1853', *Dublin University Magazine*, vol. 41, no. 246, 1853, pp. 655–62

'The South Kensington Museum', *Chamber's Journal*, 31 October 1873, p. 629

Anderson, R.J., 'The Natural History Museum, Queen's College, Galway', *Irish Naturalists' Journal*, vol. 8, 1899, pp. 125–31

Anderson, W., 'The National Gallery of Ireland', *Magazine of Art*, 1890, vol. 2, pp. 281–8

Dixon Hardy, P., 'Meeting of the British Association', *Dublin Penny Journal*, vol. 4, no. 173, 1835, p. 131

——, 'Royal Hibernian Academy', *Dublin Penny Journal*, vol. 4, no. 174, 1835, p. 136

Duret, T., 'Une Visite aux Galleries Nationales D'Irlande et D'Ecosse', *Gazette des Beaux-Arts*, vol. 25, 1882, pp. 180–3

Kane, R., *General Descriptive Guide to the Museum of Irish Industry, Dublin* (Dublin: HMSO, 1857)

Kinahan, G.H., 'Obituary: George V. Du Noyer (1817–69)', *Geological Magazine*, vol. 6, no. 2, 1869, pp. 93–5

King, W., 'Monograph of the Permian Fossils of England', *Palaeontographical Society (Monographs)*, 1850, p. 258

——, 'On *Pleurodictyum problematicum*', *Annual Magazine of Natural History*, vol. 17, 1856, pp. 11–14

MacAdam, J., *On Schools of Design in Ireland* (Dublin: Hodges & Smith, 1849)

O'Conor, C., 'The Origins of the R.I.A.', *Studies*, vol. 38, 1786, pp. 325–37

Sullivan, W.K., 'On Societies for the Promotion and Encouragement of Industrial Arts', *Journal of Industrial Progress*, vol. 6, June 1854, p. 140

Museum/Gallery Catalogues Prior to 1900

An Illustrated Catalogue of the Exhibition of Art-Industry in Dublin 1853 (London, 1853)

Armstrong, W., *Catalogue of Pictures and Other Works of Art in the National Gallery and the National Portrait Gallery, Ireland* (Dublin: The Stationery Office, 1898)

Ball, V., *Official General Guide to the Science and Art Museum, Dublin. Part I: Natural History Department in the Old Museum Building; Part II: Art and Industrial Department in the New Museum Building* (Dublin, 1890)

Catalogue of the Genuine Collection of Italian, Flemish and Other Pictures of the Late James Digges La Touche, 16 May 1764 (Dublin, 1764)

Catalogue of the National Gallery of Scotland (Edinburgh, 1894)

Catalogue of Cork Art Galleries (Cork, 1853)

Doyle, H.E., *Catalogue of Paintings in the National Gallery of Ireland* (Dublin, 1890)

General Guide to the Science and Art Museum (Dublin, 1892)

Giesecke, C., *Descriptive Catalogue of a New Collection of Minerals in the Museum of the Royal Dublin Society to which is added an Irish Mineralogy* (Dublin, 1832)

Kane, R., *General Descriptive Guide to the Museum of Irish Industry* (Dublin, 1857)

Mulvany, G., *Catalogue of Paintings in the National Gallery of Ireland* (Dublin, 1864)

O'Reilly, B., *Catalogue of the Subjects of Natural History in the Museum of the Rt. Hon. The Dublin Society* (Dublin, 1813)

Sharpe, R.B. (ed.), *The Sharpe Catalogues: A Catalogue of the Birds in the British Museum* (London, 1874–98)

Stokes, W., *Catalogue of the Minerals in the Museum of Trinity College Dublin* (Dublin, 1807)

——, *A Descriptive Catalogue of the Minerals in the Systematic Collection of the Museum of Trinity College Dublin* (Dublin, 1818)

The Art Journal, *Illustrated Catalogue of the International Exhibition 1892* (London, 1863)

The Illustrated Record and Descriptive Catalogue of the Dublin International Exhibition of 1865 (Dublin, 1865)

Wilde, W., *A Descriptive Catalogue of the Antiquities in the Museum of the Royal Irish Academy (class I–V)* (Dublin, 1857)

——, *A Descriptive Catalogue of the Antiquities in Gold in the Museum of the Royal Irish Academy (class V continued)* (Dublin, 1862)

Books prior to 1900

Anderson, J., *History of Belfast Library and Society for Promoting Knowledge, Commonly Known as the Linen Hall Library* (Belfast, 1888)

Anon, *A Museum for Your Gentlemen and Ladies or Private Tutor and Pocket Library* (Dublin, 1790)

Barnham, T.P., *Struggles and Triumphs* (Buffalo: Courier & Co., 1889)

Berkheim, C.G., *Lettres sur Paris (1806–1807)* (Heidelberg and Paris, 1809)

Bowden, C.T., *A Tour through Ireland* (Dublin, 1791)

Brown Goode, G., *Principles of Museum Administration* (New York, 1895)

Bryce, J., *Tables of Simple Minerals, Rocks and Shells with Local Catalogues of Species for the Use of Students of Natural History in the Belfast Academy* (Belfast, 1831)

Campbell, T., *An Essay on Perfecting the Fine Arts in Great Britain and in Ireland* (Dublin: William Sleator, 1767)

Colby, R.E., *Memoir of the City and North Western Liberties of Londonderry*. Parish of Templemore (Dublin: Hodges & Smith, 1837)

Desenfans, N., *A Plan, Preceded by a Short Review of the Fine Arts, to Preserve among Us, and Transmit to Posterity, the Portrait of the Most Distinguished Characters of England, Scotland and Ireland, since His Majesty's Accession to the Throne* (London, 1799)

Drummond, J.L., *Address of the President of the Belfast Natural History Society on the Opening of Belfast Museum, 1 November 1831* (Belfast, 1831)

Dunton, J., *The Dublin Scuffle: Being a Challenge, Sent by John Dunton, Citizen of London to Patrick Campbell, Bookseller in Dublin. Together with the small skirmishes of bills and advertisements … in addition containing a conversation in Ireland. Printed 1699 for the author in London* (Dublin, 1699; rpr. 2000)

Dwight, T., *The Northern Traveller and the Northern Tour* (New York: Goodrich & Wiley, 5th edn, 1834)

Edgeworth, R.L., *Practical Education* (London, 1798)

Fenn, J., *The Instructions Given in the Drawing Schools, Established in England, Scotland and Other Parts of Europe* (Dublin, 1767)

——, *The Instructions Given in the Drawing Schools Established by the Dublin Society*, 2 vols (Dublin, 1769–72)

Flower, W.H., *Essays on Museums and Other Subjects Connected with Natural History* (London: Macmillan, 1898)

Fryer, E. (ed.), *The Works of James Barry, Esq., Historical Painter* (London, 1809)

Gandon, J. and T. Mulvaney, *The Life of James Gandon Esq., with Original Notices of Contemporary Artists and Fragments of Essays* (Dublin, 1846)

Godley, R.J., *Letters from America* (London: J. Murray, 1844)

Grattan, W., *Patronage Analysed* (Dublin, 1818)

Grew, N., *Musaeum Regalis Societatis* (London, 1681)

Hyde, D., *The Revival of Irish Literature* (London, 1894)

Jamieson, A., *A Dictionary of Mechanical Science, Arts, Manufactures and Miscellaneous Knowledge* (London: H. Fisher, Son & Co. 1829)

Karsten, D.L., *A Description of the Minerals in the Leskean Museum* (Dublin, 1798)

McEvoy, J., *The Royal Dublin Society and the Citizens of Dublin: Why should Exclusiveness and Sabbatarianism be the Rule at the Glasnevin Botanic Garden, whilst under Her Majesty at Kew, Free Admission is the Rule on all Days of the Week and on Sunday?* (Dublin, 1860)

Madden, S., *Reflections and Resolutions Proper for the Gentlemen of Ireland* (Dublin, 1738)

Maguire, J.F., *The Industrial Movement in Ireland* (Cork, 1853)

Malton, J., *A Picturesque and Descriptive View of the City of Dublin 1792–99* (London: W. Fadden, 1799)

Mulvany, G., *Thoughts and Facts Concerning the Fine Arts in Ireland, and Schools of Design* (Dublin, 1847)

Museum of Irish Industry (Dublin: A. Thom. 1857)

Nichols, J. (ed.), *Letters on Various Subjects Literary, Political and Ecclesiastical, to and from William Nicholson, D.D., successively Bishop of Carlisle and of Derry, and Archbishop of Cashel*, 2 vols (London, 1809)

O'Keeffe, J., *The Recollections of John O'Keeffe* (London: Henry Colburn, 1826)

Pasquin, A., *An Authentic History of the Professors of Painting, Sculpture and Architecture who have Practised in Ireland* (London, 1796)

Patterson, R., *Introduction to Zoology for the Use of Schools, Parts 1 and 2* (London, 1849)

Plumptre, A., *Narrative of a Residence in Ireland during the Summer of 1814 and that of 1815* (London, 1817)

Pococke, C., *Pococke's Tour in Ireland in 1752, 2nd edn* (Dublin, 1891)

Raumer, F.L.G., *England in 1835: A Series of Letters Written to Friends in Germany During a Residence in London and Excursions into the Provinces* (Shannon, 1836; rpr. 1971)

Rhees, W.J., *Manual of Public Libraries, Institutions and Societies in the United States and British Provinces of North America* (Philadelphia, 1859)

Robinson, J., *Plan for the Improvements of the Fine Arts in Ireland* (Dublin, 1792)

Sproule, J. (ed.), *The Resources and Manufacturing Industry of Ireland as Illustrated by the Exhibition of 1853* (Dublin, 1853)

Smith, C., *The Ancient and Present State of the County and City of Cork* (Cork, 1750)

Talbot, E.A., *Five Years' Residence in the Canadas* (London, 1824)

Taylor, W.B., *The Origin, Process and Present Collection of the Fine Arts in Great Britain and Ireland* (London, 1841)

——, *History of the University of Dublin* (London: R. Jennings, 1845)

Thackeray, W. M., *An Irish Sketchbook, 1842* (London, 1843)

Tonna, C.E., *The Museum* (Dublin, 1832)

Twiss, R., *A Tour in Ireland in 1775* (London, 1776)

Walker, J.C., *Outlines for a Plan for Promoting the Art of Painting in Ireland: with a List of Subjects for Painters Drawn from the Romantic and Genuine Histories of Ireland* (Dublin, 1790)

Warburton, Whitelaw, et al., *A History of the City of Dublin* (London, 1818)

Ward, H.M.M., *The World of Wonders as Revealed by the Microscope* (London: Groomsbridge, 1858)

Wright, G., *Historical Guide to the City of Dublin* (London, 1825)

Wyse, T., *Education Reform* (London, 1836)

Young, A., *A Tour in Ireland 1776–79*, 2 vols, ed. A.W. Hutton (Shannon, 1780; rpr. 1970)

SECONDARY SOURCES

Theses

Carter, J., 'The Evolution of Museums as Centres for Learning: Chapters in Canadian Museology' (PhD, University of Leicester, 2000)

Jordan, P., 'The Origins and Development of Provincial Municipal Art Collections in Ireland during the Period 1930–60' (PhD, Open University, 2002)

Moore, C., 'The Life and Career in Ireland of Pieter De Gree' (BA thesis, TCD, 1989)

Rockley, J., 'Towards an Understanding of the Development of Antiquarianism and Archaeological Thought and Practice in Cork up to 1870' (PhD, UCC, 2000)

Articles in Periodicals and Journals since 1900

Aldeman. J., 'Evolution on Display: Promoting Irish Natural History and Darwinism at the Dublin Science and Art Museum', *British Journal for the History of Science*, vol. 38, no. 4, 2005

Allen, D. and R. Scholfield, 'In the Manner of One of Ireland: The Society of Arts and the Dublin Society, from the Earliest Years to 1801', *R.S.A. Journal*, 1990

Anderson, R., 'Introduction', in R. Anderson, et al. (eds), *Enlightening the British: Knowledge, Discovery and the Museum in the Eighteenth Century* (London: British Museum Press, 2003)

Archer, J.B., 'Geological Artistry: The Drawing and Watercolours of George Victor Du Noyer in the Archives of the Geological Survey of Ireland', in A. Dalsimer (ed.), *Visualising Ireland: National Identity and the Pictorial Tradition* (Boston: Faber & Faber, 1993)

Atkinson, S., 'Give Your Children Art!', *Irish Digest*, 1946

Augusteijn, J., 'The Importance of Being Irish: Ideas and the Volunteers in Mayo and Tipperary', in D. Fitzpatrick (ed.), *Revolution? Ireland 1917–1923* (Dublin: TCD, 1990)

Bannon, L., et al., 'Hybrid Design Creates Innovative Museum Experiences', *Communications of the ACM*, vol. 43, no. 3, 2005

Barrow, V., 'The National Gallery of Ireland', *Dublin Historical Record*, vol. xxxvi, 1983

Bayles, R., 'Understanding Local Science: The Belfast Natural History Society in the Mid Nineteenth Century', in D. Attis and C. Mollan (eds), *Science and Irish Culture* (Dublin: RDS, 2004)

Beaumont, E. and P. Sterry, 'A Study of Grandparents and Grandchildren as Visitors to Museum and Art Galleries in the UK', *Museums and Society*, vol. 3, no. 3, 2005

Beaumont, H. and A. Carroll, 'A Few of Our Favourite Things', *Museum Ireland*, vol. 12, 2002

Beirne, B., 'Supplement: Irish Entomology: The First Hundred Years', *Irish Naturalists' Journal*, no. 11, 1985

Bence-Jones, M., 'Ireland's Great Exhibition', *Country Life*, 15 March 1973

Bhreathnach- Lynch, S., 'The Academy of Christian Art (1929–46): An Aspect of Catholic Cultural Life in Newly Independent Ireland', *Éire-Ireland*, vol. 3, winter 1996

Black, E., 'Practical Patriots and True Irishmen: The Royal Irish Art Union 1839–59', *Irish Arts Review*, vol. 14, 1998

Bodkin, T., 'Modern Irish Art', in B. Hobson (ed.), *Saorstát Éireann: Irish Free State Official Handbook* (Dublin: Talbot Press, 1932)

Boland, J.P., 'The Future of Irish Art', *New Ireland Review*, vol. 26, no. 1, 1906–7

Borg, A., 'Theodore Jacobsen: A Gentleman', in C. Hourihane (ed.), *Irish Art Historical Studies in Honour of Peter Harbison* (Dublin: Four Courts Press, 2004)

Bourke, M., '*The Aran Fisherman's Drowned Child*', *Irish Arts Review*, vol. 6, 1988

——, 'Painting in Focus: Co-Ordinating a Touring Exhibition', *Journal of Education in Museums*, vol. 10, summer 1989

——, 'Frederic William Burton, 1816–1900, Painter and Antiquarian', *Éire-Ireland*, vol. 28, no. 3, 1993

——, 'Rural Life in Pre-Famine Connacht: A Visual Document', in B. Kennedy and R. Gillespie (eds), *Ireland: Art into History* (Dublin: Townhouse, 1994)

——, 'Innovative Approaches to Education at the National Gallery of Ireland', *Journal of the International Colloquium of Art Education in Museums*, Cologne, May 1996

——, 'The Irish Landscape through the Eyes of the Painter', in T. Collins (ed.), *Decoding the Landscape* (Galway: UCG, 1997)

——, 'Evie Hone in Her Studio: Hilda van Stockum's Portrait', *Studies*, vol. 86, no. 342, 1997

——, 'Irish Art Project Makes Cross-Border Links', *Museum Practice*, vol. 9, no. 3, 1998

——, 'Yeats, Henry and the Western Idyll', *History Ireland*, vol. 11, no. 2, 2003

——, 'Art Museums have No Boundaries: The Early Origins of Irish Museums Lead Towards New Opportunities in Learning', *ICOM Education*, vol. 18, 2004

——, 'A Growing Sense of National Identity in the Visual Arts in the Early Twentieth Century', in N. Garnham and K. Jeffrey (eds), *Historical Studies: Culture, Place and Identity* (Dublin: UCD, 2005), pp. 24–39

——, 'Partnership in Learning: Learning from Art', in *Proceedings of Committee for Education and Cultural Action* (Slovenia: ICOM, 2006)

——, 'Supporting Adult Learning and Creative Initiatives in Museums', in L. Sonne (ed.), *Cultural Heritage and Learning in the 3rd and 4th Age* (Ostersund: Nordic Centre of Cultural Heritage and Learning, 2009)

Bourke, T., 'Nationalism and the Royal Irish Academy', *Studies*, vol. 75, summer, 1986

Bright, K., 'Reflections on the Royal Dublin Society 1731–2001', *Dublin Historical Record*, vol. 56, no. 1, 2003

Cahill, M., 'The Dooyork Hoard', *Irish Arts Review*, vol. 19, no. 1, 2002

——, et al., 'James Carruthers, A Belfast Antiquarian Collector', in C. Hourihane (ed.), *Irish Art Historical Studies in Honour of Peter Harbison* (Dublin: Four Courts Press, 2004)

Cappock, M., 'Pageantry or Propaganda?,' *The Illustrated London News and Royal Visitors in Ireland* in *Irish Arts Review*, vol. 16, 2000

Carrington, F., 'The Children's Art Centre', *Bulletin of the Metropolitan Museum of Art*, vol. 13, no. 9, 1918

Carter, J.C., 'Museum Matters: A View of Our Past, a Reflection on Our Future?', in *Proceedings of the Sixth Ontario Museum Association Colloquium on Learning in Museums* (Toronto: Ontario Museums Association, 2001)

Chapman, L., 'Madame Tussaud's Years in Ireland 1804–8', *Quarterly Bulletin of the Irish Georgian Society*, vol. 24, nos. 3 and 4, 1981

Chesney, H., 'Enlightenment and Education', in J.W. Foster (ed.), *Nature in Ireland: A Scientific and Cultural History* (Dublin: Lilliput Press, 1997)

Collins, T., 'Early Teachers of Natural History', in T. Foley (ed.), *From Queen's College to National University* (Dublin: Four Courts Press, 1999)

——, 'A Note on the Life and Published Work of R.J. Anderson', *Galway Archaeological and Historical Society Journal*, vol. 56, 2004

Comerford, R.V., 'Introduction: Ireland, 1870–1921', in W.E. Vaughan (ed.), *A New History of Ireland VI: Ireland under the Union, II, 1870–1921* (Oxford: Clarendon Press, 1996)

Conforti, M., 'The Idealist Enterprise and the Applied Arts', in M. Baker and B. Richardson (eds), *A Grand Design: The Art of the Victoria and Albert Museum* (New York: Abrams and Baltimore Museum of Art, 1998)

Coolahan, J., 'Teaching in an Era of Change', *In Touch: Irish National Teachers' Organisation*, vol. 47, March 2003

Coulter, R., 'Hibernian Salon Des Refuses', *Irish Arts Review*, vol. 20, no. 3, 2003

Craig, M., 'The Society's Buildings', in J. Meenan and D. Clark (eds), *Royal Dublin Society 1731–1981* (Dublin: Gill & Macmillan, 1981)

Crookshank, A., and Knight of Glin, 'The Educational Background to the Dublin Society's Schools', *Leids Kunsthistorisch Jaarboek*, vol. 11, 1989

Csikszentmihalyi, M. and K. Hermanson, 'Intrinsic Motivation in Museums: What Makes Visitors Want to Learn?', *Museum News*, vol. 74, no. 3, 1995

Cullen, C., 'The Museum of Irish Industry: Robert Kane and education for all in the Dublin of the 1850s and 1860s', *History of Education*, vol. 38, no. 1, 2009.

Cullen, F., 'Marketing National Sentiment: Lantern Slides of Evictions in Late Nineteenth Century Ireland', *History Workshop Journal*, vol. 54, 2002

Curran, C.P., 'Archaeology', in B. Hobson (ed.), *Saorstát Éireann: Irish Free State Official Handbook* (Dublin: Talbot Press, 1932)

Curran, E., 'The National Gallery Revisited', *The Bell*, vol. 2, no. 5, 1941

——, 'World War II Revived Our Art', *Irish Digest*, 1947

Curry, K., 'William Dargan and the Worcester Shakespeare Service', *Irish Arts Review*, vol. 17, 2001

Davidson, B., et al., 'Increased Exhibit Accessibility through Multisensory Interaction', in E. Hooper-Greenhill (ed.), *The Educational Role of the Museum* (London: Routledge, 1994)

Davies, A.C., 'The Society of Arts and the Dublin Exhibition of 1853', *Journal of the Royal Society of Arts*, vol. 122, 1975

Davies, M., 'Investing in People', *Museums Journal*, vol. 105, no. 4, 2004

Davies, S., 'Renaissance: Changing the Museum Landscape in England', *Museum Ireland*, vol. 14, 2004

Dawson, G., 'The Douglas Hyde Gallery', *Irish Arts Review*, vol. 4, no. 4, 1987

De Forest, R.W., The 150th Anniversary of the Museum. *Bulletin of the Metropolitan Museum of Art* (New York: Metropolitan Museum, 1920), vol. 15, p. 124.

De Varine, H., 'Ecomuseums: Open-Air Museums', *ICOM News*, vol. 58, no. 3, 2005

Deane, A., 'Ireland's First Museum', *Belfast Municipal Art Gallery and Museum: Quarterly Notes*, vol. 25, March 1914

Dixon, F.E., 'Dublin Exhibitions, Parts 1 and 2', *Dublin Historical Record*, vol. 26, no. 3, 1973

Doyle, P., 'National Museum of Ireland: Country Life', *The Property Valuer* published by *The Irish Auctioneers & Valuers Institute/IAVI*, Autumn 2002, pp. 12–14

Drumm, S., 'The Irish Patrons of Rosalba Carriera', *Irish Architectural and Decorative Studies*, vol. 4, 2003

Duncan, C.W., 'Universal Survey Museum', *Art History*, vol. 111, 1980

——, 'From the Princely Gallery to the Public Art Museum', in D. Boswell (ed.), *Representing the Nation: A Reader, Histories, Heritage, and Museums* (London and New York: Routledge, 1999)

Dunlevy, M., 'Samuel Madden and the Scheme for the Encouragement of Useful Manufactures', in A. Bernelle (ed.), *Decantations: A Tribute to Maurice Craig* (Dublin: Lilliput Press, 1992)

Ellis, J., 'Plaster Cast Collections and Their Conservation: Some Irish Examples', *Museum Ireland*, vol. 14, 2004

Esteve-Coll, E., 'A Yearning for Learning', *Museums Journal*, vol. 93, no. 5, 1993

Fabianski, M., 'Musea in Written Sources of the Fifteenth to Eighteenth Centuries', *Opuscula Musealia*, vol. 4, no. 948, 1990

Fallon, C., The Royal Hibernian Academy and What it is About (*Art Bulletin/ebulletin*), December 2000, www.artistsireland.com

Fewtrell, M.D., 'The James Mitchell Geology Museum, University College, Galway', *Irish Naturalists' Journal*, vol. 19, 1979

Ffrench Salkeld, C., 'The Cultural Texture of a Country', *The Bell*, vol. 16, no. 2, 1950

Findlen, P., 'The Museum: Its Classical Etymology and Renaissance Geneaology', *Journal of the History of Collections*, vol. 1, no. 1, 1989

Fisher, J., 'A Powerful Vision for Irish Gallery', *Building Design*, 15 November 1996

FitzGerald, G., 'Mr. Whitaker and Industry', *Studies*, vol. 98, 1959

Foster, J.W., 'Natural History, Science and Culture', *Irish Review*, vol. 9, 1990

——, 'Nature and Nation in the Nineteenth Century', in J.W. Foster (ed.), *Nature in Ireland: A Scientific and Cultural History* (Dublin: Lilliput Press, 1997)

Freyling, C., 'Nourishing the Academy', in *Drawing Fire: Journal of the National Association for Fine Art Education*, vol. 1, no. 3, 1996

Frostick, E., 'Museums in Education: A Neglected Role?', *Museums Journal*, vol. 85, no. 2, 1985

Fyfe, G., 'Reproductions, Cultural Capital and Museums: Aspects of the Culture of Copies', *Museum and Society*, vol. 2, no. 1, 2004

Good, J. and M. Linnie, 'The History of the Early Nineteenth-Century *Coleoptera* Collection of James Tardy at Trinity College, Dublin, and the Validity of Records Based on this Collection', *Irish Naturalists' Journal*, vol. 23, no. 8, 1990

Gould, S.J., 'Cabinet Museums Revisited', *Natural History*, vol. 103, no. 1, January 1994

Greacen, R., 'Five Arts in Ireland', *Irish Digest*, November 1949

Gregory, A., 'Sir Frederic Burton', *The Leader*, vol. 1, no. 15, 1900

Guinness, D., 'An Unpublished Watercolour by James Malton from the Collection of Desmond Guinness', *Irish Architectural and Decorative Studies*, vol. 4, 2003

Hammond, J.W., 'Town Major Henry Charles Sirr', *Dublin Historical Record*, vol. 4, no. 1, 1941; vol. 4, no. 2, 1942

Harbison, P., 'Our First President, William Ashford, as Antiquarian Artist', in J. Hanley (ed.), *Royal Hibernian Academy* (Dublin: RHA, 2003)

Harper, D., 'Professor William King and the Establishment of the Geological Sciences in Queen's College Galway', in T. Foley (ed.), *From Queen's College to National University* (Dublin: Four Courts Press, 1999)

—— and M. Parkes, 'Geological Survey Donations to the Geological Museum in Queen's College Galway: 19th Century Inter-Institutional Collaboration in Ireland', *Geological Curator*, vol. 6, no. 6, 1996

Harry, O., 'The Hon. Mrs. Ward (1827–69), Artist, Naturalist, Astronomer and Ireland's First Lady of the Microscope', *Irish Naturalists' Journal*, vol. 21, no. 5, 1984

Hartfield, R., 'Challenging the Context: Perception, Polity, and Power', *Curator*, vol. 37, no. 1, 1994

Heal, S., 'Northern Ireland Nationals to get New Name and Makeover', *Museums Journal*, vol. 106, no. 2, 2006

Heaney, S., 'A Sense of the Past', *History Ireland*, vol. 1, no. 4, winter 1993

——, 'Foreword', in J. Dunne and J. Kelly (eds), *Childhood and its Discontents* (Dublin: Liffey Press, 2002)

Herity, M., 'Irish Antiquarian Finds and Collections of the Early Nineteenth Century', *JRSAI*, vol. 99, no. 1, 1969

Herries Davies, G.L., 'The Palaeontological Collection of Lord Cole, third Earl of Enniskillen (1807–86), at Florence Court, Co. Fermanagh', *Irish Naturalists' Journal*, vol. 16, no. 12, 1977

——, 'Notes on the Various Issues of Sir Richard Griffith's Quarter-Inch Geological Map of Ireland 1839–55', *Imago Mundi*, vol. 29, no. I, 1977

——, 'Geology in Ireland before 1912: A Biographical Outline', *Western Naturalist*, vol. 7, 1978

——, 'Richard Griffith and the Royal Dublin Society', in G.L. Herries Davies and R. Millan (eds), *Richard Griffith 1784–1878* (Dublin: RDS, 1980)

——, 'Irish Thought in Science', in R. Kearney (ed.), *The Irish Mind: Exploring Intellectual Traditions* (Dublin: Wolfhound Press, 1985)

——, 'William King and the Irish Geological Community', in D. Harper (ed.), *William King D.Sc. – A Palaeontological Tribute* (Galway: Galway University Press, 1988)

——, 'A Forty-Year Retrospect', in P. N. Wyse Jackson (ed.), *In Marble Halls: Geology in Trinity College Dublin* (Dublin: TCD, 1994)

——, 'Before a Blood-Stained Tapestry: Irish Political Violence and Irish Science', in D. Attis and C. Mollan (eds), *Science and Irish Culture* (Dublin: RDS, 2004)

Heslip, R., 'Museums and Public Achievement', *Museum Ireland*, vol. 13, 2003

Heywood, F., 'Survey Says Museums and Galleries Lead the Way on Customer Satisfaction', *Museums Journal*, vol. 105, no. 10, 2005

Hobsbawm, E., 'Mass Producing Traditions: Europe, 1870–1914', in E. Hobsbawn and T. Ranger (eds), *The Invention of Tradition* (Cambridge: Cambridge University Press, 2003)

Hoppen, K.T., 'The Royal Society and Ireland', *Notes and Records of the Royal Society*, vol. 20, 1965

Horton, C., 'A Light to the World', *Irish Arts Review*, vol. 21, no. 4, 2004

——, 'The Chester Beatty Library: Ireland's Museum of the Book' *Leabharlann: The Irish Library*, vol. 18, no. 1, 2008

Hoskin, M., 'Archives of Dunsink and Markree Obervatories', *Journal for the History of Astronomy*, vol. 13, 1982

Houlihan, M., 'Opening Horizons: A New Vision for Northern Ireland's National Museums and Galleries', *Museum Ireland*, vol. 10, 2000

Igoe, V. and F. Dwyer, 'Early Views of the Royal Hospital, Kilmainham', *Irish Arts Review*, vol. 5, 1988

Ireland, A., 'Robert Chambers Walker: A Sligo Antiquarian', *Journal of Irish Archaeology*, vol. 11, 2002

——, 'The First 25 Years', *Museum Ireland*, vol. 12, 2002

Jarrell, R., 'The Department of Science and Art in Control of Irish Science in the Nineteenth Century', *Irish Historical Studies*, vol. 23, no. 92, 1983

——, 'Technical Education and Colonialism in Nineteenth-Century Ireland', in N. McMillan (ed.), *Prometheus's Fire* (Kilkenny: Modern Printers, 1999)

Johnston, A.W., 'A Catalogue of Greek Vases in Public Collections in Ireland', *PRAI*, vol. 73, no. 9, 1973

Judd, D., 'Designed for Different Audiences and Different Learning Styles: The New British Galleries at the V&A', *Group for Education in Museums/GEM News*, vol. 83, 2001

Juncosa, E., 'Contemporary Collaborations' *Irish Arts Review*, 2004

Kavanagh, R., 'The First World War and its Implication for Education in British Museums', *History of Education*, vol. 17, no. 2, 1988

Kearney, F., 'Fostering Scholarship and Access,' *Visual Artists News Sheet*, January–February 2005

Kelly, A., 'Thomas Bodkin and the National Gallery of Ireland', *Irish Arts Review*, vol. 8, 1991–2

——, 'The Milltown Collection', *Irish Arts Review*, vol. 22, no. 3, 2005

Kelly, J., 'The Fall of Parnell and the Rise of Irish Literature', *Anglo-Irish Studies*, vol. 2, 1976

——, 'Francis Wheatley in Ireland, 1779–83', in A. Dalsimer (ed.), *Visualising Ireland: National*

Identity and the Pictorial Tradition (London and Boston: Faber & Faber, 1993)

Kennedy, B., 'Towards a National Cultural Policy', *Seirbhís Phoiblí*, vol. 9, no. 2, 1988

——, 'James White: A Brief Biography', in B. Kennedy (ed.), *Art is My Life: A Tribute to James White* (Dublin: NGI, 1991)

Kiberd, D., 'Learning in Museums', in M. Bourke (ed.), *Proceedings of the Symposium Learning in Museums* (Dublin, NGI, 2003)

Le Brocquy, L., 'James White', in B. Kennedy (ed.), *Art is My Life: A Tribute to James White* (Dublin: NGI, 1991)

Leaney, E., 'Missionaries of Science: Provincial Lectures in Nineteenth-Century Ireland', *Irish Historical Studies*, vol. 34, no. 135, 2005

Leerssen, J., 'The Cultivation of Culture: Towards a Definition of Romantic Nationalism in Europe', in *Working Papers. European Studies. University of Amsterdam, 2*, 2005

Leslie, S. and B. Fallon, 'Our National Gallery: A Personal History', *Irish Tatler & Sketch*, December, 1969

Lewis, G., 'The Universal Museum: A Special Case?', *ICOM News*, vol. 57, no. 1, 2004

Lindauer, M., 'What to Ask and How to Answer: A Comparative Analysis of Methodologies and Philosophies of Summative Exhibit Evaluation', *Museum and Society*, vol. 3, no. 3, 2005

Long. G., 'The Foundation of the National Library of Ireland 1836–1877', *Long Room*, vol. 36, 1991

Love, W.D., 'The Hibernian Antiquarian Society', *Studies*, vol. 51, 1962

Low, T.L., 'The Museum as a Social Instrument: Twenty Years After', *Museum News*, vol. 40, January, 1962

——, 'What is a Museum?', in C. Anderson (ed.), *Reinventing the Museum: Historical and Contemporary Perspectives on the Paradigm Shift* (Walnut Creek, Altamira Press: 2004)

Lucas, A.T., 'The National Museum: Its Place in the Cultural Life of the Nation', *Oideas: Iris na Roinne Oideachais*, vol. 1, 1968

——, 'The National Museum of Ireland', *Éire: Bulletin of the Department of External Affairs*, vol. 198, 1969

Lysaght, S., 'Themes in the Irish History of Science', *Irish Review*, vol. 19, 1996

McAvera, B., 'IMMA and the Devil's Advocate', *Irish Arts Review*, vol. 19, no. 3, 2002

McCarthy, P., 'From Torpedo Boat to Temples of Culture: Carlo Cambi's Route to Ireland', *Irish Arts Review*, vol. 18, 2002

McCrum, E., 'Irish Victorian Jewellery', *Irish Arts Review*, vol. 2, 1985

McDowell, R.B., 'The Main Narrative', in T. Ó Raifeartaigh (ed.), *The Royal Irish Academy* (Dublin: RIA, 1985)

McGonagle, D., 'The Necessary Museum', *Irish Arts Review*, vol. 8, 1991–2

MacGreevy, T., 'Fifty Years of Irish Painting 1900–1950', *Capuchin Annual*, vol. 19, 1949

McGuinne, N., 'A History of Conservation in Ireland', *Museum Ireland*, vol. 15, 2005

McKenna, S., 'Academies', in J. Hanley (ed.), *Royal Hibernian Academy* (Dublin: RHA, 2003)

McLean, F., 'Creating a Synergy between the Museum's Collection and Audience', *Museum Ireland*, vol. 15, 2005

McParland, E., 'The Royal Hospital, Kilmainham, Co. Dublin', *Country Life*, 9 and 16 May 1985

——, 'Francis Johnston, Architect, 1760–1829' *Quarterly Bulletin of the Irish Georgian Society*, vol. 12, 1986

Marsh, A., 'Dublin's Museums' , *The Bell*, vol. 4, no. 1, 1943

Marshall, C., 'A Quiet National Treasure: Gordon Lambert and the Making of a Collection', *Irish Arts Review*, vol. 15, 1999

——, 'Sustaining and Raiding the Larder: The Development of a Collection at IMMA in Its First Thirteen Years', *Museum Ireland*, vol. 14, 2004

Martin, G., 'The Founding of the National Gallery', *Connoisseur*, vol. 187, April–December 1974

Merriman, N., 'Museum Visiting as a Cultural Phenomenon', in P. Vergo (ed.), *The New Museology* (London: Reaktion Books, 1989)

Mitchell, G.F., 'Antiquities', in T. Ó Raifeartaigh (ed.), *The Royal Irish Academy: A Bicentennial History (1785–1985)* (Dublin: RIA, 1985)

——, 'Mineral and Geology', in J. Meenan and D. Clarke (eds), *The Royal Dublin Society* (Dublin: Gill & Macmillan, 1998)

Moffat, H., 'The Educational Use of Museums: An English Case-Study', *History and Social Science Teacher*, vol. 23, no. 3, 1988

Monaghan, N.T., 'Sir Karl Ludwig Metzler-Geisecke (1761–1833), Royal Mineralogist, Greenland Explorer and Museum Curator', in E. Hoch and A. Bransten (eds), *Centenary of the Geological Museum, Copenhagen University, Deciphering the Natural World and the Role of Collections and Museums* (Copenhagen: Geological Museum, 1993)

——, 'The National Museum of Ireland', in N. Buttimer, C. Rynne and H. Guerin (eds), *The Heritage of Ireland* (Cork: The Collins Press, 2000)

——, 'Frederick McCoy', in C. Mollan, W. Davis and B. Finucane (eds), *Irish Innovators in Science and Technology* (Dublin: RIA, 2002)

——, 'Modelling Nature', *Irish Arts Review*, vol. 20, no. 4, 2003

Moore McCann, B., 'A Poetry of Vision: The Rosc Exhibitions', *Irish Arts Review*, vol. 18, 2002

Moore, F., 'Young Ireland and Liberal Ideas', *Dana: An Irish Magazine of Independent Thought*, vol. 2, 1904

Murphy, P., 'Exhibitions', in J. Hanley (ed.), *Royal Hibernian Academy: One Hundred and Seventy-Fifth Anniversary Exhibition* (Dublin: RHA, 2005)

Murray, K.A., 'William Dargan', *Journal of the Irish Railway Record Society*, vol. 2, 1950–1

Netzer, N., 'Picturing an Exhibition: James Mahony's Watercolours of the Irish Industrial Exhibition of 1853', in A. Dalsimer (ed.), *Visualising Ireland: National Identity and the Pictorial Tradition* (Boston: Faber & Faber, 1993), pp. 19, 29

Nevinson, J.L., 'Antiquarians: Museums in the Eighteenth Century', *Museums Journal*, vol. 59, no. 2, 1959

Nightingale, J., 'Classical Education', *Museums Journal*, vol. 103, no. 11, 2003

Nochlin, L., 'Museums and Radicals: A History of Emergencies', B. O'Doherty (ed.), *Art in America* (New York: George Braziller, 1971)

Nolan, A., 'Innovative Approaches to Working with Young People in Healthcare Settings', *Proceedings of the Symposium Museums, Galleries and Young People*, vol. 6, 2006

Nolan, J.C., 'Income Generation for Museums: Problems and Prospects', *Museum Ireland*, vol. 1, 1991

North, F.J., 'On Learning How to Run a Museum: Lessons from Some Early Collections', *Museums Journal*, vol. 51, no. 1, 1951

O'Brien, G., 'Between a Thing and a Thought: A Brief History of the Collection', in S. Pierce and G. O'Brien (eds), *Imagining Ireland: Selected Works from the Collection of the National University of Ireland, Galway* (Galway: National University of Ireland, Galway, 2004)

O'Connor, C., 'The Dispersal of the Country House Collections of Ireland', *Bulletin of the Irish Georgian Society*, vol. 35, 1992–3

O'Connor, J.P., 'Insects and Entomology', in J.W. Foster (ed.), *Nature in Ireland: A Scientific and Cultural History* (Dublin: Lilliput Press 1997)

O'Doherty, B., 'An Tostal and the Visual Arts', *Irish Monthly*, July 1954

O'Doherty, I., 'Muse 99', in *ASTIR*, May 1999

O'Donoghue, D., 'State Within a State: The Nazis in Neutral Ireland', *History Ireland*, vol. 6, November–December 2006

O'Dwyer, F., 'Building Empires: Architecture, Politics and the Board of Works 1760–1860', *Journal of the Irish Georgian Society*, vol. 5, 2002

O'Faoláin, S., 'The New Criticism', *The Bell*, vol. 18, no. 3, 1952

O'Hagan, J.W., 'Art Museum: Collections, De-accessioning and Donations', *Journal of Cultural Economics*, vol. 22, nos. 2–3, 1998

——, 'Economics Engages Museology: The Case of Art Museums', *Museum Ireland*, vol. 14, 2004

—— and C. McAndrew, 'Restricting International Trade in the National Artistic Patrimony: Economic Rationale and Policy Instruments', *International Journal of Cultural Property*, vol. 10, no. 1, 2001

Olley, J., 'Sustaining the Narrative at Kilmainham', *Irish Arts Review*, vol. 8, 1991–92

O'Malley, C., 'Gifting the Nation', *Irish Arts Review*, vol. 20, no. 4, 2003

O'Neill, M., 'Enlightenment Museums: Universal or Merely Global?', *Museum and Society*, vol. 2, no. 3, 2004

Ó Seaghdha, B., 'Conflict Ulster Museum', *Museum Ireland*, vol. 14, 2004

Ó Tuathaigh, G., 'The Establishment of the Queen's Colleges: Ideological and Political Background', in T. Foley (ed.), *From Queen's College to National University* (Dublin: Four Courts Press, 1999)

Parkhill, T., 'The Curator as Interpreter, Interlocutor and Facilitator: The 1798 Exhibition and The Conflict Exhibition 2003', in M. Bourke (ed.), *Effective Presentation and Interpretation* (Dublin: NGI, 2004)

Parry, R.L., 'Wireless World', *Museums Journal*, vol. 106, no. 2, 2006

Peill, J., 'Heirlooms of Newbridge House', *Irish Arts Review*, vol. 20, no. 2, 2003

Pettigrew, T., 'William King (1808–86): A Biographical Note', *Newsletter of the Geological Curators Group*, vol. 3, 1980

Potterton, H., 'Obituary: James White (1913–2003)', *Burlington Magazine*, vol. 145, 2003

Pratty, J., 'New Wave Museum Web Design', *Museum Ireland*, vol. 15, 2005

Raftery, J., 'Drainage and the Past', *Oibre*, vol. 4, 1966

Reeve, J., 'Partners in Presentation: Successful Teamwork and Creative Interpretation', in M. Bourke (ed.), *Proceedings of the Symposium Effective Presentations and Interpretations in Museums* (Dublin: NGI, 2004)

Reid, G., 'Defining the Nation: Memory, Identity and Tradition in Ireland's National Museums', *Museum Ireland*, vol. 13, 2003

Rice, D., 'On the Ethics of Museum Education', *Museum News – Washington*, vol. 65, no. 5, 1987

——, 'Museum Education Embracing Uncertainty', *Art Bulletin*, vol. 77, no. 1, 1995

Robertson, B., 'The South Kensington Museum in Context: An Alternative History', *Museum and Society*, vol. 2, no. 1, 2004

Robinson, K., 'The Edo Masterwork Restored: The Chogonka Scrolls in the Chester Beatty Library, Dublin', *Irish Arts Review*, vol. 16, 2000

Rogers, M., 'Mutual Passions: A Public Museum and Private Collectors', *Apollo*, June 2005

Roholt, R. and M. Baizerman, 'Youth and Museums', *Museum Ireland*, vol. 15, 2005

Ryan, M., 'Early Irish Chalices', *Irish Arts Review*, vol. 1, no. 1, 1984

——, 'The Menagerie of the Derrynaflan Paten', *Irish Arts Review*, vol. 11, 1995

——, 'The Chester Beatty Library', *Museum Ireland*, vol. 10, 2000

——, 'Displaying Sacred Manuscripts: The Experience of the Chester Beatty Library', in Pontifical Commission for the Cultural Heritage of the Church, *Cathedral Workshops on Religious Arts and Crafts Proceedings* (Rome: Pontifical Commission for the Cultural Heritage of the Church, 2003).

Ryan, T, 'The Vicissitudes of the Royal Hibernian Academy', *Irish Arts Review*, vol. 2, no. 3, 1985

Ryan, V., 'The Crawford Municipal Gallery, Cork', *Irish Arts Review*, vol. 8, 1991–92

Saris, A.J., 'Imagining Ireland in the Great Exhibition of 1853', in L. Litvack and G. Hooper (eds), *Ireland in the Nineteenth Century* (Dublin: Four Courts Press, 2000)

Sekers, D., 'Independence Stimulates', in N. Cossons (ed.), *The Management of Change in Museums* (London: National Maritime Museum, 1985)

Seling, H., 'The Genesis of the Museum', *Architectural Review*, vol. 141, no. 840, 1967

Selwood, S., 'Profile of Museums and Galleries', in S. Selwood (ed.), *The UK Cultural Sector: Profile and Policy Issues* (London: Policy Studies Institute, 2001)

—— and S. Davies, 'English Cultural Services: Government Policy and Local Strategies', *Cultural Trends*, vol. 30, 1998

Siung, J., 'Setting Up an Education Service in the Chester Beatty Library', *Museum Ireland*, vol. 11, 2001

Smith, A., 'The New Directors', *Irish Arts Review*, vol. 10, 1994

Speers, S., et al., 'Towards Reconciliation: A Role for Museums in Divided Society', in L. Silverman and J. Hirsch (eds), *Transforming Practice: Sections from the Journal of Museum Education 1992–1999* (Washington, DC: Museum Education Roundtable, 2000)

Stanford, W.B., 'Polite Literature', in T. Ó Raifeartaigh (ed.), *The Royal Irish Academy 1785–1985* (Dublin: RIA, 1985)

Stewart, A.T.Q., 'Kings in Conflict', *Irish Arts Review*, vol. 8, 1992

Street, J., 'Learning through Culture: Impact of Phase 2 of Museums and Galleries Education Programme', *Journal of Education in Museums*, vol. 25, 2004

Strickland, W.G., 'The Carruthers' Collection, 1 Jan. 1857. Irish Antiquities', *JRSAI*, vol. 12, 1922

Teahan, J., 'Museums for the People', *Public Affairs*, vol. 5, no. 10, 1973

Tierney, M., 'Partition and a Policy of National Unity', *Studies*, vol. 24, 1935

Tipton, G., 'Art House', *Irish Arts Review*, vol. 21, no. 4, 2004

——, 'The Lewis Glucksman Gallery, Cork', *Museum Ireland*, vol. 15, 2005

Trodd, C., 'The Discipline of Pleasure; or, How Art History Looks at the Art Museum', *Museum and Society*, vol. 1, no. 1, 2004

Turner, S., 'Collections and Collectors of Note: 26. William King 1808–86', *Newsletter of the Geological Curators Group*, vol. 3, 1980

Turpin, J., 'William Orpen as a Student and Teacher', *Studies*, vol. 67, no. 271, 1979

——, 'Exhibitions of Art and Industries in Victorian Ireland', *Dublin Historical Record*, vol. 35, no. 1, 1981

——, 'The RHA Schools 1826–1906', *Irish Arts Review*, vol. 8, 1991–2

——, 'Irish Art and Design Education', *Irish Arts Review*, vol. 10, 1994

——, 'The Education of Irish Artists 1877–1975', *Irish Arts Review*, vol. 13, 1997

——, 'Introduction', in G. Willemson (ed.), *The Dublin Society Drawing Schools* (Dublin: RDS, 2000)

Walker, D., 'Dublin's Hidden Treasure', *Irish Arts Review*, vol. 4, no. 3, 1987

——, 'L'Art de Vivre: The Designs of Eileen Gray', *Irish Arts Review*, special edition 2004

Wallace, P.F., 'The Archaeological Identity of the Hiberno-Norse Town', *JRSAI*, vol. 122, 1992

——, 'Adolf Mahr and the Making of Sean P. Ó Riordáin', in H. Roche, et al. (eds), *From Megaliths to Metal: Essays in Honour of George Eogan* (Oxford: Oxbow Books, 2004)

Walsh, A., 'Change and the Northern Ireland Museums Council', *Museum Ireland*, vol. 4, 1994

Walton, J., 'Classicism and Civility', *Irish Arts Review*, vol. 21, no. 1, 2004

Waterfield, G., 'Anticipating the Enlightenment: Museums and Galleries in Britain before the British Museum', in R. Anderson, et al. (eds) *Enlightening the British* (London: British Museum Press, 2003)

Waterhouse, G., 'Goethe, Giesecke, and Dublin', *PRIA*, vol. 41, section C, 1933

Weatherup, R.M., 'Armagh County Museum, Archaeological Acquisitions. The Collection of Armagh Natural History and Philosophical Society', *JRSAI*, vol. 112, 1982

Weil, S., 'Courtly Ghosts and Aristocratic Artifacts: The Art Museum as Palace', *Museum News*, vol. 77, no. 6, 1995

——, 'From Being *about* Something to Being *for* Somebody: The Ongoing Transformation of the American Museum', *Daedalus: Journal of the American Academy of Arts & Sciences*, vol. 128, no. 3, 1999

Wheeler, T.S., 'Sir Robert Kane: Life and Work', *Studies*, vol. 34, no. 133, 1945

——, 'William Higgins, Chemist (1763–1825)', *Studies*, vol. 43, 1954

White, H.B., 'History of the Science and Art Institutions, Dublin', *Bulletin of the National Museum of Science and Art, Dublin*, 1911

White, J., 'The Visual Arts in Ireland', *Studies*, vol. 44, spring 1955

Whitfield, N., 'The Finding of the Tara Brooch', *JRSAI*, vol. 104, 1974

Whitty, A., 'The Caspar Purdon Clarke Indian and Persian Collection of the National Museum of Ireland, 1878–79', *Museum Ireland*, vol. 14, 2004

Whyte, N., 'Digging Up the Past: A Visit to Markree Castle', *Stardust*, vol. 25, no. 4, 1992

Williams, J., 'Museums as a Community Resource: Not Just Who but How', *Museum Ireland*, vol. 11, 2001

——, 'Whatever You Say, Say Nothing: The MAGNI Citizenship Project', *Museum Ireland*, vol. 14, 2004

Wynne, M., 'The Milltowns as Patrons, Particularly Concerning the Picture-Collecting of the First Two Earls', *Apollo*, vol. 49, 1979

——, 'The McNeill Bequest', *Irish Arts Review*, vol. 3, no. 4, 1986

——, 'Acquiring Irish Paintings', in B. Kennedy (ed.), *Art is My Life: A Tribute to James White* (Dublin: NGI, 1991)

Wyse Jackson, P.N., 'The Geological Collections of Trinity College, Dublin', *Geological Curator*, vol. 5, no. 7, 1992

——, 'A Victorian Landmark, Trinity College's Museum Building', *Irish Arts Review*, vol. 11, 1995

——, 'The Fossil Fishes of Bloca and the Travels in Italy of the Irish Cleric George Graydon 1791', *Museological Scientifica*, vol. 4, 1995

——, 'Fluctuations in Fortune: Three Hundred Years of Irish Geology', in J.W. Foster (ed.), *Nature in Ireland, A Scientific and Cultural History* (Dublin: Lilliput Press, 1997)

——, 'Sir Charles Lewis Giesecke (1761–1833) and Greenland: A Recently Discovered Mineral Collection in Trinity College, Dublin', *Irish Journal of Earth Sciences*, vol. 13, 1999

——, 'The Honorable George Knox (1765–1827): Parliamentarian and Mineral Collector', *Mineralogical Record*, vol. 37, no. 6, 2006

Young Lee, P., 'Musaeum of Alexandria and the Formation of the Museum in Eighteenth-Century France', *Art Bulletin*, vol. 79, no. 3, 1997

Museum/Gallery Catalogues Since 1900

Anderson R.J., *A Catalogue of Specimens in the Zoological, Botanical, Geological, Mineralogical, Ethnological and Art Collections Contained in the Museum of the University College Galway: Part 1* (Galway: Express Printing Co., 1911)

Anon, *A Festival of Young People's Art: Works of Art by Pupils from Primary and Post-Primary Schools in the Republic of Ireland and Northern Ireland* (Dublin: Department of Education, 1993)

Anon, *A Few of Our Favourite Things* (Dublin: NMI, 2002)

Art Gallery of the Corporation of London, *Catalogue of the Exhibition of Works by Irish Painters* (London: Art Gallery of the Corporation of London, 1904)

Baker, C. and T. Henry, *The National Gallery: Complete Illustrated Catalogue* (London: National Gallery Publications, 1995)

Bell, J. and M. Bourke, *Museums Matter: Accessing Ireland's Heritage* (Dublin: IMA, 2008)

Benedetti, S., *Caravaggio: The Master Revealed* (Dublin: NGI, 1993; revised edition 1999).

——, *The Milltowns: A Family Reunion* (Dublin: NGI, 1997)

——, *The La Touche Amorino: Canova and His Fashionable Patrons* (Dublin: NGI, 1998)

——, et al., *National Gallery of Ireland: Essential Guide* (London: NGI /Scala, 2008)

Black, E., *A Sesquicentennial Celebration: Art from the Queen's University Collection* (Belfast: QUB, 1995)

——, *Art in Belfast 1760–1888: Art Lovers or Philistines?* (Dublin: Irish Academic Press, 2006)

——, (ed.), *The Catalogue of Drawings, Paintings and Sculptures* (Belfast: Museums and Galleries of Northern Ireland, 2000)

——, S. Kennedy and W. Maguire, *Dreams & Traditions: 300 Years of British and Irish Painting from the Collection of the Ulster Museum* (Belfast: Ulster Museum /Smithsonian Institution Traveling Exhibition Services, 1997)

Bodkin, T., *National Gallery of Ireland: Catalogue of Oil Pictures in the General Collection* (Dublin: NGI, 1932)

Bourke, M. (ed.), *Children's Art: A Celebration* (Dublin: NGI, 1992)

——, *Drawing Studies: A Celebration* (Dublin: NGI, 2007)

Campbell, J., *Nathaniel Hone the Younger* (Dublin: NGI, 1991)

Caplan, U., *Monet, Renoir and the Impressionist Landscape* (Ottawa: National Gallery of Canada /Museum of Fine Arts, Boston, 2000)

Catalogue of Paintings Restored in the National Gallery of Ireland (Dublin: NGI, 1971)

Clarke, H. and A. O'Flanagan (eds), *75 Years of Giving: The Friends of the National Collections of Ireland: Works of Art Donated by the Friends of the Public Collections of Ireland* (Dublin: Friends of the National Collections of Ireland, 1999)

Coffey, G., *The Royal Irish Academy Collection: Guide to the Celtic Antiquities of the Christian Period Preserved in the National Museum* (Dublin: Hodges & Figgis, 1909)

Cone, P. (ed.), *Treasures of Early Irish Art 1500 BC to 1300 AD from the Collection of the National Museum of Ireland, Trinity College, Dublin, Royal Irish Academy* (New York: Metropolitan Museum of Art, 1977)

——, (ed.), *Samuel Beckett: A Passion for Paintings* (Dublin: NGI, 2006)

Croke, F. (ed.), *George Victor Du Noyer 1817–1869: Hidden Landscapes* (Dublin: NGI, 1995)

——, (ed.), *Art into Art: A Living Response to Past Masters* (Dublin: NGI, 1998)

——, (ed.), *Samuel Beckett: A Passion for Paintings* (Dublin: NGI, 2006)

Crookshank, A. and D. Webb, *Paintings and Sculptures in Trinity College Dublin* (Dublin: TCD, 1990)

Dawson, B., *Turner in the National Gallery of Ireland* (Dublin: NGI, 1988)

Dillon, S., et al., *National Gallery of Ireland Illustrated Summary Catalogue of Prints and Sculpture* (Dublin: NGI, 1988)

Dublin Museum of Science and Art: Short Guide to the Collections (Dublin, Alex Thorn & Co., 1900)

Dukes, O. and C. Marshall, *Celebrating a Decade* (Dublin: IMMA, 2001)

Dunne, T. (ed.), *James Barry 1741–1806: The Great Historical Painter* (Cork: Crawford Art Gallery/ Gandon Editions, 2005)

Fenlon, J., *The Ormonde Picture Collection* (Kilkenny: Kilkenny Castle /Dúchas, 2001)

Figgis, N., and B. Rooney, *Irish Paintings in the National Gallery of Ireland, Volume 1,* (Dublin: NGI, 2001)

Gallagher, W., *The Modern Art Collection: University College Cork* (Cork: UCC, 1998)

Guide to Belfast and the Counties of Down and Antrim by the Belfast Naturalists' Field Club (Belfast: The Linenhall Press, 1902)

Hodge, A., *Hugh Douglas Hamilton: A Life in Pictures* (Dublin: NGI, 2008)

Hunt, J., et al. (eds), *The Hunt Museum: Essential Guide* (London: Scala, 2002)

Husko, T. and A. Waiboer, *Northern Stars and Southern Lights: The Golden Age of Finnish Art 1870–1920* (Dublin: NGI, 2009)

Irish Delftware, ROSC Exhibition Catalogue (Dublin: Trinity College, Dublin, 1971)

Keaveney, R., *Master European Drawings from the Collection of the National Gallery of Ireland* (Washington, DC: Smithsonian Institution, 1983)

——, (ed.), *Views of Rome from the Thomas Ashby Collection in the Vatican Library* (London: Scala, in association with Biblioteca Apostolico Vaticana and the Smithsonian Institution Traveling Exhibition Service, 1988)

Laffan, W. and B. Rooney, *Thomas Roberts, Landscape and Patronage in Eighteenth-Century Ireland* (Tralee: Churchill Press for the National Gallery of Ireland, 2009)

Lane, H., *Catalogue of Pictures Presented to the City of Dublin to Form the Nucleus of a Gallery of Modern Art* (Dublin: RHA, 1904)

Langton Douglas, R., *Catalogue of Paintings* (Dublin: NGI, 1920)

Le Harivel, A., *National Gallery of Ireland Illustrated Summary Catalogue of Drawings, Watercolours and Miniatures* (Dublin: NGI, 1983)

——, (ed.), *National Gallery of Ireland Illustrated Summary Catalogue of Prints and Sculpture* (Dublin: NGI, 1988)

——, (ed.), et. al., *Taking Stock: Acquisitions 2000–2010* (Dublin: NGI, 2010)

——and M. Wynne, *National Gallery of Ireland Illustrated Summary Catalogue of Paintings* (Dublin: NGI, 1981)

Litton, H. (ed.), *Master European Paintings from the National Gallery of Ireland* (Dublin: NGI, 1992)

Loan Collection of Pictures by Nathaniel Hone RHA and John Butler Yeats (Dublin, 1901)

Loan Collection of Works by Sir Frederic William Burton RHA (Dublin: National Gallery of Ireland, 1900)

McArdle, A., *Yours and Mine: Thoughts on Collecting and Collections* (Dublin: IMMA, 2000)

McCrum, E., *Fabric & Form: Irish Fashion since 1950* (Belfast: Ulster Museum, 1996)

McGoogan, A., *Catalogue of Watercolours and Oil Paintings, Chalk and Pencil Drawings* (Dublin: Department of Agriculture and Technical Instruction, 1920)

MacGreevy, T., *Pictures in the Irish National Gallery* (Dublin: NGI, 1945)

McLean, J. (ed.), *Impressionist Interiors* (Dublin: NGI, 2008)

MacLochlainn, A., et al., *Science and Art 1877–1977* (Dublin: NMI, 1977)

Maguire, W.A., *The 1798 Rebellion in Ireland: A Bicentenary Exhibition* (Belfast: Ulster Museum/ Belfast City Council, 1998)

Marshall, C., *The Collection 1999–2001* (Dublin: IMMA, 2001)

Monaghan, N.T., *Guide to the National Museum of Ireland: Natural History* (Dublin: NMI, 2005)

Murray, P., *The Crawford Municipal Gallery of Art: Illustrated Summary Catalogue* (Cork: Cork VEC, 1992)

——, *George Petrie (1790–1866): The Rediscovery of Ireland's Past* (Cork: Crawford Municipal Art Gallery/Gandon Editions, 2004)

——, (ed.), *Whipping the Herring: Survival and Celebration in Nineteenth-Century Irish Art* (Cork: Crawford Art Gallery/Gandon Editions, 2006)

Muse 99: Catalogue (Dublin: NMI, 1999)

Nygaard, T., *Matisse &* (Copenhagen: Statens Museum for Kunst, 2005)

Ó Riordáin, S., *Museums: Cork Public Museum Souvenir Guide to the First Exhibition* (Cork: Cork Corporation, 1945)

O'Byrne, R., *Hugh Lane's Legacy to the National Gallery of Ireland* (Dublin: NGI, 2000)

O'Connor, A. and N. McGuinne, *The Deeper Picture: Conservation at the National Gallery of Ireland* (Dublin: NGI, 1998)

O'Donoghue, H., '… *and start to wear purple*' (Dublin: IMMA, 1999)

O'Molloy, M. (ed.), *Irish Museum of Modern Art: The Collection* (Dublin: IMMA, 2005)

O'Neill, C., *Mapping Lives, Exploring Futures* (Dublin: IMMA, 2006)

O'Riordan, C.E., *The Natural History Museum* (Dublin: Stationery Office, 1983)

Potterton, H., *The Beit Collection* (Dublin: NGI, 1988)

Quinn, S. (ed.), *Learning from Art: Catalogue with Essays* (Dublin: NGI, 2004)

Rooney, B. (ed.), *A Time and a Place: Two Centuries of Irish Social Life* (Dublin: NGI, 2006)

Rowan, A., *Art for an Institution: University Collage – Catalogue of the Art Collection of University College Dublin* (Dublin: AnCO/Irish Museums Trust Arts, 1983)

Ryan, M., *Treasures of Ireland 3000 BC to 1500 AD* (Dublin: NMI, 1983)

Schuster, P.K., *A German Dream: Masterpieces of Romanticism from the Nationalgalerie Berlin* (Dublin: NGI, 2004)

Scott, D., *The Modern Art Collection: Trinity College Dublin* (Dublin: TCD, 1989)

Surroundings: Catalogue (Dublin: NMI, 1999)

Teahan, J., *Irish Silver from the Seventeenth to the Nineteenth Century* (Dublin: NMI, 1982)

Waiboer, A. (ed.) *Gabriel Metsu: Rediscovered Master of the Dutch Golden Age* (New Haven and London: NGI in association with Yale University Press, 2010).

Wallace, P.F. and R. Ó Floinn, *Treasures of the National Museum of Ireland: Irish Antiquities* (Dublin: Gill & Macmillan, 2002)

White, J., *National Gallery of Ireland* (Dublin, NGI, 1968)

Whitty, A., *A Dubliner's Collection of Asian Art: The Alfred Bender Exhibition* (Dublin: NMI, 2008)

Wynne, M., *Later Italian Paintings in the National Gallery of Ireland: The Seventeenth, Eighteenth and Nineteenth Centuries* (Dublin: NGI, 1986)

Books Since 1900

Aalen, F., M. Stout and K. Whelan (eds), *Atlas of the Irish Rural Landscape* (Cork: Cork University Press, 1997)

Adam, T., *The Civic Value of Museums* (New York: American Association of Adult Education, 1937)

Alexander, E., *Museums in Motion* (Nashville: Association of State and Local History, 1979)

——, *Museums Masters: Their Museums and Their Influence* (Nashville, Association of State and Local History, 1983)

Allen, D., *The Naturalist in Britain* (Princeton, NJ: Princeton University Press, 1994)

Allen, N., *Modernism, Ireland and Civil War* (Cambridge: Cambridge University Press, 2009)

Allwood, J., *The Great Exhibitions: 150 Years* (London: Exhibition Consultants, 2001)

Altick, R.T., *The Shows of London* (Cambridge, MA: Harvard University Press, 1978)

Anderson, B., *Imagined Communities: Reflections on the Origins and Spread of Nationalism* (London: Verso, 1991)

Anderson, D., *A Common Wealth: Museums in the Learning Age* (London: Department of Culture, Media and Sport, 1999)

Anderson, F.H., *Francis Bacon: His Career and Thought* (Los angeles: USC Press, 1962)

Andrews, J.H., *A Paper Landscape: The Ordnance Survey in Nineteenth-Century Ireland* (Oxford: Oxford University Press, 1975)

Arnold, B., *Orpen: Mirror to an Age* (London: Jonathan Cape, 1981)

Barnard, T., *A Guide to Sources for the History of Material Culture in Ireland* (Dublin: Four Courts Press, 2005)

Bartlett, T., et al. (eds), *1798: A Bicentenary Perspective* (Dublin: Four Courts Press, 2003)

Bazin, G., *The Louvre* (New York: Harry N. Abrams, 1959)

——, *The Museum Age* (Brussels: Desoer, 1967)

Belford, B., *A Certain Genius* (London: Bloomsbury, 2000)

Bell, Q., *The Schools of Design* (London: Routledge & Kegan Paul, 1963)

Benedict, B., *The Anthropology of World's Fairs* (London and Berkeley: Scolar Press, 1983)

Berry, H., *A History of the Royal Dublin Society* (London: Longman, 1915)

Bhabha, H. (ed.), *Nation and Narration* (London: Routledge, 1990)

Blanch, S., *Peintres de Prado* (Barcelona: Ediciones Polígrafa SA, 2002)

Blau, E., *Ruskinian Gothic* (Princeton, NJ: Princeton University Press, 1982)

Bodkin, T., *Hugh Lane and His Pictures* (Dublin: Stationery Office, 1956)

——, *Four Irish Landscape Painters (1920)* (1920; rpr. Dublin: Irish Academic Press, 1987)

Bonython, E. and A. Burton, *The Great Exhibitor: The Life and Work of Henry Cole* (London: V&A Publications, 2003)

Bourdieu, P. and A. Darbel, *The Love of Art: European Art Museums and Their Public* (Cambridge: Polity Press, 1991)

Bourke, M., *Exploring Art at the National Gallery of Ireland* (Dublin: NGI, 1997)

——, (ed.), *Symposium Proceedings, The Role of Education in Museums, Arts and Heritage Venues* (Dublin: NGI, 1999)

——, *Art in Transition: Guidelines for Transition Year Teachers Using the National Gallery of Ireland* (Dublin: NGI, 1998)

—— and S. Bhreathnach-Lynch, *Discover Irish Art at the National Gallery of Ireland* (Dublin, NGI, 1999)

——, (ed.), *Symposium Proceedings, The Nature of the Education Service in Museums, Arts and Heritage Venues* (Dublin: NGI, 2000)

——, (ed.), *Symposium Proceedings, The Museum Visit: Virtual Reality and the Gallery* (Dublin, NGI, 2001)

——, (ed.), *Symposium Proceedings, Learning in Museums* (Dublin: NGI, 2003)

——, *Paul Henry and His Contemporaries: Resource Pack* (Dublin: NGI, 2003)

——, (ed.), *Symposium Proceedings, Effective Presentation & Interpretation in Museums* (Dublin: NGI, 2004)

——, (ed.), *Symposium Proceedings, Museums, Galleries and Young People* (Dublin: NGI, 2006)

——, (ed.), *Symposium Proceedings, Museums, Galleries and Lifelong Learning* (Dublin: NGI, 2008)

——, (ed.), *Symposium Proceedings, Audience Development in Museums and Cultural Sites in Difficult Times* (Dublin: NGI, 2010)

Bourke, M. and J. Bell (eds), *Museums Matter: Accessing Ireland's Heritage* (Dublin: Irish Museums Association, 2008)

Brigham, D., *Public Culture in the Early Republic: Peale's Museum and its Audience* (Washington, DC, and London: Smithsonian Press, 1995)

Bright, K., *The Royal Dublin Society 1815–1845* (Dublin: Four Courts Press, 2004)

Brown, T., *Ireland: A Social and Cultural History 1922–2002* (London: Harper Perennial, 2004)

Browne, H., *Museum of Ancient History: Report 1913* (Dublin: University College Dublin, 1913)

—— and L. McKenna (eds), *A Page of Irish History* (Dublin: Talbot Press, 1930)

Bruner, J., *The Culture of Education* (Cambridge, MA: Harvard University Press, 1996)

Bruskill, H., *Short History of the Irish Parliament House* (Dublin: Bank of Ireland, 1934)

Burt, N., *Palaces for the People: A Social History of the American Art Museum* (Boston: Little Brown, 1977)

Burton, A., *Vision and Accident: The Story of the Victoria and Albert Museum* (London: V&A Publications, 1999)

Casey, C., *The Buildings of Ireland: Dublin* (New Haven, CT: Yale University Press, 2005)

Catto, M., *A Normal School? Art & Design Matters* (Belfast: University of Ulster, 1994)

Ciolfi, L., et al. (eds), *Proceedings of the International Workshop, Re-Thinking Technology in Museums: Towards a New Understanding of People's Experience in Museums* (Limerick: University of Limerick, 2005)

Ciolfi, L. and L. Bannon, *Designing Interactive Museum Exhibits: Enhancing Visitor Curiosity through Augmented Artifacts. Proceedings of the European Conference on Cognitive Ergonomics* (Catania: Italy European Conference on Cognitive Ergonomics, 2002)

Clarke, A., et al., *Learning through Culture: A Guide to Good Practice* (Leicester: University of Leicester, 2002)

Cleary, J. and C. Connolly (eds), *The Cambridge Companion to Modern Irish Culture* (Cambridge: Cambridge University Press, 2005)

Clyde, T., *Irish Literary Magazines* (Dublin: Irish Academic Press, 2003)

Coleman, L.V., *Mousion* (Paris, 1927)

Coleman, L.V., *Manual for Small Museums* (New York: Putnams' Sons, 1927)

Conlin, J., *The Nation's Mantlepiece: A History of the National Gallery* (London: Pallas Athene, 2006)

Connolly, L., *The Educational Value of Museums* (New Jersey: Newark Museum Association, 1914)

Cooke, P., *The Containment of Heritage: Setting Limits to the Growth of Heritage in Ireland* (Dublin: Policy Institute, TCD, 2003)

Coolahan, J., *Irish Education: Its History and Structure* (Dublin: Institute of Public Administration, 1981)

Corr, S., *Caring for Collections: A Manual of Preventative Conservation* (Kilkenny: Heritage Council, 2000)

Craig, M., *Dublin 1660–1860* (Dublin: Allen Figgis, 1969)

Crooke, E., *Politics, Archaeology and the Creation of a National Museum of Ireland* (Dublin: Irish Academic Press, 2000)

Crookham, A., *The National Gallery, London: An Illustrated History* (London: National Gallery Company, 2009)

Crookshank, A. and Knight of Glin, *Ireland's Painters 1600–1940* (New Haven, C T: Yale University Press, 2002)

Csikszentmihalyi, M., *Flow: The Psychology of Optimal Experience* (New York: HarperCollins, 1990)

Cullen, F., *Visual Politics: Ireland 1750–1930* (Cork: Cork University Press, 1997)

——, *Sources in Irish Art: A Reader* (Cork: Cork University Press, 2000)

Cunningham, H., *Leisure in the Industrial Revolution c.1780–c.1880* (London: Croom Helm, 1980)

Cuno, J. (ed.), *Whose Muse? Art Museums and the Public Trust* (Princeton, NJ/Cambridge, MA: Princeton University Press/Harvard University Art Museums, 2004)

——, (ed.), *Who Owns Antiquity? Museums and the Battle over Our Ancient Heritage* (Princeton, NJ: Princeton University Press, 2008)

Daly, M., *The Famine in Ireland* (Dundalk: Irish Historical Association, 1986)

Dana, J., *The New Museum* (Woodstock: Elm Tree Press, 1917)

Davoren, A., *Come to the Edge* (Dublin: IMMA, 1999)

Dawson, B. (ed), *Hugh Lane, Founder of a Gallery of Modern Art for Ireland* (London: Scala, 2008)

De Courcy, C., *The Foundation of the National Gallery of Ireland* (Dublin: NGI, 1985)

——, *Dublin Zoo: An Illustrated History* (Cork: The Collins Press, 2009)

De Vere White, T., *The Story of the Royal Dublin Society* (Tralee: RDS, 1955)

Deane, A., *Belfast Municipal Museum and Art Gallery* (Belfast: Belfast Municipal Museum and Art Gallery, 1929)

Delors, J., *Learning: The Treasure Within* (Paris: UNESCO, 1996)

Dewey, J., *Art as Experience* (New York: Henry Holt & Co., 1934)

——, *Experience and Education* (New York: Macmillan, 1938)

——, *The School and Society* (Chicago: University of Chicago Press, 1900)

Doherty, G., *The Irish Ordnance Survey: History, Culture and Memory* (Dublin: Four Courts Press, 2004)

Dowling, P.J., *The Hedge Schools of Ireland* (Cork: Mercier Press, 1968)

Drew, A., *Framework for a System for Museums, Standing Commission on Museums and Galleries* (London: HMSO, 1979)

Duggan, C. (ed.), *I have a Museum* (Dublin: Dublin Civic Trust, 2001)

Dunlevy, M., *Dublin Barracks: A Brief History of Collins Barracks, Dublin* (Dublin: NMI, 2002)

——, *Pomp and Poverty. A History of silk in Ireland.* (New Haven, CT, Yale University Press, 2011)

Dunne, T. and W. Pressly (eds), *James Barry, 1741–1806: History Painter* (Farnham: Ashgate, 2010)

Durbin, G., et al., *A Teacher's Guide to Learning from Objects* (London: English Heritage, 1990)

Durcan, P., *Crazy about Women* (Dublin: NGI, 1991)

Elderfield, J., *The Front Door to Understanding Modern Painting and Sculpture: 1880 to the Present at the Museum of Modern Art* (New York: MOMA, 2004)

Falk, J. and L. Dierking, *The Museum Experience* (Washington, DC: Whalesback, 1992)

——, and L. Dierking, *Learning from Museums: Visitors' Experiences and the Making of Meaning* (Walnut Creek, CA: Alta Mira Press, 2000)

Fisher, M., *Britain's Best Museums and Galleries* (London: Allen Lane, 2004)

Fleming, T. and A. Gallagher, *'Even Her Nudes were Lovely': A Research Report on the Museum's Programme for Older Adults* (Dublin: IMMA, 1999)

Foster, R.F., *Modern Ireland 1600–1972* (London: Penguin, 1988)

Galard, J., *Visiteurs du Louvre* (Paris: Réunion des Musées Nationaux, 1993)

Gardner, H., *Frames of Mind: The Theory of Multiple Intelligences* (New York: Basic Books, 1983)

——, *Intelligence Reframed: Multiple Intelligences for the 21st Century* (New York: Basic Books, 1999)

Geertz, C., *The Interpretation of Cultures* (London: Hutchinson, 1975)

Gilbert, J.T., *A History of the City of Dublin,* (Shannon: Irish University Press, 1972)

Golby, T.M.S., *The Great Exhibition and Re-Reading Hard Times* (Milton Keynes: Open University, 1986)

Goldman, D., *Emotional Intelligence* (London: Bloomsbury, 1996)

Gould, C., *Trophy of Conquest: The Musée Napoleon and the Creation of the Louvre* (London: Faber & Faber, 1965)

Graburn, N., *Tourism, Leisure and Museums* (Ottawa: Canadian Museums Association, 1982)

Gregory, A., *Hugh Lane's Life and Achievement, with Some Account of the Dublin Galleries* (London: John Murray, 1921)

——, *Seventy Years 1852–1922* (New York: Macmillan, 1974)

Grey, T., *Ireland this Century* (London: Little Brown, 1994)

Griffin, D.J. and S. Lincoln, *Drawings from the Irish Architectural Archive* (Dublin: Irish Architectural Archive, 1993)

—— and C. Pegum, *Leinster House 1744–2000: An Architectural History* (Dublin: Irish Architectural Archive and OPW, 2000)

Harris, N., *Chicago's Dream, a World's Treasure: The Art Institute of Chicago, 1893–1993* (Chicago: Art Institute of Chicago, 1993)

Haywood, C., *The Making of the Classical Museum: Antiquarians, Collectors and Archaeologists* (Dublin: UCD, 2003)

Hein, G., *Learning in the Museum* (London: Routledge, 1998)

—— and M. Alexander, *Museums: Places of Learning* (Washington, DC: AAM, 1998)

Herrero, M., *Irish Intellectuals and Aesthetics: The Making of a Modern Art Collection* (Dublin: Irish Academic Press, 2007)

——, *North of the Hook* (Dublin: Geological Survey, 1995)

Hickey, N., *Reading 20th Century Irish Art: Resource Pack* (Limerick: Hunt Museum, 2004)

Hill, K., *Culture and Class in English Public Museums 1850–1914* (Aldershot: Ashgate, 2005)

Hobsbawm, E., *Nations and Nationalism* (Cambridge: Cambridge University Press, 1990)

Hobson, B. (ed.), *Saorstát Éireann: Official Handbook* (Dublin: Talbot Press, 1932)

Holroyd, M., *George Bernard Shaw* (London: Chatto & Windus), vol. 1, 1988, vol. 2, 1989, vol. 3, 1991, vol. 4, 1992

Hooper-Greenhill, E., *Museum & Gallery Education* (Leicester: Leicester University Press, 1991)

——, *Museums and the Shaping of Knowledge* (London: Routledge, 1992)

——, *Museums and Their Visitors* (London: Routledge, 1994)

—— and G. Nicol (eds), *Evaluating Creativity: Evaluation of the 10 Gallery Education Projects of Encompass 2000* (Leicester: University of Leicester, 2001)

——, et al., *Inspiration, Identity, Learning: The Value of Museums* (Leicester: Leicester University Press, 2004)

Hoppen, K.T., *The Common Scientist in the Seventeenth Century* (London: Routledge & Kegan Paul, 1970)

Horton, C., *Alfred Chester Beatty: From Miner to Bibliophile* (Dublin: Townhouse, 2003)

Hudson, K., *A Social History of Museums* (London: Macmillan, 1975)

Hughes, R., *American Visions: The Epic History of Art in America* (London: Harvill Press, 1997)

Hyland, A. (ed.), *Multiple Intelligences: Curriculum and Assessment Project* (Cork: UCC, 2000)

Impey, O. and A. MacGregor, *The Origins of Museums: The Cabinets of Curiosities in 16th and 17th Century Europe* (London: Strauss Holdings, 1985)

Ingamells, J., *The Wallace Collection* (London: Scala, 1990)

International Council of Museums, *ICOM Code of Ethics for Museums* (Paris: ICOM, 2006)

Irish Art Handbook (Dublin: Cahill, 1943)

James, K.W., *'Damned Nonsense!' The Geological Career of the Third Earl of Enniskillen* (Belfast: Ulster Museum, 1986)

James-Chakraborty, K. (ed.), *Bauhaus Culture: From Weimar to the Cold War* (Minneapolis, MN: University of Minnesota Press, 2006)

Jeffery, K. and N. Garnham (eds), *Culture, Place and Identity* (Dublin: U C D Press, 2005)

Johnston, A. and C. Souyoudzoglou-Haywood, *Corpus Vasorum Antiquorum-Ireland 1* (Dublin: UCD Press, 2000)

Kelleher, M., *The Founders of the Royal Dublin Society and Their Houses* (Dublin: RDS, 2004)

Kelly, A., *Cultural Policy in Ireland* (Dublin: Irish Museums Trust, 1989)

——, *Prelude to the Union: Anglo-Irish Politics in the 1780s* (Cork: Cork University Press, 1992)

Kennedy, B., *Dreams and Responsibilities: The State of the Arts in Independent Ireland* (Dublin: Arts Council, 1990)

Kennedy, S.B., *Irish Art and Modernism 1880–1950* (Belfast: Queen's University, Institute of Irish Studies, 1991)

Keogh, D., *Twentieth-Century Ireland* (Dublin: Gill & Macmillan, 1994, revised 2005)

Kiberd, D., *Inventing Ireland: The Literature of the Modern Nation* (London: Vintage, 1996)

——, *Irish Classics* (London: Granta, 2002)

Kolb, D., *Experiential Learning: Experience as the Source of Learning and Development* (Inglewood Cliffs, NJ: Prentice Hall, 1984)

Laffan, W., *The Cries of Dublin, Drawn from the Life by Hugh Douglas Hamilton* (Dublin: Georgian Society, 2003)

——, (ed.), *Painting Ireland: Topographical Views from Glin Castle* (Tralee: Churchill House, 2006)

Leerssen, J., *Remembrance and Imagination* (Cork: Cork University Press, 1996)

Leslie, R., *An Inquiry into the Progress and Condition of Mechanics' and Literary Institutions, Part II* (Dublin: Statistical and Social Inquiry Society of Ireland, 1952)

Lewis, G., *For Instruction and Recreation: A Centenary History of the Museums Association* (London: Museums Association, 1989)

Lincoln, S., *Mansions, Museums and Commissioners* (Dublin: OPW, 2002)

Lohan, R., *Guide to the Archives of the Office of Public Works* (Dublin: OPW, 1994)

Low, T.L., *The Museum as a Social Instrument* (New York; Metropolitan Museum of Art, 1942)

——, *The Educational Philosophy and Practice of Art Museums in the United States* (New York: Columbia University Teachers' College, 1948)

Lowenfield, V. and W. Brittain (eds), *Creative and Mental Growth* (New York: Macmillan, 1964)

Luckhurst, K., *The Story of Exhibitions* (London and New York: The Studio, 1951)

McClellan, A., *Inventing the Louvre* (Cambridge: Cambridge University Press, 1994)

——, *The Art Museum: From Boullée to Bilbao* (Berkeley, CA: University of California Press, 2008)

MacDonald, E., *The Politics of Display: Museum, Science, Culture* (London: Routledge, 1998)

McDowell, R.B. and D.A. Webb, *Trinity College Dublin: An Academic History* (Cambridge: Cambridge University Press, 1982)

McGrath, C.I., *The Making of the Eighteenth Century Irish Constitution: Government, Parliament and the Revenue 1692–1741* (Dublin: RIA, 2000)

MacGregor, A., *Ark to Ashmolean* (Oxford: Ashmolean Museum, 1988)

——, *Curiosity and Enlightenment: Collectors and Collections from the Sixteenth to the Nineteenth Century* (New Haven, CT: Yale University Press, 2007)

McHugh, R., *Davis, Mangan, Ferguson* (Dublin: Dolmen Press, 1970)

Mack, J., *The Museum of the Mind* (London: British Museum Press, 2003)

Mackin, M., *Our People, Our Times: A History of Northern Ireland's Cultural Diversity* (Belfast: NIMC, 2005)

McLean, F., *Marketing the Museum* (London: Routledge, 1997)

McParland, E., *Public Architecture in Ireland* (New Haven, CT: Yale University Press, 2001)

Mancini, J.M., *Pre-Modernism: Art World Change and American Culture from Civil War to Armory Show* (Princeton, NJ: Princeton University Press, 2005)

Mansergh, M., *The Legacy of Irish History* (Cork: Mercier Press, 2004)

Marcousé, R., *The Listening Eye: Teaching in an Art Museum* (London: HMSO, 1961)

Mason, R., *Museums, Nations, Identities: Wales and its National Museums* (Cardiff: University of Wales Press, 2007)

Matthews, G., *The Philosophy of Childhood* (Cambridge, MA: Harvard University Press, 1994)

Matthews, P.J., *Revival, the Abbey Theatre, Sinn Féin, the Gaelic League and the Co-Operative Movement* (Cork: Cork University Press, 2003)

Maxwell, C., *Dublin under the Georges 1714–1850* (London: Harrap, 1936)

Meenan, J. and D. Clarke, *The Royal Dublin Society 1731–1981* (Dublin: Gill & Macmillan, 1981)

Melton, A.W., *Problems of Installation in Museums of Art* (Washington, DC: AAM, 1935)

Miller, D.E., *City of the Century: The Epic of Chicago and Making of America* (New York: Simon & Schuster, 1996)

Miller, E., *That Noble Cabinet: A History of the British Museum* (London: British Museum, 1973)

Mollan, C. and J. Upton, *The Scientific Apparatus of Nicholas Callan and Other Historic Scientific Instruments* (Maynooth: St Patrick's College and Samton, 1994)

Moody, T.W. and J.C. Beckett, *Queen's, Belfast 1848–1949: The History of a University* (London: Faber & Faber, 1986)

Mordaunt-Crook, J., *The British Museum* (London: Allen Lane, 1972)

Moriarity, C., et al., *The Natural History Museum: Present Status and Future Needs* (Dublin, RIA, 2005)

Morrell, J. and A. Thackeray, *Gentlemen of Science* (Oxford: Clarendon Press, 1981)

Mullins, G., *Dublin Nazi No. 1: The Life of Adolf Mahr* (Dublin: Liberties Press, 2009)

Mulvihill, M., *Ingenious Ireland* (Dublin: Townhouse and Countryhouse, 2002)

Murphy, J.A., *The College: A History of Queen's/University College Cork 1845–1995* (Cork: Cork University Press, 1995)

Murray, P., *Irish Art 1770–1995: History and Society from the Collection of the Crawford Municipal Art Gallery* (Cork: Cork VEC, 1995)

Nelson, E.C. and E. McCracken, *The Brightest Jewel: A History of the National Botanic Gardens* (Kilkenny: Boethius Press, 1987)

Nesbitt, N., *A Museum in Belfast* (Belfast: Ulster Museum, 1979)

Ó Raifeartaigh, T. (ed.), *The Royal Irish Academy: A Bicentennial History 1785–1985* (Dublin: RIA, 1985)

O'Brien, E., et al., *A Portrait of Irish Medicine* (Dublin: Ward River Press, 1984)

O'Connell, D., *Picture This! Looking at Art in the Hugh Lane Municipal Gallery of Modern Art* (Dublin: Hugh Lane Municipal Gallery of Modern Art, 1997)

O'Donnell, J., *Kids Guide to Francis Bacon's Studio* (Dublin: Hugh Lane Municipal Gallery of Modern Art Gallery, 2001)

O'Donoghue, H., and A. Davoren (eds), *A Space to Grow: New Approaches to Working with Children, Primary School Teachers and Contemporary Art in the Context of a Museum* (Dublin: IMMA, 1999)

O'Grady, J., *The Life and Death of Sarah Purser* (Dublin: Four Courts Press, 1996)

O'Hagan, J.W., *The State and the Arts: An Analysis of Key Economic Policy Issues in Europe and the United States* (Cheltenham: Edward Elgar, 1998)

Pakenham, V., *The Big House in Ireland* (London: Cassell, 2005)

Patten, E., *Samuel Ferguson and the Culture of Nineteenth-Century Ireland* (Dublin: Four Courts Press, 2004)

Pears, I., *The Discovery of Painting: The Growth of Interest in the Arts in England 1680–1768* (New Haven, CT: Yale University Press, 1988)

Pearson, N., *The State and the Visual Arts: A Discussion of State Intervention in the Visual Arts in Britain 1790–1961* (Milton Keynes: Open University Press, 1982)

Perry, G. and G. Cunningham, *Academies, Museums and Canons of Art* (New Haven, CT: Yale University Press, 1999)

Pevsner, N., *Academies of Art Past and Present* (Cambridge: Cambridge University Press, 1940)

Plunkett, H.C., *Ireland in the New Century* (London: John Murray, 1904)

Pointon, M., *Art Apart: Art Institutions and Ideology across England and North America* (Manchester: Manchester University Press, 1994)

Pommier, E., *Lettres à Miranda sur les Deplacements des Monuments de l'Art de l'Italie par Antoine Quatremère de Quincy* (Paris: Paris Editions Marcula, 1989)

Praeger, R.L., *Some Irish Naturalists* (Dundalk: Dundalgan Press, 1949)

Prior, N., *Museums & Modernity: Art Galleries and the Makings of Modern Culture* (Oxford: Berg, 2002)

Purbrick, L. (ed.), *The Great Exhibition of 1851* (Manchester: Manchester University Press, 2001)

Ramsey, G., *Educational Work in Museums of the United States* (New York: Wilson, 1938)

Richardson, J., *Inside the Museum: A Children's Guide to the Metropolitan Museum of Art* (New York: Metropolitan Museum/Harry N. Abrams, 1993)

Rinaldi, C., *In Dialogue with Reggio Emilio: Listening, Researching and Learning* (London: Routledge, 2005)

Roberts, L., *From Knowledge to Narrative: Educators and the Changing Museum* (Washington, DC: Smithsonian Institution Press, 1997)

Ryan, M., *The Derrynaflan Hoard: A Preliminary Account* (Dublin: NMI, 1983)

Saumarez Smith, C., *The National Gallery: A Short History* (London: Francis Lincoln, 2008)

Schreibman, S. (ed.), *Collected Poems of Thomas MacGreevy: An Annotated Edition* (Dublin: Anna Livia Press, 1991)

Schwarzer, M., *Riches, Rivals and Radicals: 100 Years of Museums in America* (Washington, DC: AAM, 2006)

Selwood, S., et al., *Cabinets of Curiosity: Art Gallery Learning* (London: Arts Council of England, 1994)

Sheehy, J., *The Rediscovery of Ireland's Past: The Celtic Revival 1830–1930* (London: Thames & Hudson, 1980)

Simone, N., *The Participatory Museum* (Santa Cruz, California: Museum 2.0, 2010).

Somerville-Large, P., *The Story of the National Gallery of Ireland 1854–2004* (Dublin: NGI, 2004)

Sousa, J., *Faces, Places and Inner Spaces: A Guide to Looking at Art* (Chicago: Art Institute of Chicago, 2006)

Stafford, B.M. and F. Terpak, *Devices of Wonder: From the World in a Box to Images on a Screen* (Los Angeles: Getty Research Institute, 2001)

Stephens, E. (ed.), *Dublin Civic Week Official Handbook* (Dublin: Civic Week Council, Mansion House, 1929)

Stoeger, G. and A. Stannett (eds), *Museums, Key Workers and Lifelong Learning: Shared Practice in Five Countries* (Dublin: IMMA, 2001)

Sweet, R., *Antiquaries: The Discovery of the Past in Eighteenth-Century Britain* (London: Hambledon, 2004)

Taylor, B., *Art for the Nation* (Manchester: Manchester University Press, 1999)

Taylor, F.H., *Babel's Tower: The Dilemma of the Modern Museum* (New York: Columbia University Press, 1945)

——, *The Taste of Angels: A History of Art Collecting from Rameses to Napoleon* (Boston: Little Brown, 1948)

Tomkins, C., *Merchants and Masterpieces: The Story of the Metropolitan Museum of Art* (London: Longman, 1970)

Turpin, J., *A School of Art in Dublin Since the Eighteenth Century: A History of the National College of Art and Design* (Dublin: Gill & Macmillan, 1995)

Upstone, R. (ed.), *William Orpen: Politics, Sex, Death* (London: Imperial War Museum, 2005)

Usherwood, P., *Lady Butler, Battle Artist 1846–1933* (London: National Army Museum, 1987)

Viola, W., *Child Art and Franz Cizek* (New York: Reynal & Hitchcock, 1936)

Viney, M., *Ireland, A Smithsonian Natural History* (Belfast: Blackstaff Press, 2003)

Walker, D., *Modern Art in Ireland* (Dublin: Lilliput Press, 1997)

Wallach, A., *Exhibition Contradiction: Essays on the Art Museum in the United States* (Boston: University of Massachusetts Press, 1998)

Walsh, J., *The Politics of Expansion: The Transformation of Educational Policy in the Republic of Ireland, 1957–1972* (Manchester: Manchester University Press, 2009)

Waterfield, G., *Soane and After: The Architecture of Dulwich Picture Gallery* (London: Dulwich Picture Gallery, 1987)

——, *Palaces of Art: Art Galleries in Britain 1790–1990* (London: Dulwich Picture Gallery, 1991)

Weil, S., *A Cabinet of Curiosities: Inquiries into Museums and Their Prospects* (Washington, DC, and London: Smithsonian Institution, 1995)

——, *Making Museums Matter* (Washington, DC: Smithsonian Institution Press, 2002)

White, J. and K. Bright, *Treasures of the Royal Dublin Society* (Dublin: RDS, 1998)

Whyte, N., *Science, Colonialism and Ireland* (Cork: Cork University Press, 1999)

Wilson, D., *The British Museum: A History* (London: British Museum Press, 2002)

Wittlin, A., *The Museum: Its History and its tasks in Education* (London: Routledge & Kegan Paul, 1949)

——, *Museums: In Search of a Usable Future* (Cambridge, MA: MIT Press, 1970)

Wright, C., *Provincial Museums and Galleries, Department of Education and Science* (London: HMSO, 1973)

Wyse, Bonaparte O., *The Issue of Bonaparte Wyse, Waterford's Imperial Relations* (Waterford: Waterford Museum of Treasurers, 2004)

Wyse Jackson, P. N. (ed.), *In Marble Halls: Geology in Trinity College Dublin* (Dublin: TCD, 1994)

—— and E. Vaccari, *The Rev. George Graydon (c.1753–1803): Cleric and Geological Traveller* (Dublin: RIA, 1997)

Works of Reference

A Directory of Dublin for the Year 1738 (Dublin: Dublin City Library and Archive, 2000)

Breeze, G., *Society of Artists in Ireland* (Dublin: Criterion, 1985)

Clarke, M. and R. Rafaussé, *Dictionary of Dublin City Guilds* (Dublin: Dublin Public Libraries, 1993)

Hill, J.R. (ed.), *A New History of Ireland VII: Ireland 1921–1984* (Oxford: Oxford University Press, 2003)

Kors, A.C., *Encyclopedia of the Enlightenment* (Oxford: Oxford University Press, 2003)

Lalor, B. (ed.), *Encyclopedia of Ireland* (Dublin: Gill & Macmillan, 2003)

McGuire, J. and J. Quinn (eds), *Dictionary of Irish Biography* (Cambridge: Cambridge University Press, 2009)

Matthew, H. and B. Harrison (eds), *Oxford Dictionary of National Biography* (Oxford: Oxford University Press, 2004)

Moody, T.W., et al. (eds), *A New History of Ireland VIII: A Chronology of Irish History to 1976* (Oxford: Oxford University Press, 2002)

Osborne, H. (ed.), *The Oxford Companion to Art* (Oxford: Oxford University Press, 1989)

Snoddy, T., *Dictionary of Irish Artists: 20th Century*, rpr.(Dublin: Merlin, 1996)

Stewart, A.M., *Royal Hibernian Academy of Arts, Index of Exhibitors 1826–1979*. vol. I. A–G; vol. II. G–M; vol. III. N–Z (Dublin: Manton, 1986–7)

——, *Irish Art Loan Exhibitions 1765–1927, Index of Artists*. vol. I. A–L; vol. II. M–Z; vol. III: subject index (Dublin: Manton, 1990–5)

Strickland, W.G., *A Dictionary of Irish Artists*, rpr. (Shannon: Irish University Press, 1913)

Travlos, J., *Pictorial Dictionary of Ancient Athens* (New York: Praeger, 1971)

Vaughan, W.E. (ed.), *A New History of Ireland VI: Ireland under the Union 1870–1920* (Oxford: Oxford University Press, 1996)

Index

Page numbers in italics indicate illustrations or their captions. Titles of artworks can be found under the artist's name. Mc is treated as Mac.

Picture Credits

The author and publisher wish to thank the following for permission to reproduce images:

Page xviii, p.xxxii, p.9, p.158, p.163, p.166, p.168 (bottom) (Photo © NMI), p.170 (top and bottom), p.187, p.188, p.194 (top and bottom), p.197, p.198, p.199, p.201, p.202, p.323, p.325, p.326, p.329, p.333, p.337, p.339, p.340, p.345, p.346, p.348, p.350, p.352, p.399, p.403 (Photo courtesy National Gallery of Ireland), p.413, p.432, p.435, These images reproduced with the kind permission of the National Museum of Ireland; p.xxiv, p.xxvii, p.xxx, p.2 (Alfred Beit Foundation, Photo © National Gallery of Ireland), p.33, p.36, p.40, p.47, p.51, p.53, p.55, p.56, p.58, p.61, p.63, p.70, p.71 (Photographer: Roy Hewson), p.72, p.73, p.74, p.76, p.79, p.80, p.86, p.112, p.136, p.145, p.150, p.152, p.154, p.155, p.160, p.172, p.173, p.186, p.206, p.208, p.209, p.212, p.213, p.215, p.217, p.221, p.228, p.233, p.238, p.239, p.245, p.247, p.248, p.249, p.252, p.309, p.359 (main), p.361, p.363, p.364, p.368, p.370, p.371, p.384, p.386, p.392 (Photographer: Roy Hewson), p.396, p.397, p.403 (image only), p.425, p.428, Photo © National Gallery of Ireland; p.7, p.419, Archive Organization for the Construction of the New Acropolis Museum: Photo Nikos Daniilidis; p.10, Vasari, Giorgio (1511–1574): Studiolo of Francesco I. Florence, Palazzo Vecchio. © 2010. Photo Scala, Florence; p.12, p.18, p.92, Photo RMN; p.13, Firenze, Museo dell' Opificio delle Pietre Dure, Archivio Fotografico Domenico Remps, "Scarabattolo", dipinto ad olio su tela N. 1 riproduzione digitale ad alta risoluzione; p.15, The Royal Collection © 2010 Her Majesty Queen Elizabeth II; p.20, Collection Netherlands Architecture Institute, Rotterdam (NAI, Rotterdam) archive (code): RYKS; p.23, p.287, Ismael Alonso/Getty Images; p.26 (photograph by G. Whelan), p.34, Images courtesy of RDS Archives; p.44, p.64, p.65, p.66, p.159, p.168 (top), By permission of the Royal Irish Academy © RIA; p.48, Matthew William Peters, *Self portrait with Robert West*, p.101 (bottom), Henry Jamyn Brooks, Private View of the Old Masters Exhibition, Royal Academy, 1888 © National Portrait Gallery, London; p.78, Private Collection; p.82, Dublin City Council: Civic Museum Collection; p.90, Galleria Busti e Statue – Museo Pio Clementino. Photo Vatican Museums; p.96, p.107, Mary Evans Picture Library; p.99, Photo courtesy Natural History Museum, Britain; p.101 (top), By courtesy of the Trustees of Sir John Soane's Museum; p.103, London Metropolitan Archives, City of London; p.105, Courtesy of Artifice Images; p.106, © The National Gallery, London; p.115, Courtesy of the Pennsylvania Academy of the Fine Arts, Philadelphia. Gift of Mrs. Sarah Harrison (The Joseph Harrison, Jr. Collection); p.118, Smithsonian Institution Archives, Record Unit 95, image no. 2002-10677; p.121, Coloured postcard: The Metropolitan Museum of Art, NY, New York, 1905. Architects: East wing designed by Richard Morris Hunt (1827-1895); South wing designed by Theodore Weston (1832-1919). Collection of Kent Lydecker. Photograph by Irving Underhill.

New York, Metropolitan Museum of Art. © 2010. Image copyright The Metropolitan Museum of Art/Art Resource/Scala, Florence; p.122, Photograph © 2010 Museum of Fine Arts, Boston; p.123, The Art Institute of Chicago, exterior looking Northeast from opposite side of Michigan Avenue, circa 1904, C33736, The Art Institute of Chicago. Photography © The Art Institute of Chicago; p.126, The Family of Thomas Bateson, Esq. 1705-91 (1762), Strickland Lowry 1737-c.85 (attributed to) © National Museums Northern Ireland 2010. Collection Ulster Museum, Belfast. Photograph reproduced courtesy the Trustees of National Museums Northern Ireland; p.127, p. 132, p.137 © National Museums Northern Ireland 2010. Collection Ulster Museum, Belfast. Photograph reproduced courtesy the Trustees of National Museums Northern Ireland; p.133, p.134, p.300, p.301, p.302, Crawford Art Gallery, Cork; p.140 (top), Photo © Queen's University Belfast; p.140 (bottom), View of the North Wing from the lower grounds, Queen's College Cork (now University College Cork) (University Archives, UCC, UC.PH.LDSCAPE.1); p.143, Photographer: J.K. Prendergast. UCG Annual. 1915, Vol. 1, No. 3; p.146, p.230, courtesy The Board of Trinity College Dublin; p.174, Joly Collection, Exterior of the Museum of Irish Industry 1857. Courtesy of the National Library of Ireland; p.175, Davison & Associates; p.179, Image courtesy of RDS Library Archives, after original image by H. Bantry White; p.180, p.310, Dublin City Council: Civic Museum Collection. Collection Dublin City Gallery The Hugh Lane; p.181, The Dublin Metropolitan School of Art Gallery, decorated for distribution of prizes by Lord Aberdeen Lord Lieutenant, taken 27 July 1906. B.I. Tilly, the Registrar, stands by Frederick Luke, the second master, in readiness for the arrival of students and masters. NIVAL/NCAD/HISTORY COLLECTION-TURPIN DONATION. National Irish Visual Arts Library, /NIVAL/NCAD/HCTD/. NIVAL, Dublin; p.196, *Irish Builder*, 1 Dec. 1887; p.333, New Science and Art Building, Kildare Street - Perspective View, T.N. Deane R.H.A. & Son, Architects. Photo courtesy of the Irish Architectural Archive; p.219, The Royal Irish Institution, College Street. Old Masters Exhibition. Strickland, *Dictionary of Irish Artists* (1913, repr. 1969), Volume 11, plate LXII; p.225, Courtesy of the Knight of Glin/ Photo © National Gallery of Ireland; p.241, Courtesy National Gallery of Ireland Archive Collection/ Photo © National Gallery of Ireland; p.242, Photographic, The ground floor sculpture hall looking towards the stairs c.1900. Courtesy of the National Library of Ireland; p.256, © 1962 Eames Office, LLC. Photo courtesy of the Library of Congress; p.261, Visitors, a kindergarten class from Public school 116, viewing the collection of Arms and Armor. The Metropolitan Museum of Art. Photograph taken in 1913. New York, Metropolitan Museum of Art. © 2010. Image copyright The Metropolitan Museum of Art/Art Resource/Scala, Florence; p.263, Fox Photos/Getty Images; p.265, © The National Gallery, London; p.267, Bingham, George Caleb (1811-1879): *Fur Traders Descending the Missouri*, 1845. New York, Metropolitan Museum of Art. Oil on canvas, 29 x 36 x ? in. (73.7 x 92.7 cm). Morris K. Jesup Fund, 1933. Acc.n.: 33.61 © 2010. Image copyright The Metropolitan Museum of Art/Art Resource/Scala, Florence; p.269, courtesy of Andrew McClellan; p.270, Leyda, Jay (1910-1988): Alfred Barr, 1931-33. New York, Museum of Modern Art (MoMA). Gelatin silver print, 4 ? x 3 5/8 in. (12.1 x 9.2 cm). Gift of the photographer. Acc. n.: 65.1941. © 2010. Digital image, The Museum of Modern Art, New York/Scala, Florence. Courtesy of the Estate of Jay Leyda; p.272, Georges Seurat, French, 1859-1891; *A Sunday on La Grande Jatte - 1884*, 1884-86, Oil on canvas, 81 3/4 x 121 1/4 in. (207.5 x 308.1 cm), Helen Birch Bartlett Memorial Collection, 1926.224, The Art Institute of Chicago. Photography © The Art Institute of Chicago; p.273, Central Saloon looking towards Main Stairs c. 1941, a photograph. © The Trustees of the British Museum. All rights reserved; p.275, Pieter de Hooch, *A Woman and her Maid in a Courtyard* © The National Gallery, London; p.277, The interior skylight of The Solomon R. Guggenheim Museum, New York. Photograph by David Heald © The Solomon R. Guggenheim Foundation, New York; p.280, *Wilton Diptych, Richard II presented to the Virgin and Child by his Patron St John the Baptist & St Edward* © The National Gallery, London; p.281, Crowds viewing the Mona Lisa at the National Gallery of Art, Washington, January–February, 1963. National Gallery of Art, Washington D.C., Gallery Archives; p.283, 'Treasures of Tutankhamum', special exhibition at The Metropolitan Museum of Art, New York, December 20, 1978–April 15, 1979. General view of galleries with viewers of the exhibition. New York, Metropolitan Museum of Art. © 2010. Image copyright The Metropolitan Museum of Art/Art Resource/Scala, Florence; p.285, © Peter Adams; p.288, Museum Education's "The Artist's Studio: Cartouches (Blake Court); Family Gallery Walk: Ancient Worlds (Blake Court); Drop-in Workshop: Beaded Collars (Studio 18) July 21, 2000", D13655_042, The Art Institute of Chicago. Photography © The Art Institute of Chicago; p.290, UCD Collection. Photo © National Gallery of Ireland; p.292, Belfast Museum and Art Gallery. North side (originally planned as front). Botanic Gardens, 9 May 1929. © National Museums Northern Ireland 2010. Collection Ulster Museum, Belfast. *Photograph reproduced courtesy the Trustees of National Museums Northern Ireland*; p.294, *The Three Dancers* (1945), John Luke 1906–75 © National Museums Northern Ireland 2010. Collection Ulster Museum, Belfast. *Photograph reproduced courtesy the Trustees of National Museums Northern Ireland*; p.295, Exterior of Ulster Museum (2000) © National Museums Northern Ireland 2010. Collection Ulster Museum, Belfast. *Photograph reproduced courtesy the Trustees of National Museums Northern Ireland*; p.298, Discover History, Ulster Museum (2010) © National Museums Northern Ireland 2010. Collection Ulster Museum, Belfast. *Photograph reproduced courtesy the Trustees of National Museums Northern Ireland*; p.303, Sean O'Sullivan, 1906-1964, *Sir Alfred Chester Beatty (1875-1968)*. Charcoal and pencil with white highlights on card © Artist's Estate. Photo © National Gallery of Ireland; p.304, p.305, © The Trustees of the Chester Beatty Library, Dublin; p.307, p.308 (both), © The Hunt Museum, Limerick; p.311, Francis Bacon's Studio at 7 Reece Mews, London, 2001. Photograph by Perry Ogden. C-Print on aluminium, 126 x 158 cm. Collection Dublin City Gallery The Hugh Lane © 2010 The Estate of Francis Bacon/DACS, London; p.312, Michael Warren, *Beneath the bow*, 1991, oak and cor-ten steel, 12m(h), Collection Irish Museum of Modern Art, Photographer Denis Mortell, image courtesy IMMA and the artist; p.315, James Coleman, *Lapus Exposure*, 1992-94, Projected images with synchronized audio narration, Dimensions variable, Collection Irish Museum of Modern Art, Purchase, Heritage Fund, 2004. Image courtesy IMMA and James Coleman. © James Coleman; p.316, Children take part in a tour mediated by Joakim Gleisner focusing on 'St Francis Street Boys', 1994, by John Ahearn (b.1951). *Irish Museum of Modern Art Collection*; p.320, Jacques Emile Blanche, 1861-1942, *James Joyce, (1882-1941), Author*, Oil on canvas © ADAGP, Paris and DACS, London 2010. Photo © National Gallery of Ireland; p.327, Sean O'Sullivan, 1906-1964, *George Nobel, Count Plunkett (1851-1948), Scholar and Nationalist*. Graphite on paper © Artist's Estate. Photo © National Gallery of Ireland; p.347, p.351, p.431, p.433, p.436, photo Marie Bourke; p.356, Caravaggio, 1571-1610. *The Taking of Christ*, 1602, Oil on canvas. Courtesy of the National Gallery of Ireland and the Jesuit Community, Leeson St, Dublin, who acknowledge the generosity of the late Dr. Marie Lea-Wilson. Photo © National Gallery of Ireland; p.359, inset, Turner Watercolours Cabinet. Bequeathed by Henry Vaughan, 1900. Courtesy of the National Gallery of Ireland. Photo © National Gallery of Ireland; p.367,